# The Selected Papers of
# Elizabeth Cady Stanton and Susan B. Anthony

# The Selected Papers of Elizabeth Cady Stanton and Susan B. Anthony

## VOLUME III

### NATIONAL PROTECTION FOR NATIONAL CITIZENS
### 1873 TO 1880

Ann D. Gordon, EDITOR

Allison L. Sneider, ASSISTANT EDITOR

Ann Elizabeth Pfau, ASSISTANT EDITOR

Kimberly J. Banks, EDITORIAL ASSISTANT

Lesley L. Doig, EDITORIAL ASSISTANT

Meg Meneghel MacDonald, EDITORIAL ASSISTANT

Margaret Sumner, EDITORIAL ASSISTANT

RUTGERS UNIVERSITY PRESS

NEW BRUNSWICK, NEW JERSEY

LIBRARY OF CONGRESS CATALOGING-IN-PUBLICATION DATA

Stanton, Elizabeth Cady, 1815–1902.
    [Selections. 1997]
    The selected papers of Elizabeth Cady Stanton and Susan B. Anthony /
Ann D. Gordon, editor ; Tamara Gaskell Miller, assistant editor.
      p.    cm.
    Includes bibliographical references and index.
    Contents: v. 3. National protection for national citizens, 1873 to 1880
    ISBN 0-8135-2319-2 (alk. paper)
    1. Feminists—United States—Archives.  2. Suffragists—United
States—Archives.  3. Stanton, Elizabeth Cady, 1815–1902—
Archives.  4. Anthony, Susan B. (Susan Brownell), 1820–1906—
Archives.  5. Feminism—United States—History—19th
century—Sources.  6. Women—Suffrage—United States—History—
19th century—Sources.  I. Anthony, Susan B. (Susan Brownell), 1820–
1906.  II. Gordon, Ann D. (Ann Dexter)  III. Miller, Tamara
Gaskell.  IV. Title.
HQ1410.A25   1997
016.30542—dc21                         97-5666
                                                               CIP

BRITISH CATALOGING-IN-PUBLICATION information is available from the British Library.

TEXT DESIGN: Judith Martin Waterman of Martin-Waterman Associates, Ltd.
Manufactured in the United States of America

⤝⤞

Publication of this volume was assisted by a grant from the National
Historical Publications and Records Commission.

⤝⤞

Frontispiece photograph of Elizabeth Cady Stanton, 1874, photographer un-
known, and Susan B. Anthony, 1874, taken by Charles D. Mosher, Chicago.
(Department of Rare Books and Special Collections, University of Rochester
Library.)

*To the women
of the
U.S. Congress
Past, Present, and Future*

# CONTENTS

# ILLUSTRATIONS

# ✧ PREFACE

THIS IS THE THIRD IN A SERIES of volumes publishing selected papers of Elizabeth Cady Stanton (1815–1902) and Susan B. Anthony (1820–1906). Like the earlier volumes, this one builds upon the work of Patricia G. Holland, Ann D. Gordon, Gail Malmgreen, and Kathleen McDonough in preparing the microfilm edition, *Papers of Elizabeth Cady Stanton and Susan B. Anthony* (1991). The underlying search for the papers of Stanton and Anthony is described in detail in the *The Papers of Elizabeth Cady Stanton and Susan B. Anthony: Guide and Index to the Microfilm Edition* (1992).

This series brings the most important documents of that comprehensive collection to print. The *Selected Papers* focuses on the public careers of two co-workers in the cause of woman suffrage, beginning with the start of their activism in the 1840s and pursuing the story of their ideas, tactics, reputations, and impact until the end of their lives in the twentieth century. Volume three draws on the papers dating from 1873 to 1880; it documents their responses to the Woman's Crusade against liquor, the Centennial of 1876, the start of their campaign to amend the Constitution of the United States, and the end of Reconstruction.

# ❦ ACKNOWLEDGMENTS

I T IS A PLEASURE TO ACKNOWLEDGE and thank the people who made this volume possible. The title page credits the people whose work is most evident in the pages of this volume. Behind the scenes these staff members also stopped their editorial chores to execute the project's unwelcome move to new offices. With patience, skill, and high spirits, they packed tens of thousands of files, designed and decorated the new quarters, and unpacked those same files to resume work on this volume. It was a magnificent achievement. In the more usual tasks, we also had the help of Veronica A. Wilson, a graduate student at Rutgers and a former editorial assistant; of Amanda Pipkin and Erik Brandsma, our translators; and of Ivy M. Klenetsky, an undergraduate intern who made herself indispensable. Meg MacDonald came to us on a yearlong fellowship in historical editing awarded to the project by the National Historical Publications and Records Commission. As the volume neared completion, Harriet M. Sigerman joined the staff as an assistant editor.

We have acknowledged in the notes the scores of archivists, librarians, and local historians across the country who answered our queries about people and places. In New York City, Meghan Horvath located dozens of Susan B. Anthony's midwestern acquaintances in the federal census. Ellen Carol DuBois unlocked the mysteries of several manuscripts in the Huntington Library. Stacy Kinlock Sewell examined material at the Schomburg Center for Research in Black Culture. Dane Hartgrove unearthed new documents in the National Archives, and Lisa Tetrault did the same in the Wisconsin Historical Society. We also thank the staff of the Milstein Division of U.S. History, Local History and Genealogy at the New York Public Library, not forgetting those who retrieve and reshelve books when our entire staff spends the day in that splendid collection.

We also acknowledge the owners of manuscripts who allowed us to publish documents from their collections: Schlesinger Library, Radcliffe Institute, Harvard University; Harriet Beecher Stowe Center; Bancroft

Library, University of California, Berkeley; Historical Society of Pennsylvania; Massachusetts Historical Society; Chicago Historical Society; The Filson Historical Society; Sophia Smith Collection, Smith College; Jefferson County Historical Society, New York; Seneca Falls Historical Society, New York; Mabel Smith Douglass Library, Rutgers University; New-York Historical Society; Rochester Public Library; Department of Rare Books and Special Collections, University of Rochester Library; Rutherford B. Hayes Presidential Center; Huntington Library, San Marino, California; Haverford College Library; Bernhard Knollenberg Collection, Manuscripts and Archives, Yale University Library; Chautauqua County Historical Society, New York; Wisconsin Historical Society; Toledo-Lucas County Public Library; Manuscripts and Archives Division, The New York Public Library, Astor, Lenox and Tilden Foundations; Vassar College Library; and Frances E. Willard Memorial Library.

This volume was produced with major financial support from the Research Division of the National Endowment for the Humanities; the National Historical Publications and Records Commission; the Barbara Lubin Goldsmith Foundation; Patricia G. Holland; William L. Holland; and Rutgers, the State University of New Jersey. We have also received generous gifts from the following individuals: Kathleen Alaimo, Eric L. Berger, Allida M. Black, Elizabeth R. Bodine, Nadine C. Barter Bowlus, Ann D. Braude, Thomas Dublin, Elizabeth V. Faue, Carolyn De Swarte Gifford, Patricia J. Gordon, Nancy and Jesse Green, Mary M. Huth, Kathi L. Kern, Susan and Lee Lane, Kerry K. Lattimore, Margaret S. Lyons, Carol Nadell, Susan L. Pfau, Sherrill L. Redmon, Shelah Kane Scott, Fredrick E. Sherman, Kathryn Kish Sklar, and Judith Wellman.

Thanks are also due to colleagues at Rutgers: to members of the Department of History, to Mary DeMeo, to the staff of the Rutgers University Press, and to Barry Qualls.

⁓ A. D. G.

# ✍ INTRODUCTION

I N THIS VOLUME OF DOCUMENTS dating from October 1873 to September 1880, the phrase "National Protection for National Citizens" occurs late in the story. The title of Elizabeth Cady Stanton's speech to the Senate Committee on Privileges and Elections in January 1878,[1] "National Protection for National Citizens" expressed the ideal terms sought by Stanton and Susan B. Anthony for achieving woman suffrage: all citizens of the United States should be protected in their right to vote by the federal government. The phrase revived their earlier call for universal suffrage and infused it with a critique of recent judicial and political decisions that an individual's voting rights derived from state, not national, citizenship and that states could determine who qualified to vote. Most pointedly it answered the Supreme Court's unanimous opinion in *Minor v. Happersett* (1875).[2] There the Court wrote: "For nearly ninety years the people have acted upon the idea that the Constitution, when it conferred citizenship, did not necessarily confer the right of suffrage (177)." Even as amended after the war, that document did "not confer the right of suffrage upon anyone (178)." Although written to answer the question, whether a state could bar women from voting, the opinion strengthened an increasingly popular view that the federal government bore no responsibility for guaranteeing the right to vote. That view not only sanctioned women's disfranchisement by the states but also threatened black men's slim hold on their voting rights.

When Stanton spoke to the Senate committee in 1878, she insisted that "the primal rights of all citizens should be regulated by the national government, and complete equality in civil and political rights everywhere secured."[3] At a time when President Rutherford B. Hayes had withdrawn federal troops from the South, when white violence against black voters had marked the recent elections, when the Republican

---

[1] See document 133 within.
[2] Minor v. Happersett, 21 Wallace 162.
[3] See document 133 within.

party shied away from federal protection for the political rights of African-American males and states' rights Democrats controlled the House of Representatives, "National Protection for National Citizens" defined an ideal for granting woman suffrage and for continuing Reconstruction.[4]

It took time for Stanton and Anthony to define the goal they could so clearly state in 1878, in the midst of their campaign for an amendment to the Constitution. At the start of this volume in the fall of 1873, they lacked a strategy. Since 1870 they had sought suffrage by testing to what extent the Fourteenth and Fifteenth amendments redefined United States citizenship and reconfigured federal authority for voting rights.[5] When a federal circuit court convicted Susan B. Anthony in June 1873 of a federal crime for voting while being a woman, the court's opinion signaled the end of the strategy. Ward Hunt, an associate justice of the Supreme Court of the United States, wrote that voting was "a right or privilege arising under the constitution of the state, and not under the constitution of the United States."[6] But with related cases on appeal to the Supreme Court, suffragists were in a state of uncertainty rather than defeat.

As the time neared for the National Woman Suffrage Association to convene in Washington in January 1874, Stanton and Anthony weighed what to ask of Congress. With a patchwork of measures, they managed that winter to keep protest and agitation alive and remind Congress and the public yet again of women's disfranchisement, but they could not map out a route to the vote. Not until late in 1876 did they return to an earlier strategy of seeking an amendment to the Constitution that would bar states from excluding voters on the basis of their sex. The campaign they launched in 1876 lasted beyond the years documented in this volume.

[4] On the political situation, see Eric Foner, *Reconstruction: America's Unfinished Revolution, 1863–1877* (New York, 1988), 564–601; on Stanton's speech, see Ellen Carol Dubois, "Outgrowing the Compact of the Fathers: Equal Rights, Woman Suffrage, and the United States Constitution, 1820–1878," in *Woman Suffrage and Women's Rights* (New York, 1998), 81–113.

[5] This history is told in Ann D. Gordon, ed., *Against an Aristocracy of Sex, 1866 to 1873*, vol. 2 of *The Selected Papers of Elizabeth Cady Stanton and Susan B. Anthony* (New Brunswick, N.J., 2000). (Cited hereafter as *Papers*).

[6] United States v. Susan B. Anthony, 11 Blatchford 200, 204 (1873).

While Stanton and Anthony held to the principle that the federal government should enfranchise women, an alternative path was to rid state constitutions and territorial laws of the language that limited voting to males only. Twice between 1873 and 1880 state legislatures submitted such constitutional amendments to the voters for approval, and twice voters rejected the change. In advance of the vote in Michigan in 1874, Stanton and Anthony each spent weeks in the state speaking in support of the amendment as they had done in Kansas in 1867. Only Anthony ventured into the campaign in Colorado in 1877. "It is worse than folly to expect to get suffrage by the state rights plan," an exasperated Anthony wrote Stanton after the election.[7] "[T]hree times and out," she told the Iowa Woman Suffrage Association a week later; it was time "to rally to the work of petitioning Congress for a 16th amendment."[8]

⤳

Susan B. Anthony (SBA) and Elizabeth Cady Stanton (ECS) were leaders of the National Woman Suffrage Association, founded in 1869, dissolved in 1870, and revived in the summer of 1872. Based primarily on individual memberships, the association maintained a loose affiliation with suffrage societies of various sizes and capabilities in cities, states, and territories. But their ability to lead was not delimited by the strength of the National association or its affiliates. ECS and SBA were well known to a great many Americans. For one thing, the press treated them as celebrities whose actions merited coverage even from a distance. More important, they traveled year after year to deliver popular lectures and thus put faces to their names and made arguments that audiences could judge for themselves.

Their primary weapon in efforts to achieve woman suffrage was the enthusiastic response of women across the country to their calls for petitions to Congress or for other indications that women wanted to vote. Few of the respondents ever attended the National association's annual meetings or Washington conventions; some of them no doubt attended meetings in the best-organized locations, such as New York State; Chicago; Illinois; Toledo, Ohio; Michigan; San Francisco; and even tiny Oregon, Missouri. Many of them, however, met ECS and SBA

7 See document 123 within.
8 See document 124 within.

when these stars of the lecture platform came to their towns. The looseness of this network of woman suffragists helps to explain SBA's never-ending quest for a newspaper allied with the National association. Subscribers were more important than members. "[O]ut here where each county has an area of all Mass[achusetts] put together—& then <u>one</u> or <u>two</u> friends in a given town of each one of those large sections," she wrote from Iowa in 1877, a newspaper was the best way to give women ideas of something to do.[9]

The widespread appeal of their campaign for a constitutional amendment could also be traced to the energies unleashed by the emergence of a large and diverse woman's movement after the Civil War.[10] Stanton and Anthony reached out across the narrow gap that separated suffragists from advocates of temperance, Indian rights, equal wages, coeducation, access to professions, and many other causes. Their interactions with women whose primary cause was temperance recur throughout this volume, beginning with the Woman's Crusade in the winter of 1873 and 1874 and persisting through the Michigan amendment campaign, the founding of the Woman's Christian Temperance Union, the tug-of-war within the union between advocates of prayer and of suffrage, and the election of Frances Willard as union president in 1879. Announcing their amendment campaign in 1876, ECS and SBA aimed at a still wider sample of the woman's movement: "If Women who are laboring for peace, temperance, social purity and the rights of labor, would take the speediest way to accomplish what they propose, let them demand the ballot in their own hands, that they may have a direct power in the government. Thus only can they improve the conditions

[9] See document 128 within.

[10] An early synthesis of this phenomenon can be found in Eleanor Flexner, *Century of Struggle: The Woman's Rights Movement in the United States*, rev. ed. (Cambridge, Mass., 1975). Some recent studies of its component parts include: Karen J. Blair, *The Clubwoman as Feminist: True Womanhood Redefined, 1868–1914* (New York, 1980); William Leach, *True Love and Perfect Union: The Feminist Reform of Sex and Society* (New York, 1980); Ruth Bordin, *Woman and Temperance: The Quest for Power and Liberty, 1873–1900* (Philadelphia, 1981); Anne Firor Scott, *Natural Allies: Women's Associations in American History* (Urbana, Ill., 1991); Genevieve G. McBride, *On Wisconsin Women: Working for Their Rights from Settlement to Suffrage* (Madison, Wis., 1993); Sandra Haarsager, *Organized Womanhood: Cultural Politics in the Pacific Northwest, 1840–1920* (Norman, Okla., 1997).

of the outside world and purify the home."[11] Few, if any, women's organizations endorsed the campaign in this era, but many individuals unaffiliated with the suffrage movement could and did add their voices and names to it.

The division of 1869 among woman suffragists persisted in the years from 1873 to 1880, although it lost much of its emotional intensity outside of New England.[12] When state suffrage associations in Michigan and Colorado needed help with their state referenda, for example, they called in lecturers from the National association and from Lucy Stone's American Woman Suffrage Association. Limited access to the *Woman's Journal* of Lucy Stone and Henry Blackwell posed a larger problem. Stone refused to name the National Woman Suffrage Association in the paper prior to January 1880; if she consented to publish an announcement sent her by ECS or SBA, she rewrote it to say "a suffrage society" or "Miss Anthony" asks or invites. But some of her most loyal allies were crossing the divide to visit the National's Centennial Headquarters in Philadelphia in 1876, join the amendment campaign, and celebrate the thirtieth anniversary of the woman's rights convention at Seneca Falls. By 1880, Stone faced pressure from some members of the American to unite with the National.[13]

The work of the National association rested on a small group. None were more important in this period than Sara Spencer, Belva Lockwood, and Ellen Sargent in Washington, D.C. They oversaw congressional lobbying, arranged the annual conventions, and mailed thousands of tracts and petitions to post offices across the country. Sharing responsibility with ECS and SBA for laying out the association's goals in calls, memorials, and resolutions were Matilda Joslyn Gage and Isabella Beecher Hooker. To Gage and Lillie Devereux Blake fell arrangements for the association's annual meeting in New York City each spring. Gage added to her responsibilities in 1878, when she became editor of a monthly newspaper, the *National Citizen and Ballot Box*. In the

[11]  See document 100 within.

[12]  On the divisions of 1869, see *Papers*, volume 2.

[13]  Leslie Wheeler, ed., *Loving Warriors: Selected Letters of Lucy Stone and Henry B. Blackwell, 1853 to 1893* (New York, 1981), 279; Antoinette Brown Blackwell to Lucy Stone, 5 July 1880, in Carol Lasser and Marlene Deahl Merrill, eds., *Friends and Sisters: Letters between Lucy Stone and Antoinette Brown Blackwell, 1846–93* (Urbana, Ill., 1987), 218–19.

Midwest, Elizabeth Boynton Harbert, Mathilde F. Anneke, and Virginia L. Minor helped to develop ideas and organize regional meetings. By 1880, new and younger faces among the leaders brought new standards of decision making and business that would transform the association in the next decade.

✍

Although politics, travel, and lectures dominate the stories told in this volume, it is also evident that both ECS and SBA felt the pull of family obligations. Indeed, SBA seemed nearly overcome at times by her obligations. She nursed her sister Guelma McLean in Rochester until her death in 1873 and her sister Hannah Mosher in Leavenworth, Kansas, until her death in 1877, and each cold SBA caught thereafter made her worry that she too would die of consumption. Her sisters left lonely widowers and motherless children to care for, and each summer she relieved her sister Mary Anthony of the care of their aged and ailing mother, Lucy Read Anthony (1793–1880).

ECS continued to live in Tenafly, New Jersey. That her husband, Henry Brewster Stanton (1805–1887), sometimes joined her there is evident in scattered references, but perhaps more typical was the scene described by SBA at Tenafly on Christmas Eve of 1876. "Hattie, Maggie, Bob, Theodore & Kitt home to day," she wrote of five of the Stanton children, "& a splendid Roast Turkey dinner . . . but no husband & Father out to enjoy it with them—& no seeming care that there is not."[14] Also missing from the dinner table that day were the first and third of the Stanton sons: Daniel Cady (1842–1891), known as Neil, an occasional lawyer and a frequent resident at Tenafly with his mother, and Gerrit Smith (1845–1927), known as Gat, a rancher in Iowa who married there in 1875. Of those dining, Kitt or Kit was Henry Brewster, Jr., (1844–1903), still practicing law in New York City with his father. Margaret Livingston (1852–1930) graduated from Vassar College in June 1876 and lived at Tenafly until her marriage in 1878. Harriot Eaton (1856–1940) followed her sister to Vassar, entering the preparatory classes in 1871 and the college in 1874 and graduating in June 1878. Theodore Weld (1851–1925) dropped out of Cornell University in 1874

[14] SBA diary, 1876, in Patricia G. Holland and Ann D. Gordon, eds., *Papers of Elizabeth Cady Stanton and Susan B. Anthony* (Wilmington, Del., 1991, microfilm), 18:516ff. (Cited hereafter as *Film.*)

but returned to earn a bachelor's degree two years later. Robert Livingston (1859–1920), the youngest child and bedridden when this volume begins, entered Cornell in 1876 and earned his degree in 1880. By 1880, such a gathering of ECS's children as occurred on Christmas Eve was rare: Iowa was still home to Gat, and he was joined there by Margaret Stanton Lawrence after her marriage; Harriot and Theodore traveled to Europe, where both of them married in the early 1880s.

ECS retired from lecturing in the spring of 1880. Not for the first time she also resolved never to attend another suffrage convention. With considerable pride she noted the attention her children paid to the work of her lifetime. Over the sofa in Gat's parlor in Iowa, there hung lithographs of his mother and SBA, "looking earnestly at each other."[15] But it was Theodore, Maggie, and Harriot who inched their way into their mother's public life in this period—to travel, to write, and to lecture.

᭜

While the pages of this volume were being typeset, the editors learned of a small but delicious collection of letters about the Beecher–Tilton affair recently acquired by the University of Rochester. Two passing references in this volume are explicated in the newly discovered letters. In document 11 at 4 January 1874, SBA thinks it is good news that Rev. Phebe Hanaford will leave Connecticut for New Jersey; in the new letters, Rev. Olympia Brown explains to John Hooker, 11 September 1874, that Hanaford had for several years stirred up dissension in Brown's congregation and nearly succeeded in driving Brown out of Bridgeport. Letters to John Hooker from ECS, 23 September 1874, and from SBA, 2 October 1874, explain Martha Wright's reference in document 43 (3 October 1874) to a search for a missing letter: John Hooker hoped to retrieve his wife's letter to the National Woman Suffrage Association in 1872 because it contained a paragraph praising Victoria Woodhull's contributions to the suffrage movement. At least two of the new letters should be in this volume: ECS to John Hooker, 8 January 1875, and SBA to John Hooker, 20 January 1875, both of them affirming that Elizabeth Tilton had confessed her adultery to SBA.

---

[15] See document 167 within.

# ⚜ EDITORIAL PRACTICE

## PRINCIPLES OF SELECTION

This volume selects roughly ten percent of the documents available for the period of time from October 1873 to September 1880. Documents are printed in their entirety with two exceptions: entries from diaries are selected from the larger document; ECS's and SBA's contributions to meetings and pertinent discussion by other participants are excerpted from the fullest coverage available.

The high cost of producing and publishing historical editions creates an editorial imperative to bulldoze most of the trees while leaving an attractive and useful forest in place. The selection of documents to include in each volume often boils down to arbitrary choices between equally valuable items. There are, however, guidelines. Selection is governed first by the mission to document the careers of the two co-workers. Drawn from the papers of two people, the selections must next represent differences in the documentation of each one. Although writings by ECS and SBA have priority, incoming mail is included if it documents the other voice in longstanding friendships with ECS or SBA or supplies unusual evidence about their lives. The dominant stories evident in the documents of any year or era are also retained. For this volume additional decisions were made. 1) Entries from SBA's diaries were included when they provided unique perspective on her experience or best captured the pace of her daily life. 2) Speeches were assigned a higher priority in this volume than in previous ones because lecturing was the primary activity of ECS and SBA in this period. A relative scarcity of letters made it possible to devote more space to their speeches. The selections make available authoritative texts of important speeches and document significant contributions by ECS and SBA to the public debate over woman's rights. 3) A few of the National Woman Suffrage Association's petitions and memorials to Congress were included for narrative purposes even if their authorship is unclear. 4) The inclusion in this volume of one discussion where people other than ECS and SBA participate reflects the editors' conviction that in the battle of ideas waged by these women, exchanges with opponents and allies give critical evidence about political style, intellectual influences, and differences of opinion that the principals might otherwise have failed to mention.

A considerable "selection" of documents for the years of this volume occurred long before the editors began their work. With the deaths of Gerrit Smith (1874), Ann Fitzhugh Smith (1875), and Martha Coffin Wright (1875), all of whom had retained the letters they received, major sources of the letters of ECS and SBA came to an end. Another source dried up when Isabella Beecher Hooker pulled back from political life and set off for Europe in the spring of 1874. No one who took their places as friends and co-workers met the same standard of archival excellence. In addition, SBA's diaries for 1875, 1879, and 1880 are lost. There also exists an unexplained surge of copies of ECS's letters to family members in 1879 and 1880 from which the editors made a representative selection. Typed for her children from manuscripts that no longer exist, these frequent letters about life on the lecture circuit and at home are a tantalizing reminder that scores of similar letters were written in other years and lost.

## ARRANGEMENT

Documents are presented in chronological order according to the date of authorship, oral delivery, or publication of the original text. Documents dated only by month appear at the start of the month unless the context in surrounding documents dictates later placement. Documents that cover a period of time, such as diaries, are placed at the date of the earliest entry, and the longer text is interrupted for the placement of other documents that fall within the same period of time.

If a diary entry appears on the same date as another document, it is assumed that the entry was written at day's end. When two or more documents possess the same date, ECS and SBA authorship takes precedence over incoming mail, and SBA's papers appear before those of ECS unless the context dictates otherwise.

## SELECTION OF TEXT

Most documents in this edition survive in a single version. When choices were required, original manuscripts took precedence over later copies, and the recipient's copy of correspondence was used. A speech reported by a stenographer, however, took precedence over the manuscript. The newspaper to which SBA or ECS submitted a text took precedence over newspapers that reprinted it.

When letters survive only in transcripts made by editors and biographers, the earliest transcript was used as the source text. Typescripts by Harriot Stanton Blatch and Theodore Stanton took precedence over their published texts; considerable rewriting occurred between the two. Occasionally the editors created a composite text from two imperfect transcripts of the same missing original. The two sources of such a text are both indicated in the endnote, separated by a semicolon, and textual additions from the second source are set off by angle brackets.

For the text of meetings and other oral events, the official report, or in its absence, the most comprehensive coverage, is the primary source text. If reports differ widely, composite reports were created. Additions to or substitutions from a second source are set off by angle brackets. The sources are separated by a semicolon in the endnote.

The goal with speeches is to publish a text as close as possible to the version delivered at a particular date, but how to achieve that varies in nearly every case, depending on what has survived. A stenographic report of a speech is usually regarded as the most authoritative text. Two speeches in this volume (11 January 1878 and 24 January 1880) are based upon a stenographer's transcript of his notes, although, as explained at the date, the evidence on the 1878 speech is contradictory. The vast majority of the speeches are based on a local reporter's own notes. In the case of lectures delivered over and over again, the editors looked for the best—the most inclusive and comprehending—of those reports. The reports in newspapers of three major speeches (25 February 1874, 12 April 1875, and 11 May 1879) are so extensive that it seems likely the press relied on a manuscript supplied by the speaker, but no evidence of that practice has been found in these instances. ECS herself selected the newspaper report of her speech in May 1879 as a definitive text for her files and marked corrections on the clipping. In two cases in this volume (11 May 1875 and Winter 1880), the speaker's manuscript is the only text of the speech available.

## FORMAT

Some features of the documents have been standardized when set into print. The indentation of existing paragraphs was consistently set. The dateline of each letter appears as the first line of text, flush to the right margin, regardless of its placement in the original. The salutation of letters was printed on one line, flush left. Extra space in the dateline or salutation indicates the author's line break. The complimentary close of letters was run into the text itself, regardless of how the author laid it out, and signatures were placed at the right margin beneath the text. The dash is uniformly rendered even though the lengths vary in the originals.

Each document is introduced by an editorial heading or title that connects the document to ECS or SBA, except in cases of meetings at which both women participated and texts to which they both contributed.

Following the text, an unnumbered endnote describes the physical character of the document and the source or owner of the original. The endnote also identifies variants of the text, explicates unusual physical properties of the document, and explains the uses made of square brackets in the transcription. In the case of diary entries, this note appears at the end of the series. Numbered notes follow the endnote, except that numbered notes for diary entries follow each entry.

## TRANSCRIPTION

The editors strive to prepare for print the most accurate transcription that reproduces the format of the original as nearly as possible. However, the greater the remove from the author, the less literal is the representation.

LETTERS AND DIARIES. The editors retained the author's punctuation, including the absence of customary symbols; emphasis by underlining, although not occasional use of double or triple underlines; spelling and capitalization; abbreviations; superscripts; and paragraphing, or its absence. The author's form of dating was retained. Opening or closing quotation marks have been supplied in square brackets when the author neglected to enter them.

Emendations in the original text are marked by symbols to show cancelled text, interlineations, and other corrections and additions. A minimum number of exceptions were allowed when the interlineation obviously resulted from slip of the pen or thought, as when an infinitive was clearly intended but the "to" was added above the line. Strike outs and other erasures are indicated with a line through the text. Interlineations, above or below the line, are framed in up and down arrows. Text from the margin is moved into place with an editorial notation about the original location.

SBA's dashes can usually be distinguished as pauses or full stops, and the distinction is represented by spacing. The em-dash is flush to the words on either side in a pause; extra space is added after the dash at a full stop. SBA made no visible distinction when capitalizing letters "a," "m," and "w," and in haste, often lost the distinction for other letters. When her customary practice could not be found, the editors resorted to standard usage. Haste also affected SBA's ending syllables. Her rendition of "evening" became "evenng" and then something resembling "even$^g$." A similar evolution occurred with the "ly" ending. These compressions and contractions were ignored and the invisible letters supplied.

When SBA kept her diary in commercial appointment books, the printed date is set in capitals and small capitals to distinguish it from her entry.

ECS's letters contain a form of implied punctuation; if a comma or period were required and she had reached the right margin of her paper, she omitted the punctuation. Rather than supplying what she left out, extra space was introduced into the text, larger for a full stop.

SPEECHES. Two of the speeches by ECS in this volume survive only in manuscript. In order to preserve two very different kinds of evidence in these documents, indications of revisions, underlinings, and symbols were moved out of the text into textual notes. This practice allows experts concerned with composition and inscription to recover the writing process, while permitting the general reader to "hear" the speech. Despite the condition of their manuscripts, speakers introduce the necessary punctuation, pronounce the misspelled word, sound emphasis, place interlineations, omit strike outs, and expand abbreviations. In the textual notes, the alterations are listed by paragraph and line numbers, referenced to paragraph numbers printed beside the text. The textual notes employ the same editorial symbols in use elsewhere.

PRINTED TEXTS. In printed texts, obvious typographical errors have been silently corrected. When new words were substituted, the original wording was recorded in a numbered note. The original titles of articles and appeals were retained as part of the text. The practice of typesetters to use small capitals for emphasis and for highlighting the names of speakers has been ignored. To preserve the emphasis, italics have been substituted.

## ANNOTATION

In numbered notes, the editors provide the information they think necessary for readers to understand the document. In occasional editorial notes placed between documents, the editors explain events absent from the extant papers. Editorial notes placed either beneath a document's heading or interjected in the transcription provide context for texts excerpted from reports of a meeting.

To incomplete place and datelines, the editors have added, in italic type within square brackets, the best information available to complete the line. The basis for supplying a date is explained in a note.

The numbered notes principally identify references in the text, explain textual complexities, and summarize documents omitted from the edition. People are identified at the first occurrence of their names in the documents. The editors have tried to identify every person and reference, but they have not added notes simply to say "unidentified" or "not located." Biographical notes about people identified in previous volumes of this series do not recapitulate earlier information; if previous volumes contain useful references to the individual, readers are directed to them.

Documents published in this volume may be found at their date in the microfilm edition of the *Papers of Stanton and Anthony*. A citation to the film (as *Film*, reel number:frame numbers) appears in the endnote only if the document is filmed at a different date. *Film* citations are included for documents mentioned within the numbered notes.

## TEXTUAL DEVICES

[roman text]     Text within square brackets in roman type is identified in the unnumbered endnote.

| | |
|---|---|
| [roman text?] | The question mark indicates that the editors are uncertain about the text within the square brackets. |
| [roman date] | Date when a speech was delivered or an article published. |
| [*italic text*] | Editorial insertion or addition. |
| [*italic date*] | Date supplied by editors. In most cases, the basis is explained in a numbered note. |
| ⸤text⸥ | Authorial interlineation or substitution. |
| ~~text~~ | Text cancelled by the author. |
| *~~illegible~~* | Text cancelled by author that cannot be recovered. |
| \<roman\> | Addition to the source text from a second source. |

# ⚞ Abbreviations

Throughout the volume Elizabeth Cady Stanton is referred to as ECS and Susan B. Anthony as SBA.

In notes only, the National Woman Suffrage Association is abbreviated as NWSA and the National-American Woman Suffrage Association as NAWSA.

## Abbreviations Used to Describe Documents

AL   ⚞   Autograph Letter
ALS  ⚞   Autograph Letter Signed
AMs  ⚞   Autograph Manuscript
Hw   ⚞   Handwritten

## Standard References, Newspapers, and Journals

*ACAB*  ⚞   James Grant Wilson and John Fiske, eds., *Appletons' Cyclopaedia of American Biography*, 6 vols. (New York, 1886–1889)

Allibone  ⚞   Samuel Austin Allibone, *A Critical Dictionary of English Literature and British and American Authors*, 3 vols. (Philadelphia, 1854–1871)

Allibone Supplement  ⚞   John Foster Kirk, *A Supplement to Allibone's Critical Dictionary of English Literature and British and American Authors*, 2 vols. (Philadelphia, 1891)

*American Women*  ⚞   Frances E. Willard, *American Women: Fifteen Hundred Biographies with over 1,400 Portraits*, 2 vols. (New York, 1897)

*ANB*  ⚞   John A. Garraty and Mark C. Carnes, eds., *American National Biography*, 24 vols. (New York, 1999)

*Anthony*  ⚞   Ida Husted Harper, *Life and Work of Susan B. Anthony*, 3 vols. (1898–1908; reprint, New York, 1969)

*Appleton's Annual Cyclopaedia* ≪ *The American Annual Cyclopaedia and Register of Important Events of the Year 1870, 1871* (New York, 1872–1873)

*BDAC* ≪ *Biographical Dictionary of the American Congress, 1774–1971* (Washington, D.C., 1971)

Blatchford ≪ Samuel Blatchford, *Reports of Cases Argued and Determined in the Circuit Court of the United States for the Second Circuit*, 24 vols. (Auburn, N.Y., 1852–1888)

*BDAmerEd* ≪ John F. Ohles, ed., *Biographical Dictionary of American Educators*, 3 vols. (Westport, Conn., 1978)

*BDTerrGov* ≪ Thomas A. McMullin and David Walker, *Biographical Directory of American Territorial Governors* (Westport, Conn., 1984)

California Reports ≪ *Reports of Cases Determined in the Supreme Court of the State of California*, 220 vols. (San Francisco, 1852–1934)

*Compendium of the Ninth Census* ≪ Francis A. Walker, *A Compendium of the Ninth Census (June 1, 1870,) Compiled Pursuant to a Concurrent Resolution of Congress* (Washington, D.C., 1872)

*Compendium of the Tenth Census* ≪ U.S. Census Office, *Compendium of the Tenth Census (June 1, 1880,) Compiled Pursuant to an Act of Congress Approved August 7, 1882* (Washington, D.C., 1883)

Connecticut Reports ≪ *Connecticut Reports. Cases Argued and Determined in the Supreme Court of Errors of the State of Connecticut*, 150 vols. (Hartford, Conn., 1817–1966)

Court of Claims Reports ≪ *Cases Decided in the Court of Claims . . . and the Decisions of the Supreme Court in Appealed Cases*, 231 vols. (Washington, D.C., 1867–1983)

*DAB* ≪ Allen Johnson and Dumas Malone, eds., *Dictionary of American Biography*, 20 vols. (New York, 1928–1936)

*DANB* ≪ Rayford W. Logan and Michael R. Winston, eds., *Dictionary of American Negro Biography* (New York, 1982)

*DNB* ≪ Leslie Stephen and Sidney Lee, eds., *The Dictionary of National Biography*, 22 vols. (1885–1901; reprint, London, 1973)

*Dictionary of Wisconsin Biography* ≪ *Dictionary of Wisconsin Biography* (Madison, Wis., 1960)

Douglass, *Papers* ⇜ Frederick Douglass, *The Frederick Douglass Papers. Series One: Speeches, Debates, and Interviews*, ed. John W. Blassingame et al., 5 vols. (New Haven, 1979–1992)

*Eighty Years* ⇜ Elizabeth Cady Stanton, *Eighty Years and More: Reminiscences, 1815–1897* (1898; reprint, Boston, 1993)

Federal Cases ⇜ *The Federal Cases: Comprising Cases Argued and Determined in the Circuit and District Courts of the United States* . . . , 31 vols. (St. Paul, Minn., 1894–1898)

*Film* ⇜ Patricia G. Holland and Ann D. Gordon, eds., *Papers of Elizabeth Cady Stanton and Susan B. Anthony* (Wilmington, Del., 1991, microfilm)

Garrison, *Letters* ⇜ William Lloyd Garrison, *The Letters of William Lloyd Garrison*, ed. Walter M. Merrill and Louis Ruchames, 6 vols. (Cambridge, Mass., 1971–1981)

Hill's Reports ⇜ Nicholas Hill, *Reports of Cases Argued and Determined in the Supreme Court of the State of New York*, 7 vols. (Albany, 1842–1847)

*History* ⇜ Elizabeth Cady Stanton, Susan B. Anthony, Matilda Joslyn Gage et al., *History of Woman Suffrage*, 6 vols. (vols. 1–3, New York, 1881–1885; vol. 4, Rochester, 1902; vols. 5–6, New York, 1922)

Howard ⇜ Benjamin C. Howard, *Reports, Supreme Court, United States, 1843–60*, 24 vols. (Philadelphia, 1852–1861)

Howard's Practice Reports ⇜ Nathan Howard, *Practice Reports in the Supreme Court and Court of Appeals of the State of New York*, 67 vols. (Albany, 1845–1884)

Iowa Reports ⇜ *Reports of Cases in Law and Equity Determined in the Supreme Court of the State of Iowa*, 261 vols. (Davenport, Iowa, 1860–1970)

McPherson, *Hand-Book of Politics* ⇜ Edward McPherson, *A Hand-Book of Politics for 1874, 1876, 1878, 1880* (Washington, D.C., 1874–1880)

Massachusetts Reports ⇜ Horace Gray, Jr., *Reports of Cases Argued and Determined in the Supreme Judicial Court of Massachusetts*, 16 vols. (Boston, 1855–1871)

*Michigan Biographies* ⇜ *Michigan Biographies: Including Members of*

Congress, Elective State Officers, Justices of the Supreme Court, Members of the Michigan Legislature, 2 vols. (Lansing, Mich., 1924)

Michigan Reports ⚞ *Michigan Reports: Reports of Cases Heard and Decided in the Supreme Court of Michigan*, 14 vols. (Detroit, 1858–)

Mill, *Collected Works* ⚞ John Stuart Mill, *Collected Works of John Stuart Mill*, ed. J. M. Robson, 33 vols. (Toronto, Canada, 1963–1991)

Missouri Reports ⚞ *Reports of Cases Argued and Decided in the Supreme Court of the State of Missouri*, 98 vols. (St. Louis, 1835–1890)

*National Party Platforms* ⚞ Kirk H. Porter and Donald Bruce Johnson, eds., *National Party Platforms, 1840–1968* (Urbana, Ill., 1970)

*NAW* ⚞ Edward T. James, Janet Wilson James, and Paul S. Boyer, eds., *Notable American Women, 1607–1950: A Biographical Dictionary*, 3 vols. (Cambridge, Mass., 1971)

*NCAB* ⚞ *National Cyclopaedia of American Biography*, 63 vols. (New York, 1891–1984)

*NCBB* ⚞ *National Citizen and Ballot Box* (Syracuse, N.Y.)

*Papers* ⚞ Ann D. Gordon, ed., *Selected Papers of Elizabeth Cady Stanton and Susan B. Anthony*, vol. 1, *In the School of Anti-Slavery, 1840 to 1866* (New Brunswick, N.J., 1997); vol. 2, *Against an Aristocracy of Sex, 1866 to 1873* (New Brunswick, N.J., 2000)

*Past and Promise: Lives of New Jersey Women* ⚞ Women's Project of New Jersey, *Past and Promise: Lives of New Jersey Women* (Metuchen, N.J., 1990)

Peters ⚞ Richard Peters, *Reports of Cases Argued and Determined in the Supreme Court of the United States*, 17 vols. (Washington, D.C., 1828–1842)

Philadelphia Reports ⚞ Henry E. Wallace, *Philadelphia Reports*, 20 vols. (Philadelphia, 1856–1893)

*PMHB* ⚞ *Pennsylvania Magazine of History and Biography*

*Quaker Genealogy* ⚞ William Wade Hinshaw, *Encyclopedia of American Quaker Genealogy*, 3 vols. (Ann Arbor, Mich., 1936–1940)

*Register of Federal Officers* ⚞ *Register of Officers and Agents, Civil, Military, and Naval, in the Service of the United States . . .* (Washington, D.C., 1874–1883)

*RSSNY, 1852*  ⇜  *The Revised Statutes of the State of New-York, as Altered by Subsequent Legislation; . . . Prepared by Hiram Denio and William Tracy,* 2 vols. (Albany, 1852)

*Rev.*  ⇜  *Revolution* (New York)

*SEAP*  ⇜  Ernest H. Cherrington, ed., *Standard Encyclopedia of the Alcohol Problem,* 6 vols. (Westerville, Ohio, 1925–1930)

*Stanton*  ⇜  Theodore Stanton and Harriot Stanton Blatch, eds., *Elizabeth Cady Stanton, as Revealed in Her Letters, Diary and Reminiscences,* 2 vols. (1922; reprint, New York, 1969)

*Statistics of Population, Tenth Census*  ⇜  U.S. Census Office, *Statistics of the Population of the United States at the Tenth Census (June 1, 1880), Embracing Tables of the Population of States, Counties, and Minor Civil Divisions, with Distinction of Race, Sex, Age, Nativity, and Occupations* (Washington, D.C., 1883)

Sumner, *Works*  ⇜  Charles Sumner, *The Works of Charles Sumner,* 15 vols. (Boston, 1870–1883)

*Temperance and Prohibition Papers*  ⇜  *The Temperance and Prohibition Papers, Microfilm Edition,* eds. Randall C. Jimerson and Francis X. Blouin (Ann Arbor, Mich., 1977)

*Tribune Almanac*  ⇜  *The Tribune Almanac and Political Register for 1875* (New York, 1875)

*TroyFS*  ⇜  Mrs. A. W. Fairbanks, ed., *Emma Willard and Her Pupils, or Fifty Years of Troy Female Seminary, 1822–1872* (New York, 1898)

United States Reports  ⇜  *United States Reports, Supreme Court: Cases Argued and Adjudged in the Supreme Court of the United States,* 17 vols. (Boston, 1876–1883)

Wallace  ⇜  John William Wallace, *Cases Argued and Adjudged in the Supreme Court of the United States,* 23 vols. (Washington, D.C., 1866–1876)

Wisconsin Reports  ⇜  *Reports of Cases Argued and Determined in the Supreme Court of the State of Wisconsin,* 1st ser., 275 vols. (Chicago, 1853–1857)

*Woman's Who's Who 1914*  ⇜  John William Leonard, ed., *Woman's Who's Who of America, 1914–1915* (1914; reprint, Detroit, Mich., 1976)

*Woman's Bible* ✎ Elizabeth Cady Stanton, *The Woman's Bible* (1895–1898; reprint, Boston, 1993)

*Women Building Chicago* ✎ Rima Lunin Schultz and Adele Hast, eds., *Women Building Chicago, 1790–1990: A Biographical Dictionary* (Bloomington, Ind., 2001)

*WWWH* ✎ *Who Was Who in America, Historical Volume, 1607–1896,* rev. ed. (Chicago, 1867)

*WWW1* ✎ *Who Was Who in America,* vol. 1, *1897–1942* (Chicago, 1942)

*WWW2* ✎ *Who Was Who in America,* vol. 2, *1843–1950* (Chicago, 1950)

*WWW4* ✎ *Who Was Who in America,* vol. 4, *1961–1968* (Chicago, 1968)

## Archives and Repositories

CSmH ✎ Henry E. Huntington Library, San Marino, Calif.

CU-BANC ✎ Bancroft Library, University of California, Berkeley, Calif.

CtHSD ✎ Harriet Beecher Stowe Center, Hartford, Conn.

CtY ✎ Yale University Libraries, New Haven, Conn.

DLC ✎ Library of Congress, Manuscript Division (unless otherwise noted), Washington, D.C.

DNA ✎ National Archives and Records Service, Washington, D.C.

DSI ✎ Smithsonian Institution, Washington, D.C.

ICHi ✎ Chicago Historical Society, Chicago, Ill.

IEN ✎ Northwestern University Library, Special Collections, Evanston, Ill.

IEWT ✎ National Woman's Christian Temperance Union, Evanston, Ill.

IaAS ✎ Iowa State University, Ames, Iowa

KHi ✎ Kansas State Historical Society, Topeka, Kan.

KyLoF ✎ Filson Historical Society, Louisville, Ky.

MB ✎ Boston Public Library, Boston, Mass.

MCR-S ✎ Schlesinger Library, Radcliffe Institute, Harvard University, Cambridge, Mass.

MHi ✎ Massachusetts Historical Society, Boston, Mass.

MNS-S ⇜ Sophia Smith Collection, Smith College, Northampton, Mass.

MNtcA ⇜ Andover Newton Theological School, Newton Centre, Mass.

MWiW ⇜ Williams College, Williamstown, Mass.

Mi ⇜ Michigan State Library, Lansing, Mich.

MiU-H ⇜ Bentley Historical Library, University of Michigan, Ann Arbor, Mich.

NjP ⇜ Princeton University Library, Princeton, N.J.

NjPT ⇜ Princeton Theological Seminary, Princeton, N.J.

NjR ⇜ Rutgers University Libraries, New Brunswick, N.J.

NHi ⇜ New-York Historical Society, New York, N.Y.

NIC ⇜ Cornell University Library, Ithaca, N.Y.

NJost ⇜ Johnstown Public Library, Johnstown, N.Y.

NN ⇜ New York Public Library, Astor, Lenox and Tilden Foundations, New York, N.Y.

NPV ⇜ Vassar College Library, Poughkeepsie, N.Y.

NSyU ⇜ Syracuse University Libraries, Syracuse, N.Y.

NWattJHi ⇜ Jefferson County Historical Society, Watertown, N.Y.

NWefHi ⇜ Chautauqua County Historical Society, Westfield, N.Y.

OFH ⇜ Rutherford B. Hayes Presidential Center, Fremont, Ohio

OHi ⇜ Ohio Historical Society, Columbus, Ohio

OT ⇜ Toledo-Lucas County Public Library, Toledo, Ohio

PHC ⇜ Haverford College Library, Haverford, Pa.

PHi ⇜ Historical Society of Pennsylvania, Philadelphia, Pa.

PSC-Hi ⇜ Friends Historical Library of Swarthmore College, Swarthmore, Pa.

PU ⇜ University of Pennsylvania, Philadelphia, Pa.

WBB ⇜ Beloit College, Beloit, Wis.

WHi ⇜ State Historical Society of Wisconsin, Madison, Wis.

## MANUSCRIPT COLLECTIONS

Anneke Papers, WHi   M. F. Anneke Papers, Archives Division

Blackwell Papers, DLC   Blackwell Family Papers

Blackwell Papers, MCR-S   Blackwell Family Papers

ECS Papers, NjR   E. C. Stanton Papers, T. Stanton Collection, Mabel Smith Douglass Library

Gage Collection, MCR-S   Matilda Joslyn Gage Collection

Garrison Papers, MNS-S   Garrison Family Papers

NAWSA Papers, DLC   National-American Woman Suffrage Association Papers

NWSA Collection, ICHi   National Woman Suffrage Association Collection

Papers of ECS, NPV   Papers of Elizabeth Cady Stanton

Rare Books, DLC   Rare Books Division

SBA Papers, DLC   Susan B. Anthony Papers

SBA Papers, MCR-S   Susan Brownell Anthony Papers

SBA Collection, MNS-S   Susan B. Anthony Collection

Smith Papers, NSyU   Gerrit Smith Papers, George Arents Research Library

# The Selected Papers of
## Elizabeth Cady Stanton and Susan B. Anthony

1  ↝    SBA to Isabella Beecher Hooker[1]

Rochester Oct. 13/73

Dear Mrs Hooker

I am so glad you have postponed your meeting to November—fix your own date—[2] I have not & probably shall not make any engagements for that month—as I mean to be at home to <u>vote</u> <u>the</u> <u>6th</u> <u>of Nov</u>—[3] I will tell you as I have sundry others—that my first sight of the <u>Call</u> for Women's Congress was last week[4]—& I dropped all & wrote Mrs Wilbour[5]—that if my ~~left~~ name was left out because it was not wanted all right so far as I was concerned, but if from any lack of mine, I made haste to say that I surely desired to be reckoned among those who ~~illegible~~ ↑wished↓ to do all in their power for the uplifting of all womanhood in all departments of life—and that I would like to have my honorary title—"President of the National W.S. Association" precisely as she gave the other women their official titles— and I hope you & Mrs Stanton, to whom I have written this fact, will not allow the impression to go <u>out</u> or <u>in</u> that I <u>refused</u> <u>my</u> <u>name</u>— I imagine it was the <u>incident</u> of my name beginning with the first letter of the alphabet which must have placed it too near the head— What could have been the cause?— Do you know— I have sometimes felt that <u>our</u> <u>Boston</u> friends[6] & <u>Mrs</u> <u>Wilbour</u> like them, try to persuade themselves that my prosecution verdict & sentence are a <u>disgrace</u>—and that they shrink from affiliation with an adjudged Criminal—[7] I do hope you can feel out, why it is that <u>you</u> & <u>Mrs Stanton</u>—the two <u>greatest</u> <u>Woodhull</u>[8] <u>sinners</u>, are <u>more</u> <u>respectable</u> than I.— Isn't it too rich—

My Sister[9] still lingers on this side—but is the saddest sufferer from utter weariness—no feeling of <u>rest</u> by day or by night, except from anodynes— She cannot hold out many days longer—nor ↑can↓ she or we hope that she may—for every added hour is only added suffering— This <u>slow</u> death is terrible— Affectionately yours

↝    *Susan B Anthony*

    ALS, Isabella Hooker Collection, CtHSD. Envelope addressed Care President Women's Congress, Union League Hall, New York.

1. Isabella Beecher Hooker (1822–1907), the youngest child in the family of Lyman Beecher, lived at Nook Farm in Hartford, Connecticut. She presided over the state suffrage association. In 1871 and 1872, working in conjunction with ECS and SBA, she founded and led the National Woman Suffrage and Educational Committee. When the National Woman Suffrage Association reorganized in 1872, she became vice president for Connecticut. (*NAW*; *ANB*; Jeanne Boydston, Mary Kelley, and Anne Margolis, *The Limits of Sisterhood: The Beecher Sisters on Women's Rights and Woman's Sphere* [Chapel Hill, N.C., 1988]. See also *Papers* 2.)

2 SBA attended the Connecticut Woman Suffrage Association's annual meeting on 11 December 1873. See *Film*, 17:433–41.

3. The Women Taxpayers' Association of Monroe County hoped that all three thousand taxpaying women in Rochester might be persuaded to vote in the November state election, but no organizer for the effort came forward. (SBA to I. B. Hooker, 12 September 1873, *Film*, 17:287–89.)

4. The call for a Woman's Congress, dated 25 September 1873, was signed by one hundred and fifty women who were prominent professionals and reformers but not by SBA. The Congress met in New York on 14 October to exchange ideas about women's experience and found the Association for the Advancement of Women. Even her old friend Antoinette Brown Blackwell interpreted the omission of SBA's name as a choice: "Why did you refuse to recognize the Congress?" she asked in December. A report from Mary Livermore by way of Isabella Hooker confirmed SBA's suspicions: "1$^{st}$ my name began with A. and must come at head of signers to call 2$^{d}$—They would have to give me my title—& that made recognize the <u>National</u> W.S. of which I am the President and 3$^{d}$—If they let me in, ~~they~~ I could not be managed—<u>too rich</u>—" (Call to Woman's Congress; A. B. Blackwell to SBA, 10 December 1873; SBA diary, 22–23 October 1873; all in *Film*, 16:617ff, 17:294–99, 429–32; Karen J. Blair, *The Clubwoman as Feminist: True Womanhood Redefined, 1868–1914* [New York, 1980], 39–46.)

5. Charlotte Beebe Wilbour (1833–1914) was president of the New York women's club Sorosis and chair of the local arrangements committee of the Woman's Congress. Although a suffragist herself, an officer of the New York City and County Woman Suffrage Society and the National association, Wilbour carried out plans for a meeting where suffrage would not be discussed. (*NCAB*, 13:370; *New York Times*, 26 December 1914; file on C. B. Wilbour, Sorosis Collection, MNS-S. See also *Papers* 1 & 2.)

6. A sarcastic reference to leaders of the Boston-based American Woman Suffrage Association, a rival of the National Woman Suffrage Association led by ECS and SBA.

7. In June 1873 SBA was convicted of the federal crime of knowingly voting without the right to do so. See *Papers* 2.

8. Victoria Claflin Woodhull (1838–1927) carried her crusade against sexual hypocrisy to new heights in October 1872, when her newspaper, *Woodhull and Claflin's Weekly*, published charges that Henry Ward Beecher had conducted an affair with his parishioner Elizabeth Tilton. She named both ECS and SBA as sources for her story, but SBA's refusal to speak publicly about the scandal insulated her from the outcry. ECS, on the other hand, confirmed Woodhull's account and continued to credit her for the National's strategy of claiming an existing right to vote under the Fourteenth and Fifteenth amendments. Isabella Hooker also befriended Woodhull. (*NAW*; *ANB*; Lois Beachy Underhill, *The Woman Who Ran for President: The Many Lives of Victoria Woodhull* [New York, 1995]; Mary Gabriel, *Notorious Victoria: The Life of Victoria Woodhull, Uncensored* [Chapel Hill, N.C., 1998]. See also *Papers* 2.)

9. Guelma Penn Anthony McLean (1818–1873) was dying of consumption. The eldest of the Anthony children, known in the family as Gula, she married a friend of her childhood, Aaron M. McLean, and moved to Rochester around 1860. Her house on Madison Street was home to her mother as well as to her sisters Mary and Susan. (Charles L. Anthony, comp., *Genealogy of the Anthony Family from 1495–1904* [Sterling, Ill., 1904], 173, 182; Baker Genealogical Ms., SBA Papers, MCR-S. See also *Papers* 1 & 2.)

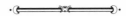

2 ~ ECS TO THEODORE W. STANTON

Tenafly, Tuesday evening, [*14? October*] 1873.

Dear Theodore:—

I have been waiting ever since the sad accident at Cornell to hear the particulars.[1] When death comes so near to us, we begin to feel some interest in philosophizing about what lies the other side. After life's brief, fitful struggle, what then? is a question that the wisest and best pause to answer. It will not be many years before, in the course of nature, your father and I will drop out of the ranks. Read Bryant's "Thanatopsis"; it is so grand and consoling in such an hour.[2] Only think of it, he wrote that poem at eighteen. With love and kisses, good night.

~ *Mother.*

~ Typed transcript, ECS Papers, NjR. Date on transcript reads "Autumn of 1873."

1. Theodore Stanton was a first-term senior at Cornell when a younger student, Mortimer Leggett, died in a hazing accident. On 16 October 1873, a

coroner's jury ruled it an accidental death. (Morris Bishop, *A History of Cornell* [Ithaca, N.Y., 1962], 132; *New York Times*, 14, 18 October 1873.)

2. In "Thanatopsis," William Cullen Bryant (1794–1878) offers assurance that in death we return to nature and connect with human history.

## 3 ⤳   SPEECH BY ECS TO THE WOMEN TAXPAYERS' ASSOCIATION IN ROCHESTER, NEW YORK

EDITORIAL NOTE: ECS addressed an evening meeting of the Women Taxpayers' Association of Monroe County at the city hall. Founded during SBA's trial in May 1873, the association identified and attempted to organize the county's taxpaying women to protest their taxation without representation. SBA stayed home from the meeting to nurse her sister.

[31 October 1873]

I am invited this evening to address the women tax-payers of Rochester, who I understand represent property in this city to the amount of nearly $7,000,000. Political economists have labored long and hard to discover some system of equitable taxation; but with all the shiftings of the burden on various classes and kinds of property, it is not yet scientifically adjusted. Sovereigns, nobles, priests and presidents, like boys tossing bean-bags in a gymnasium have played with these onerous burdens, each in turn throwing the weights from their own shoulders, on those of their less privileged neighbor. The old definition of taxation, was that portion of property exacted by the state for "public necessities" but in these days of extravagance and corruption, credit mobilier scandals and salary-grabs,[1] the tax-payers have something more to meet than "public necessities." Such "necessities" as the Tweed's, the Sweeney's and the Connolly's[2] and your commission rings in Rochester[3] and other cities have imposed heavy burdens on the tax-paying women of the Empire state, and it is time they awake to the consideration of this question.

Webster[4] defines a tax, as "a sum of money assessed on the person or property of a citizen by government for the use of the nation or state." Thus in taxing women the law pays them the compliment of recognizing in them the dignity of personality. They are "persons," "citizens," "property holders," hence enjoy the high privilege of contributing to the support of the state. Why they have no voice in deciding the rate of taxation, or who shall be tax collector, is the problem demanding solution of this age and generation.[5]

In ancient times public expenditures were drawn from the revenues of sovereigns, but when, through bad economy they found these insufficient, they demanded contributions from the nobility. The nobles, however, denied this right in a sovereign, and refused to grant the exaction. But the nobles seeing the necessity to increase the revenue in order to support the dignity of the state, or the sovereign being afraid to constrain them, they agreed to unite and lay the taxes on the people, who not belonging to the privileged orders, from want of union and power, would be obliged to yield. And here and for this reason, to a greater or less degree, the load has rested ever since. In despotisms, monarchies and republics alike, directly and indirectly the weight of taxation rests on the shoulders of the laboring masses. In England there is a wayside inn called the "Four Alls." Some satirical painter who understood the situation placed the letters A.L.L. in the middle of the sign. A clergyman, representing the church, stands on one side pointing to the letters, saying: "I pray for all"; a soldier on the other side, representing the army, says: "I fight for all"; above sits the sovereign, pointing down saying: "I rule all"; while below, bearing up the whole sign on his stooping shoulders, bows the laborer, saying: "I pay for all." Verily is this true of the women as well as men, who help to do the work of the world. Go to the rice plantations and cotton fields, and there mothers toil their lives away. Their labors freight the merchant ships for foreign lands, that bring back gold. On western prairies, too, they gather in the harvests that feed the world and watch the cattle on a thousand hills. In New England factories they work all day, with nimble fingers and keen eyes they keep time, time, with shaft, and wheel, and bar, racing with unseen powers as inexorable as death itself. In the garrets of your cities they stitch, stitch, stitch their own winding sheets. With weary brains and sad hearts they have taught presidents, senators, congressmen, our lawyers, doctors, clergymen; professors in our schools for near a century on half pay; and yet the theory is, man feeds, and clothes, and shelters woman and is her protector everywhere. Hence he pays her taxes and does her voting. "Women are our privileged class," says a recent writer. Is this true in either fact or theory? I have heard of a privileged order of "Indians not taxed" mentioned in our state and federal constitutions.[6] I have heard of a privileged order of colored men, who could vote if worth $250, and if not possessed of that sum, were not taxed.[7] I have heard of a privileged order of clergymen, $1,500 of whose property was exempt from taxation;[8] but there is no mention in any code or constitution of this fortunate type of womanhood.

In the late presidential campaign, in many of his speeches, Horace Greeley[9] dwelt on the injustice of taxation without representation. In a speech in Columbus he said: "There are many thousands in the single state of Arkansas, who being property holders and citizens, responsible, intelligent men, are forbidden to vote and hold office, while men without a penny vote away their property and bury it under enormous public debts. We think this a grievous wrong, and a wrong that ought now to be amended." I quote this to show how keenly men appreciate the degradation of "taxation without representation" for their own sex. And yet the condition of this 20,000 southern men is precisely the condition of 20,000 women in the Empire state. We, too, are citizens, responsible, intelligent, and are forbidden to vote and hold office, while men without a penny vote away our property and bury it under enormous public debts. Is it worse to disfranchise 20,000 southern men, who in the late war sought to destroy our institutions, than 20,000 loyal northern women, who gave their wealth, their husbands, brothers, sons, to save the republic? Who watched our boys in blue in hospitals, and on the battlefield, held their dying heads through the lonely watches of the night, death and carnage on every side, the cold stars only to keep them company? Are women outlaws, beneath common justice and sympathy, that no man e'er thinks to apply to them the well-established rules of equity? It is vain to press great principles of jurisprudence, constitutional law or the theory of our government, so long as political charlatans proclaim that woman knows nothing of war or glory, of justice or mercy, of freedom or equality. While the women tax-payers of Rochester listen to the echoes of '76, let them learn in all humility that the grand declarations that went booming at the mouth of the cannon 'round the world were never intended for woman's ears. "Taxation without representation is tyranny," said the grand old heroes who laid the corner stone of this republic. That was the theme for many a hot debate in the parliament of the old world, and for many an eloquent oration in the forests of the new; the theme for all our Fourth of July orations, running down through the century, inscribed on all our flags and banners, until every man and woman, boy and girl in the nation should know that "taxation without representation is tyranny."

The women of '76 who helped to fan the fires of our revolution understood these principles as well as the men by their side. James Otis[10] was indebted to his sister, Mercy Otis Warren, for many of the ideas he gave the world. Matilda Joslyn Gage[11] in a short speech said: "In 1770, six years before the declaration of independence, the women of New England made a public combined protest against taxation without representation and entered into a league. This league was formed by the married women, but the young ladies soon held an anti-tax meeting and declared publicly that they did not take this step for themselves alone, but they protested against 'taxation without representation' as a matter of principle and for the benefit of posterity." These protests were the real origin of the famous tea party in Boston harbor—a tea party generally supposed to have been inspired and conducted by men alone. Lord Coke,[12] who is good authority on this question, says "taxes cannot be laid on the people without their consent." The very act of taxing a man's property without his consent is in effect disfranchising him of every civil right, and this is woman's condition today, in denying her the right to protect her own person and property by law. She is in effect disfranchised of every civil right, for what one right is worth a rush if my inheritance, my earnings, my daily bread, may be taken from me by any privileged order, without my consent, and at their pleasure. Ah! says one, we have no "privileged orders" here, the genius of our government is opposed to all feudalism, all discriminations among citizens, all privileged orders. But what avails liberal theories, our federal constitution, our grand declaration of human freedom and equality, if with our faces to the dead past we interpret all in harmony with the customs of feudal times.

The only title to nobility there is in this country is the right of suffrage,—the ballot the only scepter of royalty. In crowning all men with this dignity, denying it to all women, we have established here the most odious form of aristocracy the world has ever seen—an aristocracy of sex, that exalts vice and ignorance, above virtue and intelligence, the unwashed, unlettered foreigner, who knows nothing of the grandeur of our free institutions, just landed on our shores, above the thousands of educated women in our public schools, who have taught American history and the United States constitution for near a century, an aristocracy that exalts brute force above moral power, the son above the mother who bore him and makes the inalienable rights of woman-hood footballs for the press, the pulpit, the bar and the bench, and for every sentimental talker and scribbler, that wants to boast his superiority to something lower down in the scale of being than he imagines himself, and this aristocracy of ours is not an imaginary line, but we can trace its legitimate results in every department of life.

First. You see it in the comparative advantages for the education of the sexes.[13] Take New York for example. We have in this state sixteen colleges and universities for boys, with 200 professors, and property to the amount of $15,000,000, besides large grants of land yearly increasing in value. Some of these colleges, founded very early in the century, have, from time to time, had large appropriations from the state, as well as generous bequests from men and women.

On the other hand, from the first settlement of the state, down to within a few years, there have been no colleges for women. There are now four—Ingham university, Elmira, Rutger and Vassar colleges,[14] and, by the gift of Henry W. Sage,[15] Cornell is now opened. Rutger has no endowment. The funds of the other three, as appears from reports to the regents,[16] amounts to about $100,000; their buildings, apparatus &c. to about $1,000,000. More than half of this is credited to Vassar college, the munificent donation of Matthew Vassar,[17] who, in thus inaugurating the greatest movement of the age, built to himself a monument more enduring than any granite or marble shafts that keep their silent watch among the dead. They only who do great deeds for the living are immortal, howe'er magnificent the tomb that marks their resting place. In considering how much has been done for men, and how little for women in this matter of education, we can fairly estimate their comparative value in popular thought, $15,000,000 against $1,100,000. And one aggravating feature of this is that women themselves have been taxed, directly and indirectly, to build and endow these colleges, while all their advantages are denied to them.

A still more aggravating and humiliating fact is that women of wealth all over this land are making bequests to institutions for boys, to the entire neglect of their own sex.

| | |
|---|---:|
| Miss Plummer gave to Cambridge university[18] | $25,000 |
| Mary Townsend to the same | 25,000 |
| Sarah Jackson to the same | 25,000 |
| Other women in sums of $1,000 | 30,000 |
| Mrs. Brown of Baltimore, to Princeton[19] | 30,000 |
| Another woman to Andover theological school[20] | 30,000 |
| Other ladies in various sums | 35,000 |
| Mrs. Garretson to a college or professional school in Illinois[21] | 300,000 |
| Mrs. Dudley of Albany to a scientific institution for men[22] | 105,000 |
| To Beloit college in Wisconsin property has been given by one lady valued at[23] | 30,000 |

And there are many more that I cannot now recall. But here we have one half a million given by women for the education of boys, showing that women themselves regard the education of boys of far more importance than their own sex.

We have heard of no bequests to Vassar or Cornell from women of wealth, and yet we are told that the mission of wives and mothers is the highest and noblest on the earth. If so, the highest, broadest, most liberal education for girls is of the first importance. Now what is the secret of this? It is plain women do not belong to the privileged order. They are a disfranchised class. Patriotism is the highest virtue, government the most exalted science; hence they whose feelings, sentiments and affections are to rise above self and family and subordinate all personal interests to the higher good of all; they who are to study political economy, jurisprudence, constitutional law, international rights and duties, the trade and commerce of the world; they who are to make and administer the laws and construct our social life, systems of education, religion and government; their education must be of primal importance. When women are a political power their education will be of equal importance with the men by their side, and never can be until then. The moment the black man was enfranchised all saw the importance of his education.

⤳ Rochester *Democrat and Chronicle*, 1 November 1873.

1. ECS names two of many corruption scandals holding national attention. In the first, the Union Pacific Railroad was charged with corrupting Congress by distributing stock to members and with pocketing the public monies for railroad construction through a cozy relationship with its fiscal agency the Crédit Mobilier of America. In the second, the Forty-second Congress closed its final session by passing a salary bill that raised congressional salaries retroactively.

2. These three Tammany Democrats—William Magear Tweed, Peter Barr Sweeny, and Richard Barrett Connolly—were principals in the Tweed Ring, the political machine that controlled New York city and county government until their corrupt practices were exposed in 1871. Tweed (1823-1878), who served on the city's board of supervisors and as a deputy street commissioner, was the party boss. Sweeny (1825-1911) was the city's treasurer. Connolly (c. 1810-1880) was the city's comptroller. (*ANB*; *New York Times*, 1 June 1880.)

3. In Rochester corruption charges focused on commissions appointed by the mayor and given authority to issue bonds for the construction of public works. (Blake McKelvey, *Rochester: The Flower City, 1850-1890* [Cambridge, Mass., 1949], 134-35, 153-59.)

4. Noah Webster (1758-1843), an American lexicographer, published *An American Dictionary of the English Language* in 1828.

5. On resistance to taxation, see Carolyn C. Jones, "Dollars and Selves: Women's Tax Criticism and Resistance in the 1870s," *University of Illinois Law Review* (1994): 265-309; and Linda K. Kerber, *No Constitutional Right to be Ladies: Women and the Obligations of Citizenship* (New York, 1998), 81-123.

6. See U.S. Const., art. I, sec. 2, and New York Const., 1846, art. III, sec. 4.

7. New York's constitution, article II, section 1, still contained language adopted in 1846 requiring that men "of color," in order to qualify to vote, must possess property worth two hundred and fifty dollars. It also stated that "no person of color shall be subject to taxation unless he shall be seized and possessed of such real estate." An amendment removing this discriminatory clause was adopted by the voters in November 1874.

8. *RSSNY, 1852*, 1:715.

9. Horace Greeley (1811-1872), editor of the *New York Tribune*, ran for president as the candidate of both the Liberal Republican and Democratic parties in 1872. ECS quotes a speech he delivered in Ohio during the campaign in which he opposed the disfranchisement of southern rebels. (*ANB*; *New York Times*, 25 September 1872. See also *Papers* 1 & 2.)

10. James Otis (1725-1783), a Boston revolutionary, and Mercy Otis Warren (1728-1814), a poet and political satirist.

11. Matilda Joslyn Gage (1826-1898) of Fayetteville, New York, who accompanied ECS to this meeting, chaired the executive committee of the National Woman Suffrage Association. ECS quotes her speech "The United States on Trial; *Not* Susan B. Anthony," delivered dozens of times in 1873, in advance

of SBA's trial for illegal voting. (*NAW*; *ANB*; *An Account of the Proceedings on the Trial of Susan B. Anthony*, p. 182, in *Film*, 17:103ff. See also *Papers* 1 & 2.)

12. Sir Edward Coke (1552–1634) was an English jurist. In fact, the words are from James Otis, *The Rights of the British Colonies Asserted and Proved* (1764), and ECS probably read them only as quoted by Charles Sumner in his 1866 speech, "Equal Rights of All," a speech on which she and SBA relied heavily for their histories of American political thought. Otis paraphrased Lord Coke. (Sumner, *Works*, 10:163.)

13. ECS presented this overview of education in New York in her speech "The Co-Education of the Sexes," delivered to the Woman's Congress on 17 October. See *Film*, 17:322–92.

14. These were Ingham University in LeRoy, founded in 1857; Elmira Female College in Elmira, founded in 1855; Vassar Female College in Poughkeepsie, founded in 1861; and Rutgers Female College in New York City, founded in 1867. ECS omitted Wells College in Aurora, founded in 1868.

15. Henry William Sage (1814–1897), a lumberman, made major donations to Cornell University, including money to open Sage College for women's education.

16. The Regents of the University of the State of New York incorporated and oversaw the state's private colleges. Their annual reports contain figures on college assets, but none could be found that match ECS's numbers.

17. Matthew Vassar (1792–1868), a brewer and banker, funded the college bearing his name.

18. That is, Harvard University. Caroline Plummer (?–1854), of Salem, Massachusetts, bequeathed twenty-five thousand dollars to endow the Plummer Professorship of Christian Morals, as a tribute to her brother. In 1861 Mary P. Townsend bequeathed five thousand dollars to the Divinity School and twenty thousand dollars to the college for scholarships for indigent students. Sarah Jackson's bequest in 1835 was to support students in the Divinity School. (Harvard University, *Endowment Funds of Harvard University, June 30, 1947* [Cambridge, Mass., 1948], 159, 212–15.)

19. Isabella McLanahan Brown (?–1885), the widow of a banker and mother-in-law of ECS's niece, gave thirty thousand dollars to Princeton Theological Seminary in 1863. (*Biographical Cyclopedia of Representative Men of Maryland and District of Columbia* [Baltimore, 1879], 74–75; Baltimore *Sun*, 23 July 1885, courtesy of Wesley Smith, Archives, NjPT).

20. Sophia Smith (1796–1870), later founder of Smith College, endowed a professorship in 1867. (*NAW*; *ANB*; research by Diana Yount, Archives, MNtcA.)

21. She no doubt meant Eliza Clark Garrett (1805–1855), not Garrettson, of Chicago, who arranged to donate a portion of her estate to establish the Garrett Biblical Institute in 1853. In 1856 this gift was valued at three hundred thousand dollars. (Mary Simmerson Cunningham Logan, *The Part Taken by Women in American History*, [Wilmington, Del., 1912], 540–42; with the assistance of David Himrod, Archives, IEN.)

22. Blandina Bleecker Dudley (1783–1863), the widow of Charles Edward Dudley, established the Dudley Observatory in Albany, New York, in 1856 and continued to support it until her death. (*ACAB*, s.v., "Dudley, Charles Edward.")

23. Sarah W. Hale of Newburyport, Massachusetts, gave title to land in Illinois to Beloit College in 1850. It was sold for thirty-five thousand dollars. (Research by Fred Burwell, Archives, WBB.)

## 4 ⤙ ECS TO ISABELLA BEECHER HOOKER

Tenafly New Jersey Nov. 3 1873

Dear Isabella

I have just returned from Rochester where I had a long talk with Susan. Tell your good husband[1] that Susan hopes to be at your State Convention & will then answer all his questions. Her name has not been mixed up in our Journals on the matter & she prefers to put nothing on paper. However to ease Mr Hooker's mind that Susan has nothing to tell more than I have already told you I would say—The denial published in Maine I never authorised, & Warrington's statement soon after in the Springfield Repub. was based on what I told him at the Tremont House in Boston.[2] I did not come out at once with a card because I did not care to fight the battle & although I knew the story was true I was not the one who told Mrs Woodhull. I never saw Mrs Woodhull a dosen times, never alone—never had any confidential talk with her: but the story Mr Tilton[3] told her & she gives to the world is mainly what <u>Mrs Tilton told Susan & Mr Tilton me & Mrs Bullard</u>.[4] The first time Susan & I met in N. York after the publication, & I had found in conversation with Saml. Wilkeson[5] that the Christian Union— Ford & Co—who publish the Life of Christ & Plymouth Church had too much money at stake to see B.[6] sacrificed & that the "lie" as they called it was to be saddled upon us women, I said to Susan let us go at once & call upon Mrs Bullard & I will lead the conversation so as to make her admit in your presence what T. T. told her & me together— she did—& we took a note of that.

Now to go back. Susan heard the story from the lips of Mrs Tilton— I from <u>him</u> at a different time & place—neither knowing what the other has heard, when we meet alone at night I tell her the whole story—& when I finished she instead of manifesting the least surprise says "Mrs Tilton told essentially the same thing to me." Victoria's story is exaggerated—rather higher colored than I heard it—but the main facts correspondend with what Susan & I had heard.

I have not a shadow of doubt of the truth. Mr Hooker is a lawyer accustomed to examine evidence. 1st—Consider that card of Bowen Tilton & Beecher[7]—in the face of all both those men had said against the latter. That shows Mr Beecher could not afford to turn his back on them. 2nd Look at the report of their last meeting in Saty's Nov. 1. Tribune[8]—with Beecher on his side Tilton dare defy him & Plymouth Church both. That investigation is a sham—a mere piece of acting. There is too much money locked up in Beecher's success for him to be sacrificed. The public especially those who have a financial interest in this matter would rather see every woman in the nation sacrificed than one of their idols of gold. They think if they can separate us one from another, prevent us writing or meeting, sowing seeds of discord all round, they can manage the public. The outrageous persecution of Mrs Woodhull in our courts[9] shows money & power behind, & she may thank Plymouth Church, Ford & Co—&c &c for all she suffered. Your persecutions in another way are as grievous & I am not willing to withold anything any longer that can help to make things easier for you either on paper or by word of mouth.

We are in the midst of a great social battle that will end in the absolute freedom of woman, & when the victory is gained we shall know that it is worth all that we have suffered. I have been crucified in this matter as much as you—have lost friends in the family & out & am vexed every day with some phase of "the Woodhull" coming up by word & letter until at times I feel like shirking everything disagreeable. But through it all I see one thing, we must stand by each other. Women must be as true to women as men are to men. Mrs Gage, Susan & I, talked over the situation & decided to hold a convention in Washington as usual about the middle of January.[10] Van Voorhees[11] Susan's lawyer promised me he would go & make a speech. We shall urge Judge Selden[12] to go. I do wish Mr Hooker would make one of his clear logical arguments on Jury Trial. Now do you & Olympia[13] get some grand guns to fire off, & let us have the best convention we ever have had.

I should like to have a great representation of the bar on our platform to discuss Hunt's[14] decision &c &c.

I send you an abstract of the speech I just made in Rochester—had a fine audience, reception &c.[15]

I hoped to see Olympia when I went up to Winsted.[16] I felt so sorry that she should have felt that I treated her coldly that I wanted to tell her how much I prised her sincerity, force, wit, everything. I have always felt that she was one of the most reliable of our women. I hope you & Olympia will feel some responsibility about the Convention & help us make it all it should be.

I start West[17] on Friday morning to be absent about six weeks—so please write me a line by return mail saying you have received this. This is the first thing I have committed to paper on this T & B matter so use it judiciously for your defense.

Persuade Mr Hooker to go with us to Washington & help us in our battle for jury trial. You see your resolution for Susan never appeared in a single paper. Can you reproduce it & send to the Woman's Journal as a part of the proceedings?[18] Write a letter & incorporate it. Some "designing woman" no doubt squelched it. Did you see my letter in The Golden Age?—[19] I wrote it in a hurry & forgot to mention you, the one of all others I would wished to have remembered. Know then it is not from want of affection, for I love you better & better every time we meet: but you will see what my object in writing it was—it was simply to praise those others ignored. With love, ever & truly yrs.

❧ E. C. Stanton.

❧ Copy in hand of I. B. Hooker, Joseph K. Hooker Collection, CtHSD.

1. John Hooker (1816–1901) was a lawyer. Like other members of the extended Beecher family, he was conducting his own inquiries into the charges lodged by Victoria Woodhull against his brother-in-law Henry Ward Beecher. He was also an outspoken critic of Justice Ward Hunt's action in SBA's trial of directing the jury to find her guilty. (Obituary Sketch of John Hooker, 73 Connecticut Reports 745; John Hooker, "Judge Hunt, and the Right of Trial by Jury," in *Account of the Trial of SBA*, pp. 206–12, *Film*, 17:103ff.)

2. In Lewiston, Maine, on 6 November 1872, clergymen asked ECS if it were true, as Victoria Woodhull claimed, that she had confirmed rumors of Beecher's affair with Elizabeth Tilton. The local paper sent nationwide a small item saying that ECS "emphatically denied the allegation, and declared her conviction that Mrs. Woodhull's statements are untrue in every particular." ECS let that statement stand until January 1873, when she told the Boston

political columnist "Warrington" that she did not deny Woodhull's charges, that she had objected only to the language Woodhull put into her mouth. "Warrington" was the pen name of William Stevens Robinson (1818-1876), who wrote principally for the *Springfield Republican*. (*New York Herald*, 7 November 1872; Massachusetts *Springfield Republican*, 10 January 1873; *NCAB*, 3:464. See also *Papers*, 2:533-37.)

3. Theodore Tilton (1835-1907) of Brooklyn, New York, was an editor, lecturer, and reformer, who enjoyed a long friendship with ECS and SBA. He and his wife, Elizabeth Richards Tilton (c. 1834-1897), had been active together in the Brooklyn Equal Rights Association and the Union Woman Suffrage Association. In 1870 Elizabeth confessed to having an affair with Henry Ward Beecher, an admission that not only launched monumental efforts to keep her confession secret but also damaged Theodore's career, beginning with his dismissal from the influential journal the *Independent* and the daily *Brooklyn Union*. In order to keep him quiet and employed as an editor, friends of Beecher were financing the weekly *Golden Age*. (*ANB*; Altina L. Waller, *Reverend Beecher and Mrs. Tilton: Sex and Class in Victorian America* [Amherst, Mass., 1982]; Federal Census, Brooklyn, 1850. See also *Papers* 2.)

4. Laura J. Curtis Bullard (c. 1834-?), who lived in Brooklyn with her parents, her son, Harold, and her husband, Enoch Bullard, was a close friend of Theodore Tilton's. She succeeded ECS as editor of the *Revolution* in May 1870. (Federal Census, 1870; city directory, 1870.)

5. Samuel Wilkeson (1817-1889), a former journalist and ECS's brother-in-law, was the secretary of the Northern Pacific Railroad and a partner in the publishing house of J. B. Ford & Company, owners of Henry Ward Beecher's journal, the *Christian Union*, and publishers of his incomplete work, *The Life of Jesus, the Christ* (1871). For more on this conversation, see 27 July 1874 below. (*ACAB*; Eugene V. Smalley, *History of the Northern Pacific Railroad* [New York, 1883], 282-86; *New York Times*, 13 March 1875; *New York Tribune*, 3 December 1889.)

6. Henry Ward Beecher (1813-1887) was the minister of Brooklyn's Plymouth Church, an influential commentator on national policy, and the first president of the American Woman Suffrage Association. (*ANB*; Paxton Hibben, *Henry Ward Beecher: An American Portrait* [New York, 1927]. See also *Papers* 1 & 2.)

7. In May 1873 Samuel Wilkeson made public a tripartite agreement to cease hostilities in the Beecher-Tilton scandal, dated 2 April 1872. Henry Chandler Bowen (1813-1896) was the publisher of the *Independent* and the *Brooklyn Union* and a member of Beecher's Plymouth Church. (*ANB*; *New York Tribune*, 30 May 1873.)

8. At a hearing about Theodore Tilton's expulsion from Plymouth Church for slandering the minister, Henry Ward Beecher took Tilton's side, arguing that he had no grievance with Tilton that the committee need consider. Later,

both men told of collaborating on that occasion to block an effort to investigate the rumors about Beecher. Successful in the short run, their claim, that Tilton left the church by his own volition and could not be subjected to its discipline, opened Plymouth Church to investigation by a denominational council and set in motion a series of hearings and trials that stretched over several years. (*New York Tribune*, 1 November 1873; Charles F. Marshall, *The True History of the Brooklyn Scandal: Being a Complete Account of the Trial of the Rev. Henry Ward Beecher* [Philadelphia, 1874], 45–46, 284–85.)

9. In the wake of her revelations about Henry Ward Beecher, Victoria Woodhull was twice jailed in New York City on charges of distributing obscene material, by which was meant her newspaper. (Underhill, *Woman Who Ran for President*, 220–38.)

10. Each January since 1869 the National Woman Suffrage Association or its close allies called a convention in Washington, while Congress was in session.

11. John Van Voorhis (1826–1905) was a Rochester lawyer and Republican who later served in Congress. He worked with Henry R. Selden to represent SBA after her arrest in 1872. (*BDAC*. See also *Papers* 2.)

12. Henry Rogers Selden (1805–1885), a former politician, former judge, and Rochester lawyer since 1859, represented SBA in her trial for illegal voting. (David McAdam et al., eds., *History of the Bench and Bar of New York* [New York, 1897], 1:472–73. See also *Papers* 2.)

13. Olympia Brown (1835–1926), an ordained Universalist minister, was pastor of the church in Bridgeport, Connecticut. She was active in the state suffrage society and a member of the executive committee of the National Woman Suffrage Association. In 1878 she moved to Racine, Wisconsin, where she lived until her death. (*NAW*; *ANB*. See also *Papers* 2.)

14. Ward Hunt (1810–1886) took his seat on the Supreme Court of the United States on 9 January 1873, and in June of that year he presided over the criminal trial of SBA in the Circuit Court for the Northern District of New York. Ruling that the right or privilege of voting arose only from state constitutions, Hunt wrote: "If the state of New York should provide that no person should vote until he had reached the age of thirty years, or after he had reached the age of fifty, or that no person having gray hair, or who had not the use of all his limbs, should be entitled to vote, I do not see how it could be held to be a violation of any right derived or held under the constitution of the United States." (*ANB*; United States v. Susan B. Anthony, 11 Blatchford 200, 204 [1873].)

15. Enclosure missing.

16. In Litchfield County, west of Hartford, Connecticut. The purpose of ECS's trip is not known.

17. To lecture in Indiana, Illinois, and Wisconsin.

18. Isabella Hooker took up the omission of SBA's name from the call to the Woman's Congress as a cause. At the meeting, she and ECS introduced a resolution of thanks to SBA for her contributions to women's advancement.

Later, she objected in a letter to Henry Blackwell to his statement in the *Woman's Journal* that SBA was absent from the congress simply because of her sister's illness. Hooker also asked Blackwell to publish SBA's letter of 13 October 1873, above. The weekly *Woman's Journal*, published in Boston by Blackwell and Lucy Stone, was at this time the only suffrage newspaper on the East Coast. (*Woman's Journal*, 22 November, 13 December 1873; I. B. Hooker to H. B. Blackwell, after 22 November 1873, NAWSA Papers, DLC.)

   19. See *Film*, 17:394.

5   ⤛   FROM THE DIARY OF SBA

[*3–9, 20 November 1873*]

MONDAY, NOVEMBER 3, 1873. Gula called for glass to look at herself— said death is stamped on my face— in her agony of weakness she cries ["]oh if I could only go to sleep & never wake again—but I must be patient to the end" then "what will you do with me—"

TUESDAY, NOVEMBER 4, 1873. It seemed every hour must end the ineffable suffering during last night—& all this day the same— Aaron[1] never left the house— Mr Porter[2] called at noon— at 11 A.M. I offered my vote again— S. Lewis[3]—the <u>tool</u> to deny & tell me my name had been struck from Register—[4] Letters from Gage & Stanton of Call for Washington Convention—

   1. Aaron M. McLean (1812–1896), Guelma's husband, was an insurance agent in Rochester. (Baker Genealogical Ms., SBA Papers, MCR-S.)
   2. Samuel Drummond Porter (1808–1881) of Rochester was first president of the Western New York Anti-Slavery Society and an old friend of the Anthony family. (Garrison, *Letters*, 4:428–29; Nancy A. Hewitt, *Women's Activism and Social Change: Rochester, New York, 1822–1872* [Ithaca, N.Y., 1984], passim.)
   3. Sylvester Lewis (?–1889), a salt manufacturer who resided in Rochester's Eighth Ward, was hired by the Democratic party in November 1872 to get out the vote and check poll lists, and he filed the complaint that led to SBA's arrest. (City directory, 1870 to 1875; *Rochester Union and Advertiser*, 27 February 1889; Rochester *Democrat and Chronicle*, 18, 19, 26, 30 November 1872, in SBA scrapbook 6, Rare Books, DLC; Rochester *Evening Express*, 29, 30 November 1872, *Film*, 16:555–56.)
   4. When SBA checked the register of voters on 15 October, she found her name still there. (SBA diary, 1873, *Film*, 16:617ff.)

WEDNESDAY, NOVEMBER 5, 1873. It is perfectly dreadful—the struggle to get out of this body— Gula about the same—only weaker & weaker

THURSDAY, NOVEMBER 6, 1873. Women Tax-Payers meeting—did not attend— These days cover us with a fearful night-mare feeling—nothing but the cry of "How long—Oh how long must this suffering continue["] & all of us perfectly powerless to relieve  gave no anodyne this night—the suffering all realized most acutely—

FRIDAY, NOVEMBER 7, 1873. Gave Sister Gula no anodyne last night nor during this day—and such a restless 24 hours—such suffering—every breath a groan— Telegram at 7 P.M. from D. R.[1] Sister Mary Luther[2] there & all coming east next week— At six this evening we were all glad to give anodyne again & she had a less suffering night—so Maggie[3] slept till her ma got up—

1. Daniel Read Anthony (1824-1904), or D. R., lived in Leavenworth, Kansas, where he published the *Leavenworth Times* and pursued careers in business and politics. (Anthony, *Anthony Genealogy*, 185-91; *United States Biographical Dictionary: Kansas Volume* [Chicago, 1879], 56-63; biographical files, KHi. See also *Papers* 1 & 2.)

2. Mary Almina Luther Anthony (1839-?), the wife of SBA's other brother, Jacob Merritt Anthony, lived in Fort Scott, Kansas. She and her children came east with members of D. R. Anthony's family. (Anthony, *Anthony Genealogy*, 173, 189; Alfred Theodore Andreas, *History of the State of Kansas, Containing a Full Account of Its Growth* [Chicago, 1883], 2:1076.)

3. Margaret McLean Baker (1845-?), the only child of Guelma McLean to reach adulthood, married George L. Baker in 1868. They lived with their young children in Rochester. (Baker Genealogical Ms., SBA Papers, MCR-S.)

SATURDAY, NOVEMBER 8, 1873. Gula under influence of anodyne since 7 last night—oblivious to all pain—but dreadfully distressed look— ate virtually nothing, a few half teaspoonfuls gruel & rice water— Maggie & self the first of night— She said it is wonderful how long life can hold out when all is gone

SUNDAY, NOVEMBER 9, 1873. [*above date*] rained all day—
    Dear Sister Guelma passed away at 5.30 this A.M.—so easily & softly as hardly to be seen—Sister Mary[1] alone at her side— Sisters Hannah[2] & Mary & niece Maggie & self—performed the last sad offices ourselves— then Mary Hallowell[3] came & spent day— Mr & Mrs Sackett

slept on ↑the↓ sofas in bedroom & back parlor [*Entries of 10–19 November omitted.*]

1. Mary Stafford Anthony (1827–1907), the youngest of the Anthony sisters, taught school in Rochester and shared the house on Madison Street with SBA, their mother, and the McLeans. (Anthony, *Anthony Genealogy*, 173; Rochester *Post Express*, 6 February 1907.)

2. Hannah Lapham Anthony Mosher (1821–1877) lived next door, at 9 Madison Street, with her husband, Eugene Mosher, and the youngest of their four children. (Mildred Mosher Chamberlain and Laura McGaffey Clarenbach, comps., *Descendants of Hugh Mosher and Rebecca Maxson Through Seven Generations* [Warwick, R.I., 1980], 311–12; Toledo *Ballot Box*, June 1877.)

3. Mary H. Post Hallowell (1823–1913), from an extended family of reformers in Rochester, was a close friend of SBA, who attempted to vote in the fall election of 1872. The National Woman Suffrage Association placed her on its executive committee in 1878. (*Quaker Genealogy*, 3:434; William F. Peck, *History of Rochester and Monroe County, New York, from the Earliest Times to the Beginning of 1907* [New York, 1908], 2:1243–44; Hewitt, *Women's Activism and Social Change*, passim. See also *Papers* 1 & 2.)

THURSDAY, NOVEMBER 20, 1873. Women Tax payers meeting—presented H. R. Selden $100. as a testimonial—[1]

Letter from Stillman urging payment of note—[2]  How like a mill stone that Revolution debt hangs about my spirit—

1. The presentation and Selden's response were reported in the *Woman's Journal*, 3 January 1874.

2. James Wells Stillman (1840–1912) loaned SBA two thousand dollars for her newspaper, the *Revolution*, in December 1869, and ECS, Anna Dickinson, and Paulina Wright Davis guaranteed the note. The son of a Rhode Island manufacturer and a graduate of the Albany Law School, Stillman came to attention as an advocate of woman suffrage in the state assembly, where he represented Westerly, Rhode Island, in 1868. He was a founder of the state suffrage association in 1869, and a year later, he signed the appeal for a union of the National and American suffrage societies. By 1873 he had opened a law office in New York City. Of all SBA's creditors, Stillman was the only one who threatened legal action, and it seems likely that he suffered losses in the Panic of 1873. She had been paying him the interest on the loan. The story continues in SBA's diary in 1874, in selections that follow. (Pages of accounts in SBA diary, 1870, 1871, 1872, 1873, *Film*, 14:173ff, 15:91ff, 888ff, 16:617ff; Francis D. Stillman, Jr., comp., *The Stillman Family: Descendants of Mr. George Stillman of Wethersfield, Connecticut, and Dr. George Stillman of Westerly, Rhode Island* [n.p., 1989]; research by Dwight C. Brown, Jr., Bradford, R.I.)

⇜ Excelsior Diary 1873, n.p., SBA Papers, DLC.

## 6 ❧ SBA TO WHITELAW REID[1]

Rochester Dec. 5th 1873

Whitelaw Reed  Dear Sir

I trust you will make honorable mention of the fact of the meeting announced in the enclosed Call, in the Tribune—[2]

I have been reading what you say of the proposed Chief Justice—[3] I met ⏊him⏊ in Oregon two years ago and heard of his comments on my lectures & our woman suffrage movement—all of them indicating a <u>coarse</u>, <u>gross</u> nature & total lack of culture— It is a most humiliating appointment—& extinguishes my last hope of any fair decision from the Supreme Court—[4] Our point of attack will have to be Congress henceforth—

Hoping that you will notice our Washington Convention, I am yours Respectfully

❧ *Susan B. Anthony*

❧ ALS, on NWSA letterhead folio for 1873, with call to Washington convention, Reid Family Papers, DLC.

1. Whitelaw Reid (1837–1912) was editor of the *New York Tribune*. He was hired as managing editor just as SBA launched the *Revolution* in 1868, and for the next few years Reid and SBA met often, though they rarely agreed on politics. Reid opposed the reelection of President Grant in 1872 and supported Horace Greeley, the Liberal Republican and Democratic candidate. (*ANB*.)

2. Omitted is the call to the Washington convention of the National Woman Suffrage Association on 15 and 16 January 1874. See *Film*, 17:421–22.

3. On 1 December 1873, the *New York Tribune* announced President Grant's selection of Attorney General George Henry Williams (1823–1910) to succeed Salmon P. Chase as Chief Justice of the Supreme Court. The nomination of this one-term senator from Oregon elicited little enthusiam. He "is so much better than many who have been authoritatively named," Reid opined, "that we receive the announcements from Washington with equanimity, if not satisfaction." A month later, Williams withdrew his name from consideration. (*ANB*; Charles Fairman, *Reconstruction and Reunion, 1864–88: Part Two*, vol. 7 of *History of the Supreme Court of the United States* [New York, 1987], 5–16, 47–61.)

4. At least three voting rights cases awaited action by the Supreme Court. In August 1873, lawyers for Virginia Minor filed her appeal of the decision by the Supreme Court of Missouri upholding the registrar of voters who refused to register Minor in 1872. Two cases from the District of Columbia were scheduled for argument before the Court on 11 December 1873. These cases, *Sara J. Spencer v. the Board of Registration* and *Sarah E. Webster v. the Judges of Election*, grew out of a large protest in 1871, in which seventy women tried and failed to vote in local elections. Their lawyers appealed the decision of the Supreme Court of the District of Columbia that women did not gain voting rights by the Fourteenth and Fifteenth amendments. (Dockets of the Supreme Court of the United States, vol. N, p. 7553, and Minutes of the Supreme Court of the United States, vol. 31, 11 December 1873, RG 267, DNA; *Papers*, 2:526n, 544, 545n.)

## 7    *~*    WHITELAW REID TO SBA

*[New York]* Dec 8 *[187]*3

Dear Miss Anthony:

I have your letter denouncing President Grant's[1] appointment for the Chief Justiceship.

Shake not your gray locks at me. I was not bought with a sugared phrase—no, with a water-gruel phrase—in a platform[2] to support what I know to be the wrong side, only to have the platform itself contemptuously ignored when its end was served. I didn't go up and down the country praising men whom I knew unfit for office, and denouncing men whom I knew to be pure and eminently able.

I was not disappointed at the selection for Chief Justice. Were you? Very truly yours,

*~*    *Whitelaw Reid*

*~* ALS, letterpress copy, Reid Family Papers, DLC.

1. Ulysses S. Grant (1822–1885) became the eighteenth president of the United States in 1869 and won reelection in 1872.

2. Reid refers to the fourteenth plank of the Republican party's platform of 1872 and the willingness of SBA to campaign for the party on the basis of its promise. The party, "mindful of its obligations to the loyal women of America," pledged to treat their demands for rights "with respectful consideration." See *Papers*, 2:501–24.

8 ᔤ SPEECH BY SBA TO THE CENTENNIAL OF THE
BOSTON TEA PARTY IN NEW YORK CITY

EDITORIAL NOTE: Six hundred people attended the New York Woman's
Suffrage Society's centennial celebration of the Boston Tea Party at
the Union League Theatre on 16 December 1873. The event kicked
off a campaign for a state law that would exempt women's property
from taxation until women could vote. Clemence Lozier, the society's
president, introduced SBA as "the greatest champion of liberty."
The text below includes coverage from the *New York Herald* and the
New York *World*, the reports that SBA deemed best.

[16 December 1873]

My friends, I stand before you to-night a convicted criminal—(applause)—tried in the United States Court, convicted by a Supreme
Court Judge in the Circuit Court of the northern district of New York,
and sentenced to pay $100 fine and costs. (Applause.) For what? For
asserting my right to representation in a government, based upon the
one idea of the right of every person governed to participate in that
government. This is the result at the close of 100 years of this government, that I, a native born American citizen, am found guilty of neither
lunacy nor idiocy, but of a crime (?)—a States Prison offence—simply
because I exercised our right to vote. If others rose to revolution
because of a stamp duty, or a tax on tea, paper or glass, some would
perhaps advocate such a measure here; but I don't propose to do so.
We shall fight it out on this line for the next 100 years. (Applause.) It is
nothing short of great outrage to attempt to govern human beings
without their consent, and take from them their property and dispose
of it without giving them any voice as to the manner of its disposition.
So, if what was said 100 years ago of the colonists was true, it is equally
true to-day of our women. Luther Martin[1] said, "Those without votes
are as absolutely the slaves of those with votes as the negroes are their
slaves."[2] There were, undoubtedly, 100 years ago, many who lived in
quiet and plenty, who would never have risen of their own accord, and
it was very likely that there were many women in the land who felt so
inclined to-day. <It was the most difficult thing in the world to make a

woman (or any one else) see a principle so long as it was not violated in her own person. She never prayed that all who had good husbands might lose them, or that the good fathers of all daughters should die, but she did know that when a woman got to be alone she got to be a woman's rights woman. When their protection went they found out.>
It is equally unjust toward woman, whether the laws affecting her are all right or all wrong. In any event, they are made for her without her consent or participation, and if they are wrong she must bear the greater burden.

After quoting Benjamin Franklin[3] on representation Miss Anthony continued— Would any one have thought that those men who thus talked and wrote would, after all, organize a government, as they did, on the blood and bones of 3,000,000 of fellow men—I mean the slaves—and exclude from participation nearly one-half the people? The United States government had better be wise in time, for these women, she thought, would not much longer submit to the tyranny of taxation without representation. Mrs. Gage and herself had been pretty well over the ground, and women were everywhere awakening to the injustice of their condition and refusing to pay the taxes. (Applause.)

Miss Anthony then gave many incidents of women, with names and residences, who had refused to pay, one of whom had not had the assessments enforced for six years past. In Rochester a committee had been to the assessment records and had copied the list of tax paying women, urging them not to submit. There were 5,000 of them, representing property to the value of $7,000,000, 400 of them living in the Eighth ward of that city alone, where the speaker also resides. The women of to-day were organized precisely as they had organized 100 years ago, and eminent lawyers all over the land would sustain the technical legality as well as the intrinsic justice of their claims. All the women need is a little courage and some cash to make the Courts themselves affirm the justice of it and accord their rights one way or the other. History tells us that the press of 100 years ago was with the people, but she was sorry to say that, with few exceptions, the press of to-day was recreant to this simplest principle of human justice and right.

<Among things denied woman was the right to sit on juries, and hence to a trial by their peers. "When I sat," she said, "in the Court at Canandaigua, and those twelve men—though they might as well have

been automatons as men—in the box, not one of them was my peer. German, French, Irish, English, intelligent, stupid, drunk, sober, each and every one was my political superior. Every human being allowed to speak in my behalf had to be selected from a class of my peers—"

Mrs. Lozier[4]—Your superiors, your superiors.

Miss Anthony—From my superiors. What do you think of the difference between the wrongs of 100 years ago and the wrongs of to-day? Judge Hunt ordered a verdict and would not allow the jury to be polled. Speaking further of woman's slavery, Miss Anthony told a story of a woman who had, as she used to say before the events to be related happened, "all the rights she wanted." She went to a dentist and was measured for a set of teeth—a full set, upper and under jaw. They fitted so badly that nervous prostration ensued and she refused payment. The dentist sued the husband, and as it was ruled that the matter—the teeth, Miss Anthony said—was one of joint interest of wife and husband, the woman was not allowed to testify to the facts. And yet the men of the nation asked them to be quiet—patient. She had been patient for the last twenty-five years. She was taxed in Washington for the license of a hall in which she and a few others had gathered to decry taxation without representation.[5] "We didn't pay it," she added. "We never will pay it any more than I shall pay the fine Judge Hunt imposed on me.">

⤨ *New York Herald*, 17 December 1873; New York *World*, 17 December 1873.

1. Luther Martin (1744–1826) was a delegate to the Constitutional Convention of 1787 from Maryland.

2. In his report to the Maryland legislature about the proposed constitution, Martin wrote that without equal voting rights individuals would be "as absolutely slaves as any negro is to his master." See Jonathan Elliot, ed., *The Debates in the Several State Conventions on the Adoption of the Federal Constitution* (1836–1845; reprint, Charlottesville, Va., 1941), 1:35

3. Benjamin Franklin (1706–1790), American statesman and scientist. In earlier speeches, SBA quoted his "Some Good Whig Principles," to the effect that "they who have no voice nor vote in the electing of representatives *do not enjoy liberty*, but are absolutely enslaved to those who have votes and to their representatives." See *Papers*, 2:573.

4. Clemence Sophia Harned Lozier (1813–1888), a successful physician in New York City, was dean and professor at the New York Medical College and Hospital for Women, which she organized in 1863. She served as president of the National Woman Suffrage Association in 1877. SBA was her guest at 361

West 34th Street on this visit to New York. (*NAW*; *ANB*; ECS, "Tribute to Dr. Clemence S. Lozier," 7 June 1888, *Film*, 26:797–800.)

5. At the Washington convention of the National association in January 1873, a policeman interrupted the proceedings with a demand that the women produce their license to hold a speculative entertainment in the city. They had none, and the meeting voted unanimously to refuse the taxation. When the officer left to consult city officials about arresting the leaders, SBA adjourned the convention. (*Film*, 16:881–85.)

## 9  ⇜  FROM THE DIARY OF SBA

[*17 December 1873*]

WEDNESDAY, DECEMBER 17, 1873. [*New York*] Good reports in all papers—World & Herald the best— Mr Stillman called to talk of Mary's offer to pay him $600— for his $1000 note against me—[1] Mrs Blake[2] called—then I called on Mrs Phelps—[3] back to tea & to train at 8 P.M. for home—

1. Mary Anthony suggested that if Stillman would accept five or six hundred dollars to settle the debt, the family might "buy it up & so end the matter—" She told her sister to "learn all you can about how little he will take to call it square—<u>donating</u> the rest to the <u>cause</u>—" (M. S. Anthony to SBA, n.d., written on A. B. Blackwell to SBA, 10 December 1873, *Film*, 17:429–32.)

2. Lillie Devereux Blake (1833–1913) was a writer whose novel, *Fettered for Life; or Lord and Master*, came out in 1874. An officer of the National association and the New York City society, she headed the effort in 1874 to exempt women from taxation in New York State. (*NAW*; *ANB*. See also *Papers* 2.)

3. Elizabeth B. Phelps (c. 1805–?), by this date a wealthy widow, participated in the New York and the National suffrage associations. A member of Sorosis, the New York women's club, and a benefactor of the *Revolution*, Phelps opened the Woman's Bureau at 49 East Twenty-third Street in 1869 to house artists' studios and offices for women's organizations and to provide overnight accommodations for women visiting the city. She and her daughter still lived at that address, although the Woman's Bureau had closed. (Federal Census, 1870; *Quaker Genealogy*, 3:250, 254; city directory, 1865 to 1874. See also *Papers* 2.)

⇜ Excelsior Diary 1873, n.p., SBA Papers, DLC.

10 ⚛ ECS TO LUCY STONE[1]

Tenafly Dec 28th 1873[2]

Dear Lucy,

Do you think it just or magnanimous to refuse to recognize the existence of an association merely because you have a personal feud with its President.[3]

I might have supposed it was because of some irregularity in its organization did I not see in your last Journal a notice of a New York state association, formed by a few persons in Brooklyn without calling any state convention, & while a state society has been in existence four years.[4]

I think the old workers who belong to this association have rendered too important services to the cause you advocate to be treated with ↑the↓ contempt you affect or feel.

For your own sake give up this petty kind of revenge as it injures you, more than you are aware in the estimation of many people whose good opinion you might prize. Too grand a work awaits the women of this generation to spend any thought or feeling on personalities. I say this in all kindness, think it over & see if high principle impels you to treat Susan as you do.[5] With kind regards   Sincerely yours

⚛ *Elizabeth Cady Stanton.*

P.S. Will you publish enclosed call[6] & much oblige all of us who hope to make the convention a success

⚛ ALS, on NWSA letterhead for 1873, NAWSA Papers, DLC.

1. Lucy Stone (1818–1893), one of the earliest advocates of woman's rights and once a close friend of SBA, edited the *Woman's Journal* with Henry Blackwell and chaired the powerful executive committee of the American Woman Suffrage Association. During the presidential campaign of 1872, Stone and Blackwell cooperated at a distance with ECS and SBA in the interest of Republican victory. ECS stayed in touch with Stone after the election, but neither Blackwell nor Stone would work with SBA. (*NAW*; *ANB*; Andrea Moore Kerr, *Lucy Stone: Speaking Out for Equality* [New Brunswick, N.J., 1992]. See also *Papers* 1 & 2.)

2. SBA arrived in Tenafly this morning for a two-day break from lecturing. In her diary on 31 December, she noted conversations with Antoinette Blackwell in Somerville, New Jersey, about Lucy Stone's "cruel aspersions of Mrs Stanton & self—& her narrow one-sided nature." (SBA diary, 1873, *Film*, 16:617ff.)

3. In keeping with its practice of not naming the National Woman Suffrage Association, the *Woman's Journal* announced that "Susan B. Anthony proposes to hold a Woman Suffrage Convention," and later, that she "calls her sixth annual" convention. (13 December 1873, 3 January 1874.)

4. ECS alludes to Lucy Stone's insistence that the National association was "irregular" in origin because it came into being at a reception without prior announcement and without a system of representation. She then refers to a New York State Woman Suffrage Association founded by friends of Stone in October 1873, just in time to send delegates to the American association's annual meeting that month. Because the original state association of the same name, founded in 1869, refused to affiliate with the American, the votes allocated to New York by the American's constitution had been cast by individuals who lived in the state rather than by delegates of a suffrage society. (*Woman's Journal*, 18 October, 20 December 1873.)

5. On 3 January, Stone wrote: "I have received an astonishing letter from Mrs. Stanton, begging me to lay aside my 'personal feud with Susan.' . . . All this because the Journal does not publish in extenso the 'Call' for their National Convention in Washington. Think of that, from <u>her</u> to <u>me</u>." (to T. W. Higginson, 3 January 1874, misdated 1873, MS.P.91.37.123, Rare Books and Manuscripts, MB.)

6. Enclosure missing.

11    ❧    SBA to Isabella Beecher Hooker and Olympia Brown

Tenafly N.J. Jan. 4th 187[4]

Dear Mrs. Hooker & Olympia

I am just back to Mrs Stanton's by last evening's train—& have read up your several letters, also Mr Hookers— And decide to run the luck of the programme you have made for me[1]—as I understand, the admission is <u>in all cases</u> to be ⟨not less than⟩ <u>25 cts</u>—whether the halls be <u>free</u> or otherwise—<u>unless</u> the <u>friends</u> of the place <u>prefer</u> to <u>make</u> up a <u>purse</u> of $25. for me, for the sake of having the admission free— But <u>I must not</u> be left to solicit subscriptions at any of my lectures— Again—as I understand—I am to have the entire nett proceeds of the 18 meetings up to $25. a lecture—and—all over $25. is to go to Mrs Hooker; that is; if the nett proceeds—over Halls, Posters, advertising & travelling expenses—should for the 18 meetings should be ↑$450.—or↓ less, then I am to have the whole—if over the $450— you have the excess & I the $450— Now that will do very well on that side—but suppose the worst—that the ↑receipts of the↓ 18 meetings taken together were less than the expenses— Am I to be the loser?— I shall have simply to trust that you will save me from such an alternative—improbable as it may seem—it may nevertheless happen— As I understand your proposition—I now say "go ahead["] & make the arrangements perfectly thorough that there may be no failure of audiences from lack of wide & full notice—

I see Phebe Ann[2] accepts Jersey City Call & leaves Conn. in the spring— Good for that—

I see T. W. H.[3] explains himself—& officially rights his position— frees himself from all responsibility for Lucy's and Harry's[4] little meannesses—

Yes—get Mr Hookers Jury article in the Independent if possible[5]— it will be just as effective for us, even more so— I shall go to Washington Monday the 12th at latest—Mrs Stanton not until Wednesday 12 noon train—reaching there at 10 P.M— The Arlington to be our head quarters—[6] Now Mark— If Olympia backs down on Washington— then Mrs Hooker must go— But Olympia must not— This is just the hour we most need her— Mrs Wilbour declines to go— So that Mrs Stanton, Gage, Blake, Lockwood[7] & Anthony will be all—if Brown & Hooker come not to the help of lord—& they must not fail him now at this last trial hour—

Send Mr Hookers article to me, care Mrs E. C. Sargent[8]—308—F— st—N.W—Washington D.C—as I shall not go to the Arlington until days of Convention—

The papers have not reached here yet—↑[in ECS hand] Yes they have↓ hope they will— Mrs Stanton has not seen them yet—though I now have one copy of each & will get her attention to them—[9]

I would dearly have loved to have had Mr Hookers article set up & printed in ship shape for my pamphlet—but it is too late now—and if I get it—on arrival at Washington will try & get the Chronicle[10] to set it up as you name & give me two or three or nine hundred—of slips of it—

I expected to find letter here from Judge Selden—with form of Memorial to Congress—but do not—[11] A letter from A. G. Riddle[12] says he shall not bring on the <u>Spencer</u> case this Winter for two reasons—1st that he is sure he would be beaten—& second, that he is not ready to make his argument before that last tribunal—so will put it off— Now in view of this—what shall we ask Congress to do for us?— Wont Mr Hooker give me his idea of Memorial or petition to Congress—for <u>we</u> must go to them <u>for</u> <u>some</u> <u>practical</u> <u>immediate</u> <u>action</u>—

I stopped here & re-read all your letters since we parted—& I believe I have answered every point— But Olympia must not fail to remember that Mrs Stanton & I feel that she <u>must</u> <u>not</u> <u>fail</u> on <u>Washington</u> Sincerely yours

~  Susan B. Anthony

P.S—N.B. I cannot help feeling that the Conn. Campaign will be a success—am <u>sure</u> it would be any other year but this[13]

[*Note in ECS hand*] Conjure Olympia to be there    I always tremble so over a convention that for one to drop out makes me miserable.

No, you must not be excused if O. B. does come. We shall have a pleasant social time at the Arlington, you must come    perhaps a hearing on the 16th amendment[14]    perhaps a reception. You have so much pluck & push, you must be there. I shall never forget how you whipped Trumbull[15] into line! do come.

[*In margin of first page, in SBA's hand*] <u>Forward to Olympia please</u>

~ ALS, on NWSA letterhead for 1873, Isabella Hooker Collection, CtHSD. Misdated "1873."

1. The Connecticut Woman Suffrage Association announced plans at its meeting in December to employ speakers for a statewide canvass and organize political clubs across the state, charged in particular with electing men to the legislature and Congress who favored woman suffrage. In letters now missing, the Hookers and Olympia Brown offered the work to SBA. (*Film*, 17:433–41.)

2. Phebe Ann Coffin Hanaford (1829–1921), a Universalist pastor in New Haven, moved to the Church of the Good Shepherd in Jersey City in 1874. (*NAW*; *Past and Promise: Lives of New Jersey Women*, 148–50.)

3. Thomas Wentworth Higginson (1823–1911) of Providence, Rhode Island, became an editor of the *Woman's Journal* at its founding in 1870. In the issue of 3 January 1874 under the heading "Personal," he announced that he was now only an editorial contributor. The earlier title "led to misapprehension." (*ANB*. See also *Papers* 1 & 2.)

4. Henry Browne Blackwell (1825-1909), known as Harry, shared editorial duties at the *Woman's Journal* with his wife, Lucy Stone. (*ANB*. See also *Papers* 1 & 2.)

5. John Hooker had looked in vain for a journal to publish his article, "Judge Hunt, and the Right of Trial by Jury," since July 1873. The *Independent*, once edited by Theodore Tilton, was a weekly journal of opinion with a large national readership.

6. The Arlington Hotel, on Vermont Avenue between H and I streets in northwest Washington.

7. Belva Ann Bennett McNall Lockwood (1830-1917), one of the National association's key allies in Washington, completed law school and gained admission to the bar in the District of Columbia in 1873. (*NAW*; *ANB*. See also *Papers* 2.)

8. Ellen Clark Sargent (1826-1911), the wife of California's Senator Aaron A. Sargent and an early advocate of woman suffrage in her home state, lived in Washington while her husband served in the Senate. She was for many years treasurer of the National Woman Suffrage Association. (Edwin Everett Sargent, comp., *Sargent Record: William Sargent of Ipswich, Newbury, Hampton, Salisbury and Amesbury, New England, U.S.* [St. Johnsbury, Vt., 1899), 218; unpublished paper by Paula Lichtenberg, San Francisco. See also *Papers* 2.)

9. Newspapers covering the Connecticut Woman Suffrage Association meeting in December.

10. The *Washington Chronicle*, a morning paper in the capital.

11. This was SBA's own memorial, below at 20 January 1874, asking Congress to remit her fine. For earlier discussion of this protest, see *Papers*, 2:618.

12. Albert Gallatin Riddle (1816-1902), a Washington lawyer, helped to plan the test of women's voting rights in the District of Columbia and acted as counsel for both Sara Spencer and Sarah Webster. A part of his letter to SBA is in *Film*, 17:895. The minutes of the Supreme Court of 11 December 1873 note that the cases were "passed for the present—On account of sickness of counsel." But a year later Riddle informed the Court that he was still not ready to argue the cases; the Court dismissed the cases and remanded them to the District of Columbia court. (*DAB*; *NCAB*, 2:371; Minutes of the Supreme Court of the United States, vol. 31, 11 December 1873, and vol. 32, 16 October 1874, RG 267, DNA.)

13. A reference to the depression settling over the nation since the collapse of banks in September 1873.

14. By the "sixteenth amendment" nineteenth-century suffragists meant their own proposal for a constitutional amendment to bar disfranchisement on account of sex.

15. Lyman Trumbull (1813-1896) was senator from Illinois from 1855 to 1873 and chair of the Judiciary Committee after 1861. ECS refers to a hearing before Trumbull's committee on 12 January 1872 at which Hooker was the chief speaker. (*BDAC*; *Film*, 15:1049-58.)

## 12 ⇝ PETITION TO THE UNITED STATES SENATE

*[12 January 1874]*[1]

To the Senate of the United states.

The undersigned respectfully ask that your Honorable body will extend to women the same protection, that colored men now enjoy in the exercise of their right to vote. As the United states constitution as it is with all its recent amendments, & laws to enforce them, does not in the opinion of Supreme Court Judges guarantee such protection in the several states,[2] we demand of Congress further legislation that shall secure to women their civil & political rights

⇝ *Elizabeth Cady Stanton*

⇝ *Susan B. Anthony*

⇝ ECS AMs, signed, Senate 43A-H20, 43d Cong., 1st sess., RG 46, DNA. Cover in ECS hand reads: "To the Senate of the United states. Petition for the protection of women    Elizabeth Cady Stanton   Susan B Anthony." Endorsed on verso: "Petition of Elizabeth Cady Stanton and Susan B. Anthony praying the passage of a law guaranteeing to women equal Civil and political rights. 1874 Jany 12, Referred to the Committee on Privileges and Elections. Mr. Sargent."

1. Senator Aaron A. Sargent introduced this petition in the Senate on 12 January, after SBA spent the night with his family. In the House of Representatives, Benjamin Butler introduced a similar petition on 13 January and asked that it be referred to the House Committee on the Judiciary, which he chaired. Senators presented most of the petitions sent to the National association by suffragists from around the country on January 19, 21, and 22. One after another senator read the words inscribed by ECS and SBA on the covers: a petition "asking for women equal protection with colored men in the exercise of their right to vote." On January 21, Senator George Edmunds challenged that summary and asked a colleague to read the petition. In fact, the petitioners sought what the National had recommended early in 1873: "a declaratory act that under the fourteenth amendment . . . women have the right to the elective franchise." The Senate did not enforce its rules about correct summaries and continued to refer the petitions to the Committee on Privileges and Elections. (*Congressional Record*, 43d Cong., 1st sess., 12, 21 January 1874, 569, 796; *House Journal*, 43d Cong., 1st sess., 13 January 1874, 229; and

House 8E 3/5/5/4, 43d Cong., 1st sess., RG 233, DNA; all in *Film*, 17:914–17, 934, 971.)

2. A reference to the decision of Associate Justice Ward Hunt of the Supreme Court in the case of SBA in the Circuit Court of the United States for the Northern District of New York.

## 13    MEMORIALS ADOPTED BY THE NATIONAL WOMAN SUFFRAGE ASSOCIATION

EDITORIAL NOTE: On 15 January 1874, SBA presided at the opening of the sixth Washington convention of the National Woman Suffrage Association in Lincoln Hall, the city's largest auditorium, at Ninth and D streets Northwest. After a few preliminaries, she read this memorial, drawn up by Isabella Hooker in December. After the convention adopted the memorial on the next day, Aaron Sargent presented it to the Senate. (*Hartford Daily Times*, 1 February 1874, *Film*, 17:928–29.)

[15 January 1874]

Whereas, Women have been denied a hearing as to their political rights at the bar of the Senate & The House, they being entirely unrepresented there in that they have had no voice in the choice of members to either body, although constituting one half the People of the United States, recognised by the Declaration of Independence & the Constitution as the only source of power, and one half the governed whose consent is necessary to all <u>just</u> government, and—

Whereas, Congress has refused, though earnestly solicited by the petitions of many thousand men & women, which petitions are now on file in the Secretaries Offices of both Houses, to so interpret the Constitution & their own Acts under it as to secure to female citizens equal political rights with the male citizens of this republic, and

Whereas, Women are thereby still subjected to many wrongs, among which is taxation without representation, a subjection declared by "The Fathers" to be an unendurable tyranny—

Therefore, We pray your Honorable Bodies to pass a law during the present session of Congress, that shall exempt women from taxation for <u>National</u> purposes, so long as they are unrepresented in National Councils.[1]

⇒ AMs in hand of Isabella B. Hooker, Committee on Finance, Tariffs and Taxes, Senate 43A–H 8.3, RG 46, DNA. Endorsed: "Petition of Mrs. Isabella Beecher Hooker & others praying for the passage of a law exempting women from taxation as long as they are unrepresented in the national counsels." Not in *Film*.

> EDITORIAL NOTE: In their resolutions, the convention condemned the conviction of SBA, supported the efforts of women to gain suffrage in the District of Columbia, opposed recent efforts in Congress to disfranchise the women of Utah, and adopted a second memorial asking for a civil rights bill, published here. ECS and SBA had focused their attention on women's civil rights by 9 January; on 12 January, they still sought advice about wording a bill. The bill took its inspiration but not its details from the civil rights bills introduced by Charles Sumner in the Senate and Benjamin Butler in the House that would bar racial discrimination in public accommodations, theaters, common carriers, and institutions of learning. Belva Lockwood corresponded with Sumner about including women in his bill, and she reported to the convention that he refused to make the change. Lockwood may have authored the text adopted by the meeting. (SBA to Gerrit Smith, 9 January 1874; SBA to Benjamin Butler, 12 January 1874; Washington *National Republican*, 17 January 1874; all in *Film*, 17:906–7, 910, 921–23.)

*Resolved*, That in national convention assembled, the women of the several States demand of Congress a civil rights bill for their protection:

1. That shall secure to them equally with colored men all the advantages and opportunities of life.

2. That shall open to them Harvard,[2] Yale, Columbia, Princeton, and all the higher institutions of learning with equal rights with colored men, to become both students and professors.

3. That shall compel the medical profession to admit women into all their colleges and societies, to practice in the hospitals, and in every way recognize them as equals precisely as they do men of color.

4. That shall open to them the law schools, with the right for married and unmarried women to practice in all our courts on the same terms with colored men; to sit upon juries, to sue and be sued, and to testify in our courts as do colored men; to be tried by a jury of their peers; and to be made eligible to all the honors and emoluments of the bar and bench.

5. To be admitted to all theological seminaries on equal terms with colored men; to be recognized in all religious organizations as bishops,

elders, priests, deacons; to officiate at the altar and preach in the pulpits of all churches, orthodox or heterodox; and that all religious sects shall be compelled to bring their creeds and biblical interpretations into line with the divine idea of the absolute equality of women with the colored men of the nation.

6. That women, equally with colored men, shall be protected in all their uprisings and down-sittings and in all their outgoings and incomings; that they be admitted to theatres and hotels alone; that they may walk the streets by night or day; ramble in the forests, or beside the lakes and rivers, as do colored men, without fear of molestation or insult from any white man whatsoever; and that women, the same as colored men, shall have equal place and pay in the world of work; be admitted into whatever trade or occupation they desire as apprentices, journeymen, masters; and if any white man refuse to work beside a woman as an equal he shall suffer fine and imprisonment, precisely as if he refused to work beside a colored man.[3]

&#8766; Washington *National Republican*, 16 January 1874.

1. Dated 16 December 1873, the manuscript sent to the Senate was signed by SBA, ECS, Isabella Beecher Hooker, Ruth C. Denison, C. A. Jewell, Jennie F. Jewell, Susan A. Edson, M.D., Caroline B. Winslow, M.D., Sara J. Spencer, Ellen C. Sargent, Emily Rogers, Belva A. Lockwood, and Kate C. Harris. Aaron Sargent presented the memorial on 22 January 1874. (*Congressional Record*, 43d Cong., 1st sess., 830.)

2. The *National Republican* reported Howard, rather than Harvard, University.

3. The bill found no sponsor in the Forty-third Congress.

14 &#8766; SBA TO LILLIE DEVEREUX BLAKE

Washington D.C. Jan 18th 1874

Dear Mrs Blake

Don't delay letting me know about Albany[1]—you see, it will take me a day & a night to get there—so if your day is Thursday[2]—I must leave here Wednesday A.M. at latest— and then remember that I speak at Manchester Connecticut Saturday night the 24th—so it will not do to have Albany Friday—& then I have not a day again until after Feb. 15th

& that will bring us so nearly to Washingtons 22[d] Feb. as to spoil the hearing— So make Mrs Stanton & Mrs Gage your backers at Albany— & let me off altogether—

The more I do here the more I find to do—& if I were not advertised in Ct. I should stop here a few weeks to push the District Suffrage[3] & my petition—but Mrs Barnard[4] says she will take my petition in hand— so you see that will make it go—& Mrs Spencer[5] will push the District—

Gen Butler[6] was most gracious yesterday—presents petition[7] tomorrow & gives us hearing Tuesday A.M— Sincerely yours

↝ *Susan B Anthony*

↝ ALS, on NWSA letterhead for 1873, NWefHi.

1. After petitioning the New York State legislature for "a law exempting the property of women from taxation so long as they shall be denied the privilege of the ballot," Blake awaited announcement of a hearing. See *Film*, 17:933. See also *History*, 3:412-13.

2. That is, 22 January.

3. The long-standing lobby to gain woman suffrage in the District of Columbia dominated the National's work in Washington this January. As Sara Spencer explained to the convention, the Supreme Court of the District of Columbia determined in two voting rights cases in 1871 that by the Fourteenth Amendment women gained "the capacity to become voters," but only by action of Congress could they gain the vote. While *Spencer v. Board of Registration* and *Webster v. Judges of Election*, on appeal, awaited action by the United States Supreme Court, six hundred women petitioned Congress to place "the constitutional rights of the women of this District, as declared by the highest judicial tribunal, under the protection of the legislative power." (Washington *National Republican*, 16 January 1874, *Film*, 17:919-20.)

4. Helen M. Barnard, a government clerk and journalist in Washington, helped to organize the first suffrage association in the District of Columbia in 1867. Hopes that she would edit a new newspaper for the National association were dashed in the fall of 1873, when the financial panic wiped out pledges of support. (*Register of Federal Officers*, 1867, p. 42, 1871, p. 160; *Woman's Journal*, 4 May 1872. See also *Papers* 2.)

5. Sara Jane Andrews Spencer (1837-1909) ran the Spencerian Business College in Washington with her husband, Henry Caleb Spencer, and emerged by 1871 as a leader among the city's suffragists. Although Henry Spencer complained in 1873 that "Woman's Rights Doctrines" had broken up "the peace of his family," Sara Spencer led the National association's efforts in Washington until 1880. (*WWW1*; *Representative Men of Maryland and District of Columbia*, 426-27; *The Diary of James A. Garfield*, eds. Harry James Brown and Frederick D. Williams [East Lansing, Mich., 1967], 2:176. See also *Papers* 2.)

6. Benjamin Franklin Butler (1818–1893) of Massachusetts won election as a Republican to the House of Representatives in 1866 and served until 1875. He was returned for one term in 1877. In the Forty-third Congress he was chairman of the House Committee on the Judiciary. Butler may have attended the reception at the Willard Hotel for delegates to the National's convention on 17 January. (*BDAC*. See also *Papers* 2.)

7. That is, the petition for suffrage in the District of Columbia.

## 15 ⨺ SBA TO ISABELLA BEECHER HOOKER

Washington Jan 18th 1874

My Dear Mrs Hooker

How I did wish you were here to enjoy all— But the best & hardest comes now, Gen. Butler is bound to put the question of Woman Suffrage, <u>pure</u> & <u>simple</u> to the House <u>first</u>—& that will be on <u>striking Male</u> from the District of Columbia suffrage clause— He will present the Petition to the House tomorrow—& if possible get consent to have it read & make speech—then it will go to Judiciary Com—& Tuesday A.M. he gives us a hearing before his Committee—& do you pry the Gods to help me— And Senator Sargent[1] will do the same for us in the Senate—

Then 2[d]—Loughridge[2] of Iowa is to present my petition to Congress to remit my fine—& thus pass censure on Judge Hunt—& Butler will bring in Bill for that—& Sargent push it in Senate the same way—thus you see—the work of agitation is likely to go on here—& though it looks as if I ought to stop here a month & work with the members—I am booked for Ct. & cant—

As to your member Hawley[3]—he will loose his life by <u>saving</u> it—<u>or</u> <u>trying to</u>— Senator Fenton[4] of N.Y. has <u>one</u> <u>foot</u> on our side of the fence—& many members of both houses are <u>almost</u> <u>persuaded</u>—& with a little stronger tide will wash over t̶h̶e̶ to our help—

<u>Mrs</u> Sargent is just the same excellent sound sense woman—splendid—and the dear children one & all very very sweet—[5] But the rest when I come— Shall it be direct to <u>your</u> <u>home</u>?— Miss Burr[6] will stop here a few weeks—

I did not read Mr Hookers letter— Judge Selden drew up my

petition, which was most admirable—then we all <u>crucified</u> poor Judge Hunt over & over again so many times that I thought we would spare from Mr Hookers spear— I will hand you the paper when I come—

I do not yet know if I shall be at Albany Thursday— But will reach you by <u>Friday night</u> if possible—but surely Saturday A.M— Have letter waiting me at Mrs Dr Loziers—361—West 34th st—New York   With ever so much love, though hastily

⇒ *Susan B. Anthony*

⇒ ALS, on NWSA letterhead for 1873, Olympia Brown Papers, MCR-S.

1. Aaron Augustus Sargent (1827-1887) represented California in the House of Representatives from 1861 to 1863 and again from 1869 to 1873, when he entered the Senate. He did not, in this session, take up the cause of suffrage in the District of Columbia. (*BDAC*. See also *Papers* 2.)

2. William Loughridge (1827-1889), a Republican, served in the House of Representatives from 1867 to 1871 and from 1873 to 1875. With Benjamin Butler, he wrote a minority report of the House Judiciary Committee in 1871 sustaining the claim that women were already voters under the Fourteenth and Fifteenth amendments. (*BDAC*.)

3. Joseph Roswell Hawley (1826-1905), a former governor of Connecticut and the president of the United States Centennial Commission, served in the House of Representatives from 1872 to 1875 and again from 1879 to 1881, when he entered the Senate. (*BDAC*.)

4. Reuben Eaton Fenton (1819-1885) was elected to the Senate from New York in 1869 and served until 1875. On 15 January 1874, he presented a petition for suffrage from women in western New York, but he told ECS that she had his "sympathy for efforts" to elevate women but not yet to enfranchise them. (*BDAC*; *Congressional Record*, 43d Cong., 1st sess., 663; R. E. Fenton to ECS, 15 January 1874, and ECS to Editor, *Golden Age*, 20 January 1874, *Film*, 17:918, 945-46.)

5. The children were: Ellen, or Ella, Clark (1854-1908); Elizabeth (1857-1900); and George Clark (1860-1930).

6. Frances Ellen Burr (1831-1923), Connecticut's senior advocate of woman suffrage, was the sister of the publisher of the *Hartford Times*, the state's leading Democratic paper. While in Washington, she filed reports of the convention to the *Times*, delivered what ECS described as "one of the best speeches ever made on our platform," and testified before the House Judiciary Committee in favor of woman suffrage in the District of Columbia. (Charles Burr Todd, *A General History of the Burr Family*, 4th ed. [New York, 1902], 305; *New York Times*, 10 February 1923; *History*, 2:538-43; ECS to Editor, *Golden Age*, 20 January 1874.)

## 16 &#x223D; FROM THE DIARY OF SBA

[*18-19 January 1874*]

SUNDAY, JANUARY 18, 1874. At Mrs Sargents—Washington

B. F. Butler presented petition   600— names for Suffrage in D.C.[1] Dawes[2] of Mass. offered bill for W.S. in the District— President Grant sent in name of Morris R. Wait[3] of Toledo O. for Chief Justice—good— Put my petition in hands of W$^m$ A. Loughridge of Iowa— <u>this was done the 19$^{th}$</u> —

This P.M. Mr & Mrs. S[argent] & self rode all over Washington  my first ride over the city though I have been here every winter the past 6 years— Phebe Couzens[4] & I called on Mrs Barnard—[5]

1. On 19 January, Norton Parker Chipman, the delegate to the House of Representatives from the District of Columbia, not Butler, presented the petition for woman suffrage in the District. It was referred to the Judiciary Committee. (*Congressional Record*, 43d Cong., 1st sess., 770.)

2. Henry Laurens Dawes (1816–1903) of Massachusetts was elected to Congress in 1857, served in the House of Representatives until 1875, and entered the Senate that year. Dawes acted for Butler in presenting H.R. No. 1353 to strike "male" from the qualifications for voting in the District. (*BDAC; Congressional Record*, 43d Cong., 1st sess., 765.)

3. Morrison Remick Waite (1816–1888) of Ohio was notified on 19 January 1874 of his selection to fill the vacancy left by the death of Salmon P. Chase as Chief Justice of the Supreme Court. He served from 1874 to 1888. (*ANB*.)

4. Phoebe Wilson Couzins (1839–1913) of St. Louis was the first woman to enter law school at Washington University. Since her graduation in 1871, she worked primarily as a lecturer. On hand for the founding of the National Woman Suffrage Association in 1869, Couzins took part in most of its meetings through the decade. (*NAW; ANB*.)

5. At 1104 L Street, Northwest.

MONDAY, JANUARY 19, 1874. Mrs H. M. Barnard will look after my petition in both Houses—

&#x223D; Excelsior Diary 1874, n.p., SBA Papers, DLC. Letters in square brackets expand abbreviations.

## 17   PETITION OF SBA TO CONGRESS

EDITORIAL NOTE: Henry Selden's petition for SBA asked Congress to remit the fine imposed by Associate Justice Ward Hunt at her trial in June 1873—in effect, to review his decision. William Loughridge presented the petition in the House of Representatives on 20 January, and Aaron Sargent presented it in the Senate on 22 January 1874. Both houses referred the petition to their judiciary committees, and those committees issued reports later in the year. The reports provide succinct histories and precedents for the action sought by SBA. (*Congressional Record*, 43d Cong., 1st sess., 795, 830; House, Committee on the Judiciary, *Susan B. Anthony. Report to Accompany Bill H.R. 3492*, 25 May 1874, 43d Cong., 1st sess., H. Rept. 608, Serial 1625, and *Susan B. Anthony. Report*, 16 June 1874, 43d Cong., 1st sess., H. Rept. 648, Serial 1626; Senate, Committee on the Judiciary, *Report to Accompany Bill S. 391*, 20 June 1874, 43d Cong., 1st sess., S. Rept. 472, Serial 1587.)

[*20 January 1874*]

To the Congress of the United States.

The petition of Susan B. Anthony, of the city of Rochester in the county of Monroe and state of New York, respectfully represents:

That prior to the late Presidential election your petitioner applied to the board of registry in the Eighth ward of the city of Rochester, in which city she had resided for more than 25 years, to have her name placed upon the register of voters, and the board of registry, after consideration of the subject, decided that your petitioner was entitled to have her name placed upon the register, and placed it there accordingly.[1]

On the day of the election, your petitioner, in common with hundreds of other American citizens, her neighbors, whose names had also been registered as voters, offered to the inspectors of election, her ballots for electors of President and Vice President, and for members of Congress, which were received and deposited in the ballot box by the inspectors.

For this act of your petitioner, an indictment was found against her by the grand jury, at the sitting of the District Court of the United

States for the Northern District of New York at Albany,[2] charging your petitioner, under the nineteenth section of the Act of Congress of May 31, 1870, entitled, "An act to enforce the rights of citizens of the United States to vote in the several states of this union, and for other purposes," with having "<u>knowingly</u> voted without having a lawful right to vote."[3]

To that indictment your petitioner pleaded not guilty, and the trial of the issue thus joined took place at the Circuit Court in Canandaigua, in the county of Ontario, before the Honorable Ward Hunt, one of the Justices of the Supreme Court of the United States, on the eighteenth day of June last.[4]

Upon that trial, the facts of voting by your petitioner, and that she was a woman, were not denied—nor was it claimed on the part of the government, that your petitioner lacked any of the qualifications of a voter, unless disqualified by reason of her sex.

It was shown on behalf of your petitioner on the trial, that before voting she called upon a respectable lawyer and asked his opinion whether she had a right to vote, and he advised her that she had such right; and the lawyer was examined as a witness in her behalf, and testified that he gave her such advice, and that he gave it in good faith, believing that she had such right.[5]

It also appeared that when she offered to vote, the question, whether, as a woman she had a right to vote, was raised by the inspectors, and considered by them in her presence, and they decided that she had a right to vote, and received her vote accordingly.

It was shown on the part of the government, that on the examination of your petitioner before the commissioner on whose warrant she was arrested,[6] your petitioner stated that she should have voted if allowed to vote, without reference to the advice of the attorney whose opinion she had asked; that she was not induced to vote by that opinion; that she had before determined to offer her vote, and had no doubt about her right to vote.

At the close of the testimony, your petitioner's counsel proceeded to address the jury and stated that he desired to present for consideration three propositions, two of law and one of fact:

First— That your petitioner had a lawful right to vote.

Second— That whether she had a right to vote or not, if she honestly believed that she had that right, and voted in good faith in that belief, she was guilty of no crime.

Third— That when your petitioner gave her vote she gave it in good faith, believing that it was her right to do so.

That the two first propositions presented questions for the Court to decide, and the last a question for the jury.

When your petitioner's counsel had proceeded thus far, the Judge suggested that the counsel had better discuss in the first place the questions of law;[7] which the counsel proceeded to do, and having discussed the two legal questions at length, asked leave then to say a few words to the jury on the question of fact. The Judge then said to the counsel that he thought that had better be left until the views of the court upon the legal questions should be made known.[8]

The district attorney thereupon addressed the court at length upon the legal questions,[9] and at the close of his argument the Judge delivered an opinion adverse to the positions of your petitioner's counsel upon both of the legal questions presented, holding, that your petitioner was not entitled to vote; and that if she voted in good faith in the belief in fact that she had a right to vote, it would constitute no defense—the ground of the decision on the last point being that your petitioner was bound to know that by law she was not a legal voter, and that even if she voted in good faith in the contrary belief, it constituted no defence to the crime with which she was charged.

The decision of the Judge upon those questions was read from a written document, and at the close of the reading the Judge said, that the decision of those questions disposed of the case, and left no question of fact for the jury, and that he should therefore direct the jury to find a verdict of guilty. The judge then said to the jury that the decision of the Court had disposed of all there was in the case, and that he directed them to find a verdict of guilty; and he instructed the clerk to enter such a verdict.

At this time, before any entry had been made by the clerk, your petitioner's counsel asked the Judge to submit the case to the jury, and to give to the jury the following several instructions:

First— That if the defendant at the time of voting, believed that she had a right to vote, and voted in good faith in that belief, she was not guilty of the offence charged.

Second— That in determining the question whether she did or did not believe that she had a right to vote, the jury might take into consideration as bearing upon that question, the advice which she received from the counsel to whom she applied.

Third— That they might also take into consideration as bearing upon the same question, the fact that the inspectors considered the question, and came to the conclusion that she had a right to vote.

Fourth— That the jury had a right to find a general verdict of guilty or not guilty, as they should believe that she had or had not been guilty of the offense described in the statute.

The Judge declined to submit the case to the jury upon any question whatever, and directed them to render a verdict of guilty against your petitioner.[10]

Your petitioner's counsel excepted to the decision of the Judge upon the legal questions, and to his direction to the jury to find a verdict of guilty; insisting that it was a direction which no court had a right to give in any criminal case.

The Judge then instructed the clerk to take the verdict, and the clerk said, "Gentlemen of the jury, hearken to your verdict as the court hath recorded it. You say you find the defendant guilty of the offence charged. So say you all."

No response whatever was made by the jury either by word or sign. They had not consulted together in their seats or otherwise. Neither of them had spoken a word, nor had they been asked whether they had or had not agreed upon a verdict.

Your petitioner's counsel then asked that the clerk be requested to poll the jury. The Judge said, "that cannot be allowed, gentlemen of the jury you are discharged," and the jurors left the box. No juror spoke a word during the trial, from the time when they were empannelled to the time of their discharge.[11]

After denying a motion for a new trial, the Judge proceeded upon the conviction thus obtained to pass sentence upon your petitioner, imposing upon her, a fine of one hundred dollars, and the costs of the prosecution.

Your petitioner respectfully submits, that in these proceedings she has been denied the rights guarantied by the constitution to all persons accused of crime, the right of trial by jury, and the right to have the assistance of counsel for their defence. It is a mockery to call her trial a trial by jury;[12] and unless the assistance of counsel may be limited to the argument of legal questions, without the privilege of saying a word to the jury upon the question of the guilt or innocence in fact of the party charged, or the privilege of ascertaining from the jury whether they do or do not agree to the verdict pronounced by the court in their name, she has been denied the assistance of counsel for her defence.

Your petitioner, also, respectfully insists, that the decision of the Judge, that good faith on the part of your petitioner in offering her vote did not constitute a defence, was not only a violation of the deepest and most sacred principle of the criminal law, that no one can be guilty of crime unless a criminal intent exists; but was also, a palpable violation of the statute under which the conviction was had; not on the ground that good faith could, in this, or in any case justify a criminal act, but on the ground that <u>bad faith</u> in voting was an indispensable ingredient in the offence with which your petitioner was charged. Any other interpretation strikes the word "knowingly," out of the statute, the word which alone describes the essence of the offence.

The statute means, as your petitioner is advised, and humbly submits, a <u>knowledge</u> in <u>fact</u>, not a knowledge falsely imputed by law to a party not possessing it in fact, as the Judge in this case has held. Crimes cannot either in law, or in morals, be established by judicial falsehood. If there be any crime in the case, your petitioner humbly insists, it is to be found in such an adjudication.

To the decision of the Judge upon the question of the right of your petitioner to vote she makes no complaint. It was a question properly belonging to the court to decide, was fully and fairly submitted to the Judge, and of his decision, whether right or wrong, your petitioner is well aware she cannot here complain.

But in regard to her conviction of crime, which she insists, for the reasons above given, was in violation of the principles of the common law, of common morality, of the statute under which she was charged, and of the Constitution; a crime of which she was as innocent as the Judge by whom, she was convicted, she respectfully asks, inasmuch as the law has provided no means of reviewing the decisions of the Judge, or of correcting his errors,[13] that the fine imposed upon your petitioner be remitted, as an expression of the sense of this high tribunal that her conviction was unjust.

Dated January 12, 1874.

⇜ *Susan B. Anthony.*

&#x1F852; MsS, House 8E 3/5/4/5, 43d Cong., 1st sess., RG 233, DNA. Endorsed: "Petition of Susan B. Anthony For remission of Fine imposed for voting Jan. 20, 1874. Refer to the Judiciary Commttee. W Loughridge."

1. SBA registered on 1 November and cast her ballot on 5 November 1872. The board of registry and the inspectors of election were one and the same: Edwin T. Marsh and Beverly Waugh Jones, Republicans, and William B. Hall, Democrat. See below at 18 February 1874.

2. For the indictment of 24 January 1873, see *Film*, 16:1000–1004. It appears also in *Account of the Trial of SBA*, pp. 1–4, *Film*, 17:103ff.

3. Section 19 of "An Act to enforce the Right of Citizens of the United States to vote in the several States of this Union, and for other Purposes," under which SBA was indicted and convicted, opens with this phrase: "That if at any election for representative or delegate in the Congress of the United States any person shall knowingly . . . vote without having a lawful right to vote." Prosecution and defense differed about the term "knowingly." Henry Selden argued that if SBA lacked the right to vote, "she has been guilty of no crime, if she voted in good faith believing that she had such a right. . . . [I]t is incumbent on the prosecution to show affirmatively, not only that the defendant knowingly voted, but that she voted *knowing that she had no right to vote*." Richard Crowley, for the prosecution, insisted "that the true meaning of the word 'knowingly,' as used in the statute, was only that the party charged should know that she was at the time engaged in the act of voting." (31 May 1870, *U.S. Statutes at Large* 16 [1870]: 140–46; *Account of the Trial of SBA*, p. 51; unidentified clipping in *Film*, 17:99.)

4. See *Account of the Trial of SBA*, pp. 5–85.

5. SBA consulted Henry Selden, and he was the witness referred to. See *Account of the Trial of SBA*, p. 14. At her initial examination, SBA insisted she consulted Selden only after registering to vote. See *Papers*, 2:537–39.

6. On 29 November 1872, SBA was examined in Rochester before William C. Storrs, Commissioner of the Circuit Court of the United States for the Northern District of New York, who issued the warrant for her arrest. Storrs (?–1873), a resident of Rochester, held the appointed position for fifteen years. (City directory, 1872; Richard T. Halsey, transcriber, *Tombstone Inscriptions from the Old Section of the Mt. Hope Cemetery, Rochester, N.Y.*, typescript, 1987; SBA, *Account of the Trial of SBA*, p. 125; *Papers*, 2:531–33, 537–39.)

7. See *Account of the Trial of SBA*, pp. 17–19.

8. The report in *Account of the Trial of SBA* omits the steps that the petition here describes. After the conclusion of Henry Selden's presentation on questions of law, the *Account* proceeds to Justice Hunt's reading of, in his own words, "a brief statement in writing." (p. 59.)

9. Richard Crowley (1836–1908) of Lockport, New York, was appointed United States District Attorney for the Northern District of New York in March 1871 and reappointed in 1875. He later served in Congress from 1879 to 1883. Omitted from the *Account of the Trial of SBA*, Crowley's speech was

later published as *Woman Suffrage Question. United States Circuit Court, Second Circuit, Northern District of New York. The United States vs. Susan B. Anthony. Argument of Richard Crowley, U.S. District Attorney* . . . (Lockport, N.Y., n.d.). A newspaper's synopsis of the speech is in *Film*, 17:99. (*BDAC.*)

10. *Account of the Trial of SBA*, pp. 66–68.

11. Richard Crowley disputed this account of the jury's role. He wrote to Congressman Lyman Tremain: "The jury concurred with the judge. There was no dissent by word or sign. On the contrary, when asked by the clerk to hearken to their verdict that they found the defendant guilty, in accordance with the usual form, I saw several of them nod approval, and it was after the verdict was received and entered, according to my recollection, that the defendant's counsel asked to have the jury polled." (R. Crowley to L. Tremain, 8 June 1874, in House, Committee on the Judiciary, *Susan B. Anthony. Report*, 16 June 1874, 43d Cong., 1st sess., H. Rept. 648, Serial 1626, p. 4.)

12. This was the point made by John Hooker about the trial, that Justice Hunt's order of a verdict of guilty "was so remarkable, so contrary to all rules of law, and so subversive of the system of jury trials in criminal cases, that it should not be allowed to pass without an emphatic protest." In July 1874, the *Albany Law Journal* reversed its earlier support of Hunt's action: "In effect, Miss Anthony had no trial by jury," the editors wrote. "She had only a trial by Judge Hunt. This is not what the constitution guarantees her." Hunt's precedent stood, however, until 1882. ("Judge Hunt and the Right of Trial by Jury," in *Account of the Trial of SBA*, p. 206; *Albany Law Journal*, 18 July 1874; Fairman, *Reconstruction and Reunion, Part Two*, 225.)

13. No appeal was available in federal criminal cases, unless two judges presided at the trial and certified their disagreement about the outcome. Justice Hunt alone had the power to decide if errors in the case warranted a new trial, and he rejected Henry Selden's request.

18　⤳　FROM THE DIARY OF SBA

[*20–21 January 1874*]

TUESDAY, JANUARY 20, 1874. Washington D.C.— Hearing before the House Judiciary Committee— F. Miller,[1] S. J. Spencer, B. A. Lockwood— F. E. Burr, P. W. Couzens, & self—all crowded into 45 minutes—[2]

Found letters at house—so took the 9. P.M. train for New York—

1. Francis Miller (1829–1888), a Washington attorney, was Albert G. Riddle's associate counsel in the District of Columbia voting rights cases. Miller's testimony on this occasion was published as *Argument before the Judiciary Committee of the House of Representatives upon the Petition of 600 Citizens*

*Asking for the Enfranchisement of the Women of the District of Columbia, Jan. 21, 1874* (1874). The title misdates the hearing. (*Yale Obituary Record 1888*, from Archives, CtY. See also *Papers* 2.)

2. SBA "sat at Gen. Butler's right hand, and acted as lieutenant to that officer in managing the proceedings," but she declined to speak when she learned that committee members needed to report to the floor of the House in less than an hour. (*Film*, 17:947–49.)

WEDNESDAY, JANUARY 21, 1874. [*Albany, N.Y.*] Reached New York at 7 A.M. and breakfasted with Mrs Murray—[1] then had a short call with Mrs Phelps—& took Cars for Albany at 10.30—

Found Mrs Blake on board— I went direct to Phebe Jones[2] & dined & then to Lydia Mott's[3]—she is better—but very feeble & bad cough—

1. Margaret Cady Livingston Murray (1809–1909), a distant cousin of ECS and early activist for woman's rights, ran a boardinghouse on Twenty-third Street where SBA often stayed. (Howland Davis and Arthur Kelly, comps., *A Livingston Genealogical Register* [Rhinebeck, N.Y., 1995], chart N8; Catherine Bryant Rowles, *Tomahawks to Hatpins: A History of Johnstown, New York* [Lakemont, N.Y., 1975], 83–86; city directory, 1874. See also *Papers* 2.)

2. Phebe Hoag Jones (1812–1881), a widow who lived at 87 Columbia, was a longtime activist in the reform community at Albany. (SBA speech at funeral, *Film*, 22:38; unidentified clipping, SBA scrapbook 9, Rare Books, DLC. See also *Papers* 1 & 2.)

3. Lydia Mott (1807–1875), at 105 Columbia, had provided a stopping place for SBA and countless other reformers for many years. She took charge of meetings and lobbying at the state capital for the antislavery and woman's rights movements. (Thomas Clapp Cornell, *Adam and Anne Mott: Their Ancestors and Descendants* [Poughkeepsie, N.Y., 1890], 134, 219; *History*, 1:744–45n; *Woman's Journal*, 28 August 1875; obituaries in SBA scrapbook 8, Rare Books, DLC. See also *Papers* 1 & 2.)

≈ Excelsior Diary 1874, n.p., SBA Papers, DLC.

19 ⇝ TESTIMONY OF SBA BEFORE THE JUDICIARY COMMITTEE OF THE NEW YORK ASSEMBLY

EDITORIAL NOTE: Lillie Blake spoke first at this hearing before the Judiciary Committee of the New York Assembly and a large audience of legislators and women in the Assembly Chamber at the state capitol.

[22 January 1874]

The principal speaker of the evening, however, was Susan B. Anthony. This veteran in the work was greeted with tumultuous applause, which having subsided, she said it was no new thing for her to appear before this Legislature in behalf of the cause of Woman. Thirty years ago[1] she, with Lucretia Mott,[2] Ernestine L. Rose,[3] and others, came down to Albany to plead for some changes in the laws respecting women. At that time a married woman owned neither property nor her children; if she earned fifty cents by washing or whitewashing, the man who employed her must pay it to her husband, although that husband lay drunk in the house all the time she was at work. If it was paid to her the husband could bring suit and collect it the second time. Over her children she had no control; the husband could will away her unborn child, even, and she had no power to prevent it.

The history of the change in the laws was briefly given, but enough had not been done. Woman would never be secure in the possession of her property until she could protect it by the ballot. She referred to the great injustice of taxing women without allowing them representation. In Rochester a Women Tax-payers' Association had been formed, whose demand was either representation or freedom from taxation. The women of Rochester pay one-fifth of the taxes assessed upon the city. Yet when they attempt to exercise their rights of representation they are subject to fine and imprisonment. They were banding together to resist this oppression. Then matters would be brought to a crisis and it would be an ugly thing to do to enforce this taxation upon those who were denied representation. It had never been a very popular idea in a free country. For years they had asked for the ballot; now they presented the other horn of the dilemma; they asked to be exempt from taxation. Petitions on the same subject had been presented in Congress, and if there were any here whose back bones were weak and needed strengthening, she would say that Benj. F. Butler, Chairman of the Judiciary Committee of the House of Representatives, had promised that these two questions should be brought this winter squarely before the House: shall women have the ballot, if not, shall they be exempt from taxation?

There were some signs of the times which were very favorable. Our Vice-President[4] is a Woman's Rights man, the speaker had just come from Washington, where she had a very encouraging talk with the President.[5] He thought he should be given some credit for appointing so many women in the post office department. She was satisfied with the new Chief Justice, as she knew he was all right on this great question. Coming nearer home she said that she understood the Speaker of the Assembly[6] was in favor of Woman Suffrage. This announcement was hailed with prolonged cheers and calls for Husted. General Husted replied that Miss Anthony was perfectly correct in the statement.

&#x223d; *Woman's Journal*, 21 February 1874.

1. Twenty years, not thirty, had passed since SBA first testified before a legislative committee in Albany on 2 March 1854. See *Papers*, 1:261–63.

2. Lucretia Coffin Mott (1793–1880) of Philadelphia signed the call to the woman's rights convention at Seneca Falls in 1848, and she often joined New York activists in their campaigns thereafter. Mott did not, however, testify with SBA in 1854. (*NAW*; *ANB*. See also *Papers* 1 & 2.)

3. Ernestine Louise Siismondi Potowski Rose (1810–1892), born in Poland and married in England, moved to New York in the 1830s. She was one of the first women to petition for reform in the laws regarding married women's property. In March 1854, she testified before committees of both the assembly and the senate. (*NAW*; *ANB*; Yuri Suhl, *Ernestine L. Rose and the Battle for Human Rights* [New York, 1959]. See also *Papers* 1 & 2.)

4. Henry Wilson (1812–1875), former Republican senator from Massachusetts, was the vice president in Ulysses S. Grant's second administration. Wilson paid a visit to the National Woman Suffrage Association's convention on 16 January 1874 but declined to make a speech. (*BDAC*; *Film*, 17:921–23, 926.)

5. Several newspapers reported this encounter, which occurred when President Grant met SBA while taking a walk on Pennsylvania Avenue. She suggested that he solve his difficulties over the selection of a chief justice by nominating ECS, according to one report; she recommended Henry Selden, according to another. (Boston *Commonwealth*, 24 January 1874; unidentified and undated clipping, SBA scrapbook 8, Rare Books, DLC.)

6. James William Husted (1833–1892) of Westchester County was the Republican Speaker of the House. Active in politics since 1857, he entered the legislature in 1869 and served, with one year's break, until 1891. In the 1880s, Husted was a strong advocate of granting municipal suffrage to New York women. (*NCAB*, 25:53; *History*, 4:853–56.)

## 20 &#x223D; FROM THE DIARY OF SBA

*[22, 27, 30 January 1874]*

THURSDAY, JANUARY 22, 1874. Allbany—N.Y— Hearing before the Assembly Judiciary Committee   Prince[1] Chairman

Had Assembly chamber packed— Mrs Blake spoke first—then I—& lastly Mrs Gage—all chimed in together well

Was dreadfully cut down this A.M.—by letter to my Sister Mary with Stillman's to her—threatening to sue the four givers of the note—if the whole $1000— was not paid by Feb. 1st—and I had to spend hours in writing— begged Stillman to accept the $100— I could now pay him & wait my possibilities—& Mrs Stanton to go to N.Y. & loan it & pay it & <u>trust</u> <u>me</u>— [*Entries for 23-26 January omitted.*]

1. LeBaron Bradford Prince (1840-1922) entered the assembly as a Republican from Queens County in 1870 and served until his election to the state senate in 1875. After 1878, Prince made his home in New Mexico, where he served as chief justice and territorial governor. (W. H. McElroy and Alexander McBride, *Life Sketches of the Government Officers and Members of the Legislature of the State of New York for 1876* [Albany, N.Y., 1876], 77-79; *BD TerrGov.*)

TUESDAY, JANUARY 27, 1874. Willimantic[1]

John L. Hunter Esq[2]
Dr. F. L. H. Willis ⎫
Love M. Willis[3] ⎬        Glenora Yates Co—N.Y.
                    ⎭
Mrs Julia A. K. King[4]—stopped here—
Father W. Hayden—[5]
L. J. Fuller & son William—[6]

Spiritualists Hall—packed house—& many left for want of room—

Got letters here, from J. W. Stillman on the $1000. note—he is bound to sue the <u>givers</u> of it—& Mrs Stanton writes my sister Mary that <u>my</u> <u>family</u> <u>ought</u> to pay it—& they don't see with her— they got none of the good from the Revolution—& Mrs Stanton got a great deal— [*Entries for 28-29 January omitted.*]

1. This small manufacturing center in Windham County was the third stop in Connecticut for SBA and Isabella Hooker, after speaking in South Manchester and Rockville. They spoke in Excelsior Hall, built by the town's spiritualist society in 1868. For coverage, see *Film*, 17:981.

2. John Lathrop Hunter (1834–1903), originally of Maine, moved to Willimantic to practice law in 1871. He was active in the state Democratic party. (*Commemorative Biographical Record of Tolland and Windham Counties, Connecticut* [Chicago, 1903], 132–34.)

3. Frederick Llewellyn Hovey Willis (1830–1914), who was driven from the Harvard Divinity School for his spiritualism in 1857, earned a medical degree and taught in the New York Medical College for Women before settling in Rochester and Glenora. His wife was Love Maria Whitcomb Willis (1824–1908). (Edith Willis Linn and Henri Bazin, eds., *Alcott Memoirs, Posthumously Compiled from Papers, Journals, and Memoranda of the Late Dr. Frederick L. H. Willis* [Boston, 1915], 11–18, 61; Emma Hardinge, *Modern American Spiritualism: A Twenty Years' Record of the Communion between Earth and the World of the Spirits*, 3d ed. [New York, 1870], 173–85; Charles Eugene Claghorn, *Biographical Dictionary of American Music* [West Nyack, N.Y., 1973].)

4. Julia A. K. King (c.1826–?) was, in 1870, the head a household with three children. (Federal Census, 1870.)

5. Probably William Benjamin Hayden (1816–1893), a Swedenborgian clergyman and critic of spiritualism. (Oscar Fay Adams, *A Dictionary of American Authors* [Boston, 1897].)

6. Probably Lucius J. Fuller (c. 1821–?) and William C. Fuller (c. 1846–?), druggists in Willimantic. (Federal Census, 1870.)

FRIDAY, JANUARY 30, 1874. Norwich—Ct—[1] Mrs E. P. Treadway[2]

Stopped with Mrs A. H. Hakes[3]—who keeps a boarding school— Had splendid <u>free</u> Audience—1000—or more— Sent $200. P.O. orders to Mrs Phelps—New York—& Telegraphed J. W. Stillman to call on her & get it—and wrote her to try & stop him from suing Mrs Stanton, A. E. Dickinson[4] & P. W. Davis—[5]

1. After speaking in Putnam and Danielsville, SBA and Hooker reached this manufacturing city on the Thames River.

2. Elizabeth P. Webb Treadway (c. 1829–1910) married Charles F. Treadway in 1848 but lived alone in Norwich by 1861, supporting herself as a teacher and later as proprietor of a variety store. In 1871 she started the Norwich Circulating Library. (*Vital Records of Norwich, 1659–1848*, pt. 2 [Hartford, Conn., 1913], 934; city directory, 1861, 1871, and *Norwich Bulletin*, 8 March 1910, courtesy of Diane Norman, Otis Library, Norwich, Conn.)

3. The identity of SBA's hostess is unknown.

4. Anna Elizabeth Dickinson (1842–1932) of Philadelphia was one of the nation's most sought after lecturers during and after the Civil War, when she was also a close friend of SBA. By 1874, her platform career was on the decline, and she had distanced herself from SBA. (*NAW*; *ANB*. See also *Papers* 2.)

5. Paulina Kellogg Wright Davis (1813–1876), who called the first National Woman's Rights Convention in 1850 and helped to organize the New England Woman Suffrage Association in 1868, also loaned SBA money to publish the *Revolution*. She was the National Woman Suffrage Association's vice president for Rhode Island. (*NAW*; *ANB*. See also *Papers* 1 & 2.)

⚘ Excelsior Diary 1874, n.p., SBA Papers, DLC.

## 21 ⚘ SBA to Benjamin F. Butler

Rochester—N.Y.   Feb. 18, 1874

Hon. B. F. Butler   My Dear Sir

I am just home,[1] and find the <u>Court</u> report of my trial has not been sent you yet— My Lawyer says it shall go to you tomorrow, without fail—he waited to <u>print</u> it— I do hope you will be able to push it to the point of discussion in the house, and if possible a vote—

Now—I want you to tell me what <u>the</u> <u>inspectors</u>[2] who took my vote, had better do—they were find $25. & costs—& like myself refused to <u>pay</u>— The U.S. Marshall[3] now threatens serve upon them a "body prosecution," I believe they call it—at any rate to put them in jail if they do not at once pay it—their day of grace expires to day—

I ought to have put a petition before Congress or the President for them— I want their fine remitted—and that without any concession on their part, that they have committed a crime—

My counsel suggests that they allow themselves to go to jail—and then go out on the <u>limits</u>[4]—that ~~thus~~ ↑in this↓ way they can remain free any length of time— Now will you give the matter a thought and tell me what course you think the best one to make the most <u>healthful</u> <u>agitation</u>— You see Judge Hunt has put the <u>ban</u> on all Judges of Election—by this conviction & sentence,—and I want it removed if possible—

I ↑am↓ hoping you are pushing the District Suffrage Bill— We are giving you so many points to urge forward, that I hope & trust you will not weary of us—

Can you send me ten or 20 or more copies of my petition? Respectfully, Gratefully

           ⤳   *Susan B. Anthony*

⤳ ALS, Benjamin F. Butler Papers, DLC.

1. She concluded her eighteen meetings in Connecticut at Glastonbury on 14 February and reached Rochester on the sixteenth.

2. The inspectors, all residents of the Eighth Ward, were found guilty of registering women who were not eligible voters and accepting their ballots, in violation of the Enforcement Act of 1870. Their trial immediately followed SBA's in June 1873, and it is included in *Account of the Trial of SBA*. William B. Hall, described as a young man, resided at 13 West Troup and worked as a clerk. He was the Democrat of the group. (City directory, 1871 to 1873.) Edwin T. Marsh (c. 1840–?), a Republican, was selected by the city council just before the 1872 election to fill a vacancy. A veteran who spent ten months in Confederate prisons and a letter carrier through 1873, Marsh had recently gone into business as a druggist. (City directory, 1871 to 1874; Federal Census, 1860.) Beverly Waugh Jones (1848–1879) was a roofer, who lived at 13 West Atkinson. Voters in the ward elected him to be an inspector of election, and at the time of the voting incident, he had been four years in the post. (City directory, 1872, 1873; Halsey, *Tombstone Inscriptions of the Mt. Hope Cemetery.*)

3. Deputy United States Marshal Elisha J. Keeney (1810–1874) was in charge. Keeney, who had twice been Rochester's chief of police before the war, was the marshal assigned to SBA in 1872 and 1873. Richard Crowley, the United States District Attorney, issued the writ of capias ad satisfaciendum, signed on 3 February 1874. SBA means "body execution," the seizure of a person to enforce a judgment for the payment of a fine. SBA learned that New York law barred federal authorities from executing the same writ on a woman. (*Rochester Union and Advertiser*, 12 May 1874; Halsey, *Tombstone Inscriptions of the Mt. Hope Cemetery*; Rochester *Evening Express*, 26 February 1874, SBA scrapbook 8, Rare Books, DLC; SBA to Isabella B. Hooker, 17 February 1874, and SBA to B. F. Butler, 26 February 1874, *Film*, 17:987–95, 1015–19.)

4. That is, to be bailed out.

·⟨⟶⟩·

## 22 ➷ FROM THE DIARY OF SBA

[*19–20 February 1874*]

THURSDAY, FEBRUARY 19, 1874. At Home— Mother a little better—[1] Letter from Carter & Thompson[2]—Anna E. Dickinson's Lawyers— asking what I proposed to do about the Stillman note—showing that she would not loan a dollar to me—to save the suit—any more than Mrs Davis or Mrs Stanton—not one of them felt the slightest responsibility to aid me— Sister Mary went into school to day—& left mother in my charge

1. Lucy Read Anthony had fallen soon after Guelma's death. Through December and January, she suffered acute pain and grew weaker. Mary Anthony sent daily reports of her condition while SBA lectured in Connecticut, and SBA concluded it was "clearly her last sickness." Lucy Anthony, however, lived until 1880. (SBA diary, December 1873, January, February 1874, *Film*, 16:617ff, 17:491ff.)

2. Alfred G. Carter and John A. Thompson practiced law at 150 Nassau Street, New York City. (City directory, 1875.)

FRIDAY, FEBRUARY 20, 1874. At Home— Mother a little more comfortable— Letter from Sister Annie[1]—all well there—

Went down town before dinner—bought the rose blankets—& rubber water bottle for Mother— back to lunch—found Huldah Anthony[2] here—& so went to niece Maggies— Harry better[3]—but looks puny & is weak—

Got off letter to J. W. Stillman—with check of $600— principal— $11— interest & 18 Costs of suit to collect— Loaned $500— of Sister Mary to pay it up— Now all my debts are to Mother & Mary[4]

1. Anna E. Osborne Anthony (1845–1930), married to Daniel R. Anthony since 1864, lived in Leavenworth, Kansas. (Anthony, *Anthony Genealogy*, 185; *U.S. Biographical Dictionary: Kansas Volume*, 56–63. See also *Papers* 1 & 2.)

2. Huldah Griffin Anthony was the widow of Asa Anthony, a distant cousin of SBA's father, and one of Rochester's Quaker reformers since 1842. Her daughter-in-law joined SBA in voting in 1872, and she herself attended at least one meeting of the Women Taxpayers' Association. (Anthony, *Anthony Gene-*

*alogy*, 120–21; Hewitt, *Women's Activism and Social Change*, 61; Records of Saratoga Monthly Meeting and Queensbury Monthly Meeting, PSC-Hi.)

3. Henry Anthony Baker, born 1870, was the older son of George L. and Margaret McLean Baker.

4. Earlier in the month, she sent two payments to Stillman of one hundred dollars each. See SBA diary, 1874, February accounts.

❧ Excelsior Diary 1874, n.p., SBA Papers, DLC.

23 ❧ BENJAMIN F. BUTLER TO SBA

Washington, D.C., Feb 22, 1874.

My Dear Miss Anthony:

There are no copies of your petition printed     Petitions are not usually printed[1]

I have drawn a report in your case and submitted it to the Committee; it is under discussion.

In regard to the inspectors of Election I would not, if I were they, pay, but allow any process to be served, and I have no doubt the President will remit the fine if they are pressed too far. I am Yours Truly

❧ *Benj F Butler*

❧ LS, on letterhead of the House of Representatives, HM 10555, Ida Harper Collection, CSmH.

1. The Senate did print the petition. *Petition of Susan B. Anthony*, 43d Cong., 1st sess., Sen. Mis. Doc. 39, Serial 1584.

24 ❧ "WOMAN'S WHISKY WAR": LECTURE BY ECS
TO THE RADICAL CLUB OF PHILADELPHIA

EDITORIAL NOTE: ECS spoke to a regular meeting of the Radical Club of Philadelphia in their meeting rooms at 333 Walnut Street about the Woman's Crusade against the liquor trade. This new protest had spread like a fire, from Wisconsin in 1873 to western New

York in late December, and into Ohio, Indiana, Illinois, and Iowa by mid-January 1874. In the usual instance, bands of praying women, encouraged by ministers in each town, marched on saloons to demand that the proprietors sign a temperance pledge and destroy their supplies of liquor. Before the movement slowed later in the year, more than nine hundred crusades took place across the country. ECS repeated this speech in Detroit on 27 March, by which time the crusades had swept across Michigan. (Jack S. Blocker, Jr., *"Give to the Winds Thy Fears": The Women's Temperance Crusade, 1873–1874* [Westport, Conn., 1985]; Genevieve G. McBride, *On Wisconsin Women: Working for Their Rights from Settlement to Suffrage* [Madison, Wis., 1993], 55–60, 315; *Film*, 17:1043–44.)

[25 February 1874]

This movement is now rousing much thought among the people, filling large space in our daily journals.

The friends of temperance receive the news with gladness; whisky dealers with fear and trembling; and philosophers hesitate to express an opinion, and respond to all inquiries, "Let us wait and watch."

Radical clubs,[1] I suppose, are organized to send forth a certain sound on all movements and questions that from time to time force themselves on public consideration. Hence it is proper to express an opinion here on the wisdom of the present attack on King Alcohol.

I notice it is called in all our journals "the woman's war." This settles one question, that women will fight, choosing their own weapons and mode of warfare. After black men fought in the late rebellion the nation gave them freedom and the ballot, because it was said they had earned it. If this severe contest with rumsellers, by night and day, in rain and sleet and snow, earns the ballot for women, so far so good. I notice the clergy of all orthodox denominations sustain the movement, actually countenance women in preaching, praying and singing to promiscuous assemblies in the public streets, "instead of asking questions of their husbands and influencing them at home," thus obeying the injunctions of Paul.[2]

If this demonstration, carried on by leading women in the several churches, forever settles the question of woman's right to speak and act for the public good, and compels Brooklyn Presbyteries,[3] school boards[4] and that ilk to reverse their decisions, there is another point gained.

I suppose those of us here assembled are all agreed on the general question of intemperance, that it is a social, moral, political calamity, sapping the very foundations of national virtue, strength and prosperity. Statistics show that most of the crime and pauperism in the country can be traced directly to the dram shops—for drunkenness is to-day our great national vice. Its victims fill our poor-houses, jails, prisons, asylums and hospitals. The deaf, the dumb, the blind, the insane paupers and orphans are all the legitimate children of alcohol in some form. Many of the terrible accidents by land and sea can be traced to the same cause. Its victims cower at every hearthstone—in our pulpits, editorial chairs and legislative assemblies, shadowing all our lives.

The taxes on whisky, its sale and license, occupy a large space annually in our statutes. But nothing effective has as yet been accomplished for the repression of intemperance.

If, then, women, with exhortations, psalms, prayers, faith and enthusiasm, can end all this in a grand pentecostal outpouring of the spirit of God, as well as whisky barrels and demijohns, why should there not be a grand national rejoicing from Maine to Texas? This might be the best way yet suggested of celebrating the Centennial, a national holiday which the people of your State seem just now in danger of bearing its responsibilities and glories quite alone.[5]

Instead of taxing the nation $20,000,000 for a demonstration in Philadelphia, would it not be better to save $100,000,000 by a universal crusade on dram shops, wine cellars and distilleries?

This is one view of the case, but there is another, and quite as important, in summing up the principles of just government.

So long as the nation legalizes the manufacture, importation, and sale of whisky, and licenses its agents all over the land to deal it out to the people, by what right is the war carried on and the traffic made disreputable? It is not wise to play fast and loose in this way with principles of equity, and confuse unthinking minds as to the province of law.

If dram selling and distilling are crimes against the higher law, let us say so in our statute books, and act accordingly. If the traffic promotes the best interests of the nation, and is so respectable a branch of business that whisky dealers may be deacons and elders in churches, Congressmen, State legislators, leaders of ton, why disturb the dramshop keepers? They but carry out the policy of Deacon Jones and the Hon. John Doe.

This "whisky war," as now waged, is mob law, nothing more nor less, and neither church influence, psalms nor prayers can sanctify it. Though we may wink at mob law in a good cause, we are educating the people to use it in a bad one.

Here, where we have no popes or kings, no royal family or apostolic descension, nothing in our human relations to call out reverence and awe, law to our people should be a holy thing, and the ballot-box the holy of holies.

As every man and woman in this republic are sovereigns in their own right, responsible for the laws and constitutions, we should see that they keep pace with the public sentiment of the people. It is the right and duty of every woman to use her moral power in every way for the safety of her country and the preservation of republican institutions, and at every election, municipal and national, seal her power and make it effective by casting her vote into the ballot-box.

It is fatal in a republic to educate the people into a contempt for constitutions and laws, especially as they themselves constitute the government and hold the power to amend constitutions and repeal laws.

The trouble is, American citizens do not yet appreciate the dignity of their position nor the responsibility that self-government involves.

What should we say of an individual who made a set of rules to regulate his every-day life, and then trampled them all under foot? We should say that he was incapable of self-government. What shall we say of a people who have legislated nearly a century on alcohol as a factor in their political, religious, commercial and social relations, who, instead of revising their statutes and vigorously enforcing their laws, ignore the personal and property rights of one class of their citizens, and send their women into the byways and sinks of iniquity and vice in towns and cities to pray down the evils and crimes they vote up?

We should say such people are incapable of self-government.

If the hour has come when men see that the "moral necessity" of the nation demands woman's help, let it be asked and given in line with law. Let her be recognized as a component part of the legislative, judicial and executive branches of the government.

I would rather, by my vote and voice in the laws, regulate the whisky traffic and uniformly protect the people against the rapacity of liquor dealers, than by an occasional spirit of enthusiasm make the obscure dram-seller odious and set one drunkard on his feet again. I consider it a cruel waste of woman's strength, influence and enthusiasm to be forever patching the rents man so recklessly makes in the world of morals.

I would rather, with the purse in my own hand, buy a good substantial suit of clothes for my boy, put his feet in the best English stockings, double heels and toes, and with the ballot in my own hand secure free-trade, good cloth and stockings at low prices, than to spend my days patching the cheap things that paterfamilias might purchase under his system of protection.

It is a degradation of the religious element in woman to use it exclusively, as men do now, to mitigate by indirect influences the crimes of their making, instead of, by direct power, preventing them.

Instead of teaching a higher moral code in our pulpits, and sealing it at the ballot-box, as the matrons of this Republic have a right to do, shall woman, insulted by a Brooklyn Presbytery and Boston School Board, be granted no higher mission for good than as humble petitioners at the feet of drunkards and rumsellers in a dram shop.

Shall woman's political sagacity as to war, finance, and social life always manifest itself in scraping lint, saving pennies and fishing for drunkards in the muddy parts of our cities?

Woman's sympathy in great national calamities needs some other expression than prayers and tears.

We have had sympathy enough poured out from heartbroken mothers, wives and daughters, to sober every drunkard in the universe; but sympathy as a civil agent is vague and powerless until caught and chained in logical, irrefragible propositions, and coined into State law. The dignified way for women to express their opinions on all questions of national policy is in convention, in the halls of legislation, in the pulpit, in the press, and at the fireside, and vote them at the ballot-box, conscientiously and religiously as the most sacred duty the American citizen can execute.

Mobs in the streets, on the sidewalks, or crowding into halls and neighbors' houses, are all alike to be deplored. The den of the rumseller, in a by-lane, with law and the Constitution on his side, and the American flag over his head, is, in one sense, as sacredly intrenched as the wine-bibbing nabob in his palace in Fifth avenue, who treats our sons and daughters to champagne and sherry. We must take from both the protection of the flag, the law and public sentiment, and when every psalm and prayer is backed by a vote the devil himself will begin to tremble. But he will laugh in his sleeve at woman's influence so long as, by law, gospel and public sentiment, she is a slave in the State, the church and the home.

There is a body of women in this country who believe that they have the right of suffrage, and that the best interests of the nation demand the recognition of their rights.

How would it be for them to commence a campaign of singing and prayer in all the State Legislatures and at the National Capitol, interrupting the regular business, until their wrongs were redressed.

Much of the business done under these domes is as depleting to the national treasure as the whisky traffic, and it might be as beneficial to public morals to bring our representatives, as dram sellers, to repentance.

But without some form of government we should have anarchy. Hence, we patiently submit to unjust laws, until, by educating public sentiment, we can repeal them.

When laws and customs are so oppressive as to be no longer endured; when resistance is general as to carry everything before it, then a movement rises to the dignity of a revolution; anything short of this is mob law, and, in the end, does more harm than good.

The lesson these women in Ohio are learning to-day they will teach their sons at their hearthstones. They practically say to them now, votes, laws, constitutions are nothing, when you see evils and crimes go forth with songs and prayers and a "thus saith the Lord" in your mouth, and turn and overturn at your good pleasure. Shall labor thus settle its wrongs with capital in our mines, manufactories and metropolis? Shall those interested in sailors' rights besiege every tyrannical captain and keep him in harbor until his heart is softened?[6] Shall prison reformers pitch their tents within those gloomy walls until they melt the strong keepers and iron doors and set the victims free?[7]

There is a better way to a higher civilization than this, and that is to organize the faith, enthusiasm, spirituality, moral power of woman, and, in combination with the best qualities of manhood, incorporate it with the laws and constitutions of the Republic. We need this united thought to-day in government. "A military necessity" eight years ago demanded the enfranchisement of the black man. A "moral necessity" now demands the enfranchisement of woman, and there is a poetic justice in the nation's slaves thus being at last its saviors.

⤙ *Philadelphia Inquirer*, 26 February 1874.

1. Philadelphia's Radical Club was founded by Edward M. Davis and shared rooms with the Citizens' Suffrage Association. At the time of its dissolution in 1876, Davis described it as promoting "the doctrine of equal political rights without regard to color, sex or nationality"; opposing "idolatry in the worship of days or books or people"; and upholding "the rights of conscience as firmly for those with whom we differ as for those who agree with us." (*Philadelphia Inquirer*, 21 December 1876; Timothy Messer-Kruse, *The Yankee International: Marxism and the American Reform Tradition, 1848–1876* [Chapel Hill, N.C., 1998], 117.)

2. 1 Cor. 14:34–35. The apostle Paul commanded women to keep silent in churches and learn instead from their husbands at home.

3. The Presbytery of Brooklyn, New York, had reopened its investigation of teaching by Sarah F. Smiley at the Lafayette Avenue Presbyterian Church. An incident in 1872, when Smiley preached a sermon, led the General Assembly of the Presbyterian Church to restate its rule that women not "teach and exhort or lead in prayer in public and promiscuous assemblies." Late in 1873, Smiley returned to Brooklyn to lead an evening lesson, and the Presbytery found the church in violation of the denominational rule. (*Golden Age*, 20 January 1872, 2 February 1874, the latter in *Film*, 17:984–85; *Woman's Journal*, 17 February, 16 March 1872, 31 January 1874; *New York Times*, 24 April, 20 May 1872, 28 January, 15 April 1874; Lois A. Boyd and R. Douglas Breckinridge, *Presbyterian Women in America: Two Centuries of a Quest for Status* [Westport, Conn., 1983], 98–100. See also *Papers*, 2:624, 636n.)

4. Three of Boston's wards elected women to the school committee in 1873, but when the time came for them to take their seats, the committee, on the advice of the city's solicitor, declared them ineligible to serve. Repeated efforts to reverse that decision and protests by male voters kept the story in the news through January and February 1874. In June the legislature passed an act to declare women eligible, and the women were reinstated. (*Woman's Journal*, 27 December 1873, 3, 17, 31 January, 7, 14, 21, 28 February 1874; *History*, 3:289–90.)

5. In 1871, Congress created the Centennial Commission to plan an international exposition in Philadelphia to celebrate the anniversary of the Declaration of Independence, but the legislation stipulated that the federal treasury would not fund the event. Due in large part to the economic depression that began in 1873, the commission had trouble raising money beyond the 1.5 million dollars appropriated by Pennsylvania and Philadelphia. In February 1874, city and state officials requested financial assistance from the federal government. (John Henry Hicks, "The United States Centennial Exhibition of 1876" [Ph.D. diss., University of Georgia, 1972], 27–31, 38–47.)

6. Postwar protests by American seamen against their lack of civil rights on land and sea drew national attention in the press. Congress passed the Shipping Commissioners Act of 1872, but dramatic reports of brutality aboard ship

were numerous in 1873. (J. Grey Jewell, *Among Our Sailors* [New York, 1874]; Richard H. Dillon, *Shanghaiing Days* [New York, 1961], 127, 139-70.)

7. Prison reformers organized themselves nationally by 1870 and internationally by 1872 to investigate conditions, develop strategies for reforming inmates, and wrest control of penal institutions from politicians. ECS was drawn to their ideas, as she was to many examples of the application of social science to social problems. She frequently visited prisons, notably in San Francisco, Cook County, and Jackson, Michigan, and among her papers is a manuscript "Prison Life," a speech or article endorsing reform, written circa 1876. (Blake McKelvey, *American Prisons: A History of Good Intentions* [Montclair, N.J., 1977], 64-115; *Film*, 18:1109-42; *Eighty Years*, 303-6.)

## 25    ⚭    FROM THE DIARY OF SBA

*[25 February, 2-3 March 1874]*

WEDNESDAY, FEBRUARY 25, 1874. [*Rochester*] Beverly W. Jones arrested this A.M. & taken to Jail—[1] His Father paid his fine & he was soon out— Marsh arrested in P.M.—and I called at Jail about 6 P.M[2] Then walked through Snow to Judge Selden's—he was gone—then walked to Democrat office[3]—& home at 10— couldn't bear to leave Marsh in that dolorous place over night— [*Entries for 26 February–1 March omitted.*]

1. Deputy Marshal Elisha Keeney made the arrests. William Hall turned himself in on 26 February. (Rochester *Evening Express*, 26 February 1874, SBA scrapbook 7, Rare Books, DLC.)

2. Signing the register that recorded the prisoners' many visitors, SBA wrote: "In an American Bastile for practically recognizing the right of consent to the governed— So be of good cheer—" (Visitors' Register of Edwin T. Marsh and William B. Hall, SBA Collection, MNS-S.)

3. The next morning, the Rochester *Democrat and Chronicle* published the text of Benjamin Butler's 22 February letter to SBA, above. On this day SBA also telegraphed Butler about the arrests. See *Film*, 17:1007-8.

MONDAY, MARCH 2, 1874. Left Dansville[1] at 7 A.M. for Rochester— went direct to Jail—took a 9.30 breakfast in the Inspectors cell— Mrs Truesdell[2] had sent basket of lunch & pail of coffee— Hall & Marsh keep up good cheer—but Marsh's business is suffering & his wife[3] is threatening to pay the fine— Thence to Van Vhooris office & to

Marshall Keeneys to get boys out on limits— Sent Telegram to Crowley—
He [*illegible*] at 1— Telegram from Senator A. A. Sargent saying
President was making out Papers to release the Inspectors—[4] Inspec-
tors bailed out on the limits at 6 P.M.[5]

Uncle Humphrey Anthony[6] & son Willie came at night—

1. She spoke on 28 February at Our Home, the water-cure in Dansville,
New York, and stayed until this morning. In the register at the jail, she noted
that her audience decided to petition the president for the release of the
inspectors; "The indignation of the people was intense." (Visitors' Register,
SBA Collection, MNS-S.)

2. Sarah Cole Truesdale (1837–1890), a neighbor of the Anthonys on Madison Street and the wife of a lawyer, was indicted with SBA for voting. Her
husband visited the prisoners on this date. (Peck, *History of Rochester and
Monroe County, N.Y.*, 1:641; city directory, 1872; correspondence with Mrs.
George Truesdale Clarke, Rochester, N.Y.)

3. Esther E. Marsh (c. 1849–?).

4. A. A. Sargent to SBA, 2 March 1874, *Film*, 17:1020. The telegram arrived
at midday. President Grant's pardon was dated March 3, but several days
passed before it reached Rochester. (*History*, 2:949.)

5. Samuel D. Porter and Alonzo L. Mabbett offered bail for the inspectors.
According to local papers, Elisha Keeney refused to admit them to bail;
Richard Crowley told the federal commissioner he would not advise him what
to do; the commissioner decided he lacked authority to act; and finally, the
county sheriff sought legal opinion about his own authority to release the men.
(Rochester *Democrat and Chronicle*, 3, 4, 5 March 1874.)

6. Humphrey Anthony, Jr., (1818–1896) was the youngest brother of SBA's
father. He brought with him the tenth of his thirteen children, William Winton
Anthony (1860–1904). (Anthony, *Anthony Genealogy*, 171, 221, 223.)

TUESDAY, MARCH 3, 1874. City Election— Marsh & Jones re-elected to
the office of Inspector by a good majority vote—thus has the 8th Ward
rebuked Judge Hunt by honoring the boys— The day was perfectly
beautiful— I did not attempt to vote—as Sylvester Lewis scratched my
name off the register list last fall—

Beautiful spring day— Eugene[1] took Humphrey about to see the
City—

1. Eugene Mosher (1819–1894) married SBA's sister Hannah in 1845. His
family lived next door to the house inhabited by SBA, Mary, and their mother.
(Chamberlain and Clarenbach, *Descendants of Hugh Mosher*, 128–29, 311–12.)

⚹ Excelsior Diary 1874, n.p., SBA Papers, DLC.

## 26  &#x5E1;  ISABELLA BEECHER HOOKER TO ECS

Hartford [*Conn.*] March 13, [*1874*]

Dear Mrs Stanton

You know I am expecting to sail early in May—so it is impossible that I should help about the meeting in any way.[1] But there are women enough & to spare I should say in & near New York. To begin with you & Susan are a host—& I wouldn't mind carrying on a Convention with us three alone—by judicious interchange, repartee & management we could keep a house interested one day at least & that is all you need to undertake— I told Susan to try hard for a church & that would save expense—& taking advantage of this temperance crusade, & the deep religious feeling underlying it I think you can get a church. I cannot at all agree with the views you expressed at Philadelphia— I believe a pentecostal outpouring is upon us, today & women are the anointed ones at last—& ~~they~~ ↑there↓ is no end to the gifts that are being bestowed. If we are not to speak ~~with~~ ↑in↓ foreign tongues we are to speak with inspiration in our own & all hearts are to give way before us.[2] I enclose a few words I said at a New Haven meeting on this subject[3]—& pray you beware how you overlook the love of the Heavenly Father in thus bringing the most conservative & fastidious women of the land to a sense of their ↑own personal↓ responsibility for the corruptions of the day. Every one of these women is on her way to the polls—& they will shame us by their prayerful enthusiasm & take the victory out of our hands if we are not up to our high duty of making them welcome in our midst & giving them praise for their work.

I send you copy of a letter just recd. from my sister in law Sarah Beecher ~~whose~~ ↑the rich & aristocratic↓ widow of my brother George[4]—whose only son is settled in the old aristocratic presbyterian church of old Joshua Wilson—the man who prosecuted & persecuted my father for heresy.[5]

"Our church is the church from which all reforms must go forth—times are changed since Dr Joshua Wilson & your father were pastors in the first & second Presbyterian churches in Cincinnati!! The great prayer meeting on the social question is held in our church[6] & the Woman's temperance meetings are being held there from <u>two to five every</u> day, the body of the church being filled. Nannie[7] is a famous worker (my nephew is just married to this Nannie—a very rich girl from Pittsburg—handsome & accomplished also & from ↑one of↓ the most aristocratic old families of Ohio)—enters as earnestly into religious & church work as she ever did into the gaieties of the world & fashionable life. We had purchased tickets for three for the whole course of Proctor's astronomical lectures,[8] attended three & ~~af~~ preferred attending the temperance meetings rather than the remaining lectures.

["]I think you who are living east can form no conception of the intense & deep spiritual engrossment of this woman's movement. Too deep for emotional excitement, a very quiet & subdued feeling, the very earnest & constant prayer for Heavenly wisdom—just a breathing out of the soul to Christ either in silent or verbal prayer, or in singing 'Nearer My God to Thee'[9] & such like hymns. It is like the old old revivals, or crusades in the olden times. I never witnessed such earnestness & solemnity. It is a question whether this work can be carried on in our great cities: but as Dr Hatfield[10] says—'if it is God's work, & he is persuaded that it is, surely it matters not. He certainly can work in the city—numbers more or less matter not to Him.'

["]Those dignified, conservative & proper ladies in Hillsboro never dreamed of such notoriety.[11] My sister Martha & Mrs Thompson of the number![12] I can think of nothing but the walls of Jericho!—so small the means, so wonderful the result.[13]

["]Thanks for your kind & earnest letter on the social question & the <u>Book</u>—(my little book on Womanhood[14] which I sent to Dr Hatfield & her son—& ordered my publishers to send many copies right out there & advertise for sale— I also offered to give two weeks to speaking & organising resistance to the proposed license law—~~but~~ ↑&↓ Dr. Hatfield tho' ~~illegible~~ ↑strongly↓ opposed to suffrage wrote me that if they had not carried the day at once he should have sent for me—& praised my book)—which we like much & are sure that it will do great good. I was told at Clark's book store[15] that it was having a good sale, & our copy has been lent constantly & every one endorses it most entirely"

No dear friend—you are mistaking the signs of the times for once, as it seems to me—& old Joel in the heavens is rejoicing at last in the fulfillment of his prophetic words of three thousand years ago. "I will pour out my spirit upon all flesh; & your sons & your <u>daughters</u> shall prophecy, your old men shall dream dreams, your young men shall see visions—& also upon the servants & upon the <u>handmaids</u> in those days will I pour out my Spirit."[16]

I should run the May Convention on this new enthusiasm & point the way to the permanent establishment of woman's power in government as the only renovator of public morals.

Miss Burr is of my mind in the practical part of these suggestions, at least, though she is a spiritualist & freest kind of a universalist—& if her expenses can be paid will help to the best of her ability— She would write a capital temperance speech—with political bearings—& give it with unction—but she is so modest I cannot convince her that it would be worth her expenses. Susan must do that & set her right to work. Then Olympia[17] is at her best on temperance & would I am sure take hold with a will—so trim your sails to the breeze my friend & your May meeting will eclipse all its predecessors.

I write on a gallop—have so much to do in preparation for Europe—because I am determined to take over assorted papers & speeches & sermons & ~~get~~ ↑use↓ every opportunity to teach there as well as learn that we ~~may~~ women may help each other as if there were no ocean between. Canon Kingsley[18] visits my nephew here today & preaches tomorrow— I shall get well acquainted with him & confide to him that ↑while↓ I have no disposition to be <u>buried</u> in Westminister Abbey or any where else just at present, I should have no objection to <u>preach</u> there or in any other church big or little he may choose to offer. Good bye & much love from your attached friend

✎ *Isabella B. Hooker*

I have just read my letter to my husband & he likes it so much he wants it preserved. At first I was very doubtful of this temperance movement—but carefully avoided saying a word to any but him—now we are both sure of gracious purposes underneath an apparent fanaticism. I Send it to Susan at once—& if you think best to Mr Davis[19] at the Philadelphia friends—they must believe that the Spirit has many ways of working. By the way what a wonderful letter Judge Edmonds published in The Herald[20]—surely we shall all cross the deep without a shadow of apprehension—& with almost a longing ~~from~~ for those strong loving arms that are to bear us away from sorrow & pain to the everlasting hills of light & peace.

❦ ALS copy, Isabella Hooker Collection, CtHSD.

1. Isabella Hooker's disagreements with her family about the Beecher-Tilton scandal led her to make an extended trip to Europe, where she stayed until the fall of 1875. Her departure in May precluded helping with the National's annual meeting in New York City.

2. An allusion to 1 Cor. 14.

3. Neither meeting nor newspaper clipping has been identified.

4. Sarah Sturges Buckingham Beecher (1817–?), the widow of George Beecher (1809–1843), lived in Cincinnati from 1873 to 1879, while her son, George Buckingham Beecher (1841–1925), preached at the city's First Presbyterian Church. (James Buckingham, comp., *The Ancestors of Ebenezer Buckingham, Who Was Born in 1748, and of His Descendants* [Chicago, 1892], 29, 59–60, 138–39; *Yale Obituary Record 1927*, from Archives, CtY; Roger W. Clark, "Cincinnati Crusaders for Temperance: 1874," *Cincinnati Historical Society Bulletin* 32 [Winter 1974]: 185–99.)

5. In 1835, Joshua Lacy Wilson (1774–1846), pastor of Cincinnati's First Presbyterian Church, charged Lyman Beecher (1775–1863), of the Second Presbyterian Church, with heresy.

6. By "the social question," Sarah Beecher meant debate about licensing or regulating prostitutes and houses of prostitution. Cincinnati's Board of Aldermen was considering such an ordinance, but public resistance to regulation won out. (Henry J. Wilson and James P. Gledstone, *Report of a Visit to the United States, as Delegates from the British, Continental, and General Federation for the Abolition of Government Regulation of Prostitution* [Sheffield, England, 1876], 5; Aaron M. Powell, *State Regulation of Vice. Regulation Efforts in America. The Geneva Congress* [New York, 1878], 48, 84.)

7. Nannie Price O'Hara Beecher (1850–?), of Allegheny City, Pennsylvania, and Hillsboro, Ohio, married George B. Beecher in November 1873. She was at the head of a band of crusaders in April 1874 when a policeman shoved the women to hurry them along, but she avoided arrest in May, when forty-three women were rounded up. (Buckingham, *Ancestors of Ebenezer Buckingham*, 138–39; Clark, "Cincinnati Crusaders for Temperance," 191, 196–97, 199.)

8. Richard Anthony Proctor (1837–1888), an English astronomer, lectured in the United States in the winter of 1874.

9. This popular hymn by the English Unitarian poet Sarah Flower Adams was first published in 1841.

10. Robert M. Hatfield, the pastor of St. Paul's Methodist Episcopal Church in Cincinnati, supported the Woman's Crusade and, in the protest against regulating prostitution, used his pulpit to urge men and women to "rise up as a unit on this question and to forever crush it out." Before moving to Ohio, Hatfield served several churches in Chicago. (Matthew Simpson, ed., *Cyclopaedia of Methodism*, 4th ed. [Philadelphia, 1881]; Bessie Louise Pierce, *A History of Chicago* [New York, 1940], 2:291–92, 439; *New York Times*, 23 February 1874.)

11. The crusade in Hillsboro, Ohio, began in December 1873, and though it was not the first instance of praying women pitted against the liquor traffic, Hillsboro became known as the cradle of the crusade.

12. Martha Hale Buckingham Trimble (1820–1890) was married to William H. Trimble, a lawyer and politician in Hillsboro. Her sister-in-law, Eliza Jane Trimble Thompson (1816–1905), led the crusade in that town. (Buckingham, *Ancestors of Ebenezer Buckingham*, 29, 62–65; John Farley Trimble, *Trimble Families in America* [Parsons, W.Va., 1973], 39, 45–46; *NAW*; *ANB*.)

13. Reference to the taking of the city of Jericho in Josh. 6.

14. Isabella Beecher Hooker, *Womanhood: Its Sanctities and Fidelities*, published by the Boston firm of Lee and Shepard in 1874, included a discussion of Josephine Butler's campaign against the Contagious Diseases Acts, England's laws regulating prostitution.

15. Robert Clarke and Company, 65 West Fourth Street, Cincinnati.

16. She quotes the Old Testament prophet, from Joel 2:28.

17. That is, Olympia Brown.

18. Charles Kingsley (1819–1875), Canon of Westminster and a founder of Christian Socialism, arrived in the United States early in February and reached Hartford on 14 March. According to the *Hartford Courant*, 16 March 1874, he was the guest of Charles Enoch Perkins (1832–1917), Hooker's nephew through her half-sister Mary Beecher Perkins. The paper also reported that the announcement that Kingsley would preach at Trinity Church was in error. (*Charles Kingsley: His Letters and Memories of His Life*, ed. Frances Eliza Grenfell Kingsley [New York, 1877], 459; *WWW1*.)

19. Edward Morris Davis (1811–1887), a son-in-law of Lucretia Mott and a noted reformer, was the leading figure in Philadelphia's Radical Club and its Citizens' Suffrage Association. (Anna Davis Hallowell, *James and Lucretia Mott: Life and Letters* [Boston, 1884]; *Philadelphia Inquirer*, 28 November 1887. See also *Papers* 1 & 2.)

20. *New York Herald*, 6 March 1874. John Worth Edmonds (1799–1874) was a prominent judge in New York and a well-known spiritualist. The *Herald* published his transmission of a spirit letter from the late Rufus W. Peckham, another New York judge. (McAdam, *Bench and Bar of New York*, 1:317–18.)

27 &#x223D;   ECS TO SISTER G.[1]

Tenafly N.J. March 16th [*1874*]

Dear sister G.

Name of person & town shall be sacredly kept. I wish to use the fact to show that women can do a radical work in temperance by providing better amusement for boys than society provides.[2]

These praying bands are not exactly to my taste. Lifting humanity up to a higher plane is to be done by the slow process of education, which can be accomplished not by praying, but <u>working</u>.

I am going to Detroit[3] to speak the 26th & will stop & spend a night with you either going or coming if you will tell me where to find you, & then I can ask all the questions I need, but in the mean time write me all you have the patience to do, as I wish to use it, & something might happen to prevent me from seeing you. This temperance revival, I am glad to see for some reasons, though I do not approve the mode of warfare.

The women who are leading the war will not be easily remanded to silence, & as the churches now endorse the singing, praying, & preaching in the most public places, I trust we shall hear no more of "promiscuous assemblies"   One thing is certain "the moral necessities" of the hour demand the best thought & action of all true women.

What times these are in which we live, bribery, corruption & fraud everywhere! It is sad to lose such men as Sumner just now when true men are so scarce.[4] With kind regards for you & daughter   as ever sincerely yours

&#x223D;   *E. C. Stanton.*

&#x223D;   ALS, Gratz Collection (Case 7 Box 20), PHi.

1. This correspondent remains unidentified.

2. Speaking on 27 March about the Woman's Crusade, ECS referred to programs for boys in Detroit and Boston. She later included accounts of the work of Buffalo's Charlotte Mulligan to provide boys with instruction and amusement in her lecture "Our Boys." (*Film*, 17:1043–44, 45:75–125.)

3. She was scheduled by her agent to deliver her lecture "The Coming

Girl," but her trip coincided with the legislature's decision on 23 March to submit to the voters a constitutional amendment for woman suffrage. Joining discussions in Detroit about how to campaign for its passage, ECS chose to lecture on woman suffrage instead. Local women arranged for ECS to speak again about temperance on March 27. In Michigan, where the Woman's Crusade flourished at the time of ECS's visit, collaboration between crusaders and suffragists was particularly strong. (Harriette M. Dilla, *The Politics of Michigan, 1865–1878* [New York, 1912], 150–52; Virginia Ann Paganelli Caruso, "A History of Woman Suffrage in Michigan" [Ph.D. diss., Michigan State University, 1986], 61–64; Blocker, *"Give to the Winds Thy Fears,"* 168; Catharine A. F. Stebbins to Lucy Stone, *Woman's Journal*, 18 April 1874, *Film*, 17:1042.)

4. Charles Sumner (1811–1874), senator from Massachusetts since 1851, died on 11 March. An eloquent advocate of equal civil and political rights, he championed the rights of African Americans but would not take up the cause of women. Hearing news of his death, Lucy Stone remarked to her daughter, "'Well, . . . I don't know that Woman's Suffrage owes much to Mr. Sumner'"; and SBA wrote in her diary, "the noblest Roman of all the senators—he was true to the negro—but never uttered a public word for Equal rights to woman—" (*ANB*; *Growing Up in Boston's Gilded Age: The Journal of Alice Stone Blackwell, 1872–1874*, ed. Marlene Deahl Merrill [New Haven, Conn., 1990], 230; SBA diary, 11 March 1874, *Film*, 17:491ff.)

## 28    ⤳    SBA to Mathilde Franziska Anneke[1]

Rochester Apr. 13th 1874

Madam M. F. Anneke   My Dear Friend

Now, once more, will you give our National anniversary at New York a letter—setting forth the state of our movement in Wisconsin—[2] I received your articles on the Radical Democracy[3] during the last year—also the Washington letter from them & from the Free Thinkers—[4] But as we have no newspaper to report our meetings—no public notice of their reception could be given—  If I should get nothing further from you or them—I will present the same two documents at our May meeting—& try & get the N.Y. city papers to make note of it

The dear Lilie Peckham[5]—how my thought always goes out to her when my eye turns to Milwauke & Madam Anneke—  Hoping to get your good word of the Woman Suffrage Cause in Wisconsin in time for our Convention I am With Love

⤳    *Susan B. Anthony*

P.S. The report of my trial for voting will soon be ready—then I shall forward you a copy— S. B. A

&#8766; ALS, Anneke Papers, WHi. Not in *Film.*

1. Mathilde Franziska Giesler Anneke (1817–1884), educator and author, had been active in woman's rights in the United States since shortly after her arrival from Germany in 1849. She was a founding member of the Wisconsin and National suffrage associations, and she raised one of the largest contributions made to help SBA meet the costs of her trial in 1873. Anneke was also active in German radical and free-thought circles in Milwaukee and nationally. Anneke's undated letter to "My dear friend," which SBA answers, is in Anneke's papers. (*NAW*; *ANB*; Henriette M. Heinzen and Hertha Anneke Sanne, "Biographical Notes in Commemoration of Fritz Anneke and Mathilde Franziska Anneke," in Anneke Papers, WHi; Annette Bus, "'Reason Commands Us to Be Free': Mathilde Franziska Anneke, Early German-American Feminist" [M.A. thesis, City University of New York, 1984].)

2. For the annual meeting of the National Woman Suffrage Association on May 14 and 15.

3. Radical Democracy was a political society of German-Americans hoping, in the words of their message to the National Woman Suffrage Association, "to bring a reorganization of our republican institutions according to radical democratic principles." Reflecting the values of its founder, Karl Heinzen, those principles included equal rights for women. Heinzen was about to transfer the group's headquarters out of New York City to Milwaukee, where the local radicals became its executive committee and Anneke its secretary. Heinzen and Anneke believed that the future of their mission to remake American republicanism lay in forging alliances with American radicals. They began to work with the National Woman Suffrage Association in 1872, sending delegates and letters of encouragement to the meetings. That effort continued, and Radical Democracy made similar overtures to the National Liberal League at its founding in 1876. Their message to the Washington convention congratulated suffragists on the change in public opinion about their cause, assured them that German-American views were growing more favorable, and expressed confidence "that ere long the banner of universal freedom and equality shall wave" throughout the United States and even "into the stagnant political and social atmosphere beyond the waters." (Carl Wittke, *Against the Current: The Life of Karl Heinzen (1809–80)* [Chicago, 1945], 199–228; Karl Heinzen to M. F. Anneke, 23 April 1874, and M. F. Anneke for Radical Democracy to National Woman Suffrage Association, 10 January 1874, both in Anneke Papers, WHi; Boston *Der Pionier*, 15 January, 12 February, 14 May 1873, 30 April, 21 May 1874, 8 January 1875; National Liberal League, *Equal Rights in Religion; Report of the Centennial Congress of Liberals* [Boston, 1876], 54–55; M. F. Anneke to SBA, 30 September 1872, and to ECS, 31 December 1872, these last two in *Film*, 16:476–77, 607–8.)

4. The Freethinkers' Society in Milwaukee, a branch of the Internationalen Bund Freier Gemeinden, was another center of German-American radicalism and support for woman suffrage, in which Anneke worked closely with Karl Doerflinger. At their instigation the Milwaukee and Wisconsin branches of the league adopted a platform endorsing woman suffrage and proposed it to the international. (*Platform and Constitution for an International Union of Liberal Societies*, undated broadside, c. 1872, SBA scrapbook 4, Rare Books, DLC; M. F. Anneke to SBA, 30 September 1872; Marshall G. Brown and Gordon Stein, *Freethought in the United States: A Descriptive Bibliography* [Westport, Conn., 1978], 95–98.)

5. Elizabeth, or Lily, Peckham (1843–1871) attended the founding of the Wisconsin Woman Suffrage Association in 1869, and in the short span before her sudden death in October 1871, she became a practiced public speaker on woman's rights. (*Dictionary of Wisconsin Biography*; *Woman's Journal*, 21 October 1871.)

## 29 ➸ FROM THE DIARY OF SBA

[*16–17, 26 April 1874*]

THURSDAY, APRIL 16, 1874. [*Rochester*] Beautiful spring day— H. H. Day & St John of St Louis from Industrial Congress sitting here called this A.M—[1]

Letter from Sara J. Spencer of D.C. Reform school for girls[2] and D.C. Suffrage bills—[3]

sent Stillman note to A. E. D[ickinson]—1122 Vine st—Phila—to day—by her order through her agent O. G. Bernard—138—8th st New York—[4] The note is paid & receipted—

1. The Industrial Congress of the United States convened on 14 April for a four-day meeting on how to coordinate labor agitation nationwide. Horace H. Day and Andrew Warner St. John were two of three delegates from the secret Industrial Brotherhood. Day (1813–1878), best known for his inventions to manufacture rubber products and schemes to utilize the waterpower of Niagara Falls, was well known among reformers as a spiritualist and a proponent of forming a new political party through which labor unions could find a voice. He worked with the National Labor Union from 1868 to 1871, took part in the founding of the Labor Reform party in 1872, signed the call for Victoria Woodhull's Equal Rights party in 1872, met with founders of the Greenback party later in 1874, and convened a meeting to launch an antimonopoly party

in 1875. St. John (c. 1840–?), who headed the Industrial Brotherhood from its headquarters in Carthage, Missouri, was an influential figure at the Industrial Congress. His model of labor organization won acceptance, and the body formed at this meeting took over the name "Industrial Brotherhood." By 1882, he was a partner in a Greenback party newspaper in Carthage. (*Workingman's Advocate*, 25 April 1874; John R. Commons et al., *History of Labour in the United States* [1918; reprint, New York, 1966], 2:126, 161–70; John R. Commons et al., eds., *A Documentary History of American Industrial Society* [Cleveland, Ohio, 1910], 9:270–73, 239; *Woodhull and Claflin's Weekly*, 25 May 1872; *New York Tribune*, 27 August 1878; Terence V. Powderly, *Thirty Years of Labor, 1859–1889* [1890; reprint, New York, 1967], 59–71; *The History of Jasper County, Missouri* [1883; reprint, Clinton, Mo., 1979], 5, 241, 291.)

2. At the urging of Sara Spencer in 1873, the District of Columbia legislature approved the establishment of a girls' reform school, and in the first session of the Forty-third Congress, Spencer sought federal funds to construct buildings for the school. She kept the National Woman Suffrage Association apprised of her progress, and in May the association resolved to urge Congress to action. Congressman James H. Platt reported Spencer's bill from the Committee on Public Buildings and Grounds on 26 May, the House debated it on 2 June, but Congress adjourned before scheduling a vote. Spencer resumed her efforts in the first session of the Forty-fourth Congress. (43d Cong., 1st sess., A Bill Providing for the Construction of Buildings for the Use of the Girls' Reform School in the District of Columbia, 26 May 1874, H.R. 3498; *Congressional Record*, 43d Cong., 1st sess., 4477–82; New York *World*, 16 May 1874, *Film*, 18:11; S. A. Spencer to James A. Garfield, 9 June 1874, Garfield Papers, DLC.)

3. SBA learned from Benjamin Butler on 15 April that in the current session, only a report on the District suffrage bill would be presented. (SBA diary, 1874, *Film*, 17:491ff.)

4. Oscar G. Bernard (c. 1843–1882) was Anna Dickinson's new manager, trying to revive her speaking career and later promoting her theatrical career. (*New York Times*, 5 June 1882; Giraud Chester, *Embattled Maiden: The Life of Anna Dickinson* [New York, 1951], passim.)

FRIDAY, APRIL 17, 1874. Trial pamphlets done to day—mailed copy to Mrs Gage Hooker & Stanton—[1]

dropped into Industrial Congress—gave me privilege of the floor— & invited me to speak—told them degraded labor of women made them quite as heavy a milstone round working mens necks as that of the "Heathen Chinese"—[2]

1. *An Account of the Proceedings on the Trial of Susan B. Anthony, on the Charge of Illegal Voting, at the Presidential Election in Nov., 1872, and on the*

*Trial of Beverly W. Jones, Edwin T. Marsh and William B. Hall, the Inspectors of Election by Whom Her Vote Was Received* (Rochester, 1874).

2. SBA and "ladies with her" were admitted to the congress in the morning and invited to speak late in the afternoon. Lewia C. Smith of the Women Taxpayers' Association spoke first. The women were present when the congress adopted as one of its principles that "the importation of all servile races" be prohibited and the Burlingame Treaty that governed Chinese immigration be abrogated or at least modified. (*Workingman's Advocate*, 25 April 1874.)

SUNDAY, APRIL 26, 1874. Mother had severe attack of pain through right shoulder—which made it impossible for her to lie down—so sat up & rested head on arm chair with pillow— no relief until after breakfast—then quite smart again— Snow a foot deep last night— Mother, with wish of Mary & Hannah & consent of Aaron cancelled my $1000. note in consideration of my staying at home—through the illness of herself & Sister Gula—during 1873–1874—

✎ Excelsior Diary 1874, n.p., SBA Papers, DLC. Letters in square brackets expand abbreviation.

30 ✎ SBA TO DANIEL R. ANTHONY

*[before 5 May 1874]*

I like the *Times'* article on the women's whisky war.[1] So long as women continue to be the mothers of whisky tainted children, no amount of emotional prayers or tears will ever root out the infernal appetite. Emerson[2] says, "God answers only such prayers as men themselves answer." After ignorant mothers have transmitted to their children the drunkard's appetite,—God cannot answer their prayers to save them from gratifying it.

But this crusade will educate the women who engage in it to use the one and only means of regulating or prohibiting the traffic in liquor—that of the ballot. So soon as they find this crusade experiment a failure, which they surely and very soon will—precisely as all spasmodical, sensationalistic religious efforts are always transient and fleeting—they will realize the enduring strength and usefulness of the ballot. This temperance crusade is only a spasm. But however little permanent good may come of this movement, it is good in itself, because anything is better for women than tame submission to the evils around them, and when they find kind words, entreaty and tears avail nothing, they will surely try the virtue of stones—ballots—to bring down the grand demon that makes their homes a desolation.

&#x2E17; *Leavenworth Times*, 5 May 1874. Filmed at [Winter? 1874].

1. It is difficult to know to which article in her brother's paper, the *Leavenworth Times*, SBA responded. Though he advocated temperance, D. R. Anthony opposed prohibition and consequently did not endorse the Woman's Crusade. His evenhanded coverage of the movement, however, earned him compliments from local crusaders. An editorial on 10 April, as the marches waned, expressed his belief that social ills, unlike political ills, could not be "banished by an instant uprising"; they required "the slow, unyielding progress of better civilization and better thought." But, he wrote, the crusades did focus public attention on "the waste of wealth and humanity which marks the pathway of the drunkard." A male contributor, writing at the height of the local crusade in March, concluded that "the greatest and best result to flow from the present excitement is, that it will convince the women of the importance of the suffrage." A critical editorial from the Rochester, New York, *Evening Express*, reprinted in the *Times* on 30 April, reminded readers that crusaders' tactics reflected "woman's sufferings from intemperance and her political disqualifications." (*Leavenworth Times*, 11, 13, 24 March, 10, 12, 30 April 1874.)

2. Ralph Waldo Emerson (1803–1882), essayist and philosopher. SBA used this quotation often, but its source is unidentified.

31 &#x2653; VIRGINIA L. MINOR AND FRANCIS MINOR[1] TO SBA

No. 2652 Olive Street, St. Louis, May 7th 1874

My Dear Miss Anthony

I find it impossible to send you anything yet for the Convention there really has been nothing done in this State, except a few speeches by Miss Cousins, in some cases for the edification of empty benches.[2] Will try & get M[r] M. to write a few lines just for the looks of the thing.

Thanks for your so called "Trial"[3]   I wish every woman in the land could read it. You defended yourself nobly & there is no better proof of it than the failure of the press to report it, the same thing is being repeated in M^rs Lockwoods case.[4] Make a note of the Court of claims acting as counsel before the Supreme Court in her case. Please send me another copy of the Trial, as it is impossible to get any one to buy, I shall circulate mine as soon as I have one in its place. I enclose my help towards the Convention, are you all not going to make some demonstration at the Centennial? Yours truly

⇜ *Virginia L. Minor.*

Dear Miss Anthony—

I have really nothing to add, as Mrs Minor thought I would, unless it be to say, that what she referred to in Mrs Lockwood's case was, a paragraph we saw in the newspapers to the effect, that the Judges of the Court of Claims intended to consult with the Judges of the Supreme Court about her case—of course they would represent their view of the case, and adversely to Mrs L— I don't think the S.C. Judges ought to know anything of a case ouside the regular course of reaching them. Wishing you every possible success, I am very truly yours

⇜ *Francis Minor*

⇜ ALS, on stationery imprinted with address, HM 10556, Ida Harper Collection, CSmH. Francis Minor to SBA on verso.

1. Virginia Louisa Minor Minor (1824–1894) and Francis Minor (1820–1892) of St. Louis developed the legal argument in 1869 that the Constitution guaranteed women's right to vote. In order to test their view, they sued the election official who refused to register Virginia to vote in 1872. The case, *Minor v. Happersett*, was on the docket of the Supreme Court of the United States awaiting review. (*NAW*; *ANB*; alumni records, Archives, NjP; *St. Louis Republic*, 21 February 1892; *Woman's Journal*, 5 March 1892. See also *Papers* 2.)

2. The Woman Suffrage Association of Missouri, founded by Virginia Minor and others in 1867, was the oldest woman suffrage society in the country, but it became a shadow of its former self by 1874. Between 1869 and 1871, Lucy Stone and her allies drove Minor from office, overturned an agreement to keep the society neutral, and affiliated it with the American Woman Suffrage Association. The state's best-known suffragists, Minor and Phoebe Couzins, worked alone until the National association organized a Missouri affiliate in 1879. (*Woman's Journal*, 3 October 1874; Phoebe Couzins to Editor, *St. Louis Republican*, 29 September 1874, in unidentified and undated clipping, SBA scrapbook 8, Rare Books, DLC; Rebecca N. Hazard to Lucy Stone, 19 April 1875, with clipping from *St. Louis Daily Globe*, 18 April 1875, NAWSA Papers, DLC; *History*, 3:604–7.)

3. She refers to the pamphlet, *Account of the Trial of SBA*.

4. When Belva Lockwood sought admission to the United States Court of Claims in April 1874, the court doubted it could admit her but took her application under consideration. On 11 May 1874, the court ruled that "a woman is without legal capacity to take the office of attorney," and that the judiciary could not overturn "immemorial usages" governing the role of women. Nonetheless, Lockwood could seek review of the decision by the United States Supreme Court. (*New York Times*, 12 May 1874; In re Mrs. Belva A. Lockwood, ex parte, 9 Court of Claims Reports 346, 355, 356 [1873]; *Woman's Journal*, 23 May 1874; Madeleine B. Stern, *We the Women: Career Firsts of Nineteenth-Century America* [New York, 1963], 211-15, 362-65.)

## 32 ⤳ FROM THE DIARY OF SBA

*[11–18 May 1874]*

MONDAY, MAY 11, 1874. [*New York*] Left home at 10 A.M—first for three months— If Mother can only be careful & quiet—but she so longs to see everything & do something— It seems sad enough to leave them so lonely—only Aaron & Mother & Mary— Miss Baker[1] board there but we cannot take her into our hearts as one of family some way—though nice, smart & pleasant—too self conscious to be acceptable—

1. Ellen S. Baker, a school teacher who boarded for several years with the Anthonys, voted in the election of 1872 and was convicted along with SBA. Earlier diary entries make clear that the distance between Baker and SBA resulted from Baker's friendship with Aaron McLean. SBA dreaded the possibility that her brother-in-law might remarry, and she thought it unseemly that he occasionally escorted Baker to public events. (City directory, 1871 to 1874; 30, 31 March, 1, 6 April 1874, SBA diary, *Film*, 17:491ff.)

TUESDAY, MAY 12, 1874. Left Belvidere House[1] this A.M.—too much Lager Beer, Tobacco smoke & Onions smell—finally settled at Westminster—room 197—$2. per day—

Saw Mrs Hallock[2] & Phelps both promised to come this eve to work up report— Mrs Blake too occupied—but none came—

1. SBA first checked into the Belvedere House, at 19 Irving Place, and then the Westminster Hotel, on Sixteenth Street near Union Square.

2. Frances Virginia Robinson Dietz Hallock (1819-1898) was an officer of the National and the New York City and County suffrage associations. (Robinson

Genealogical Society, "Robinson Genealogy. Thomas Robinson of Guilford, Connecticut," typescript, 7:25–26, NN; Shirley V. Anson and Laura M. Jenkins, comp., *Quaker History and Genealogy of the Marlborough Monthly Meeting, Ulster County, N.Y., 1804–1900* [Baltimore, 1980], 60; *Woman's Journal, 3* December 1898; *History,* 3:405, 410. See also *Papers 2.*)

WEDNESDAY, MAY 13, 1874. At Westminster   Mr & Mrs Rose[1] called— glad enough to see the grand old pioneer once more—

Rev Olympia Brown arrived at noon—so hope of force enough to go through the Convention comes with her[2]

Preliminary meeting at Mrs Dr. Loziers this P.M—   Mrs Martha Wright[3] called at Westminster—she stops at St Nicholas[4]—at 10 P.M—

1. William Ella Rose (c. 1813–1882) was an English jeweler and silversmith who came to the United States with his wife, Ernestine Rose, in 1836. (Suhl, *Ernestine Rose,* passim.)

2. SBA learned on 8 April that ECS would miss the annual meeting. Instead, she agreed to attend the Michigan Woman Suffrage Association meeting on 6 May and lecture in the state for a month in support of the constitutional amendment. "I fired back hot shot–" SBA wrote in her diary, "but ended by saying if she could affort to desert our National ship at this hour—we could afford to let her—" (SBA diary, 1874.)

3. Martha Coffin Pelham Wright (1806–1875), sister of Lucretia Mott, lived in Auburn, New York. Active in the woman's rights movement since the convention at Seneca Falls in 1848, Wright was the founding president of the New York State Woman Suffrage Association. (*NAW; ANB.* See also *Papers* 1 & 2.)

4. On Broadway, between Broome and Spring streets.

THURSDAY, MAY 14, 1874. Irving Hall—New York[1] Anniversary Meeting of the National Woman Suffrage Association

Preliminary meeting at 10 A.M—

First session of Con—at 2 P.M. Very fair audience of excellent people— Mrs Rose sat on platform as of old—it was such a strength   Antoinette Brown Blackwell[2] sent note that she would speak for us—first time since 1869

1. At the corner of Irving Place and Fifteenth Street. For coverage of this meeting, see *Film,* 18:10–15.

2. Antoinette Louisa Brown Blackwell (1825–1921) was the first American woman to be ordained a minister. Her friendship with SBA in the 1850s had been damaged by the division among suffragists; Blackwell remained loyal to her college classmate and sister-in-law Lucy Stone. She began to repair the

breach in 1873, when she arranged a lecture for SBA and hosted her in Somerville, New Jersey. (*NAW*; *ANB*.)

FRIDAY, MAY 15, 1874. National W.S.A. Annual meeting—Irving Hall—New-York—

Audiences larger—but <u>no</u> letter from Mrs Stanton—though she promised sure to send one back—to compensate in a measure for her absence—

O. B. Frothingham[1] & A. L. Brown Blackwell spoke this P.M.—[2]
Mrs M. C. Wright made President for coming year

1. Octavius Brooks Frothingham (1822–1895) was a leading Unitarian minister in New York. The press treated his as the major speech at this meeting. (*ANB*; New York *World*, 16 May 1874, *New York Tribune*, 16 May 1874, *Film*, 18:11, 14.)

2. Blackwell spoke on "Evolution applied to the Woman Question." She explained in a letter to Lucy Stone that she spoke for the National association "because they are anxious now to be respectable and proper, and I am desirous they should; and would like to help them. Some of their elbows were apparently quite ready to give me a poke; but if they did, it was not hard enough to hurt; and it was really a good meeting." (21 May 1874, in Carol Lasser and Marlene Deahl Merrill, eds., *Friends & Sisters: Letters between Lucy Stone and Antoinette Brown Blackwell, 1846–93* [Urbana, Ill., 1987], 184.)

SATURDAY, MAY 16, 1874. Settled up at West minster—& moved to Dr Loziers—it is a shame—that I spent at Hotels $22— I did it to be with the strangers who should come—& not one save Olympia Brown stopped with me—so lost my cash & gained no society of friends— rained all day—

Letter from Sister Mary   Mother keeps smart—

SUNDAY, MAY 17, 1874. New York— At noon called at Dr. Millers[1]—41 West 26th   Saw Dr J. C. Jackson Jr[2]—& Geo. F. Train[3]—then to Brooklyn—met E. A. Studwell[4]—his wife died a year ago—then to Cousin Semantha Lapham's[5] to diner—146 Jorolamon st.— Cousin Ellen Squire[6] came after dinner—but oh the Smoke Smoke—Henry, Lucian & Johnny[7]—all together—the sitting perfectly saturated,—nauseating every breath— How can women endure such smells a life-time— Slept in Grandma Lapham's[8] bed—& sheet was saturated with snuff as well as smoke from the sitting room—had a good visit with Nellie & Semantha in spite of smells—

1. Eli Peck Miller and his wife operated the Home of Health Water-Cure on West Twenty-sixth Street. (Harry B. Weiss and Howard R. Kemble, *The Great American Water-Cure Craze: A History of Homeopathy in the United States* [Trenton, N.J., 1967], 153.)

2. James Hathaway Jackson (1841–1928), the son of James Caleb Jackson, worked at his family's water-cure in Dansville, New York. He might, at this date, have been a student at Bellevue Hospital Medical College, from which he graduated in 1876. SBA always assumed he was James C., Jr. (*WWW2*; William D. Conklin, comp., *The Jackson Health Resort: Pioneer in Its Field* [Dansville, N.Y., 1971], passim.)

3. George Francis Train (1829–1904), once a successful financier and founder of the *Revolution* in 1868, now lectured for his living. He spent five months of 1873 in jail for publishing excerpts from the Bible that met Anthony Comstock's definition of obscene, and in order to avoid the potentially embarrassing trial, a state judge declared Train not guilty by reason of insanity. (*DAB*; Willis Thornton, *The Nine Lives of Citizen Train* [New York, 1948]. See also *Papers* 2.)

4. Edwin A. Studwell (1837–?), a New York Quaker, businessman, and abolitionist, became business manager of the *Revolution* after SBA sold the paper in 1871. Mary Merritt Studwell (1835–1873), the daughter of suffrage activists from Brooklyn, married Edwin in 1862. (Garrison, *Letters*, 5:186–88, 410–12, 461; *Quaker Genealogy*, 3:226, 305. See also *Papers* 2.)

5. Semantha Lapham Vail Lapham (1826–1905) was a second cousin and childhood friend of SBA. She married her cousin Henry Griffith Lapham (1822–?) in 1846 and moved from Danby, Vermont, to Brooklyn's Joralemon Street. (*Quaker Genealogy*, 3:198, 332; Bertha Bortle Beal Aldridge, *Laphams in America* [Victor, N.Y., 1953], 182–83; *Friends' Intelligencer* 62 [1905]: 124; William Penn Vail, *Moses Vail of Huntington, L.I. Showing His Descent from Joseph (2) Vail* [n.p., 1947], 224. See also *Papers* 1.)

6. Ellen Hoxie Squier (1833–1904), known as Nellie, was a first cousin of SBA and the daughter of Hannah Anthony Hoxie. She and her husband, Lucien Bertrand Squier (1829–1904), lived in Brooklyn. (*Friends' Intelligencer* 61 [16 January 1904]: 40; Anthony, *Anthony Genealogy*, 191, 197; *Quaker Genealogy*, 3:173.)

7. In addition to Lucien Squier and Henry Lapham, SBA blames John Jesse Lapham (c. 1852–1911), the oldest son of Semantha and Henry Lapham. (*New York Times*, 12 February 1911.)

8. Her great-grandmother, Hannah Sherman Lapham (1726–1799), was also great-grandmother to both Semantha and Henry Lapham. (Aldridge, *Laphams in America*, 27.)

MONDAY, MAY 18, 1874. Called on Mrs Rose   spent two hours very pleasantly—& bade her good bye—probably the last parting in this world—& she thinks there will be no meeting in the next—but I hope &

believe she will find that there is life beyond the river of death—[1] She sails for England the 30<sup>th</sup> inst— She is a glorious spirit—

Dined at dear Mrs Loziers, called on Mrs Phelps, then Mrs Blaked & dined at Cousin Geo. Caldwells,[2] & to Depot at 8 & Bridgeport at 10. and to Rev. Olympia Browns ready to begin Connecticut work on the morrow—[3]

1. For SBA's record of Rose's opposition to spiritualism in 1854, see *Papers*, 1:271–72.

2. George Caldwell (c. 1808–?), who married SBA's first cousin Eleanor Read Caldwell, was a trustee of the Canajoharie Academy when SBA taught there in the 1840s. He lived at 450 Lexington Avenue with his wife, two sons, and a nephew. (Federal Census, 1850; city directory, 1874. See also *Papers* 1 & 2.)

3. Olympia Brown arranged eleven additional lectures for SBA in Connecticut, beginning at New Milford on 19 May and ending at Bridgeport on 7 June. (SBA to O. Brown, 6 May 1874, *Film*, 17:1063–66.)

&#x223d; Excelsior Diary 1874, n.p., SBA Papers, DLC.

## 33  &#x223d;  "WOMAN SUFFRAGE": SPEECH BY ECS IN GRAND RAPIDS, MICHIGAN

EDITORIAL NOTE: Luce's Hall, on Monroe Avenue in Grand Rapids, filled to capacity to hear ECS as her month-long campaign across Michigan drew to a close. Working from 6 May 1874 until early June, she was the first national figure to join local suffragists in their efforts to mobilize voters in every township, county, and congressional district to support the proposed amendment. The campaign offered a "golden opportunity," in the words of Henry Blackwell, for the national movement; "Michigan is now to be the battleground of political reform." The *Woman's Journal* treated the campaign as the major national story and tracked editorial opinion in the state's newspapers. Dozens of men and women from outside the state followed ECS's lead; in mid-June the New England Woman Suffrage Association sent two organizers into Michigan to work until the election; and suffragists in Boston, Philadelphia, and St. Louis raised money for speakers and pamphlets. (*Woman's Journal*, 2 May 1874.)

[30 May 1874]

She commenced by attaching to her line some of Rev. J. Morgan Smith's "corks,"[1] touching the policy or impolicy of extending the ballot to women. He regarded the proposed step as revolutionary, and he hated revolutions. She supposed therefore that if he had lived in 1776 he would have hated the revolution which separated this country from Great Britain; or on the same principle he must have opposed the cause of emancipation and equal rights in 1860 because that led to our recent internal revolution. But she claimed that the Woman Suffrage movement was not revolution; that on the contrary it was a step forward toward full recognition of the principles of our Declaration of Independence—another movement in progression toward securing equal rights for all.

Again, he said the question was comparatively new and not sufficiently discussed. In that she claimed he was mistaken. It had been discussed for thirty years. Women had been enfranchised, partially, in England, Russia, France[2] and in this country and are voting now. It was curious that he had heard nothing of that.

Thirdly, J. M. S. argued that the premises were insufficient; the claim that women were needed to purify or improve the morals of politics was not conclusive; that but few political questions involve the element of morality. But she claimed that all questions of law were also questions of morals—and besides she placed the demand for Woman Suffrage on the ground of right.

Fourth, he said the women did not want the ballot. That she contended was not the real question—it was, Does the public good require that women should vote? And it was a lame objection at best. If women do not want to vote, what is the use of keeping up the fence against them? Because some do not want to vote is no reason why others should be forbidden.

We claim to have a republican form of government, and its central idea is self-government. It is based upon the theory that governments derive their just powers from the consent of the governed, and women as well as men are the governed, and are governed without their consent as long as they are not allowed to vote. It is an insult to women, she claims, to say that they don't want to vote—when the rag-tag and bob-tail of our own and all other countries are invited to vote, provided they are males, are not intelligent women humiliated?[3]

They talk about woman's sphere, and all that, said the speaker, but woman does not wish to be dictated to as to what shall be her sphere, she is to decide her own sphere; she is demanding the rights that are hers by nature. But the male objector says, "we don't want to be governed by women." Very well, the women will retort, "we don't want to be governed by men." "It is a poor rule that won't work both ways."[4] Self-government for both sexes is what we want—equal freedom for both and an equal voice in prescribing the laws. Many objectors, the speaker said, are now claiming that republicanism is a failure, that the ballot should be restricted rather than extended, and some of them openly oppose republicanism. But she claimed that we had not given republicanism a fair trial; she had full faith in it; but instead of simple republicanism we have established an odious aristocracy—the aristocracy of sex. They say the ballot degrades men—Charles Sumner said it was the columbiad of liberty.[5] The idea of republican equality and equal sovereignty in citizenship is what gives us distinction and respect in the old world. In demanding the ballot for women, we are just working up to pure republicanism. Sumner at first opposed amending the constitution, on the ground that the constitution as it was gave all citizens equal protection in their rights. The amendments put in specific language the definition of citizenship and the rights of citizens which Sumner claimed the constitution already gave.

Women are citizens, yet are denied one privilege of citizens, the right to vote. They are taxed without representation, and that is tyranny. There is a woman in New York who regularly refuses to pay her taxes. When the collector comes she puts her attachable chattels out of sight, shuts the door against him, and from some safe position in an upper window fires the Constitution and Declaration of Independence at him till he is glad to retreat, and pay her tax himself.[6] She would advise all women who are taxed and not allowed to vote to disobey the law and refuse to pay. For suffrage is a natural right—the right to protect one's person and property by law. Being a divine right, it is as much woman's as man's right.

The talk about women being so much above men, celestial, ethereal, and all that, is sentimental nonsense. The real woman is not up in the clouds nor among the stars, but down here upon earth by the side of man. She is on the same material plane with man, striving and working to support herself. But the constitution or law which denies to her the ballot while allowing it to the most degraded of men, classes women with idiots and criminals, and insults every woman in the State. Man treats woman as if she were made solely for his use and service. The speaker denied such ownership, such vassalage, and wanted to vote because she wanted to be an independent sovereign in the land. The civil rights bill, she asserted, gives to the blacks rights which are denied to the women of the land.

It has been asserted that women in politics will degrade politics—also that politics will degrade women. But see what women have done in the Western Territories; look into the public schools, and the colleges; everywhere that woman has of late years taken parts in the affairs of life and society which used to be denied to her—is there any degradation there? On the contrary there has been a marked improvement, elevation instead of degradation. Go into a room where a dozen men and no women are talking; their language and tone are coarse and perhaps sensual. Take a dozen women together; they are not so refined in language and conduct as when men are present. The great rule is that the sexes in company have an elevating and refining influence upon each other. What is politics? The science of government, providing for the safety, peace and prosperity of the community, the State, or the nation. Ought there to be anything demoralizing or degrading about that? On the contrary is it not among the highest pursuits of civilized society? But, says the objector, it will not do for the sexes to be mixed up promiscuously at elections, and political caucuses and conventions. Indeed are they not pretty well mixed in this hall to-night? Did the Creator make a mistake in bringing men and women together into the world? Ought he to have decreed that they should not be mixed in the family, that one family should be all males and another all females? Is the family worse for having both boys and girls in it? There is no danger that women will corrupt politics or that politics will corrupt them. But when the women vote they will be pretty sure to demand better and cleanlier places for voting. Law should be a holy thing and the ballot box the holy of holies.

It is claimed that the ballot for women will divide the family, or merely duplicate the voting. But it produces unpleasantness in the family now. Give two dogs a bone and they will fight over it. But give them two bones and there is peace immediately. Woman would not be so bothered and perplexed over the finance question as men are. She would see at once that all the talk of specie currency and gold basis, knowing that there was not one-half or one-quarter enough specie in the country for the purpose, is the merest twaddle.[7] [She'd give her note to pay the plaguey debt and have done with it, of course.—*Rep.*]

In conclusion the speaker insisted that it was not only the right but the duty of woman to vote; that she had equal interest with man in all the affairs of government and society. She spoke of the filthiness and otherwise uncomfortableness of prisons, with an intimation that with a little woman's work in their management they would be made more like flowery beds of ease. She thought the cause would soon triumph in Michigan. She hoped the constitutional amendment would be adopted this year. The great Democratic party had gone down. The Republican party must also decay. Another and progressive party must succeed, in which the women will take part. The twenty millions [whew!] of disfranchised women must yet come to the front, and with the pure and good men reform the government. The Methodists had the other day indorsed Woman Suffrage.[8] The Grangers were all going for it.[9] Success was not far distant.

At the close Mrs. Stanton asked the women who wished to vote to make it manifest by rising. There were three or four hundred in the audience and some forty or fifty of them rose.

❧ *Grand Rapids Daily Eagle*, 1 June 1874. Square brackets in the original.

1. Joseph Morgan Smith (1833–1883), a graduate of Yale College, was called to the First (or Park) Congregational Church in Grand Rapids in 1863. Through his column, "Corks," in the *Grand Rapids Democrat*, Smith campaigned against the suffrage amendment, and ECS used his arguments as a foil for her own. After hearing ECS lecture, Smith corrected her: "we have forty-five reasons against female suffrage instead of the five to which she spoke. The points on which the whole question turns at last are: 1st, Is suffrage a natural right or a political privilege? . . . Second, The effect of suffrage upon the nature of woman." On neither point, he claimed, had she proved the argument. (*History of Kent County, Michigan* [Chicago, 1881], 1132–33; *Grand Rapids Democrat*, 31 May 1874.)

2. In England, the Municipal Corporations Act (1869) and the Elementary Education Act (1870) allowed women partial suffrage. The franchise was restored to taxpaying women in cities, and women were allowed to vote in school elections. Russian women voted in some municipal and county elections. Her inclusion of France is unexplained. (Helen Blackburn, *Women's Suffrage: A Record of the Women's Suffrage Movement in the British Isles, with*

*Biographical Sketches of Miss Becker* [1902; reprint, New York, 1970], 91–94, 108; *Woman's Journal*, 25 April 1874; *History*, 3:844–48, 850, 915.)

3. In the *Grand Rapids Democrat*, 5 June 1874, J. Morgan Smith devoted his column to this phrase. "Perhaps Mrs. Stanton is more of an aristocrat than she imagines. . . . Though not above the vote, she is above the voter. . . . We call the attention of our foreign fellow-citizens to this language of the honorable missionary."

4. Writing in 1837, James Fenimore Cooper thought this "healthful maxim" would be known to his readers. However, modern scholars trace its appearance in print to Cooper's published letter. (*The Letters and Journals of James Fenimore Cooper*, ed. James Franklin Beard [Cambridge, Mass., 1964], 3:281; Wolfgang Mieder, Stewart A. Kingsbury, and Kelsie B. Harder, eds., *A Dictionary of American Proverbs* [New York, 1992], 518.)

5. "The Equal Rights of All," delivered in the United States Senate on 5 and 6 February 1866, during debate on the Fourteenth Amendment, in Sumner, *Works*, 10:224. The columbiad was a large cannon.

6. This story also appeared in ECS's 1867 lecture "Reconstruction." See *Papers*, 2:34.

7. ECS refers to political debates about whether the government ought to resume the gold standard for currency after suspending it during the Civil War. She aligns herself with those who argued that the supply of gold and silver was insufficient to serve the nation's financial needs. The debate had intensified in April, when President Grant vetoed the Inflation Bill of 1874, which was designed to ease the economic depression with a modest increase in the supply of paper currency or greenbacks. Critics charged that the increase would cause inflation. The reporter's aside refers to federal debt in the form of treasury bonds sold to finance the Civil War. The currency debate was linked to the question whether the principal on those bonds should be repaid in gold or greenbacks. (Irwin Unger, *The Greenback Era: A Social and Political History of American Finance, 1865–1879* [Princeton, 1964], 17, 43, 234–45; Gretchen Ritter, *Goldbugs and Greenbacks: The Antimonopoly Tradition and the Politics of Finance in America* [New York, 1997], 36–37, 96–98.)

8. The Michigan Conference of the Methodist Episcopal Church commended the legislature for submitting woman suffrage to the voters and taking "a step towards a higher and purer administration of the government of our country." (*Ypsilanti Commercial*, 6 June 1874.)

9. Farmers and their families organized into local units of the Patrons of Husbandry, or Grange, in nearly every state by 1873, and in the upper Midwest, the Grange was a significant economic and political force. By 1875, six hundred local granges operated in Michigan. Because it granted full membership to women, the Grange seemed a likely ally in suffrage campaigns. At its January and May meetings in 1874, the National Woman Suffrage Association commended the Patrons of Husbandry for giving a wide recognition to women and educating them for future political responsibilities. However, at the national

and state levels, the Grange kept its distance from the suffrage movement. Some local granges in Michigan endorsed the constitutional amendment; the Marshall Grange, for example, scheduled a discussion of woman suffrage on 16 May, the day after ECS spoke in that town, and voted thirty-nine to eleven in favor of the amendment. (D. Sven Nordin, *Rich Harvest: A History of the Grange, 1867–1900* [Jackson, Miss., 1974], 29; Donald B. Marti, *Women of the Grange: Mutuality and Sisterhood in Rural America, 1866–1920* [Westport, Conn., 1991], 10–11, 107–11; *Film*, 17:919–23, 18:12; Marshall *Democratic Expounder and Calhoun County Patriot*, 7, 14, 21 May 1874; *Woman's Journal*, 26 September 1874.)

## 34 ⤙ ECS TO SBA

June 1st. 1874— (Ionia [*Mich.*]—wherever that may be)[1]

You have no idea how these people have work'd me. Every night, & twice on Sunday, has been the rule, straight thro', with speeches in prisons, asylums, schools &c &c & talking in the intervals. I am so tired to-day I am ready to drop. Mrs. Hazlitt[2] has persecuted me ever since I came into the state, starting annoying things in the papers. We couldn't imagine,[3] at first, the source, or the spirit that prompted it, but found her out at last. She wants all the money that is spent in her own pocket, & evidently has an idea that the State of Michigan should be there too.[4]

If you will be at home abt. the 12th. I speak in Perry, Wyoming Co. returning.

Yesterday I spoke twice in Grand Rapids to 1000 people, in the Opera House—[5] As it was Sunday, I gave the Bible Argument. We had the regular services, two clergymen officiating.[6] There is great interest & enthusiasm on the question every-where, thro' out the State but they are not doing the educational work we did in Kansas.—[7] Theodore sails for Europe Wednesday[8] Mrs. Voorhees[9] gave him $500. for the trip, & I just sent him two.— When I return I intend to stop & spend a day with Martha Wright send her this, as I am too tired to write another line. Yrs. as ever

⤙ E. C. S.—

⤙ Copy in hand of M. C. Wright, Garrison Papers, MNS-S.

1. In the evening of 1 June, ECS spoke in Ionia, thirty-four miles east of Grand Rapids. (*Ionia Sentinel*, 5 June 1874.) The query was no doubt added to the place line by Martha Wright when she copied the letter.

2. Mary Adelle Brown Hazlett (1837–1911), a staunch Republican of Hillsdale, came to prominence in the Michigan suffrage movement in 1870 as an effective lecturer and a leader who wanted the Midwest to steer clear of the divisions among eastern suffragists. For several years she presided over the independent Northwestern Woman Suffrage Association. Named to the state executive committee for the campaign of 1874, Hazlett opposed the presence of lecturers from out of state. (Richard Illenden Bonner, ed., *Memoirs of Lenawee County, Michigan, from the Earliest Historical Times* [Madison, Wis., 1909], 2:564–66; with assistance from Mitchell Public Library, Hillsdale, Mich. See also *Papers* 2.)

3. "We" probably includes Catharine Stebbins of Detroit, who traveled with ECS for parts of this campaign, and her husband, Giles Stebbins.

4. For an example of ECS's troubles with the press, in this case brought on by her praise for Democrats, see the Battle Creek *Michigan Tribune*, 28 May 1874. Lucy Stone also saw Hazlett as a source of trouble in Michigan, but she linked ECS and Hazlett together. "I was sorry when I found that Mrs. S. was to be in Michigan," she wrote to her agent, Margaret Campbell, "for she is utterly indiscreet. But it seems to me that, in another way Mrs. Hazlett will do as much harm. Between the two, will *the cause* be ground to powder?" Stone objected in particular to ECS's "attacks on the Republican party." (13 June 1874, in Leslie Wheeler, ed., *Loving Warriors: Selected Letters of Lucy Stone and Henry Blackwell, 1853–1893* [New York, 1981], 250.)

5. Powers Opera House, on Pearl Street.

6. According to the Grand Rapids *Evening Post*, 6 June 1874, she spoke in the morning at the Universalist Church, where the Rev. Richmond Fisk, Jr., (1836–1916) introduced her, and in the afternoon at the Opera House. Fisk was an officer of the state suffrage association meeting in May. In the afternoon, he and ECS were joined by Charles M. Temple, who served as minister of the Westminster Presbyterian Church for three years from 1872. ECS's standard Sunday speech, "The Bible Position of Woman," was reported at length on another occasion in the *Kalamazoo Daily Telegraph*, 18 May 1874. (*NCAB*, 10:199; *New York Times*, 30 January 1916; *History of Kent County, Mich.*, 888.)

7. In 1867, when Kansas voters faced a referendum on amending the constitution to enfranchise women. See *Papers* 2.

8. Theodore Stanton left Cornell during his senior year to study in Paris.

9. Jane Cowenhoven Voorhees (1792–1874) lived in Wilmington, Delaware, with her son-in-law, Allen Voorhees Lesley. ECS visited the family in 1871. (*Biographical and Genealogical History of the State of Delaware* [Chambersburg, Pa., 1899], 1:181; *Papers*, 2:427–29.)

·◖━━━━◗·

35   ᨞   SBA TO BENJAMIN F. BUTLER

Rochester, N.Y., June 11<sup>th</sup> 1874

Hon. B. F. Butler   Dear Sir

Thanks for the report on petition—[1] Saw a copy in Albany—but find none here— Will you please send me a few copies— Will get into our papers in full & have it struck off in tract form to circulate— I wish I had a thousand dollars to print & circulate your report & the Senate discussion on Pembina Territory—[2]

I do not comprehend your Committee's action on the D.C. suffrage petitions—when you so possitively assured me you would bring the House to a vote on that question—

But I am too glad for what <u>you have</u> done in the House on my petition & the La↑w↓yer bill,[3] & for what Sargent has done in the Senate—to wonder or ask why more has not been done—

Will you send me a number of ↑copies of↓ your report—also the copy of the Congressional Record that has your speech or motion in—

I saw an item that <u>Colora[do]</u> is still asking to be admitted as a <u>sta[te]</u>—[4] Don't fail to move to amend [so?] as to ensure woman suffrage— By such means the agitation [will?] be kept alive—

I have watched the reports of your illness with great anxiety—[5] I hope you are quite well again—& may live to see woman politically emancipated & that by your own powerful help— With many thanks Respectfully yours

᨞   *Susan B. Anthony*

᨞ ALS, on letterhead of John Van Voorhis's law office, Benjamin F. Butler Papers, DLC. Letters in square brackets obscured by docket.

1. On 25 May, Butler introduced a report and bill, H.R. No. 3492, to remit SBA's fine. He argued that Justice Hunt's decision to enter a verdict of guilty, without submitting the case to the jury, set a dangerous precedent, and concluded that Congress should "sustain in its integrity the common-law right of trial by jury" by granting SBA's petition. Although the press understood Butler to speak for the Judiciary Committee, SBA may have known he would write a minority report to force action. (Her acknowledgment of his

plans for a minority report did not specify in which cause he would write one.)
After considerable publicity for Butler's report and an outraged letter from the
prosecutor, Richard Crowley, on 8 June, asking Lyman Tremain to vindicate
the judge, Tremain submitted a rival report from the committee on 16 June.
Butler and Tremain could not agree which one spoke for the minority. In his
report, Tremain denied that Congress had the authority to condemn and
censure a judge by remitting a fine, and he defended Hunt's right to direct the
jury to convict. Minutes of a committee meeting on 19 June read that the
committee would take up the matter of SBA's petition "(either for present
consideration or to lay the same over) as to which matter two proposed reports
(No's 608 & 648) have been printed but as to which subject matter no final
determination has yet been had. We consent to the foregoing resolution, and
that, if consented to by all present, it be entered in the minutes of this day's
proceedings, June 19, 1874." The Senate Committee on the Judiciary also
divided. George F. Edmunds, for the majority, doubted the truthfulness of
SBA's petition and denied that the Senate had the legal right to interfere. For
the minority, Matthew Carpenter wrote that Congress had a duty "to declare
its disapproval of the doctrine asserted, and the course pursued" with respect
to the role of a jury in SBA's case, especially in light of the failure to provide
for appeals to the Supreme Court in federal criminal cases. (SBA to B. F.
Butler, 22 April 1874, *Film*, 17:1059–60; *Independent*, 11 June 1874; *Golden
Age*, 13 June 1874; *Woman's Journal*, 20 June 1874; *Congressional Record*, 43d
Cong., 1st sess., 25 May, 16, 20 June 1874, pp. 4243, 5066, 5265; 43d Cong.,
1st sess., A Bill for the Relief of Susan B. Anthony, 25 May 1874, H.R. 3492;
House, Committee on the Judiciary, *Susan B. Anthony. Report to Accompany
Bill H.R. 3492*, 25 May 1874, 43d Cong., 1st sess., H. Rept. 608, Serial 1625;
House, Committee on the Judiciary, *Susan B. Anthony. Report*, 16 June 1874,
43d Cong., 1st sess., H. Rept. 648, Serial 1626; Committee minutes, House 8E
3/5/4/5, 43d Cong., 1st sess., RG 233, DNA; Senate, Committee on the Judiciary, *Report to Accompany Bill S. 391*, 20 June 1874, 43d Cong., 1st sess., S.
Rept. 472, Serial 1587.)

2. On May 28, when a bill to create the Territory of Pembina out of the
northern portion of Dakota Territory came up for consideration, Senator
Aaron Sargent moved an amendment to require universal suffrage and prompted
a major debate on woman suffrage. In a roll call vote, the first of five Senate roll
calls on woman's rights between 1874 and 1880, the amendment failed nineteen to twenty-seven. The bill itself also failed. When it was revived in the
second session of the Forty-third Congress, its sponsor proposed that all
citizens of the United States have the right of voting and holding office, but
opponents of organizing new territories defeated the measure again. An edited
record of the debate of 28 May 1874 is reproduced in *History*, 2:545–82.
(*Congressional Record*, 43d Cong., 1st sess., 4331–45; 43d Cong., 1st sess., A
Bill to Establish the Territory of Pembina, 3 December 1873, S. 44; 43d Cong.,
2d sess., A Bill to Establish the Territory of Algonkin, as Amended, 21
December 1874, S. 44.)

3. In the wake of the decision by the United States Court of Claims that a woman could not practice law in federal courts, Belva Lockwood petitioned Congress to bar such discrimination. Butler, in the House, and Roscoe Conkling, in the Senate, presented her petition. On 1 June, Butler reported a bill drafted by Lockwood, and it was ordered to a third reading by a vote of ninety-five to sixty-six. (*Congressional Record*, 43d Cong., 1st sess., 18, 25 May, 1 June 1874, pp. 3999, 4215, 4447.)

4. On 28 May 1874, Colorado's congressional delegate reported a bill to enable the territory to organize as a state. This followed several failed attempts to gain statehood since 1863, and it took Congress a year to approve the new measure. (*Congressional Record*, 43d Cong., 1st sess., 4345; Jerome C. Smiley, ed., *History of Denver: with Outlines of the Earlier History of the Rocky Mountain Country* [1901; reprint, Denver, Colo., 1978], 494–98.)

5. Butler fell ill in May and was bedridden for a month.

## 36 &#x223D; MARTHA COFFIN WRIGHT TO SBA

Auburn [*N.Y.*] June 25th 1874

My dear Susan—

I have written the call as you request, ↑(if you think best to use it)↓ but unless you are well assured of speakers, I fear a convention during the hot Summer will be as great a failure as the last at Saratoga & Niagara were—& you will hardly admit that it is better to have met & failed, than not to meet at all—[1] Mrs. Gage was here when your letter came, & she thought October would be a more suitable time, never mind if it was not the exact date of the first or other meetings— She said she should have to recruit at the sea shore, ↑& could not be there,↓ & she doubted whether Mrs. Stanton, in her exhausted condition would be able to be there—she hoped therefore that you wd. defer it— I tell you this, tho' of course if you feel assured that a convention would be successful & plenty of speakers ready, you will go on— I would be with you, if I could leave home at that time, but I am expecting a house full of company, & might not be able to get away.— Let me know your decision.—

Now I must tell you about the recent Prohibition Convention here— on the 23rd—[2] Mrs. Gage was cordially welcomed as a delegate from Onondaga & politely conducted to the platform, when she rose to speak, amid general applause; the whole audience rising, when she reached the platform—some objection was then made, but it was over-ruled by a large majority—& the proposition made to waive the discussion until after she had spoken— she made a good speech, & it was very evident that the audience was mainly in her favor—only one persistently opposing. She was invited to remain on the platform. The last Resolution was about as non-committal as you wd. ~~accept~~ expect—gratefully commending the women who had devoted all their powers to the overthrow of intemperance, & hoping they wd keep on influencing their husbands & brothers & sons, & others who have the ballot "until such time as <u>they</u> shall be endowed with the same legal privileges as their fellows."—

During the recess Mrs. Gage prepared a substitute wh. she offered when the Resolution was read for discussion, in the afternoon— Quite an animated debate followed, & one or two pretty thoro' W. Suffrage speeches were made, but as no conclusion seemed likely to be reached, the matter was at last referred back to the Com. & Mrs. Gage placed on that Com.— Finding the opposition too strong there, she did as a gentleman behind us advised her to do, if that was the case—"bring in a minority report & we will all sustain you—" The result was that a substitute for both ↑(by Mr. Hammond of Onondaga)↓[3] was adopted— "Resolved   That we hail with devout thankfulness to God, the great uprising among the women of our land, to put away the liquor nuisance from among us, & that we renew our pledge to put the ballot into the hands of women when we shall have power to do so, thus enabling them to vote as well as pray against the giant curse of the world."

Mrs. Gage's, wh. was not adopted was "Resolved, That as all reforms in this country are at last settled at the ballot box, and as the only permanent & efficient aid woman can give the temperance cause must be thro' her vote, we therefore earnestly demand a recognition of woman's political right as a means of bringing about the final triumph of the temperance cause."

It was unexpected to me, as it was gratifying to see the enthusiasm of the audience on that question, & the deference paid to Mrs. Gage who received the unlooked for homage from one & another, as she passed out, at the close of the meeting, with commendable dignity & modesty—

Even should nothing come of this convention and politicians sneer at the nominations &c— &c— that such a discussion was possible marks a gratifying advance in public sentiment. There was scarcely another woman present ↑beside ourselves↓ (two or three at the far end of the hall)    I supposed that many of the women recently active in prayer meetings & in a few public meetings would have been there.

The Convention over we had a good long day to talk & a little drive—our only regret being that you were not here with us— I hope you will find it possible before long to come—

I have a letter from Flora—[4] she arrived in Johnstown on the 10th. after a fatiguing journey & her dear little Anne (the oldest) was taken very ill on her arrival at her mother's[5] requiring great care & watchfulness, but she is pretty well now— The journey, with the heat & dust, & a long walk on her arrival, were too much for her— We hope to have them here soon—& Will ↑is coming↓ on the 1st Aug.—Ellen & childn. also—[6]

[*sideways on first page*] Mrs. Gage left us this morning & my very first business was to write this letter.— Perhaps you never can get to the end of it to receive renewed assurances of very sincere regard  Yrs

&#x1F5E9;  *M. C. Wright*

&#x1F5E9; ALS, Garrison Papers, MNS-S.

1. Earlier letters about this plan are missing. The New York State Woman Suffrage Association, about to mark its fifth anniversary on 13 July 1874, followed an antebellum custom of calling summer meetings at such resorts as Saratoga Springs and Niagara Falls. The failures noted by Wright were probably the meetings in 1870, at Saratoga on 28 July and Niagara Falls on 2 August, although SBA thought the first of those a success. (SBA diary, 1870, *Film*, 14:173ff.)

2. Temperance advocates and prohibitionists from New York met at Auburn's Academy of Music on 23 June to found a state Prohibition party and nominate candidates for office. Preceding Matilda Gage's remarks, the delegates debated whether the party should endorse woman suffrage. (New York *World*, 24 June 1874.)

3. Reporters at the meeting omitted Mr. Hammond's given name. Probably this was Charles Addison Hammond (1825-?). Active in temperance work before the Civil War and at one time the preacher in Gerrit Smith's Church of Peterboro, Hammond helped to organize the Onondaga County branch of the state woman suffrage association. (Smith Papers, NSyU; *Rev.*, 26 February, 19 March, 18 June, 20 August 1868, in *Film*, 1:59, 82, 186, 260; Federal Census, 1870.)

4. Flora McMartin Wright (1843-1898), a niece of ECS, married Martha Wright's son, William Pelham Wright (1842-1902), in 1869. Their daughter

Anna McMartin Wright was born in 1870. On a visit to the Cady homestead in New York, Flora had journeyed from Drayton Island, Florida, where she and her husband were orange growers. Flora served as vice president for Florida of the National Woman Suffrage Association through the 1870s. (Wright genealogical files, Garrison Papers, MNS-S; Orrin Peer Allen, *Descendants of Nicholas Cady of Watertown, Mass., 1645–1910* [Palmer, Mass., 1910], 174.)

5. Margaret Chinn Cady McMartin (1817–1902) and her husband, Duncan McMartin, lived at this time on a farm in Iowa but spent time in the summer in Johnstown, New York. (Allen, *Descendants of Nicholas Cady*, 174; *TroyFS*; *Portrait and Biographical Record of Jasper, Marshall and Grundy Counties, Iowa* [Chicago, 1894], 371–72; genealogical notes courtesy of Barbara McMartin, Canada Lake, N.Y., and Barbara Wood McMartin, Beaman, Iowa.)

6. Ellen Wright Garrison (1840–1931), the second daughter of Martha and David Wright, married William Lloyd Garrison, Jr., in 1864 and lived in Boston. Agnes Garrison was born in 1866, Charles Garrison was born in 1868, and Frank Wright Garrison was born in 1871. (Wright genealogical files, Garrison Papers, MNS-S.)

## 37 ⋙ HANNAH BRADLEY COMSTOCK[1] TO SBA

No 11 College Street   New Haven [*Conn.*] July 25, 1874

Dear Miss Anthony

I have been from home two or three weeks, but just returned & find your letter awaiting me, also a fresh one from Mrs Hooker which I have sent to Miss Burr, then it is to go to Mrs Brown then to you.

I cannot learn that the Legislature have done any thing for us, but on account of absence have lost the reading of some of the papers, the body a↑d↓journ to day.[2]

We were not well repoted by the papers, or rather I should say the reports were very me↑a↓gre, what they said was respectful & all that— but evidently they all tried to dispose of us in the shortest way possible.

How are you feeling on the Beecher Tilton question? & how does it look to you.[3] I wish I knew how you felt & what you thought of it—just to think of Mr Beecher's & Mrs Tiltons denial of every thing. My sympathy is very strong for Mr Tilton & I would gladly help him & hope if he has any friends they will stand by him in this hour of his deep trial. Has not the time come when we women must stand boldly up shoulder to shoulder & be willing to face the storm. We cannot look to man for help, they are determined to keep us as we are if they can—& I some times think our deliverence will come only through blood. What the end of this great social upheaving will be, no human being can tell surely the reality & the beginning of the storm are terrible. God rules & in Him is light and no darkness at all—but to me at times there is thick darkness. Will Mrs Stanton speak for Mr Tilton if called on, & shall you my dear friend— I do sincerely hope that the real truth in the matter may come out— I feel for them all—but there is terrible guilt some where oh may it rest where it belongs—

Are you well & rested—you seemed tired and worn when I parted from you, I wish I could help you. Let me hear from you occasionally if only a few lines.

Mrs Sheldon[4] is away for the rest of the summer—Olympia too gone I suppose to Elmira Water cure[5] to remain until after her confinement—Mrs Hooker in Europe & I feel alone here with no one to enlighten me. Affectionately your friend

❧   *Hannah M. Comstock*

❧ ALS, Olympia Brown Papers, MCR-S. Was enclosed in SBA to Olympia Brown, 6 August 1874, below.

1. Hannah M. Bradley Comstock, who may have joined Olympia Brown in canvassing Connecticut, served on the executive committee of the state association and as secretary of the New Haven association. She married Lafayette Comstock in 1833. Once a carriage maker, Lafayette was by this date a real estate broker, and the couple boarded on College Street. Their daughter Cornelia Comstock Nicoll was also active in the New Haven association. (John Adams Comstock, *A History and Genealogy of the Comstock Family in America* [Los Angeles, Calif., 1949], 294; city directories, 1872, 1874, 1876; minutes of Connecticut WSA annual meetings, 30 September 1872, 11 December 1873, *Film*, 16:478–84, 17:436–41.)

2. Although petitions were not mentioned in plans for the Connecticut canvass nor by SBA while she took part in it, another participant, Sarah Perkins, indicated that the lecturers circulated petitions, presumably to the state legislature. (*Woman's Journal*, 7 March 1874.)

3. Henry Ward Beecher convened a committee of Plymouth Church members in June 1874 to investigate the charges and insinuations made against him by Theodore Tilton. Within weeks of its first meeting, members of the committee and witnesses turned to rival newspapers to publish competing claims and documents about the case. The *Brooklyn Daily Argus*, 21 July, carried Theodore Tilton's sworn statement to the committee; the *Brooklyn Daily Eagle*, 23 July, published Beecher's denial of everything that connected him

dishonorably with Elizabeth Tilton; and on the same day, it carried Elizabeth Tilton's denial that she had ever been guilty of adultery with Beecher. All three statements can be found in Marshall, *True History of the Brooklyn Scandal*, 112–29, 177–88.

4. Abby E. Barker Sheldon served with Hannah Comstock on the executive committee of the Connecticut Woman Suffrage Association. The wife of the lawyer and reformer Joseph Sheldon, she lived in New Haven. (Edward E. Atwater, ed., *History of the City of New Haven to the Present Time* [New York, 1887], 251–52; *WWW1*, s.v. "Sheldon, Joseph"; minutes of Connecticut WSA annual meetings, 30 September 1872, 11 December 1873.)

5. Awaiting the birth of her first child, Olympia Brown took up residence at the Elmira Water-Cure, under the care of Dr. Rachel Brooks Gleason, a specialist in women's health and prenatal care. (Jane B. Donegan, *"Hydropathic Highway to Health": Women and Water-Cure in Antebellum America* [Westport, Conn., 1986], 85–110.)

## 38 ❧ INTERVIEW WITH ECS IN TENAFLY

*[27 July 1874]*[1]

An *Argus* reporter called on Mrs. Elizabeth Cady Stanton, at her residence, in Tenafly, N.J., this morning, for the purpose of eliciting facts in the Great Scandal.

"I am perfectly willing to be interviewed," remarked the lady, with a smile.

"Can you tell me when you first learned of this affair, Mrs. Stanton?"

"I have a shocking poor memory for dates, and will, therefore, not endeavor to fix the exact time; I think, however, it was a year before Mrs. Woodhull published her statement that I knew of the matter.[2] Not all the details, you understand, which have since come to light, but the story in substance."

"And are you willing to tell in what manner you came possessed of this knowledge?"

"Certainly. Some time—I think it was in the Fall of the year, though I won't be positive—while Mrs. Bullard was still connected with the *Revolution*, Susan B. Anthony, Mr. and Mrs. Tilton, Mrs. Bullard, and myself, were in Brooklyn together. It was afternoon, and after calling at the office of the *Revolution*, Mr. Tilton and myself accompanied Mrs. Bullard to her residence, and remained to dinner.

"Through some misunderstanding, Miss Anthony went with Mrs. Tilton, and dined with her instead of us. There was some feeling on the part of Mrs. Tilton in regard to this, although it was quite unintentional on my part. Well, at the table—no one was present but Mrs. Bullard, Mr. Tilton, and myself—Theodore told the whole story, of his wife's faithlessness.[3] As I before observed, he did not go into the details; but the sum and substance of the whole matter he related in the hearing of Mrs. Bullard and myself. We were reformers. He gave us the story as a phase of social life."

"This was the first you had heard of it?"

"This was the first. The next evening, hearing that Miss Anthony was a little piqued at me for leaving her on the day before, I returned to my home here in Tenafly. To my surprise, I found Susan awaiting my arrival. That evening, when we were alone, I said to her: 'Theodore related a very strange story to Mrs. Bullard and me, last evening.' Then I recounted to her all that he had told us. Miss Anthony listened attentively to the end. Then she said: 'I have heard the same story from Mrs. Tilton.' We compared notes, and found that by both man and wife the same story had indeed been told."

"What were the particulars of Mrs. Tilton's confession?"

"I will tell you how it was made. When Mr. Tilton returned home that evening, some angry words—growing out of the separation in the afternoon—passed between him and his wife. Both became intensely excited. In the heat of the passion, and in the presence of Miss Anthony, each confessed to the other of having broken the marriage-vow. In the midst of these startling disclosures, Miss Anthony withdrew to her room. Shortly after she heard Mrs. Tilton come dashing up the stairs, and Mr. Tilton following close after. She flung open her bedroom door, and Elizabeth rushed in. The door was then closed and bolted. Theodore pounded on the outside, and demanded admittance, but Miss Anthony refused to turn the key. So intense was his passion at that moment that she feared he might kill his wife if he gained access to the room. Several times he returned to the door and angrily demanded that it be opened. 'No woman shall stand between me and my wife,' he said. But Susan, who is as courageous as she is noble, answered him with the words, 'If you enter this room it will be over my dead body!' And so the infuriated man ceased his demands and withdrew. Mrs.

Tilton remained with Susan throughout the night. In the excitement of the hour, amid sobs and tears, she told all to Miss Anthony.

"The whole story of her own faithlessness, of Mr. Beecher's course, of her deception, and of her anguish, fell upon the ears of Susan B. Anthony, and were spoken by the lips of Mrs. Tilton. The next morning, Mr. Tilton told Susan never to enter his house again. She told him she should enter whenever she chose; but I believe she did not go there again."[4]

"By Mr. Tilton's cross-examination," observed the reporter, "it appears that Mrs. Tilton was far from friendly to Miss Anthony.[5] How could she have made this confession to her?"

"On the contrary, Mrs. Tilton thought a great deal of Miss Anthony, of Mrs. Bullard, and all those ladies. I was very intimate with her before Mrs. Woodhull's thunderbolt. At the time of our first knowledge of the affair, Mr. Wilkeson also heard of it. He besought the ladies not to make it public. To him it was a matter of money. He was a stockholder in Plymouth Church, in the *Christian Union*, and in 'The Life of Christ.' Now, the destruction of Mr. Beecher would be the destruction of all of these. As Mr. Wilkeson expressed it, 'It would knock the Life of Christ higher than a kite.' Hence his concern in keeping the matter secret."[6]

"Did Miss Anthony ever speak to Mr. Beecher of the matter?"

"Often. She asked him if he knew how affairs stood with Mr. and Mrs. Tilton. He said that he did. Mrs. Hooker went to Mr. Beecher and plead with him to come out and take a manly stand.[7]

"She told him all this had come from his having married a woman whom he hated.[8] He made answer to her by saying, 'Belle, I have lived a lie for forty years; don't ask me to act the truth now!'"

Mrs. Stanton expressed her willingness to appear before the Committee and testify to the above facts.[9]

✎ *Brooklyn Daily Argus*, n.d., in Beecher-Tilton scrapbook 7, Main Reading Room, NN. Filmed at 26 July 1874.

1. This interview, from an undated clipping, was extensively reprinted and reported by morning and afternoon papers on 28 July 1874. The *Chicago Tribune*, 28 July, and *Woodhull and Claflin's Weekly*, 8 August, credited the *Argus* of 27 July.

2. Victoria Woodhull published her revelations about Beecher's affair in late October 1872. ECS and SBA probably learned about the affair two years

earlier, not the one year she claims here. It is difficult to date the events because many pages are missing from SBA's diaries of 1870 and 1871. Reference below to Laura Bullard's tenure as editor of the *Revolution* places events between June 1870 and mid-October 1871, though Bullard spent nearly a year of that time in Europe. ECS and SBA may have known as early as mid-August 1870 that there was trouble in the Tilton household, and they certainly did by early October. By January 1871 Francis Moulton and Theodore Tilton were including ECS and SBA in their discussions of how to manage Henry Ward Beecher. (SBA diary, 19 August, 3, 5, 10 October 1870, 9 January 1871, *Film*, 14:173ff, 15:91ff.)

3. In a subsequent interview with the same reporter, after New York newspapers ridiculed Tilton's idea of good table talk, ECS amended this description. He talked "in the library, after dinner." (*Film*, 18:72–73.)

4. This report of SBA's evidence was a bombshell. The public had not yet linked her to the scandal, and no other outsider had heard a confession from Elizabeth Tilton that could undermine her defense of Henry Ward Beecher before the investigating committee. Under the subhead "Call Susan," the *New York Herald*, 28 July 1874, reprinted an item from the *New Haven Palladium*: "If Miss Susan B. Anthony knows anything about the Beecher scandal, with which her name is now becoming mixed, she should be asked to testify before the committee. Whoever lies, that good old girl will tell the truth."

5. Angry that Tilton's sworn statement appeared in the press without their agreement, the investigating committee released an edited transcript of his two-day cross examination for publication in the *Brooklyn Daily Eagle*, 27 July. See also Marshall, *True History of the Brooklyn Scandal*, 130–77. The reporter refers to answers Tilton gave while the committee steered him to talk about Victoria Woodhull. On one occasion they asked: Had his wife complained about people who visited their house? Her mother complained about ECS and SBA. Had his wife complained of the presence of ladies at the house? Not that he could recall. "Q. Not of Mrs. Stanton nor Susan Anthony? A. She said she would consider it an insult if they came to the house; I do not remember of any others" (142).

6. When Samuel Wilkeson was called as a defense witness for Beecher in the trial on Tilton's charges of adultery in 1875, Tilton's lawyer asked him if he had said this about the *Life of Christ*, and he denied it. But his flippant answers led Beecher's lawyers to ask him again in their redirect examination. In the second telling, Wilkeson admitted saying, "if these imputations and charges against Mr. Beecher are true, and if they become public, the *Life of Christ* is of course knocked higher than a kite." He went on to say, "Mrs. Stanton utilized a part of that—" before the lawyers cut him off. (*New York Times*, 13 March 1875; *Theodore Tilton vs. Henry Ward Beecher, Action for Crim. Con. Tried in the City Court of Brooklyn* [New York, 1875], 2:309, 313–15.)

7. Isabella Hooker proposed, in a letter of 1 November 1872, that Henry

Ward Beecher admit his relationship with Elizabeth Tilton and defend himself as a reformer in the realms of love and marriage. She must have mentioned this to ECS, because her letter to her brother was only made public on 21 August 1874 by Frank Moulton. Beecher's reply was not part of the record released to the press. (New York *Daily Graphic*, 21 August 1874; *Brooklyn Daily Eagle*, 21, 22 August 1874; Marshall, *True History of the Brooklyn Scandal*, 332.)

8. Eunice White Bullard Beecher (1812–1897) married Henry Ward in 1837. (*WWWH*; *New York Times*, 9 March 1897.)

9. On the likelihood of ECS saying this, see notes at 6 August 1874 below.

## 39 &#x223d; ECS TO SBA

Tenafly, July 30, 1874.

Offended Susan,—[1]

Come right down and pull my ears. I shall not attempt a defense. Of course I admit that I have made an awful blunder in not keeping silent so far as you were concerned on this terrible Beecher-Tilton scandal. The whole odium of this *scandalum magnatum* has, in some quarters, been rolled on our suffrage movement, as unjustly as cunningly; hence I feel obliged just now to make extra efforts to keep our ship off the rocks. There was never anything so base and cowardly as that statement of some of Beecher's supporters, building a footstool for him to stand upon out of the life, character, aspirations, and ambition of a large circle of reputable women. This terrible onslaught on the suffrage movement has made me feel like writing for every paper daily. From the silence on all sides, I saw it was for me to fight alone. I have in fact written several articles, *incog.*, in the *Graphic*.[2] But I am too silent when I know I should be thundering against this wholesale slaughter of womanhood. When Beecher falls, as he must, he will pull all he can down with him. But we must not let the cause of woman go down in the smash. It is innocent.

&#x223d; *Stanton*, 2:145–46.

1. Although SBA's message to ECS is lost and the pages of her diary from 22 to 27 July and 3 to 6 August were removed, there are clues to her reaction to ECS's interview. While she stayed with Eliab Capron in Oneonta, New

York, on 30 July, SBA "learned that Mrs Stanton had given her version of Mrs Tiltons confidences with me to the Caprons last March— It is marvelous how she has talked over these people with everybody—" She did not yet know that on 28 July D. R. Anthony released a statement asserting that his sister told him essentially the same story repeated by ECS. Confronted with that news by a reporter who chased her down in Unadilla, New York, on 31 July, SBA refused to confirm or deny the reports. "But this I will say and thank you to repeat: Provided I did tell it them—which I do not admit—if my brother and Mrs. Stanton have said what has been accredited to them, it was a very ungracious thing in them to do. No one is able to repeat what another says, and correctly represent the speaker. To attempt it is invariably to do injustice." One reporter thought to ask ECS on 31 July if she had heard from SBA since her interview appeared; "I have," she replied. "She has been on a lecturing tour, and has been very unwilling to say anything about the matter. She considered it would be a breach of confidence." (SBA diary, 30 July 1874; *Utica Morning Herald and Daily Gazette*, 1 August 1874; interview with *Brooklyn Daily Argus*, 31 July 1874, reprinted in *Woodhull and Claflin's Weekly*, 15 August 1874; all in *Film*, 17:491ff, 18:70–73.)

2. These articles in the New York *Daily Graphic* remain unidentified. The author of two columns signed "Inquirer," on 23 and 30 July 1874, knew ECS's version of events but drew quite different conclusions from the scandal and placed some of the blame on the individualism promoted by "the woman's rights agitation." For opinions about the Inquirer's identity, see Richard Wightman Fox, *Trials of Intimacy: Love and Loss in the Beecher-Tilton Scandal* [Chicago, 1999], 377 n30, and Barbara Goldsmith, *Other Powers: The Age of Suffrage, Spiritualism, and the Scandalous Victoria Woodhull* [New York, 1998], 489.

## 40     SBA TO OLYMPIA BROWN

Rochester Aug 6, 1874

My Dear Olympia

Your note is here— how I did want to go to Elmira & <u>gabble</u> with you on my way home from Otsego Co.[1]—but I couldn't the trains ran so provokingly on that route—so I had to go clear back to Albany to get home <u>Monday</u> night last—which I was bound to accomplish—because my Sister Mary was waiting my arrival, that she might start for Kansas—which she did Tuesday night—to be gone the entire month—so you see I am <u>fixed</u> for No. 7. Madison street until she gets back—[2] But you must not get homesick— You must be <u>asy</u> in your <u>mind</u>—& if you cant be at Elmira & could be back at home I'd just pack up & go— I am dreadfully disappointed that <u>you</u> are disappointed with the Elmira Water Cure— I hope the second week will prove more satisfactory,— as to the little girl—there is no fear of that—<u>boy</u> though it should be—[3] The little woman boarding at my Sisters—not nearly so large as you— but just as <u>close</u> built—just as <u>firm</u> ↑built↓ & plucky as you—has a <u>little</u> <u>"girl"</u> two weeks old—& got through the ordeal <u>splendidly</u>—never even made <u>one</u> <u>groan</u>— My sister said she was a perfect wonder for self control—everybody prophesied a <u>hard time</u> for her—but she just went right through it like a queen—& so will you—so don't be uneasy— If you want me to slip down in September after my sister gets home—I will come cheerily—for it does seem pretty lonely for you there <u>without</u> <u>John</u> <u>Henry</u>—[4] Do you think <u>Susan</u> could in any fill the vacancy?

Well—Well aint they getting deeper & deeper into the mud there in Brooklyn—& was there ever such a needless heedless foot splashed into the mud as that of E. C. S.—& her boast that she belongs to a family of <u>lawyers</u>—[5] Isn't it perfectly killing— Well I do hope, whoever else wants to plunge in—they'll go <u>alone</u>—& not drag in everybody else they ever saw or spoke to—on that or any other subject—

I had a very good week with Mrs Perkins[6] in Otsego Co.—averaged only $9. a night—that is netted only that—but we had three rainy nights out of the six—and my expenses were tremendously large—having to go clear down to Albany to get to & from— But My—she <u>talks</u> as much about <u>walking</u> <u>with</u> <u>God</u>—& praying & faithing with Jesus—as does our friend Isabella— By the way here is a note from dear Mrs Comstock—[7] So soon as you get Hookers second letter send it on to your friend & lover

﹏ S. B A.

﹏ ALS, Olympia Brown Papers, MCR-S.

1. SBA lectured in this central New York county for six nights, beginning on 27 July in Cooperstown and returning to Rochester on 3 August. (SBA diary, 1874, *Film*, 17:491ff.)

2. Mary Anthony returned from Kansas on 8 September, late for the start of the school year. For two days, SBA substituted for her as principal of the No. 2 School, noting in her diary, "Got along very well—" (SBA diary, 6–7 September 1874.)

3. Brown gave birth to Henry Parker Willis on 14 August.

4. John Henry Willis (1825–1893) married Olympia Brown in April 1873. A member of her congregation in Weymouth, Massachusetts, he moved his grocery business to Bridgeport, Connecticut, when he married. (*Portrait and Biographical Album of Racine and Kenosha Counties, Wisconsin* [Chicago, 1892], 702-3.)

5. In a second interview with the *Brooklyn Daily Argus* on 31 July, ECS explained that she would not testify before the hand-picked investigating committee of Plymouth Church: "I belong to a family of lawyers, and I have great respect for the law. When the case comes before a civil court I shall willingly appear if summoned." (*Film*, 18:72-73.)

6. Sarah Maria Clinton Perkins (1824–1905) was living in Cooperstown, New York, when she invited SBA to join her on a local lecture tour that combined temperance with woman suffrage. Her ambition to learn to lecture was encouraged by Phebe Hanaford, among others, and she toured Connecticut with Olympia Brown in February 1874. Perkins was licensed to preach in the Universalist church in 1877 and ordained a year later, but she was best known for her work in the temperance movement. (*SEAP*; *American Women*; Phebe Hanaford, *Daughters of America; or, Women of the Century* [Boston, 1883], 432-40; *Woman's Journal*, 7 March 1874.)

7. See 25 July 1874 above. On a sheet of Hannah Comstock's letter, SBA added a postscript to this letter of 6 August. "Well—what more shall I say— only that I long to hear from you often—& to know that you are getting on nicely—& the '<u>girl</u>' proves splendid—it wont <u>pay</u> if she doesn't— S. B. A."

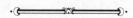

# 41 &#x5c; ECS to Alonzo J. Grover[1]

Tenafly, N.J., Aug. 24, 1874.

Dear Friend: You ask, in a recent letter, my views of the great social earthquake that has recently jarred so many theories and reputations that once stood firm.

I have a double interest in this sad page of domestic history; first, because it involves great principles of social ethics; second, because those who have accidentally been forced to illustrate our ignorance of these principles are among my personal friends.

To those who take a surface view of "the scandal," it is probably "prurient," "disgusting," "nauseating," as our refined Metropolitan press affects to consider it, although the first news sought for by the reading public, by gentlemen and ladies alike, has, I presume, during the last two months, been "the Plymouth Church investigation." This, to my mind, is an evidence, not of a depraved popular taste, but of a vital interest in the social problems that puzzle and perplex the best of us.

The true relations of man and woman, the foundations of the family and home, are of more momentous importance than any question of State, or Church, can possibly be. Hence the intense interest roused to every new page of social history,—summoning some Darwin, Spencer, or Tyndall,[2] to a fearless investigation of the sources of our present social evils, and their scientific remedy.

The true social code, whatever it is, must be the same for both sexes. If the testimony given in this case be all true, and it be proven that such men as Henry Ward Beecher and Theodore Tilton find the marriage laws of the State of New York too stringent, both being in discordant marriage-relations, might it not be well to review the laws, as well as their violations?

To compel unhappy husbands and wives, by law and public sentiment, to live together, and to teach them that it is their religious duty to accept their conditions, whatever they are, produces, ever and anon, just such social earthquakes as the one through which we are now passing.

Whilst the many are eager to discover the facts in this one case, let the few seek for those laws which, if obeyed, would prevent like cases in the future.

If all our homes were unroofed, many a husband might be painted in darker colors than Theodore Tilton, and many a wife weaker than his, and many a man more perplexed and miserable than "the Great Preacher." Hence we have, all alike, a deeper interest in this "scandal" than the guilt or innocence of the actors.

Society has played fast and loose with the religious conscience of woman long enough, educating her faith in one code of morals and her affections in another,—thus leaving her ever liable to, in an hour of weakness, so betray the man she fain would save.

The lesson for "advanced thinkers"—for such men as Henry Ward Beecher—to learn is, the necessity of teaching the women in their circle of friends, if from no higher motive than their own protection, the man-philosophy, such as Leckey teaches in his History of Morals,[3] if that is the ultimatum of man's wisdom.

In this way only can woman maintain her self-respect and true dignity, while living under the same moral code by which man governs himself. To educate woman's conscience in the line with the generally-received views of social morals, in the latitude in which she lives, and then tempt her to sin against her conscience and public opinion, is making cowards and hypocrites of men and women on every side. In spite of the various relations in which men and women of all ages have lived, and still live, there must be a true condition; and, to my mind, it seems that might be found, *with love and equality*,[4] in a true marriage of one man to one woman. The trouble with the man-philosophy in all these matters is, that the best interests of woman have never entered into the consideration of the whole question.

What a holocaust of womanhood we have had in this investigation! What a football the Committee, the lawyers, Mrs. Beecher, and her husband, have made of Elizabeth R. Tilton![5] What statements and counter-statements they have wrung from her unwilling lips, then like a withered flower, "the Great Preacher" casts her aside, and tells the world "she thrust her affections on him unsought,"[6]—the crowning perfidy in that bill of impeachment that blackens every one who dared to hear or tell the most astounding scandal of the nineteenth century!

In common with the rest of the world, members of the National Woman's Suffrage Association heard and repeated the scandal, as other men and women did; and, forsooth, Mr. Beecher dubs them "human hyenas" and "free-lovers,"[7] though his own sister was one of the number, and who, by letters and conversations that, through him and his brother, were published to the world, is represented as "insane," "deluded," "weak-minded."[8] Those who know Mrs. Tilton—her natural diffidence, delicacy, and refinement—will readily believe her true story, that, through months of persuasion and argument, her love was sought and sealed.

Bewildered, racked, tormented, tempest-tossed in the midst of misery and weakness, in her last act on leaving home, and in her statement before the Committee, a touch of grand womanhood is revealed, after all. In the face of law, gospel, conventionalism, ready to leave her home forever, she says: "Theodore, the end has come; I will never take another step by your side." And to her brother,[9] in announcing her decision, she said: "I have always been treated as a non-entity,—a plaything,—to be used or let alone at will; but it has always seemed to me I was *a party* not a little concerned."[10]

Thus leaving husband, children, home, she went forth to vindicate the man she loved,—making his friends her friends, his God her God! With what withering cruelty, then, his words must have fallen on her heart: "She thrust her affections on me unsought"; though a mutual confession of love is revealed in the course of the investigation, and recognized in the verdict.[11]

Those who know Isabella Beecher Hooker must be equally surprised with his treatment to her. Brilliant, gifted, and clear-minded, her excellent advice to her brother, to confess his life and justify it by his theories, which she had heard him many times enunciate,[12] prove her a straightforward, strong character, but not a "free-lover," "weak-minded," or "insane."

I have known Mrs. Hooker well enough and long enough to testify that she is neither. But,—in the clashing of interests, ambition, and revenge among men,—mothers, sisters, wives, and daughters are readily sacrificed.

Coming up through four years of the agony and despair Mr. Beecher so pathetically describes, who is surprised to see in him so little sense of justice towards those who, from no fault of their own, became cognizant of the whole sad story. To blacken such characters as Susan B. Anthony and Laura Curtis Bullard,[13] Bessie Turner[14]—an unreliable servant, a self-confessed tool for whomsoever might choose to use her—is the main witness against Mr. Tilton, and his friends who chanced to visit his house.

Her statement in regard to Miss Anthony was false, and of me was exaggerated beyond all bounds. She said before the Committee that I *frequently* played chess with Mr. Tilton until 3 o'clock in the morning; as if she, who was never half-awake in the daytime, could spend her nights in watching. Through all the years of our acquaintance, I played chess once with Mr. Tilton, finished the game at 12 o'clock, and retired,—making a note of it the next day in the *Revolution*, which I was then editing.[15]

You ask if it is possible for Mr. Beecher to maintain his position in face of the facts. His position will be maintained *for* him, as he is the soul and centre of three powerful religious rings, as he tells you himself in his statement:[16]

1. Plymouth Church;
2. The *Christian Union*;

3. "The Life of Christ."

As church-property is not taxed, its bonds, in the hands of the wealthy men of that organization, are valuable, and the bondholders, alive to their financial interests, stand around Mr. Beecher, a faithful, protecting band, not loving truth and justice less, but their own pockets more. They are shrewd enough to know that, in Mr. Beecher's downfall, their bonds would be of little value.

Next, the *Christian Union*,—a dull paper that represents no new thought in morals, religion, or politics,—that floats on the name of Beecher, in spite of Mrs. Stowe's heavy Scripture-lessons and Edward Beecher's theological antiquities.[17] "The Great Preacher" seldom gilds its pages with his brightness. If then, his good name is shadowed, another circle of suffering stockholders would be brought to grief.

As to "The Life of Christ," in the words of one of the fold,[18] that would, indeed, be blown "higher than a kite" were the author proved an unworthy shepherd, betraying the flock he was set to watch. I have heard that he was paid $20,000 for that work before he put pen to paper. Then he ground out one volume, which the English market refused to touch until the second was forthcoming; and thus the whole investment hangs by the eyelids, until Mr. Beecher is whitewashed and sees fit to finish the work. With such wealthy circles of influence in Brooklyn and New York, all depending on the vindication of Mr. Beecher's honor and honesty, you will readily understand the number, strength, and activity, of his partisans, and the reason why the tone of the Metropolitan press differs so widely from that throughout the country.

Under such circumstances, justice for Mr. Beecher is quite impossible. When the friends of Mr. Beecher thought they had silenced Mr. Moulton, our city press toasted him as a brave, generous, refined gentleman; but, as soon as he opened his mouth to tell the whole truth, he became a blackmailer and conspirator.[19]

If the secret history of this tragedy is ever brought to light, we shall have such revelations of diplomacy and hypocrisy in high places as to open the eyes of the people to the impossibility of securing justice for any one when money can be used against him.

When a refined gentleman and scholar like Theodore Tilton can be hurled in a day from one of the proudest positions in the country,—the able editor of a great journal,—and become a target for the jibes and jeers of the nation, without one authenticated accusation of vice or crime against him, all young men are specially interested in knowing whether his downfall is the result of a lack of moral rectitude in himself, or those who counseled his dethronement. They who try to see Theodore Tilton vindicated do but maintain the claims of common justice for those who have not the money to buy it.

I have long known Mr. Tilton and Mr. Moulton, and visited them frequently in their pleasant homes, and seen them under trying circumstances, and know they are not the base, unreliable men represented in Mr. Beecher's statement. However, when this matter is thoroughly sifted in the civil courts, truth may be made to appear.[20] With kind regards,

         ❧ *Elizabeth Cady Stanton.*

❧ *Chicago Daily Tribune*, 1 October 1874, reprinted from the *Earlville Transcript*.

1. Alonzo J. Grover (1828–1891) was editor and publisher of the *Earlville Transcript* in Illinois, for which he lined up ECS, Edward Davis, and Matilda Gage as contributing editors. An old friend of Parker Pillsbury, with whom he toured for the American Anti-Slavery Society in 1852, Grover settled in Earlville in 1854 to practice law. He and his wife were founding members of the state's first woman's rights association in 1855 and joined the suffrage movement after the war. His letters appeared in the *Revolution*, and he wrote several pamphlets, including *The Bible Argument against Woman Stated and Answered from a Bible Standpoint*, published in 1870 by the Cook County Woman Suffrage Association. By 1880 he had moved to Chicago, and within the decade he settled in Kansas. Grover urged SBA also to write her account of the scandal for his paper. (Alfred Theodore Andreas, *History of Chicago, from the Earliest Period to the Present Time* [Chicago, 1884], 3:693; Parker Pillsbury, *Acts of the Anti-Slavery Apostles* [Concord, N.H., 1883], 339–43, 349–52; *Rev.*, 3 December 1868, 18 February 1869, and SBA diary, 9 September 1874, *Film*, 1:380, 467–68; 17:491ff; obituary in Atchison [Kan.] *Champion*, 13 February 1891, in SBA scrapbook 17, Rare Books, DLC.)

2. These scientific writers who purported to explain social as well as natural phenomena and traced sexual inequality to evolutionary science were Charles Robert Darwin (1809–1882), naturalist; Herbert Spencer (1820–1903), philosopher; and John Tyndall (1820–1893), physicist. (Louise Michele Newman, *White Women's Rights: The Racial Origins of Feminism in the United States* [New York, 1999], 22–55.)

3. William Edward Hartpole Lecky (1838–1903), British historian, published the *History of European Morals from Augustus to Charlemagne* in 1869. ECS may allude to Lecky's view that man need not, indeed should not, be

limited to a lifelong marriage for his sexual satisfaction. His "appetite" was "far greater than the well-being of man requires." Lecky approved of men's short-term connections with women other than their wives; such "have always subsisted side by side with permanent marriages." As much as he deplored prostitution, he understood the prostitute to be "ultimately the most efficient guardian of virtue" in the family (2:281–82, 283, 348–49).

4. The *Tribune* printed "quality."

5. Eunice Beecher befriended Elizabeth Tilton as early as 1870 in order to reinforce her loyalty to Henry Ward Beecher. Her role was discussed in Theodore Tilton's cross-examination before the committee. (*Brooklyn Daily Eagle*, 27 July 1874, and Marshall, *True History of the Brooklyn Scandal*, 133–36, 147.)

6. Beecher used this phrase in his second, and more reckless, statement to the investigating committee on 13 August. About a conversation with Frank Moulton in 1871, he recalled for the committee how he thought aloud: "Should I pour indignation upon the lady? Should I hold her up to contempt as having thrust her affection upon me unsought?" (*Brooklyn Daily Eagle*, 14 August 1874, and Marshall, *True History of the Brooklyn Scandal*, 265–66.)

7. In the same statement, Beecher traced the rumors about his behavior to "one wing of the Female Suffrage party," centered around Victoria Woodhull. Continuing the thought, he recounted how Theodore Tilton and Frank Moulton, in their efforts to manage the rumors, kept up "friendly relations with the group of human hyenas." (Marshall, *True History of the Brooklyn Scandal*, 272–73.)

8. On 10 August 1874, the pro-Beecher *Brooklyn Daily Eagle* published letters by George H. Beecher and Edward Beecher impugning Isabella Hooker; other papers published them the next day. Getting right to the point about the trustworthiness of her opinion, George wrote of Hooker's "strange fascination" with Victoria Woodhull and described her views on marriage as "somewhat similar to those of Mrs. Woodhull, though not so gross." Her behavior in a family argument showed "a wild and excited state of mind." Perhaps most important, he emphasized that Hooker's only sources for her belief in Henry's guilt were ECS, SBA, and Woodhull. George H. Beecher was not, as ECS assumes, a brother of Henry Ward, but his family connection is not known. Edward's letter, written to his sister in 1872, accused her of "laboring with all your might to ruin Henry," and, he continued, "[a] greater delusion is not possible" than the pretense that she acted out of love for her brother. Edward Beecher (1803–1895), formerly a pastor in Galesburg, Illinois, moved to Brooklyn in 1871 to be with his brother. (*ANB*.)

9. Joseph Richards (c. 1836–?) of Brooklyn. (Federal Census, 1850.)

10. Both quotations come from Elizabeth Tilton's statement to the public, published in the *Brooklyn Daily Eagle*, 23 July 1874, and Marshall, *True History of the Brooklyn Scandal*, 186, 188.

11. The investigating committee's exoneration of Beecher, which ECS could

not have seen in full by the time she wrote this letter, detected an "overshadowing affection for her pastor" on the part of Elizabeth Tilton and a "warm friendship for Mrs. Tilton" on the part of Beecher. (*Brooklyn Daily Eagle*, 29 August 1874, and Marshall, *True History of the Brooklyn Scandal*, 406-32.)

12. See notes above at 27 July 1874. For Isabella Hooker's objections to ECS's portrayal in this letter of her conversations with Henry Ward Beecher, see her letters from Paris to SBA, 18 February 1875, and to ECS, 28 February 1875, *Film*, 18:319-25, 328-41.

13. Theodore Tilton's long-standing friendship with Laura Curtis Bullard was brought to the attention of the investigating committee and through them to the press by Beecher's supporters, including Elizabeth Tilton.

14. Elizabeth A. Turner (c. 1851-?), known as Bessie and previously named Lizzie McDermott, moved into the Tiltons' household in 1863 or 1864 as a servant, and stayed until 1870, when Beecher paid for her education at a female seminary. Intensely loyal to Elizabeth Tilton, Turner testified against Theodore to the committee, offering details about his domestic life and visitors. The committee released her testimony to the press on 22 August. Asked about Tilton's relations with ECS and SBA, Turner testified: "He seemed to think a great deal of Mrs. Stanton and Miss Anthony; I saw her sitting on his lap on one occasion when I was coming into the parlor, and she jumped up pretty quick.

"Q. Miss Anthony? A. Susan B. Anthony.

"Q. What was his conduct with Mrs. Stanton? A. Well, I never saw him caressing her, but he used to be alone with her a great deal in his study. They used to play chess until two or three o'clock in the morning. Frequently they were up until after the family had gone to bed quite late."

SBA learned of the testimony from a reporter on 24 August and marveled, "everybody who refuses to aid Beecher, or blacken Tilton—is to be made wholly bad." (*T. Tilton vs. H. W. Beecher*, 1:443, 2:466, 489-91, 559; *Brooklyn Daily Eagle*, 22 August 1874; Marshall, *True History of the Brooklyn Scandal*, 393; SBA diary, 1874, *Film*, 17:491ff.)

15. See *Rev.*, 2 July 1868, *Film*, 1:200. She described it as a match "to decide the superiority of sex" but refrained from saying who won.

16. In his statement of 13 August. See Marshall, *True History of the Brooklyn Scandal*, 255-56.

17. Harriet Beecher Stowe (1811-1896), a prolific author, was critical of her sister Isabella Beecher Hooker and intensely loyal to her brother Henry Ward Beecher during the scandal. On the extensive Beecher family involvement in the *Christian Union*, see Joan D. Hedrick, *Harriet Beecher Stowe, A Life* [New York, 1994], 370-73. (*ANB*.)

18. Her brother-in-law, Samuel Wilkeson. See note at 27 July 1874.

19. Francis D. Moulton (1836-1884), a Brooklyn businessman and college friend of Theodore Tilton, came to be known as the "Mutual Friend" for his part in the Beecher-Tilton scandal. All parties to the dispute confided in him,

and most of them entrusted him with the documents in the case. Beecher and
Moulton parted ways on 4 August, when Beecher decided that Moulton had
taken sides with Theodore Tilton. He lashed out at Moulton in his statement
of 13 August, portraying him as a blackmailer who extorted money from
Beecher to aid Tilton. Moulton rebutted Beecher in his statement of 21
August, in the New York *Daily Graphic*, but he held back his harshest
assessment until 11 September, when his final statement appeared in the same
paper. Both of Moulton's statements are also in Marshall, *True History of the
Brooklyn Scandal*, 307-79, 448-505. (*New York Times*, 5 December 1884;
Hibben, *Henry Ward Beecher*, passim; Fox, *Trials of Intimacy*, passim. See
also *Papers* 2.)

20. Earlier in August 1874, Theodore Tilton filed suit against Henry Ward
Beecher, charging him with criminal conversation and alienation of affections,
or, in other words, with adultery. This civil trial was delayed until early 1875.
For a discussion of the meaning of criminal conversation and its application to
Tilton's case, see Laura Hanft Korobkin, *Criminal Conversations: Sentimen-
tality and Nineteenth-Century Legal Stories of Adultery* (New York, 1998).

## 42 ❦ FROM THE DIARY OF SBA

*[24-27 September 1874]*

THURSDAY, SEPT. 24, 1874. [*Grand Rapids, Mich.*] Left Rochester for
the Michigan Woman Suffrage campaign—[1] Dewitt & Mary Ann[2] in
company as far as Harrisburg Canada—when they left to go to Preston
to visit the Perines—Mary, Billings & Joseph—[3]

Had a pleasant ride— after they left I took out the Graphic & read
T. T.s last statement—[4] it is appalling in its exposures of the lying &
deceit practiced all round among them—

Took Sleeping Car at Detroit for Grand Rapids

1. SBA left Rochester on short notice, when she received a letter on September 23 saying she "was engaged for Friday night" in Grand Rapids. (SBA
diary, 1874, *Film*, 17:491ff.)

2. William Dewitt McLean (1814–1892) of Greenwich, New York, and Mary
Ann McLean Pitcher (1819–1892) of South Branch, New Jersey, arrived in
Rochester on 14 September to visit their brother Aaron McLean. (Baker
Genealogical Mss., SBA Papers, MCR-S; Crisfield Johnson, *History of Wash-
ington County, New York* [Philadelphia, 1878], 499; Federal Census, 1880,
Somerset County, N.J.; SBA diary, 1 February 1892, *Film*, 29:655ff; SBA
diary, 1874.)

3. Cousins of the McLeans with whom SBA was acquainted since childhood, these were Mary Crocker Perine (1813-1904) and her brothers, Moses Billings Perine (1815-1898) and Joseph S. Perine (1820-1880). The brothers resided in Doon, Ontario, at the time of their deaths. (Howland Delano Perrine, comp., *Daniel Perrin, "The Huguenot," and His Descendants in America: of the Surnames, Perrine, Perine, and Prine, 1665-1910* [South Orange, N.J., 1910], 227, 339.)

4. Theodore Tilton released this statement through the New York *Daily Graphic*, 18 September 1874. Also in Marshall, *True History of the Brooklyn Scandal*, 515-96. Opponents of the suffrage amendment in Michigan had seized upon the Brooklyn scandal by mid-summer. The *Woman's Journal's* weekly survey of editorials in the state picked up references to free love as the inevitable consequence of woman suffrage by August 8. Tilton's mention of SBA in this last statement ensured that her connection to the scandal was fresh in people's minds. In mid-October, one editor offered the fact that suffragists did not order SBA to leave the state as proof that greater sexual freedom was their aim. (*Woman's Journal*, 8, 22, 29 August 1874; *Big Rapids Magnet*, 1 October 1874; Marshall *Democratic Expounder and Calhoun County Patriot*, 15 October 1874.)

FRIDAY, SEPT. 25, 1874. reached Grand Rapids at 6 A.M— found Mrs Marion Carr Bliss[1] at her home—Park place house— She is a most earnest & energetic woman— It was not to lecture <u>this</u> evening—but to meet with their Executive Committee that I was so sumarily commanded hither

Judge Withe,[2] their City President, was present—Mr. Hine[3] of Lowell, Mr & Mrs Briggs[4] & others— a Mrs Immen[5]—wife of a merchant called—beautiful woman— it said her husband actually beats her—

1. Marian Carr Bliss (c. 1839-?), a delegate to the state suffrage meeting in May, was named to the committee charged with organizing Kent County for the canvass, and she invited SBA to the state. Bliss moved to Grand Rapids in 1867, when her husband, Zenas E. Bliss, a doctor and distinguished military surgeon in the Civil War, opened a new practice there. Marian Bliss served on the advisory committee of the National Woman Suffrage Association in 1876 and 1878 and was named to the executive committee in 1879. By 1880, she had moved to Ann Arbor. (F. A. Barnard, *American Biographical History of Eminent and Self-Made Men . . . Michigan Volume* [Cincinnati, Ohio, 1878], 12; *History of Kent County, Mich.* 428; *Grand Rapids Daily Eagle*, 24 April 1877; *Film*, 4:875-76, 21:182-84; Federal Census, 1870.)

2. Solomon Lewis Withey (1820-1886), not Withe, was appointed judge of the United States District Court for the Western District of Michigan in 1863 and served until his death. (Judicial Conference of the United States, Bicentennial Committee, *Judges of the United States*, 2d ed. [Washington, 1983].)

3. James Willson Hine (1846–?), a Republican who served as recording secretary of the state senate during the recent special session, was editor of the *Lowell Journal*, in a town nineteen miles from Grand Rapids. He came out in support of the suffrage amendment in early May, and he exchanged papers with the *Woman's Journal* throughout the campaign. (*Michigan Biographies*; *History of Kent County, Mich.*, 434–35; *Woman's Journal*, 2 May 1874.)

4. Edward L. Briggs (1830–?), a farmer, surveyor, and timber agent, was seeking reelection to the state assembly from Kent County as a Republican. His wife, Cordelia T. Fitch Briggs, held office in the Grand Rapids, Michigan, and National suffrage associations in the 1880s, while she also cooperated with the American association. (Franklin Everett, *Memorials of the Grand River Valley* [1878; reprint, Grand Rapids, Mich., 1984], 9–10; Albert Baxter, *History of the City of Grand Rapids, Michigan* [New York, 1891], 511–12; *History*, 3:184, 530, 956–57, 4:24, 432, 755.)

5. Loraine Pratt Immen (1840–1927) married Frederick Immen (1837–1908) in 1860, after teaching school for four years. She attended the state suffrage meeting in May 1874 as a delegate from Grand Rapids, and was, in 1885, president of the city's suffrage society. In the interval, she studied elocution and gained some renown as a lecturer. She was noted too for her support of women's clubs and charities in Grand Rapids. (*American Women*; *History*, 3:530; Edward Harvey Mohneke, comp., Kent County, Michigan, Cemetery Records, typescript, vol. 2, Mi; city directory, 1874–75.)

SATURDAY, SEPT. 26, 1874. Grand Rapids—Mich   Spoke in Luce's Hall—large audience—though a heavy shower just at 7 Oclock— Gave my <u>argument</u>—friends seemed pleased—some said there had been no lecture before that had made so many votes—

Judge Withe did not come to introduce me—so Mrs Bliss bravely walked on to the platform and officiated—& she did it in a most dignified manner—

Found Mrs Stone of Kalamazoo[1] at the rooms on our return— Mr Geo. Stickney of Grand Haven[2]—the State W.S. sec'y came down to hear me speak

1. Lucinda Hinsdale Stone (1814–1900) and her husband, James A. B. Stone, were founders and leaders of the Michigan Woman Suffrage Association. Formerly head of female education at Kalamazoo College, where her husband was president until 1863, Stone often hosted ECS and SBA in Kalamazoo. (*NAW*; *ANB*.)

2. George H. Stickney (1838–1916), a businessman and banker, was named treasurer and secretary to the executive committee in charge of the state campaign. (*History of Ottawa County, Michigan, with Illustrations and Biographical Sketches of Some of Its Prominent Men and Pioneers* [Chicago,

1882], 41, 48, 49; Daughters of the American Revolution, Holland, Michigan, Cemetery Records, Ottawa County, Northern Half, typescript, 1943, Mi; Grand Haven *Daily Tribune*, 18 October 1916; *Woman's Journal*, 10 October 1874.)

SUNDAY, SEPT. 27, 1874. Did not go out to Church— Messrs Foster[1]— Editor of the Post—and Mr Stickney came—and we mapped out plan of work for me through the campaign to Nov. 3<sup>d</sup> [*Entries for 28 September–19 October omitted.*]

    1. David Nathaniel Foster (1841–1934) moved to Grand Rapids in 1873 to found the *Evening Post* and left in 1877 for New York. He was a delegate to the state suffrage convention in May. (*NCAB*, 41:49–50.)

&#128;❦ Excelsior Diary 1874, n.p., SBA Papers, DLC.

## 43 ❧ MARTHA COFFIN WRIGHT TO ECS

Auburn [*N.Y.*] Oct. 3rd. 1874

My dear Mrs. Stanton—

    Aggravating old things, those Postal cards![1] Why didn't you write me a nice letter, when I never had heard a word from you, since I had your room prepared & yr promise to come & see me— However yr. card explains that, but I did want very much to see you after my long absence in Florida, & the great disappointment of yr. absence from the Con. in May— I felt as if I should sink, the evening before, when Susan dear energetic indomitable Susan told me that you wd. not be there; but we did have a pretty good anniversary for all. It was gratifying for a pious Temperance saint[2] to come forward & acknowledge that their efforts were powerless, without the ballot.— You wd have been pleased with her little speech—

    I dreaded inexpressibly the greatness thrust upon me, knowing so well my own limitations in the matter of speech making, when that seems to be considered one of the essentials for a Presiding officer, & I knew that you were so much more suitable, & Susan had filled the place so well, but my protests were unheeded—so with dreadful misgivings I look forward to our next meeting—the chances being ↑however↓

that I may not be present—as I shall have to be in Boston with Ellen a part of Dec. & Jany.—[3]

I hoped to hear of you in Johnstown during the summer, & perhaps have a visit from you while Flora & her family were with us.— you wd have loved that dear little Cady baby[4] & the sensible little Anne— Her mother feared she would not get along well with other little ones, having been so much by herself, but she was the best one among them, & she & little Frank Garrison were almost inseparable rarely getting into trouble— Frank whispered something to her once & they both started, & ran as fast as they could, till they got almost to the Post office Anne's father saw them start, but he had to get his coat on, & then wait for a funeral to pass the crossing, wh. gave them an advantage wh. they enjoyed— They tried it once last yr— D[5] sd to Anne, in Florida, "What made you run away with little Frank, in Auburn?"— She sd "I didn't run away with him—he runned away his self, & I runned away my self"— Perhaps he wd. have sd. "The woman tempted me, & I did <u>run</u>":—but you see Anne put it on independent womans rights ground. We were very sorry to have them leave, the very day after the arrival of Eliza & family,[6] but Flora's sister[7] had also arrived—so they all hurried off, Will returning to be with his sisters a little longer    He could not be contented, however in this solitude, after W<sup>m</sup>[8] & Ellen & children had all gone, & his father in Phila. so he returned to Johnstown ↑last Tuesday↓ to spend a wk with Flora & the children, & return here for one more week.— You can imagine how still & deserted the house seems— I take refuge in constant occupation, & find plenty to do, but it is rather a choking sensation, it must be confessed, when the last carriage drives off & you return to deserted rooms— my first occupation usually is to prepare them to 'welcome the coming' after speeding the parting guest.[9] Our plan of returning to Florida this Fall is "<u>knocked higher than a kite</u>" ↑(like the Life of Jesus)↓ by Ellen's prospect for Dec.— We enjoyed exceedingly the time we spent there last Winter.—

↑As to the Beechers matters↓ It will take considerable time to make up the time in one's reading, sacrificed in going over <u>that pack</u> of <u>lies</u>— It will require more than human ingenuity ever to get at the truth— Wasn't it rather amusing to see the alacrity with which Mrs. Howe[10] assumed the case to be forever settled, & sang her song of rejoicing.

Do write to me & tell me all yr plans, & whether yr son[11] is improving— I feel very sorry for him & for you, in all yr anxiety for him—

Give my love to him [*sideways on first page*] & to yr other children—
My sister mourns the death of our dear Anna Hopper[12] & a few weeks
later, ~~her~~ ↑Anna's↓ only son Issac T.—of Typhoid fever, his death
quite unexpected till a day or two before— My tho'ts are much with
that sorrowing household—only Edward H. & his daughr. Maria left.—
her illness wd not have surprised us, after so many mos. of nursing &
anxiety.— With regards to Mr Stanton   Affy Yr. friend

           ✍ *M. C Wright*

I am glad for dear Mrs. Hooker to be away from all the excitement of
the Brooklyn controversy—

Mrs. Gage sent me Mr Hooker's letter & yr. added lines, asking
information concerning Mrs. Hooker's letter to a Convention— I have
no remembrance of any such letter— I wish they cd. be perfectly
indifferent—to the misrepresentations of enemies—it is easy eno' to
<u>live down</u> falsehood— There are no such haters in the world as <u>pious
haters</u>. Poor Mrs. Beecher can hardly make up her mind whether she
has a happy home or the reverse, when her dear friends who wd. 'scorn
to tell a lie' make exactly opposite statements:[13]—but none of them
quite come up to the energetic language of the vigorous Mrs. Morse!—[14]
I didn't think her 'dear son' wd. have lived to return to the welcoming
arms of Plymouth Ch.—

✍ ALS, Papers of ECS, NPV. Endorsed by ECS to SBA, "a pleasant letter
from Martha Wright."

1. Penny postal cards were introduced in 1873.

2. Amanda Halstead Deyo (1838–?) spoke to the meeting about prohibition
and woman suffrage. A Quaker from Dutchess County, New York, and the
mother of two girls, Deyo was best known for her promotion of peace. She
became active in the Universal Peace Union after the war and represented it at
the Universal Peace Congress in Paris in 1889. By then she had left the Society
of Friends to be ordained, in 1886, as a Universalist minister. That career took
her from New York to Pennsylvania and, by the 1890s, to California. (*American Woman*; *Quaker Genealogy*, 3:100; Catherine F. Hitchings, "Universalist
and Unitarian Women Ministers," *Journal of the Universalist Historical Society* 10 [1975]: 60; *New York Herald*, 17 September 1874; *New York Tribune*, 17
September 1874; *History*, 3:422, 4:128, 496.)

3. Ellen Wright Garrison was expecting a child.

4. Edith Livingston Wright, daughter of Flora McMartin and Will Wright,
was born on 25 February 1874.

5. David Wright (1805–1897), a lawyer in Auburn, married Martha Coffin in 1829.

6. Eliza Wright Osborne (1830–1911), a daughter of Martha and David Wright, lived in Auburn with her husband, David Munson Osborne (1822–1886), and their four children: Emily, born in 1853; Florence, born in 1856; Thomas Mott, born in 1859; and Helen, or Nelly, born in 1864. Eliza Osborne was active in the New York State Woman Suffrage Association. (Wright genealogical files, Garrison Papers, MNS-S; Garrison, *Letters*, 6:214n; *Woman's Journal*, 12 August 1911.)

7. Elizabeth McMartin (1846–1941) or, according to one source, Elizabeth Cady McMartin, was, like her sister, a graduate of Miss Porter's School in Farmington, Connecticut. Sometime in 1874 she married Charles Hume Baldwin, formerly the Presbyterian minister in Johnstown. (*Jasper, Marshall and Grundy Counties, Iowa*, 272; *Class of Sixty-Three, Williams College, Fortieth Year Report*, from college archives, MWiW; genealogical notes courtesy of Barbara McMartin, Canada Lake, N.Y., and Barbara Wood McMartin, Beaman, Iowa.)

8. William Lloyd Garrison, Jr., (1838–1909) was a businessman in Boston. (*New York Times*, 13 September 1909.)

9. Alexander Pope, "The Odyssey of Homer," book XV, lines 15–16: "True friendship's laws are by this rule express'd, / Welcome the coming, speed the parting guest."

10. Julia Ward Howe (1819–1910) was president of the American Woman Suffrage Association and an editor of the *Woman's Journal*. In the issue of 22 August 1874, her editorial, "End of the Beecher-Tilton Controversy," opened with the epigram, "Now praised be great Apollo!" Howe poured praise on Henry Ward Beecher and dismissed Theodore Tilton as "an American anomaly, a common, smart man, in a position of eminence and command, utterly unfit for him." (*NAW*; *ANB*.)

11. Beginning in October 1873, Bob Stanton, then fourteen years old, was treated for a "hip disease," spending at least four months in bed, with eight pounds attached to his left leg to free the hip joint. A postcard from ECS informed SBA in mid-March 1874 that he was dressed and downstairs for the first time in months. (SBA diaries, 3 October, 28 December 1873, 3 January, 10 March 1874, *Film*, 16:617ff, 17:491ff.)

12. Anna Mott Hopper (1812–1874), a daughter of Lucretia Mott, died on 3 August, and her son, Isaac Tatem Hopper (1855–1874), died on 15 September. This left the widower, Edward Hopper (1812–1893), a lawyer in Philadelphia, and a daughter, Maria Hopper (1845–1899). (Cornell, *Adam and Anne Mott*, 323–24; *Quaker Genealogy*, 2:801; *Friends' Intelligencer* 31 [1874]: 425, 489; 53 [1893]: 503, and 56 [1899]: 27.)

13. Wright may refer to a letter in the *Chicago Tribune* on 1 October and the *New York Times* and other papers on 2 October, made available by a friend of Eunice Beecher's from Chicago. Beecher wrote that "until my good and noble and most pure husband has rest from these cruel persecutions I have no heart

for anything but that little I am privileged to do for him in protecting him from needless interruption."

14. Joanna S. Richards Morse (c. 1819–?) of Brooklyn was the mother of Elizabeth Tilton. By her "dear son," however, Wright means Henry Ward Beecher. Beecher's request that Morse call him "son" and Morse's compliance were made known by a letter included in Frank Moulton's last statement, in New York *Daily Graphic*, 11 September 1874, and Marshall, *True History of the Brooklyn Scandal*,

## 44 ⇒ ECS TO MARTHA COFFIN WRIGHT

[*Tenafly, 10? October 1874*][1]

Dear Martha

As I read your nice long letter my conscience reproached me all the way, to think I had sent you "an aggravating old postal card" And now as to morrow is the Lord's day & I wish to start the week with a clean conscience, I will write you as long a letter as you wrote me, & will try to imitate your beautiful chirography So Mrs President you intend to dodge all the conventions you can, of course with Eliza, Ellen, Flora & Fanny[2] you will always be furnished with unanswerable excuses! Rest assured the indomitable, unswerving Susan will not thus let you slip through her fingers. Do you know I am so nervous at the very thought of a convention, that I count the months, weeks & days before its approach, just as I used to do the advent of the various men children I have brought into the world. It is such a task to make them run smoothly to fill up the time with <u>good</u> <u>speaking</u>, to choke bores such as "Wolfe" & Walker,[3] I am always racked with anxiety. I hope & pray Susan does not propose to march us all to Washington this winter. These biennial attacks are too much. I hear Susan is in Michigan but I have not had a letter from her in a long time. Bob is rapidly improving. He can almost run on crutches. His legs are perfectly straight, & the same length, & Dr Wood[4] pronounces him entirely cured. He has been very happy & hopeful through all his trials. I have never heard him complain through all his confinement. He walks out, & rides out every day, plays on the guitar & reads everything from the Political History of New York down to the "The New York Weekly.["][5]

I had letters from Theodore (my fourth son) last evening, from Paris where he is now studying   He hopes to remain abroad two years, to perfect himself in French & German. Maggie & Hattie are in Vassar doing finely. My eldest son, & Bob are all we have at home now. I have two engagements near Phila the last of this month, & may spend a night with dear Lucretia.

When a few years ago at one of the American Conventions they made an onslaught on Susan because she said Lucy was not "legally" married,[6] did not your husband say Susan was right. That as they repudiated the marriage laws, or accepted the fact under protest, they were civilly but not legally married. I remember we three that is David you I had some talk about it, what was our conclusion on this point or what does David say now   I have a copy of Lucy's protest. As you say Julia Ward's "Now be praised great Apollo"!! was rather premature.[7] The richest thing the Woman's Journal has said in many a day, is Lucy & Blackwell having rescued the woman movement from the disgrace into which the rest of us had dragged it.[8] What a blessing! It was worth while for the little [*sideways on first page*] Englishman to come three thousand miles to do so grand a thing. Well I think our movement has always been respectable   I am sorry to hear of Edward Hoppers affliction. I hope it will not have a bad effect on Lucretia   Have you seen any of E. M. D's [*continued on new sheet*] postal cards. I use all he sends me so as to keep the great financial frauds before the people[9]   It does seem to me this question will never be perfectly clear to me so that I can answer all the arguments. I often start off quite <u>ably</u> when lo! I am asked some question that I cannot answer. Still hope sustains me, & I read & think as opportunity offers. An occasional visit to the fount of knowledge 333 Walnut is quite encouraging. I wrote a long letter on the Beecher question for a western friend, <u>which</u> <u>is</u> <u>in</u> <u>print</u>,[10] scraps flying through the eastern press, disjointed & disconnected & full of typical errors [*sideways in margins*] When I get the whole of it I will send it to you   ever yours

               ✒   E C S.

I hope to have a glimpse of Will Flo & the babies before they go south. They all tell me that baby is perfection. As I am accused of making that match I am charmed to have babies & oranges all prove a success. I thought Ellen had decided on the French number, too bad that you cannot go to Florida.[11]

⚒ ALS, Garrison Papers, MNS-S.

1. ECS notes that she writes on a Saturday. The tenth was the first Saturday after she received Wright's letter of October 3.

2. That is, Eliza Wright Osborne, Ellen Wright Garrison, Flora McMartin Wright, and the wife of Martha's son Francis, or Frank, Wright, Fanny Rosalie Pell Wright (1848–1892).

3. John B. Wolfe, or Wolff, and Mary Edwards Walker (1832–1919). Wolfe, a member of Section 12 of the International Workingmen's Association in New York City, attended suffrage meetings in Washington and New York off and on until at least 1885 and took part in the National's anniversary meeting in May 1874. He was also active in the Universal Peace Union and the American Labor Reform League. (*Film*, 13:280–84, 290–94, 507–10, 15:326–27, 335–39, 597–98, 16:101–2, 18:12; *New York Times*, 8, 9 May 1871; *History*, 4:59; Samuel Bernstein, *The First International in America* [New York, 1962], 90; Messer-Kruse, *The Yankee International*, 248.) Mary Walker, a physician, was a leading dress reformer who defied public opinion and endured numerous arrests for wearing trousers. She attended most of the Washington suffrage conventions, making something of a nuisance of herself by interrupting the proceedings. Far too often, in the opinion of ECS, Walker attracted a disproportionate amount of attention from the press. (*NAW*. See also *Papers 2*.)

4. Possibly James Rushmore Wood (1813–1882), a New York City surgeon with a speciality in bones and joints. (Howard A. Kelly and Walter A. Burrage, *Dictionary of American Medical Biography* [New York, 1928].)

5. *Political History of the State of New York* was a title sometimes applied to the multi-volume work by Jabez D. Hammond, *The History of Political Parties in the State of New York* (1846–1852). Or, Bob Stanton might have read the two volumes of John Romeyn Brodhead, *History of the State of New York*, which was published in a revised edition in 1874. The *New York Weekly News* appeared from 1855 to 1886.

6. At the annual convention of the American Woman Suffrage Association, 23 November 1870. See *Papers*, 2:376–79. The protest signed by Lucy Stone and Henry Blackwell at their wedding in 1855 was published at the time and in *History*, 1:260–61.

7. Responding to this letter, Wright asked: "<u>Why</u> Appollo—nobody knows, unless because he keeps a <u>lyre</u>." (3 November 1874, *Film*, 18:133–38.)

8. In a second celebration of Henry Ward Beecher's vindication, entitled "Beecher Acquitted," in the *Woman's Journal*, 5 September 1874, the English-born Henry Blackwell laid blame for the entire episode on a conspiracy of Theodore Tilton, Victoria Woodhull, and Francis Moulton to promote free love. He went on to boast: "Five years ago the editors of this paper assisted in rescuing the good cause of Woman Suffrage from the attempted control of these very men and their associates." For another reaction to this boast and the implication that the National Woman Suffrage Association was the party of free love, see the unsigned column, "'The Rescue.'—A Bit of History.—Free

Love," in the *Earlville Transcript*, 1 October 1874, in M. J. Gage scrapbook, MCR-S. Martha Wright suspected ECS wrote the column. (M. C. Wright to ECS, 3 November 1874.)

9. Edward M. Davis was a longtime critic of the gold standard and advocate of currency reform. His postcards with Greenback slogans have not been found; his Citizens' Suffrage Association sold similar propaganda in the form of envelopes imprinted with woman suffrage mottoes. (*Rev.*, 4 February 1869, *Film*, 1:456; ECS to E. M. Davis, 9 April 1874, *Film*, 17:1051–52.)

10. See above at 24 August 1874.

11. By "French number," ECS means three children (close to the birthrate in France) rather than four (a bit less than the rate in the United States). But she also alludes to contraception; American writers credited France with mastering contraceptive techniques in advance of other countries and labeled as "French" many devices for reproductive control. (Janet Farrell Brodie, *Contraception and Abortion in Nineteenth-Century America* [Ithaca, N.Y., 1994], 184–86, and Linda Gordon, *Woman's Body, Woman's Right: A Social History of Birth Control in America* [New York, 1976], 48, 149.)

45 ❧ FROM THE DIARY OF SBA

[*20–21 October 1874*]

TUESDAY, OCTOBER 20, 1874. Adrian [*Mich.*] Opera House[1]

Found Mr & Mrs Burton Kent[2] at Depot—the same good people I stopped with 5 years ago— Miss Maggie Thompson—the teacher—is now wife of Dan'l Benedict—[3] She introduced me nicely—asked for collection to pay $30 hall—got $20.— & forgot to tell me it was lacking—so nothing more was got— several Gents contributed a dollar each—

1. See *Film*, 18:124–25. SBA interrupted her tour on 12 October to attend a meeting of the Illinois suffrage association in Chicago. The trip also took her out of Michigan during the annual meeting of the American Woman Suffrage Association in Detroit. While changing trains in Adrian on 19 October, she discovered that no preparations were made for her lecture the next evening, so she stopped to hire a hall and order the printing of a poster.

2. Burton Kent (1814–?) and Caroline A. Palmer Kent (c. 1824–?) hosted SBA on 8 April 1870. Burton Kent, a Republican and the surveyor of Lenawee County, retired from farming before the war and moved into Adrian. (*Portrait and Biographical Album of Lenawee County, Mich.* [Chicago, 1888], 654–55; SBA diary, 1870, *Film*, 14:173ff; Federal Census, 1870.)

3. Daniel Benedict (c. 1832-?) grew up in Adrian, the son of a leading trader in furs, and was in the grocery business himself. By introducing SBA to her audience in 1874, Maggie Thompson Benedict (1846-?) repeated the part she played when SBA spoke in Adrian in 1870, when she boarded with the Kents. In March 1874, Maggie Benedict was among the leaders in Adrian's crusade against the saloons, and in 1880, she and Caroline Kent signed a petition to the Republican party, attesting to their desire to vote. (*Adrian Daily Press*, 21 April 1876; SBA diary, 1870; *Film*, 4:868; Annie Turner Wittenmyer, *History of the Woman's Temperance Crusade* [Boston, 1882], 620; Federal Census, 1870.)

WEDNESDAY, OCTOBER 21, 1874. Hillsdale—Hill. Co. Opera House—
Stopped—Mrs E. S. Samm—[1] Freeman Clough[2] took responsibility of my lecture— "Will Carlton"[3]—Michigans young poet—author of Betsey & I are Out—introduced me very handsomely— Mrs J. B. Norris—[4] Mrs———Gallaher—[5] Miss [*blank*] Mead[6]—whom I used to see in Leavenworth with Mother Haviland & the Freedmen—lives at Hillsdale    Opera House packed long before 7. so people were going away—it was estimated that 2,000 people had to go— The Hillsdale Standard—Repub. had announced that the local Com. Mr Penfield[7] at head—a stationer—↑that the friends of W.S. in H.↓ did not wish Miss to speak at H.— But the vast turn out didn't look much that way—[8] [*Entries for 22-26 October omitted.*]

1. Elizabeth Stafford Samm (1837?-1918) was the second wife of Michael Samm, a German immigrant who settled in Hillsdale. She was a local delegate to the state association's meeting in May, and she joined the canvass as a lecturer. In 1880, she earned a medical degree from the University of Michigan. (Milton M. Ferguson et al., *150 Years in the Hills and Dales: A Bicentennial History of Hillsdale County, Michigan* [Hillsdale, Mich., 1976], 1:329-30, 2:189; Louise Hawkes, Jack C. Northrup, and Kathleen M. Dawley, comps., Cemetery Records of Hillsdale County, Michigan, vol. 1: City of Hillsdale, Hillsdale Township, Friends of Mitchell Public Library, typescript, 1983, 1987, p. 121, Mi; Hillsdale County Records, Michigan State Library, typescript, 1867, 3:514, Mi; *Woman's Journal*, 26 September 1874; Federal Census, 1860, 1870.)

2. Freeman Clough (1823-1903) was a grocer who lived in Hillsdale from 1868 to 1887. (Federal Census, 1870; on-line family records in possession of editors.)

3. Will Carleton (1845-1912) worked as a journalist after graduation from Hillsdale College in 1869, until he made his reputation as a poet. "Betsy and I Are Out," a humorous look at marriage and divorce, was published first in 1871 and included in Carleton's 1873 collection of *Farm Ballads*. (*DAB*; *NCAB*, 2:505-6.)

4. Elizabeth M. Kinney Norris (1828–?) immigrated to Michigan with her parents, married fellow New Yorker Jason Bates Norris in 1856, and settled on a farm in Woodbridge Township near Hillsdale. Jason Norris held numerous local offices and entered the Michigan lower house as a Republican in 1871. (*Portrait and Biographical Album of Hillsdale County, Mich.* [Chicago, 1888], 280–81; Elon G. Reynolds, comp., *Compendium of History and Biography of Hillsdale County, Michigan* [Chicago, 1903], 169–70.)

5. Margaret Fingland Gallaher (1832–1915) was the widow of the late pastor of Hillsdale's First Presbyterian Church, Frederick R. Gallaher, and the mother of two young girls. (Ferguson, *150 Years in the Hills and Dales*, 2:150; Hawkes, Northrup, and Dawley, Cemetery Records of Hillsdale County, Mich., 1:124.)

6. Mary Jane Ford Mead (1822–1902) and Laura Smith Haviland (1808–1898) ran the Freedmen's Home in Leavenworth, Kansas, where SBA met them in 1865. (Laura Haviland, *A Woman's Life Work: Labors and Experiences of Laura S. Haviland* [Chicago, 1887], 361–79; *NAW* and *ANB*, s.v. "Haviland, Laura Smith"; Mitchell Public Library, Hillsdale, Mich.; *Papers*, 1:537, 547.)

7. Here in Adele Hazlett's hometown, the newspaper announced that easterners with "objectionable isms" were not welcome and that the local committee rejected arranging a lecture for "that 'relict of Methuselah,' Susan B. Anthony." Lewis R. Penfield, an alderman, school board member, and proprietor of a bookstore in Hillsdale, co-signed the letter refusing to arrange SBA's lecture because she would "do the cause more harm than good." He served on the executive committee of the Woman Suffrage Association of Hillsdale. (*Hillsdale Standard*, 13 October 1874, SBA scrapbook 8, Rare Books, DLC; Albert Dickerman et al. to William M. Ferry, 9 October 1874, Ferry Family Papers, MiU-H; *History of Hillsdale County, Michigan, with Illustrations and Biographical Sketches* [Philadelphia, 1879], 102, 113.)

8. From Hillsdale, SBA proceeded to Coldwater, Three Rivers, Niles, and Marshall.

≈ Excelsior Diary 1874, n.p., SBA Papers, DLC.

46   ≫   SPEECH BY SBA IN JACKSON, MICHIGAN

[27 October 1874]

Miss Anthony began her speech by asking the question why it was that in the face of the utterances of our forefathers relative to all men being born free and equal, taxation without representation, government deriving its just powers from the consent of the governed, that one-half of the people are denied any voice in the workings of the government, and answered the query by saying that society upheld a false theory relative to woman's place in the world, which thus makes it safe to violate these governmental maxims as regards women, which no one would dare do in the case of any class of men. This theory is that women are created primarily for man's happiness, and secondarily for her own. The new dispensation proposed to reverse this and put her on the level of man in this regard. It is claimed that man is born to support and protect women, and so he will care for those to whom he is closely allied. But millions of women working in factories, stores, schools, house service, give the lie to the claim of support, and married women do enough work to far more than earn their living. The trouble was not that woman did not work enough, but that their earnings went to their husbands. She spoke of the laws regulating division of property on the death of the husband, and said a law was wanted where man and wife should stand as copartners and each one have the disposition of the property on the death of the other. As to legal protection no woman was ever tried by her peers, for the blackest, most ignorant or most brutal juror was her political superior. She brought forward the millions of women in the world driven by poverty and man's neglect to a life of shame as examples of man's protection of woman outside of his immediate circle. Having thus laid down some of the evils to which woman is liable, she proceeded to show how, in her opinion, the ballot would remove all these evils. It would raise her in the estimation of a government, as was shown by the change of policy of the English parties after the ballot had been given to the workmen.[1] It was not exactly a fair issue that woman didn't want to vote, for neither did the negroes in this country or the workmen of England ask to vote, still the ballot proved a priceless boon to them. She showed that it was the votes of the trades union men that gained them their many concessions and gave a number of instances where unions of women had failed to receive from Legislatures what men's unions had no difficulty in obtaining, justice. She took a vote of the audience and a large number of men said they intended to vote "yes" in November on the suffrage amendment, only a few scattering "noes" were heard. She said this was the way wherever she had spoken. To the workingmen she would say that they could not afford to degrade any laboring class, and showed how the work of women at the wages she gets keeps down wages of men in the same branch of industry.

It was a fallacy that women's wages were regulated by supply and demand, any more than the slave labor before the war was unpaid for the same reason.[2] She wanted the ballot put in woman's hands so that self-interest will cause political parties to look out for her interest. She contrasted the condition of negroes before the war and since as an illustration of what the ballot will do for its possessors. She closed by urging the men in the audience to vote in favor of woman suffrage next Tuesday, and called for a rising vote, when a large number arose in favor and only one in opposition to the measure, the largest proportion keeping their seats.

&#8460; Jackson *Daily Patriot*, 28 October 1874, in SBA scrapbook 8, Rare Books, DLC.

1. In this speech, as in her best-known lecture, "Woman Wants Bread, Not the Ballot," SBA relied on the example of recent British political history to illustrate a connection between economic needs and political rights and demonstrate how voting rights could transform the political landscape. Reporters' synopses and paraphrases of her speeches often muddled her own imperfect grasp of the history, but the outlines of her interpretation are evident. Here she refers to the Reform Act of 1867, which nearly doubled the number of voters in parliamentary elections and inaugurated a period of social reform as Liberals and Conservatives appealed to the interests of their new constituents. (Angus Hawkins, *British Party Politics, 1852–1886* [New York, 1998], 109–11, 131–40; Eugenio F. Biagini, *Liberty, Retrenchment and Reform: Popular Liberalism in the Age of Gladstone, 1860–1880* [Cambridge, England, 1992].)

2. The text reads "unpaid by for the same reason."

## 47  &#8460;  From the Diary of SBA

[*27 October, 3–4 November, 15–17 December 1874*]

TUESDAY, OCTOBER 27, 1874. Jackson Union Hall— Mrs Judge Livermore[1] Mary T. Lathrop[2]

Stopped with Mrs Livermore—introduced by Rev. [*blank*] M^cCarty[3]— Mrs Conable[4] sat on platform—Mrs Lathrop made Finance appeal at beginning—raised $16— at close I made one—& got——— $10.50 for Trials[5]

Had packed house three times size of Senator Chandlers—[6] It made the Methodist Mrs Lathrop & Conable <u>Shout Glory</u>—they said— they hadn't the slightest hope of an audience—but Jackson proved no exception to all my meetings thus far—

Mothers Cousin Benjamin Reads Widow[7] came forward to see me— she with two daughters lives at Napoleon—a few miles from J[ackson] her son in law <u>Pryne</u> was with her—[8] A Mr Brown[9]—whose wife is a Temperance Lecturer—very earnest— [*Entries for 28 October-2 November omitted.*]

1. Sarah E. Safford Livermore (c. 1829-?) was the second wife of Fidus Livermore, a lawyer, former judge, and the Democratic candidate for the legislature. During the war, she was made vice president of the Ladies' Aid Society in Jackson. (Helen F. Lewis, comp., *Southeastern Michigan Pioneer Families: Especially Jackson County and New York Origins* [Rhinebeck, N.Y., 1998], 249; Jackson County Marriages [Michigan], 1833-1870, As Recorded in the County Clerk's Office, typescript, Mi; *Michigan Biographies*, s.v. "Livermore, Fidus"; *History of Jackson County, Michigan . . . History of Michigan* [Chicago, 1881], 1:146, 162, 236-37, 343.)

2. Mary Torrans Lathrap (1838-1895) petitioned Michigan's constitutional convention for woman suffrage in 1867, helped to found the Michigan Woman Suffrage Association in 1870, and was charged with organizing suffrage societies in Jackson County for the campaign of 1874. A former teacher and a licensed preacher in the Methodist Episcopal church, Lathrap was prominent in the Woman's Crusade in Jackson, and she attended the founding of the Woman's Christian Temperance Union after the fall election. Thereafter she focused her attention on the temperance movement, leading the Michigan union for many years. (*American Women*; *SEAP*; *The Poems and Written Address of Mary T. Lathrap, with a Short Sketch of Her Life*, Julia R. Parish, comp. [N.p., 1895]; *History*, 3:516n.)

3. Joseph Hendrickson McCarty (1830-1897), of the Methodist Episcopal Church, helped women in Jackson launch their crusade against liquor in the spring of 1874. He attended the founding of the Michigan Woman Suffrage Association in 1870, when he lived in Saginaw. (Simpson, *Cyclopaedia of Methodism*; *History*, 3:516n; *Woman's Journal*, 12 September 1874.)

4. Cadelia Newkirk Connable (c. 1825-?), not Conable, the wife since 1843 of Edwards J. Connable of the Jackson Fire Clay Company. When SBA lectured in Jackson in 1870, Connable, as president of the local suffrage association, introduced her to the audience. (*History of Jackson County, Mich.*, 1:614; SBA diary, 9 April 1870, *Film*, 14:173ff; Federal Census, 1870.)

5. The blank should read $12.50 as the collection at Jackson totaled $28.50. In addition, she sold copies of *Account of the Trial of SBA*.

6. Zachariah Chandler (1813-1879), Michigan's Republican party boss and

a United States senator since 1857, was in disfavor with the state party, and in January 1875, the legislature ended his career in the Senate. He had voted in favor of Aaron Sargent's amendment to implement universal suffrage in Pembina Territory, but according to a report in the *Woman's Journal*, 14 November 1874, he refused to cast a ballot for or against the suffrage amendment on election day. (*BDAC.*)

7. This Benjamin Read was probably the son of Lucy Read Anthony's uncle Benjamin Read (1770-1841), who died in Sparta, New York. The younger Benjamin (c. 1813-?) and his wife Elizabeth Allen Read (c. 1813-?) moved to Michigan from Mount Morris, New York, before 1860, and by 1868, lived in Columbia Township, Jackson County, where they helped to organize the Clark's Lake Baptist Church. In 1870, Betsy Read, as she was known, accompanied her husband and three daughters to SBA's lecture in Jackson. The census of that year listed an Eva Read, age fourteen, and two boys in the household. (Read Genealogical Ms., SBA Papers, MCR-S; Perrine, *Daniel Perrin and His Descendants*, 275-76; *History of Jackson County, Mich*, 1:787; SBA diary, 9-10 April 1870; Federal Census, 1870.)

8. Hulburt James Perrine (1837-1904) was married in 1860 to Sarah Eliza Read (1838-1895). When SBA spoke in Jackson in 1870, he took her to call on the Reads. Like his in-laws, he moved to Michigan from New York. (Perrine, *Daniel Perrin and His Descendants*, 275-76.)

9. Amos H. Brown (c. 1811-?) and Ann Brown (c. 1811-?), both born in New York, came to Michigan as children and married there, raising a family on their farm in Parma. Ann Brown and Mary Lathrap were described as "indefatigable workers in the temperance cause" in the city of Jackson. (Lewis, *Southeastern Michigan Pioneer Families: Jackson County*, 46; Paul R. Peck, *Early They Came*, [N.p., 1978], 340; *History of Jackson County, Mich.*, 1:242-43, 2:1081-82; Wittenmyer, *History of the Temperance Crusade*, 631.)

TUESDAY, NOVEMBER 3, 1874. <u>Election</u> <u>Day</u>— returned from Pontiac to Detroit[1]—found Mrs Stebbins,[2] Boothe,[3] Gardner[4] & other women working at the polls— Dined at Mrs Smiths—the Stebbins— spent P.M. at Cousin Benjamin Anthony's—[5]

1. After speaking at Jackson on 27 October, SBA went on to Lansing, Owosso, Flint, and Pontiac.

2. Catharine Ann Fish Stebbins (1823-1904), a participant in the woman's rights conventions of 1848, grew up in Rochester, New York, and settled in Detroit with her husband, Giles Badger Stebbins (1817-1900), a prominent antislavery and spiritualist lecturer. Catharine Stebbins was an activist in city and state suffrage associations as well as the National Woman Suffrage Association, and she accompanied ECS on her tour in May 1874. She also reported on state activities for the *Woman's Journal*. Giles Stebbins joined the statewide canvass as a lecturer. (*American Women*; *History*, 3:47-48, 523-25;

research by Jean M. Czerkas, Rochester, N.Y.; Garrison, *Letters*, 5:326n; Giles B. Stebbins, *Upward Steps of Seventy Years, Autobiographic, Biographic, Historic* [New York, 1890]. See also *Papers* 2.)

3. Mrs. Boothe or Booth is unidentified. She joined Catharine and Giles Stebbins at the founding of the American Woman Suffrage Association in 1869. (*History*, 2:759n.)

4. Nannette Brown Ellingwood Gardner Smith (1828–1900), renowned for her success at registering and voting in Detroit's Ninth Ward in 1871, married George Bliss Smith (1820–1874), a fellow member of the Detroit suffrage association, in February 1873. They lived at 327 Howard Street. Smith and her daughter, Sarah M. Gardner, decorated their polling place and worked there on election day to hand out ballots marked for approval of the amendment. (Genealogical records, Nannette B. Gardner Papers, MiU-H; city directory, 1874; *Woman's Journal*, 14 November 1874. See also *Papers* 2.)

5. Benjamin Mason Anthony (1822–1877), a second cousin, assisted SBA in organizing the canvass for universal suffrage in New York in 1867, before he moved to Detroit. He was a traveling salesman, living at 79 Winder Street. (Anthony, *Anthony Genealogy*, 137; SBA to B. M. Anthony, 4 April 1867, *Film*, 12:111; city directory, 1874 to 1876; *Detroit Free Press*, 9, 11 May 1877.)

WEDNESDAY, NOVEMBER 4, 1874. From Detroit to Rochester— Took Cars at 8.40—and reached home at 10.25 P.M.

[*added later*] The newspaper returns show Woman Suffrage lost—3 or 5 to 1—[1] what better could be expected every whiskey maker, vender drinker, every gambler every Libertine every ignorant besotted man against us—& then the other extreme—every narrow selfish religious bigot—[2]

1. The amendment lost, in the final tabulation, by 40,077 to 135,957, winning approval only in tiny Emmet County in the north, where forty-one of the seventy-five men who voted on the measure indicated their approval. The amended constitution also failed, in an election where Republicans narrowly held on to the governorship, and Democrats gained strength in the legislature. Suffrage lost quite uniformly across the state, though the results were better in the more populous counties, where suffragists organized most effectively. Even in Wayne County, where the state's leading newspaper spewed antisuffragism and the liquor industry mobilized against the amendment, twenty-five percent of the voters approved it. Voters in two of Detroit's wards approved the amendment: in the "respectable," native-born Fifth and the heavily Irish Eighth.

T. W. Higginson suggested in the *Woman's Journal* that the Beecher-Tilton scandal cost thousands of votes. ECS and SBA had noted weaknesses in the canvass itself—insufficient emphasis on education and inadequate organization. Getting supporters to the polls to pass out the ballots marked for a "yes" vote proved difficult everywhere. The failure of political parties to endorse the measure and activate party machinery in its favor also cost votes. But most of the blame fell on liquor interests and German immigrants, two groups often joined in the public imagination.

The election appeared to many voters to be a referendum on liquor, or as one Detroit voter explained, it was another step in the Woman's Crusade. Indeed, Matilda Hindman, organizer for the American Woman Suffrage Association, campaigned with the slogan "Temperance and Woman Suffrage are inseparable." Anecdotal reports from different counties indicated that saloonkeepers and others in the liquor trade put men at the polls on election day to work against woman suffrage. At one Detroit polling place, "there were five men who did little else than distribute anti-Suffrage ballots," according to W. N. Hudson in the *Detroit Advertiser and Tribune*.

When the campaign opened, Henry Blackwell predicted victory in Michigan precisely because it lacked the immigrant population that stymied suffragists in Massachusetts; all the liberty-loving New Englanders had migrated to the state, he lamented. But when it came time to explain the defeat, there were enough immigrants to take the blame. In Ann Arbor's Second Ward, Detroit's Ninth Ward, and the city of Grand Haven, observers singled out German opposition to account for defeat; they "were our most determined foes."

To some observers this collision of interests between woman's rights and the "whiskey and beer element" told a larger truth about the state's class structure; to G. M Taber of Detroit, the election proved that "the intelligent classes of Michigan voted for Woman Suffrage, and the ignorant masses against it." (*Tribune Almanac, 1875*, 86–87; *Woman's Journal*, 2 May, 14, 28 November, 5 December 1874.)

2. Entries from 4 November to 14 December omitted. Most of this time SBA visited with her family in Rochester, interrupting her stay for a ten-day lecture tour in northern New York. She left home for Washington on 8 December to get advice about holding the annual convention in January, and she stopped in Philadelphia on her return. ECS thought "that the Beecher scandal had made it unwise for us to attempt" the meeting, SBA noted in her diary on 9 December, but Edward Davis and Lucretia Mott told her to go ahead. (SBA diary, 1874, *Film*, 17:491ff.)

TUESDAY, DECEMBER 15, 1874. [*Tenafly*] From Philadelphia to New York—at 11 A.M. Anna Thomson[1]—very feeble—in company ↑with me↓ to Jersey City— I reached Tenafly at 4 P.M—& found a warm welcome To work to get out Call for Jan Con. at Washington

1. Anna Thomson (1806–1885) of Philadelphia and her sister, Mary Adeline Thomson, had been friends of SBA since the three met at the national woman's rights convention in Philadelphia in 1854. They often hosted SBA when she visited the city. (*Friends' Intelligencer* 42 [1885]: 697; *Anthony*, 1:122, 2:264,

814; *History*, 3:468n; with assistance of the Estate of J. Edgar Thomson, Philadelphia.)

WEDNESDAY, DECEMBER 16, 1874. At Tenafly  Wrote letters for Washington National Convention—got off 30 or 40

Rode to Englewood with Bob—he is still lame—but hopes to gain use of his leg—

THURSDAY, DECEMBER 17, 1874. At Tenafly  Wrote again all day—both Mrs S & self—

And had a long, long talk

⤳ Excelsior Diary 1874, n.p., SBA Papers, DLC.

## 48 ⤳ ECS TO ANTOINETTE BROWN BLACKWELL

Tenafly N.J. Dec 18th [*1874*]

Dear Mrs Blackwell,

Our friend Susan arrived here from Washington a few days since, having just made arrangements for a convention there on the 14th & 15th of January. We are busy writing letters to our friends in all directions asking them to attend the con. or to send letters & contributions. Is it possible for you to be there & make one of your best speeches. We always have large & enthusiastic audiences there. I have seen Lincoln Hall literally packed three day[s in] succession. How of[ten] I have sat & lookin[g at?] those immense au[diences] & felt the hour h[ad] come for woman [&?] the woman for [the?] hour had not [yet] appeared. Our sp[eakers?] all seem so th[in? &?] feeble, compared [to?] ↑the↓ glowing eloquence of all classes of men under similar oppressions. The fact is women have no self-respect. I wish you would make it a point to go to Washington this year. Aside from the needed public work, it would afford you an opportunity to take your daughter[1] & show her our rulers in counsel in that magnificent Capitol. As to expenses we have written to all our rich friends for contributions to the convention & what we get, will pay expenses as far as it goes. But rich women will give their thousands to churches, charities, & institutions of learning for boys, & their fives to their own sex. With kind regards for yourself, Husband,[2] & daughters.

AL, Blackwell Papers, MCR-S. Square brackets surround words cut away with signature.

1. The Blackwells had five daughters, ranging in age from five to twenty-four: Florence, born 1856; Edith, born 1860; Grace, born 1863; Agnes, born 1866; Ethel, born 1869. (Elizabeth Cazden, *Antoinette Brown Blackwell: A Biography* [Old Westbury, N.Y., 1983].)

2. Samuel Charles Blackwell (1823–1901), a brother of Henry Blackwell and a businessman in New York and New Jersey, married Antoinette Brown in 1856.

## 49   FROM THE DIARY OF SBA

[*18–19 December 1874*]

FRIDAY, DECEMBER 18, 1874. Left Tenafly at 12 noon—for New York—Lunched at Mrs Phelps—she not in—then down town to Associated Press Office—found that the N.Y. papers had rejected Washington despatch of fact of our January Convention—no doubt to punish us all for Mrs Stantons interference in the Beecher Tilton scandal—against Beecher— The whole N.Y. Press seems subsidized to him— Dined with Mrs Phelps— Mrs Blake & Winchester[1] met me there—talked up the Wash. Con. & then slept at Mrs Lozier's <u>new</u> house—in New York[2]

1. Margaret E. Winchester, a trustee of the New York Medical College and Hospital for Women, served on the executive committee of the American Equal Rights Association and contributed money to its campaigns. By 1870, she and her husband, Jonas Winchester, owner of a drug company, were living at separate addresses in New York City. (City directories, 1865 to 1872.)

2. Clemence Lozier moved to 238 West Fourteenth Street. (City directory, 1875.)

SATURDAY, DECEMBER 19, 1874. [*Albany, N.Y.*] Had warm reception by Mrs Lozier this A.M. She told me prospect that her Women's Medical College to which she has given 13 years hard work—and $16,000 dollars seemed about to be "gobbled" up by the <u>men</u> doctors—to go out of control of women altogether—[1]

Took 10.30 train for Albany—arrived at 2.30 P.M—found my dear friend Lydia[2] nice & bright—but very weak— Phebe Jones spent the evening with us—

1. The New York Medical College and Hospital for Women, founded by Lozier in 1863, bought property on Lexington Avenue in 1874 in order to expand its facilities. Because the value of the new property exceeded the amount allowed in the corporation's charter, the trustees turned to the legislature for an amendment. But, in the words of the institution's historian, "with the increased educational facilities there came increased responsibilities in the business management and maintenance of the institutions, and it was deemed necessary to make some changes in the personnel of the board of trustees, which prior to 1875 had been composed of women, by replacing some of them with persons of the opposite sex." At the same time, the trustees organized a group of "Hospital Managers"—volunteer women to raise funds and "look to the welfare and comfort of the unfortunates" brought to the hospital for care. (William Harvey King, ed., *History of Homeopathy and Its Institutions in America* [New York, 1905], 3:134–35.)

2. Lydia Mott.

↩ Excelsior Diary 1874, n.p., SBA Papers, DLC.

## 50 ⇝ ANTOINETTE BROWN BLACKWELL TO ECS, WITH ECS TO SBA

Somerville [*N.J.*] Dec 21 1874

Dear Mrs. Stanton

I am glad you and Susan will hold the Washington Convention and am ready most sincerely to wish you the highest success. But I cannot attend; and it may be as well to say frankly what you will both understand whether it is said or not, that the desire to do so is not strong enough to override the inevitable obstacles. It may not seem to you that the Washington movement is shadowed by some of the antecedents of that great "duel in the dark";[1] but to me so it is.

Well, let that go! That we are all sincerely interested in a common work there is no doubt; and in the presence of a great multitude of willing listeners, the feeling which you so strongly express often comes uppermost in my heart. Yet I dont believe it is true after all. There are thousands of "women for the hour" at every fresh turn in life. We dont need one preeminent over all others, but a multitude keeping abreast, as they should in a democratic movement. It is like the civil war. That had no genius, but many men of effective tallent. So we and our work are well enough as they are; and the right result will come uppermost. No one need fear that we shall fail of a final triumph.

Is it possible that it is a year since Susan was here?[2] Well, if there was more real work to show for the time spent that would be satisfactory! But this morning on the mountain, in its beautiful snowy wrappings, is bright enough to drive away even, "it might have been."[3]

I shall look with interest for the reports of your convention, and shall follow with lively interest and some <u>sisternal</u> solicitude all your other movements as publicly reported.

The husband and daughters unite in sending good wishes to you and yours—the visitor Susan included.

We are just off for the first sleigh ride    Yours always sincerely
⚞ *A. B. Blackwell*

⚞ ALS, Blackwell Papers, MCR-S.


### ECS to SBA

*[Tenafly, c. 23 December 1874]*

I am so vexed with myself to think that I should have laid myself open to such a supercillious reply. Gerrit[4] sends $25 & Mrs Bullar[5] $20, nearly enough to pay for you & me & quite if we are invited to stay with friends

I shall [write?] Mrs Sargent & Stebbins about con. I have not put pen to paper since the girls returned. It has been one hurry & hurrah to get their clothes washed & mended [*sideways on first page*] & now a grand dinner for Christmas with presents company &c &c I go to Connecticut Tuesday. With love    Did Mrs Blake say she would write notices to papers. You must do what you can I shall have but little time to do anything

⚞ AL, written on sheets of letter above, Blackwell Papers, MCR-S. Square brackets surround an illegible word.

1. A reference to the division between the American and National associations.

2. Since SBA lectured in Somerville, New Jersey, on 30 December 1873 and stayed with the Blackwells.

3. John Greenleaf Whittier, "Maud Muller": "For of all sad words of tongue or pen, \ The saddest are these: 'It might have been!'"

4. Gerrit Smith (1797–1874), ECS's first cousin, was a reformer and philanthropist whose donations had helped the woman's rights movement since the 1850s. He lived in Peterboro, New York, but arrived in New York City on 24 December 1874, suffered a stroke on the twenty-sixth and died on the twenty-eighth. ECS went north to Peterboro for his funeral. (*ANB*; ECS to Elizabeth Smith Miller, 7 January 1875, *Film*, 18:252–60. See also *Papers* 1 & 2.)

5. That is, Laura Curtis Bullard.

## 51 &#x219A; SBA TO SIR[1]

Tenafly N.J. Jan. 12/75[2]

Dear Sir

I have ordered the Express to leave <u>two</u> packages of books with you— Will you please pay the charge on them—& I ↑will↓ settle with you on my arrival on Wednesday—& will also make a payment on the hall rent.

Now as to the <u>Hall</u>— Please be sure & have it thoroughly <u>heated</u>— to go into a cold hall just <u>chills</u> & <u>kills</u> a meeting— So dont fail to give us a <u>well</u> <u>warmed</u> <u>room</u> <u>to</u> <u>begin</u> <u>with</u>—

Then, <u>without</u> <u>fail</u>—please—give us a <u>carpet</u> <u>on</u> <u>the</u> <u>platform</u>— With a dozzen <u>easy</u> chairs & a sofa—if possible—and three or four small tables along the front—<u>not</u> that great long one—put that please, on the floor in front of the platform for the Reporters—

Then can you not give us a flag or two over the platform—& make the hall <u>wear</u> <u>a</u> <u>lady</u>-<u>like</u> appearance generally—for though we are <u>strong</u>-<u>minded</u> we do not wish to have things about us look <u>manish</u>—

<u>Especially</u>— Do have the hall <u>floor</u> <u>cleaned</u> throughly—also the <u>ante</u> <u>rooms</u>— They were <u>simply</u> <u>filthy</u> last year—we had them just after some sort of <u>tobacco</u> <u>spitting</u> <u>performance</u>— So please give us every thing clean as silver, and all in real <u>woman</u> <u>housekeeping</u> order—& we will not ↑only↓ pay our rent promply—but say a thousand thanks beside—[3] Respectfully yours

&#x219A; *Susan B. Anthony*

&#x219A; ALS, Papers of SBA, NPV.

1. SBA addressed the manager of Washington's Lincoln Hall.

2. SBA returned to Tenafly in the New Year. Details about her schedule thereafter are scarce because her diary for 1875 disappeared after Ida Harper used it in writing her biography. Harper's extracts from the original are in *Film*, 18:247.

3. When the National association's meeting opened, the press reported "several improvements" to Lincoln Hall: "Brand new matting has been put down in the aisles, a new carpet adorns the platform, while upon it a sofa and a number of easy chairs have been placed for the use of the ladies. A large American flag is festooned above the stage." (Washington *Evening Star*, 14 January 1875, *Film*, 18:271–72.)

52   REMARKS BY ECS TO THE NATIONAL WOMAN SUFFRAGE ASSOCIATION

EDITORIAL NOTE: ECS opened the seventh Washington convention of the National Woman Suffrage Association at Lincoln Hall on 14 January with a eulogy for Martha Coffin Wright, the National's president, who died in Boston after a short illness on 4 January. She then made these remarks.

[14 January 1875]

This is the seventh annual convention we have held in Washington to discuss the rights of self-government for one half the people. This meeting comes at a most auspicious moment, when the entire nation is wide awake to this great principle of American independence, now being trampled under foot in the State of Louisiana.[1] Self-government is the great subject now that occupies the press and the people—the theme for eloquent speeches and debates in Congress and every State Legislature. Democrats and Liberal Republicans[2] alike are proclaiming the inalienable rights of the people harmoniously together. At such a crisis, in view of the grand principles they are just now so earnestly enunciating, one would think these liberty-loving statesmen might now be easily converted to our ideas, and demand the right of self-government for women too. Such a step would be in line with their present position. They need adopt no new principle. Only extend the rights they now demand for the people of Louisiana to the women of their own States. Hon. Carl Schurz,[3] in his great speech just delivered in the Senate, points out the danger of infringing on the constitutional rights of the people. He clearly sees the danger in Louisiana. But the question is, if the danger arises from educating the people to violate the principles of our government, is it not as dangerous, in the case of twenty millions of women, as the Legislature of Louisiana? If it is the principle these gentlemen—Democrats and Liberal Republicans—are so earnestly defending, they should make eloquent protests on our platform to-day, and point out the violation of all the great principles of republican Government in denying us a voice in the laws and rulers that govern us, in the right of trial by jury, and representation while taxed to support the State.

~ Washington *National Republican*, 15 January 1875, in SBA scrapbook 8, Rare Books, DLC.

1. A bitter, partisan argument about Reconstruction opened in January 1875, after federal troops in Louisiana protected Republican legislators against Democratic efforts to settle a disputed election by force. In Congress and the nation, Democrats and Liberal Republicans used the occasion to attack President Grant and promote their view that southern states should be left to govern themselves without federal intervention. Their impassioned speeches, as ECS notes, celebrated self-government and the sanctity of voting rights. (William Gillette, *Retreat from Reconstruction, 1869–1879* [Baton Rouge, La., 1979], 104–35; Joe Gray Taylor, *Louisiana Reconstructed, 1863–1877* [Baton Rouge, La., 1974], 304–39; Ella Lonn, *Reconstruction in Louisiana after 1868* [New York, 1918], 292–307, 319–38.)

2. Appalled by the spoils system that flourished under the Grant administration and intent on returning the South to the control of white southerners, the Liberal Republican party formed in 1872 and nominated Horace Greeley for president. In the Forty-third Congress, four senators and four representatives identified themselves as Liberal Republicans.

3. Carl Schurz (1829–1906) of Missouri, the most prominent German-American politician in the country, served in the Senate from 1869 to 1875. A force in building the Liberal Republican movement and a sharp critic of the Grant administration, he was also a firm opponent of woman suffrage. Speaking to the Senate on 11 January, Schurz deplored the use of troops in Louisiana and called for legislation to "secure to the people of the State of Louisiana their rights of self-government under the Constitution." (*BDAC*; *Congressional Record*, 43d Cong., 2d sess., 365–72.)

53    RESOLUTIONS ADOPTED BY THE NATIONAL
         WOMAN SUFFRAGE ASSOCIATION

EDITORIAL NOTE: There is no record of who served on the resolutions committee at this meeting. SBA read the resolutions at the opening session of the convention. ECS's handwritten texts of the fourth, fifth, and seventh resolutions are in *Film*, 18:279–81.

[14–15 January 1875]

*Resolved*, That the assumed power to restrict the fundamental rights of citizenship is the recognition of an inequality of rights among citizens; the establishment of political caste; essentially monarchical in spirit; and hence, fatal to the principle of self-government.

*Resolved*, That the assumed power of all male citizens to restrict the rights of all female citizens is based on the lowest power of force, and is unworthy the sons of American mothers.

*Resolved*, That we rejoice in the fact that there can be no security of liberty for any class while the most sacred rights are denied to one-half of the people, for in this law of divine justice we see our emancipation. The moral necessities of the nation must ere long compel that justice for woman that the military and political necessities secured for black men.

*Resolved*, That as the duties of citizens are the outgrowth of their rights, a class denied the common rights of citizenship should be exempt from all duties to the State. Hence the Misses Smith[1] of Glastonbury, Conn., and Abby Kelley Foster,[2] of Worcester, Mass., who refused to pay taxes because not allowed to vote, suffered gross injustice and oppression at the hands of the State officials, who seized and sold their property for taxes.

*Resolved*, That to deny the right of suffrage to the women of the nation is a dangerous innovation on the rights of men, since the assumed right to deny the right to one class is the implied right to deny it to all others.[3] Acting on this principle New Hampshire abridges the rights of her citizens by forbidding Catholics to hold office,[4] and Rhode Island abridges the rights of her citizens by forbidding foreigners to vote, except on a property qualification.[5]

*Resolved,* That proper self-respect and the best interests of humanity at large should lead those women who believe that their civil and political equality lies at the basis of all reform to give their best thought, time, and money to the elevation, education, and enfranchisement of their own sex, as of far more importance than all church or charitable interests, peace, prison, or temperance reforms, Indian policies,[6] national fairs, or centennial birthdays,[7] which now absorb the activities of the large majority of all women.

*Resolved,* That our thanks are due to the Hon. A. A. Sargent and the other nineteen Senators who voted for Woman Suffrage in Pembina, and to the 40,000 brave men who went to the polls and voted for Woman Suffrage in Michigan.

*Resolved,* That in the death of Martha C. Wright, the president of our Suffrage Association, Dr. Harriot K. Hunt,[8] the first woman in the country who entered the medical profession, the Rev. Beriah Green,[9] and the Hon. Gerrit Smith, steadfast advocates of Woman Suffrage, we have in the past year been called to mourn the loss of four most efficient and self-sacrificing friends of our movement, women and men alike true to the great principles of republican government.

❧ *Woman's Journal,* 23 January 1875. Printed in part in *History,* 2:583.

> EDITORIAL NOTE: On January 15, Carrie Burnham, a delegate from Philadelphia's Citizens' Suffrage Association, introduced a separate resolution about the centennial of American independence to be celebrated on the Fourth of July 1876.

*Whereas:* The government of the United States, though professedly based on the principle of equal rights for all:—the consent of the governed—taxation and representation inseparable—disfranchises one-half its people. And

*Whereas:* It now proposes to celebrate its centennial birth day, as a free government, inviting the monarchies of the old world to join in the festivities, while the women of the country have no share in its blessings. Therefore

*Resolved:* That the National Woman Suffrage Association will hold a convention in Philadelphia on July 4, 1876, to protest against such injustice, unless Congress shall in the meantime secure to woman the rights, privileges, and immunities of American citizens.

*Resolved:* That we cordially invite all women in the old world and the new to cooperate with us in promoting the objects of the convention in 1876, and in order to defray its expenses we request them to forward without delay one dollar each to Mrs. Ellen C. Sargent, Treasurer National Woman Suffrage Association, 308 F. street, N.W. Washington, D.C. As the enfranchisement of woman would be the most fitting way of celebrating this great event in our nation's history, women suffragists throughout the country should now make an united effort with Congress and all state legislatures to act on this question, that when the old liberty bell rings in the dawn of the new century we may all be free and equal citizens of a true republic.

⚞ New York *Golden Age*, 22 January 1875. Printed in part in *History*, 2:583–84.

1. Abby Hadassah Smith (1797–1878) and her sister, Julia Evelina Smith (1792–1886), were the best-known tax protesters of the 1870s. After their refusal to pay taxes levied late in 1873, the tax collector seized seven of their cows. A few months and another tax bill later, he seized land. Astute publicists and agitators, the Smith sisters gained wide and sympathetic coverage in the press. (*NAW*; *ANB*; Kerber, *No Constitutional Right to Be Ladies*, 81–92, 107–12; Julia E. Smith, *Abby Smith and Her Cows, with a Report of the Law Case Decided Contrary to Law* [1877; reprint, New York, 1972]; *History*, 3:336–37.)

2. Abigail Kelley Foster (1810–1887) and her husband, Stephen Foster, refused to pay taxes on their farm until Massachusetts recognized Abby's right to vote. In the winter of 1874, the city of Worcester took title to the farm, but the Fosters remained in residence. They continued their protest until 1880, when Stephen's ill health forced them to settle with city officials. (*NAW*; *ANB*; Dorothy Sterling, *Ahead of Her Time: Abby Kelley and the Politics of Antislavery* [New York, 1991], 367–72. See also *Papers* 1 & 2.)

3. At this sentence, ECS's handwritten text reads: "a dangerous innovation on the rights of all citizens: since the assumed ~~right~~ power to deny this right to one class, is the implied power to deny it to all others."

4. New Hampshire Const. of 1792, secs. 14, 29, 42. The offending qualifications were removed in 1877.

5. Rhode Island Const. of 1842, art. II, sec. 1. George F. Edmunds and the Senate Committee on the Judiciary rejected a claim by Rhode Island residents that the provision violated the Fourteenth and Fifteenth amendments. (*Congressional Globe*, 41st Cong., 2d sess., 19, 20, 26 May 1870, pp. 3605, 3649, 3828; McPherson, *Hand-Book of Politics for 1874*, 215–16.)

6. This list reflects a range of new ways women entered political life after the Civil War, especially in charitable and reformatory projects. In particular, they joined with men to focus on the rights of Native Americans, whom they hoped to civilize, Christianize, and protect. (Robert Winston Mardock, *The Reformers and the American Indian* [Columbia, Mo., 1971], 199–200.)

7. Through the official Women's Centennial Executive Committee, headed by Elizabeth Duane Gillespie, women established a network of local committees across the country after 1873 in order to raise funds to cover costs of the centennial celebration and of their own Woman's Building and exhibits. (Mary Frances Cordato, "Toward a New Century: Women and the Philadelphia Centennial Exhibition, 1876," *PMHB* 107 [January 1983]: 113–35.)

8. Harriot Kezia Hunt (1805-1875) practiced medicine in Boston, where her annual protests against paying her property taxes were legendary. (*NAW*; *ANB*.)

9. Clergyman and reformer Beriah Green (1795-1874) was a prominent New York abolitionist who toured with ECS and SBA in the winter of 1861. (*ANB*.)

## 54  ⇝  MEMORIAL TO CONGRESS FROM THE NATIONAL WOMAN SUFFRAGE ASSOCIATION

[15 January 1875]

A MEMORIAL TO THE CONGRESS OF THE UNITED STATES, FROM THE
NATIONAL WOMAN SUFFRAGE ASSOCIATION IN CONVENTION
ASSEMBLED AT WASH. D.C. JAN 14TH & 15TH 1875.[1]

Honorable Gentlemen,

More than a decade of years has already passed, since the Women of this Nation sent their first petitions to Congress, asking for the abolition of Slavery[2] and their own enfranchisement. During the darkest days of the War, we who now appeal to you for the redress of our wrongs, rolled up the largest petition ever sent into Congress, for emancipation[3] which was then the vital issue of the Republican party. On the presentation of that petition signed by 300,000 men & women from all the Northern States, Charles Sumner made the most eloquent speech of his life.[4]

This great work accomplished, we next appealed for our own enfranchisement, but our petitions laid on the table, or under the table, ridiculed, or ignored, found no eloquent champion in either House, to press their serious consideration.[5]

While at the polling booths, in the Courts, & legislative assemblies, representatives of all nations in varied foreign accents, demand the

Constitutional liberties our Fathers declared & defended, native born American Women have thus far petitioned for their rights of self-government, in vain.

Though the Federal Constitution declares all persons citizens, and Suffrage their natural right, yet are we denied the privilege of exercising it. Though the Fathers declared "taxation without representation, tyranny," yet is our property taxed without our consent. And while suffering all the disabilities of a disfranchised class, our Fathers, Husbands, Brothers, sons, cannot plead ignorance of the evil results of class legislation, for their debates in Congress show that they understand the logic of republican principles.

The most triumphant vindication of the right of self-government ever made in the Federal Capitol, was Senator Sumner's great speech on "Equal Rights to all," the echo of whose voice is still heard round the world.[6] His argument, though made for the black man, logically proved the equal right of Woman to the power & protection the ballot gives. May the Statesman on whom the mantle of Charles Sumner shall fall, finish the work he left undone, & unfurl again the republican banner with "equal rights for woman too."

Daniel Webster[7] in one of his great debates, said, "It is well for us ever and anon to pause in the midst of party strife and consider the fundamental principles on which our government is based." Much as we have deplored the conflicts, that compelled us again & again, to review the grounds of our constitutional liberties, but for the vigilance these very dangers aroused, we should have drifted back to the old tyrannies from which we sprung. Those who have watched our leading statesmen, must see, that in these seasons of peril,[8] the nation has ever had its faithful witnesses to testify for the right of self-government. In the debates on the Missouri Compromise and the Fugitive Slave Bill, on the admission of Texas, Kansas, Nebraska, and Pembina, on the 13th, 14th & 15th Amendments, and the Dist. of Columbia Suffrage bill, and now on the Louisiana troubles, we have had brave Senators and representatives, who steadily demanded the recognition of the right of self-government as the only solution of all these vexed problems of National life. Nor need we go back to Adams, Seward, Giddings, Wade, Lovejoy, Julian, Stevens[9] or Sumner for examples; for the speeches that Democrats & Liberals are making in Congress, this very hour, on the Louisiana difficulties, are equally conclusive as to the right of all citizens to self-government.

And all we ask, gentlemen, is that you now apply these principles, so long & so well understood,—to the Mothers, Wives, Daughters and Sisters of the Republic.

We ask you to give us a Civil Rights Bill, that shall open to us the trades and professions; the Colleges & Churches; the Hotels & places of amusement.[10] We ask the right to protect ourselves by law;—that the rights of person & property may be the same for all United States citizens, that our government may be homogeneous from Maine to California.

Having battled for years to establish national freedom from chattel Slavery,—we ask you now for National protection from all class-legislation, by extending the right of Suffrage to every citizen under our flag.

The questions of Federal or State rights, centralization or local governments, specie basis or greenbacks, all involve the same principle. The time has come for the American people to choose,—despotism or Freedom,—a ruling class or self-government,—a financial ring or a national currency;—luxuries for the few, or the necessaries of life for all.

Some of our leading Constitutional lawyers have expressed the opinion, that Congress has the right to exempt from taxation all citizens denied the right of representation, in the several States; hence while so denied, we appeal to our representatives to be released from these burdens so onerous & unjust.

The right of Congress to regulate suffrage in the district & the Territories, is equally pronounced, hence we ask you to remove the political disabilities of Woman, wherever the United States has jurisdiction, and thus set an example of justice to all the States of the Union.

The Declaration of Independence, the Federal Constitution, the essential elements of republican government are all based on the equal rights of citizens, and opposed to the popular assumption that Special legislation is needed to give the citizen the right to vote. The logical conclusion is just the reverse; the right of self-government inheres in the people, and the right to vote cannot be denied except on account of age, idiocy, lunacy or crime.

It is the violation of this principle that plunged us into a bloody civil war, and as long as we continue class legislation in any form, we cannot have national peace & prosperity. Judge Hunt's decision in the case of Susan B. Anthony, that a citizen is not a voter because of sex, is not less infamous than Judge Taney's decision in the case of Dred Scott,[11] that a man was not a citizen because of color.

And Judge Taney remained on the bench without rebuke <u>then,</u> for the same reason that Judge Hunt remains on the bench without rebuke <u>now</u>: the class outraged, in both cases, had no voice in the government. The Democratic party ignored the rights of black men in 1860, just as the republican party ignores the rights of women in 1875. But as human rights were verified in the case of the black man, & became the vital issue of the grandest political party that has ever existed in our government; so shall human rights be again verified in the case of Woman, another & far more important issue for the party of the future, to triumph, we hope, in 1876, when we shall round out the first century of our national life.

*Elizabeth Cady Stanton,*

*Catharine A. F. Stebbins,*

*Ellen C. Sargent,*

*Susan B. Anthony,*

*Abby P. Ela,*[12]

*Amanda M. Smith.*[13]

Ms in unknown hand, Senate 43A-H20, 43d Cong., 2d sess., RG 46, DNA. Endorsed "Memorial of the Woman's Suffrage Association in Convention Jan'y 15th, 1875, praying for equal political rights for all citizens without regard to sex. 1875 Feby 8. Referred to the Com. on Privileges and Elections. Mr. Sargent."

1. SBA read this memorial aloud on the second day of the convention and moved its adoption. For ECS's authorship of the text, see her article, "Washington Convention," *Film,* 18:282. Senator Aaron Sargent presented the memorial to the Senate on 8 February 1875. Four days later, William Loughridge presented it to the House of Representatives, where it was referred to the Committee on the Judiciary. (*Congressional Record,* 43d Cong., 2d sess., 1049, 1231.)

2. This manuscript, in an unknown hand and retained in the records of the Senate, differs in a few particulars from the other known copy, in an undated clipping from the Detroit *Truth for the People,* in SBA scrapbook 8, Rare Books, DLC. In the Detroit text, this phrase reads: "asking for the emancipation of the colored race".

3. The Detroit text reads: "for the abolition of slavery".

4. On this work through the Women's Loyal National League, see *Papers* 1, and for presentation of their petition in the Senate, see *Film*, 10:719–21. Charles Sumner's speech on that occasion, "Prayer of One Hundred Thousand. Speech in the Senate, on Presenting a Petition of the Women's National League, Praying Universal Emancipation by Act of Congress, February 9, 1864," is in Sumner, *Works*, 8:80–83.

5. For the petition for universal suffrage circulated by ECS, SBA, and Lucy Stone in 1865, and its problems in Congress, see *Papers*, 1:566–67, 572–75.

6. "Equal Rights of All," Sumner, *Works*, 10:115–237.

7. Daniel Webster (1782–1852), lawyer and statesman.

8. The phrase "in these seasons of peril" is omitted from this sentence in the Detroit text.

9. All champions of abolition, these men were: John Quincy Adams (1767–1848) of Massachusetts, sixth president of the United States and member of Congress; William Henry Seward (1801–1872) of New York, senator from New York and secretary of state in the cabinets of Abraham Lincoln and Andrew Johnson; Joshua Reed Giddings (1795–1864), congressman from Ohio; Benjamin Franklin Wade (1800–1878), congressman from Ohio and a leader of the radical Republicans; Elijah Parish Lovejoy (1802–1837), antislavery editor of Illinois who was murdered while protecting his printing press from a mob; George Washington Julian (1817–1899), congressman from Indiana and sponsor of a sixteenth amendment for woman suffrage in 1869; and Thaddeus Stevens (1792–1868), congressman of Pennsylvania and chair of the Joint Committee on Reconstruction.

10. Congress passed the Civil Rights Act for African Americans on 1 March 1875.

11. Roger Brooke Taney (1777–1864) was chief justice of the Supreme Court of the United States when the court issued its opinion in *Dred Scott v. Sandford* (1857), ruling that African Americans were not citizens of the United States but a subject race with only such rights and privileges as the dominant race chose to grant them.

12. Abigail P. Ela (?–1879) of New Hampshire was Abigail Kelley, an abolitionist and the mother of three children, at the time of her marriage to Jacob Hart Ela in 1845. After giving birth to three more children, she became an invalid, remembered by friends for entertaining reformers and politicians while "wrapped in shawls and propped up by pillows." When Jacob Ela served in Congress from 1867 to 1871, Abby Ela was an organizer of the New Hampshire Woman Suffrage Association, aligned with Boston. Jacob Ela's appointment as Fifth Auditor of the Treasury in 1872 and their more permanent settlement in Washington coincided with Abby's emergence as an officer in the National Woman Suffrage Association. (Stebbins, *Upward Steps of Seventy Years,* 112–13; Franklin McDuffee, *History of the Town of Rochester, New Hampshire, from 1722 to 1890*, ed. and rev. Silvanus Hayward [Manchester, N.H., 1892], 2:409–19; *History*, 2:425, 482, 3:368, 370, 378.)

13. Amanda M. Smith, who otherwise appears in the papers only as a signator to the petition for suffrage in the District of Columbia in 1874, lived in Washington. She was still associated with the National Woman Suffrage Association in 1878, when a local paper reported that she would host Helen Cooke at her home on Fourteenth Street during the Washington convention. (*Film*, 17:943; Washington *National Republican*, 7 January 1878, in SBA scrapbook 8, Rare Books, DLC.)

## 55   SBA TO ISABELLA BEECHER HOOKER

Tenafly N.J. Jan. 20, 1875

My Dear Mrs Hooker

I am just back thus far from our 7^th Washington Convention— And a perfect jam of people with no <u>single</u> <u>man</u> <u>on</u> <u>the</u> <u>platform</u>—save the <u>old</u> gent. Lockwood,[1] at whose appearance the <u>crowd</u>—the <u>curiosity</u> seekers—seemed quite as much amused, as at the artistic presentation of <u>Dr</u> <u>Mary</u> <u>E.</u> <u>Walker</u>[2]—both of whom seemed careful to come on late & to get the most conspicuous seat on platform— But on the whole we got on <u>very</u> <u>well</u> with <u>the</u> <u>fleas</u> of this Convention— Phebe Couzens & Mrs Stanton were the <u>stars</u>[3]—though Carrie S. Burnham[4] gave the law & its origin—citizenship and its rights & duties with greater power than any one has ever done before—with practice in speaking—Miss B. is destined to fill a most important niche among the <u>heavy</u> <u>artillery</u> of our platform— But oh, my dear Mrs Hooker we do miss your presence & your help more than I can tell— That Connecticut campaign last February—one year ago—taught me more of your real worth & power than I had ever before known— And I was so glad to hear through Miss Burnham of Phila—that you had said in letter to E. M. Davis that you were coming back next autumn—and to work the following 10 months as never before to make woman free & equal, when the <u>old</u> <u>bell</u> <u>shall</u> <u>ring</u> in the new century— You will see by the enclosed resolution that we have already set the wheels in motion for a <u>grand</u> <u>gathering</u> of the women at Philadelphia July 4^th 1876—to <u>protest</u> against the outrage of our exclusion from equality of rights—unless, by the Gov't's decreeing justice to women—we may turn it into a grand celebration—a jubilee— I find Mrs S. & I in ↑our↓ hurry to get off letters to the newspapers have sent off every copy of our <u>Centennial resolution</u>—but so so soon as it comes out in the Golden Age[5]—we will send you a copy—then I hope <u>you</u>—as the Foreign Correspondent of the National Woman Suffrage Association—will get as many of the foreign woman suffragists interested in <u>our</u> <u>Centennial</u> <u>Screech</u> <u>for</u> <u>freedom</u> as you possibly can—or as I told the Convention—unless Congress should send forth the decree for our protection—it would be "<u>Woman's Centennial growl</u>"— And I am so glad you have your eye on that historic day & year—& I wish you could be here in New York at our coming May Anniversary meeting— May 13$^{th}$ & 14$^{th}$ 1875—but since you cannot be present in body—I hope you will not fail to be present in spirit—1$^{st}$ in a letter to be read in public & <u>printed</u> in <u>papers</u>—which must be short and full of things the <u>newspaper</u> <u>men</u> will <u>deem</u> ↑of <u>interest</u> to↓ their readers—the second— in a letter to be read to the <u>elect</u>—the few of us—like Mrs Stanton, Gage, Brown, Lozier, Phelps, Sargent, Davis &c. &c. who <u>have</u> the <u>helm</u> of our good <u>national</u> <u>craft</u> in hand—as to resolutions on <u>theories</u> & facts—plans of work for the year &c— But I need not suggest what we want from you;—you are full of thought and waiting only the time to come home to rush into the thick of the good fight again—& we shall all be so glad to have you once more with us so full of hope & faith the good time of freedom & equality is surely coming to women in 1876—

You will see our noble President—Martha C. Wright has gone from our midst—she was so staunch a friend— Last May—when she knew all my strong supports were absent—Mrs Stanton in Michigan, Mrs Gage not able to come, Mrs Hooker in Europe—though far from able to make the trip—she at the last moment and unexpectedly to me came—and after 10 Oclock the night before Con. opened presented herself to me at Westminster Hotel—& oh how rejoiced I was— Olympia had just come—& we felt we two had [*in margin*] the burden on us—

Never was there such general recognition of the <u>right</u> of our demand—<u>nobody</u> <u>denies</u> <u>it</u>— It is <u>inertia</u>—<u>dead</u> <u>inertia</u>—that we have to plough through—if it only would take on <u>life</u> & <u>fight</u>—we could sooner overcome it—far—

The Michigan <u>40,000 votes</u> was really a wonderful success—a triumph—whenever before, on first trial—did 40,000 of a sovereign class freely vote to share their power with a <u>subject</u> <u>class</u>?—never—never— the fact is without precedent— So I count Michigan a <u>grand triumph;</u>—<u>not a failure</u>— You see, to educate <u>only</u> <u>15,000</u> <u>more</u> of the sovereigns of Mich. & we should have a majority there— But we now pass on from Mich. to Iowa—whose Legislature last winter passed the proposition to submit—& which proposition is to be ratified by their next Legislature—one year from now—of which there is not a shadow of a doubt—since ~~such~~ ↑a similar↓ ratification was lost ~~four~~ ↑three↓ years ago by only one vote,—~~and~~ the Republican Party state Convention, last May, voted approvingly on the proposition,—~~and~~ the Methodists, the Universalists, and the ↑state↓ Masonic Lodge—say nothing of the Granges and Patrons of Husbandry—The Good Templars & other Temperance organizations of the state—all of them having passed resolutions in favor of Woman Suffrage—[6] All these ↑are but↓ straws;— ↑still they↓ make me feel hopeful of Iowa—and that it is the duty of our National Society to see to it that that state shall be thoroughly canvassed during the 20 months now left us to work there—

Because of the disagreeable newspaper thrusts, to the effect that Michigan did not want any outside help from the east or the west—I, as Chair. of Ex. Com. failed to go to their state W.S. Ex. Com. and show them how to do the work— It was Mrs Hazzlett—they said, who instigated all the repulse of Mrs Stanton, Phebe Couzens & myself— yes and the Boston wing too—she didn't want any one her superior to go into the state,— So now—I propose that the National Society shall mother Iowa & help her ↑on↓ to her ↑two↓ feet—

Now dear Mrs Hooker, dont forget, nor fail to have a good public and private letter here for our May meeting— And with best love & wishes for you & your "Ned"[7]—I am as ever Sincerely

⇜   *Susan B. Anthony*

[*sideways on first page*] Theodore—[8] How do you do— Well I hope— & making haste to Editorial chair— You may read & hand to Mrs Hooker   With Love— S.B.A.

⇜ ALS, Isabella Hooker Collection, CtHSD.

1. Ezekiel Lockwood (c. 1830–1877) married Belva McNall in 1868. A dentist in Washington and a chaplain during the war, he became a partner in his wife's endeavors, heading her school while she studied law, joining her in court while she pursued admission to the federal bar, and serving as a notary public in her law office. (Stern, *We the Women*, 209, 216; *NAW*, s.v. "Lockwood, Belva Ann"; city directory, 1875.)

2. Mary Walker's velvet pantaloons and contentious behavior dominated

press coverage. When permitted to address the convention, Walker chided those in attendance for their mistreatment of her and offered a resolution demanding that Congress "pass an act defining the clothes proper for a woman to wear." (Washington *Evening Star*, 14, 15 January 1875, and Washington *National Republican*, 16 January 1875, *Film*, 18:271–73, 276.)

3. Phoebe Couzins spoke on the "Social Trinity," described by ECS as "one of the most touching appeals for woman's influence in the moral, spiritual, and aesthetic parts of our nature, ever uttered on the subject." The press did not report ECS's principal speech at the meeting. (Washington *National Republican*, 15 January 1875, and *Golden Age*, 22 January 1875, *Film*, 18:275, 282.)

4. Caroline, or Carrie, Sylvester Burnham (1838–1909), a schoolteacher and student of law in Philadelphia, was a member of the Citizens' Suffrage Association. Barred from voting at city and county elections in October 1871, Burnham argued her own case before the justices of the state supreme court in 1873. She married Damon Kilgore in 1876. (*NAW*; *ANB*; Elizabeth K. Maurer, "The Sphere of Carrie Burnham Kilgore," *Temple Law Review* 65 [1992]: 827–56; Washington *National Republican*, 15 January 1875, and *Golden Age*, 22 January 1875.)

5. Theodore Tilton launched the weekly New York *Golden Age* on 4 March 1871 and edited it until July 1874, when William T. Clarke replaced him for the journal's final year. ECS supplied articles on a regular basis.

6. In March 1874, the state legislature voted to submit a constitutional amendment for universal suffrage to Iowa voters. The proposed amendment could not be put to a popular vote until November 1876, after a new state legislature approved the measure a second time. At the prompting of local suffragists, Iowa Republicans adopted a plank favoring submission of the amendment. The other groups named by SBA endorsed woman suffrage. In 1872, the measure failed in the state senate by two votes, not by one. (*History*, 3:619–22; McPherson, *Hand-Book of Politics for 1874*, 233; *Woman's Journal*, 26 September, 3, 10 October 1874; Louise R. Noun, *Strong-Minded Women: The Emergence of the Woman-Suffrage Movement in Iowa* [Ames, Iowa, 1969], 217–18.)

7. Edward Beecher Hooker (1855–1927), the son of John and Isabella Hooker, accompanied his mother to Europe. (Anne Throne Margolis, *The Isabella Beecher Hooker Project: Guide/Index* [Hartford, Conn., 1979], 71.)

8. That is, Theodore Stanton. Later a correspondent in Paris for American papers, Stanton may have intended this trip to launch his career. (Department of Archives, NIC.)

56 &#8620; THEODORE TILTON TO ECS

Brooklyn, [*N.Y.*,] Jan^y 20 187[5]

Private

My dear Mrs. Stanton,

My friend Judge Morris,[1] who passed his legal examination before your father, & who is a great admirer of your father's most brilliant daughter, wants you to come to court and say that Elizabeth & I had a happy home, for years, as you knew it to be. This testimony will be ladylike to give on your part, and will be a great benefit to me, while it cannot but reflect credit at the same time on Elizabeth. I have no power to summon you, as you live out of the state. But remember how much I would do for you, if you were in the supreme trial of your life. If you will come, drop me a line saying so, and I will then send you word when—so as to put you to no inconvenience.[2] Everything prospers thus far. Ever yours,

&#8620; *T. T.*

&#8620; ALS, on letterhead of Morris & Pearsall, Counsellors at Law, ECS Papers, DLC. Tilton incorrectly wrote "1874."

1. Samuel Decatur Morris (1823–1909) was a distinguished lawyer and Democratic politician in Brooklyn who attended Rutgers College before beginning the study of law in 1849. Daniel Cady (1773–1859) served on New York's supreme court from 1847 to 1855, where he would have examined Morris at the time of his admission to the bar. Morris represented Tilton in his civil suit against Henry Ward Beecher for criminal conversation. The case was postponed several times in 1874. From its opening on 4 January 1875, *Theodore Tilton v. Henry Ward Beecher* played to a packed crowd in the chambers of Brooklyn City Court until early July. (*New York Times*, 1 November 1909; Rutgers College alumni files, NjR.)

2. ECS did not testify.

·◁▬▬▶·

57 → SBA TO ELLEN WRIGHT GARRISON

Tenafly N.J.—Jan. 22/75

My Dear Ellen

How almost constantly my thought has turned to you since the shock of your Mothers death first came to me—it was at Albany, I had gone into our friend Phebe Jones, on way to Lydia Motts—when Mrs ~~Ellen~~ Mellen—wife Rev. Mellen[1] formerly of Auburn—Said to me how sad to think that Mrs Wright is gone— I said what Mrs Wright— she answered of Auburn— I said no—it cant be— I have just had a letter from her—and she is in Boston.— Yes, and she died there.— I was struck dumb— And ever since it has seemed as if all the rest of us older workers were doomed to pass over the dark river ere we reach the goal of freedom here.— Dear as are her two last letters to me—I know how precious they will be to you—so I enclose them—[2]

Twelve years ago—when my dear Father[3] died—aged 69—in the full strength & vigor of body & mind—precisely as was your dear Mother— it seemed to me the world and everybody in it must stop— It was months before I could recover myself—and at last it came to me, that the best way I could prove my love & respect for his memory, was to try to do more & better work for humanity than ever before—and from that day to this the feeling, in my triumphs and defeats, that my Father rejoiced and sorrowed with me—has been a constant stimulus to urge me ever to rally to new effort— May you even more fully come to the realization the ever present benediction of your precious Mother—

How sad for your Father to make his Florida visit alone—and dear Lucretia Mott—Edward M. Davis writes is very despondent—how little any of us dreamed she wold be left to mourn her sister Martha— So it is—and how strange that we are never ready to let go our loved ones— Since I have seen you I seen my eldest Sister borne away from among us—and it has seemed as if a part of myself had been wrenched away— All I can say is I know the deep valley you are passing through—

Give my love to your William L. and kisses for your little ones[4]—and best love & reverence to your Father Garrison and Mother[5]—and to your own dear Father—when you write & Sister Eliza[6] my regards & sympathy— How all alone Eliza will fell with no Mother's to run to— and how sad & lonely it will ever seem to me to pass through Auburn— I am very sorry now I failed to visit your Mother last Fall as I had hoped—

How good & true she always was—and what a tower of strength I always felt her to be on the platform with us—and never more so than last May, when she went to New York, as she said, just to sit by me— because Mrs Stanton was in Michigan—and she knew how <u>weak</u> I would feel without her presence Well—there is none other to fill her place—unless it shall be one of her daughters—so calm—so self-poised— so equal to every emergency—

Ellen, whenever you go to Auburn again—do come to Rochester— I would so love to see you once more—and then those beautiful volumes of Whitier's Poems[7] have never yet had your name inscribed within— Once more Farewell with Love & Sympathy

⤝ *Susan B. Anthony*

⤝ ALS, Garrison Papers, MNS-S.

1. William Roland Greenville Mellen (c. 1822–c. 1896) ministered to the Unitarian Society of Albany for a year, beginning in 1874. From 1851 to 1855, he served at the First Universalist Church in Auburn, New York, where he knew the Wrights. His wife is unidentified. (*Christian Register*, 9 January 1896; Elliot G. Storke, *History of Cayuga County, New York* [Syracuse, N.Y., 1879], 207; with assistance of Clifford Wunderlich, Andover-Harvard Theological Library.)

2. One of these was M. C. Wright to SBA, 6 December 1874, *Film*, 18:215–18.

3. Daniel Anthony died 25 November 1862.

4. That is, William Lloyd Garrison, Jr.; the children Agnes, Charles, and Frank; and the new baby born on 5 December 1874, William Lloyd Garrison III.

5. William Lloyd Garrison (1805–1879) and Helen Eliza Benson Garrison (1811–1876) lived near their son and daughter-in-law in Roxbury, Massachusetts. Once the leading voice for the immediate emancipation of slaves, Garrison in retirement was still active as a reformer in Massachusetts and a commentator on national politics. (*ANB*. See also *Papers* 1 & 2.)

6. Eliza Wright Osborne.

7. To celebrate SBA's fiftieth birthday in 1870, Ellen Garrison presented her with a volume of poems by John Greenleaf Whittier (1807–1892), the Quaker poet and abolitionist editor. (E. W. Garrison to SBA, 15 February 1870, *Film*, 14:609.)

58 ⇒ ECS TO SBA

Chicago,[1] February 16, 1875.

Dear Susan:

I have been in Chicago for some three days and such a rush of people you never saw. I had a magnificent audience at the Grand Opera House, which was packed, with people on the stairs, sidewalks and even out into the street, who could not get into the building.[2] I was in the depths all night and the day before lest the speech should not be up to the occasion, and when I saw the crowds in the street and, from behind the scenes, that immense concourse in the auditorium, I did feel like running! There is a shrinking devil in me from some timid old ancestor that plunges me into the valley of humiliation just when I should be on the mountain tops. But when I was fairly launched and every eye on me, I could feel the pluck and pathos slowly rising and I went through the ordeal with credit to myself and to you; for I believe you are always quite as anxious about me as I am myself. Bradlaugh,[3] who sat on the platform, pronounced "Our Boys" worth giving.[4]

I was a week speaking in Iowa and I found a large number of grand women in every town, all of whom expressed a desire to see you.[5] The people in the country towns are crazy to hear lectures. When I arrived in Alden,[6] managers came at once from two adjoining towns and invited me to lecture on Sunday. So at one o'clock that afternoon I went six miles off and spoke at three o'clock, and in the evening I held forth in the other town. One night people came twenty miles to hear me. I had a hard time with snow blockades but missed only two appointments. When the day was before me, I twice took a sleigh and went twenty miles on one occasion and thirty-eight on another, and successfully filled engagements. At this last place, the audience despaired of me, though I telegraphed I was on the way in a cutter. They did not believe it was possible for me to get through. However, when I stepped on the platform in travelling dress, but supperless, the audience, from miles around, was on the spot and ready to listen.[7] These splendid people are hungry, hungry, and I always feel that what I have to say is inadequate. Oh, for more power to give out the truth! Lovingly,

⇒ *Elizabeth Cady Stanton.*

&#x2E5C; Typed transcript, ECS Papers, NjR. Variant in *Stanton*, 2:146–47.

1. On 12 February, ECS arrived at the Sherman House at the corner of Clark and Randolph streets. (*Chicago Tribune*, 13 February 1875.)

2. This Grand Opera House was located at 51 Clark Street. Another building with the same name opened in 1880. According to the *Chicago Tribune*, hundreds of people were "unable even to squeeze inside the door or gain standing-room for a single foot" on 14 February to hear ECS. (*Film*, 18:314–16.)

3. British reformer Charles Bradlaugh (1833–1891) "listened intently," according to the *Chicago Tribune*. He was in Chicago to deliver the farewell lecture of his second American tour. (Hypatia Bradlaugh Bonner, *Charles Bradlaugh: A Record of His Life and Work by His Daughter* [London, 1902], 2:5.)

4. For the manuscript of this, one of ECS's most popular lectures, see *Film*, 45:75–125.

5. It is likely that this second paragraph of the transcript came from a later letter. ECS probably went to Iowa only *after* lecturing in Chicago. There are a few fixed points in her schedule: she left Tenafly about 25 January; she spoke in Ohio on 5 and 6 February; she reached Chicago on 12 February to lecture two days later; and she spoke in Eldora, Iowa, on 25 February, en route to Council Bluffs. (*Canton Repository* [Ohio], 5, 12 February 1875; *Chicago Tribune*, 13 February 1875; *Woman's Journal*, 3 April 1875.)

6. A village in central Iowa on the Iowa River.

7. In her reminiscences, ECS described the difficulties of traveling through Iowa in deep snow in what is probably her tour of 1875. (*Eighty Years*, 261–62.)

## 59 &#x223D; SBA to Elizabeth Boynton Harbert[1]

Chicago Ill[2]—March 15 1875

Dear Lizzie

I hope you will not come into the City tomorrow— For the meeting is post[poned][3] & I have to go to Earlville [to sp]eak tomorrow night—[4] When they do hold their annual <u>state</u> meeting <u>do</u> <u>you</u> come in—& accept the office of <u>President</u>—so as to <u>save</u> the <u>Society</u> from falling into the <u>wrong</u> <u>hands</u>— Mrs <u>Jones</u>[5] is <u>bound</u> not to <u>hold</u> the office—& some of the <u>Boston</u> <u>sympathizers</u> want to make Mrs Campbell[6]—the President— <u>Now</u> if <u>you</u> <u>will</u> <u>take</u> <u>the</u> <u>post</u>—it will save the society from being <u>run</u> into the Boston Depot— Sincerely yours

&#x2E5C; *Susan B. Anthony*

～ ALS, on NWSA letterhead for 1874, Box 2, Elizabeth Harbert Collection, CSmH. Square brackets surround letters obscured by a blotch on paper.

1. Elizabeth Morrison Boynton Harbert (1843–1925) met SBA in 1870 when she organized her lecture in Crawfordsville, Indiana. After marriage to William S. Harbert later that year, Harbert moved to Des Moines, Iowa, and became a leader in the state suffrage movement, particularly during the campaigns to amend the constitution in 1872 and 1874. In the latter year, the Harberts settled in Evanston, Illinois, just north of Chicago. Again Harbert became a leader in her new home, assuming the presidency of the Illinois Woman Suffrage Association in 1876. With the advent in 1877 of her column, the "Woman's Kingdom," in the Chicago *Inter-Ocean*, a major Republican newspaper in the Midwest, she gained a wide circle of influence. (*American Women*; *NCAB*, 18:232; *Women Building Chicago*; SBA diary, 13 June 1870, *Film*, 14:173ff.)

2. SBA delivered her new lecture, "Social Purity," in Chicago's Grand Opera House on Sunday evening, March 14. (*Film*, 18:344–54.)

3. This was a meeting to discuss Illinois Woman Suffrage Association politics.

4. Earlville, in LaSalle County, Illinois, was the home of SBA's cousin, Susan Hoxie Richardson, where SBA stopped nearly every year to visit and often to lecture. There, in 1855, Richardson founded the first woman suffrage society in Illinois, and more recently, Alonzo J. Grover published the *Earlville Transcript*.

5. Jane Grahame Jones (?–1905), who hosted SBA at her home on Prairie Avenue during her stay in Chicago, was a founding member and officer of the Cook County and Northwestern suffrage associations, an officer of the National association since 1871, and president of the Illinois association. Despite her misgivings, Jones presided over the state society until May 1876. By that time the Joneses had moved to Europe for a stay of several years. (*The Book of Chicagoans: A Biographical Dictionary of Leading Living Men of the City of Chicago* [Chicago, 1911], s.v. "Jones, Fernando"; Andreas, *History of Chicago*, 2:588–89; *History* 3:580, 585–86, 589; *Woman's Journal*, 13 May 1876. See also *Papers* 2.)

6. Margaret West Campbell (1827–1908) was a lecturing agent for the American Woman Suffrage Association and affiliated state associations. When Campbell was elected chairman of the Illinois Woman Suffrage Association's executive committee in February 1874, Lucy Stone wrote to congratulate her and urge her to "bring that State into shape." But Campbell seldom remained in one place long. Even as SBA wrote this letter, Campbell was planning to leave Chicago. She spent the rest of the year lecturing in Iowa, Indiana, Nebraska, and Colorado. (L. Stone to M. W. Campbell, 30 March 1874, in Wheeler, *Loving Warriors*, 249; *Woman's Journal*, 28 February, 4 April 1874, 13 March, 26 June 1875, 28 July 1894, 12 December 1908; *History*, 2:766, 3:269, 622.)

## 60 &#8474; ECS to Elizabeth Smith Miller[1]

Elroy Wisconsin[2] March 15<sup>th</sup> [*1875*]

Dear Lizzie

I was shocked & surprized yesterday to read in a western paper of the death of Cousin Nancy.[3] That journey to Peterboro must have been too much for her. I should like to know all about those last days & hours but must wait until I return home as I cannot tell you where to write me. Well the last link is broken Peterboro can never be to us what it was. I find myself continually regretting that I have not seen more of them the last few years    A visit there was always to me such a benediction    How many times Cousin Gerrit & I have walked & talked ~~leaning~~ in that quiet spot where they now rest side by side, leaning on his Father's monument, how often we have speculated about what lay beyond. Now they have penetrated the veil, but can they return & tell us of the mysteries they have solved? That is the question, not answered yet to my entire satisfaction, but one we naturally put to ourselves again & again as our loved ones in turn disappear to come to us no more    I know the void in your life these losses have made. Such a Father & Mother few children are called to mourn. I look in vain for words to comfort & console, time only reconciles us to the inevitable.

One thing I can do pour out more love & sympathy, write oftener to my dear Julius & cement our long friendship with stronger ties while our lives last. I shall lose no opportunity to see you & write to you. With much love & sympathy good night ever your

&#8474; *E. C. S.*

&#8474; ALS, Smith Family Papers, Manuscript Division, NN.

1. Elizabeth Smith Miller (1822–1911), the daughter of ECS's cousins Gerrit and Ann Smith, was a close friend since girlhood and an officer of state and national suffrage associations. She moved between New York City and a lakeside house in Geneva, New York. Since 1851, ECS and Miller had called each other Johnson and Julius after characters in a show by the Christy Minstrels. Julius was the wit, while Mr. or Missur Johnson played the philosopher. (*NAW*; *ANB*.)

2. ECS was scheduled to lecture in Eau Claire on 10 March; nothing else about her Wisconsin itinerary is known.

3. Ann Carroll Fitzhugh Smith (1805–1875), known as Nancy, returned to her home in Peterboro, New York, after the death of her husband in New York City in December, and there, according to the *Woman's Journal*, "the arctic climate of the Peterboro hills was fatal to her." (*Woman's Journal*, 20 March 1875.)

## 61 ⇝ "SOCIAL PURITY": LECTURE BY SBA IN ST. LOUIS

EDITORIAL NOTE: Speaking in the Star Lecture Course at Mercantile Library Hall, SBA chose to deliver a new lecture that she introduced in Chicago on 14 March. Like most of SBA's lectures, "Social Purity" evolved from earlier texts. She spoke on "Social Evil" on her West Coast tour in 1871, and in 1874, "Relations of Woman to the Temperance Cause" was one of her titles. Both speeches found their way into "Social Purity." In later years, a similar speech bore the titles "Moral Influence vs. Political Power" and "Why Temperance Women Should Vote." This report from a paper in St. Louis is the most comprehensive text of the speech still available. After her appearance in Chicago in March, the *Chicago Tribune* printed a generous report but that one chiefly summarized the first half of the lecture. The text published by Ida Harper in her biography of SBA omits statistics and illustrative examples and also incorporates material added to "Social Purity" after 1875.

"Social Purity" drew sharp criticism for its subject matter. The Springfield, Missouri, *Weekly Patriot* thought SBA handled social vice "so plainly as to be quite objectionable to many"; a reporter in Berlin, Wisconsin, said the speech abounded in "filth and nastiness." The furor surrounding her lecture in St. Louis was linked to the testimony emerging in the case of *Tilton v. Beecher*, on the one hand, and to the division among suffragists, on the other hand. Local partisans of the American association and the editor of the *St. Louis Daily Globe* agreed that in "Social Purity" SBA advocated the free love doctrines evident in the Brooklyn courtroom. The *Globe* predicted that SBA's "bombshell" of a lecture would be "the occasion of a very formidable secession movement" among suffragists and warned that suffrage would fail if the movement did not repudiate "all the advocates of free love and divorce." Some suffragists stayed away from Virginia Minor's open house welcoming SBA to the city, and it was reported after the speech by critics that "the National side . . . want it understood that it was not a suffrage document, but a sort of ex parte, extra judicial effort of Miss Anthony." (*Film*, 15:729, 836–37, 18:209–10, 344–54, 708, 19:692, 25:152–5, 29:276–78; *St. Louis Daily Globe*, 11–12, 14–19 April 1875; Rebecca N. Hazard to Lucy Stone, 19 April 1875, NAWSA Papers, DLC.)

[12 April 1875]

It needs no apology, friends, for woman to speak or work for social purity. Though, as a class, women are much less frequently given to the vices of drunkenness and prostitution than men, it is freely conceded that they are by far the greater sufferers—compelled, by their position in society, to depend on man for subsistence, for food, for clothes, and shelter, for every chance, even, to earn a dollar, they have no way of escape from the besotted victims of appetite and passion with whom their lot shall chance to be cast. They must endure, if not actually embrace, those twin vices embodied, as they so often are in the person of husband and lover, father and brother, employer and employe, and no one doubts that the suffering of the sober, virtuous woman in legal subjection to the presence and mastership of a drunken libertine, husband and father over herself and her children, not only from physical abuse, but from spiritual shame and mortification must be such as wretched man himself cannot possibly comprehend.

But it is not my purpose to harrow your feelings by any attempt at depicting the horrible agonies of mind or body that grow out of these monster social evils. They are but too well-known already. Scarcely a family throughout our whole proud land but has had its hopes and happiness marred by one or other or both. That these evils exist, we all know; that something must be done, we as well know; that the old methods have failed, that man alone has proved himself incompetent to eradicate, or even regulate them, is equally evident, and therefore it shall be my endeavor to prove to you that we must now adopt new measures and new forces to accomplish the desired end. First, of their present status. Forty years of efforts of men alone to suppress the evils of intemperance, give us the following appalling figures: Six hundred thousand common drunkards, which, allowing our population to be forty millions, and ten millions out of the forty to be men and boys old enough to be common drunkards, gives us one common drunkard to every seventeen moderate drinkers and total abstinence men, and one woman out of every seventeen the wife of a common drunkard.[1] Then, granting to each of these six hundred thousand common drunkards not only a wife, but four children as well—and a drunkard seldom has less—we have three millions of the women and children of this nation helplessly and hopelessly bound to this vast army of low, groveling victims of appetite.[2] In many States now—and twenty years ago in all of them, the old common law of England prevailed as regards marriage, the Blackstonian idea which was that husband and wife are one—and that one the husband.[3] Under the old law, all these millions of women and children, bodies and souls, belong to the drunken head of the family.

The wife, person, services, wages, property, all belong to the husband, to do with as he pleased; her children were his absolutely, he could compel his wife to go out to service to pay his whisky debts and if any employer paid her the price of her day's work, he could sue that employer on to-morrow and compel him to pay it to his drunken self a second time. He could apprentice out her sons to rum-sellers, or her daughters to brothel-keepers and she had no redress in law. The wife was dead in law, and only the husband lived in the statute books. Out of these six hundred thousand common drunkards, one hundred thousand had families; one hundred thousand families annually witness some one of their number going down to the horrible death of delirium tremens.[4] Two hundred thousand—one out every thirty-six drunkards are actual paupers, supported at the public expense.[5] Nine-tenths of all the crimes committed throughout the country result from intemperance, and forty millions of the hard earnings of the sober and thrifty are spent annually to punish and support these criminals, and probably not nine-tenths but ninety-nine one hundredths of all the poor, aided by public and private charity, are directly or indirectly the victims of intemperance.[6] Three-fourths of the insane throughout our entire country are made so by drunkenness.[7] There are forty thousand idiots in the United States, a ratio of one idiot to every thousand persons,[8] and three-fourths of these idiots are the children of drunken parents. Dr. S. S. Howe,[9] on careful inquiry into the parentage of three hundred cases of idiocy, found one hundred and forty-five of them were the children of acknowledged drunken parents. Dr. Wilbur,[10] of our New York State Asylum, records that the ratio of idiots is continually increasing in the United States. The annual cost of support to idiots in our Asylum is $200 per capita, which, supposing the whole forty thousand to be properly cared for, would make an annual cost of $8,000,000, and $6,000,000 for the support and education of the idiot offspring of drunkenness; $1,500,000,000 are annually expended for intoxicating liquors, which makes an average $37.50 for every man, woman and child in the nation.[11] The last Presidential election showed eight millions of voters and over, all supposed to be male citizens and over twenty-one years of age.[12] Therefore, those who must purchase $1,500,000,000 worth of liquors, which makes the annual cost $187.50 for each voter, enough to support a small family, you perceive. Thus, to feed this enormous abnormal appetite for whisky, and punish, support and educate the criminals, paupers, idiots, lunatics and deformed victims, untold millions and billions of dollars of the hard earnings of the honest and industrious people are extorted from them annually by legal taxation and voluntary contribution, until figures reveal the fearful fact that the cost of whisky to the nation is far greater than that of all the necessaries, comforts and luxuries of life. Not only the cities, towns and counties enrich their coffers from licensing the sale of this archdestroyer of men, but the National Government itself feeds and fattens upon its manufacture and traffic. The internal revenue receipts for the past fiscal year was, in round numbers, one hundred and two millions of dollars; from distilled and fermented liquors, fifty-nine millions of dollars; from tobacco, thirty-three millions; total from liquors and tobacco, ninety-two millions; from all other sources, bank deposits, bank circulation, adhesive stamps, penalties, etc., etc., only ten million dollars were collected.[13]

Thus, you perceive, the government gets eight dollars from these two articles, manufactured and sold for the gratification of the bad vices of men, to every one dollar from all useful and healthful sources.

The roots of this giant evil, therefore, are not merely moral and social, but they extend deep and wide into the political and financial structure of the government, and when women shall intelligently and seriously set themselves about the work of uprooting this traffic, they will find something more than tears and prayers needful for the task. Moral, social, financial, political influence and power are all needed and must all of them be united into one earnest, energetic and persistent force. The failure of man's efforts alone to suppress the social evil is quite as apparent, and the facts and figures are even more appalling. The prosecutions in our courts for breach of promise, for divorce, marital infidelity, bigamy, seduction, rape—the newspaper reports of every day and every year of scandals and charges of wife murder, abortions and infanticide, are perpetual reminders of man's incapacity to cope successfully with this monster evil of society.

The statistics of New York show the number of professional prostitutes of that city to be over 20,000[14] and add to this the thousands and tens of thousands of Boston, Philadelphia, Washington, New Orleans, St. Louis, Chicago and San Francisco, and all the cities from ocean to ocean, and what a horrible array of the women of this nation is sacrificed to the insatiate Moloch[15] of lust. And yet more. This myriad of wretched women, publicly known as prostitutes, constitute but a small portion of the numbers who actually tread the paths of vice and crime. As the oft broken ranks of the vast army of common drunkards are filled from time to time by the enlisting under its banner of some boasted moderate drinker, so are the ranks of professional prostitution filled and replenished by disappointed, deserted, seduced, unfortunate women who can no longer hide the terrible secret of their lives. And in the language of the report of your Board of Health, "It is a great mistake to class all fallen women together in one sweeping censure of contempt, as if they were all absolutely vile and irreclaimable";[16] and now I add to that, not only are they quite as good in the average as the tenfold greater number of male prostitutes who visit them, but many of them are angels of purity in comparison. (Applause.)

In 1869 the good Catholic women of New York established a foundling hospital, the first that had ever been established in that city. At the close of the first six months Sister Irene[17] reported thirteen hundred little waifs laid in the basket at the door. That meant thirteen hundred young women, beautiful or ugly, educated or ignorant, from the four-story brown stone fronts of Fifth avenue or the low cellars or rickety garrets of Five Points, not yet fully abandoned; that meant thirteen hundred of the daughters of New York, with trundling hands and breaking hearts, trying to bury their sorrow and their shame from the world's cruel gaze; that meant thirteen hundred mothers' hopes blighted and blasted, thirteen hundred Rachels weeping for their daughters, because they were not.[18] Nor is it woman alone that is thus fearfully sacrificed. For every betrayed woman there is always the betrayer—

man. For every abandoned woman there is always one abandoned man and often more. It is estimated that there are fifty thousand professional prostitutes in London[19] and Dr. Ryan calculated that there are four hundred thousand persons in that city, directly and indirectly connected with them, and that the record of the City Council, shows an expenditure of $40,000,000.[20] All attempts to describe the loathsome and contagious disease this vice engenders, stagger human language. The Rev. W. G. Eliot[21] of your city says: "Few know the terrible nature of the disease in question and its fearful ravages, not only among the guilty, but the innocent. Since its first recognized appearance in Europe in the fifteenth century, it has been a desolation and a scourge. In its worst forms it is so subtle that its course can with difficulty be traced. It poisons the constitution, and may be imparted to others by those who have no outward and distinguishable marks themselves. It may be propagated months and years after it seems to have been cured. The purity of woman and the helplessness of infancy alike afford no certainty of escape. In England, taking the medical result of 1855, out of four hundred and sixty-eight deaths of females from this terrible disease, three hundred and eighteen were children under five years of age." M. W. Holland, who only estimates the number of prostitutes in the whole kingdom at fifty thousand, says that in one year this terrible disease is contracted by 1,650,000 individuals. During a period of seven years and three months, the English army, numbering 44,611 men, gave each year 8,092 cases of this disease—one out of every five soldiers. During the same period of years, the Royal Marine on the home post, 28,000, gave each year twenty-eight hundred cases, one out of ten.[22] Thus, in a period of seven years the English army and Royal Marines numbering 72,611 men, gave 16,244 cases, showing that 5,673 of them were under first presentation for treatment of this disgusting disease. The statistics of the Continent, principally of Paris, are still more fearful, and those of our own country are making most rapid progress.

And yet, with all these facts, our newspapers are plastered over with advertisements alluring young men, as well as young women, into the idea that this is a curable disease;[23] and all legislative attempts to set back this fearful tide of social corruption have proved even more fatal and disastrous than have those for the suppression of intemperance.

To license certain persons to keep brothels and grog shops, is to throw around them the shield and protection of the law, and thereby to blunt the edge of all moral and social efforts against them. I need only cite you to your own experiment in St. Louis to know how little it does towards elevating the morals of the community,[24] and the work of woman is not to lessen the severity or certainty of penalty of the violation of the social law; but the work of woman is and must be to prevent that violation by the rule of the cause that leads to it. The causes are directly the reverse with the sexes. The acknowledged incentive to this vice, on the part of the man, is his own abnormal passion, while on the part of the woman it is freely conceded to be destitution and absolute want of the necessaries of life. In this conclusion all the students of the social-evil problem of both countries agree. Lecky, the great historian and European moralist, says that the statistics of prostitution show that the great proportion of those women so fallen have been thus impelled by the most extreme poverty, in many instances verging on starvation.[25] Thus, while woman's want induces her to pursue this vice, man's love of the vice leads him into it and holds him to it at the cost of the last dollar for himself and family; and whilst statistics show no lessening of the passional demands on the part of man, they reveal a most frightful increase of the temptations and necessities on the part of woman to supply them. In the olden time, when the daughters of the family, as well as the wife, were occupied in useful and profitable work in the household, getting the meals and washing the dishes three times every day of every year, doing the baking and the brewing, the washing and the ironing, the whitewashing and soap making, the mending and making of clothes for the entire family, making the butter and the cheese, doing the carding and the spinning and the weaving of the cloth, when everything to eat, to drink and to wear was manufactured in the home, almost no young woman went out to work for a livelihood, all were supported in the home; while now, when nearly all these handicrafts, turned over to machinery and men, tens of thousands, nay, millions of women in both hemispheres are suddenly thrown into the markets of the world to earn their own subsistence, and society, ever slow to change its condition, presents to these millions but few and meagre changes; only the barest necessities and oftentimes not even those can be purchased with proceeds of the most excessive and exhausting labor. Hence the price of virtue for the homeless, friendless, penniless woman, is either a scanty larder, a faded wardrobe, a rickety garret, and the scorn and neglect from the more fortunate of her sex, and nightly, as weary and worn from her day's toil, she winds her way through the dark alleys to her still darker abode, where only cold and hunger await her, she sees on every hand and every turn the gilded hand of vice and crime outstretched, beckoning her to food, and clothes, and shelter; whispering to her, in softest accents, "Come with me, and I will give you all the comforts, pleasures and luxuries that love and wealth can bestow." And it is to reject temptations such as these that the myriads of struggling, suffering and working women are called and since the vast multitudes of human beings, women like men, are not born to the courage or conscience of the martyr, can we wonder that so many of these poor women fall, that so many accept ease and comfort at the expense of spiritual purity and peace? Clearly, then, the first step towards solving this problem is to lift this vast army of poverty stricken women who now crowd our cities above the temptation to sell themselves for food and shelter, either in or out of marriage. To do that, girls, like boys, must be educated to some lucrative employment; women, like men, must have equal chances in all trades and professions, clerkships and offices of the country. Women, like men, must not only have fair play in the world of work and self-support, but, like men, must be eligible to all the honors and emoluments of society and of government; and the only possible way of accomplishing this great change, this perfect revolution in the position of women, is to accord to them equal power in the making, shaping and controlling the circumstances of life; that equal power is vested in the ballot; the first step therefore is to perfect women in the exercise of their inherent, personal, citizen's right to vote. (Applause.) The old maxim says: "virtue and independence go hand in hand." Alexander Hamilton said, one hundred years ago, "Give to a man a right over my subsistence, and he has a power over my whole moral being."[26] No one doubts the truth of this assertion as between man and man, while as between woman and man not only almost no one believes it, but almost everyone scouts it. And yet it is the effect of man's position of his right over the woman's subsistence, that gives to him the power to dictate to her a moral code, vastly higher and purer than the one he chooses for himself; and not less true is it that the effect of woman's dependence on man for her subsistence renders her utterly powerless to exact from him the same high moral code that he demands from her.

Of the eight millions of women over twenty-one years of age in the United States eight hundred thousand—one out of every ten—are unmarried and fully one-half of the entire number of women of the United States, or four millions, support themselves, wholly or in part, by the industry of their own hands and brains;[27] and all of those married or single who go out to support themselves in the world, have to ask men, either as individual, a committee or government to give them the poor privilege of hard work and poor pay, which at best is allotted to any. The tens of thousands of poor but respectable young girls soliciting schools, copying clerkships, shop work, must be stared in the face by men, not always righteous and pure, and often receive in response, what?

You work for a living! You are too pretty. You ought to be married. An insult, of course, but nevertheless women have to meet it at every turn. When I was publishing my newspaper, the *Revolution*, in New York, a few years ago, a beautiful young girl from the State of Connecticut came in and told me her story. Her father was a farmer in moderate circumstances. He had desired her to marry a neighboring farmer's son. She had refused to do so from the fact that she did not love him, and then she felt too much pride and self respect to allow her to remain under her father's roof and be supported by him. She tried to find employment at home. It was impossible. She then resorted to an advertisement in the New York *Herald*, which thousands of young girls have done before her and since. She advertised for a place as teacher, governness or seamstress. She brought me thirteen letters which she had received in reply to this advertisement, and out of those thirteen twelve of them had a direct or implied insult to her virtue. Only one of them was couched in high and honorable language. What a commentary on man's protection of woman!

And it is precisely such a gauntlet that every girl who comes to St. Louis, Chicago or New York has to run when she goes to solicit work in the shops or offices of our great cities. Now, what we must have everywhere is women employers as well as employes. We must have women employers, women superintendents, committees and legislators everywhere, ere a poor girl who is compelled to seek the means of subsistence, shall always find good, noble women. Nay, more than that, we must have women ministers, lawyers and doctors; that wherever women go to seek spiritual or legal counsel they will be sure to find the best and noblest of their own sex to minister to them. When in

Washington Territory, four years ago, I met the Pixley Sisters, as they were called, a theatrical troupe.[28] They were playing there before crowded houses every night for a week, while the Territorial Fair was going on. They were fatherless, young girls, the eldest scarcely eighteen. Their mother had married an unprincipled, thriftless stage man[29]<ager who had educated them for the business, put them on the stage, and had taken the lion's share of their earning. Miss Annie had at last determined to start for herself. So long as she was under this man's rule she was insulted by both managers and employes, but as a manager she had only received respect. Now that the men she employed were dependent upon her for their salaries she said, "Not a single dog of them has ever insulted me." These sisters occupied a room next to Miss Anthony, and late at night a knock was heard at their door and some poor wretch begged for two bits, just two bits, because he was sick and wanted some medicine. But Miss Annie was obdurate. She evidently had little faith in the man's needs; told him he had gambled away his money; that he should not have a penny, but to go to bed and behave himself. Miss Anthony was evidently not the only woman who rejoiced over this turning of the tables; but she asked very particularly what the indignities might not have been which a woman would have had to have suffered had she been obliged thus to appeal to a man even for her rightful dues. Pecuniary independence, she argued, was moral power. It not only enabled the possessor to control morals, but it was happiness.

Here she quoted one of George Sand's heroes, who never had been happy until when turned out of his rich uncle's house he was obliged to support himself. All luxury was gone, but he wrote to a friend that he had always suffered from being in a dependent position without knowing it, until he had learned [that]> independence is happiness. No man should depend upon another, not even upon his own father. By "depend" I mean "obey" without examination; yield to the will of anyone whomsoever.[30]

In one of our Western cities, a few years ago, I once met a beautiful young woman, a successful teacher in one of its public schools. She was an only daughter, who had left her New England home and all its comforts, luxuries and culture. Her father was a member of Congress, and could not only bring to her the attractions of Boston society and the cultivation of Boston, but also the attractions of Washington society. That young girl said to me, "the happiest moment of my life was when I received in my hands my first month's salary for teaching school." Not long afterward I met her father in Washington, and spoke to him of his noble daughter. "Yes," said he, "you women's rights people have robbed me of my only child, and left the home of our old age sad and desolate. Would to God that the notion of supporting herself had never entered her head." Now, had that cultured young girl left the luxury and the attraction of that New England home for marriage, instead of money, had she gone out to be the light and joy of her husband instead of her own, had she but chosen another man instead of her father to decide for her all her pleasure and occupations, had she but taken a position of dependence instead of independence, neither the father nor the girl would have felt the change.

To accomplish this reform, pure women must not only refuse to associate with impure men, but, finding themselves deceived in their husbands, they must refuse to continue in the marriage relation with them. (Applause.) We have had quite enough of the sickly sentimentalism that counts woman a hero and a saint for remaining the wife of a drunken libertine husband, thereby diseasing herself and poisoning the life-blood of the young beings that grow out of her unholy alliance.

A young girl proved herself a very efficient and attractive copyist to a down-town lawyer in New York. She had neither father nor mother or a home. Her employer spoke of her and her good qualities to his wife. The wife, therefore, acceded to his proposition to bring her into their comfortable home, and soon learned to love her as a daughter. All seemed right for a time. The girl proved a real blessing in her love, care and protection of the little ones, and yet another passage through the dark valley of the shadow of death brought to that mother another darling to love and to do for. Meantime, the interest of the lawyer and husband grew into a passion, and that lovely, lonely young girl had fallen a victim to his winning appeals. The wife neither saw nor knew the situation, but the girl was panic-stricken. She knew not what to do, nor whither to go. She decided to seek counsel of a woman who is known as the friend of the poor and unfortunate of her sex. To her she told her sad story. The tears started bitterly to her eyes, and weeping, she cried, "What can I do? To remain is but continued shame to me and cruelty to his wife. To go out and seek work is to have my crime follow me. Whether I go or stay I am ruined. I am a hated thing to his wife and to the world." An excellent woman and devoted wife, whose husband had the reputation of not being altogether immaculate, said to me, "I lost my faith in Mrs. B., when she repeated to me the story of this girl, and that she really didn't know how to advise her." "Well," said I, "what would you have said to her?" "Why," said she, "I would have told her to flee from that man and that home." "But what would you have told her to flee to," said I. "Better that she should have starved in the streets than destroy the peace of that wife and mother, and bring reproach and shame upon those children."

"Do you not see," said I, "how hedged about was the way of that poor girl? How, ninety-nine chances out of a hundred, there was nothing before her but to go from bad from worse, to flee from the ills she suffered there to those she knew not of. How she would be questioned as to whom she had lived with, why she had left, and how the lawyer, when applied to as to her character, would give a significant wink to his fellow-companion that would betray the young girl's weakness. How the good woman, the wife and mother, divining some of the causes of the sudden departure, would intimate to another wife, who sought a recommendation, that the girl's only fault was that of pleasing the men too well."

Now, what I would have the girl do in such a case would be to go to that woman and wife and reveal to her her story and her shame; and what I would have that woman and wife do would be precisely what she would have another wife and mother do for her daughter, were she thus left helpless, alone in the world and betrayed by some other woman's husband, and that surely would not be to proclaim her weakness on the house-tops, and thrust her out upon the world's bleak poverty and despair, there to be left a prey, not only to her husband, but for every vulture that feeds and fattens on woman's virtue. No, no. Instead I would have that good wife hold that husband criminal, forbid him the pleasure of her house and her home; banish him from her bed and her board; suffer not her children to breathe the breath of the betrayer. But then how could she? Not only her house and home, her bed and board, her children and herself, all belong to that bad man, and like a poor girl who got away from home, she too must go out into the cold, hard world, penniless and alone to have the finger of suspicion and scorn pointed at her, and to be followed by reproach for inhumanly abandoning her children. Notwithstanding, so long as the wife is held innocent in continuing to live with a libertine and every young girl whom he inveigles into his net becomes an outcast, whom no other wife will tolerate in her house, there is and there can be no hope of solving the problem of prostitution, as long as experience has shown that these poor, houseless, homeless girls, cannot be relied on, as a police force, to hold all husbands true to their marriage vows.

Here and there they will fall, and whenever they do the wives must make their husbands suffer for their infidelity, as the husbands never fail to do when their wives weakly or wickedly yield to the blandishments of another man. Had it been a wife or mother who had lost herself in the charms of a young man, an employe, think you the young man alone would have been banished from that house and home. No, under those circumstances the wife would have been made the target. The shame and crime would have been hers, to be proclaimed before all Israel and the sun, and penniless and childless, she, like a poor, seduced girl would have been thrown out upon the world's rude gaze; there, with her ninety-nine chances out of a hundred to go from bad to worse.

Now, why is it that a man can thus hold woman to his high code of morals, and punish her for every departure, while she is so helpless, so powerless to check him in his career of licentiousness? As his power comes out of his right over her subsistence, her lack of power grows out of her dependence on him for her bread, for every comfort and every luxury of life. Therefore, before marriage will cease to be a free pass to bad men into the hearts of good women, good women must be told to support themselves by the industry and energy of their own hands and brains. Their houses and homes must be theirs by law. Their persons and children must be theirs by law. In Sioux City, Iowa, four years ago on my way to California, I stopped to speak, and a few nights before the good wives had burned down a house of ill-fame in which their husbands had placed half a dozen demi-mondes, which they had just imported from St. Louis, your own city.[31] (Applause.) How much better would it have been if these women had refused to recognize those unprincipled libertine husbands, instead of wreaking their vengeance upon those half dozen poor, deluded girls. But then, how could they expect to go out penniless and alone? The persons, services, children, of each and every one of those women belonged by law, not to herself, but to her unfaithful husband. Hence her only redress lay in outraging her husband's guilty partner, rather than in banishing him from her home. The New York *World* in a recent article says: "As long as the human race has existed it has had the function of marrying and rearing its young. If it does not know what the reformers call the relations of the sexes, the human race is a complete failure; if it has not learned here it is unteachable." Now, the true relation of the sexes can never be learned until woman is free and equal with man, any more than the true relation of the races could have been learned while the negro was enslaved to the Caucasian. Neither in making nor executing the laws regulating the relation of the sexes has woman ever had the slightest voice. The laws for marriage and divorce, for adultery, breach of promise, seduction, rape, bigamy, abortion and infanticide were all made by men alone. Men alone decide who are guilty of violating those laws and what shall be their punishment. The judge, jury and advocate are all men. I am glad to see that in your State you have set an example to the world of admitting women to the bar, and that in your State to-day you have a lawyer that can plead the cause of every woman.[32] (Applause.)

<She protested against women occupying themselves so much in homes for the friendless, asylums, hospitals and other charitable associations. It is women's dependence and subjection that produces the evils which these institutions are established to meet, and it is for emancipation that women should work. {Speaking of the woman's crusade, she said that she favored it only because she believed that the women would thus see the impossibility of working a reform in that way, and at the same time see that it can be accomplished by the ballot, and that alone.} If the ballot was in their hands they could easily compel an enforcement of the laws against liquor selling on Sunday, etc. Give woman the ballot for a fulcrum, and she will move the moral world.

Three great necessities had been laid upon the nation. First, a military necessity at the time of the rebellion; second, a political necessity, which brought about the emancipation of the negro; and now, a third, a moral necessity, to enfranchise the women of all classes. The nation stood to-day, morally, at a dead-lock, as it did before it declared for the emancipation of the negro, or during the rebellion, when it was obliged to acknowledge the necessity of military power. (Applause.)

Towards the close Miss Anthony alluded to her recent trial for exercising the elective franchise, and her conviction and fine. You all remember, she said, my prosecution for having taken my citizen's right to vote and the judgment pronounced against me by Judge Hunt, of the Supreme Court, brought up there to Washington for that purpose, and who denied my citizen right to a jury in order to take the case into his own hands and pronounce me guilty. Until he did pronounce me guilty he did not allow me to say a word. Then he asked, "Prisoner, have you anything to say why sentence should not be pronounced?" I said, "If you please, your Honor," and I went on to mention several reasons why sentence should not be pronounced. Then the court said: "I don't propose to listen to an argument." "But I do propose to recite some of the reasons why sentence should not be pronounced." Then I stated my reasons, and what I think he will remember to the day of his death, for no man ever learned anything after he got on the Supreme Bench of the United States. Then I sat down, and he told me to stand up, and he pronounced a fine on me of $100 and costs. Then I said: "May it please the court, I have got no stocks, no real estate, no bonds: all I have got is a debt of $10,000 on my Revolution. It is my purpose to work until I pay that debt, principal and interest, but if I live as long as Methuselah,[33] I won't pay a cent of that unjust penalty you have pronounced against me." The court only said: The court will not commit you until the costs are paid, and ordered my discharge. He was glad to git rid of me. (Laughter.)

In conclusion, Miss Anthony called attention to the fact that the Dred Scott case had gone to the Supreme Court from Missouri, and had been overturned by the people afterwards; and the Minor case just decided by the Supreme Court had also come from Missouri; to which fact might be attached considerable significance.>[34]

⇒ *St. Louis Globe*, 13 April 1875; *St. Louis Democrat*, 13 April 1875; *St. Louis Daily Times*, 13 April 1875; all in SBA scrapbook 8, Rare Books, DLC. Word in square brackets added by editor.

1. The *St. Louis Daily Globe*, 14 April 1875, challenged this and other statistics in SBA's speech: she "convinces us," the editor wrote, "that she is not exempt from the common feminine failing of making wild work with figures." Her figures are difficult to trace to her sources. Similar statistics abounded in the literature of reform; reformers concerned with temperance, prostitution, incarceration, crime, disease, insanity, idiocy, and women's labor, all incorporated numbers into their arguments in the belief that better

statistics would result in better policy. The figure of 600,000 drunkards in the United States was accepted by many advocates of temperance. See, for example, Thomas Lape, *Statistics of Intemperance*, no. 28 of National Temperance Society and Publication House, *Temperance Tracts* (New York, n.d.), p. 2; and Jane E. Stebbins, *Fifty Years History of the Temperance Cause* (Hartford, Conn., 1874), 22.

2. SBA's figure of three million family members can be calculated by simple multiplication, but it resembles a different construction of the problem in Sumner Stebbins, *The Fruits of the Liquor Traffic, and the Results of Prohibition*, unnumbered tract in *Temperance Tracts*, p. 6. Stebbins put the number of drunkards at one million, their children at two million, and "the mothers, wives, sisters, and daughters" at three million. He was making the point that women, though rarely intemperate, were not spared the evils of drink.

3. William Blackstone (1723–1780), in his basic text on English common law, described the effect of marriage on women: "By marriage, the husband and wife are one person in law: that is, the very being or legal existence of the woman is suspended during the marriage, or at least is incorporated and consolidated into that of the husband; under whose wing, protection, and *cover*, she performs every thing." To rid American state law of this principle was the central objective of the antebellum woman's rights movement. (William Blackstone, *Commentaries on the Laws of England in Four Books* [New York, 1841], 1:355.)

4. Temperance advocates circulated different estimates about the annual death rate from alcohol, sometimes within the same essay. As an alternative to SBA's figure of 100,000, the lower figure of 60,000 was also accepted. For 60,000, see Lape, *Statistics of Intemperance*, 1; S. Stebbins, *Fruits of the Liquor Traffic*, 9, 11; J. Stebbins, *Fifty Years of the Temperance Cause*, 22; and Charles H. Fowler in W. H. Daniels, ed., *The Temperance Reform and Its Great Reformers. An Illustrated History* [New York, 1878], 567. For 100,000, see *May I Drink Moderately?* no. 14 of *Temperance Tracts*, p. 2; J. Stebbins, *Fifty Years of the Temperance Cause*, 169; Frances E. Willard in Daniels, *Temperance Reform*, 340.

5. Some temperance advocates referred to a count, made in 1863, of 200,000 paupers in the State of New York alone, but others reported that number as a national figure. The federal census of 1870 counted 116,102 paupers supported at some time in the preceding year in all the states and territories. (*Compendium of the Ninth Census*, 531.) At "one out of every thirty-six drunkards," the arithmetic does not work. Of the 200,000 paupers in New York, it was reported that seven-eighths of them were brought to poverty by alcohol. Below, SBA accepts the figure that 99/100 of the poor were the victims of intemperance. For comparable numbers, see Lape, *Statistics of Intemperance*, 4; J. Stebbins, *Fifty Years of the Temperance Cause*, 173; Charles H. Fowler in Daniels, *Temperance Reform*, 576.

6. Nine-tenths was the most common of many fractions circulated about the

proportion of crimes attributable to or influenced by liquor. See Lape, *Statistics of Intemperance*, 1; Charles H. Fowler in Daniels, *Temperance Reform*, 575–76; William M. Thayer, *The Fruits of License*, no. 52 in *Temperance Tracts*, p. 4. As for costs, SBA's figure seems low. Authorities in Massachusetts estimated the public costs of responding to problems caused by drink in 1868 to be three million dollars in that one state. Jane Stebbins thought it cost $200 million a year to "pay for all these woes and calamities" of drink. A national estimate that included the cost of crime, pauperism, and litigation associated with intemperance arrived at a figure of $356 million annually. (William M. Thayer, *Rum and Taxation under License*, no. 70 in *Temperance Tracts*, pp. 3–4; J. Stebbins, *Fifty Years of the Temperance Cause*, 169–70; S. Stebbins, *Fruits of the Liquor Traffic*, 11.)

7. Jane Stebbins thought only one-half of the instances of insanity were caused by drink. (*Fifty Years of the Temperance Cause*, 339.)

8. According to the *Compendium of the Ninth Census*, 632, there were 24,527 idiots in the United States in 1870.

9. By S. S. Howe is meant Samuel Gridley Howe (1801–1876), the husband of Julia Ward Howe, who taught that idiocy resulted from a violation of natural laws, especially intemperance. His statistics can be found in *On the Causes of Idiocy; Being the Supplement to a Report by S. G. Howe and the Other Commissioners . . . to Inquire into the Condition of the Idiots of the Commonwealth, Dated February 26, 1848* [1848; reprint, New York, 1972], 28–29. (*ANB*; Harold Schwartz, *Samuel Gridley Howe, Social Reformer: 1801–1876* [Cambridge, Mass., 1956], 137–47.)

10. Hervey Backus Wilbur (1820–1883) was the director of the New York State Asylum for Idiots in Syracuse. The costs per pupil at the asylum were reported by the State Commissioners of Public Charities in 1873 to be $208. The commissioners also reported figures on the proportions of the insane and idiots in the population. SBA's numbers are close to the national figures for insane (37,382, or 1:1031), which appeared just above the proportion of idiots at 1:1572. (*DAB*; Board of State Commissioners of Public Charities of the State of New York, *Sixth Annual Report* [Albany, N.Y., 1873], 32, 81.)

11. Retail liquor sales of $1,483,491,865 for the fiscal year ending 30 June 1867 were reported by the special commissioner of revenue, David A. Wells, and widely reprinted. See, for example, Lape, *Statistics of Intemperance*, 7; William Goodell, *Drunkenness and "Moderate" Drinking*, no. 68 of *Temperance Tracts*, p. 2; and *Chicago Tribune*, 21 February 1874. SBA's calculation of per capita expenditures is made with census figures for 1870.

12. The official count was 6.5 million voters in the presidential election of 1872. (McPherson, *Hand-Book of Politics for 1874*, 228.)

13. The amounts are those receipts reported for the fiscal year ending 30 June 1874, in U.S. Treasury Department, *Annual Report of the Secretary of the Treasury on the State of the Finances for the Year 1874* (Washington, D.C., 1874), xxviii.

14. The figure is one published by the Unitarian minister and editor Henry W. Bellows in the *Liberal Christian*, 15 April 1871. For a discussion of more realistic and lower estimates, see Marilynn Wood Hill, *Their Sisters' Keepers: Prostitution in New York City, 1830–1870* (Berkeley, Calif., 1993), 30–31.

15. An Old Testament deity whose demands for sacrifices were often associated with lust.

16. William L. Barrett, *Prostitution in Its Relation to the Public Health* (St. Louis, Mo., 1873), 13; this was a reprint of the Sixth Annual Report of the St. Louis Board of Health of which Barrett was the health officer. SBA substituted "irreclaimable" for "irredeemable" in the original report.

17. Sister Irene (1823–1896), born Catherine Fitzgibbon, established the New York Foundling Hospital in 1869. Rapid growth in the numbers of abandoned infants left to its care caused the hospital to move several times in its first few years. By this date it was located at Third Avenue and Sixty-eighth Street. (*DAB*.)

18. A paraphrase of Jer. 31:15, where Rachel, weeping for her children, "refused to be comforted for her children, because they were not."

19. This estimate, made in 1793 by Patrick Colquhoun, a police magistrate, came into question long before SBA wrote this speech, particularly by Michael Ryan (1800–1841), an English physician, who published *Prostitution in London, with a Comparative View of That of Paris and New York* in 1839. Colquhoun's estimate, however, appeared in William W. Sanger, *The History of Prostitution: Its Extent, Causes, and Effects Throughout the World* (1859), 358, and William Acton, *Prostitution Considered in Its Moral, Social, and Sanitary Aspects in London and Other Large Cities and Garrison Towns* (1857, 1870), 3. The number is repeated in Barrett, *Prostitution and Its Relation to the Public Health*, 4.

20. The conclusion of this sentence, from Ryan onward, is taken from Barrett, *Prostitution and Its Relation to the Public Health*, 4, although Barrett gives the expenditures of the London City Council as "two hundred millions of francs."

21. William Greenleaf Eliot, Jr., (1811–1887) was the chancellor of Washington University and pastor emeritus of the Unitarian society in St. Louis, a church he founded in 1834. He led the successful opposition to the city's system of licensing prostitution. Eliot wrote a series of articles, based on his research about regulation and licensing of prostitution in Europe, for the *St. Louis Globe* in March 1873. They were later published as a pamphlet: *A Practical Discussion of the Great Social Question of the Day* (New York, 1879). SBA quotes a passage on page 7. (*ANB*.)

22. These three sentences, beginning with M. W. Holland, came from Bartlett, *Prostitution and Its Influence on the Public Health*, 4, with only minor adjustments. The data, describing conditions from 1830 to 1836, appeared also in Sanger, *History of Prostitution*, 357, and in part in Acton, *Prostitution*, 66.

23. See Hill, *Their Sisters' Keepers*, 30, for a discussion of the ineffective but heavily advertised "cures."

24. St. Louis was the only American city in this era to adopt the European system of licensing and inspecting prostitutes. Its Social Evil Ordinance of 1870 inspired public health officials elsewhere in the United States to pursue similar legislation. As a consequence of the persistent campaign against regulation headed by William Eliot, the city's residents became quite familiar with the moral, medical, and legal issues surrounding prostitution. In response to the campaign, the state legislature nullified the ordinance in the winter of 1874. (John C. Burnham, "The Social Evil Ordinance—A Social Experiment in Nineteenth Century St. Louis," *Bulletin of the Missouri Historical Society*, 27 [April 1871]: 203-17; Burnham, "Medical Inspection of Prostitutes in America in the Nineteenth Century: The St. Louis Experiment and Its Sequel," *Bulletin of the History of Medicine* 45 [May 1971]: 203-18.)

25. Lecky, *History of European Morals*, 2:286. The text reads "statistics of prosecution"; Lecky wrote "prostitution."

26. Alexander Hamilton (1755-1804) wrote in *Federalist Papers*, no. 79, that "a power over a man's subsistence amounts to a power over his will."

27. SBA's numbers on women, marriage, and work do not match the federal census of either 1860 or 1870. By 1870, the number of females sixteen and older was about 11 million, and the number of families was 7.5 million. Not until 1880 did the census collect data on women's occupations by marital status. Nonetheless, SBA's argument was well known. The Census Bureau acknowledged that its methods failed to account for the work of women. Eight million women between the ages of sixteen and fifty-nine were not assigned any occupation, and in a long note to the *Compendium of the Ninth Census*, the superintendent laid out a series of calculations he thought established how many of those women kept house, had some gainful occupation not accounted for, or truly did not work. By 1878, women's organizations launched a campaign for improvements in how data would be collected for the census in 1880. In the words of a resolution passed by the National Woman Suffrage Association in 1879, "In the taking of the ninth census 12,000,000 of women were overlooked as laborers and producers, the life-long silent, thankless, unpaid toil of the housekeepers counting for nothing in the production of the wealth of the country." (*Compendium of the Ninth Census*, 597-603; Senate, *Memorial of Mary F. Eastman, Henrietta L. T. Woolcott, and Others, Officers of the Association for the Advancement of Women, Praying That the Tenth Census May Contain a Just Enumeration of Women as Laborers and Producers*, 15 June 1878, 45th Cong., 2d sess., S. Mis. Doc. 84, Serial 1786; *NCBB*, June 1879, *Film*, 20:778-88.)

28. The Pixley Sisters, Annie, Minnie, and Lucy, performed at fairs while SBA toured the Northwest in 1871. At the time, SBA noted their ages as eighteen, sixteen, and twelve. (SBA dairy, 21 September 1871, *Film*, 15:91ff, and *Papers*, 2:561, 572, 578n.)

29. A small section of SBA's clipping of this speech is lost, and although she marked it as from the *St. Louis Daily Globe*, it is not in surviving copies of that

paper. Her story about the Pixley sisters is completed, within the angle brackets, from the report in the *Chicago Daily Tribune*, 15 March 1875.

30. She quotes the title character in the opening scene of George Sand, *Monsieur Sylvestre* (1865): "Non, il ne faut pas qu'un homme dépende d'un autre homme, cet homme fût-il son propre père. Dépendre, c'est à dire obéir sans examen à des volonté quelconques!" George Sand was the pen name of Armandine Aurore Lucille Dupin (1804–1876), French novelist and sexual radical.

31. SBA made no mention of this episode when she stopped at Sioux City in 1871 en route to California, but in 1877 she noted new developments. "Spoke in same Opera House as six years ago—when on way to California & the Legal wives burned House of Ill fame—& now Jury were out 15½ hours & returned verdict of '<u>not guilty</u>'—for Madame Shaw—a <u>notorious</u> Brothel keeper—" (SBA diary, 14 June 1871, 8 November 1877, *Film*, 15:91ff, 19:12ff.)

32. That is, Phoebe Couzins. Here the *Globe* abruptly ended its report of the speech: "The remainder of Miss Anthony's address, equally good with the foregoing, is crowded out by press of other matter." A briefer report in the *St. Louis Democrat*, with one addition from the *St. Louis Daily Times*, complete the text.

33. In Gen. 5:27 Methuselah is described as living for 969 years.

34. The United States Supreme Court decided the case of *Virginia Minor v. Reese Happersett* on 29 March 1875, with the unanimous opinion "that the Constitution of the United States does not confer the right of suffrage upon anyone" and that the power of states to define the qualification of voters was supreme. (21 Wallace 162, 178 [1875].)

## 62 ❧ ARTICLE BY ECS

[8 May 1875]

### "NOTHING NEW."

One criticism uniformly made on woman suffrage speeches, discussions, and conventions, is "there is nothing new to be said." I notice in a London letter to a New York journal, the writer, in speaking of the recent discussion in the House of Commons on the "Woman's Disabilities bill," says, "the same old arguments were made to do duty once more"; "it is not a topic on which much that is new remains to be said."[1]

This mode of dealing with the woman question, whenever and

wherever brought forward, has become so stereotyped with reporters, that although new views are being constantly presented, they invariably say "the same old arguments were reported."

Woman's true position in the state, the church, and the home, is by no means as yet satisfactorily explored. And while John Stuart Mill,[2] Herbert Spencer, Darwin, and Dr. Clarke differ, there must be room for argument without saying "the same old thing." When we took the new departure on the Fourteenth Amendment,[3] on equal marriage, and divorce laws, and social freedom; when we traced our disabilities to the canon law, making the church and not the state responsible for woman's degradation—reporters said, "the same old arguments."

But granting the truth of what they say, in discussing fundamental principles of human rights, why should woman be expected, like a kaleidoscope, to present an endless variety of views to subjects that men present in the same old way? Woman's right to self-government admits of no better argument than the fathers made against King George, and the smitten slaves against their masters.

All questions that are frequently up for discussion have a few salient points that are uniformly presented, varied simply by the style and arrangement of the speaker.

I notice that men—white, black, foreign and native—in all their convocations—political, religious, reformatory, commercial, educational, agricultural, social, and scientific—say the same old things their fathers said before them. But the press reports them, one and all, respectfully, without ever telling the world that these same old men met together and said the same old things.

In the debate on self-government in Louisiana in Washington last winter, the Congressional record reported all our representatives respectfully, and the press of the nation said "amen" to the same old arguments on "state rights" we have had from John C. Calhoun to Thomas Bayard,[4] of Delaware; and not one criticism was made on the personal appearance of the Senators, nor the lack of novelty in their arguments. George W. Curtis,[5] in his recent speech at Concord, reviewed the same old historical ground, pointed the same moral of national life, and painted the same bright hopes of our future, greatness and prosperity, that so many have done before him, and he has so frequently done himself.

Carl Schurz, at his late complimentary dinner, pointed out the same old dangers to free institutions, the treachery of political parties, and the selfishness of leaders who recklessly sacrifice country to party.[6] Yet in both cases the press reported what they said, without telling the world these men have "nothing new to say," or that "the old arguments were made to do duty once more."

In reporting religious services, performed in the same way for centuries, it is not said, "the Rev. Dr. Humdrum gave us an essay on the same old doctrine Luther[7] preached centuries ago, and made 'the same old service do duty once more.'"

In notices of theatres, operas, and concerts, the people are not told that Theodore Thomas, Louise Kellogg, Charlotte Cushman, Booth and Rignold[8] gave them the same old airs, operas and dramas that Macready, Siddons, Hayden, Mozart, Malibran and Jenny Lind[9] gave us long ago.

In noticing the ups and downs of the stock market and gold in Wall street, reporters do not say that the same old men gathered in the exchange, and made themselves princes and paupers in the same old way. Under the head of "shipping intelligence" the movements of steamers are respectfully and concisely stated. The *Adriatic*, the *Scotia*, the *Hohenzollern* sailed yesterday with so many passengers. No one thinks of saying the same old ship sailed out of the same old harbor on time by the same old clock in the City Hall. A man-of-war is never ridiculed for having done good service for thirty years, with the same old guns, fired the same old way. Even the almanac, the humblest form of literature, speaks of the sun, moon, and tides rising and going down with dignity, without hinting that they have done the same thing from the beginning, and hence there is no peculiar interest to be attached to their movements as they have "nothing new" to offer, unless it be an eclipse that envelops all Nature in darkness.

But if the shadow of any great social tragedy be cast on the woman suffrage disk, instead of giving the public a new interest in finding out woman's true status before the law, they blame the movement for the transient darkness instead of the chance meteor passing between it and the sun.

Now the moral of all this, Mr. Editor, is that the women who propose to assemble in New York on the 11th of May[10] to discuss the right of self-government, wish to be treated with the same respect

extended to the planets, ships, artists, speculators, ministers, statesmen as above mentioned, and neither more nor less.

New York *Golden Age*, 8 May 1875.

1. ECS quotes George Washburn Smalley (1833–1916), London correspondent for the *New York Tribune*. In a recent dispatch, he complained of the lack
of originality in arguments for and against the Women's Disabilities Removal
Bill, a measure that would extend suffrage in parliamentary elections to women
on the same terms as men. When first introduced in 1870, the bill was voted
down in the House of Commons, but members of Parliament sympathetic to
suffrage continued to introduce versions of the bill. In April 1875, it was again
rejected. (*New York Tribune*, 28 April 1875; Blackburn, *Women's Suffrage in
the British Isles*, chart I, 103–140.)

2. John Stuart Mill (1806–1873), philosopher, economist, and member of
Parliament, championed women's political equality. In his book *The Subjection of Women* (1869), Mill argued that women's subordination hindered
social progress. Herbert Spencer rejected Mill's arguments in the belief that
man had evolved into a superior being. Spencer's evolutionary theories, along
with those of Charles Darwin, influenced the American physician Edward
Hammond Clarke (1820–1877), author of the controversial bestseller, *Sex in
Education; Or, A Fair Chance for the Girls* (1873). Clarke believed that higher
education on the model of men's colleges overtaxed women and endangered
their reproductive health. (*ANB*, s.v. "Clarke, Edward Hammond"; Michael
St. John Packe, *The Life of John Stuart Mill* [New York, 1954], 431–34;
Newman, *White Women's Rights*, 29–42, 86–95.)

3. By the New Departure, ECS refers to the militant strategy adopted in
1870, to insist that women had an existing, constitutional right to vote and
need only act on it. In the same period, ECS returned to her antebellum
themes of women's self-sovereignty in marriage, divorce, and sexual relations.
(Ellen Carol DuBois, *Woman Suffrage and Women's Rights* [New York, 1998],
98–108; *History*, 2:407–520; *Papers* 2.)

4. Vice president and South Carolina congressman, John Caldwell Calhoun
(1782–1850) was an early champion of states' rights. Thomas Francis Bayard
(1828–1898) of Delaware carried on the tradition, most recently in several
speeches against federal intervention in Louisiana. He also led the opposition
to Senator Sargent's proposal for universal suffrage in the Territory of Pembina.
He succeeded his father as Democratic senator in 1869 and served until 1885.
He was the nephew of Edward Bayard, ECS's brother-in-law. (*BDAC*.)

5. George William Curtis (1824–1892), author and lecturer, spoke at the
hundredth anniversary celebration of the skirmish between British soldiers
and American minutemen at Concord. (*New York Tribune*, 20 April 1875;
*ANB*.)

6. At a dinner held in his honor at Delmonico's in New York City. (*New
York Tribune*, 28 April 1875.)

7. German religious reformer and founder of Protestantism, Martin Luther (1483–1546).

8. Contemporary American performers, these were: conductor Christian Friedrich Theodore Thomas (1835–1905); singer Clara Louise Kellogg (1842–1916); actress Charlotte Saunders Cushman (1816–1876); actor Edwin Thomas Booth (1833–1893); and actress Catherine Mary Reignolds (1836–1911).

9. Great artists of the past, these were: English actor William Charles Macready (1793–1873); English actress Sarah Kemble Siddons (1755–1831); Austrian composers Franz Joseph Haydn (1732–1809) and Wolfgang Amadeus Mozart (1756–1791); French singer Maria-Felicita Garcia Malibran (1808–1836); and Swedish singer Jenny Lind (1822–1887).

10. For the anniversary meeting of the National Woman Suffrage Association. ECS delivered a speech similar to this article at the convention. Despite her admonition, journalists who covered the meeting for the *New York Herald* and the *World* accused participants of telling the "same story" every year. (New York *World*, 12 May 1875, and *New York Herald*, 12 May 1875, *Film*, 18:403, 405.)

63   "SELF-GOVERNMENT": SPEECH BY ECS TO THE NATIONAL WOMAN SUFFRAGE ASSOCIATION

EDITORIAL NOTE: ECS presided over the daylong anniversary meeting of the National Woman Suffrage Association in the Masonic Temple in New York City, during which the association resolved that Congress should "take the necessary steps to secure an amendment to the Constitution that shall prohibit the several States from disfranchising citizens of the United States on account of sex." She delivered this speech during the afternoon session. (New York *World*, 12 May 1875, *Film*, 18:403.)

[11 May 1875]

¶1 In Washington last winter, our representatives entertained the people, with a long debate on the excellence, the safety the necessity of self government in Louisiana. Even such conservative democrats as Senator Bayard (of Delaware) and Hon Eli Saulsbury[1] argued stoutly for the principle of self-government as the corner stone of a republic, the great experiment in the laboratory of nations, our Fathers told the world in 76 they proposed to try. But we all know that the greatest difficulty in making any experiment is the right kind of apparatus, and skillful hands to use it. These two conditions achieved and any principle can be illustrated.

¶2　The statesmen, who proposed to make our national experiment, of self government, labored under two difficulties. 1$^{st}$ They did not believe the principle themselves, they had been born, and bred under kingcraft, and priestcraft, and though they declared the equality of the human family, in a moment of inspiration, they could not see how the theory could be put into practise. 2$^{nd}$ They did not understand the apparatus: how to adjust the necessary elements, that entered into the experiment. Blinded with their educational prejudices, they threw out of their experiment, what they considered the most dangerous elements: men who could not read, men who did not possess $250, black men, and women, which made the problem not one of self-government, but of another form of aristocracy.

¶3　Men who would not submit to King George, who would not be represented by Lord North, and the Earl of Chatham,$^{2}$ to have their commerce, manufactories, and taxes regulated by others, who threw off the British yoke, and declared their right to govern themselves;—their liberties achieved, they at once fastened their broken chains, on all they considered inferior to themselves, and incapable of resistance. And thus, after having declared a republic to the world, we have spent nearly a century, of our national life in the anomalous position, of trying to convince ourselves, that self-government is possible, that a republic is better than a despotism, a monarchy or an empire. Commencing with an aristocracy of education, property, color, sex, we have advanced step by step, recognizing the right of the ignorant man, the poor man, the black man to govern himself. One more step remains to be taken and we reach the goal of equal humanity:—the right of self-government, must now be secured to the mothers of the race.

¶4　But here, the grand army of the republic come to a dead stand. Republicans, Liberals, and Democrats alike halt. It is one thing say they to enfranchise different classes of men and quite another to grant the right of self-government to women!! Why!! cannot intelligent, refined, well educated women, who neither smoke, nor chew, nor drink, nor lie, nor steal, nor swear, who govern households, train children, and servants, teach school, lead choirs, and prayer meetings, who are missionaries to the heathen, successful physicians, lawyers, preachers, editors, artists, why cannot such women govern themselves? Are they not as well fitted for the blessings, and privileges of a republican form of government as the freedmen of the south, the foreigner who cannot read his a.b.c's, nor add two and two, the drunkard, who cannot walk a straight line to the ballot box, or a politician, who does not know, that the best interests of the country, are of primary importance, to party success. Do you say such classes, are better fitted for self-government, than the best developed woman, that their influence in building up a republic is more desirable more potent than hers? "No! no! cries chivalry, that is not a fair way to present the question. The main argument, that underlies the opposition to woman's enfranchisement, is that woman is unfit for the work proposed. Governments are founded on force, violence, war, and consequently need the strong arm, the rugged will, the coarse nature, to administer them;—that the right to make laws, and rule, implies the possession of power to enforce obedience, and the inability of woman to do the one, is the reason why she should not do the other, in short that woman with finer organization, and diviner sympathies, is sadly out of her sphere, when laboring in these low material departments."

¶5   Which I ask you argues the most exalted status in a citizen, to have a voice in the laws that govern her, or to be subject to the will of others? If a property holder, to have her property rights left wholly to the discretion of others; or to have a voice in choosing tax-gatherers and assessors? If a criminal, to be tried, imprisoned, hung, ignorant of law, to have her personal rights left to the discretion of others; or to have a voice in the code, Judge, Jury, sheriff and forms of punishment? Can the lowest type of manhood govern women better than they can govern themselves? Self-government is the experiment we propose, and we believe educated women are better fitted for it than ignorant men. The statistics of vice and crime everywhere show that all classes of women govern themselves, better than men do, and their government over others, in the home, the schools, prisons, asylums, whenever, and wherever tried, compares favorably with man's attempts in the same line. But the primal question is not, whether we are fit to govern other people, to rule the state, the church and the home, but whether in nature we have the right to govern *ourselves*; whether *our* best interests, *our* happiness and developement, would be better secured in following out our own tastes, wishes, wills, in making laws for ourselves, in harmony with our own nature, choosing our own rulers, in a word, whether we should be happier as sovereigns or subjects;—pursuing life, liberty, and happiness in *our* way, or to have all classes of men arbitrarily governing us.

¶6　When by way of palliation, men say women do not desire this liberty, they libel human nature at large. All men and women, formed in the image of their creator, a part of the infinite, prefer to follow their own will to any outside power. Childhood is one long struggle against arbitrary power, one continued protest in favor of self-government;—and the health, happiness and developement of children are found in the exact ratio of the freedom and self-controul in which they are educated. Show me a child that is snubbed, cribbed, crippled, thwarted in every way, and I will show you incapacity, weakness, disease, misery. I never saw a happy man, woman, or child that did not to a greater or less degree enjoy the right of self-government. Thinking people are recognizing this divine principle, in all forms of government. As we advance in civilization, we find there are higher sentiments in the human soul to appeal to than fear. We are beginning to teach self-government in our schools, substituting the monitor for the whip. There is one school in New England, where the pupils constitute the government, executive, legislative, judicial.[3] They make and administer their own laws, organize their courts, try offenders, and decide their punishment, the teacher frequently appearing in court to mitigate the sentence of the offender.

¶7　Even in prisons, the principle of self-government is being tried, by shortening the term of the criminal on good behaviour, and it has already proved most salutary.[4] The state in this experiment practically says to the prisoner, bring yourself into line with law, make the experiment of self-government, and you shall secure your liberty in one third less time. The appeal to this living principle, in every soul works like magic, a new dignity, and self respect inspires the most hopeless, indifferent, hardened criminals.

¶8　And here is the ground of our hope, for the safety and stability of republican institutions:—the desire for self-government is founded in nature. Everybody likes it for himself and herself better than any other form yet tried. The most sorry growler against universal suffrage, and republican institutions, does not desire to be disfranchised himself, nor to be the subject of an arrogant majority, or monopoly of a king, emperor, or despot. Consider it settled then that self-government is the next step in civilization, and that in common with the rest of the world women prefer it to any form of subjection.

¶9    But can they govern *others*? The experience of life shows they can. Blackstone says the elements of sovereignty are three: wisdom, goodness, and power.[5] No one doubts the wisdom and goodness of woman, and if we substitute moral power for brute force woman has all the elements of sovereignty, for the moral, scientific, period into which we are now entering. The infancy of the human race, the merely material animal age is passed, the moral, the artistic, the aesthetic, the spiritual is now dawning upon us. And with the coming of the new day woman will take her true place. We hear the notes of preparation from every land and clime, we see the forces gathering on every side. And England our mother country takes the lead. Just as younger nations are about to snatch the material sceptre, that has so long ruled the world, from her iron hand, she clothes herself with new power, and leads the way to freedom and equality. She first declares that on her soil no slave can breathe, that on her throne woman may reign and rule and that all her daughters who support the state shall have a voice in her government. Think of it in the last election in England 400,000 women went to the polls and voted.[6] On the "woman's disabilities bill" in the House of Commons 152 vs. 187 votes were given to extend the rights of English women still farther, and Disraeli voted for the bill, and should any party exigency arise, says the Tribune correspondent, he may make it a party question.[7]

¶10    Thus is England again leading the greatest moral question of the hour, while America professing self-government, failed to secure it to the black race until forced by war and is to day denying to the daughters of the pilgrims the most sacred rights for which their fathers fought and bled and died. While celebrating her Concord, Lexington and Centennial birthday, she denies 20,000,000 of her people the right of self-government, the rights of person, property, trial by jury, representation, and to testify in a court of justice against a husband, the last crowning insult to wifehood, motherhood, and womanhood. Nothing more touching, and dramatic has transpired in that Brooklyn Court than the woman's appeal to be heard in her own defence. Ruled out of court as a witness by some technicality of law Elizabeth Tilton determined to be heard through a letter to the Judge,[8] and rising like an apparition in their midst, she addressed the Judge, passed a letter to the counsel and requested that it be read aloud.[9] "I ask, says she, for a few words in my own defence." "I feel very deeply the injustice of my position before the law and before the court now sitting." "My soul cries out before you." Ah! from how many women the same hopeless, helpless wail is echoed round the world, and no one heeds their cry. The men in power mock their griefs, like the Judge who coolly returned the letter and pointed the victim to the law, a law that his coadjutors quote with respect, sustain and perpetuate, a law that is a disgrace to the statute books, to the lawyer who pleads it and to the Judge whose ruling is based on the narrowest interpretation of the letter and spirit.[10] The great social earthquake, now convulsing two continents, bears many lessons of solemn import for women. We see the need of strong character, independence, equality, in the home; the advantage of place and power in the world of work; and credit in the church, and the state. It has shown that as women represent no political, or church organizations, no commercial monopolies, nor monied aristocracies, their character is considered of but little value, as compared with men who represent all these interests. Woman fills so small a place in the trades and professions, that no political religious financial or social crash is precipitated when she falls, hence her sins of omission or commission are nothing in the scale of morals, unless she drags some luminary from the Heavens with her. The exalted position of wife and mother of which we hear so much is counted as nothing against all these material interests. A married woman's character is not of sufficient value in the eyes of the law, to admit of defence even in a court of justice. Was there ever a tragedy that more completely illustrated the helpless, hopeless condition of married women under the law, than the one now passing before us. Dragged into court by the quarrels of men, by laws made by men, accused of falsehood, cowardice, dishonor, adultery, ridiculed, scarified, and condemned by the press of the nation, and yet not allowed one word in her own defence. Such is the dignity the law confers on the wife, and these legal gentlemen have such profound respect for these old statutes that have come down to us from the barbarous ages, that the natural right of a woman to self-defence is as nothing thrown into the scale against these obsolete statutes, at war with every principle of justice, and with all the advance legislation of the state of New York for the last twenty five years.

¶11    Here is work for the women of New York, to see that "the statute of May 10<sup>th</sup> 1867 which expressly declares the wife to be incompetent as a witness for or against her husband" be repealed.[11] Let no woman in the state of New York say she has all the rights she wants so long as any wife is subject to such insult and injustice. On what principle of equity may a husband accuse his wife before all Israel and the sun of any crime in the calendar, and she be denied the right to testify in her own defence. Mr Evarts[12] who is just now so blind to the danger of infringing on the rights of one class of citizens lest the rights of all should thereby be imperilled, said in his speech at the great meeting at Cooper Institute on the Louisiana question, "I do not exactly like the form of argument addressed to citizens of the United States,—as we all are,—on this question: that we must not be careless or unconcerned about this action in Louisiana, for it may be repeated in New York. I do not like that form of argument to citizens. I tell you fellow citizens of the United States, that when it is done in one state, it is done in all. The United States in its frame of government is vital in every part, and cannot be hurt in one part, without injury to all."[13] And just as the safety of the United States depends on a careful observance of the rights of the state, so the safety of the several states depends on a careful observance of the rights of the citizen. Here is a point in this question of justice to woman that Mr Evarts never considered.

¶12    When the people are educated into the idea that they can trample on all the sacred rights of an American citizen in the person of a married woman, to deny her the right of representation in the government, to a voice in the laws, while compelled to pay taxes and the penalty of her crimes, the right of trial by a jury of her peers or to testify in a court of justice in her own defence, they can easily go a little farther and infringe on the rights of other classes.

¶13    Can 20,000,000 citizens in the United States be treated as women are, all the most sacred rights of citizens violated, without injury to the republic? Is not the right of a woman to self-government in New York as sacred as that of a man in Louisiana? Does not the violation of these rights in one class of citizens compromise our principles of government as certainly as in the other? In denying to Susan B. Anthony the right of trial by Jury, in the United States circuit court of New York, to Virginia Minor the *right* to vote in Missouri, in the supreme court of the U.S., and to Elizabeth R. Tilton, the right to testify in her own defence, in the superior court in Brooklyn N.Y., the women of the whole nation have been outraged, defrauded and degraded, and the vital principles of our government in the persons of these women have been trodden under foot.

¶14   The question of woman's enfranchisement is one of national life. In the settlement of her status, our great American idea of individual rights, our great protestant idea of individual conscience and judgement, our theory of self-government, are all on trial. Let me read you a few extracts from the speeches of our United States senators in the debate on Louisiana. Republicans, Democrats, Liberals were all united on the vital principle of self-government. We need not go back to Jefferson, Hancock, or Adams, Patrick Henry[14] or James Otis, when the senators from Illinois, Delaware and New Jersey so nobly echo their declarations at this very hour.

¶15   Hon Eli Saulsbury of Delaware said[15]

> I do not unite in the cry that these men of Louisiana ought to have tamely surrendered their liberties even at the dictation of the President of the United States. Why, sirs, if they had done so, they would have been far less worthy of freedom than our fathers who, at the command of King George and even at the dictates of the British Parliament, were not willing to be made slaves; and in uttering this sentiment that I am glad they would not tamely consent to be slaves, I but give expression to the noble sentiments of Pitt in the British Parliament, when he declared: "I rejoice that America has resisted. Three millions of people so dead to all the feelings of liberty as voluntarily to submit to be slaves would have been fit instruments to make slaves of the rest."

Take notice, Mr Saulsbury tells us that people denied the right of self-government are "slaves," and "slaves" in any nation are a dangerous element, continually undermining the freedom of the rest. And yet when we assert that the women in this republic are "slaves," men smile incredulously; when we assert that the irresponsible, unrecognized, misdirected power of woman to day is dangerous to the state, women smile incredulously. And yet it is easy to show that women are "slaves" according to the definition of statesmen of all periods, and being such are "fit instruments" to make slaves of the rest. The social intrigue, the religious bigotry, the political infidelity, that mark this hour cannot be remedied while woman remains in subjection. Hence I plead her right to self- government: her right to vote on the laws, and rulers, of this republic.

¶16   On this point the Hon John A. Logan of Illinois said[16]

> Sir, I ask you what is citizenship in this country if not the right of selecting by your ballot the men who shall exercise the functions of office under the laws in this land. If that right is denied, I ask you where is the great boast of American citizenship in this country? Once it was said that the proudest thing that could be uttered by a citizen of Rome was that he thanked his God that he was a Roman citizen. Why did he do this? Because in those days the rights that Rome gave her citizens were protected. For that reason the boast went forth of citizenship; but in this country where we boast of American citizenship, I ask you what becomes of the boast if the greatest right that inheres to the citizen under the laws and Constitution of our country is denied? What is there then for the citizen to boast of?

Now it is clear to my mind that the reason women are treated with the contempt they are, by the press, the pulpit, in the courts, and the world of work, is because they are not recognized as political equals. But while consenting to different forms of class legislation, eloquent statesmen in all nations, echo and reecho, the grand idea, that all rights centre in the sovereignty of the individual, and that governments are safe and stable only as these are recognized and protected.

¶17   The Hon F. T. Frelinghuysen of New Jersey in the Louisiana debate said,[17]

In the violation of that simple law of right and wrong which is written in letters of light on the shrine of creation, and on all our heads, you may read the downfall of the generations of nations that have figured upon earth. The crimes of the Roman republic were lost in the greater crimes of the empire. The revolutions of France, the vibrations between anarchy and tyranny in the Greek republics, only prove that no matter what be the form, government cannot be maintained but by maintaining virtue.

¶18　　Our fathers, when they laid the foundations of this nation, made a compromise with vice, and it well-nigh cost the life of the Republic. Too patriotic to inscribe upon the pages of their Constitution that word which is the sum of all iniquities; too logical, when establishing a government based on the equality of man, to recognize different grades of citizenship or civil privileges, they yet did tolerate slavery; and the result has been that for every tear-drop that in response to the lash of the task-master has trickled down the cheek of man, there has been demanded a drop of the heart's blood of the sons of those who thus struck hands with a great national wrong.

¶19　　We should learn wisdom by experience. We have come to a national epoch. The rebellion is over; there has been enough of suffering and of torture; the storm is passed, but the current still runs strong. There are animosities, antagonisms, hostility; and the question for us is whether, come weal or woe, we will stand by the right, or whether we will suffer the Republic to drift away to that destruction which has met every nation that did not withstand the tide of vice.

¶20　　The people of our country have inscribed on their Constitution three principles: universal freedom, universal suffrage, universal citizenship. There they are. They are the trophies of the war. To purchase them three hundred thousand young men, as good as any of us, lie to-day cold and stark in death. Time has brought its alleviations, but to-day thousands of hearts are shrouded in sorrow. We

Senators at yonder rostrum have assumed the solemn obli-
gation to do all we can to maintain and enforce in letter and
in spirit those three great amendments of the Constitution.
Has it been done? Is it being done? Is there a citizen of the
North who would to-day be willing to live under such
citizenship as the colored people of the South are subjected to?

¶21   In direct opposition to this broad declaration by Mr Frelinghuysen,
Chief Justice Waite in his opinion on the case of Virginia L. Minor
tells us that these three principles, universal freedom, universal
suffrage, universal citizenship are not inscribed in the constitution,
and that a republican form of government means nothing in particular: that the status of the original thirteen states varied on the question of suffrage, the citizens right was based on property, education,
color, sex, birth, naturalization, that in one state only was universal
suffrage recognized and that was in New Jersey,[18] and that poor little
state, looking back and seeing how far she was ahead of all her
sisters, returned in haste to share the protection of their company,
and thus the only attempt at a genuine republic was nipped in the
bud, to bloom no more for a century. The decisions of the Supreme
Court on the several cases brought by women, demanding the right
to vote under the 14th amendment, have all been decidedly retro-
gressive in their tendency, so much so, that in this strenuous effort,
to prove that woman has no new guarantees of liberty by the amendments, there is danger lest the rights of the black man be imperilled
also.[19] Even Chief Justice Taney in his decision in the Dred Scott
case gave more scope, power dignity to the term "citizen" than Chief
Justice Waite now does.[20]

¶22   But these laws, and constitutions, our rulers would fain have us
believe are so unbending and unchangeable, are susceptible of more
liberal interpretations, when there shall arise a mind broad and
grand enough to take the responsibility of bending these stiff necked
statutes to human necessities, or sweeping them away altogether
when opposed to the great principles of justice and equality, as Lord
Mansfield[21] did in the Somerset case, when rising in his majesty
above the puny interpretations that puny men had for centuries put
on puny statutes, he gave the man his freedom and declared that by
the spirit of English law no slave could breath on British soil.

ᔨ AMs, ECS Papers, DLC.

1. Eli Saulsbury (1817–1893) of Delaware succeeded his brother as Democratic senator in 1871 and served until 1889. (*BDAC.*)

2. Evoking the views of colonists at the time of the American Revolution, ECS names George III (1738–1820), king of England; Frederick North, second Earl of Guilford (1732–1792), known as Lord North, the prime minister of England from 1770 to 1782; and William Pitt, Earl of Chatham (1708–1778), a member of Parliament who opposed taxation of the colonies.

3. This experiment at the Gardiner Lyceum in Maine was described (as a failure) by Jacob Abbott in *The Teacher. Moral Influences Employed in the Instruction and Government of the Young*, rev. ed. (New York, 1873), 59–61. (Research assistance from the subscribers to the internet discussion group H-Education.)

4. As an expression of the idea that prisons be reformatory, the practice of commuting sentences for good behavior while in prison spread after the war into twenty-three states and federal prisons by 1869 and into the South and Far West in the 1870s. (McKelvey, *American Prisons*, 76, 81, 109.)

5. William Blackstone wrote "that government should be reposed in" the people most likely to exhibit these qualities, which he further defined as "wisdom, to discern the real interest of the community; goodness, to endeavour always to pursue that real interest; and strength or power, to carry this knowledge and intention into action." (*Commentaries on the Laws of England*, 1:33.)

6. British election returns revealed that women enfranchised under the Municipal Franchise Act took advantage of their rights, voting in roughly the same proportion as their male counterparts. (Patricia Hollis, *Ladies Elect: Women in English Local Government, 1865–1914* [Oxford, England, 1987], 33–34; *Woman's Journal*, 6 June 1874.)

7. ECS again quotes George W. Smalley's report in the *New York Tribune*, 23 April 1875. Benjamin Disraeli (1804–1881) became prime minister in February 1874. His Conservative party did not follow his example; a majority of its members of Parliament opposed the disabilities removal bill. (*Woman's Journal*, 24 April, 1, 22 May 1875.)

8. Joseph Neilson (1813–1888) served on the Brooklyn City Court from 1849 to 1883. (McAdam, *Bench and Bar of New York*, 1:426–27.)

9. ECS borrows the phrase "like an apparition" from the *New York Tribune*'s description of the sensational scene in court when Elizabeth Tilton rose from her seat to call to the judge and place a letter in his hands. Although the judge denied her request that the letter be read aloud, it was widely published in the press. ECS quotes the words with which Tilton proclaimed her innocence and pleaded for the opportunity to testify on her own behalf. (*New York Tribune*, 4 May 1875; *Chicago Tribune*, 5 May 1875; *T. Tilton vs. H. W. Beecher*, 3:323, 355.)

10. The judge denied Elizabeth Tilton's request to be heard in the trial on

the basis of "An act to enable husband and wife, or either of them, to be a witness for or against the other." Section two of the act excepted from its provisions "any action or proceeding instituted in consequence of adultery." (*Laws of New York, 1867*, chap. 887.)

11. ECS quotes the written reply of Judge Neilson to Elizabeth Tilton's request to testify in the trial. The judge erroneously claimed that the law applied only to wives and not to husbands. (*Chicago Tribune*, 5 May 1875.)

12. William Maxwell Evarts (1818–1901), former attorney general in the administration of Andrew Johnson, acted as chief counsel for Henry Ward Beecher in *Tilton v. Beecher*. He and his associates in the case declined to call Elizabeth Tilton to the stand. (*ANB*.)

13. Evarts spoke on 11 January at a meeting called to protest the use of federal troops in the Louisiana election dispute. For varied reports of his speech, see *New York Tribune*, 12 January 1875; *New York Herald*, 12 January 1875; New York *World*, 12 January 1875; *New York Times*, 12 January 1875.

14. American revolutionaries, Thomas Jefferson (1743–1826) of Virginia, who became the third president of the United States; John Adams (1735–1826) of Massachusetts, who became the second president of the United States; John Hancock (1737–1798) of Massachusetts; and Patrick Henry (1736–1799) of Virginia.

15. *Congressional Record*, 43d Cong., 2d sess., 16 January 1875, 519. ECS clipped his speech from that source and inserted it in her manuscript, as she did with the further quotations from the congressional debate below.

16. John Alexander Logan (1826–1886) of Illinois was a Republican senator from 1871 to 1877 and again from 1879 until his death. He spoke on 14 January 1875. (*BDAC*; *Congressional Record*, 43d Cong., 2d sess., 450.)

17. Frederick Theodore Frelinghuysen (1817–1885), Republican of New Jersey, served in the Senate from 1866 to 1869 and 1871 to 1877. He spoke on 15 January 1875. (*BDAC*; *Congressional Record*, 43d Cong., 2d sess., 489.)

18. To this point ECS paraphrases a part of Chief Justice Morrison Waite's decision in which he argued that the standard for ascertaining what was meant by the constitutional guarantee of a republican form of government in the states was to be found in the original constitutions of the states, all of which excluded one or more class of citizens from the suffrage. New Jersey's constitution of 1776, in force until 1844, permitted adult inhabitants to vote, if they met the property qualifications. In 1807, however, the legislature disfranchised women, African Americans, and aliens by a simple law that limited the franchise to white male taxpaying citizens. (Minor v. Happersett, 21 Wallace 162, 175 [1875]; *History*, 1:447–51; Judith Apter Klinghoffer and Lois Elkis, "'The Petticoat Electors': Women's Suffrage in New Jersey, 1776–1807," *Journal of the Early Republic* 12 [Summer 1992]: 159–93.)

19. In *Minor v. Happersett*, Waite wrote that the Fourteenth Amendment "did not add to the privileges and immunities of a citizen. . . . No new voters

were necessarily made by it." As for other cases, ECS may refer to the federal district court decision in *United States v. Susan B. Anthony* (1873). Similar readings of the Fourteenth Amendment appeared also in decisions on women's voting rights cases by state supreme courts in California, Pennsylvania, and Missouri that upheld the right of states to define the qualifications of voters. See Ellen R. Van Valkenburg v. Albert Brown, 43 California Reports 43 (1872); Carrie S. Burnham v. Louis Lunning et al., 9 Philadelphia Reports 241 (Pa. Sup. Ct. 1871); and Minor v. Happersett, 53 Missouri Reports 58 (1873).

20. Chief Justice Roger Taney wrote that the term citizens "describe[s] the political body who, according to our republican institutions, form the sovereignty, and who hold the power and conduct the Government through their representatives." To Waite, the term simply "convey[ed] the idea of membership of a nation, and nothing more." (Dred Scott v. Sandford, 19 Howard 393, 404 [1857]; Minor v. Happersett, 21 Wallace 162, 166 [1875].)

21. In 1772 chief justice of the Court of Kings Bench, William Murray, Earl of Mansfield (1705–1798), freed the slave James Somersett, who was brought to England from Virginia, ruling that in the absence of positive law creating slavery, slaves could not lawfully be kept in England.

## Textual Notes

| | | |
|---|---|---|
| ¶1 | *l*.5 | the principle ↑of self-government↓ as the corner stone |
| | *l*.6 | great experiment in the labratory |
| ¶2 | *ll*.3–4 | born, and bred ~~in~~ ↑under↓ kings↑craft↓, and priests craft , |
| ¶3 | *ll*.8–9 | of our national ↑life↓ in the anomolous position, |
| | *ll*.13–14 | to govern himself, one more step |
| ¶4 | *ll*.2–3 | It is one thing ↑say they↓ to enfranchise |
| | *ll*.9–10 | editors, artists, ↑why↓ cannot such women govern |
| | *ll*.13–14 | to the ballot box, ~~nor~~ a politicain, |
| ¶5 | *l*.1 beg. | Which ↑I ask you↓ argues the most exalted |
| | *l*.22 | happier as sovreigns or subjects; |
| ¶6 | *l*.1 beg. | When by way of paliation, |
| | *ll*.6–7 | & ↑the↓ health happiness & developement ↑of children↓ are found in the exact ~~ration~~↑of↓ the |
| | *l*.20 | sentence ~~on~~ of the offender. |
| ¶8 | *l*.8 | next step ~~of~~ ↑in↓ civilization |
| ¶9 | *l*.2 | the elements of sovreignty are three |
| | *ll*.5–6 | the elements of sovreignty, for the moral, scientific, period of ~~the race~~ ↑history↓ into which we are now entering [*and further emended*] period ~~of history~~ into which |
| | *ll*.14–15 | She ↑first↓ declares that on her soil no slave can breath, |
| | *ll*.19–20 | House ↑of Commons↓ 152 ↑vs. 187↓ votes were given |

¶10    *ll*.10–11    more touching, & ~~tragic~~ ↑dramatic↓ has transpired

        *ll*.14–17    she ↑addressed the Judge↓ passed ~~it~~ ↑a letter↓ to the counsel & requested ~~the~~ ↑that↓ it be read aloud. "I ask, says she, for a few words in my own defence"

        *ll*.27–30    We see the need of strong character independence, equality, in the home the advantage of place & power in the world of work, & credit:—in the church, & the state.

        *ll*.39–40    A ↑married↓ womans character is not of sufficient value

        *ll*.45–46    cowardice, dishonor adultery, ridicule, scarified,

¶11    *l*.3    witness for or against her husband be repealed"

        *l*.7    any crime in the calender,

        *ll*.10–11    in his speech at the great ~~Cooper~~ ↑meeting↓ at Cooper

        *l*.14    this action ↑in↓ Louisiana

        *l*.16

¶13    *ll*.2–3    sacred rights of citizens violated without injury to the republic.

        *l*.4    as that of a man in Louisiana.

        *l*.6    as certainly as in the other.

        *ll*.7–8    in the United States circuit ↑court of New York↓

¶14    *l*.6    Republicans, Democrats Liberals were all

¶15    *l*.16    Mr Saulsbury tell us

        *ll*.19–21    are "slaves" men smile incredulously, when we assert that ↑the↓ irresponsible unrecognized ↑misdirected↓ power of woman

        *ll*.25–26    religious bigotry, the political infidelty, ↑that mark this hour↓

¶16    *l*.21    centre in the sovreignty of the individual

¶21    *ll*.2–3    the case of Virginia L. Miner tell us that the↑se↓ three

        *ll*.7–9    on property education, color, sex, birth naturalization, that in one state ↑only↓ was universal suffrage

        *l*.19    Even ~~Judge~~ ↑Chief Justice↓ Taney

¶22    *l*.3    when there ↑shall↓ arises a mind

        *l*.10    no slave could breath on British soil

## 64   INTERVIEW WITH ECS IN TENAFLY[1]

*[before 17 July 1875]*

An interviewer sat on a wicker settee opposite Mrs. Stanton in a rustic arm chair, apart from the company, on a recent afternoon, and after some conversational skirmishing around the main object of the visit, Mrs. Stanton substantially said:

The trial of Henry Ward Beecher for adultery, which has so tediously nauseated the whole country, I believe to have been a salutary medicine which has produced three distinct beneficial effects.

### ITS EFFECT ON WOMEN.

It has knocked a great blow at the priesthood. All over this country women had a reverent respect for clergymen; a loving, clinging confidence in them, like that of the sick and long-troubled woman who said of Christ: "If I can but touch the hem of His garment I shall be safe."[2] It is a lesson well learned by women and by the world that the woman of this trial, precisely by "touching the hem of his garment," and even though only touching the hem of his garment, shattered her household, her home, and her hopes, beclouded her children, lost her else unattacked and happy obscurity, and has appeared before all Christendom, draggling!

This unhappy and exciting lawsuit has struck a great moral blow at the weakness of women. It brought before men's attention a truth which has faced them up like a picture held before their eyes, how utterly weak the women are who stand in fear of men, and feel obliged to use their husbands as confessors. It has taught men the need of women being strong-minded and self-poised for men's own protection. If Mrs. Tilton had been such a woman, she would not have been making these confessions, which themselves are largely the origin of the priest's publicity as an accused adulterer. It has knocked a blow at the subordination of the state of wifehood. The weakness of this wife has taught men that domestic security is more reliable when there are individuals in the home than when there is only one intellect in the house, and that one the husband's. This muddle never could have happened if Mrs. Tilton had been a grand, strong-minded, self-poised woman. Men will not forget that for their own safety, that in all associations of men with women, better a strong, self-poised woman than the weakling who is to-day domineered by this man's magnetism, and to-morrow by that; confesses here, retracts there, and re-confesses and re-retracts.[3]

### EQUALIZING MEN AND WOMEN.

Another prominent effect of this trial, said Mrs. Stanton, is that it has been a strong pull toward making the standard of tolerated and reputable behavior of women and men equal. Here are a woman and a man, an accused adulteress and an accused adulterer. Plymouth Church, 3,000 strong, have stepped in advance of all past ages, and their public regard and social treatment is the same of the woman as of the man. For once in the history of the world, since the Christian era, fellowship has been given to a woman the same as to a man in the same circumstances.[4] Plymouth Church merits no thanks. Plymouth Church did not reflect what it was doing. Plymouth Church did not know it, nor care. It is doing it all, in its blind zeal to protect a man. But the moral epoch has come in geological history when a man cannot be protected without the woman is protected too; and on the self-same social plane is given the good right hand of fellowship. But while the Plymouth Church zealots have socially upheld Mrs. Tilton to bolster up Beecher, legally they have trodden her under foot, gagged her, caged her, and guarded her. Beecher stands for a large moneyed interest—for Plymouth Church, the *Christian Union*, and the "Life of Christ." The protection of Beecher means the preservation of capital invested in a very wealthy society, a newspaper, and a book enterprise. A woman, on the contrary, stands for nothing. No matter if Mrs. Tilton were sacrificed, nor how many women. They would sacrifice any number of women.

As to the "guilty or not guilty," said Mrs. Stanton, "I have all along said that what Henry Ward Beecher would swear to I should believe."[5]

It is true that Mrs. Tilton told all this same story to Susan Anthony at several times, years ago; and Theodore Tilton to me. And what man could have stood the ordeal of six months' search by every means for all that could be found against him, and come out as clear as Theodore

Tilton has! And what have they found? As a journalist, that he was honorable. With women? They proved that he knew Mrs. Woodhull; but what if he did?[6] The effort to put him down has only made conspicuous a wonderfully clean, upright character.

### A PERFECT HOME.

Mrs. Stanton said that she had some years ago found the Tilton home perfect; as lovely a home as she ever saw; everything harmonious—the furniture, and arrangement, servants, and all; and carried on without friction, and no loud command; Mrs. Tilton devotedly affectionate to Theodore, and he demonstratively fond of her. They were a couple, ill adapted to each other for joint lives. "Both are too solely sentimental," said Mrs. Stanton. "There needs a dash of common sense. Each had an exaggerated notion of what the other should be."

As for the fear entertained of a demoralizing effect from these scandalous details filling the newspapers for six months, Mrs. Stanton did not so regard it. There never was a trial for adultery of such length, that was so clean. There were but two points that could be clawed at by the fastidious—the ankle scene,[7] and the sitting down to discuss the paternity of one of the children.[8] It has not, as is said, demoralized the young girls and boys of every family that buys a newspaper; for there was so much of it that the children would not read it; and if they did, it only familiarized them with the inevitable inference, that a woman could be accused of adultery, could forsake her husband and home, to throw herself on the side of her accused paramour, and be sustained in society and protected by Plymouth Church.

Mrs. Stanton said that she had read the reports all through—every word of the testimony, of counsel, and judge, although it had been a great bore to do it; for she wished to view the whole, from beginning to end; because the influence of this trial was greater upon the world, and in this respect different from other trials of ecclesiastics on the same charge, on account of the characters being more prominent. These two men were universally known. This man accused of adultery was the most popular clergyman in the world.

❧ New York *Sun*, 17 July 1875.

1. Two weeks after a divided jury failed to reach a verdict in Theodore Tilton's civil suit against Henry Ward Beecher, a reporter visited ECS at

home in Tenafly, where she was surrounded by husband and children while preparing for her next lecture tour. Describing ECS as a "faithful wife, unfailing housekeeper, and good mother of many children," the unnamed reporter remarked that if a person ignorant of ECS's background were to see her, he might mistake her for an "ordinary" woman. (New York *Sun*, 17 July 1875.)

2. Matt. 9:21.

3. Under pressure from her husband and Henry Ward Beecher, Elizabeth Tilton alternately confessed to adultery, retracted her confession, and recanted her retraction. Over the course of a couple of days in December 1870, she did all three. This pattern persisted throughout the scandal, shaping public perception of Elizabeth Tilton. (Fox, *Trials of Intimacy*, 97–98, 170–74.)

4. Elizabeth Tilton was housed and supported by members of Plymouth Church throughout the investigation and trial. She remained a member of the Church until 1878, when she was excommunicated for publicly announcing that her denial of adultery had been a lie.

5. Beecher caused a stir when he took the witness stand on 1 April 1875, by refusing to swear on the Bible due to "conscientious scruples." (*Chicago Tribune*, 2 April 1875; *T. Tilton vs. H. W. Beecher*, 2:729.)

6. The nature of Theodore Tilton's relationship with Victoria Woodhull became a major focus of the trial. Beecher's lawyers subpoenaed three of Woodhull's former servants and all of her correspondence with Tilton in their effort to prove intimacy between the two and show that they conspired to publish the scandal. Tilton claimed that he befriended Woodhull, at Beecher's behest, with the goal of keeping her quiet. (*Chicago Tribune*, 3 February, 13 May 1875; *New York Times*, 26 March 1875; *T. Tilton vs. H. W. Beecher*, 1:412–15, 2:583–618, 3:508–10.)

7. ECS refers to Tilton's claim that he once caught Beecher sitting near Elizabeth, his hand under her dress touching her lower leg. He described this incident, popularly known as the "ankle scene," before the Plymouth Church investigating committee in 1874. (*Brooklyn Daily Eagle*, 27 July 1874; Marshall, *True History of the Brooklyn Scandal*, 154–55.)

8. Theodore Tilton testified about a conversation with Beecher in 1872 to date the beginning of his adulterous relationship with Elizabeth Tilton. According to his testimony, the purpose of their meeting was to ascertain the paternity of Ralph Tilton, born 21 June 1869. Beecher declared the story "a monstrous and absolute falsehood." (*Chicago Tribune*, 3 February 1875; *New York Tribune*, 6, 7 April 1875; *T. Tilton vs. H. W. Beecher*, 1:411–12; 2:797.)

65   ☞   ARTICLE BY ECS

[11 September 1875]

## GREENBACKS OR GOLD.

I have looked in vain thus far in your radical and progressive journal for a few flashes of light on the financial discussion now agitating the country. As this is not a question of dollars and cents merely, but one of the gravest humanitarian problems of our day and generation, I would suggest that it might be a great benefit to your readers to have your views on this subject.

As popular thought is now turned to this question of finance, and it is likely to control our next Presidential election, it is a happy time for those who understand the subject to teach our people its principles. As you are neither a politician, nor a religious bigot, a bondholder nor a pauper, you are in a good position to give us the moral, religious, and social necessities of "cheap money for the people,"[1] if in the range of human possibilities such a thing can be done. As women may be called upon to vote at no distant day, as Congressmen and Senators on some finance bill, it is important for us to understand these knotty questions of political economy. As a class, we have neither time nor taste, to plod through dull octavo volumes to find out the nature, use, and power of money. It is man's sphere to dig, to delve, and give the woman the result of his researches. Now do not refer us to Adam Smith, Say, Law, Ricardo, John Stuart Mill, or Carey;[2] but in a few graceful editorials give your countrywomen an insight into this money question. I have been reading what the wise men on both sides say, and have become so muddled and distracted that I am forced to the conclusion either that "these men" do not know what they are talking about, or that the science of finance is too vast for a woman's comprehension.[3]

The latter conclusion, after all I have claimed for the sex, seems so humiliating that with each returning day, I begin with renewed zest the consideration of the question. In glancing over the metropolitan journals every morning, I never pause now to read the deaths and marriages, but hasten to find the financial manna and feed myself and children; for unfortunately the youth of my household are continually pushing me with questions about this "greenback riddle," and accusing me of gravitating to the "rag money" side of the question.[4] An ordinary self-respect will drive any person seeking truth to the side most easily comprehended; and I must confess that in reading Butler, Kelley, Carey, Drew, Phillips, Davis,[5] The Indianapolis *Sun*, and Kellogg's monetary system,[6] glimmers of light flash across my mind that McCulloch, Reverdy Johnson, and Nasby shed not.[7] This "gold basis" talk is to me quite incomprehensible, and I can see no reason why money should have an intrinsic value. Captain Canot[8] says, in his recollections of the slave trade, that in his time the money of Africa was human beings. If the philosophers who maintain that money should have intrinsic value are correct, those Africans had the best possible currency, for human beings are of higher intrinsic value than any precious metals. Indeed there is nothing else strictly speaking that has intrinsic value.

There is not so much difference between the African using his spices, and the Caucasian his specie, as at first sight appears. For those who control the specie make slaves of those who have their labor only to dispose of, as effectually as the slave traders do of the African; only the money traders do it in a finer, less palpable way. The unanswerable objection to the use of gold and silver as money is, that the quantity is so limited, that it can be monopolized by a few speculators who make it their business to control it. But our hard money men do not propose to substitute gold for greenbacks, but another kind of paper.[9] Now I cannot understand why a paper currency, issued by the government, based on the wealth of the nation which cannot fail, at a low rate, is not better than the paper of banks, at a high rate of interest, based on the honor of monopolies, rings and corporations, as uncertain as the sands of the sea, and that fail periodically, bringing want and disappointment to all classes. Is there a sure, safe system of finance, that has not the word "fail" in its vocabulary? If there is such a system what are its laws, and where are they laid down so plainly that even a woman can read and understand them? Whoever will be the interpreter of these hidden mysteries to the daughters of this republic will make himself a public benefactor.

⤳ New York *Golden Age*, 11 September 1875.

1. The phrase refers to paper currency. Advocates of government-issued paper understood it to expand economic opportunities by increasing the supply of money and credit and, at the same time, to break monopoly control of the money supply. (Ritter, *Goldbugs and Greenbacks*, 62–109.)

2. ECS lists the authors of classic studies of political economy and monetary policy: Adam Smith (1723–1790) of Scotland; Jean-Baptiste Say (1767–1832) of France; John Law of Lauriston (1671–1729) of Scotland; David Ricardo (1772–1823) of England; and Henry Charles Carey (1793–1879) of the United States. She includes John Stuart Mill for his *Principles of Political Economy* (1848).

3. On her quest for information, see ECS to Benjamin Butler, 12 December 1874; William D. Kelley to ECS, 13 December 1874; and W. W. Phelps to ECS, 13 December 1874; all in *Film*, 18:219–23.

4. Critics of greenbacks used this term.

5. Here ECS names reformers and politicians who popularized schemes for expanding the nation's money supply with paper currency. After Benjamin Butler, she lists: William Darrah Kelley (1814–1890), Republican congressman from Pennsylvania (*BDAC*); either Henry C. Carey or Samuel Fenton Cary (1814–1900), a labor reformer and former congressman from Ohio, who ran for vice president on the Greenback party ticket in 1876 (*BDAC*); John G. Drew of New Jersey, a labor reformer active in the Industrial Brotherhood, who published two books on currency and political economy in 1874 (Unger, *Greenback Era*, 110, 305; *Workingman's Advocate*, 25 April 1874); Wendell Phillips (1811–1884), the abolitionist orator, whose postwar interest in labor reform led him to the advocacy of greenbacks (*ANB*); and probably Edward M. Davis.

6. The newspaper, the *Indianapolis Sun*, was promoting the organization of a Greenback party to run candidates in the election of 1876. Edward Kellogg, *A New Monetary System: The Only Means of Securing the Respective Rights of Labor and Property, and of Protecting the Public from Financial Revulsions* was the work of Kellogg's daughter, Mary Kellogg Putnam, published first in 1861 and in new editions until 1884. Kellogg (1790–1858) supplied the postwar reformers with the rationale for government-backed currency that expanded in proportion to economic growth. When Mary Kellogg Putnam became the financial editor of the *Revolution* in November 1868, she made "Kelloggism" the main topic of discussion in her pages of the paper. (Unger, *Greenback Era*, 94–100, 293–95; Ritter, *Goldbugs and Greenbacks*, 5; Timothy Hopkins, *The Kelloggs in the Old World and the New* [San Francisco, 1903], 1:349.)

7. ECS lists advocates of currency backed by gold. Hugh McCulloch (1808–1895), secretary of the treasury in the administrations of Lincoln and Johnson, contracted the supply of greenbacks after the war as a step toward returning

the nation to the gold standard (*ANB*); Reverdy Johnson (1796–1876), a noted lawyer and Democrat, insisted that the Constitution recognized only gold and silver as legal tender (*ANB* and R. Johnson to Editor, *New York Tribune*, 14 August 1875); and David Ross Locke (1833–1888), a journalist and satirist, used his character Petroleum V. Nasby to ridicule an expansion of the money supply with paper currency (*ANB*; John M. Harrison, *The Man Who Made Nasby, David Ross Locke* [Chapel Hill, N.C., 1969], 230).

8. Theodore Canot was the pseudonym of Théophile Conneau, a sea captain in the illegal trade in slaves, who published *Adventures of an African Slaver* (New York, 1854). Explaining the trade's penetration of African society, he wrote, "MAN, *in truth, has become the coin of Africa, and the 'legal tender' of a brutal trade*" (127). ECS criticizes the conservative position that money must have intrinsic value, as in the case of gold or silver.

9. ECS refers to bank notes issued by private, national banks. The notes, in circulation at the same time as greenbacks, were secured by government bonds. Under the terms of the Resumption Act of 1875, bank notes were replacing greenbacks in preparation for a return to the gold standard in 1879. Critics, echoed here by ECS, emphasized that control of paper money gave enormous economic power to the banks. While reformers saw a dangerous monopoly in the system, conservatives argued that currency expansion and contraction were better managed by private entities responding to markets than by government and politicians. (Ritter, *Goldbugs and Greenbacks*, 78–96.)

## 66  ✥  SBA to Mathilde Franziska Anneke

Rochester Sept. 27, 1875

My Dear Friend  Madam Anneke

A Postal Card just received asks me if I ever sent on to you a letter written by Mrs Stanton in answer to yours to her of Aug. 2$^{\text{d}}$—[1] I thought it a <u>copy</u> of what she had sent to you in reply—and have made haste to dig it out of my large pile of letters received & hastily read & laid away for leisure to properly attend ↑to↓—such a <u>whirl</u> has been my life the past five months—[2] It now looks ↑as↓ if more quiet times awaited me, but who can tell what things lie very near in the unseen future— My brother—the Col. who was shot at Leavenworth Last May—has just left us—he & his wife, & my younger brother who has nursed him all through his terrible ordeal have been with us the past three weeks—& my brother youngest child of 3 years[3]—that I brought home with me last July—has gone with them—so we are all alone

My Agent[4]—writes me that I am to Lecture in Milwaukee some Sunday P.M—during the coming Winter—then I hope to meet you— I passed through your City the last of April—no first of May last—had 3 hours there—wanted to see you very much—but found you too far off—so called on my old townswoman—Mrs Sarah Ford ———[5] cant remember her married name—& Mrs Mary Stout Roddis—[6]

All that our National W.S. Association has proposed for the Centennial at Philadelphia—is a meeting of protest to be held in that city as nearly on the 4th of July as is practicable— I think on the 4th itself if we can possibly secure a place— Your idea of an address to the People—signed by 2 or 3 millions—would be splendid ↑to be ready then—↓ but if signed by only a few thousands—it would seem weak— I have very little hope or faith in our women rolling up an immense list of names for their own freedom—if we wanted them to do the Herculean task for negro men—Irish men or any class of the superior sex—they would all, as one earnest woman, rush to the work—

I am glad you do ↑not↓ get discouraged with the seeming neglect of Mrs Stanton or me—but it is seeming—for I am interested in all you say—always—& shall ever be grateful for all your thought for me personally in my efforts to establish the principle of woman's equality of rights— With kindest regards I am as ever my dear Friend  Yours Sincerely

        ⤳ *Susan B. Anthony*

P.S.—Do you not think women should hold a grand mass meeting of indignation & protest in Philadelphia July 4th 1876— There will many many women there—& if we should thoroughly advertise the place where Madam Anneke Stanton & all the leading woman suffrage were to speak we should have a crowd— All I should fear would be that our own women speakers would not be prepared to shout for freedom as valliantly as did Patrick Henry & Sam Otis[7] of old—but for themselves—they seem so listless—it is hard to keep in the patience with them. If it were possible to rouse, even our woman suffrage ↑women↓ to ↑take↓ hold of the work ↑of↓ circulating a good address—a tremendous "Centennial growl" of the Women of the United States, I should be delighted & ready to join in the work right heartily—

And, with as little faith as I have in the success as to getting <u>large</u> <u>numbers</u> interested in getting signatures, if I could see with my ↓own↓ eyes <u>just</u> <u>the</u> <u>right</u> <u>words</u> of <u>protest</u> & <u>rebuke</u> that this nation needs—I should be in favor of doing all we could to get it before the people— I should want it <u>restricted</u> to the <u>one</u> <u>point</u> of <u>shutting</u> <u>one</u> <u>half</u> <u>the</u> <u>people</u>—<u>women</u>—out from Equal rights, civil & political—with the other half—men—

But whoever would attempt to write could hardly fail to bring in the 19 <u>other</u> failures of the government to <u>practice</u> its principles—of Equal rights to all—Land Monopoly—& every other great question—every one ↑of↓ which <u>men</u> <u>should</u> include in <u>their</u> protests & demands—but for <u>us</u> <u>women</u>—<u>abject</u> <u>slaves</u> to the ruling class—to demand this or that reform—in the <u>same</u> <u>paper</u> or <u>address</u> <u>with</u> the demand for <u>our</u> <u>political</u> <u>freedom</u>—seems to <u>let</u> <u>our</u> <u>claim</u> <u>down</u> to the <u>level</u> of the others—as only <u>one</u> of <u>many</u> <u>wrongs</u>—[8] Whereas I feel it, and want ever so to express it—as the <u>one</u> & <u>great</u> <u>wrong</u> <u>of</u> <u>the</u> <u>Nation</u>—that must—like negro slavery, be put away, before it will be possible for the nation to purge itself of any, or all of its other sins— ~~But~~ ↑Therefore↓ I wait to see <u>Woman's</u> <u>Political</u> <u>enslavement</u> set forth singly and separately from everything else—in the most glowing colors so as to startle every one who reads the document into recognition of the <u>Nation's</u> <u>crime</u> <u>against</u> <u>woman</u> & <u>the</u> <u>race</u>— Now cannot you get precisely such an address written & send me the copy— If your association and ours could <u>unite</u> <u>on</u> the same address, the two together would be stronger than either alone—

I shall be at home two or three weeks longer—then I go into Iowa to begin the Canvass of that state, preparatory to the election of <u>Nov.</u> <u>1876</u>—when the question of W.S. is to be voted upon there— I intend to work in that state mainly the coming year—

⤚ ALS, on NWSA letterhead for 1875, Anneke Papers, WHi.

1. Anneke, in a letter now missing, proposed a collaboration between Radical Democracy and the National Woman Suffrage Association to prepare a protest in advance of the Centennial celebration. A month later, ECS wrote a reply and mailed it and Anneke's letter to Matilda Gage with instructions that both be sent on to SBA. Gage answered Anneke on 12 September, full of enthusiasm for a protest with thousands of signatures but cautious about the expense. She asked if Radical Democracy would foot the bill for one thousand copies and proposed that writing begin right away. Gage also wrote to ECS

and SBA, but those letters are missing, as is her postcard prompting SBA to write this reply. ECS's letter of 6 September, finally mailed to Anneke as an enclosure with this letter, said the idea was good for "agitation," but that women paying any attention to the Centennial was "absurd." (ECS to M. F. Anneke, 6 September 1875, and M. J. Gage to M. F. Anneke, 12 September 1875, Anneke Papers, WHi. The ECS letter is not in *Film*.)

2. While SBA attended the National's May meeting, D. R. Anthony was shot in Leavenworth and believed to be fatally wounded. The bullet, fired at point-blank range as Anthony and his wife left an opera, severed an artery near his collarbone, and obituary tributes appeared in papers across the country. Leavenworth newspapers reported on 14 May that "[t]elegraphic dispatches have been sent to different parts of the country inquiring the whereabouts of Miss Susan B. Anthony, but as no response has yet been received, it is supposed that none of these have reached her." SBA left New York for Kansas and remained for nine weeks to nurse her brother in what the medical profession regarded as a remarkable recovery. Dr. Tiffin Sinks began a regimen of uninterrupted compression on the artery that continued until the end of August. Members of the family took turns at the job, with SBA doing her share until she returned East in late July. Days after she returned, she learned that her old friend Lydia Mott had survived the summer in her long battle with consumption but was failing fast. SBA left for Albany to nurse Mott until her death on 20 August. (*Anthony*, 1:470-71; clippings in SBA scrapbook 8, Rare Books, DLC; *U.S. Biographical Dictionary: Kansas Volume*, 61-62.)

3. D. R. Anthony visited Rochester with Anna O. Anthony and his younger brother, Merritt. SBA brought her niece Susan B. Anthony to Rochester in July. Susie, the youngest daughter of D. R. and Anna Anthony, was born in 1872.

4. Henry L. Slayton, SBA's new agent, had offices on LaSalle Street in Chicago that served his law practice and his lecture agency. He renamed his business Slayton's Lecture Bureau in 1876, and by 1880 moved his offices into Central Music Hall. Slayton represented SBA and ECS until at least 1880. (City directories, 1875 to 1880.)

5. Sarah Ford Austin was a childhood friend of SBA from Washington County, New York. She and her family moved to Ann Arbor, Michigan, in the 1840s, and there she married Robert N. Austin in 1849. Robert Austin became a prominent lawyer in Milwaukee, and Sarah, the mother of three children, took a leading role in the city's wartime relief work. By 1874 Sarah and Robert Austin lived at different addresses in the city. (Mary Ann McLean to SBA and Mary S. Anthony, May 1850, and SBA diary, 6 April 1865, in *Film*, 6:1049-52, 10:928ff; Alfred Theodore Andreas, *History of Milwaukee, Wisconsin, from Pre-Historic Times* [Chicago, 1881], 1:610, 669, 745, 749; city directory, 1874 to 1878.)

6. Mary Stout Roddis (c. 1820-?) was another friend from Washington County who also married and moved to Milwaukee by 1850. The widow of

Thomas R. Roddis, she operated a boarding house in the 1870s. SBA noted meeting her daughter Mary. (Mary Ann McLean to SBA and Mary S. Anthony, May 1850, and SBA diary, 31 March 1877, in *Film*, 6:1049-52, 19:12ff; Federal Census, 1870; city directory, 1875-76.)

7. SBA confounds two revolutionaries of Massachusetts, James Otis and Samuel Adams (1722-1803).

8. SBA assumed that Radical Democracy hoped to gain the National's endorsement of the twenty objectives of reform in its platform, including woman suffrage. Gage assumed, when she replied on 12 September, that this would be a protest "against the celebration of our so-called <u>republican</u> centennial with woman unrecognized as a voting citizen." (M. F. Anneke to My dear friend, c. April 1874, and M. J. Gage to M. F. Anneke, 12 September 1875, Anneke Papers, WHi; Union of the Radicals of North America, *Platform and Constitution of a New Party, Agreed upon at a Convention, Held at Philadelphia, June 28th, 29th, & 30th, 1876* [Philadelphia, 1876].)

## 67 ⟿ SBA TO ISABELLA BEECHER HOOKER

Rochester Oct. 12, 1875—

My dear friend Mrs Hooker

I guess I do wish I could just step into Olympia's home with you & chat ↑over↓ every thing & everybody about our work—but I can not go east now—though I expect to do so the last of this month & then may possibly be able to see you—[1] About Iowa— If you two can see any other places of greater importance—just tell me— I do not believe in getting suffrage by <u>state</u> <u>action</u>—but it is the ↑only↓ way the politicians will allow us to <u>agitate</u> the question— So I accept it of necessity—not choice.— Madam Anneke has asked Mrs Gage to write an appeal to Congress to be presented the coming session—[2]

Do you see any way we can <u>even</u> <u>hope</u> to make Congress look at us—

Shall we hold our Convention at Washington next January? It is a most expensive luxury, to <u>me</u> at least.— If we could drive some <u>practical</u> <u>work</u> upon Congress— But the Supreme Court has pronounced its fiat against ↑U.S.↓ citizenship entitling us to suffrage— If we could get Congress to <u>pass</u> a proposition for a Constitutional amendment—it would be good—then we could go to the <u>state</u> <u>Legislatures</u>—even if it took ten years to move three fourths of them to ratify—it would be better than <u>state</u> action—

But I only drop this to say to you & to Olympia that I should be <u>very</u> <u>very</u> glad to be with you this week— With best love to ye both & yer good husbands too.— I am as ever   your sincere friend

✍ *Susan B. Anthony*

✍ ALS, Isabella Hooker Collection, CtHSD.

1. At Olympia Brown's house in Bridgeport, Connecticut. SBA was scheduled to speak in New Hampshire at the end of October.

2. The plan had developed. Mathilde Anneke had shown Matilda Gage's letter of 12 September to her co-worker Karl Doerflinger, and he disagreed with Gage. A memorial with signatures should first go to Congress, and if Congress failed to notice it, then a protest for the Centennial would be appropriate. Anneke conveyed that message to Gage on 30 September and asked her to prepare a memorial capable of "awaking the whole woman world to a cry for justice!" She also pledged money to print one thousand copies. Although Gage did not tell Anneke until 6 November, she disagreed with this plan. The congressional session was too long to learn how the memorial was received in time to circulate a protest before the Fourth of July. Nonetheless, she drafted both documents. (K. Doerflinger to M. F. Anneke, 25 September 1875; M. F. Anneke to M. J. Gage, 30 September 1875; and M. J. Gage to M. F. Anneke, 6 November 1875; all in Anneke Papers, WHi.)

## 68 ➤ SBA TO MATILDA JOSLYN GAGE

Rochester Oct. 21$^{st}$ 1875

My Dear Mrs Gage

I thought I had answered every point you say I am remiss in— I like Madam Annekes plan of protest & demand this winter—as I thought I wrote <u>you</u> as well as Mrs Stanton, Mrs Hooker & the Madam Anneke— but I want it to be on the one & <u>sole</u> <u>point</u> of <u>women</u> <u>disfranchised</u>— separate & alone—and <u>not</u> mixed up with—or one of—19 <u>other</u> <u>points</u> of <u>protest</u>—each all of the 19 good & proper perchance—but the very moment we put Temperance, Land Monopoly, Labor & Capital, anything, however good & needed—we sink ~~our~~ ↑<u>woman's</u>↓ claim <u>to</u> equality of rights civil & political down the common level of the others— whereas we must keep our claim first & most important overshadowing every other—

Mrs Stanton answered me that she agreed with me—just woman &

her disfranchised— Leaving the other 19 demands of the Old Liberty to wait our free emancipation—

And Mrs Hooker is wide awake for the most vigorous attack upon Congress we have ever made—and I am sure you are the one to write the protest— Like Mrs Stanton I do not want to stop the ↑Rebels—nor any more do I the↓ Irishmen or negroes—or drunken vagabonds—↑for↓ I am glad they all have the right—only I want mine too ↑my sex to have it too—↓[1]

And our National must prepare the address—& then if the Radical can adopt all right—but I should hardly expect them, if they were to draw up the address, to do other than make woman suffrage one of their demands—but if we draw it up—& they adopt & work for it—why they will help us very much— The National should take half or perhaps more of the cost of printing the document— There were several persons who pledged money at the May Anniversary—and it will help— one was Mr Wilcox Father[2]—another was a Lady from Flushing— Then beside the National & Rad. Dem's—the Philadelphia Citizen Suffrage Society[3]—Mr E. M. Davis will help—& the San Francisco— California State Society too—Mrs Wallis[4] of Mayfield—& Mrs Gordon[5] of Stockton represent it— So I say get the right thing for Memorial—& get it printed—& set afloat as soon as possible—but Mrs Hooker

⟿ AL incomplete, on NWSA letterhead for 1875, SBA Papers, DLC.

1. This sentence appears to answer Gage on the point of her opposition to an act of general amnesty for Confederate leaders to restore their political rights. At the National's convention of 1874, held just after President Grant recommended and the House of Representatives passed such a bill, she introduced a resolution condemning it. "It raised a breeze," in the words of the *Washington Chronicle*, and ECS, among many others, opposed adoption. "[I]t was in particularly bad taste," ECS said, "for woman suffragists, who are clamoring for representation and for the ballot, to call for its denial to any part of the nation." Although the reporters present agreed that the resolution was soundly defeated, Gage wrote on a clipping in her scrapbook, "Not so. Mrs. Stanton spoke against it several times but the vote was nearly equal." Stopped in the Senate in 1874, general amnesty was a top priority in 1875 for the Democratic majority in the House of Representatives. (*Washington Chronicle*, 16 January 1874; Washington *National Republican*, 16 January 1874; and *Hartford Daily Times*, 1 February 1874; all in *Film*, 17:919–20, 924–25, 928–29; *History*, 2:542; Jonathan Truman Dorris, *Pardon and Amnesty under*

*Lincoln and Johnson: The Restoration of the Confederates to Their Rights and Privileges, 1861–1898* [Chapel Hill, N.C., 1953], 362–92.)

2. Albert Oliver Willcox (1810–c. 1897) was a New York merchant, an abolitionist, a Democrat, and a lifetime supporter of woman suffrage. He was the father of Hamilton Willcox. At Gage's request, he sent ten dollars to the National on this occasion. (*ACAB*; *History*, 4:295; M. J. Gage to Isabella B. Hooker, 23 December 1875, Isabella Hooker Collection, CtHSD.)

3. The Citizens' Suffrage Association of Philadelphia was founded in 1872 in anticipation of a constitutional convention in Pennsylvania in order "to obtain Suffrage for Women and secure it to all Citizens." Among its members were Lucretia Mott, Edward M. Davis, Carrie Burnham, Damon Kilgore, and Robert Purvis. (*History*, 3:461–64; tracts of the association in SBA scrapbooks 4 and 8, Rare Books, DLC. See also *Papers* 2.)

4. Sarah Armstrong Montgomery Green Wallis (1825–1905) lived in Mayfield, Santa Clara County, with her third husband, Joseph Sawyer Wallis. An early subscriber to the *Revolution* and a founder of the suffrage movement in California in 1868 and 1869, she presided over the contentious meeting to organize a state society in 1870. She and Laura Gordon were among those who stopped efforts to ally the society with the American association and won a decision to remain independent for one year. From that moment on through the 1870s, California's suffragists organized and reorganized competing societies that reflected local disputes over difficult personalities, free love, and domineering men. Wallis remained with the group that traced its roots to the 1870 founding, hosted ECS and SBA in 1871, reported its work to the National association, and incorporated in 1873, while she was president. (*Women's Heritage Museum News* 3 [26 August 1987], 1; Pioneer Roster Submission, Native Daughters of the Golden West, San Francisco, vol. 67, p. 215; Hubert Howe Bancroft, *History of California* [San Francisco, 1890], 4:743; *History of Santa Clara County, California* [San Francisco, 1881], 590; *History*, 3:751, 753, 757, 765; *San Francisco Chronicle*, 17, 18 May 1871, *Film*, 15:605–6; San Francisco *Pioneer*, 8 May 1873; *New Northwest*, 17 July, 14 August 1874; *Woman's Journal*, 13 February 1875; *Papers*, 2:293–95.)

5. Laura De Force Gordon (1838–1907), the leading organizer for woman suffrage on the West Coast, was at this time editor and publisher of the *Sacramento Weekly Leader*. (*NAW*; *ANB*; Robert J. Chandler, "In the Van: Spiritualists as Catalysts for the California Women's Suffrage Movement," *California History* 73 [Fall 1994]: 188–201, 252–54. See also *Papers* 2.)

## 69   SBA TO MATILDA JOSLYN GAGE

Rochester Nov. 3, 1875

Dear Mrs Gage

I like the general import of your protest—but cannot possibly make any verbal criticisms—I am overwhelmed with thought & writing for tomorrow night—[1] I know you will get it right— I find here Mrs Hookers letter— Now if she doesn't take hold & you should be too ill to attend to Washington—I don't see how it can be possible to hold a Con. there— For I have been so long kept out of Iowa—that I feel that there is too little time to do the half I hoped— There is force in what Mrs Hooker says about <u>no</u> Convention—<u>seeming</u> to be a surrender— Still if she can't give <u>time</u> <u>nor</u> <u>money</u>—nor <u>you</u> <u>cant</u> give <u>money</u>—nor Mrs Stanton—why what then— Why, simply, <u>Susan</u> shoulder the risk again— Well I don't propose to do it this time—not that I should be much afraid but that I could make ends meet—within 75 or 100 dollars—& that to come out of my own pocket—but I cant give the necessary time this winter—because I feel it a <u>better</u> <u>use</u> <u>of</u> <u>it</u> to stay & work in Iowa— But without me—you & Mrs Blake—& Olympia & Mrs Hooker & Stanton—& think she will be back east about that time— ought to be able to carry the Con. through—

But dear a me don't everything look dark & dreary—<u>ahead</u>— Mrs Stanton is to be in Milwaukee[2] <u>Sunday</u>—the 7th—if possible start on your letter with protest—so she & Madam A. can go over it together—[3]

I am so sorry you have such a <u>sorry</u> beginning of the winter[4]—my cold has passed off—but I am in constant fear lest another will come to me—the weather is the sort to bring colds— Mrs Wrights newspaper clippings are all packed away safely in a box—also her letters—she had all of mine & Mrs Stanton's & others carefully saved together—but none of them are to be touched until Ellen & I can sit down together— & sort them out—because so many of them will have <u>private</u> as well as public matter in them—but they will be kept safe—& will help us in our history—[5]

  AL, Anneke Papers, WHi.

1. Back from New Hampshire, she delivered her lecture "Social Purity" in Rochester. She left home again the next day to begin her winter tour, including a return to the campaign in Iowa. See *Film*, 18:487.

2. ECS delivered her lecture "Home Life." See *Film*, 18:489.

3. SBA returned the first draft of the protest to Gage, who amended it before mailing a text to Mathilde Anneke on 6 November, too late to reach ECS in Milwaukee. This second draft based women's claim to voting rights on the Declaration of Independence and the Constitution, asserted that women were "<u>disfranchised</u> and debarred from exercising their natural rights of self-government," pronounced the Centennial celebration "a mockery and deceit of all peoples," and called upon "the assembled nations to hearken to our cry against falsehood and oppression as it rings to high heaven." Gage complained bitterly about SBA's lack of attention to her protest and blamed her for the fact that it did not reach ECS in time to get her advice. Anneke and the Radicals were silent for a month, Isabella Hooker forgot to acknowledge its receipt, and Carrie Burnham sent word from Philadelphia that she did not like it at all. Unnamed friends feared it was "too strong" and might "frighten away some people." In the meantime, Radical Democracy abandoned the idea of a memorial to Congress and asked that the protest be printed in German and English. Pressed with work and uncertain how to pay for the protest, Gage set it aside. In Washington in late January, Sara Spencer revised Gage's draft of the protest before the National's convention adopted it for use on the Fourth of July. This text "protest[ed] against the Government of the United States as an oligarchy of sex" and "against calling this a Centennial celebration of the independence of the people of the United States." Anneke later wrote her own protest for the Wisconsin Woman Suffrage Association. (M. J. Gage to M. F. Anneke, 6 November 1875, 4 December 1875, 10 January 1876, and Declaration of Principles and Protest [incomplete], Anneke Papers, WHi; M. J. Gage to I. B. Hooker 22 November 1875, 11, 23 December 1875, and Declaration of Principles and Protest, Isabella Hooker Collection, CtHSD; M. J. Gage to Thomas C. Gage, 26 January 1876, Matilda Joslyn Gage Collection, MCR-S; Washington *National Republican*, 29 January 1876, *Film*, 18:731–33; *Woman's Journal*, 22 July 1876.)

4. Gage had put aside the memorial and protest in October when she suffered from congestion of the lungs. (M. J. Gage to M. F. Anneke, 6 November 1875, Anneke Papers, WHi.)

5. In this, the earliest mention of plans for a history of woman's rights, SBA refers to sorting the papers of Martha Wright with her daughter Ellen Garrison.

70   ECS TO ISABELLA BEECHER HOOKER

St Charles Ill.[1] Nov. 12th [1875]

Dear Mrs Hooker,

I am quite ashamed that I have allowed so long a time to pass by without giving you a hearty welcome to your home again, but when I first heard of your return I was so busy getting ready for my western trip that all the amenities of life were indefinitely postponed   Now from the far off prairie accept my love & greeting. I was rejoiced to hear through Susan that you came back as enthusiastic as ever in our suffrage struggle, & that you felt equal to taking the Washington Convention on your well rested shoulders. Before making the final decision let us review our forces & see on whom we can depend with certainty. Does Olympia Brown say she will <u>positively</u> be there? Will Phebe Couzins & Miss Burnham? Can we find any men who will come bringing honor & dignity to our platform? Mrs Gage our President presides well, & is always good for a speech. With these we might fill one day & evening & perhaps a one day convention is enough   Susan, I believe intends to remain in the west, & I may do the same. You & Mrs Gage must take the responsibility of deciding what is best to do.[2] Mrs Jones of Chicago[3] intends to be there & Madame Anneke thought she might also. The forces necessary for a good convention seem to me so inadequate that my courage always oozes out at the approach of one, & yet I know that by the foolishness of preaching[4] the car of progress is made to move on. But your enthusiasm, & complacency always restores my equilibrium, somewhat so I hope to feel quite brave again when I meet you, & join with you in the songs of freedom as of yore. I trust you are still sound on "the referendum"[5] I have †had↓ charming weather thus far, good audiences, & easy travelling. If you can write me a few lines on the receipt of this, direct to me Care of Gerrit Smith Stanton Woodbine Harrison Co Iowa[6] I shall be there a week after the 20th until the 28th of Nov   With kind regards for Mr Hooker & yourself. Sincerely yours as ever

  E. C. Stanton

⤙ ALS, Isabella Hooker Collection, CtHSD.

1. A village west of Chicago.

2. With ECS and SBA in the Midwest and Matilda Gage in charge for the first time, plans for the Washington convention were confused. Twice in December Gage reached the conclusion that the convention would not be held, and it was not until early January that she issued a call to the meeting. Gage did "not really believe Susan would allow a convention to come off without returning to it." In that she was wrong. (SBA to Olympia Brown, 3 November 1875, ECS to I. B. Hooker, 28 November 1875, *Film*, 18:476–79, 498–501; M. J. Gage to I. B. Hooker, 22 November, 23 December 1875, Isabella Hooker Collection, CtHSD; and M. J. Gage to M. F. Anneke, 10 January 1876, Anneke Papers, WHi.)

3. Jane Grahame Jones.

4. 1 Cor. 1:21.

5. A similar jest about the referendum as a test of radicalism is found in ECS's letter to Hooker on 14 June 1872, shortly after the convention of the Equal Rights party nominated Victoria Woodhull for president. Brushing aside SBA's criticism of Hooker's enthusiasm for the convention, ECS wrote: "I don't know what she means at all nor do I care so long as you are sound on the 'Referendum' Minority representation & graduated taxation." (*Papers*, 2:512.)

6. Gat Stanton acquired three hundred acres in Harrison County, near Woodbine, in 1867, but when he left the farm in 1888, he dated his term as a "stockman on the western plains" to 1873, the year he settled down to stay. (G. Smith Stanton, *"When the Wildwood Was in Flower." A Narrative Covering the Fifteen Years' Experiences of a Stockman on the Western Plains, and His Vacation Days in the Open* [New York, 1909]; G. S. Stanton to Gerrit Smith, 30 July 1870, 21 June 1871, 18 September 1874, Smith Papers, NSyU.)

71 ⇝ SBA TO MATILDA JOSLYN GAGE

Clarinda [*Iowa*][1] Jan 19/76

Dear Mrs Gage

Now do you go strait to Mrs Stanton's & both of you sit down together & map out the work of the Wash. Con. and the plan of the Philadelphia Centennial Pow wow— Mrs Sargent writes again urging me to go on to W—but I had taken your letter as the final <u>no</u>—and gone ahead & filled in my time with engagements    I give you the principal points

Jan. 24<sup>th</sup> Bedford—Iowa
     27<sup>th</sup> Garden Grove "
     31— Albia
Feb  1— Ottumwa
     7— Washington—

I have letter to day— The Doctors pronounce my Sister Hannah Mrs Mosher—going the way our dear Sister Mrs M<sup>c</sup>Lean went—& she is leaving all at home to go to <u>Denver</u>—& I feel that I must drop all go with her—[2] It is too cruel to see her going down— I am dreadfully hampered—but am going to try to hold myself to the rack of work until I get my neck out of the yoke of the Revolution debt— Now do go <u>to</u> Mrs S. & she wont say no to <u>you</u>—but if you just write she may feel she can't & say so on paper—but if you go & look her in the face with your appeal just as I always do—she <u>wont</u> <u>say</u> <u>no</u>—her love & benevolence & all will lift right along to help you right royally—just as she always has me—when I have had a Con. on my shoulders—

Mrs Sargent says they have got nearly enough money raised to pay the Hall rent—and if you fail to raise enough to cover expenses—send to me & I will do as much as I said in my last—if you need me to—[3] I haven't a P.O. order on hand now—so send on without again—but don't <u>miss</u> <u>me</u>— You are all strong & can get on splendidly without me— Affectionately

                                  &#x00248; *Susan B. Anthony*

&#x00248; ALS, SBA Papers, DLC.

1. SBA reached Iowa in December, took a break in Kansas for the holidays, returned to Iowa on 15 January, and spoke twice in this town in the southwestern corner of the state. She continued to lecture in Iowa through 8 April, although by then, the state senate had defeated the woman suffrage amendment and thus brought the anticipated campaign to a close. (*History*, 3:622; *Woman's Journal*, 19, 26 February, 4 March, 1 April 1876.)

2. Denver was a destination for people suffering from pulmonary disease, but at this time, Hannah Mosher went only as far as Leavenworth, Kansas.

3. SBA's "last" letter is missing. She sent fifty dollars toward convention expenses. (Washington *National Republican*, 29 January 1876, *Film*, 18:731-33.)

·⊂⊃═══⊃═⊂═══⊃·

72   ⤳   FROM THE DIARY OF SBA

[*4–8 March 1876*]

SATURDAY, MARCH 4, 1876. Left Savannah[1] at 8 A.M—reached Leavenworth at 11. Sister Hannah met me at door looking much better than last fall—5 lbs heavier—[2] Sister Annie in bed—been sick for a month— tampering with herself[3]—& was freed this A.M. what ignorance & lack of self-government the world is filled with

   1. SBA lectured the previous night in this Missouri town.

   2. Hannah Mosher was staying at the home of their brother D. R. Anthony.

   3. That is, inducing an abortion.

SUNDAY, MARCH 5, 1876. Left Leavenworth at 4.30 on R[ock] I[sland] Train for Cameron—[1] Sister came down stairs to 3 P.M. dinner   Arthur[2] called—   Sister Hannah made Custard for desert—   Brother D. R. seems anxious & overtaxed—   O if he could only not drive so much business & so hard—   Dr. Sinks[3] examined H's lungs—not seriously diseased he says

   1. At Cameron Junction, she caught the Hannibal & St. Joseph Railroad to Chillicothe, Missouri.

   2. Arthur Anthony Mosher (1851–1932), Hannah's oldest son, moved to Leavenworth in 1870 to learn the insurance business from his uncle D. R. Anthony. He took over and expanded the business, and at the start of 1877 was transferred by the Travelers Insurance Company to St. Louis. He married Martha Beatrice Brown in 1875, and she gave birth to their son Arthur Byron on 17 March 1876. (Anthony, *Anthony Genealogy*, 183; *Insurance Times*, February 1891, in SBA scrapbook 17, Rare Books, DLC.)

   3. Tiffin Sinks (1834–?) moved to Leavenworth in 1856, after training at the Medical College of Ohio in Cincinnati. In 1876 he was president of the Kansas Medical Society. (Andreas, *History of Kansas*, 285, 434, 453.)

MONDAY, MARCH 6, 1876. Chillicothe Mo. J. S. Funk[1] Dr. [*blank*] Wilcox[2]

   regular warm spring rain to day— at 7. P.M. cold & snowing hard— small audience 200—though—   Mrs Col. S. B. Taylor of Brookfield here—[3]

1. Jacob S. Funk (c. 1842-?) was a lumber dealer and secretary of the board of education in Chillicothe, the seat of Livingston County. He and his wife were both born in Pennsylvania. (A. J. Roof, *Past and Present of Livingston County, Missouri: A Record of Settlement, Organization, Progress and Achievement* [Chicago, 1913], 1:278-79; Federal Census, 1870.)

2. M. H. Wilcox (1840-?) grew up in Rochester, New York, where he studied dentistry. After eight years in practice in Corning, New York, he went west, moving often until he arrived in Chillicothe in 1872 and built a successful practice. In 1890 he joined the faculty of the Chillicothe Normal School. (Roof, *Past and Present of Livingston County, Mo.*, 1:312; *History of Caldwell and Livingston Counties, Missouri* [St. Louis, 1886], 1159-60.)

3. At 15 April 1876 in her diary, SBA named S. E. Taylor, a colonel, as the person in Brookfield, Missouri, in charge of her lecture. She described spending the Saturday night with the Taylors and attending their church on Sunday. Mrs. Taylor, she noted, was "an English lady." (SBA diary, 1876, *Film*, 18:516ff.)

TUESDAY, MARCH 7, 1876. Left Chillicothe at 4 A.M. arrived Cameron Junction & breakfasted—& found my trunk not sent— Leavenworth 10.30— Sister Annie better—but looks very slim— she will rue the day she forces nature— Hannah brighter & better—but raises what shows disease sure—

WEDNESDAY, MARCH 8, 1876. Left—Leavenworth on the 4.30 R[ock] I[sland] train— wrote Sister Mary & mailed it on board—[1] Sister Hannah going to start for Denver next week— she feels very much encouraged—gained 6 lbs—in six weeks— arrived Allerton at 11.30—& slept there—till 9 A.M—[2]

1. On all important mail routes, the United States Post Office provided services for rail passengers to buy stamps and send mail.

2. She was picked up at Allerton, Iowa, and driven the last five miles to lecture in Corydon, Iowa, on March 9.

⚞ The Standard Diary 1876, n.p., SBA Papers, DLC. Letters in square brackets expand abbreviations.

·(&#x2508;&#x2508;&#x2508;&#x2508;&#x2508;&#x2508;&#x2508;&#x2508;)·

## 73   "WOMAN WANTS BREAD, NOT THE BALLOT": LECTURE BY SBA IN MILWAUKEE, WISCONSIN

EDITORIAL NOTE: At an afternoon event in Milwaukee's Academy of Music, "crowded to its utmost capacity," SBA delivered "Woman Wants Bread, Not the Ballot," her best-known lecture for two decades. The speech, first delivered in 1875, evolved from earlier lectures entitled "Work, Wages and the Ballot"; "The False Theory"; and "The Power of the Ballot"; and it bore strong similarities to her lecture "The Workingman and His Strikes," below at 6 September 1877. No manuscript of the speech survives, and SBA's biographer Ida Harper claimed none ever existed. Although many newspapers reported the lecture, none provided a full text, and Harper created what she called an abstract of the lecture "from scattered notes and newspaper reports." This report from Milwaukee is one of the best available.

[19 March 1876]

She said in brief: Disfranchisement is political, industrial, and moral degradation. Thirty years ago the workingmen of England were in the habit of holding bread meetings. At one in Manchester John Bright[1] said to them, "You want the ballot to bring you cheap bread," and they, not believing, broke the meeting up in a row. Yet the great disciple of labor was right, as events have since proved. When George Thompson[2] and others came over to talk against slavery here the Southerners said, "Go home, you have worse slavery at home in your factories than we have," and there was a spice of truth in the taunt. Everywhere disfranchisement means industrial degradation and it is as true of the Chinamen on the Pacific Coast as it is of the women of the United States. John Stuart Mill advocated a bill to give every person who paid £7 taxes a right to vote.[3] It was bitterly opposed and finally passed so as to exclude women. Robert Lowe[4] sprang up the moment the bill passed and said it would be necessary to educate these people or they would be dangerous. Here is an example of a bitter enemy being forced to aid the lower classes because they need the right to vote.

You say that women are extravagant and not more honest than men. Well, if it is so it comes from their position. They are slaves, and so long as a woman must account rigidly for every dollar she spends, she will deceive. We are all selfish, and self-interest rules the world. If we would have woman do her whole duty as a citizen, we must make her rights and duties equal to man's.

Here in the Northwest every man, no matter how poor, may vote, and each may reach the highest position accorded to any citizen. In many of the older States there was a property qualification, but the Democratic leaders under Jefferson and Jackson set to work to remove this objection, and thus secured the votes of foreigners and working-men.[5] Horace Greeley worked for years to educate these people to believe that the Whig party would do more for them than the Demo-crats.[6] They came over, and the Republican party was victorious. These gave the ballot to the negroes, and they to-day vote for that party.

The Democrats who seem to have no leader now are not trying yet to convince the negroes that they will help them if they vote with them. Till they do this they cannot hope to regain power for more than one term unless the Republicans behave so badly that we'll be glad to take anybody in their place.

A disfranchised class must always follow revolutionary methods. There is no other course left to them, and I am always glad when I see a disfranchised class rise in rebellion. (Applause.) The parties fear the laboring men, and they never dare to go against the platforms made by the workingmen. In 1868, the National Labor Congress met and put a greenback plank in their platform.[7] A little later the Democrats met and made a greenback platform and nominated a hard-money candidate to run on it. The Republicans made a platform that no one could under-stand and nominated a man who had no financial policy.[8] If the Demo-crats had run on the greenback platform honestly and the Republicans had run a hard-money candidate, the former would have been success-ful. But they both got on the fence and the Republicans won. But we always see the same truckling spirit in both parties.

There was a strike in California. The miners struck; the capitalists hired Chinamen; the miners drove them out; the capitalists asked Gov. Haight[9] to send on militia and protect their men; he did and the Chinamen worked. I said he would not be elected again and people laughed at me. Well, the election came on and he was beaten by 6000 majority. It was because the voters of that State knew that in a struggle between capital and labor Gov. Haight would side with capital. Your farmers in the West are just waking up to the importance of studying political matters. I always feel like blessing the Grangers, for they did one thing never done before in a political move; they took the women with them. If they could have taken the women to the ballot-box they would not have been sold out as they have been. Men's trade's unions are successful generally, when they strike, but women never are. I have seen but one good fight made by women. It was in Troy. The girls in the collar-laundry business to the number of 500 struck, and lay idle for thirteen weeks.[10] Their money, as a union, was used up, and they had to go back to work at lesser rates than before. I passed through there the next year and talked with the girls. "Miss Kate," said I, to a bright Irish girl, who was president, "why did you fail?" She said, "I think it was because the editors ridiculed us." They would not have done it if they had been men and could vote.

Kate said she thought the capitalists had bribed the editors with $10,000. She didn't think that the capitalists couldn't bribe the editors if the bricklayers were on the strike, for they could vote. If these 500 girls had votes, the papers would have stood by them to the end. If you women do not want to vote, I want you to think of the workingwomen of the country who need protection from the greedy capitalists. They must have it. (Applause.)

See the change it has wrought in the condition of the negro. And do not forget that it was a military necessity, and not our sense of justice that freed the slaves. A political necessity gave them the ballot. There was not a State in the Union at the beginning of the war that would give the negro the right to vote. Iowa was the only one that did it freely.[11] Now all the avocations of life are open to them. They sit in Congress, practice in the Supreme Court, fill our schools and colleges, ride on cars and live in hotels.

In 1865 I was in Kansas and a great meeting of negroes was held in Leavenworth.[12] A list of speakers containing all the leading names of that place were down on the programme for speeches. Not one of them came, and I had to make the first speech. I told those colored men that if they had votes all these men would be there, and Senators Pomeroy and Jim Lane[13] would be foremost among them. Well, in 1870 I was there again and there was another meeting. Then Mr. Revels[14] was in Congress, and when he came a delegation of Republicans met him with a band and took him in state to a sumptuous suite of rooms in the Planters' Hotel.[15] Five years before he lived in Leavenworth, but he was unnoticed. Why this change? The ballot was the cause.

I wonder that these men who scribble so much in newspapers don't read history. They think that the same laws of justice and right that apply to men don't apply to women. They will learn.

To return to the meeting in Leavenworth. Shortly after it I met the Governor and senators, and they all admitted that they had been at the meeting, and my brother said there were so many office-seekers there that there wasn't room for each of them to say "fellow-citizens." The negroes can vote.

No matter how low men are their wants are heeded and their requests are treated with respect by the politicians. No matter how high and noble women are their requests are treated with disrespect. In New York we tried to enforce the Sunday liquor law.[16] From every side word came that the officers could not undertake to do their duty because they would lose votes by it. The District-attorney of Rochester wouldn't shut up a beer-garden because he said he'd lose the German vote and that would defeat him. If those women could have told him that though he lost 5000 German votes he would gain the votes of 10,000 honest fanatical women he would have done his duty.

In Chicago 18,000 women petitioned against the repeal of the Sunday liquor law, and their prayer was disregarded.[17] Now the office-holders would just as lief be elected by women's votes as by these indecent men. When a woman tells a man she doesn't want to vote, he knows she lies. I didn't mean to say that word, but it came out. All women want to vote. Women are what men make them. They talk of poor Mrs. Belknap,[18] but she never took a dollar that her husband didn't want her to. Yet all the editorial scribblers in the country are abusing her. They talk of chivalry, and say that men were made to take care of women. There are half a million of women in this country working in factories; half a million more are in other professional employments. In your State a woman can't enter the Supreme Court.[19] Think what one little infinitesimal judge can do. In all, 2,000,000 women are doing for themselves, besides 1,000,000 servant-girls. Not only are women taking the places of men, but men are going into woman's sphere. The best milliners and dressmakers now are men. In the West, Chinamen wait at table, and when I was in Astoria[20] my chambermaid was a Chinaman. What I ask of you is to make it possible for these working women to make a living as easily and as honestly as men. The temptation of marrying for a home should be removed from women. Pecuniary dependence destroys all sense of respect.

You say that man protects woman. Let us see. Man holds the keys to everything. How long can a woman keep the servant girl if the man doesn't like her? Lecky says the professional prostitutes of a world are driven to it by poverty.[21] In New York there are 50,000 prostitutes. Man refused to each a chance to earn easily an honest living and then offered to her the gilded hand of vice. A few years ago the good sisters of New York opened a foundling hospital and in the first six months 1300 little babies were brought to their doors.[22] All of which shows that 1300 women were not protected. Men may protect their wives and daughters, but they take no care of other men's wives and daughters.

Here changes come rapidly, and it may be that the daughter of some of my hearers may yet come to join these classes through the stress of want. I beseech you to help to lift woman to a place in which she can help herself in the battle of life. She needs the ballot as a protection to herself; it is a means and not an end. Until she gets it she will not be satisfied, nor will she be protected. Labor, then, every woman of you, till she gets the right to a voice in making the laws that apply to her as well as to men.

Miss Anthony was repeatedly applauded.

～ *Milwaukee Sentinel*, 20 March 1876.

1. John Bright (1811–1889), a member of Parliament almost continuously from 1843 until his death, championed the Reform Act of 1867. In the 1840s, however, Bright, as a leader of the Anti-Corn Law League, argued that free trade and lower-priced bread were more important at that moment than parliamentary reform and wider suffrage. He tried in many contentious meetings to bridge the divide between the middle-class league and the working-class Chartists, telling Chartists that they needed cheap bread and could wait for the franchise, while telling the league that it must support parliamentary reform. Neither side was convinced. In 1858, Bright made the reform of parliamentary elections one of his major goals. (*DNB*; Norman Longmate, *The Breadstealers: The Fight against the Corn Laws, 1838–1846* [New York, 1984], 81–95; Herman Ausubel, *John Bright, Victorian Reformer* [New York, 1966], 11–12.)

2. George Thompson (1804–1878) was a fiery British orator who toured the United States to oppose slavery.

3. Although these were not the precise terms of the Reform Act of 1867, SBA refers to Mill's failed attempt to amend the bill to enfranchise women on the same terms as men.

4. Robert Lowe (1811–1892) was a vociferous opponent of extending suffrage through the Reform Act of 1867 and a strong supporter of the Education Act of 1870 to expand elementary education. (Michael Stenton and Stephen Lees, eds., *Who's Who of British Members of Parliament: A Biographical History of the House of Commons* [Atlantic Highlands, N.J., 1976], 1:244; D. W. Sylvester, *Robert Lowe and Education* [Cambridge, England, 1974], 28–29, 118–19.)

5. The antebellum Democratic party, drawing its inspiration from Thomas Jefferson and Andrew Jackson (1767–1845), the seventh president of the United States, defined the franchise as a right of white and male citizens which should not be restricted to property owners.

6. SBA credits Horace Greeley with wooing traditional Democratic voters into the new Republican party when it superceded the Whig party in the 1850s.

7. The National Labor Union drew up its own platform in advance of the Democratic National Convention in 1868 and pledged to support only those candidates who endorsed the platform. SBA argues that labor thus influenced the decisions of the major political parties, especially with regard to monetary policy. For her own involvement with the story she tells, see *Papers*, 2:150–52.

8. The Democratic platform favored repaying the national debt in paper currency, but the candidate, Horatio Seymour (1810–1886), advocated that the bonds be repaid in gold. Ulysses S. Grant, the Republican candidate, showed little interest in public finance.

9. Henry Huntley Haight (1825–1878), Democratic governor of California from 1867 to 1871, called out the state militia in June 1871 to put down a strike by Amador County miners. Later that year, he lost his bid for reelection. (*ANB*; Alexander Saxton, *The Indispensable Enemy: Labor and the Anti-Chinese Movement in California* [Berkeley, Calif., 1971], 58, 91; *New York Times*, 26, 27 June 1871.)

10. From May to September 1869, members of the Troy Collar Laundry Union went on strike for higher wages, but the workers returned to their jobs without a raise and with their union dissolved. SBA met with Kate Mullaney (1845?–1906), an organizer of the union and the strike, in Troy, New York, in 1870. For an earlier telling of this event, see *Papers*, 2:325. (*Rev.*, 17 February 1870, *Film*, 2:264; Carole Turbin, *Working Women of Collar City: Gender, Class, and Community in Troy, New York, 1864–86* [Urbana, Ill., 1992], 94–97, 107, 155–63.)

11. In fact, both Iowa and Minnesota voted to enfranchise black men in 1868, before the Fifteenth Amendment required it.

12. On 1 August 1865; see *Papers*, 1:552.

13. The first senators from Kansas, these were James Henry Lane (1814–1866) and Samuel Clarke Pomeroy (1816–1891). Both Republicans, they entered the Senate together in 1861. Lane served until his death; Pomeroy was replaced in 1873. (*BDAC.*)

14. Hiram Rhoades Revels (1827?–1901) was a minister of the African Methodist Episcopal Church in Leavenworth when SBA lived there in 1865. A resident of Mississippi after the war, he was elected to the state senate in 1869 and to the United States Senate in 1870. (*ANB.*)

15. Built in 1856 to serve proslavery guests, the Planters' Hotel at Shawnee and Main streets was an elegant and popular establishment in Leavenworth.

16. During the Woman's Crusade in Rochester in the spring of 1874. After the police began to enforce the Sunday closing law, antiprohibition forces presented an extensive petition opposing the closing of beer and ale rooms on the Sabbath. (McKelvey, *Rochester: The Flower City*, 140–41; Wittenmyer, *History of the Temperance Crusade*, 518–20.)

17. Women in Chicago gathered sixteen thousand names on a petition to the city council against the repeal of a law requiring saloons to close on Sunday. When fifty women left the council's chambers on 16 March 1874, they were met by a mob in the corridors and nearby streets, and with help from the police, they walked through the crowd back to the Clark Street Methodist Episcopal Church. The council repealed the law. (Andreas, *History of Chicago*, 3:857–58; Wittenmyer, *History of the Temperance Crusade*, 399–405.)

18. Amanda Tomlinson Bower Belknap, the wife of Secretary of War William Worth Belknap (1829–1890) and a queen of Washington society, was discovered in early March 1876 to be supporting her social supremacy with bribes paid her for the privilege of controlling an Indian trading post. Although the secretary rushed to resign his office on 2 March, the Democratic House of Representatives went ahead with impeachment proceedings to expose the corruption of the Grant administration. In April 1876, ECS made Mrs. Belknap the centerpiece of her speech "Women in Washington," about the "butterflies" who were "creature[s] of man's fancy" but doomed to extinction. (William S. McFeely, *Grant: A Biography* [New York, 1981], 427–36; *ANB*, s.v. "Belknap, William Worth"; *Film*, 18:763.)

19. Wisconsin's state supreme court ruled in February 1876 against admitting Rhoda Lavinia Goodell to its bar. The practice of law by a woman, the chief justice wrote, would be "treason against" the law of nature, not to be encouraged by public policy. At Goodell's behest, the legislature passed a law a year later on the admission of women to all of the state's courts, and in 1879, Goodell gained admission to the supreme court. (Catherine B. Cleary, "Lavinia Goodell, First Woman Lawyer in Wisconsin," *Wisconsin Magazine of History* 74 [Summer 1991]: 242–71; Ada M. Bittenbender, "Woman in Law," in *Woman's Work in America*, ed. Annie Nathan Meyer [New York, 1891], 218–44; In re Motion to Admit Miss Lavinia Goodell to the Bar of This Court, 39 Wisconsin Reports 232 [1875].)

20. In Washington Territory, during her tour of the Northwest in 1871.

21. Lecky, *History of European Morals*, 2:286.

22. On New York prostitutes and this report of Sister Irene and the New York Foundling Hospital, see notes above at 12 April 1875.

## 74   From the Diary of SBA

[*7–11 May 1876*]

SUNDAY, MAY 7, 1876. Into Rochester—<u>Home</u> arrived at 4.30 P.M— found sister Mary, niece Louise & nephew Wendell[1] at Depot—with bright welcome & an equally warm one from Mother at No 7— & then Mary Dobbin[2] Ditto— brother Aaron up at Batavia—& Mary & Sarah & William Hallowell[3] called—to welcome me—

    1. Helen Louise Mosher (1862–?) and her brother Wendell Phillips Mosher (1858–1946) were the younger children of Hannah and Eugene Mosher. They moved into 7 Madison Street with their father when their mother left for Leavenworth and Denver. Louise, as she was known, still attended school. Wendell left Rochester for Chicago late in 1876 or early 1877 to learn book-keeping at the Albert F. Dickinson Seed Company. (Chamberlain and Clarenbach, *Descendants of Hugh Mosher*, 312, 550; Aldridge, *Laphams in America*, 223; SBA diary, 4, 6 April, 7 September, 2 November, 13 December 1877, *Film*, 19:12ff.)

    2. Mary Dobbins was a servant in the Anthony house. SBA first mentioned her in August 1873, on an occasion when she and Mary "swept parlors & bedroom" together. Dobbins continued in the family's employ until her marriage to John Joseph Birmingham in September 1878. The couple moved to Buffalo, and SBA wrote ungraciously in her diary, "It seems a great relief to have the change from the reign of Mary Dobbins over the kitchen—" (SBA diary, 8 August 1873, 25–27 September 1878, *Film*, 16:617ff, 19:791ff.)

    3. Mary Hallowell was joined by her husband, William R. Hallowell (1816– 1882), a businessman in Rochester, and Sarah L. Kirby Hallowell Willis (1818–1914), a sister of Amy Post and another Rochester reformer. In 1873, Sarah Willis was a founding officer of Rochester's Women Taxpayers' Association. (Hewitt, *Women's Activism and Social Change*, passim; Peck, *History of Rochester and Monroe County, N.Y.*, 2:1243–44; *Quaker Genealogy*, 3:483, 489, 507; *Papers*, 1:81.)

MONDAY, MAY 8, 1876. Saw brother A[aron] only at Dinner—very bland & sociable—it is such a pity—his delusion & snare with any woman save his <u>own</u> <u>wife</u> dear Gula— Can we ever get used to it so as not to feel cut & hurt—

TUESDAY, MAY 9, 1876. Left Rochester at 5.30 P.M—last night—arrived New York—at 7 this A.M— Found Mrs Gage at Mrs Loziers all ready for work— Mrs Blake had <u>Tin</u> wedding reception this eve—[1] I went with Mrs L—rain poured— Mrs Gage did not go [*added later*] Merritt[2] & Mary L's boy born this day—weighed 10 lbs—light hair—blue eyes—

1. Lillie Blake celebrated the tenth anniversary of her marriage to Grinfill Blake.

2. Jacob Merritt Anthony (1834–1900), the youngest of SBA's siblings, known always as Merritt, and Mary Luther Anthony had lived in Fort Scott, Kansas, since 1869. According to a later entry in her diary, SBA learned on 26 June of the birth of their fourth child, Luther Burt Anthony, known as Burt. (Anthony, *Anthony Genealogy*, 173, 189; Andreas, *History of Kansas*, 2:1076; *Woman's Journal*, 23 June 1900.)

WEDNESDAY, MAY 10, 1876. National Woman Suffrage Association Masonic Hall—New York—[1]

small audience—and no work systematized & ready— Mrs S. J. Spencer the real helper—very efficient—& earnest—Julia & Abby Smith present in P.M.—terrible pouring rain in evening—

1. At 114 East Thirteenth Street. Matilda Gage presided at the National's meeting, and Lillie Blake presided at the New York State meeting. For coverage of both events, see *Film*, 18:768–76. One among the many resolutions called upon women to hold protest meetings on the Fourth of July "to declare themselves no longer bound to obey the laws in whose making they have had no voice" and "to demand justice for the women of this land." (*Film*, 18:772–73.)

THURSDAY, MAY 11, 1876. New York State W.S. Association Masonic Hall—New York—

Pleasant day—but audiences still small all day—evening larger—but got good reports in papers—the [one?] result of Convention—

⚝ The Standard Diary 1876, n.p., SBA Papers, DLC. Letters in square brackets expand abbreviations or indicate uncertain words.

75    SBA to Laura De Force Gordon

New York May 15th 1876.

My Dear Laura

Our National Woman Suffrage ↑Centennial↓ Head Quarters are at 705 Arch street—Philadelphia—Penn—[1] Mrs M. Joslyn Gage—Mrs Stanton, myself & others—we hope Mrs Gordon—will be on hand to receive, entertain, & instruct—visitors—and we hope all the friends will report themselves at our W.S. Head Quarters— Lodgings & meals can be had in the building at reasonable cost—

We shall hold meeting of protest in our rooms on the 4th July—at 12 noon—to shout our protest against the denial of our individual right of consent—and ↑shall↓ very soon send out an appeal to the woman suffrage women of the country—for every state—county—township— to assemble in their respective localities at same hour of same day—to join with us in spirit—& to mail their protests—written or printed to us—at earliest moment—[2]

Then at a later date—we mean to hold in a large Hall—a Mass Convention—to issue our ↑womans↓ Declaration of Independence— now do you make ↑rouse↓ the women to make the welkins ring on your pacific slope— are you coming over— Hope you can— Wish we here had money—but we haven't—can barely get through ↑each↓ with our ↑her↓ own expenses— affectionately—

     SBA

I am just appointed Editor of the woman suffrage department of an immense Encyclopedia—the grandest ever published—am to give the defenition to woman suffrage—& biographical sketches of all the lead- ing women in it—& I want yours—& you must write it—no puff—just the bare facts—of your life work in the fewest words possible—not over one square of your newspaper—that is all ↑the space↓ they have given me—and such a nothing in it— I have just been to the man publishing it[3]—& pointed out to him how far from full justice any man could define our ↑the↓ aim of our movement—or ourselves—& he at saw the fact—& made me the sole umpire in the matter—so send me on your briefest—& yet best statement of the main points of your life work— Let me hear from you once more—it seems an age since I retired from movement work— ↑I↓ am out of debt—thank God—& free once more to go ahead—[4] Please don't mention the fact of my editorship to any of the Boston ring—so it will go back there— How are you— S. B. Anthony

❧ ALS, on NWSA letterhead for 1875, Laura D. Gordon Collection, CU-BANC.

1. This proved to be a premature announcement. SBA thought she had finally settled the arrangements on 13 May, when she signed a contract with Mrs. W. L. Webster to rent rooms found by Edward M. Davis at this address, not thinking that under Pennsylvania law a married woman could not sign a contract without her husband's consent. Word that Mr. Webster objected reached SBA while she was en route to Boston on 16 May. Matilda Gage and a committee of the Citizens' Suffrage Association began the search for rooms in February but had nothing large enough lined up before the National's May meeting. (SBA diary, 13, 16 May 1876, *Film*, 18:516ff.) There is an incomplete account of the search for rooms in *History*, 3:16–18. See also M. J. Gage to Isabella B. Hooker, 1, 4, 14, 16 February, 7 March 1876, Isabella Hooker Collection, CtHSD; telegram from E. M. Davis to SBA in *New York Herald*, 12 May 1876, *Film*, 18:769; and *Philadelphia Inquirer*, 22 March 1876.

2. Dated 1 June 1876, the multipurpose appeal described the National Woman Suffrage Parlors, announced plans to issue a Declaration of Rights on the Fourth of July, and urged "the women of the whole land, on that day, in meetings, in parlors, in kitchens, wherever they may be," to join in the protest. It also mentioned plans to publish a history of woman's rights. (*Film*, 18:790–92.)

3. Alvin Jewett Johnson (1827–1884) made his name and fortune as a publisher of atlases before he launched *Johnson's New Universal Cyclopaedia, A Scientific and Popular Treasury of Useful Knowledge* in 1874. He had published two of the projected four volumes and was completing the third, when SBA met with him on this date. All of SBA's contributions—those she wrote and those she solicited from others—went into the fourth volume. (She misunderstood this for a time and thought she could recommend names to be added to volume three.) Volume four consists of alphabetical entries from *S* to *Z* and a large alphabetical appendix. Within the first part, SBA's initials appear on entries for ECS and the doctor Mary F. Thomas as well as on the long entry "Woman's Rights," which she and ECS wrote together. SBA solicited at least three other entries in that section. Most of her work is evident in the appendix. Her initials follow the entries for Mathilde Anneke, Amelia Bloomer, Olympia Brown, Sarah and Angelina Grimké, Abby Hutchinson, Clemence Lozier,

Virginia Minor, Lydia Mott, Ernestine Rose, and Sara Spencer. Through her efforts to identify significant women and find writers for the entries, she added at least twenty more biographies of women noted for advancing woman's rights to this section. (*Funeral Services of Alvin J. Johnson: At No. 9 East Sixty-fourth Street, New York, Saturday, April 26, 1884* [N.p., 1884]; SBA diary, 15 May 1876, SBA to Isabella B. Hooker, 3 August 1876, and SBA to Caroline H. Dall, 5 August 1876, *Film*, 18:516ff, 951–54, 961–65.)

4. On 10 March 1876, SBA noted in her diary that she sent the last payment on her loan from Mary Anthony, "which closes up Revolution debt—"

## 76   ᔦ   FROM THE DIARY OF SBA

[*24–28 May 1876*]

WEDNESDAY, MAY 24, 1876. In Phila— Spent day in hunting rooms[1]— in P.M. attended Radical Club at 333. Walnut st—[2] Mr Davis absent— Mich. Copper mines— met Judge Westbrook[3]—& with him fixed upon 1431 Chestnut as rooms—

Letter from Sister Mary—fear Sister Hannah is not improving—& hence that she must be losing—

1. For the Centennial Headquarters. Matilda Gage discovered the loss of the rooms on Arch Street when she arrived in Philadelphia on 16 May but, as she told her son, waited for SBA to solve the problem. The Chestnut Street location consisted of a large parlor for meetings, other rooms for social conversation, and sleeping rooms. (M. J. Gage to Thomas C. Gage, 22 and 23 May 1876, Gage Collection, MCR-S.)

2. For coverage, see *Film*, 18:788–89.

3. Richard Brodhead Westbrook (1820–1899), a New York lawyer, writer, and former minister, was the husband of Henrietta Paine Westbrook (1835–1909), the recording secretary of the National Woman Suffrage Association in 1875. Richard Westbrook was a freethinker and later president of the American Secular Union. Henrietta Westbrook, who changed her name to Payne, circulated and perhaps wrote one of the many protests about celebrating the Centennial while women lacked suffrage. She graduated from the Woman's Medical College of Pennsylvania in 1881. (Sidney Warren, *American Freethought, 1860–1914* [New York, 1943], 171–72; Allibone Supplement; New York City directory, 1877 to 1879; *Philadelphia Inquirer*, 22 March 1876; *New York Times*, 17 October 1909; with assistance of Joanne Grossman, Archives, MCP Hahnemann University, Philadelphia.)

THURSDAY, MAY 25, 1876. 1431 Chestnut st—Phila Pa National Woman Suffrage Parlors— slept in them for the first time this night— wrote Sister Mary— Mr & Mrs Judge Westbrook called—

FRIDAY, MAY 26, 1876. Dear Lucretia Mott called at 2 P.M.—really our first call—so her name must go first into Centennial Autograph Book—[1] went with her to see the English Gentlemen—Wilson & Gledstone[2]— on Legislation on Social evil—

1. This leather-bound book, now at the Onondaga Historical Association, Syracuse, N.Y., was expressly made for the National Woman Suffrage Association to be signed by callers at the Centennial Headquarters and any other supporter who sent in her signature for mounting on the pages.

2. Henry Joseph Wilson (1833–1914) and James Paterson Gledstone, both prominent in the British campaign to repeal the Contagious Diseases Act, toured the United States on behalf of the Federation for the Abolition of the State Regulation of Vice. SBA may have heard them at a private gathering; in their *Report of a Visit to the United States*, Wilson and Gledstone noted a meeting in a house "one evening, where we had an informal but useful conversation" (25). (Stenton and Lees, *Who's Who of British Members of Parliament*, 2:377; Allibone Supplement.)

SATURDAY, MAY 27, 1876. Messrs Wilson & Gledstone at, 11— Only Mr Wilson called—gave account of English Laws for Licensing & registering Prostitution—most demoralizing—[1] going to New York & Boston—& then return here June 12th— Mr G. & self went to Musical Fund Hall to meeting to open exposition Sundays[2]

1. One in a series of public discussions scheduled at the Centennial Headquarters, interest in this event was, according to the *Report of a Visit to the United States*, "increased by the presence of the venerable Mrs. Lucretia Mott, who spoke with great earnestness of the importance of our mission" (25–26).

2. Although SBA wrote "Mr," she went to the meeting with Matilda Gage. It was but one of many meetings to protest the Centennial Commissioners' decision to close the exposition on Sundays. Secularists and working people objected to the government enforcing a religious holiday and thereby excluding wage earners from the fairgrounds. (Boston *Index*, 4, 18 May 1876.)

SUNDAY, MAY 28, 1876. Did not go to Church—wrote & felt unsettled all day— at eve—Mrs G. & self called on the Purvis'—Robert in Washington the daughters—Hattie & Georgie at home[1]—both feeble—

1. Robert Purvis (1810–1898), a prominent African-American abolitionist

and one of the few who argued that the rights of his daughters were as important as those of his sons, was a regular participant in meetings of the National Woman Suffrage Association. (*DANB*; *ANB*.) Harriet Purvis (1839–?) and Georgiana B. Purvis (c. 1850–1877), who lived in their father's house outside Philadelphia, were heirs to their parents' interest in equal rights for women and African Americans. Hattie, who was still alive in 1903, held office in the Pennsylvania and national suffrage movements until the turn of the century. (Garrison, *Letters*, 5:96n; Rosalyn Terborg-Penn, *African American Women in the Struggle for the Vote, 1850–1920* [Bloomington, Ind., 1998], passim; Register of Interments in Friends' Fair Hill Burial Ground, PHi.)

&#x224B; The Standard Diary 1876, n.p., SBA Papers, DLC.

## 77 &#x223D;  SBA to Sarah Langdon Williams[1]

Philadelphia, Pa., June 7th 1876.

My Dear Mrs Williams

Do send your Ballot Box to our Centennial Parlors—that I may see what you are saying. I hope you can get our circular in this months issue[2]—Mrs Gage sent you a copy, she told me, some days ago—also to the Boston Woman's Journal—but, of course, that righteous sheet will not allow our name to deface its fair page—[3] Do you write up the duty of every woman to hoist her flag of Equal rights flag to the mast head— Are you coming to the big show—it is simply wonderful—no words can describe it— Our <u>largest</u> <u>meeting</u> will be the 19th & 20th of July—[4]

Cant you send us some little emblem for Ohio—for Toledo Woman Suffrage Society— We have just ordered a dozzen little bits of flags to put in the Chandelier—to have mottoes printed on them— Lucretia Mott was in & said put on one—"<u>Call no man master</u>"— "These are the times that try women's souls"—is to be another—have a different expression on every flag— Mrs Stanton is not here yet—but will be next week—& we shall feel so much stronger & certain that we are right when she comes—

And Mrs Williams—will you not gather up as many $5. contributions as possible & send on—for the History—as well as smaller or larger contributions to help defray our heavy expenses here—

I feel that I must go through this terrible strain this centennial summer—though neither my purse nor my head, heart or hands are at all equal to it— My dear sister is still in Denver—hoping & hoping to get strength to overcome her cough—but I <u>fear</u> & <u>fear</u>—& long to spend these summer days with her—lest they may be the very last ones she may be permitted to stay on earth— But duty says <u>stand by your guns</u> at Philadelphia—so I am here— And I hope the friends not compelled to stand here at the front during these broiling days—will send us their sympathy & material aid— Affectionately

Susan B. Anthony

ALS, on Centennial Headquarters letterhead, Mss. Coll. 18—Women's Movement Papers, Local History and Genealogy Department, OT.

1. Sarah R. Langdon Williams (1822–1902), a former teacher, a widow, and a journalist, edited the new monthly paper the *Ballot Box*, first published in April 1876 by the Toledo Woman Suffrage Association in Ohio. Williams joined the Toledo association at its founding in 1869. Despite a tendency on the part of Ohio's state association to identify with the American Woman Suffrage Association, the Toledo society allied itself with the National. Williams served on the executive committee of the National from 1873 to 1879. (*In Search of Our Past: Women of Northwest Ohio* [Toledo, Ohio, 1987], 1:51–53; Clark Waggoner, ed., *History of the City of Toledo and Lucas County, Ohio* [New York, 1888], 641, 654; *History*, 3:503–4.)

2. This was the appeal dated 1 June 1876.

3. The *Woman's Journal* neither printed the circular nor mentioned the Centennial Headquarters.

4. To commemorate the anniversary of the Seneca Falls woman's rights convention.

## 78   SARAH LANGDON WILLIAMS TO SBA

Toledo, O., June 10, 1876.

. . . There is a power invisible which is working through all this. . . . I have thought of some appropriate mottoes for the little banners. Give us for Ohio, "We know we are right"; also, "No compromise with wrongs." I wish you would send me two or three more copies of the protest to send away.[1]

Sarah R. L. Williams

Toledo *Ballot Box*, August 1876.

1. By the protest Williams means a text circulated by the National association since early May that indicted the United States for failing to realize a
republican form of government and *"protest[ed]* before the assembled nations
of the world against the centennial celebration, as an occasion for *National*
rejoicing." Enfranchisement of the nation's women, it concluded, "is the only
act of justice . . . worthy of the occasion you propose to celebrate." Americans
were asked to sign the protest and return it to Edward Davis. The papers of
ECS, SBA, and Matilda Gage say nothing about the writing of this text, and it
differs both from the one adopted by the National in January and from that
issued on the Fourth of July. SBA had it in hand at a meeting in Chicago on 2
May. (*Protest. National Woman Suffrage Association. To the Men of the United
States in Celebration of the Nation's Centennial Birthday, July 4th, 1876,* c. 1
May 1876, and Special Meeting of the Illinois Woman Suffrage Association, 2
May 1876, *Film,* 18:764–67.)

## 79 &#x223d; ELIZABETH BOYNTON HARBERT TO SBA

Evanston, Ill., June 16, 1876.

Weary and dusty, having just returned from the convention, I attempt to write you a line.[1] Surely our cause was effectually advanced by
means of agitation, at least. . . . The varied influences at work did not
seem to conflict.[2]

&#x223d; *Lizzie B. Harbert*

&#x223d; Toledo *Ballot Box,* August 1876.

1. Pursuant to the National's decision to make a third attempt to place a
woman suffrage plank into a national party platform, Harbert and Sara Spencer attended the Republican National Convention in Cincinnati, carrying
with them a memorial written by Matilda Gage and SBA that incorporated
language for the platform. As presented to the delegates, the proposed plank
read: "Resolved, That the right to the use of the ballot inheres in the citizens
of the United States." According to Gage, who accused SBA of sabotaging her
work on the memorial by omitting her name and sending the wrong text, it
should have gone on to say, "and we pledge ourselves to secure the exercise of
this right to all citizens, irrespective of sex." (The National later circulated the
longer text with Gage's name restored.) Harbert and Spencer appeared before
the committee on resolutions, chaired by Joseph R. Hawley; George F. Hoar
presented the memorial to the full convention; and Spencer followed with a
ten-minute speech to the delegates. (*Film,* 18:814–21; *Ballot Box,* July 1876;

M. J. Gage to Thomas C. Gage, 4, 16, 20, 28 June 1876, Gage Collection, MCR-S.)

2. She refers to the presence of representatives from the American association at the convention. Henry Blackwell told them to rewrite their plank, "to add 'irrespective of sex'"; otherwise "the public would never dream that women were included." He also observed that Spencer "looked well & did no harm." (H. B. Blackwell to L. Stone, 16 June 1876, in Wheeler, *Loving Warriors*, 254; *Woman's Journal*, 24 June 1876.)

## 80 ⇝ SBA TO ELIZABETH BOYNTON HARBERT

Philadelphia, Pa., June 19th 1876.

My Dear Lizzie B. H.

Was glad to get your hurried note—but the newspapers had told all the good accomplished by you & Mrs Spencer— I really believe you two young women <u>got more concessions</u>—than any of <u>older heads could</u> possibly have extorted— I imagine the <u>Plank</u> is <u>Harry Blackwells very words</u>—it sounds just like him—[1] At our National meeting at New York—Delegates were appointed—no A <u>Campaign Committee</u>[2]—& we—that is Mrs <u>Gage & I</u>—delegated the persons to go to Cincinatti— & also to St Louis—[3] Now the latter are—Phobe Couzens—Rev. O. Brown—Virginia L. Minor & Eliz. A. Meriwether—[4] Miss Couzens left here last night—Olympia writes she will go— She is now at her Sisters[5]—227—Leavitt street—Chicago—& will go from thence to St Louis— Mrs Stanton got her Thursday last—& with Mrs Gage has the address to the Democratic Convention done & it is ↑in↓ printers hands— they are now grinding out our <u>Declaration of Rights</u>—for the 4th of July—[6] ↑Will send both to you so soon as done↓ You did splendidly at C. both of you—it was too bad that both should have had to (<u>seemingly</u>) neglect babies to be there—still it is good too—[7] do send us a flag or banner with some nice inscription on it— I wish you could pop in to our receptions—Tuesday & Friday evenings— You see the [*written in margin*] Journal doesn't know we are here

⇝ AL, on Centennial Headquarters letterhead, Box 2, Elizabeth Harbert Collection, CSmH.

1. After praising "Republican legislatures" for advances in woman's rights,

the plank concluded: "The honest demands of this class of citizens for additional rights, privileges, and immunities should be treated with respectful
consideration." Henry Blackwell did take credit for the text. "Our resolution," he wrote his wife, "was adopted except the last clause for which
'respectful consideration' was substituted." To readers of the *Woman's Journal* he opined that the platform was "far in advance of that of 1872" and "an
important indication of progress." Sarah Williams pointed out in the *Ballot
Box* that right after the party promised "respectful consideration" in 1872,
Republican officials arrested SBA for voting; the editor of the Detroit paper
*Truth for the People* pronounced the plank "the sneaking homily of dema-
gogues discoursing upon the matter of the etiquette due to woman civilly
asking the possession of rights." (*National Party Platforms*, 54; H. B. Blackwell
to L. Stone, 16 June 1876, in Wheeler, *Loving Warriors*, 254; *Woman's
Journal*, 24 June 1876; *Ballot Box*, July 1876; *Truth for the People*, n.d., in M.
J. Gage scrapbooks, MCR-S.)

    2. For members of the campaign committee, see appendix B.

    3. To the Democratic National Convention 27 June. Phoebe Couzins ad-
dressed the convention and presented the National's memorial. (*Film*, 18:830–
40.)

    4. Elizabeth Avery Meriwether (1824–1917) of Memphis, Tennessee, ap-
pealed to the Democratic convention on behalf "of the women of the South,"
seeking a pledge from the party to secure "the right to equality before the law"
to every citizen, "not only to the black men so recently lifted from the condition of slavery, but to the 20,000,000 women of America." The appeal was
consigned by Elizabeth Saxon of New Orleans. Meriwether, who was the
author of romanticized tales about slavery and the Old South and the wife of
a Ku Klux Klansman, took a particular interest in women's economic and legal
rights. As a taxpaying owner of property, she had ventured in 1871 to vote in
a local election and succeeded. By 1879 she was a featured speaker at meetings
of the National Woman Suffrage Association. (Kathleen Christine Berkeley,
"Elizabeth Avery Meriwether: 'An Advocate for her Sex': Feminism and
Conservatism in the Post-Civil War South," *Tennessee Historical Quarterly*
43 [Winter 1984]: 390–407; *History*, 3:153–54, 180n, 181n, 184n, 193, 822;
*Memphis Avalanche*, 25 June 1876, in M. J. Gage scrapbooks, MCR-S.)

    5. Oella Brown Schuyler (1837–1921) attended both Mount Holyoke and
Antioch colleges with her sister Olympia before marrying William H. Schuyler
in 1858. By 1880 she was living in Ann Arbor, where her daughter Orielle
attended the University of Michigan. In her new home, Schuyler was active in
the local woman suffrage movement. (Charlotte Coté, *Olympia Brown: The
Battle for Equality* [Racine, Wis., 1988]; University of Michigan, *Catalogue of
Graduates, Non-Graduates, Officers, and Members of the Faculties, 1837–1921*
[Ann Arbor, Mich., 1923]; *NCBB*, May 1880, *Film*, 21:166; with assistance of
Peter Carini, Mount Holyoke College Archives, and Scott Sanders, Archivist,
Antiochiana, Antioch College.)

6. According to Gage, who was still fuming over her experience writing the memorial to the Republican party with SBA, she and ECS were each working alone "<u>before</u> we begin to combine." Sara Spencer arrived to join the writing team on 23 June, "putting her idea of Declaration & protest on paper," according to SBA's notation in her diary, and on the next day, taking the drafts by ECS and Gage and writing her own text from them. On 28 June, Gage described the writing as "a <u>very hard task</u>. I have been made nearly ill over it, but we hope to have it done to-day." By 2 July, the text was ready for Spencer to engross, while ECS, SBA, and Gage prepared printed copies for mailing. (M. J. Gage to Thomas C. Gage, 16, 20, 28 June 1876, Gage Collection, MCR-S; SBA diary, *Film*, 18:516ff.)

7. Both Spencer and Harbert were the mothers of young children, but SBA also alludes to the common claim that voting would cause mothers to abandon their babies. Sara Spencer regaled the National's meeting in May 1876 with a story about trying to vote in 1871: "I returned home in thirty minutes," she told the audience. "Nothing had happened to the baby in that time. The same day I left the baby a whole hour to go to market, and nobody said a word about that." (*Film*, 18:768.)

## 81 ⤳ ECS TO MATHILDE FRANZISKA ANNEKE

Philadelphia, Pa., July 1<sup>st</sup> 1876.

Dear Friend

We intend to issue Woman's Declaration of Independence on the 4<sup>th</sup> of July. It is to be lithographed, framed, & signed by those who inaugurated the movement for woman's enfranchisement, & the most prominent worker in our cause in each state. If you wish to represent your state send your name to us plainly written on a slip of thin paper, as soon as possible as we are in haste to complete the work    Sincerely yours

⤳ *Elizabeth Cady Stanton*

⤳ ALS, on Centennial Headquarters letterhead, Anneke Papers, WHi.

## 82 ⚟ Declaration of Rights of the Women of the United States

[4 July 1876]

DECLARATION OF RIGHTS
OF THE
WOMEN OF THE UNITED STATES
BY THE
NATIONAL WOMAN SUFFRAGE ASSOCIATION,
JULY 4TH, 1876.

While the Nation is buoyant with patriotism, and all hearts are attuned to praise, it is with sorrow we come to strike the one discordant note, on this hundredth anniversary of our country's birth. When subjects of Kings, Emperors, and Czars, from the Old World, join in our National Jubilee, shall the women of the Republic refuse to lay their hands with benedictions on the nation's head? Surveying America's Exposition, surpassing in magnificence those of London, Paris, and Vienna,[1] shall we not rejoice at the success of the youngest rival among the nations of the earth? May not our hearts, in unison with all, swell with pride at our great achievements as a people; our free speech, free press, free schools, free church, and the rapid progress we have made in material wealth, trade, commerce, and the inventive arts? And we do rejoice, in the success thus far, of our experiment of self-government. Our faith is firm and unwavering in the broad principles of human rights, proclaimed in 1776, not only as abstract truths, but as the corner stones of a republic. Yet, we cannot forget, even in this glad hour, that while all men of every race, and clime, and condition, have been invested with the full rights of citizenship, under our hospitable flag, all women still suffer the degradation of disfranchisement.

The history of our country the past hundred years, has been a series of assumptions and usurpations of power over woman, in direct opposition to the principles of just government, acknowledged by the United States at its foundation, which are:

*First.* The natural rights of each individual.

*Second.* The exact equality of these rights.

*Third.* That these rights, when not delegated by the individual, are retained by the individual.

*Fourth.* That no person can exercise the rights of others without delegated authority.

*Fifth.* That the non-use of these rights does not destroy them.[2]

And for the violation of these fundamental principles of our Government, we arraign our rulers on this 4th day of July, 1876,—and these are our

### ARTICLES OF IMPEACHMENT.

*Bills of Attainder* have been passed by the introduction of the word "male" into all the State constitutions, denying to woman the right of suffrage, and thereby making sex a crime—an exercise of power clearly forbidden in Article 1st, Sections 9th and 10th of the United States Constitution.[3]

*The Writ of Habeas Corpus,* the only protection against *lettres de cachet,*[4] and all forms of unjust imprisonment, which the Constitution declares "shall not be suspended, except when in cases of rebellion or invasion, the public safety demands it,"[5] is held inoperative in every State in the Union, in case of a married woman against her husband,—the marital rights of the husband being in all cases primary, and the rights of the wife secondary.[6]

*The Right of Trial by a Jury of One's Peers* was so jealously guarded that States refused to ratify the original Constitution, until it was guaranteed by the 6th Amendment.[7] And yet the women of this nation have never been allowed a jury of their peers—being tried in all cases by men, native and foreign, educated and ignorant, virtuous and vicious. Young girls have been arraigned in our courts for the crime of infanticide; tried, convicted, hung—victims, perchance, of judge, jurors, advocates—while no woman's voice could be heard in their defence. And not only are women denied a jury of their peers, but in some cases, jury trial altogether. During the war, a woman was tried and hung by military law,[8] in defiance of the 5th Amendment, which specifically declares: "no person shall be held to answer for a capital or otherwise infamous crime, unless on a presentment or indictment of a grand jury, except in cases . . . of persons in actual service in time of war." During the last Presidential campaign, a woman, arrested for voting, was denied the protection of a jury, tried, convicted and sentenced to a fine and costs of prosecution, by the absolute power of a judge of the Supreme Court of the United States.[9]

*Taxation Without Representation,* the immediate cause of the rebellion of the Colonies against Great Britain, is one of the grievous wrongs the women of this country have suffered during the century. Deploring war, with all the demoralization that follows in its train, we have been taxed to support standing armies, with their waste of life and wealth. Believing in temperance, we have been taxed to support the vice, crime, and pauperism of the Liquor Traffic. While we suffer its wrongs and abuses infinitely more than man, we have no power to protect our sons against this giant evil. During the Temperance Crusade, mothers were arrested, fined, imprisoned, for even praying and singing in the streets, while men blockade the sidewalks with impunity, even on Sunday, with their military parades and political processions. Believing in honesty, we are taxed to support a dangerous army of civilians, buying and selling the offices of government and sacrificing the best interests of the people. And, moreover, we are taxed to support the very legislators, and judges, who make laws, and render decisions adverse to woman. And for refusing to pay such unjust taxation, the houses, lands, bonds, and stock of women, have been seized and sold within the present year, thus proving Lord Coke's assertion, "that the very act of taxing a man's property without his consent, is, in effect, disfranchising him of every civil right."[10]

*Unequal Codes for Men and Women.* Held by law a perpetual minor, deemed incapable of self-protection, even in the industries of the world, woman is denied equality of rights. The fact of sex, not the quantity or quality of work, in most cases, decides the pay and position; and because of this injustice thousands of fatherless girls are compelled to choose between a life of shame and starvation.

Laws catering to man's vices have created two codes of morals in which penalties are graded according to the political status of the offender. Under such laws, women are fined and imprisoned if found alone in the streets, or in public places of resort, at certain hours. Under the pretence of regulating public morals, police officers seizing the occupants of disreputable houses, march the women in platoons to prison, while the men, partners in their guilt, go free.

While making a show of virtue in forbidding the importation of Chinese women on the Pacific coast for immoral purposes,[11] our rulers, in many states, and even under the shadow of the National Capitol, are now proposing to legalize the sale of American womanhood for the same vile purposes.[12]

*Special Legislation for Woman* has placed us in a most anomalous position. Women invested with the rights of citizens in one section— voters, jurors, office-holders—crossing an imaginary line, are subjects in the next. In some states, a married woman may hold property and transact business in her own name; in others, her earnings belong to her husband. In some states, a woman may testify against her husband, sue and be sued in the courts; in others, she has no redress in case of damage to person, property, or character. In case of divorce, on account of adultery in the husband, the innocent wife is held to possess no right to children, or property, unless by special decree of the court. But in no state of the Union has the wife the right to her own person, or to any part of the joint earnings of the co-partnership, during the life of her husband. In some States women may enter the law schools and practice in the courts; in others they are forbidden. In some universities, girls enjoy equal educational advantages with boys, while many of the proudest institutions in the land deny them admittance, though the sons of China, Japan and Africa are welcomed there.

But the privileges already granted in the several states are by no means secure. The right of suffrage once exercised by women in certain States and Territories, has been denied by subsequent legislation. A bill is now pending in Congress to disfranchise the women of Utah, thus interfering to deprive United States citizens of the same rights, which the Supreme Court has declared the National Government powerless to protect anywhere.[13] Laws passed after years of untiring effort, guaranteeing married women certain rights of property, and mothers the custody of their children, have been repealed in States where we supposed all was safe.[14] Thus have our most sacred rights been made the football of legislative caprice, proving that a power which grants, as a privilege, what by nature is a right, may withhold the same as a penalty, when deeming it necessary for its own perpetuation.

*Representation for Woman* has had no place in the nation's thought. Since the incorporation of the thirteen original states, twenty-four have been admitted to the Union, not one of which has recognized woman's right of self-government. On this birthday of our national liberties, July 4th, 1876, Colorado, like all her elder sisters, comes into the Union, with the invidious word "male" in her Constitution.[15]

*Universal Manhood Suffrage*, by establishing an aristocracy of sex, imposes upon the women of this nation a more absolute and cruel despotism than monarchy; in that, woman finds a political master in her father, husband, brother, son. The aristocracies of the old world are based upon birth, wealth, refinement, education, nobility, brave deeds of chivalry; in this nation, on sex alone; exalting brute force above moral power, vice above virtue, ignorance above education, and the son above the mother who bore him.

*The Judiciary of the Nation* has proved itself but the echo of the party in power, by upholding and enforcing laws that are opposed to the spirit and letter of the Constitution. When the slave power was dominant, the Supreme Court decided that a black man was not a citizen, because he had not the right to vote; and when the Constitution was so amended as to make all persons citizens, the same high tribunal decided that a woman, though a citizen, had not the right to vote.[16] Such vacillating interpretations of constitutional law unsettle our faith in judicial authority, and undermine the liberties of the whole people.

*These Articles of Impeachment Against Our Rulers* we now submit to the impartial judgment of the people.

To all these wrongs and oppressions woman has not submitted in silence and resignation. From the beginning of the century, when Abigail Adams, the wife of one President and the mother of another, said, "we will not hold ourselves bound to obey laws in which we have no voice or representation,"[17] until now, woman's discontent has been steadily increasing, culminating nearly thirty years ago in a simultaneous movement among the women of the nation, demanding the right of suffrage. In making our just demands, a higher motive than the pride of sex inspires us; we feel that national safety and stability depend on the complete recognition of the broad principles of our government. Woman's degraded, helpless position is the weak point in our institutions to-day; a disturbing force everywhere, severing family ties, filling our asylums with the deaf, the dumb, the blind, our prisons with criminals, our cities with drunkenness and prostitution, our homes with disease and death.

It was the boast of the founders of the republic, that the rights for which they contended, were the rights of human nature. If these rights are ignored in the case of one half the people, the nation is surely preparing for its own downfall. Governments try themselves. The recognition of a governing and a governed class is incompatible with the first principles of freedom. Woman has not been a heedless spectator of the events of this century, nor a dull listener to the grand arguments for the equal rights of humanity. From the earliest history of our country, woman has shown equal devotion with man to the cause of freedom, and has stood firmly by his side in its defence. Together, they have made this country what it is. Woman's wealth, thought and labor have cemented the stones of every monument man has reared to liberty.

And now, at the close of a hundred years, as the hour hand of the great clock that marks the centuries points to 1876, we declare our faith in the principles of self-government; our full equality with man in natural rights; that woman was made first for her own happiness, with the absolute right to herself—to all the opportunities and advantages life affords, for her complete development; and we deny that dogma of the centuries, incorporated in the codes of all nations—that woman was made for man—her best interests, in all cases, to be sacrificed to his will.

We ask of our rulers, at this hour, no special favors, no special privileges, no special legislation. We ask justice, we ask equality, we ask that all the civil and political rights that belong to citizens of the United States, be guaranteed to us and our daughters forever.

&#x22FE; Circular, National Woman Suffrage Association, *Declaration of Rights of the Women of the United States . . . July 4th, 1876* (N.p., n.d.).

1. In London in 1862, Paris in 1867, and Vienna in 1873.

2. Matilda Gage created this list of principles for her congressional testimony in favor of woman suffrage in the District of Columbia in January 1876, and she used it again in the call to the National's annual meeting in May. (*History*, 3:12; *Film*, 18:761.)

3. The ninth section bars Congress from passing any bills of attainder or ex post facto laws, and the tenth extends the prohibition to the states. This point was central to the argument made by Francis and Virginia Minor since 1869. In the words of their brief to the Supreme Court, the states inflicted on women "the bar of perpetual disfranchisement, where no crime or offense is alleged or pretended, and without 'due process of law.'" This amounted to "a 'bill of

attainder' of the most odious and oppressive character." (*History*, 2:408–9, 720.)

4. Official letters authorizing imprisonment without trial.

5. U.S. Const., art. I, sec. 9.

6. The authors raise one of the residual problems of coverture, pointing out that the husband's common law right to confine his wife took precedence over a married woman's individual right to obtain a writ of habeas corpus. For differing views of how courts treated this conflict of rights, see Rollin C. Hurd, *A Treatise on the Right of Personal Liberty, and on the Writ of Habeas Corpus*, 2d ed. (Albany, N.Y., 1876), 21–35, 449–52, and Hendrik Hartog, *Man and Wife in America: A History* (Cambridge, Mass., 2000), 150–52.

7. Within the Bill of Rights, adopted after the Constitution was ratified.

8. Mary Jenkins Surratt (1823–1865), considered on slim evidence to be a co-conspirator with John Wilkes Booth in the plot to assassinate Abraham Lincoln, was tried before a military commission rather than a civil court. Surratt's lawyers obtained a writ of habeas corpus on the grounds that civilians could not be tried before such a commission in peacetime, but General Winfield Scott Hancock refused to turn over the prisoner, and President Andrew Johnson suspended the writ of habeas corpus. Surratt was hanged in July 1865. (*NAW*; *ANB*.)

9. That is, SBA.

10. Like the quotation from Lord Coke at 31 October 1873, above, this one uses the words of James Otis, who referred to Lord Coke while discussing taxation of the colonies. Again the authors' source was likely Charles Sumner's "Equal Rights of All," in Sumner, *Works*, 10:164.

11. On 3 March 1875, President Grant signed a bill outlawing the importation of Asian prostitutes. (Andrew Gyory, *Closing the Gate: Race, Politics, and the Chinese Exclusion Act* [Chapel Hill, N.C., 1998], 71.)

12. In March 1876, George Willard of Michigan introduced a bill in the House of Representatives to expand the powers of the Board of Health of the District of Columbia. Although the bill made no mention of prostitution, opponents of licensing feared that the board would use its new powers to introduce medical inspection and licensing of prostitutes. The bill died in committee. (Wilson and Gledstone, *Report of a Visit to the United States*, 6–7, 21; Powell, *State Regulation of Vice*, 78–82; 44th Cong., 1st sess., A Bill to Further Define and Regulate the Powers and Duties of the Board of Health of the District of Columbia, 1 March 1876, H.R. 2440.)

13. The authors refer to H.R. 3723, a bill proposed in June "to regulate elections and the elective franchise in the Territories." This bill, pending in the Committee on Territories, proposed to disfranchise women in Utah and Wyoming. It replaced an earlier bill (H.R. 3101) that called for women's disfranchisement only in Utah. Women had been voting in Utah since 1869, in Wyoming since 1870. (*Congressional Record*, 44th Cong., 1st sess., 10 April, 12 June 1876, pp. 2357, 3765.)

14. Reference is made to New York's Married Women's Property Act of 1860 as amended in 1862. By the amendments, women lost equal guardianship of their children and were left with only veto power over decisions on apprenticeship and the appointment of testamentary guardians. In addition, the provisions of the 1860 law that made husbands and wives equal with regard to realty in cases of intestacy were overturned, restoring the privileges husbands had previously enjoyed. (*Papers*, 1:475–76; Norma Basch, *In the Eyes of the Law: Women, Marriage, and Property in Nineteenth-Century New York* [Ithaca, N.Y., 1982], 207–8, 236–37; *Laws of New York, 1862*, chap. 172.)

15. Colorado Const. of 1876, art. VII.

16. *Dred Scott v. Sandford* (1857) and *Minor v. Happersett* (1875).

17. The phrase appeared in a letter by Abigail Smith Adams (1744–1818) to her husband, John, on 31 March 1776. (*The Book of Abigail and John: Selected Letters of the Adams Family, 1762–1784*, eds. L. H. Butterfield, Marc Friedlaender, and Mary-Jo Kline [Cambridge, Mass., 1975], 120–21.)

## 83 ⤳ ECS TO ISABELLA BEECHER HOOKER

Philadelphia, Pa., July 5th 1876.

Dear Mrs Hooker,

Yours received. There is room plenty for your name.[1] I send you by to days mail two papers telling you all about the grand times we had yesterday, which I have not the time now to write out fully, but suffice it ↑to↓ say our hopes were more than realized in all respects. As you will see by the papers, Susan walked up to Mr Ferry[2] the presiding officer on Independence square the moment Richard Lee[3] finished reading the Dec of 1776, & presented ours of 1876. It had been engrossed on a large piece of parchment signed by a dozen of us. It was nicely rolled up, & tied with red, white, & blue ribbons   Mr Ferry rose up made a graceful bow & received it, although he & Gen Hawley had forbidden us even to present it, a ceremony that would not occupy a <u>single minute</u>.[4] But you will read it all in the papers so to your letter. You ask who prepared the documents   Mrs Gage & Susan wrote the republican address before I came, & I wrote the Democratic incorporating their suggestions   Mrs Gage & Susan & Mrs Spencer all made suggestions & points for the Declaration & I put it together in my language, when each one criticised & improved. A splendid work has been accomplished here, both public & social. We have receptions twice a week, the parlors are always crowded, & calls at all times. We send every visitor away loaded with tracts & new ideas. Our meeting in Dr Furness[5] church on the 4th was the most enthusiastic earnest, yea solemn meeting we ever had, continuing nearly five hours with un-abated interest, Lucretia Mott in her 84th year presiding, I doing all the business of chairman for her[6]     She was so full ↑of the subject, its memories & promises↓ that she made half a dozen speeches full of wit & wisdom. Everything went off so well, no bores, no misunderstand-ings, no halting, & the Hutchinsons[7] seemed to be inspired in their sweet songs. The atmosphere was so peculiar that every one said this place seems like the very gate of Heaven. After one of Lucretias sweet-est appeals the Hutchinsons started impromptu "Nearer my God to thee" the whole congregation joining in. Think of people standing in the aisles five hours, & when we chanted the benediction no one was satisfied to go. I wish you could have been here, & the women all spoke so well, our dear little Phebe[8] surpassed herself.

I am glad you & Mr Hooker have been educating Connecticut legislators.[9] Am much obliged for Mr Hookers appeal, I have not had time to read it having been all day rolling up & directing documents from Maine to California. "Boston" held a meeting here that did not create a ripple on the surface. Cold barren & unprofitable, the press scarcely noticed it, while day after day all we have done has been heralded. They celebrated the third because the women of New Jersey had once voted & were then robed of the privilege!! Was there ever anything so absurd. Everybody said what a stupid idea & what a stupid meeting. We wanted them to sign the Declaration but they would not consent that there names should go down to posterity with ours.[10] Well good night no time for more, ever yours

⤙  *E.C Stanton*

⤙ ALS, on Centennial Headquarters letterhead, Isabella Hooker Collec-tion, CtHSD.

1. ECS asked Hooker to sign the Declaration of Rights. (1 July 1876, *Film*, 18:850–52.)

2. Thomas White Ferry (1827–1896), as acting vice president of the United States, presided at the ceremonies on the Fourth of July. He entered the Senate as a Republican in 1871 and served until 1883. When he spoke during the Pembina debate, he recalled his support for woman suffrage in the state

legislature as early as 1856 and welcomed the opportunity "to prove my consistency by voting for woman suffrage to-day." (*BDAC*; *History*, 2:568.)

3. Richard Henry Lee (?–1902), a grandson of one of Virginia's delegates to the Continental Congress and an officer in the Confederate Army, was selected to read the Declaration of Independence. (George Norbury MacKenzie, *Colonial Families of the United States of America* [1907; reprint, Baltimore, 1966], 311–19.)

4. There are several accounts of the negotiations between representatives of the National Woman Suffrage Association and Joseph R. Hawley for the Centennial Commission in advance of the Fourth of July. The National received tickets to attend the ceremonies at Independence Hall, but Hawley refused ECS's request for permission to present the Declaration of Rights to the dignitaries on the stage. In the end, SBA, Lillie Blake, Matilda Gage, and Sara Spencer surprised the presiding officer, walking to the stage, placing the Declaration into his hands, and distributing printed copies to the audience as they departed. Sara Spencer told the story in a speech on the Fourth, in *Ballot Box*, August 1876. Matilda Gage wrote an account for the same paper at the same date, and her recollections along with ECS's inform *History*, 3:27–31. ECS retold the story in *Eighty Years*, 310–14, and Lillie Blake's account is in Katherine Devereux Blake and Margaret Louise Wallace, *Champion of Women: The Life of Lillie Devereux Blake* (New York, 1943), 123–26.

5. William Henry Furness (1802–1896) led Philadelphia's First Unitarian Society from 1825 to 1875, when he became pastor emeritus. The church was located at 1426 Pine Street. (*ANB*.)

6. For coverage of this meeting, see *Film*, 18:859–61.

7. John Wallace Hutchinson (1821–1908), one of the original Hutchinson Family Singers who first performed at gatherings of reformers in 1843, continued the tradition with his wife, children, and grandchildren. In the summer of 1876 he visited Philadelphia with his wife, Frances Burnham Patch Hutchinson (1822–1888); his daughter, Viola Gertrude Hutchinson Campbell (1847–?), and her child; his son, Henry John Hutchinson (1844–1884); and his brother, Asa Burnham Hutchinson (1823–1884). (John Wallace Hutchinson, *Story of the Hutchinsons (Tribe of Jesse)*, ed. Charles E. Mann [Boston, 1896], 2:56–63; *Woman's Journal*, 8 July 1876.)

8. That is, Phoebe Couzins.

9. John and Isabella Hooker were supporting a bill before the Connecticut legislature that would entitle taxpaying women to vote in city, borough, town, and school district elections. John Hooker's tract in favor of the bill went to every legislator, and Isabella Hooker addressed a special committee session called to consider the issue. (*Woman's Journal*, 24 June, 12 August 1876.)

10. The American Woman Suffrage Association met 2 July 1876 in Philadelphia's Horticultural Hall to commemorate the centennial of the granting of suffrage to women in New Jersey with speeches about the loss of those rights in 1807. (*Woman's Journal*, 8 July 1876.)

## 84 ❧ RUTH CARR DENISON[1] TO ECS, SBA, ET AL.

Washington, D.C., July 7, 1876.

I hasten to send you heartfelt greetings for that grand Declaration and Protest of the Women of the United States.

I ask myself, was there anything done on the 4th of July, 1876, better adapted to the time and occasion? *No, indeed!* It came to me yesterday; and it is almost worn out. It would do you good to hear the comments. "So good," "So dignified," "So truthful," "So creditable to a band of noble women," &c., &c. Please send me a few more as soon as you can.

❧ *Ruth Carr Denison*

❧ Toledo *Ballot Box*, August 1876.

1. Ruth Carr Denison (c. 1829–?), the wife of William O. Denison, a clerk in the Treasury Department, became involved in the suffrage movement as one of the women who attempted to register and vote in 1871. Upon meeting her that winter while lobbying Congress, Isabella Hooker described Denison as "a woman of uncommon ability & real influence," from whom she learned "how to work upon people" in Washington. Denison held many offices in the National association thereafter, becoming auditor in the 1880s. In 1876 and 1877, she was a member of the National's congressional committee. (Federal Census, 1870; city directories, 1870 to 1880; *History*, 3:813, 956, 4:27, 567–68n; I. B. Hooker to SBA, 11 March 1871, *Film*, 15:452–73. See also *Papers* 2.)

## 85 ❧ SBA TO OLYMPIA BROWN

[*Philadelphia*] July 9, 1876

Dear Olympia

Your Postal here— You did just right—though it was a pentecostal occasion—[1] This is to say—we have thrown up all idea of a Convention the 19 & 20 of July— the weather here is simply intolerable—only a seven times seven heated furnace could match it— So it is <u>no</u> <u>Conven-</u>

tion—[2] Mrs Stanton declares she will not come into this <u>oven</u> again—
Mrs Gage is going home in a very few days—& I shall get out of the city
the moment I can get safe arrangements here—as to letters & correspondence— it is simply killing—beats New York altogether—[3] Sincerely yours

&#x1f43a; *Susan B. Anthony*

P.S—We ought to hold our Con in October—right away after the Womans
Congress[4]—but alas where is the woman to take the responsibility on
her head & heart & <u>purse</u>— Echo answers where?—

&#x1f43a; ALS, Olympia Brown Papers, MCR-S.

1. Brown had not come to Philadelphia for the Fourth of July meeting.
2. In its place, the Citizens' Suffrage Association held a commemoration of
the Seneca Falls convention on the nineteenth, and SBA hosted a reception in
honor of Lucretia Mott on the twentieth. (SBA to Friend, 18 July 1876;
*Philadelphia Inquirer*, 20 July 1876; *Ballot Box*, August, September 1876; all
in *Film*, 18:920–22, 929–32.)
3. ECS returned to Tenafly on the sixth, and Matilda Gage left for home on
the fourteenth. SBA closed the Centennial Headquarters and left for Tenafly
on the twenty-first. (SBA diary, July 1876, *Film*, 18:516ff.)
4. Scheduled to meet in Philadelphia on 4 October 1876.

# 86 &#x1f43a; ANNA JOHNSON IRVINE[1] TO SBA

Oregon, Mo., July 11, 1876.

My Dear Miss Anthony:—The Declaration of Rights read lately by
yourself at the Centennial celebration in Philadelphia, has stirred the
hearts of many women, I hope, all over the country. History will some
day write that act as corresponding, in many things, to the little scene
in Boston harbor, over 100 years ago. I send a few signatures to the
document, all good and honest women. If you have on hand any
circular copies of the paper, please send me some soon, and I hope to
send you from this little corner of the world a long list before the
Summer is ended.

Women themselves must come to the front. So long as we wait for the courtesy and gallantry of the other sex to enfranchise ours, just so long we shall not have justice. A recent leading editorial in the St. Louis *Times* comments on the late declaration at Philadelphia as though twenty-five or thirty women were all that could be found calling for equality.[2] To combat such heresy, nothing could be better than to scatter abroad, at certain periods, full lists of the subscribers, week after week. In a few months with proper effort, you could enroll an army that would be invincible if actuated by your spirit. Hoping that in your day the goal will be won, I am Yours, very truly,

             ⚞ *Anne K. Irvine*

⚞ Toledo *Ballot Box*, August 1876.

     1. Anna Keturah Johnson Irvine (1837–1918) moved to Oregon, Missouri, from Council Bluffs, Iowa, at the time of her marriage to Clarke Irvine, a lawyer and, later, newspaper editor. She was the mother of three boys. Her involvement with the National association followed a visit by ECS in 1875 to lecture in the town. ECS recalled her "surprise at meeting so large a circle of bright, intelligent women" there. They were members of a successful small-town club called the Woman's Union that Irvine helped to found in 1872. In advance of the National's meeting in St. Louis in 1879, the Irvines signed the call to organize the Holt County Woman Suffrage Association and select a delegate to the meeting. In the 1880s, Annie Irvine continued to write letters to the National's meetings, contributed material for the Missouri chapter of the *History of Woman Suffrage*, and became a member of the National's executive committee. She is invariably referred to as "Anne R. Irvine" in the *History*. (*United States Biographical Dictionary: Missouri Volume* [Chicago, 1878], 161–62; Elizabeth Prather Ellsberry, *Cemetery Records of Holt County, Missouri* [Chillicothe, Mo., n.d.], 72; Eileen Derr, *Gone Home: Directory of the Deceased and Items of History of Holt County, Missouri, 1837–1981* [Maysville, Mo., 1981], 194, 453, 454; *History*, 3:19, 119, 144, 607–10, 957, 996, 4:24.)

     2. On 9 July, the *St. Louis Times* followed up a favorable news story about woman suffragists at the Centennial with an editorial that opened: "The women have had their Centennial say—that is, several of them have made a few remarks upon the occasion." A "few agitators" could not change the minds of men who believed that women did not want to vote.

87 &#x223D; ECS TO SARAH LANGDON WILLIAMS

Tenafly, N.J., July 22, 1876.

Dear Mrs. Williams:—I have read several numbers of the *Ballot Box* with great interest, and I must say it is the best Woman Suffrage journal that we have yet had, unless I except Miss Anthony's *Revolution*. I hope western women will now give you the generous patronage you so well deserve. In travelling extensively through the Western States, and to the extreme northern point of Texas, I have found Western and Southern women deeply interested in our demands, and all asking for some paper advocating our principles. As we had no really liberal, national journal, taking a fair view of the situation, without local prejudices and partialities, I could not heartily respond in recommending any until I saw the first number of the *Ballot Box*. Now, said I, here is a paper to meet the demands of Western women, and for those associations in the East that have no organ to herald what they do and say. We have decided, in the Executive Committee, to make the *Ballot Box* the organ of the National Woman Suffrage Association, and we shall do all in our power to keep you well informed of what is done, and to extend your circulation. I believe Miss Anthony has already sent you her list of subscribers to the *Revolution*, and Mrs. Gage a report of our last most successful meeting in Philadelphia.[1] Your friend, Mr. Abbott[2] of the *Index*, says of that meeting:

> The best and most spirited meeting of woman suffragists we ever attended was that of the National Woman Suffrage Association at Philadelphia, on the Fourth of July 1876. Mrs. Mott, Mrs. Stanton, Mrs. Lockwood, Mrs. Spencer, Miss Couzins, and a New York lady whose name we did not catch,[3] all made excellent speeches; but Miss Anthony carried off the palm by her rebellious speech, giving an account of her judicial battle with Judge Hunt and her audacious presentation of the "Declaration of Rights" in Independence Hall on that very morning, in defiance of

the authorities of the occasion. It was the "pluckiest" address we ever listened to. Miss Anthony set an example of energy and determination worthy of all imitation by the Liberal League.

Thus you see how completely Susan is overshadowing the whole of us. Even the editor of the *Woman's Journal*, with whom Miss Anthony has long had "an unpleasantness," is now so impressed with the great national work she has been doing for eight years, before Congress, in the courts, at the polls, everywhere, that she always reports the doings of the National Woman Suffrage Association under the head, "Miss Anthony's Meeting."[4] Now, while we are all devout worshippers of the beloved sister Susan, we do not wish future generations to suppose that she carried the suffrage movement in her pocket, and that such women as Lucretia Mott, Ernestine L. Rose, Matilda Joslyn Gage, Belva Lockwood, Dr. Clemence Lozier, Lillie Devereux Blake, Phoebe Couzins and Sara Andrews Spencer, supplied no enthusiasm, muscle or money for the work.

I will send you, in a few days, a long list of names of prominent women I have met in my travels, that the forthcoming number, containing the report of the Philadelphia meeting on the 4th, may be extensively circulated. I sincerely hope you may be able to keep your *Ballot Box* so well stuffed that you may never know a vacuum in pigeon hole or purse, ever sustained with nice contributors and greenbacks as good as gold. Ever yours,

&#x224b;    *Elizabeth Cady Stanton.*

&#x224b; Toledo *Ballot Box*, August 1876.

1. *Ballot Box*, August 1876, *Film*, 18:861.
2. Francis Ellingwood Abbot (1836–1903) founded the weekly *Index* in 1870 in Toledo, Ohio, and moved it to Boston in 1873. Trained as a Unitarian minister, Abbot broke with his denomination over its reliance on revelation and doctrine rather than science as the basis of its Christianity. He helped to found the Free Religious Association in 1867, and through the *Index*, he sought to promote secularism, particularly in the administration of government. He was in Philadelphia in July 1876 to attend the Centennial Congress of Liberals, called to organize the National Liberal League. His report on the National's meeting appeared in *Index*, 13 July 1876. (*ANB*; Sydney E. Ahlstrom and Robert Bruce Mullin, *The Scientific Theist: A Life of Francis Ellingwood Abbot* [Macon, Ga., 1987].)
3. This was Lillie Blake.

4. In the latest instance of the refusal to name the National Woman Suffrage Association in the *Woman's Journal*, an article on the Fourth of July reported that "Miss Anthony's society held a public meeting in the Church of Dr. Furness on the fourth inst. . . ." Not until 3 January 1880 did the editors acknowledge the National's existence by name. (15 July 1876.)

## 88 &#x224B; LUCY STONE TO ECS

Dorchester, [*Mass.*] Aug 3, 1876

Mrs. Stanton

I have erased the closing line in the notice of the "Universal Encyclopedia" as it was not true. I have never lived in Kansas. I have nothing to add.[1]

I do not add my name to the "Declaration" because, as I had nothing to do with its presentation, it would be wrong to say so. I think it is an admirable paper and my only regret about it was the sensational manner of presenting it.[2]

In regard to the History of the Woman's Rights Movement,[3] I do not think it <u>can</u> be written by any one who is alive to-day. Your "wing" surely are not competent to write the history of "our wing," nor should we be of yours, even if we thought best to take the time while the war goes on; rations, recruits and all are to get as we go.

There will come a time when this greatest of all the world movements will have made its history and <u>then</u> it can be written. I do not wish to have any hand in the present one.

The complete set of the *Woman's Journal* can be sent you for the purpose you desire, for three dollars a volume.[4] The regular price is five dollars. Six volumes would cost eighteen dollars. Do you want them?

&#x224B; *Lucy Stone*

&#x224B; Transcript in hand of I. P. Boyer, Blackwell Papers, DLC.

1. Two letters to Lucy Stone and H. B. Blackwell preceded this reply. ECS and SBA wrote to Stone on 30 July, and ECS wrote to Blackwell on 31 July. With the first letter, they enclosed page proofs of the biographical entry on Stone for *Johnson's Cyclopaedia* and told her that Alvin Johnson would insert whatever revisions she made. Stone was among those originally selected for inclusion in the work; at "Blackwell, Lucy Stone" in volume one, readers are

referred to "Stone, Lucy." ECS and SBA were editing the entry provided to them. (*Film*, 18:946–48)

2. ECS asked Lucy Stone to sign the Declaration of Rights. Although Stone declined, she did not condemn the National's Fourth of July. It was a "cute thing Mrs. Stanton and Susan did on the 4th July," she wrote to a friend. "They told John Hutchinson that they 'meant to go down to history with doings of the 4th July 1876'—and so they will. By the use of Lucretia Mott's name, they got the use of the church of Dr. Furness, and they made a really good meeting, and good will come of it. I have dreaded the effect of their presence in Philadelphia. But they seem to be on their good behavior." (L. Stone to Margaret Campbell, 19 July 1876, in Wheeler, *Loving Warriors*, 254–55.)

3. Stone answers two different suggestions that she collaborate on the movement's history. On 30 July, ECS requested "thirty lines concisely stating what you have done since 1870" to be included in the woman's rights entry for *Johnson's Cyclopaedia*. On 31 July, she described the one-volume history and suggested to Blackwell that the American association contribute a chapter about its activities and members.

4. ECS asked: "Could you sell us a complete copy of the Woman's Journal from the beginning that we may know what your wing have done?"

## 89 ⤝ ECS TO LUCY STONE

[*Tenafly*], Aug 4th 1876.

Mrs Lucy Stone   Dear Madam,

Yours received. In your notice for Encyclopedia the same number of words must be substituted. You struck out twenty eight. Shall I substitute the following, "After her marriage she lived in privacy in New Jersey for several years. In 67. she canvassed Kansas on woman suffrage In 70. established the 'Woman's Journal' in Boston." It would derange the whole page to strike out without replacing something.

As to the Declaration to sign it you do not necessarily endorse its presentation at Independence Hall. I took no part in those proceedings. Gen Hawley sent the officers of our association tickets for the platform. When it was first proposed that Mrs Mott & I should present the declaration immediately after the one of 76 was read, I wrote to Gen. Hawley making that request   As he refused, I felt I could not do it. Accordingly Lucretia Mott & I went to the church to open the

meeting at 12 o'clock, where I read The Declaration. I think you are
mistaken in your views of a history. Those of us now living can collect
the facts of the last thirty years & would be more interested in doing so,
&#8593;more easily&#8595; than those who come after us. Our partisan's on either
side could not do justice to us more than we can now do each other. I
wish you & Mr Blackwell would write a chapter say of ten pages octavo
volumn concisely stating your work for the last eight years, & a biographical sketch of yourself & Antoinette to go in precisely as you
write it. We shall have chapters of the movement ~~from~~ &#8593;in&#8595; England,
France, Germany Sweden written by parties in those countries. I must
consult Mrs Sargent & Gage about the purchase of the Journal & will
let you know in a few days. respt yours

&#x21DC; *Elizabeth Cady Stanton*

&#x21DC; ALS, on Centennial Headquarters letterhead, place uncorrected, NAWSA
Papers, DLC.

## 90 &#x21DD; ECS TO ISABELLA BEECHER HOOKER

Tenafly N.J., Aug 6th 1876.

Dear Mrs Hooker

Susan just brought the enclosed letter[1] to me & I suggested that
perhaps it might have more weight with Paulina with a word from you
& me. I certainly always understood that Paulina gave that money to
The Revolution at the time she became editor. Now I have written
Paulina for a donation to the History. As Susan cannot return the five
hundred now   Paulina better call it her donation to the history & let
that go as her subscription & thus the same sum can be twice credited
to her, for the cause. You & I know how faithfully & selfsacrificing
Susan has been all her life to the various reforms. She is free not[2] of
debt if we can settle this matter. Have you been to see Paulina lately? I
have not seen her since last January.[3] I went west soon after & did not
return until three weeks ago, & now Susan has loaded me with labors
that cannot be accomplished before Christmas. After my children return to their respective schools in September I want you to come &

visit Susan & me as she will remain with me until the history is finished. If you can do go & see Paulina & get this matter settled. As Susan read me this letter it brought tears to my eyes. Did your husband get our letters. All these exasperating reports have their origin in that Boston clique.[4] Sincerely yours

✒ *Elizabeth Cady Stanton*

✒ ALS, on Centennial Headquarters letterhead, place corrected, Isabella Hooker Collection, CtHSD.

1. Enclosure missing. It was probably SBA's reply to a request from Paulina Wright Davis that she repay Davis's loan of five hundred dollars made in August 1869 to meet the costs of publishing the *Revolution*. Already a writer for the paper at that date, Davis became one of its corresponding editors the following January and remained at the post until SBA sold the paper in May 1870. (Promissory note, 4 August 1869, and *Rev.*, 6 January, 26 May 1870, *Film*, 2:214, 375, 13:625; P. W. Davis to Gerrit Smith, 4 November 1869, Smith Papers, NSyU.)

2. ECS knew that SBA was "free now of debt," despite what she wrote here.

3. ECS visited Davis in December 1875. See her reminiscences and obituary of Davis, in *History*, 1:283–89, and *Film*, 18:1052.

4. These reports are unexplained.

91 ✒ ANTOINETTE BROWN BLACKWELL TO SBA

Somerville [*N.J.*] Aug 14 '76

Dear Susan

There is the Cyclopedia notice—packed to order like meat in an egg shell; exactly 10 words more, as you said.[1]

Mr. Blackwell promises to write and forward you shortly a longer sketch of his wife.[2] We agree with you that when one is to be written up, the better it is done, the better the result. You know what part I took in the woman movement after we began to work together. That section of the question we will leave to you.

I sincerely hope you will make a good and wide statement of the subject; and that every woman will help you as she can with items. Lucy hates being written about. She declined or but half complied when I asked her for certain facts not long ago, as she thought I might "print em." You see I am a little in the biographical line also just now—not in a way to interfere with you however. One worker never hinders another in my opinion—at least not while there is as wide a field as at present. I am making studies of women chiefly not in the suffrage movement, at least directly. As Miss Mitchell, in last "New Century," Miss Herschel, etc.[3]

Let me say what I wanted to say at Phila, if I could have managed to meet you there, and have had burning on my conscience a good while—that I thank you for the course you took before the public on the Beecher matter. On your view of the question, it seemed to me eminently wise. That is not condemning Mrs S. She judged for herself as she was entitled to do. Give my love to her and keep for yourself the unchanged old time belief, that you follow your own conscience

⇜ Nette

[*in margin of first page*] If you are to have, as I suppose, good steel portraits, I will send you a photo. Wood cuts are an abomination. A. L. B B.

⇜ ALS, Blackwell Papers, MCR-S.

1. Due to Lucy Stone's uncooperative responses, Blackwell stepped in and amended Stone's entry for *Johnson's Cyclopaedia*.

2. Blackwell refers to her own husband, Samuel Blackwell. When ECS requested a biographical sketch from Elizabeth Harbert for the history, she wrote: "you must get your husband to write you up eloquently & concisely, as those who love us can only do." No doubt ECS phrased her request to Antoinette Blackwell in the same fashion. (ECS to E. B. Harbert, 30 July 1876, *Film*, 18:942–45.)

3. *New Century for Woman*, 5 August, 9 September 1875. Only the biographies of American astronomer Maria Mitchell (1818–1889) and English astronomer Caroline Lucretia Herschel (1750–1848) bore Blackwell's name. This weekly paper, edited by Sarah Hallowell and financed by the Women's Centennial Committee, was published in Philadelphia during the exposition.

92 &#x267A; FROM THE DIARY OF SBA

[*26 August–3 September 1876*]

SATURDAY, AUGUST 26, 1876. [*Tenafly*] This evenings mail brought note from Kate Stanton[1]—that Mr Davis wished Mrs Stanton to be at P. W. Davis funeral[2]—so she Telegraphed Mr. D. that she & Susan would reach there Monday A.M—

1. Kate Sands Stanton (1838–?) of Rhode Island became a lecturer for woman's rights and active suffragist in 1870, while she was a law student in Providence. The daughter of former congressman George A. Stanton and a distant cousin of Henry Stanton, she later practiced homeopathic medicine. (William A. Stanton, *A Record, Genealogical, Biographical, Statistical, of Thomas Stanton, of Connecticut, and His Descendants, 1635–1891* [Albany, N.Y., 1891], 456; Charlotte Field Dailey, ed., *Rhode Island Woman's Directory for the Columbian Year, 1892* [Providence, R.I., 1893]. See also *Papers* 2.)

2. Paulina Davis died on August 24. Her husband, Thomas Davis (1806–1895), served for one term in the House of Representatives in 1853 as an antislavery Democrat. After several unsuccessful campaigns to return to Congress, he won election to the state senate in 1877. (*BDAC*.)

SUNDAY, AUGUST 27, 1876. Mrs Stanton and self, took train at 5.30 this P.M. for N.Y. called an hour with Mrs Phelps—then Sleeping car for Providence—

MONDAY, AUGUST 28, 1876. Arrived Providence at 5.10 A.M— Theodore Tilton at Thomas Davis— Funeral at 2 P.M. Mrs Stanton & self spoke— I read from Theo. Parkers Diary—his feelings of loneliness from his unpopular beliefs—[1] It was a sad funeral— Had not seen T. T. since the Dem. Con of /72—at Baltimore—[2] Mr Davis handed me P. W. D's note—[3]

1. For coverage of the funeral, see *Film*, 18:1005. Theodore Parker (1810–1860), clergyman, author, and reformer, came into conflict with Unitarian colleagues over his Transcendentalism. Excerpts from his journals were incorporated into *Life and Correspondence of Theodore Parker*, ed. John Weiss (1864).

2. Tilton attended the Democratic National Convention in 1872 as a sup-

porter of Horace Greeley; SBA and Isabella Hooker went there to seek the party's support for woman suffrage. See *Papers*, 2:507–14, 516.

3. See *Film*, 13:625.

TUESDAY, AUGUST 29, 1876. Spent forenoon looking over Mrs Davis' papers & letters—found but very little of any use to our history— marvelous <u>how</u> very little— Took 2 P.M. train & slept at Dr Bayards[1]— only Sam'l Wilkerson there— Hadn't seen him since he <u>testified</u> on the Beecher Tilton—scandal—& he acted ashamed—as he ought to feel—[2]

1. Edward Bayard (1806–1889), who married ECS's sister Tryphena Cady, was a distinguished physician in New York. He lived at 8 West Fortieth Street with several other members of the Cady family. (*Cleave's Biographical Cyclopaedia of Homeopathic Physicians and Surgeons* [Philadelphia, 1873], 51; *New York Times*, 1 October 1889; city directory, 1876.)

2. Samuel Wilkeson testified at length against Theodore Tilton at the trial in 1875. Alleging to quote Tilton, he told the court that SBA "was a morbid old maid; that she was an old maid in whom the suppression of the sexual instinct had brought morbid disease of the imagination; that she had morbidly imagined what she said; that there was not a word of truth in it, and that it was wholly a fabrication of the imagination, wholly so." (*New York Times*, 13 March 1875; *T. Tilton v. H. W. Beecher*, 2:309–10.)

WEDNESDAY, AUGUST 30, 1876. Spent A.M. in looking among publishers for our History— Mrs S. at Mrs E. B. Phelps— Lunched with Mrs Phelps—& came back to T[enafly] on the 1. P.M. train—found sundry letters—all well at home—

THURSDAY, AUGUST 31, 1876. At Tenafly— Miss Helen L. Potter[1] came over & spent the day— She personates me in her entertainments this Season—my answer to Judge Hunt, Why Sentence should not be pronounced—

1. Helen L. Potter enjoyed great success for at least a decade as an impersonator of popular lecturers and stars of the stage, including ECS and SBA. She developed a system of notation to record the sounds, pitch, and timing of her subject's public speech and the gestures employed with each phrase, and she created costumes and makeup for each of her characters. Speaking of one of her impersonations, her agent recalled that her costume was "so well chosen and so well arranged, and his peculiarities of voice and manner so faithfully represented, that the audience often forgot it was a personation." Potter lived in New York City by 1880 and was still there at the turn of the century. (J. B. Pond, *Eccentricities of Genius: Memories of Famous Men and Women of the Platform and the Stage* [New York, 1900], 170–71; Helen Potter,

*Helen Potter's Impersonations* [New York, 1891]; Federal Census, 1880; city directory, 1881.)

FRIDAY, SEPTEMBER 1, 1876. Mrs E. B. Phelps came over & spent the day with Mrs. S.— The England Girls[1] came just before Lunch time—

    1. Julia England (c. 1856–?) was a daughter of Isaac W. England, owner of the New York *Sun* and a resident of Bergen County, New Jersey. After the death of his first wife in 1871, England married Mary Paddock, whose own children from an earlier marriage joined the household. According to SBA's notation below, at 3 September, Julia arrived with her stepsister, Lizzie Paddock. Lizzie was not in the household by 1880. (Federal Census, 1880; *New York Tribune*, 26 April 1885; *Eighty Years*, 322–23.)

SATURDAY, SEPTEMBER 2, 1876. Kitt—(Henry Jr) staid at home—all went to the Palisades[1] in the A.M. Andrew Paddock[2] came— No letter from home or Sister Hannah—but one from dear Mrs Duniway[3]—from Mount Pulaska—Ill—

    1. A rock wall rising to a height of five hundred feet, the Palisades form the western shore of the Hudson River north of New York City in New Jersey's Bergen and Hudson counties. From the west, roads allowed access to the wooded summit.

    2. Andrew Paddock (c. 1858–?) was another stepchild of Isaac England, whose name was given as Andrew England in the 1880 census.

    3. Abigail Jane Scott Duniway (1834–1915) of Portland, Oregon, was the towering figure in woman suffragism in the Northwest from 1871 until her death, wielding power through her newspaper, the *New Northwest*, and her frequent trips around the region to help local activists. She traveled east to attend the Centennial Exhibition, lecturing and gathering subscriptions for her newspaper along the way. (*NAW*; *ANB*; Ruth Barnes Moynihan, *Rebel for Rights: Abigail Scott Duniway* [New Haven, Conn., 1983].)

SUNDAY, SEPTEMBER 3, 1876. At Tenafly—N. Jersey— The England girls—Lizzie Paddock & Julia E. here at Mrs Stantons—

    My heart is heavy—as if some great sorrow were pressing down upon me— The prospect of getting a history at all satisfactory seems lessening—

&#8766; The Standard Diary 1876, n.p., SBA Papers, DLC.

93 &#x22B4; SBA TO ISABELLA BEECHER HOOKER

Tenafly Sept. 4, 1876

My Dear Mrs Hooker

You will have learned, doubtless, that Mrs Stanton and myself went over to Providence and were present at the funeral of Mrs Davis— We left here Sunday nights train & reached there at 5.10 Monday A.M.— and the services were at 2 P.M.— We were very, <u>very</u> glad we went, too—as we were the <u>only</u> Woman Suffrage friends from a distance— The Unitarian Minister[1] read the beatitudes & made a few excellent remarks—had known her for 20 years— Then Mrs Stanton spoke 15 or 20 minutes in the most touching manner & matter of the dead & her sacrifices for woman—& made an earnest appeal to the women present to try to so live & work as to leave an easier path for the women who shall follow them—

Then I read a paragraph from the Diary of Theodore Parker—where he was so deserted by all his old friends because of his heretical beliefs—how alone—how ostracised—and closed with a few words on the <u>illusion</u> of <u>life</u>—seeking ever to find a full & true communion with some other soul—but that as we come into the world alone & go out alone—so in ~~the~~ ↑our↓ deepest & holiest lives—each one of us must live ↑alone↓— each one who was true to himself  herself "must tread the wine press alone"[2] and the work of the true teacher should be to dispel ↑this illusion from↓ the minds of the young— ~~of this~~ Theodore Tilton— when lecturing at Providence—last Winter—had called on Paulina in her sick room—& she had made him promise to come to her funeral— & when he saw the telegram of her death—he took first train—& reached there Saturday A.M.—but he declined to speak— Paulina looked very natural—and draped & festooned with illusion lace[3]—all according to her own order— She looked very beautifully too— Mr Davis seemed & said he was very glad we had come— They <u>expected</u> Mrs Stanton—because Paulina had made her promise to go to her the moment she saw she was gone—but they did not expect me—& you know how embarrassing it must have been for me to go—but I just said it is my duty—not one of the Old Boston W.S. women will pay this last tribute of respect I said—& <u>I will</u>—be my reception what it may— ~~but~~ ↑and↓ it was very kind—nay more cordial— Mrs Hine,[4] after breakfast called me one side & told me Paulina had left word for the $500— to be cancelled—& that she as well as myself & you & the rest—always understood it was not to be returned unless The Revolution became a rich or paying paper—and the morning we left Mr Davis put the old note into my hands & said that is all settled— Thus I was doubly paid for going over—

Now if you have <u>mentioned</u> <u>about</u> <u>the note to any</u> of <u>your</u> <u>friends,</u> please do Paulina the kindness the justice to say she left the matter settled— I cant tell you what a relief it is to me that <u>Mr</u> Davis spoke so <u>cheerfully,</u> ↑and↓ <u>whole souled</u>—when he handed me the note— It was all right and just as he expected it to be when the money was given— But oh what torture the poor woman had been ↑in↓ the three years since her return from Europe—she fell into a comitose state a week before she passed away—it was a great relief to the living as well as the dead when the end came— I have seized this first moment to tell you about the $500— I really do not ↑know↓ whether she knew about our letters—but think she did—but no matter—it is all right now—

Mrs Stanton is fitting her "<u>Bob</u>." off for Cornell now—& Theodore returns there as <u>Tutor</u>—for the coming year— Harriot returns to Vassar—& Maggie is to remain at home—they are lovely girls—& a real joy to their mothers heart. With kind regards—Mrs Stanton joining— to Mr Hooker—& a great deal of love to yourself  I am Sincerely yours

✎ *Susan B. Anthony*

✎ ALS, Isabella Hooker Collection, CtHSD. Envelope addressed to Hartford, Connecticut.

1. Augustus Woodbury (1825-1895) became the pastor of the Westminster Congregational Church (a Unitarian society) in Providence in 1857. He read from Matt. 5:3-12. (Adams, *Dictionary of American Authors*; *ACAB*; Allibone; city directory, 1876.)

2. Isa. 63:3.

3. Illusion lace is a thin and transparent tulle or delicate net.

4. Kate Hines (c. 1835-?) was the housekeeper in the Davis household. (Federal Census, 1870.)

## 94 ➢ FROM THE DIARY OF SBA

[*4–7 September 1876*]

MONDAY, SEPTEMBER 4, 1876. One of my terrible head colds came on & grows on me

TUESDAY, SEPTEMBER 5, 1876. Darning stockings for boys with Mrs Stanton—all history work broken

WEDNESDAY, SEPTEMBER 6, 1876. Letter from Sister Hannah of Aug 24th—says she breathes easier but cough is worse & very hard & dry— & she can get nothing satisfactory to eat—all looks bad—[1]

  1. Hannah Mosher was still in Colorado, ordered by a doctor to stay there until she conquered a cold. On 2 August, SBA admitted to her diary, "I fear there is no cure for her." Hannah returned to Leavenworth on 1 October.

THURSDAY, SEPTEMBER 7, 1876. The England girls left this A.M.— So now we settle back a little—cold better to day—the first I have come to tower write since Sunday last—have felt miserable enough—just seems as if all of us were to follow dear Gula—& not very long after

❦ The Standard Diary 1876, n.p., SBA Papers, DLC.

## 95 ➢ CLARA BARTON[1] TO SBA

Danville [*N.Y.*] Sept. [*13*] 1876[2]

Dear Susan B Anthony

  I want to thank you for your kind letter of sympathy.[3] I knew I should have it from generous heart if you knew me ill but it was sweet to hear you say it if only on paper and through space. I am better, recovering slowly, "resting out" they tell. I have presented your good messages to Dr Jackson[4] and family and am loaded down with theirs in return, a visit from you would be dearly prized by them, if ever <u>time</u>

came to you to make it. I congratulate you with all my heart on the health and strength that still enables you to remain at your post— It is the survival of the fittest—and God be praised— I wish the next Centennial might find you yet at work and indeed it will only that "the veil so thin, so strong"[5] may hide from mortal view

But I too, must "to business."

I thank you for the courtesy which prompts you to invite my little story for your big book, and such as it is. I send it,[6] but I perceive that you cannot accept it for its too great length, and I cannot make it less, and cannot consent to have any other person shorten it. I have gone over & over and cut and whittled until it is a bare skeleton, of major bones, it cannot spare one more and stand up— I have clipped conjunctions and prepositions regardless of connection, and it has not an adjective in it. The sweetest and best things are all left out. I have put the four hardest years worth of my life into words. I cannot ~~do any better with it~~ cut ~~any~~ more and have it in any manner fit to go to the world but as that will be no loss to the world and no trouble to me it is not a matter to be deplored    This is the first ~~instance~~ time in my life under all similar calls which have been made on me that I have ever written or permitted a word to go, and this is only because Susan B Anthony asks it, and it is for women— But Masterless as our Susan she cannot <u>create</u> <u>space</u>, and if it is not accorded her she cannot control it. ~~In the~~ I see by actual count that my article contains in stead of 200 words 3 which I am morally certain you cannot accept, and as I cannot consent to the cutting of a sentence, there can be no way but to leave it out, and I enclose stamps for you to return it to me which you will greatly oblige me by doing— With congratulates and warmest and best wishes for your success in all things ~~and~~ I remain your sincere friend

⤜ AL copy, Clara Barton Papers, DLC.

1. Clara Barton (1821–1912), noted for her aid to soldiers during and after the Civil War, returned to relief work under the International Red Cross Committee in 1870, during the Franco-Prussian War. While abroad, she suffered a breakdown and returned to America, moving to the Dansville, New York, Water-Cure in 1873. Her successful campaign to establish the American National Red Cross began in 1877. (*NAW*; *ANB*.)

2. Barton wrote from Dansville, not Danville. The day of the month on which she wrote is noted in SBA's reply, below at 19 September 1876.

3. SBA to Clara Barton, 22 August 1876, *Film*, 18:989–93.

4. James Caleb Jackson (1811–1895) was an early abolitionist and journalist and the head physician at the Dansville Water-Cure. (*ANB*.)

5. From Harriet Beecher Stowe's poem "Only a Year," written about the death of her one-year-old child in 1849. The stanza reads: "The veil, the veil— so thin, so strong / Twixt us and thee / the mystic veil, when shall it fall / That we may see!"

6. Enclosure omitted. Her sketch for the encyclopedia is in *Film*, 18:1022–25.

## 96 ✒ SBA to Frances E. Willard[1]

Tenafly N.J. Sept. 18th 1876

My Dear Frances Willard

I saw by the newspapers a few days since, that you had <u>spoken</u> out for suffrage as a power to help on your hearts hope & work for Temperance—and thought to drop a word of cheer to you at the moment but failed to do so— On Friday evening the 15th inst—I went into New York to attend a Woman Suffrage reception at Mrs Dr Loziers—238 West 14th st—in honor of our dear Scotch friend, Mrs Margaret E. Parker[2]—and from her I had a most delightful recital of the night of your first public committal— I rejoice that at last you have obeyed the "inner light" as we Quakers say—<u>the "divine</u> inspiration" I say—and put under your feet all the timid conservative <u>human</u> counsels, I feel sure you will find great peace and strength in your obedience to your <u>own</u> highest convictions—rest assured the <u>higher</u> & <u>highest</u> <u>truths</u> never come to us <u>too</u> <u>soon</u> for us to give to the world— We should hold ourselves the faithful mediums of the divine; it is only by such faithfulness that we shall be continued and counted <u>worthy</u> ~~the~~ instruments to the higher work waiting, ever, for willing hearts to do— Hence, now, I know the Good Father blesses you with a serener feeling, than you have known during the months previous, that you were halting & waiting—postponing the utterance you better convictions bade you make— <u>I know</u> the breaking ↑the spell,↓ the declaring yourself has brought <u>peace</u> & comfort to you—and that new blessings are showering down upon your <u>soul</u>—no matter how many ↑of the↓ weak, timid, <u>short sighted</u> may send you deprecating words— Now, you are to go forward—now the <u>Red Sea</u> <u>opens</u> to pass you through—now you ↑are the one that⁴ shall put the ten thousands to flight—³ I wish I could see you & make you feel my gladness, not only for your sake, personally, but for the <u>cause sake</u>—for Temperance & <u>Virtue's</u> sake—for Woman's sake.—

Tomorrow Tuesday P.M. Dear Mrs Parker, and dear Mrs Lozier—(if ever ↑you↓ go to N.Y. City again, ~~to~~ go to Mrs Lozier's—her house, her home & her heart are all open to receive you—)

&#x223d; AL incomplete, on Centennial Headquarters letterhead, place corrected, IEWT, from *Temperance and Prohibition Papers.*

1. Frances Elizabeth Caroline Willard (1839–1898) announced her support for woman suffrage at a temperance meeting in Old Orchard Beach, Maine, in August 1876. Formerly president of the Evanston College for Ladies in Illinois and dean of the Woman's College of Northwestern University, Willard had joined veterans of the Woman's Crusade in founding the Woman's Christian Temperance Union in 1874. She became its corresponding secretary as well as president of the local union in Chicago, but she met resistance within the national organization to her ideas about votes for women. After speaking in Maine, she took her plan for what she called the Home Protection ballot to the Illinois state union in September, to the Woman's Congress in mid-October, and only then to the national union later in that month. (*ANB*; Mary Earhart, *Frances Willard: From Prayer to Politics* [Chicago, 1944]; Ruth Bordin, *Frances Willard, A Biography* [Chapel Hill, N.C., 1986]; *Woman's Journal*, 26 August, 2 September 1876.)

2. Margaret Eleanor Walker Parker (1828–1896) of England and Scotland was saluted at this event as a woman suffragist and president of the British Woman's Temperance Association. During her visit she was also elected president of the short-lived Woman's International Temperance Association, founded at a meeting in Philadelphia. (*SEAP*; Willard, *Woman and Temperance*, 114–18; *Film*, 18:1026, 1045).

3. An allusion to Exod. 14:21–15:21.

97 &#x223d; SBA TO CLARA BARTON

Tenafly N.J. Sept 19^th 1876.

My Dear Friend   Clara Barton

Yours of 13^th inst is before me— I can't consent to leave your poor skeleton so denuded of flesh & blood— You shall double it or more— if need be to round it out handsomely— I would like the copy two or three times back of this cutting & clipping— What a life yours has been— I have the power to command more space & now say double it— Your facts crowded together so break my back, tire my head & hands—no—no—you shan't be crowded into the same space ↑—a thousandth part of the same space↓ of a man who never did a tithe for his country to what you did—[1]

I am very, very sorry to have so taxed you while you are so illy able to do hard work— It is beautiful work you did—not one other woman has comprehended what I wanted, or been able to do it—except dear Mrs. C. I. H. Nichols[2] of Vermont— Yours is capitally done—only I want to ↑you↓ put on its clothes again— I did ↑not↓ mean to have the poor bones all left bare,— ↑But↓ I didn't dream you had so many, ↑and↓ such mammoth ones either—

I am so glad you are gaining strength—& hope you may yet live to ↑do↓ as work for woman's emancipation as you did for the slaves & the soldiers— How gloriously our movement would go on, if it had the like of your hand, brain & heart to organize systematize, vitalize & marshall its forces— Do get well, my dear, & come to ↑the↓ help of the weary & worn in the service for woman— Then beyond the Cyclopedia articles— Mrs Stanton & I are writing a history of our w.s. movement down to the close of this Centennial year—and you will remember that we suspended all woman suffrage work during the war—and organized a Women's Loyal League & rolled up a mammoth petition of 300,000 ~Co~ ↑asking↓ Congress to emancipate slavery—hence we shall have a Chapter on the War, & in that, we not only wish to tell what we did at home—but ↑what↓ you & others ↑did↓ on the field of battle—and more still—we are to give personal sketches of the leading women—with their pictures—Steel engravings—and we want your first long article of yourself—with your woman's rights expressions and actions since the war, ↑added—↓ for our history— If you will give ↑your↓ picture & sketch to us—we will put you in the record—& your face shall go down with dear Lucretia Motts, Mrs Stantons—Antoinette Brown Blackwells— &c. &c.— I feel sure you will not deny me these.

Mrs Stanton bids me enclose her love to you—and both of us return best regards to the Doctor & family—With gratitude if he & they are helping you to new life— Hoping soon to hear from you—affectionately

⇝ *Susan B. Anthony*

P.S—I shall hold on to this copy—until I hear from you—as you probably have the former copies—for I dare not run the risk of losing this—If you have not preserved a copy & want this to work from—let me know & it shall go to you at once— S. B. A.

⤝ ALS, on Centennial Headquarters letterhead, place corrected, Clara Barton Papers, DLC. Envelope addressed to "Our Home" Dansville N.Y.

1. Barton replied that she would try to "galvanize the bones into sufficient life to take on a small coat of flesh." Her unsigned biography appears in *Johnson's Cyclopaedia*, 4:1564. (C. Barton to SBA, 23 September 1876, *Film*, 18:1043–44.)

2. Clarina Irene Howard Nichols (1810–1885) was a pioneer in woman's rights agitation, in Vermont as early as 1847 and in Kansas where she settled in 1854. In December 1871, she moved to Mendocino County, California. Her biography appears in *Johnson's Cyclopaedia*, 4:1627. (*NAW*; *History*, 1:171–200. See also *Papers* 1 & 2.)

## 98  ⤜   ECS TO ELIZABETH BOYNTON HARBERT

Tenafly N.J. Sept 29th [*1876*]

Dear Friend,

As Susan & I are one & that one is Susan, I feel that my letters from you are answered. However your letter this evening moves me to say a word myself. Your feeling about not leaving your children is right.[1] Let no one tempt you to do it. Overtaxed as you are do not let any one induce you to take such a journey as from Chicago to Newark with a baby unless it is absolutely necessary.[2] With three children, & housekeeping, no one should ask you to do another thing.

As to the sketch I think it is better for you to rewrite & condense.[3] It must not be more than one quarter as long as it now is. You would like to keep the extracts &c &c therefore it is best to be scissored by you then us. We intend to get as complete a history as one volumn octavo can give:—the sketches of persons must be <u>very</u> <u>brief</u>, only the most important facts can have place. We are already swamped with material. My head turns to look at it. Everybody amplifies. Now let me advise you as I would my own daughter; whilst you are having young children, rest, take your ease, or you ↑will↓ not be able to give the necessary vitality to your children, neither will you have the necessary strength to give them the needed care. As we bring children into the world without consulting them, it is our duty to give them sound minds in sound bodies, perfect physical training, a good education & something to begin life with. The old idea that children are under such obligations to parents should give place [*concluded sideways in margins of first page*] to the higher, that the obligations of the parents are ten fold & begin with conception, are momentous during the antinatal period & when I may ask are they not greater than the childs can ever be? Yours sincerely

➷    Elizabeth Cady Stanton

➷ ALS, Box 7, Elizabeth Harbert Collection, CSmH. In *Film* at 29 September 1880.

    1. These were: Arthur Boynton Harbert, born 1871; Corinne Boynton Harbert, born 1873; and Elizabeth Boynton Harbert, born 1875.

    2. To attend the meeting of the National Woman's Christian Temperance Union on 25 October.

    3. ECS earlier asked Harbert for a biographical sketch to be included in the history. "Crowd as much as possible into the smallest space," she directed, "& let us have it within a month." (30 July 1876, *Film*, 18:942–45.)

## 99  ➷  ECS TO THE EDITOR, *INDEX*[1]

[Tenafly, before 9 November 1876]

Woman is held in bondage to-day by the complete perversion of the religious element of her being. I have long seen this, and tried to do the best I could by liberal interpretations of the Bible; but that, I find, amounts to very little so long as the priest, with holy unction, teaches the opposite. I have travelled very extensively through the Western States, through California, Texas, etc. Everywhere the devotion of women to their churches is really pitiful; and when oppression is accepted as the will of God, where can we open the argument? A devout, complacent slave is as pitiful, as exasperating, whether on a Southern plantation or in an Orthodox congregation. I had thought that with political freedom woman might get rid of her superstition, as man has. Higher education in science and philosophy is doing something for the rising generation of girls; but, as you say, these religious superstitions make their subjection after all certain. There is not, I believe, an Orthodox woman on our platform; there may be, but I do not recall one just now. Now what can we do to get the suffrage movement "out of the ruts, and base it on universal truths?" The very idea you express of woman's ownership of herself we declared in the closing sentence of our Fourth of July Declaration. One thing we should do, and that is to identify ourselves with the struggle you and a few others are now making for free religion, to avert the danger to our schools, our Constitution, in fact to freedom in all directions. Though I am not well enough informed to write the articles referred to, yet I will write from time to time on anything suggested by the articles in your journal, which I read regularly with much pleasure. I am busy just now writing a history of the suffrage movement; when that is done, I intend to look into the religions and their effect on woman's condition. I have no objection to be enrolled among your correspondents.

❧ Boston *Index*, 9 November 1876.

1. Prefacing this letter, Francis Abbot remarked that "these striking passages from Mrs. Stanton's very kind acceptance" of his invitation to become an editorial contributor to the *Index* were "too profoundly wise and instructive to be buried in a merely private letter." Abbot issued his invitation after ECS wrote a lengthy letter on women and the Bible, published in *Index*, 28 September 1876, *Film*, 18:1046.

100   ❧   APPEAL BY THE NATIONAL WOMAN SUFFRAGE ASSOCIATION, WITH PETITION

Tenafly, N.J., Nov. 10, 1876.[1]

APPEAL

FOR A

SIXTEENTH AMENDMENT.

To the Women of the United States:

Having celebrated our Centennial birthday with a National jubilee, let us now dedicate the dawn of the Second Century to securing justice to Woman.

For this purpose we ask you to circulate a petition to Congress, just issued by the "National Woman Suffrage Association," asking an amendment to the United States Constitution, that shall prohibit the several States from disfranchising any of their citizens on account of Sex. We have already sent this petition throughout the country for the signatures of those men and women who believe in the citizen's right to vote.

To see how large a petition each State rolls up, and to do the work as expeditiously as possible, it is necessary that some person, or society in each State and District should take the matter in charge, print, and send out petitions to reliable friends in every county, urging upon all thoroughness and haste. When the petitions are returned, they should be pasted together, neatly rolled up, the number of signatures marked on the outside, with the name of the State, and forwarded to Sara Andrews Spencer, Chairman of our Congressional Committee, corner of L. and 7th street, Washington, D.C. On the 16th and 17th of January, 1877, we shall hold our 8th Annual Convention[2] at the Capitol and ask a hearing on our petition before Congress.

Having petitioned to our law-makers, State and National, for years, many from weariness and despair have vowed to appeal no more; for our petitions, say they, by the tens of thousands, are piled up mid the National archives unheeded and ignored.[3] Yet, it is possible to roll up such a mammoth petition, borne into Congress on the shoulders of stalwart men, that we can no longer be neglected or forgotten. Statesmen and politicians, alike, are conquered by majorities. We urge the women of this country to make now the same united effort for their own rights, that they did for the slaves at the south, when the 13th amendment was pending. Then a petition of over 300,000 was rolled up by the leaders of the suffrage movement, and presented in the Senate by the Hon. Charles Sumner. But the leading statesmen who welcomed woman's untiring efforts to secure the black man's freedom, frowned down the same demands when made for herself. Is not liberty as sweet to her as to him? Are not the political disabilities of Sex as grievous as those of color? Is not a civil rights bill that shall open to woman the college doors, the trades and professions—that shall secure her personal and property rights, as necessary for her protection, as for that of the colored man?

And yet the highest judicial authorities have decided that the spirit and letter of our National Constitution are not broad enough to protect

Woman in her political rights; and for the redress of her wrongs they remand her to the State. If this Magna Charta of Human Rights can be thus narrowed by judicial interpretations in favor of class legislation, then must we demand an amendment that in clear, unmistakable language, shall declare the equality of all citizens before the law.

Women are citizens, first of the United States, and second of the State wherein they reside: hence, if robbed by State authorities of any right founded in nature or secured by law, they have the same right to national protection against the State, as against the infringements of any foreign power. If the United States government can punish a woman for voting in one State, why has it not the same power to protect her in the exercise of that right in every State? The Constitution declares it the duty of Congress to guarantee to every State a republican form of government, to every citizen equality of rights. This is not done in States where women, thoroughly qualified, are denied admission into colleges, which their property is taxed to build and endow; where they are denied the right to practice law and are thus debarred from one of the most lucrative professions; where they are denied a voice in the government, and thus while suffering all the ills that grow out of the giant evils of intemperance, prostitution, war, heavy taxation and political corruption, stand powerless to effect any reform. Prayers, tears, psalm-singing and expostulation are light in the balance, compared with that power at the ballot box that converts opinions into law. If Women who are laboring for peace, temperance, social purity and the rights of labor, would take the speediest way to accomplish what they propose, let them demand the ballot in their own hands, that they may have a direct power in the government. Thus only can they improve the conditions of the outside world and purify the home. As political equality is the door to civil, religious and social liberty, here must our work begin.

Constituting as we do one-half the people, bearing the burdens of one-half the National debt, equally responsible with man for the education, religion and morals of the rising generation, let us with united voice send forth a protest against the present political status of Woman, that shall echo and re-echo through the land. In view of the numbers and character of those making the demand, this should be the largest petition ever yet rolled up in the old world or the new;—a petition that shall settle forever the popular objection that "Women do not want to vote." On Behalf of the National Woman Suffrage Association.

ᢞ *Elizabeth Cady Stanton, Pres.*

ᢞ *Matilda Joslyn Gage, Chairman Ex. Com.*

ᢞ *Susan B. Anthony, Cor. Sec.*

Newspapers please copy.

## PETITION FROM VERSO

N.B. Circulate this Petition thoroughly; have the names written plainly with ink, by each person, on one side of the sheet only. When this sheet is filled, paste on another. When you have obtained all the names possible, roll up and carefully direct to the President of your State W.S. Society, or to the resident Congressional Committee, Sara Andrews Spencer, Chairman, corner of L. and 7th streets, Washington, D.C. All our Petitions must be returned to Washington by the 10th of January, 1877.

## PETITION FOR WOMAN SUFFRAGE.

To the Senate and House of Representatives,

  In Congress Assembled:

The undersigned Citizens of the United States, Residents of the State of [*blank*] earnestly pray your Honorable Bodies to adopt measures for so amending the Constitution as to prohibit the several States from Disfranchising United States Citizens on account of Sex.

MEN: | WOMEN:

ᢞ Circular, Henry Rowe Schoolcraft Papers, DLC.

1. Matilda Gage arrived in Tenafly about the first of November for a fortnight's stay, and SBA returned from Rochester on November 4. SBA indicated in her diary that this appeal was completed and copied for the printer much earlier on October 4, before her sojourn in Rochester. (Mary E. Paddock Corey, "Matilda Joslyn Gage: Woman Suffrage Historian, 1852–1898" [Ph.D. diss., University of Rochester, 1995]; SBA diary, 1876; *Film*, 18:516ff.)

2. In fact, the National association's *ninth* Washington convention was slated for January. The count began with the convention of 1869, called by the Universal Franchise Association. Confusion over numbering the meeting of 1877 carried over into the call to the meeting (next document) and SBA's notation in her diary. Perhaps the authors overcorrected Gage's mistaken reference to the convention of 1876 as the "Ninth Annual Convention" in her call to that meeting. (*Film*, 18:761–62.)

3. Congressional records were kept at this time in the Capitol Building, in offices, attics, basements, and various storage rooms.

101  &#8631;  CALL TO THE WASHINGTON CONVENTION OF THE NATIONAL WOMAN SUFFRAGE ASSOCIATION

Tenafly, N.J., Nov. 10, 1876.

The Eighth Annual Convention of the National Woman Suffrage Association will be held in Lincoln Hall, Washington, D.C., January 16th and 17th, 1877.

As by repeated judicial decisions, Woman's right to vote under the 14th Amendment has been denied, we must now unitedly demand a 16th Amendment to the U.S. Constitution, that shall secure this right to the Women of the Nation.

In certain States and Territories where Women had already voted, they have been denied the right by legislative action. Hence it must be clear to every thinking mind that this fundamental right of citizenship must not be left to the ignorant majorities in the several States; for unless it is secured everywhere, it is safe nowhere.

We urge all Suffrage Associations and friends of Woman's Enfranchisement throughout the country to send delegates to this Convention, freighted with mammoth Petitions for a 16th Amendment. Let other proposed amendments be held in abeyance to the sacred rights of the Women of this Nation. The most reverent recognition of God in the Constitution would be justice and equality for Woman.[1] On behalf of the National Woman Suffrage Association,

    &#8631;  *Elizabeth Cady Stanton, Pres.*

    &#8631;  *Matilda Joslyn Gage, Chair. Ex. Com.*

    &#8631;  *Susan B. Anthony, Cor. Sec.*

N.B. Letters should be addressed to the Secretary, Susan B. Anthony, Tenafly, N.J., and contributions to the Treasurer, Ellen Clarke Sargent, 1732 De Sales street, Washington, D.C.

Editors please copy.

⚞ Circular, WHi.

1. Dozens of proposals for a sixteenth amendment came before the first session of the Forty-fourth Congress. Many of them concerned the manner of electing senators and the president, but at least three proposals looked for ways to prohibit the distribution of tax revenue to religious institutions for schools or any other purpose. The text alludes to an additional proposal, rejected by the House Committee on the Judiciary in the Forty-third Congress but still a subject of considerable agitation, to amend the Constitution to acknowledge "Almighty God and the Christian religion." (McPherson, *Hand-Book of Politics for 1874*, 57–58, and *Hand-Book of Politics for 1876*, 127–33.)

## 102 ⤳ SBA to Elizabeth Boynton Harbert

Tenafly N.J. Nov. 12/76

My Dear Friend

Yours of the 7th is here— I mail your first sketch[1] with this—have just returned to Mrs S's from a month's visit at home. I put a few names of friends that I can think of into the roll with the sketch— They[2] lost all they records in the great fire in /71 & have never really enrolled their membership since— I am glad you are going to re-suscitate the movement in Ill—but <u>don't</u> call it re-<u>organize</u>—just call the annual meeting— appeal to every friend in the state to come up to it in person or by letter—elect your new officers—put new life into everything & everybody—as is befitting the beginning of our new century— Will send you package of our <u>National</u> W.S.A's Call for Wash. Con. 16 & 17 Jan./77— with form of Petition & Appeal to circulate it—from which you will learn the <u>practical</u> point upon which we urge all the friends of W.S. throughout the Union to concentrate all their energies— <u>The State's rights</u> plan of getting our right to vote is wholly impracticable— you can never <u>convert</u> a <u>majority</u> of the rag tag & hob-tail of Chicago to vote in favor of <u>woman's equality</u> with <u>them</u>— Nor ↑can↓ we ever educate the Constituency of John Morrissey[3] in the 6th Congressional District of N.Y. City to vote <u>yes</u>— So <u>that</u> <u>mode</u> of getting the suffrage is perfectly hopeless—as well as perfectly discordant with the fundamental principles of our Constitution & of our assertions as to the <u>points</u> gained by the war & reconstructi[on] Legislation— So I do hope all the friends will see that the <u>true</u> <u>thing</u> to do at this hour is to demand submission of a 16<sup>th</sup> amendm't by Congress to the several Legislatures— If all will take hold in right good earnest—we can carry into Congress—at time of our Con. at Washington—the grandest petition ever seen— Now you go into the work heartily—set all Illinois to work—have all the petitions of your State sent in to you—& you be made the Ill. delegate to the Wash. Con. & to be one of the Committee to go before Congress with the petition— Do you see—what a grand petition & appeal we can make to Congress by all joining—giving a strong pull, a short pull & a pull all together!!— This is the best plan for <u>local</u> & <u>state</u> as well as National agitation— I know the time is short— but if all will seize the idea & go to work, we can make the grandest discussion and the most <u>generall[y]</u> & specially & widel[y] [*rest of line torn away*] agitation & [*rest of line torn away*]

Let me hear from you as soon as you get the petitions & Appeal— Sincerely yours

&#x223d;   *Susan B. Anthony*

—P.S. Wont Miss Willard represent Ill. at our Wash. Con. and let us announce her as one of our speakers—ask her—beg her—

&#x223d; ALS, on Centennial Headquarters letterhead, place corrected, Box 2, Elizabeth Harbert Collection, CSmH. Letters in square brackets lost at margin.

1. See 29 September 1876 above.
2. SBA refers to the Illinois Woman Suffrage Association.
3. John Morrissey (1831–1878), the 1858 world heavyweight boxing champion and principal owner of the racetrack in Saratoga Springs, New York, was elected as a Democrat to the House of Representatives in 1866 and 1868. (*BDAC.*)

·⊙━━━━━━━━⊙·

## 103 &#8766; SBA TO CAROLINE HEALEY DALL[1]

Tenafly N.J. Nov 24/76

My Dear Mrs Dall

Your Postal of yesterday is here— I wish you had given your <u>number</u>, as well as said you were <u>avenue</u> not street— Have had this matter of yours sealed up & directed all this time—but postponed mailing—until I should ↑see↓ Cyclopedia proof to see if we had our points correct—but that has not come yet— Have seen the first proof of our "<u>Woman's Rights</u>" item—found a good many links left out—& supplied them—but dare say many more will reveal themselves when it is too late to fill them in—[2]

It now seems probable—almost sure—that <u>The Appleton's</u> will publish our History—[3] I took them over Preface—Introduction—& first 6 or 8 chapters—& they think it will make a very interesting book— Dear, dear—but what a herculean undertaking—instead of <u>Christmas</u> seeing it done—it will be months yet—

Well you doubtless see I am to lecture in Boston Sunday the 3^d of Dec—on "<u>Woman</u> & the 16^th amendment"— Pray the Gods to help me to get just the best possible argument for us women— I shall not leave here until Friday A.M. Hope I shall be able to see you—

How I do wish it could be as in the olden time—that the <u>Ex. Committees</u> of the state & New England societies would be called together—& we all together study <u>how</u> to <u>press</u> on the good work— I have made no engagement for Monday the 4^th—& if you can see any way to help me to meet some of the <u>real</u> <u>workers</u>—not "<u>dogs in the manger</u>" sort of people—I should love to see them— Sincerely yours

&#8766; *Susan B. Anthony*

&#8766; ALS, on Centennial Headquarters letterhead, place corrected, C. H. Dall Collection, MHi.

1. Caroline Wells Healey Dall (1822–1912) of Boston became active in the woman's rights movement in the 1850s, making a speciality of detailed progress

reports on changes in the law, education, and employment. After Dall visited Centennial Headquarters in June 1876, she and SBA exchanged several letters, including SBA's request that Dall write up her biography for *Johnson's Cyclopaedia* and the history. Although Dall wrote on a corner of that request in August, "Of course I absolutely decline to do anything asked in this letter," her unsigned biography appears in the appendix to *Johnson's Cyclopaedia*. (*NAW*; *ANB*; SBA to C. H. Dall, 9 July, 5 August 1876, *Film*, 18:884–87, 961–65. See also *Papers* 1 & 2.)

2. See *Film*, 20:620–23.

3. D. Appleton & Company of New York. It is not known which chapters were submitted to the publisher in 1876. At the time, the authors envisaged their history as one volume detailing the movement up to the centennial year and including biographies and portraits of woman's rights leaders. The plan had changed by 1878, when Matilda Gage published chapters in the monthly *National Citizen and Ballot Box*. Complete in 1878 were an introduction exploring the historical condition of women, a section on women journalists, and descriptions of early movement work in New York and Ohio.

## 104    SBA to Isabella Beecher Hooker

61 Hawthorn street  Chelsea—Mass—[1] Dec. 6/76

My Dear Mrs Hooker

How cheering, how like a balmy breeze, ↑is↓ your letter of the 4th inst— I wanted to stop to see—but could get started in time[2]—& now I cannot go to you, until I get through in Boston & vicinity— I had a good audience Sunday night—[3] Stopped at the Tremont House[4] over Sunday & Monday—but not a "<u>Saint</u>" of the "<u>Hub</u>" called on me, nor attended my lecture[5]—nor did one of them, when I spoke in Parker Fraternity last May—[6] But I am half inclined to look upon Lucy's Saintly face this P.M.—as she is to address the W.S. Club of Chelsea at 3 Oclock— Do you think the radiance would dazzle my poor eyes?—[7] I lecture here Thursday night— In ↑the↓ <u>Paine</u> <u>Course</u>, again, in Boston—Sunday the 10th then at Lynn, Salem &c during next week— & at <u>Florence Mass</u>—Sunday the 17th— If I should have a day before or one after the 17th—I will slip down to Hartford— Or if I am not compelled to return east for more lectures will come to you the 18th from Florence on my way to New York—

For I am & have been longing to see you once more as well as you to see me— I can assure you—

I long for you to be at the front of the battle again— Affectionately
⇒ *Susan B. Anthony*

Regards to Mr Hooker—when he returns— I shall be glad to see him too—

⇒ ALS, on Centennial Headquarters letterhead, place corrected, Isabella Hooker Collection, CtHSD.

1. The address of Annie C. Cheney.

2. En route to Boston, SBA lectured in Bridgeport, Connecticut, visited with Olympia Brown, and then journeyed straight to Boston.

3. At the corner of Tremont and Beacon streets. The *Woman's Journal* office was at 3 Tremont Place at the rear of the hotel.

4. She spoke at Paine Memorial Hall on Appleton Street in a lecture series organized by Boston's free-thought Investigator Society. See *Film*, 18:1094–96.

5. SBA kept a clipping, probably from the *Boston Investigator*, of a letter to the editor by "T. W. G.," who praised her lecture in Paine Hall but expressed sorrow "not to see any of the prominent women's rights advocates present— such as Wendell Phillips, James Freeman Clarke, Mr. Blackwell, Mrs. Livermore, Lucy Stone, Julia Ward Howe, and others. I hope they were not afraid of going to an Infidel Hall, or of being mixed up with heretics, but perhaps the Women Party study policy and so are divided into cliques and rings like the Republicans and Democrats." (SBA scrapbook 8, Rare Books, DLC.)

6. On 21 May 1876. See *Film*, 18:786–87.

7. SBA underestimated her opponent. She wrote in her diary later this day: "The Woman Suffrage Club of Chelsea—met at Parlors of Mrs Strickland— Mrs Cheney & Mrs Osgood asked Lucy Stone if it would be agreeable to have Miss Anthony invited to be present—<u>Lucy said no</u>—so I was left at Mrs Osgoods." (SBA diary, 1876, *Film*, 18:516ff.)

## 105 ⇒ FROM THE DIARY OF SBA

[*10–16 December 1876*]

SUNDAY, DECEMBER 10, 1876. [*Chelsea, Mass.*] Paine Hall—Bread & Ballot[1]

Mrs Ricker[2] came over to Cheneys[3] to dinner & went with me to Paine Hall—dreadfully cold & windy—small audience— went home with W[m] & Ellen Wright Garrison—[4]

1. See *Film*, 18:1102.

2. Marilla Marks Young Ricker (1840–1920) of New Hampshire was an early protestor against taxation without representation in Durham, and she voted in local elections in 1871. She began to attend meetings of the National association in 1875 and held office in succeeding years. At the end of the decade, she settled in Washington to study with Albert G. Riddle and practice law. (*NAW*; *ANB*.)

3. Annie, or Anna, C. Cheney (c. 1842–1882) and Perley C. J. Cheney (c. 1839–?) hosted SBA at their home at 61 Hawthorn Street, Chelsea. A war hero from Vermont's First Cavalry Regiment, Perley Cheney worked at this time as a salesman in Boston. Annie Cheney, a former subscriber to the *Revolution*, belonged to the Chelsea Woman Suffrage Association and the New England Woman's Club. In 1877, she was named a vice president of the National Woman Suffrage Association. (*Rev.*, 28 January 1869, *Film*, 1:444; Federal Census, 1870; Boston and Chelsea city directories, 1876, with assistance of Chelsea Public Library; *Woman's Journal*, 15 July 1882.)

4. At 32 Linwood, Roxbury.

MONDAY, DECEMBER 11, 1876. Salem—Mrs Mary G. Ward—[1]

called at Mr Garrisons in A.M. Sarah Southwick[2] there—long talk on Repub. Party—& Woman Suffrage—

Small audience at Salem— my old associate—Daniel B Hagar[3] of Canajoharie present—& gave me highest compliment for my argument—

1. Mrs. Mary G. Ward lived at 2½ Federal Street in Salem, according to the city directory of 1878. (Research assistance from Kathy Flynn, Peabody Essex Museum, Salem, Mass.)

2. At Rockledge, 125 Highland Street, Roxbury. Sarah Hussey Southwick (1821–1896), from a distinguished family of abolitionists, kept house for Garrison for six months after the death of his wife. She served as an officer of the National Woman Suffrage Association from 1872 to 1874. (Garrison, *Letters*, 5:272n; 6:11, 271n.)

3. Daniel Barnard Hagar (1820–1896) was principal of the Salem State Normal School from 1865 to 1896 and a prominent educator. SBA worked with him at the Canajoharie Academy, where he was principal for five years in the 1840s. His wife, Mary Bradford McKim Hagar, also taught at Canajoharie until December 1848, when the couple departed for Norwich, New York. (SBA to Anthony family, 15 April 1847, and SBA to Daniel R. Anthony, 19 December 1848, in *Film*, 6:654–57, 849–50; *BDAmerEd*, though it errs in marriage date. See also *Papers* 1.)

TUESDAY, DECEMBER 12, 1876. Mrs Ward took me to Prof. Hagar's school—State Normal—200 girls—then to call on Mrs. H[agar] & thence to call on Richie Remond—[1] Charles & wife dead—Mrs Putnam—

& Sarah P. in Florence Italy—only Richie & Susan at Salem— the P.M. went to Peabody—to Womens Temp. meeting[2]

1. Maritcha Juan Remond (1818–?), who owned a hair salon with her sister Cecelia Remond Babcock, was one of the eight children of a prominent African-American family in Salem that also included Charles Lenox Remond (1810–1873), Caroline Remond Putnam (1826–?), Sarah Parker Remond (1824–1894), and Susan H. Remond (1814–?). SBA knew Charles the best; they toured together for the American Anti-Slavery Society and the American Equal Rights Association, and she recalled his wife, Elizabeth Thayer Magee Remond (c. 1837–1872). Before Sarah moved to England and Italy, where she practiced medicine, she too toured with SBA. Caroline Putnam, a partner in her sisters' Salem business, moved abroad to live with Sarah. By 1894, Maritcha had also emigrated to London. Susan Remond carried on her father's trade as a caterer and stayed in Salem. (*DANB* and *ANB*, s.v. "Remond, Charles Lenox" and "Remond, Sarah Parker"; Dorothy Burnett Porter, "The Remonds of Salem, Massachusetts: A Nineteenth-Century Family Revisited," *Proceedings of the American Antiquarian Society* 95, pt. 2 [October 1985]: 259–95; Sibyl Ventress Brownlee, "Out of the Abundance of the Heart: Sarah Ann Parker Remond's Quest for Freedom" [Ph.D. diss., University of Massachusetts, 1997]. See also *Papers* 1 & 2.)

2. This was a local Woman's Christian Temperance Union, founded in December 1875. Describing her audience, SBA wrote: "They hear the word vote—& are scared—but when they listen to a full exposition of its uses & powers—they grasp the ballot." (D. Hamilton Hurd, comp., *History of Essex County, Massachusetts* [Philadelphia, 1888], 2:1028; SBA to Elizabeth B. Harbert, 23 December 1876, *Film*, 18:1103–8.)

WEDNESDAY, DECEMBER 13, 1876. Returned to Boston—Slush & Snow— called at 7 Groten st—on Lydia Maria Child[1]—then to Mrs Rickers— 27. Motte st—& then to Ellen Wright Garrisons— found Mrs Phelps daughter[2] there—very afraid I would publish something of her Mothers insanity in our History

1. Lydia Maria Francis Child (1802–1880), a professional writer and early editor for the American Anti-Slavery Society, wrote the influential *History of the Condition of Women, in Various Ages and Nations* (1835). She was boarding on Groton (not Groten) Street. (*NAW*; *ANB*.)

2. This was a daughter of Charles Abner Phelps and Phoebe Harris Phelps, and presumably it was the daughter with whom Phoebe Phelps fled her marriage in 1860. SBA transported mother and daughter from Albany to a safe house in New York City. The daughter was later seized by her father's agents in Philadelphia and returned to Boston. According to their father's obituary in 1902, there were two daughters alive and in Boston: Florence L. Phelps and

Delia Clark Phelps. (*Papers*, 1:456-58; obituary of Charles Phelps, from *Boston Globe* files, courtesy of Lynn Sherr.)

THURSDAY, DECEMBER 14, 1876. Took the 11 A.M. train for Hartford— found Mrs Hooker glad to see me—first meeting since the B[eecher] & T[ilton] scandal— both <u>Mrs</u> & <u>Mr</u> Hooker thoroughly believe Mr B. guilty of the ↑first↓ charge & of <u>perjury</u> & that the burden of guilt will eventually be too great—& that he will <u>confess</u>.

FRIDAY, DECEMBER 15, 1876. At Hartford— Mrs H. read me her Spiritual experiences & illuminations—thinks herself a medium—[1] Said Martha C. Wright tried to get control of her to talk to me— but could not entirely— Spirits reveal to her that <u>she</u> is to be President in 1880— & S. B. A. to be her Sec'y of the Interior—!!—the only woman in her cabinet—

    1. Long interested in spiritualism, Isabella Hooker's visions of her dead mother during her travels in Europe completed her conversion and convinced her that she was a medium. (Margolis, *Isabella Beecher Hooker Project*, 34-39.)

SATURDAY, DECEMBER 16, 1876. Spent Friday night at the Burrs[1]— Ellen F. Burr—believes she hears <u>rapps</u>—& feels <u>great comfort</u> in spirit presences   She took me to Depot at 10 A.M.—reached Florence at 2 P.M. Stopped with dear Elizabeth Powell Bond—[2]

    1. Probably at the home of Alfred E. Burr, Ellen's older brother, on Main Street. (City directory, 1876.)
    2. Elizabeth Macy Powell Bond (1841-1926), a sister of Aaron Powell and active in New York State reforms as a young woman, directed the department of physical culture at Vassar College from 1865 to 1870, before her marriage to Henry Herrick Bond in 1872. The Bonds lived in Florence, Massachusetts, north of Hartford. She became dean of Swarthmore College in 1886. (*NCAB*, 6:365; Franklin Ellis, *History of Columbia County, New York* [Philadelphia, 1878], 347; Emily Cooper Johnson, *Dean Bond of Swarthmore, A Quaker Humanist* [Philadelphia, 1927].)

&#x2767; The Standard Diary 1876, n.p., SBA Papers, DLC. Letters in square brackets expand abbreviations.

# OPERA HOUSE, MASSILLON.

**ELIZABETH CADY STANTON.**

## Saturday Evening, Feb'y 6, 1875.

### LECTURE, "OUR GIRLS."

*This poster advertised a lecture by Elizabeth Cady Stanton in Massillon, Ohio. The portrait is credited to William Dreser, a lithographer in business in New York, and it may have been provided by the agency that arranged Stanton's tours. W.J. Morgan & Co., Lithographers, Cleveland, produced the poster.*

(Courtesy of the Massillon Museum, East Massillon, Ohio.)

*Aaron Augustus Sargent (1827–1887),*
*Republican senator from California*
*from 1873 to 1879, led efforts in the*
*United States Senate to expand women's*
*rights and gain woman suffrage.*
*Undated photograph.*
(Library of Congress.)

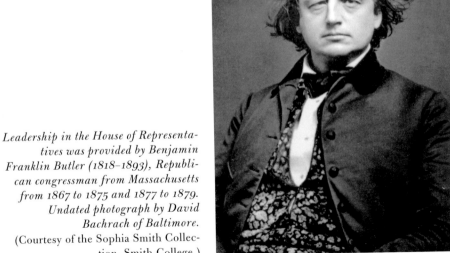

*Leadership in the House of Representa-*
*tives was provided by Benjamin*
*Franklin Butler (1818–1893), Republi-*
*can congressman from Massachusetts*
*from 1867 to 1875 and 1877 to 1879.*
*Undated photograph by David*
*Bachrach of Baltimore.*
(Courtesy of the Sophia Smith Collection, Smith College.)

*A staff artist sketched Elizabeth Cady Stanton speaking to the Senate Committee on Privileges and Elections on 11 January 1878 for the New York Daily Graphic of 16 January 1878. Isabella Beecher Hooker peers in from the right. The man seated to Stanton's left is unidentified; to his left and around the table are committee members Angus Cameron, John Mitchell, Bainbridge Wadleigh, George Hoar (with chin in hand), Benjamin Hill, Eli Saulsbury, and Samuel McMillan. Chairman Wadleigh, Stanton recalled, "took special pains to show that he did not intend to listen. . . . It was with difficulty I restrained the impulse more than once to hurl my manuscript at his head."*
Engraving by Philip G. Cusachs.

At their Centennial Headquarters in central Philadelphia, Susan B. Anthony and Elizabeth Cady Stanton welcomed hundreds of visitors to the Centennial Exposition in the summer of 1876, offering them comfortable seating, cultural events, and literature from the National Woman Suffrage Association. In this letter from the headquarters, Stanton asks John Russell Young of the New York Herald to report on Anthony's interruption of Fourth of July festivities at Independence Hall to present the National's Declaration of Rights. Although dated "July 3ᵈ," the letter was written on July 5. (From John Russell Young Papers, Library of Congress.)

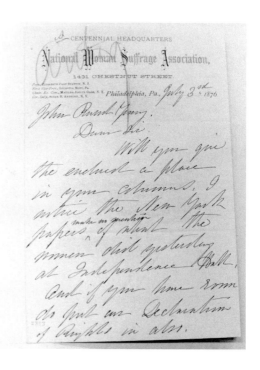

*Issued by her brother, publisher of the* Leavenworth Times, *this press pass allowed Susan B. Anthony free admission to the fairgrounds at the Centennial Exposition. She made use of it on only four occasions in May and June.*
(Courtesy of the Rochester Public Library.)

*The Perry House and buildings, Garland City, Colorado, 1877 or 1878, photographed by F. C. Warnky. Built as a construction camp for workers on the Denver & Rio Grande Railway in 1877, Garland City existed for a year before its buildings were moved further west along the track to Alamosa. Susan B. Anthony reached the town by train on 17 September 1877 and spoke to voters in the hotel dining room, urging them to approve the woman suffrage amendment to Colorado's constitution.*
(Denver Public Library, Western History Collection.)

*Belva Ann Lockwood (1830–1917) gained admission to the bar of the District of Columbia in 1873, but the federal courts refused to admit any woman to practice. After intense lobbying alongside the National Woman Suffrage Association, Lockwood pushed legislation through Congress to open the courts. Undated photograph by Charles Milton Bell, Washington, D.C.*
(Courtesy of the Sophia Smith Collection, Smith College.)

*Ellen Clark Sargent (1826–1911) served as treasurer of the National Woman Suffrage Association and a member of its Resident Congressional Committee while she resided in Washington during her husband's term as senator from California. Photograph dating from about 1890.*
(Reproduced by permission of The Huntington Library, San Marino, California.)

*Elizabeth Morrison Boynton Harbert
(1843–1925) came to the attention of
Susan B. Anthony in Indiana and went
on to become a leader in Iowa and
Illinois. The Illinois Woman Suffrage
Association elected her president in
1876, and a year later, the Chicago*
Inter-Ocean *named her editor of a
weekly column, the "Woman's Kingdom," that was read by women across
the Midwest. Engraving by John
Chester Buttre, 1885, from a photograph by Aitkin.*
(From E. C. Stanton, S. B. Anthony, and
M. J. Gage, *History of Woman Suffrage*.)

*Matilde Franziska Giesler Anneke
(1817–1884), a writer, teacher, and
political activist, came to the United
States after the German Revolution of
1848. An officer of the National Woman
Suffrage Association from 1869 until
her death, she built coalitions of
suffragists with German-American
radicals and freethinkers, and from her
home in Milwaukee, she organized
Germans and other urban immigrants
into the Wisconsin suffrage association.
Photographed by J. Ganz in Zurich,
where Anneke lived from 1860 to 1865.*
(Image WHi-3701, Wisconsin Historical
Society.)

*Matilda Joslyn Gage (1826–1898), photo-*
*graphed by Matthew Brady in 1876.*
(Schlesinger Library, Radcliffe Institute,
Harvard University.)

*Lillie Devereux Blake (1833–1913),*
*engraving by Frederick Girsch, 1882.*
(From E. C. Stanton, S. B. Anthony, and
M. J. Gage, *History of Woman Suffrage.*)

*Clemence Sophia Harned Lozier*
*(1813–1888), undated photograph*
*by Veeder, Albany, New York.*
(Library of Congress.)

*Three of the most prominent suffragists from New York State between 1873 and 1880 were*
*Matilda Gage of Fayetteville, near Syracuse, and Dr. Clemence Lozier and Lillie Blake of New*
*York City. All held office in the National Woman Suffrage Association and its state*
*counterpart. All had professional careers.*

*Susan B. Anthony, photographed by J. H. Kent of Rochester, New York, about 1877. (Courtesy of Department of Rare Books and Special Collections, University of Rochester Library.)*

*Helen L. Potter is here dressed to deliver her impersonation of Susan B. Anthony, probably about 1877, when her career as a popular entertainer was at its peak. (From Helen Potter's Impersonations.)*

*Describing how to be Anthony on the stage, Potter wrote: "Take short steps upon entering and retiring from the platform. Throw the wrap or shawl over the chairback and sit down, but never lean back. Intense natures like hers sit forward. Make few gestures, and those of the emphatic sort only, and leave the platform the minute you are done speaking."*

*This page from Elizabeth Cady Stanton's manuscript of "The Bible and Woman Suffrage" illustrates her habit of recycling pages from her lectures. Once the twenty-something page of a sequence now lost, the sheet elsewhere served as page "30" and "38b" before she pasted "44" onto her sheet and obscured an insertion of Vashti's name. The manuscript is very like the speech included in this volume at 11 May 1879. The markings of a typesetter, evident only on recycled pages, date from an earlier use. When she spoke in May 1879, she ended Tennyson's line with "out" rather than making the correction to "forth."*
(Elizabeth Cady Stanton Papers, Library of Congress.)

*Elizabeth Cady Stanton in a cabinet photo by Henry Rocher, Chicago. Inscribed by Stanton on verso to Robert Purvis, 27 August 1880.*
(Minneapolis Public Library, Huttner Collection.)

*Harriet Purvis (1839–?), a daughter of Robert Purvis, joined her parents in reform and like them became a friend of Elizabeth Cady Stanton and Susan B. Anthony. A member of the Philadelphia Female Anti-Slavery Society while a teenager, Hattie held office in the American Equal Rights Association in her twenties, and worked with the National Woman Suffrage Association. This picture originally appeared in Ida Husted Harper,* Life and Work of Susan B. Anthony. (Courtesy of Rosalyn Terborg-Penn.)

*The Holland Union Literary Association in western New York advertised Susan B. Anthony and her best-known lecture, "Woman Wants Bread, Not the Ballot," for an engagement on 30 March 1880. Anthony scheduled all her lectures close to home that spring in order to be near her mother who died in Rochester on April 3.*
*(Courtesy of the Holland Historical Society, Holland, New York.)*

## 106 ⤳    SBA to Robert G. Ingersoll[1]

Tenafly N.J. Jan. 1, 1877

Hon. R. J. Ingersol   Dear Friend

Will you honor our Woman's Cause by making one of your clear cut arguments at our Washington Convention the 16th & 17th inst?— I hope you will be able to say <u>yes</u>, without an if—but, if it is utterly impossible for you to be present—you will not, I am sure refuse to write us a letter—Setting forth the duty of the national government to protect women ↑in↓ the enjoyment of equality of rights, civil and political, against any & all invidious discriminations in the different states—

Now, please, do not fail to have your letter in Washington in ample time to be read at our Convention—

I am very, very glad that we are to have "<u>Bob</u>" Ingersol—& <u>his</u> "<u>Gods</u>" to Champion our Woman's Cause in the next Congress— Mrs Stanton & all her <u>immortal</u>—or <u>mortal</u>, as the case may—seven have been reading your "<u>Gods</u>" with great delight[2]—& her daughter Hattie, to day, at dinner rebuked her Mother for speaking somewhat disparagingly of the "<u>Devil</u>"—& said I agree with "Bob" Ingersol— The Devil is about the best friend we have.— So with a "Happy New Year" to yourself & wife & children—and another <u>hope</u> <u>that</u> ↑you↓ will <u>speak</u> for us, <u>if</u> <u>possible</u>—& write us a <u>letter</u> <u>any</u> <u>way</u>—I am Sincerely yours—

⤳   *Susan B. Anthony*

⤳ ALS, Centennial Headquarters letterhead, place corrected, Robert G. Ingersoll Papers, DLC.

1. Robert Green Ingersoll (1833–1899), orator and lawyer, was in Washington not, as SBA wrote, because he was entering Congress, but because he expected an appointment from Rutherford B. Hayes in recognition of his major role in the Republican campaign. Religious opposition to his secularism ended hopes of a position in the administration, but Ingersoll decided to move to Washington anyway. SBA first met him in Peoria, Illinois, at a county suffrage convention on 15 March 1870, where he delivered "a most splendid speech." He was married to Eva Amelia Parker Ingersoll (1840–1923) and was the father of two daughters, Eva Robert (1863–1928) and Maud Robert (1864–1936). (*ANB*; *New York Times*, 3 February 1923, 29 August 1928, 13 February

1936; Orvin Larson, *American Infidel, Robert G. Ingersoll: A Biography* [New York, 1962], 52, 85, 102, 120–29; *Woman's Who's Who 1914*, s.v., "Brown, Eva R. Ingersoll," and "Ingersoll, Maud R."; SBA diary, 1870, *Film*, 14:173ff.)

2. The Stantons were reading Ingersoll's *The Gods, and Other Lectures*, first published in 1874. Harriot Stanton alludes to the lecture "The Gods," in which Ingersoll described devils as sympathetic teachers of humanity, in contrast to gods who ordered terrible punishments.

## 107 ᨌ WILLIAM LLOYD GARRISON TO SBA

Roxbury [*Mass.*] Jan. 4, 1877.

(Private.)

Dear Miss Anthony:

I have received your letter of the 1st instant, with the printed slips enclosed therein.[1] Miss Southwick joins with Frank[2] and myself in reciprocating your kind wishes for "a happy new year."

You desire me to send you a letter, to be read at the Washington Convention of the National Woman Suffrage Association, in favor of a petition to Congress, asking that body to submit to the several States a 16th Amendment to the Constitution of the United State, securing suffrage for all, irrespective of sex. On fully considering the subject, I must decline doing so, because such a petition I deem to be quite premature. If its request were complied with by the present Congress—a supposition simply preposterous—the proposed Amendment would be rejected by every State in the Union, and in nearly every instance by such an overwhelming majority as to bring the movement into needless contempt. Even as a matter of "agitation," I do not think it would pay. Look over the whole country, and see in the present state of public sentiment on the question of woman suffrage what a mighty primary work remains to be done in enlightening the masses, who know nothing and care nothing about it, and, consequently, are not at all prepared to cast their votes for any such thing. I think it is a mistake to look for a favorable consideration of the question on the part of legislators, under such circumstances. More light is needed for the popular mind, ab initio.[3] Yours for the right,

ᨌ *W^{m} Lloyd Garrison.*

⤳ ALS, HM 10564, Ida Harper Collection, CSmH.

1. See *Film*, 19:414–17.

2. Francis Jackson Garrison (1848–1916), the youngest of the Garrison children and still single, worked at the Riverside Press in Cambridge. (Garrison, *Letters*, 6:18.)

3. From the beginning.

108  ⤳  FROM THE DIARY OF SBA

[*16–22 January 1877*]

TUESDAY, JANUARY 16, 1877. 8̶ ↑9↓^th Washington National W.S. Convention—Lincoln Hall—[1] Mrs Stanton President— She & self stopped at Senator Sargents—[2] Mrs Gage, Mrs Blake & Miss Couzins present— Belva A. Lockwood made an excellent speech on the Supreme Court— Streets very sloppy—but audiences good— Dr Mary Walker on hand first one & on the platform before we arrived— A. H. Riddle spoke this evening—[3]

1. On the confusion over which convention this was, see note above at second document, 10 November 1876. For coverage of the meeting, see *Film*, 19:427–40.

2. At 1733 DeSales Street, Northwest.

3. That is, Albert G. Riddle.

WEDNESDAY, JANUARY 17, 1877. ~~Eighth~~ ↑Ninth↓ Washington National W.S. Convention.

Rainy to day—still the audiences splendid— nothing seems ordinarially pleasant to me—the speaking not equal—but it is doubtless myself—

THURSDAY, JANUARY 18, 1877. Washington— Worked on the Petitions at Mrs Spencers until 3. P.M.[1] then went with her to the House—to get them in the hands of M.C. there are 23 States represented—[2]

1. They organized the petitions for a sixteenth amendment by state and copied seven thousand names to provide a duplicate set of petitions for the Senate. (SBA to Isabella B. Hooker, 20 January 1877, *Film*, 19:448–55.)

2. For a description of this visit to the House of Representatives, see below at 24 January 1877. The petitions came from California, Colorado, Connecticut, District of Columbia, Illinois, Indiana, Iowa, Kansas, Kentucky, Maine,

Massachusetts, Michigan, Minnesota, Missouri, New Hampshire, New Jersey, New York, Ohio, Oregon, Pennsylvania, Rhode Island, Vermont, and Wisconsin.

FRIDAY, JANUARY 19, 1877. Petitions from 23 states presented in the H.R. this A.M.—by 23 different members—[1] also a unanimous report of the Judiciary Committee on Mrs Lockwoods petition for removal of legal disability of women to practice law—[2]

Mrs Stanton left for home this A.M.—

1. *Congressional Record*, 44th Cong., 2d sess., 752–53, 755. At the request of the speaker, the House gave unanimous consent to receive the petitions one by one. They were referred to the Committee on the Judiciary.

2. The Supreme Court considered Belva Lockwood's petition for admission to practice on 6 November 1876 and immediately denied it. Lockwood then renewed her plea to Congress to allow women to practice in the federal courts. Her bill, H.R. 4435, was introduced on 16 January. The Committee on the Judiciary did not report on this day; rather, while members presented petitions for the sixteenth amendment, George Hoar told the House that the committee would submit the bill soon. (*Congressional Record*, 44th Cong., 2d sess., 661, 752.)

SATURDAY, JANUARY 20, 1877. Petitions presented in the Senate[1]—Mr Sargent leading off & making a nice little speech—followed by 22 other Senators—[2] Dawes of Mass. made approving remarks—[3] Cameron of Penn.[4] made disagreeable comments showing he was an opponent—

1. *Congressional Record*, 44th Cong., 2d sess., 762–63. The petitions were referred to the Committee on Privileges and Elections.

2. Aaron Sargent ended his remarks with the observation that woman suffragists "should not be left to the Herculean labor of applying to the States in detail. The colored man would never have had a vote, left to that process. Congress should fairly submit the question to the people, as is its custom in such matters; and the people can be safely trusted to decide it rightly." (*Congressional Record*, 44th Cong., 2d sess., 762.)

3. Henry Dawes, who entered the Senate in 1875, observed "that the subject-matter of this petition is engaging the attention of both political parties in my own State to some extent, and that the members of both political parties are committing themselves to it." (*Congressional Record*, 44th Cong., 2d sess., 762.)

4. Simon Cameron (1799–1889), Republican from Pennsylvania until his resignation in March 1877, suggested that the many petitions should have been combined into one to save the Senate's time. (*BDAC*; *Congressional Record*, 44th Cong., 2d sess., 763.)

SUNDAY, JANUARY 21, 1877. Went to Mrs Spencers again & worked on petitions all day—[1] at eve called on Mrs Lockwood & bid Mrs Gage, Mrs Ricker & Mrs L. Good Bye— Mrs Gage did not return my kiss— but turned her cheek— Thence to ↑see↓ Robert Purvis[2]—found him very ill—but better—seemed very glad to see me— Found Miss Couzzins at Mr Sargents—she staid all night

1. Seven hundred to a thousand petitions arrived too late to be prepared for the initial presentation in Congress. These were presented in the Senate and House on 30 January 1877. (*Congressional Record*, 44th Cong., 2d sess., 1095–96, 1118, 1121, 1122.)

2. At the home of his son, Charles B. Purvis, a doctor and professor at Howard University, who lived at 1118 Thirteenth Street, Northwest. The younger Purvis attended the National's convention. (City directory, 1877.)

MONDAY, JANUARY 22, 1877. Left Washington on the 7.40— Northern Central route[1]—this evening— Went to Mrs Spencers at 10 & worked on Convention report until 5 P.M.[2] then back to Mr Sargents to dinner & off for home—

1. By the Northern Central Railway through Pennsylvania and western New York, she could travel overnight to Rochester.

2. That is, the report in the *Ballot Box*.

⤳ The Standard Diary 1877, n.p., SBA Papers, DLC.

109 ⇒ ECS TO THE EDITOR, *BALLOT BOX*

Tenafly, N.J., Jan 24 [*1877*].

Dear Editor:—If the little *Ballot Box* is not already stuffed to repletion with reports from Washington, I crave a little space to tell your readers that the convention was in all points successful. Lincoln Hall, which seats about fifteen thousand people,[1] was crowded every session; the speaking was good, order reigned; no heart-burning behind the scenes, and the press vouchsafed "respectful consideration."

The resolutions you will find more interesting and suggestive than that kind of literature usually is, and I ask especial attention to the one for a national convention, to revise the constitution, which, with all its amendments, is like a kite with a tail of indefinite length, still to be lengthened.[2] It is evident a century of experience has so liberalized the minds of the American people, that they have outgrown the constitution, adapted to the men of 1776. It is a monarchical document with republican ideas engrafted in it, full of compromises between antagonistic principles. An American statesman remarked, "that the civil war was fought to expound the constitution on the question of slavery,"— expensive expounding![3] Instead of further amending and expounding, the real work at the dawn of our second century is to make a new one. Again I ask the attention of our women on the education resolution.[4] After much thought it seems to me we should have education compulsory in every State of the Union, and make it the basis of suffrage, a national law, requiring that those who vote, after 1880, must read and write the English language. This would prevent ignorant foreigners voting in six months after landing on our shores, and stimulate our native population to higher intelligence. It would dignify and purify the ballot box, and add safety and stability to our free institutions. Mrs. Jane Grey Swisshelm,[5] who had just returned from Europe, attended the convention, and spoke very well on this point.

Belva A. Lockwood, who had recently been denied admission to the Supreme Court of the United States, although a lawyer in good practice for three years in the Supreme Court of the District, made a very scathing speech, reviewing the decision of the court. It may seem to your disfranchised readers, quite presumptuous for one of their number, to make those nine wise men on the bench, constituting the highest Judicial authority in the United States, subjects for ridicule, before an audience of the sovereign people; but when they learn the decision in Mrs. Lockwood's case, they will be reassured as to woman's capacity, to cope with their wisdom.[6]

To arrive at the same conclusion with these judges, it is not necessary, said Mrs. Lockwood, to understand constitutional law, nor the history of English jurisprudence, nor the inductive, nor deductive modes of reasoning, as no such profound learning, or processes of thought, were involved in that decision, which was simply this, "There is no precedent for admitting a woman to practice in the Supreme Court of the United States, hence Mrs. Lockwood's application cannot be considered."

On this point Mrs. Lockwood showed that it was the glory of each generation to make its own precedents. As there was none for Eve in the garden of Eden, she argued there need be none for her daughters on entering the college, the church, or the courts. Blackstone—of whose works she inferred the judges were ignorant—gives several precedents for women in the English courts.[7] Mrs. Lockwood having also been checkmated in the Court of Claims, a lady speaking of that Bench, consisting of five judges, remarked, "One is almost blind, one is lame, one is consumptive, one so narrow that he looks at all great principles through his microscope, and the last is the successor of a dead man, who fills less space on the bench than his predecessor now fills under the sod." Charles O'Conor,[8] a distinguished member of the New York bar, was quite as severe on our sex, when he was asked, what he thought of Judge Hunt? "Judge Hunt, said he, why, I think he is a very ladylike Judge."

After listening to these charcoal sketches of the Washington Judiciary, some ladies visited the Supreme Court, opera glass in hand, and reported that branch better looking than their decisions indicated; the committee on the Court of Claims have not yet reported.

As Mrs. Lockwood—tall, well proportioned, with dark hair and eyes, regular features, in velvet dress and train, with becoming indignation at such injustice, marched up and down the platform, and rounded out her glowing periods, she might have fairly represented the Italian Portia at the bar of Venice.[9] No more effective speech was ever made on our platform.

Matilda Joslyn Gage, whose speeches are always replete with historical research, reviewed the action of the Republican party towards woman, from the introduction of the word "male," into the 14th Amendment of the constitution, down to the celebration of our national birthday in Philadelphia, when the declaration of the mothers was received in contemptuous silence, while Dom Pedro[10] and other foreign dignitaries looked calmly on. Mrs. Gage makes as dark a chapter for the Republicans, as Mrs. Lockwood for the Judiciary, or Mrs. Lillie Devereux Blake for the church. She had been an attentive listener during the trial of the Rev. Isaac See,[11] before the Presbytery of Newark, New Jersey, hence she felt moved to give the convention a chapter of ecclesiastical history, showing the struggles through which the church was passing with the irrepressible woman in the pulpit. Mrs. Blake's Biblical interpretations and expositions proved conclusively that Scott's and Clarke's[12] commentaries would at no distant day be superceded by standard works from woman's standpoint. It is not to be supposed that women ever can have fair play as long as men only write and interpret the scripture; make and expound the law. Why would it not be a good idea, for women to leave these conservative gentlemen alone in the churches? How sombre they would look with the flowers, feathers, bright ribbons, and shawls, all gone; black coats only kneeling and standing, and with the deep-toned organ swelling up, the solemn bass voice heard only in awful solitude; not one soprano note, to rise above the low dull wail and fill the arched roof with triumphant melody. One such experiment, from Maine to California, would bring these bigoted Presbyteries to their senses. Miss Phoebe Couzins, too, was at the convention, and gave her new lecture, "A Woman Without a Country," in which she shows all that woman has done to make this country what it is from fitting out ships for Columbus,[13] to sharing the toils of the great exposition, without a place of honor in the republic for the living, or a statue to the memory of the dead.

A. G. Riddle and Francis Miller, members of the Washington bar, spoke ably and eloquently as usual, the former on the 16th Amendment and the Presidential aspect, modestly suggesting that if 20,000,000 women had voted they might have been able to find out for whom the majority had cast their ballots.[14]

Mr. Miller recommended State action, advising us to concentrate our forces in Colorado, as a shorter way to success, than Constitutional amendments.[15] His speech, roused Susan B. Anthony to the boiling point, for if there is anything that exasperates her, it is to be remanded, as she says, to John Morrissey's constituency, for her rights. She contends that if the United States authorities could punish her for voting in the State of New York, they hold the same power to protect her here in the exercise of that right. Moreover she said we have two wings to our movement. The American Association is trying the State rights method. The National Association is trying the Constitutional method, which has emancipated and enfranchised the African, and secured to the race all their civil rights; to-day, by this method, they are in the courts, the colleges, the halls of legislation in every State in the Union, while we have puttered with State rights thirty years, without a foothold anywhere, except in the territories, and it is now proposed to rob the women of their rights in those localities. As the two methods do not conflict and what is done in the several States, tells on the nation, and the national work reacts again on the State, it must be a good thing to keep up both kinds of agitation.

In the middle of November, The National Association sent out thousands of petitions, and appeals for the 16th Amendment, which were published and commented on extensively by the press in every State in the Union. Early in January they began to pour into Washington at the rate of a thousand a day, coming from twenty-six different States.[16] It does not require much wisdom to see that when these petitions were placed in the hands of the representatives of their several States that a great educational work was accomplished at Washington, and public sentiment there has its legitimate effect throughout the country, as well as that already accomplished in the rural districts, by the slower process of circulating and signing the petitions.

The present uncertain position of men, and parties, has made politicians more ready to listen to the demands of their constituents, and never has Woman Suffrage been treated with more courtesy in Washington.

To Sara Andrews Spencer we are all indebted, for the great labor of receiving, assorting, counting, rolling up and planning the presentation of the petitions. It was by a well-considered coup d'etat that with her brave coadjutors, she appeared on the floor of the House at the moment of adjournment, and there without circumlocution, gave each member a petition from his own State. Even Miss Anthony, always calm in the hour of danger, on finding herself suddenly whisked into those sacred enclosures, mid a crowd of stalwart men, spittoons and scrap baskets, when brought vis-a-vis with our champion, Mr. Hoar,[17] she hastily apologized for the intrusion, to which the Hon. gentleman promptly replied, "I hope Madame, yet to see you on this floor, in your own right, and in business hours too." Then and there the work of the next day was agreed on, the members gladly accepting the petitions. As you have already seen, Mr. Hoar made the motion for the special order which was carried, and the petitions presented. Your readers will be glad to know, that Mr. Hoar has just been chosen, by Massachusetts, as her next Senator, that gives us another champion in the Senate. As there are many petitions still in circulation, urge your readers to keep sending them until the close of the session, to Mrs. Spencer, as we want to know how many women are in earnest on this question. It is constantly said "women do not want to vote." Forty thousand told our representatives at Washington in a single day that they did![18] What answer? Yours sincerely,

                   ⇜ *Elizabeth Cady Stanton*

⇜ Toledo *Ballot Box*, February 1877. Also in *History*, 3:65–67.

    1. Fifteen hundred was closer to the capacity of Lincoln Hall.

    2. Matilda Gage, SBA, Belva Lockwood, Edward Davis, Charles Purvis, and Jane Swisshelm made up the committee on resolutions. ECS refers to the resolution reading: "the safety and stability of free institutions and the protection of all United States citizens in the exercise of their inalienable rights . . . are not guaranteed by the present form of the Constitution of the United States; therefore, . . . it is the duty of the several States to call a national convention to revise the Constitution of the United States." (*Ballot Box*, February 1877, *Film*, 19:434–35.)

    3. This sentence, including its quotation, comes from Karl Heinzen, *What Is Real Democracy? Answered by an Exposition of the Constitution of the United States* (Indianapolis, Ind., 1871), 15.

    4. The text of the resolution that ECS describes can be found below in her letter dated before 24 May 1877.

    5. Jane Grey Cannon Swisshelm (1815–1884) published antislavery papers before the war and a Radical Republican paper in Washington, D.C., at the war's end. After losing a federal job, she divided her time between Pittsburgh and Chicago, continued to write, publishing articles in the *Woman's Journal*, *Chicago Tribune*, and *Pittsburg Commercial-Gazette*, among others, and made occasional appearances in the suffrage movement. In the early 1870s she was active in the Illinois Woman Suffrage Association, and in 1872 and 1874, she campaigned in Iowa to press for a constitutional amendment. When she attended the National's meeting in January 1877, she had just returned from a trip to Europe. Always argumentative and independent, Swisshelm grew more conservative and cranky as the decade progressed, and by 1878 she turned her acerbic pen against suffrage activists. (*NAW*; *ANB*; Noun, *Strong-Minded Women*, 205–6, 215–19; *Woman's Journal*, 20 January 1872, 16 May 1874; *New York Tribune*, 8 June 1876, 14 February, 17 April, 13 June 1878; *Chicago Tribune*, 15 October 1874, *Film*, 18:118–20. See also *Papers* 1.)

    6. In its unpublished opinion, the Supreme Court stated that "none but men are permitted to practice before [the Court] as attorneys and counsellors. This is in accordance with immemorial usage in England, and the law and practice in all the States until within a recent period, and that the Court does not feel called upon to make a change until such a change is required by statute or a more extended practice in the higher courts of the States." (Fairman, *Reconstruction and Reunion, Part One*, 1366–67.)

    7. Lockwood repeated her review of English precedents in her brief to the Senate, 7 March 1878, citing the examples of Queen Victoria; Eleanor, wife of

Henry III; Queen Elizabeth I; and Anne Clifford, countess of Dorset, Pembroke, and Montgomery, who inherited the office of sheriff from her father in 1643. (Blackstone, *Commentaries on the Laws of England*, 1:255; *History*, 3:106–8.)

8. Charles O'Conor (1804–1884), a prominent Democrat and rival of Ward Hunt, was counsel to Jefferson Davis and helped to break the Tweed Ring in New York City. For an earlier telling of this story, see *Papers*, 2:626. (*ANB*.)

9. The heroine of William Shakespeare's *Merchant of Venice*, Portia disguised herself as a lawyer to defend a friend against Shylock. Her name became synonymous with female attorneys.

10. Dom Pedro II (1825–1891), emperor of Brazil, attended the Fourth of July ceremonies in Philadelphia in 1876.

11. Isaac McBride See (1829–1902), a graduate of Rutgers College and the Theological Seminary of New Brunswick, was a Dutch Reformed minister who served the Wickliffe Presbyterian Church in Newark, New Jersey, from 1872 to 1878. Lillie Blake recounted his recent church trial after he was charged by the Presbytery of Newark with disobeying biblical injunctions against women preaching in church because he allowed two members of the Woman's Christian Temperance Union to speak from his pulpit in October 1876. Blake and Matilda Gage were among the many women who crowded the proceedings in a show of support for See. (John Haven Raven, comp., *Biographical Record. Theological Seminary, New Brunswick, New Jersey, 1784–1934* [New Brunswick, N.J., 1934], 97, with assistance of Kenneth J. Ross, Presbyterian Historical Society, Philadelphia; Lois A. Boyd, "Shall Women Speak? Confrontation in the Church, 1876," *Journal of Presbyterian History* 56 [Winter 1978]: 281–94; *History*, 3:484–88.)

12. Thomas Scott (1747–1821), an English clergyman known as "the Commentator," published *The Holy Bible, with Explanatory Notes, Practical Observations, and Copious Marginal References* between 1788 and 1792. Adam Clarke (1762–1832), an Anglo-Irish Methodist, published *The Holy Bible, with a Commentary and Critical Notes* between 1810 and 1826. (Allibone.)

13. Isabella (1451–1504), Spanish queen of Castile from 1474, supported the explorations of Christopher Columbus (1451–1506).

14. The presidential election of 1876 was not settled: within days of the election, Democrat Samuel J. Tilden of New York claimed victory on the basis of the popular vote, but Republican Rutherford B. Hayes believed that there were enough electoral votes in dispute to give him the victory. At the time of the National's meeting, congressional committees were discussing the creation of an electoral commission to settle the election. Not until 29 January was the commission approved, and not until 2 March was Hayes declared the winner.

15. Article 7, section 2 of Colorado's first state constitution directed that the assembly "shall, at the first session thereof, and may at any subsequent session, enact laws to extend the right of suffrage to women of lawful age, and

otherwise qualified according to the provisions of this article. No such enactment shall be of effect until submitted to the vote of the qualified electors at a
general election, nor unless the same be approved by a majority of those
voting thereon." At its first session in January 1877, the assembly agreed to
send the question of woman suffrage to the voters in October.

16. ECS errs; by all counts, petitions came from twenty-three states.

17. George Frisbie Hoar (1826–1904) of Massachusetts served as a Republican in the House of Representatives from March 1869 to March 1877, when he
took his seat in the Senate. In 1871, he was a member of the Massachusetts
Republican convention that endorsed woman suffrage. A strong supporter of
most woman's rights measures in the Senate, Hoar gave only qualified support
to the sixteenth amendment because he favored amending state constitutions
rather than the federal one. (*BDAC*.)

18. Ten thousand was the usual estimate of petitioners.

## 110 &sect; ARTICLE BY SBA

[February 1877]

### THE HISTORY.

The proposed history of the woman suffrage movement is progress-
ing slowly; the work grows on the hands of its editors—much time and
labor have been expended in getting the material together. Mrs. Stanton
and Mrs. Gage are steadily at work upon it, but it will hardly be ready
to go into the hands of the publisher before Autumn.[1] So, friends, be
ready with your $5 when that time comes. Some friends have already
sent us the money and the book shall go to them in due time.

&sect; *Susan B. Anthony.*

&sect; Toledo *Ballot Box*, February 1877.

1. In fact, they had no publisher. D. Appleton & Company informed SBA
in January that the firm would not undertake such an expensive job in hard
times; she still hoped they would do it when the times got better. (SBA diary,
12–13 January 1877, *Film*, 19:12ff.)

111  →  FROM THE DIARY OF SBA

[*11–14, 17 March 1877*]

SUNDAY, MARCH 11, 1877. At Vincennes Ind[1]—at 9 A.M. the porter brought me 3 letters—one from Mr Burton[2]—Princeton—one from brother Aaron M. L. written the 6th inst—saying he thought sister H[annah]'s Louise ought to go to her—that sister had but a little while to stay & Louise should have her company & counsel—while she was able to enjoy & give & one from sister Mary—the same date—[3] Answered brother A. that I had long felt that Louise should be sent to her mother—

1. SBA lectured in Illinois for two months with occasional forays into Indiana. About twenty-five miles from her next engagement, Vincennes, a junction of major railroads, was a good location in which to spend a weekend without lectures.

2. J. Ralph Burton was a young lawyer who moved to Gibson County, Indiana, in 1873 and stayed four years, before settling in Abilene, Kansas. He was SBA's contact for a lecture in Princeton, Indiana, on 8 March. Though she had set out from Mount Carmel, Illinois, that day to travel to Princeton by ferry and train, she missed the engagement: "rained & no ferryboat at landing got into a skiff & was rowed half over the Wabash when the driver shouted the train is gone—so all was lost—& I set back." (*History of Gibson County, Indiana: With Illustrations Descriptive of Its Scenery* [Edwardsville, Ill., 1884], 96; SBA diary, 8 March 1877, *Film*, 19:12ff.)

3. Letters crossed in the mail. On 6 March, SBA heard from Hannah Mosher, who told her to keep lecturing, but SBA concluded that Hannah was "failing very rapidly." On the same day, SBA wrote Mary Anthony in Rochester to take Louise out of school and let her go to her mother at once. (SBA diary, 6 March 1877.)

MONDAY, MARCH 12, 1877. Robinson—Ill— $25—[1] Geo. W. Harper[2]

Left Vincennes at 4.45 A.M. after almost no sleep—got up & dressed at 3 & sat & rocked & worried because I couldn't sleep—[3] Trains & Engines crashing by almost constantly— Mr Haper met me at depot—rain pouring— Miss Mary Buntin[4]—Ed. & Pub. of the "Rural Republican"—and <u>Mrs</u> Maria J. Isom[5]—a Dry Goods & Notion Merchant—from Lawrenceville—Lawrence Co. Ill—came up to hear me—20 miles—

1. SBA indicates that the terms of her employment at Robinson guaranteed her this sum. On other occasions, for example below at 19 March, she indicates what fraction of ticket sales would be hers. On the basis of these earnings, she then paid her agent his commission.

2. George W. Harper (c. 1838–1928), who first apprenticed himself to a printer in 1853, founded the Robinson *Argus* in 1863 and published it for more than six decades. He stayed in contact with SBA, writing her as late as 1902. (William Henry Perrin, ed., *History of Crawford and Clark Counties, Illinois* [Chicago, 1883], 80, 83, 238; Federal Census, 1870; *Film*, 20:714–15, 720–23, 42:683–84; on-line list of veteran burials, Crawford County, Illinois, in possession of editors.)

3. The Paris & Danville Railroad ran one train daily from Vincennes to Robinson, twenty-five miles to the northwest. The town was the seat of Crawford County.

4. Mary Buntin (c.1851–1880) purchased the *Rural Republican* from her father, "the pioneer printer" of Lawrence County, in 1874 or 1875 and published it until her premature death. (*Combined History of Edwards, Lawrence and Wabash Counties, Illinois* [Philadelphia, 1883], 135; Bessie Irene Black, *Cemeteries of Lawrence County, Illinois* [Bridgeport, Ill., 1976], 261.)

5. Mariah Isom (c. 1850–?), in 1870, lived with a one-year-old son in the household of a lawyer in Lawrenceville. (Federal Census, 1870.)

TUESDAY, MARCH 13, 1877. Effingham—Ill  $25—  H. C. Painter[1]

Left Robinson at 6.35 A.M.—but little good sleep—breakfasted at Marshall—[reached?] Effingham at 1 P.M—[2] Mr & Mrs Painter & Mrs Kepler[3] called at Etna Hotel to see— cold & cloudy—almost rain—very muddy—about 100 in my audience—the very best—all 50 & 75 cts—so the young men Mr ——— Thompson,[4] Painter & [*blank*]—paid expenses—

Got letter here from sister Mary—brother Aaron had telegraphed brother D. R. if they should send Louise to Leavenworth—& he had replied Hannah said she better remain in school—so I wrote Mary, Aaron & Eugene—that I could not go on lecturing unless Louise went—

1. Henry C. Painter (1845–?), a printer, moved to Effingham in 1873 to publish and edit the local paper, the *Republican*. He married Amanda Eskridge (1842–?) in 1868. Amanda Painter was active in the town's lyceum. (William Henry Perrin, ed., *History of Effingham County, Illinois* [1883; reprint, Evansville, Ind., 1972], 60–61, 94, 157–58.)

2. SBA boarded the Paris & Danville Railroad northbound again for a thirty-mile ride to Marshall, where she changed to the St. Louis, Vandalia, Terre Haute, & Indianapolis Railroad into Effingham, another county seat. For coverage of her lecture there, see *Film*, 19:472.

3. Although SBA wrote the name as "Kepler," it is likely she met Ada Harriet Miser Kepley (1847–1925), a longtime resident of Effingham who was active in the woman's rights, suffrage, and temperance movements and the first American woman to graduate from law school. Her husband, Henry B. Kepley, an attorney, was a founder of the local lyceum. (*ANB*; Perrin, *History of Effingham County, Ill.*, 42–44, 157.)

4. Possibly this was Wesley Thompson (1845–?), a medical doctor whose family were druggists in Effingham. He returned to town in 1877 after seven years pursuing his other vocation as a horticulturalist in Nebraska, and he helped found the local lyceum. (Perrin, *History of Effingham County, Ill.*, 73–74, 157.)

WEDNESDAY, MARCH 14, 1877. Neoga—Ill— $30— J. L & W F. Allison—[1]

Left E. on 11 A.M. freight train—[2] stopped at ↑with↓ Mr Tracy Kingman & Mrs Carrie Johnson Kingman[3]—Mrs K. quite deaf—but a very intelligent— Mrs W. J. Lemon[4] of Mattoon there to visit—had a nice time—large audience— two Postals from Slayton begging me to let him go on with my engagements to first of May—[5] I feel that I ought to say <u>no</u> on my own account, as well as sister Hannahs—for I am getting dreadfully tired— [*Entries for 15–16 March omitted.*]

1. The Allison brothers owned the *Neoga News* in 1875 and 1876; a local historian referred to them as "J. L." and "W. H." In 1870, Jackson Allison (c. 1817–?) and William Allison (c. 1820–?) were farmers in Neoga. (*Counties of Cumberland, Jasper and Richland, Illinois: Historical and Biographical* [Chicago, 1884], 169, 328; Federal Census, 1870.)

2. The Illinois Central Railroad connected Effingham and Neoga, about thirty miles to the northeast.

3. Tracy Kingman (1830–1910), who owned considerable land in Neoga, was born in New York, raised in rural Illinois, and married in Chicago in 1871. Carrie, or Caroline, Johnson Kingman (1849–1932) grew up in Indiana. (Cumberland County Historical Society, *Cumberland County History* [Greenup, Ill., 1968], 35; Violet Butler McCandlish and Mary Todd Greeson, comps., *Cemeteries of Cumberland County, Illinois* [Toledo, Ill., 1970], 1:15.)

4. Probably Maggie Lemon (c. 1842–?), the wife of William Lemon, a grocer in Mattoon. (Federal Census, 1870.)

5. SBA informed Henry Slayton in late February of her need to stop her tour and go to Leavenworth to be with her sister. (SBA diary, 24 February 1877.)

SATURDAY, MARCH 17, 1877. Newman—Ill— $30— C. V. Walls[1]

Left Pana at 4. A.M.—breakfasted at Decatur & reached N at noon— might just as well have slept & come by way of Matton by daylight—

getting at 4 P.M.—[2] Found letters from sisters Hannah & Mary—both saying Louise was going to Leavenworth—

1. Cicero V. Walls (c. 1848-1917) owned and edited the Newman *Independent*, a Republican paper, until 1884. (*County of Douglas, Illinois. Historical and Biographical* [Chicago, 1884], 244; Federal Census, 1880, with assistance of Joan A. H. Sanders; additional assistance of Douglas County Museum, Tuscola.)

2. SBA lectured at Pana the previous evening. She describes a trip on the Illinois Central to Decatur, where she changed trains to take the Indianapolis, Decatur & Springfield Railway fifty miles east to Newman. She rejected an alternate and probably shorter route through Mattoon.

ᔓ The Standard Diary 1877, n.p., SBA Papers, DLC. Square brackets indicate uncertain words and expanded initials.

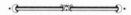

## 112 ᔥ SBA TO LAURA DE FORCE GORDON

On the "War Path" [*Newman, Ill.*]  March 18, 1877

My Dear Laura

Is it possible that I have been so neglectful of you, my dear friend?— I can hardly believe ⸢it⸣— Yes, your letter was received, but not in time to be <u>read</u> at the Convention—but it <u>is</u> published in the March number of "<u>The Ballot Box</u>"—[1] Your <u>innocence</u> of <u>all</u> our work & workers— causes me to believe that <u>your</u> <u>name</u> <u>was</u> not among those I sent to Mrs Williams—3,000 of them too—for her to send her "Ballot Box" with the report of our Philadelphia Centennial 4th of July—also report of our Wash. Con. & the Petitions— I now write her to send you the Jan. Feb. & March numbers of the B.B.—that you may have all— If you have not subscribed for the B.B. do so at once—& get all the friends to do so likewise— It is a live paper & represents <u>our</u> <u>National</u> Society— & if Mrs Spencer has not sent you Petitions—it is because your name has slipped out—somehow— I pass your letter on to Mrs Gage—[2] Mrs Stanton ⸢is⸣ on the "War Path" too in Ohio—[3] I have spoken six nights out of every seven for the past <u>seven weeks</u> & have about as many more before me—so am up to my ears in packing & unpacking  getting to & from trains—& to & from lecture halls—

Am carry↑ing↓ everybody for the 16<u>th</u> <u>Amendment plan</u>— If we can but rouse the friends to roll up a million of signatures to our petition— I believe we can get our proposition through the next Congress

<u>No</u> <u>don't</u> <u>come over this Spring</u>—[4] Work there in California— rolling up the petitions—& then bring ↑them↓ over next winter & help present them— Don't you see <u>thats</u> <u>the</u> <u>time</u> that we shall want you— <u>I</u> <u>am</u> <u>not</u> <u>going</u> <u>back</u> to the <u>May</u> <u>Meeting,</u> <u>even</u> because I can do <u>more</u> & <u>better work</u> <u>here</u> <u>stumping</u>—& <u>I think</u> <u>Mrs Gage</u> will decide not to hold the <u>May</u> <u>meeting</u> this spring—for the reason that we are all at work <u>away</u> <u>from</u> New York— <u>Our</u> <u>Wash</u> <u>Con.</u> and <u>Congressional</u> <u>Work</u> have come to be the <u>main</u> <u>things</u>— So bend every thing to coming ~~over~~ to ↑the↓ <u>1878</u> <u>Jan.</u> Convention & get ~~over~~ ↑<u>there</u> too↓ at leat <u>two</u> <u>weeks</u> <u>before</u> its date—<u>so</u> as to be <u>on time</u>—

Give my love to all the friends & tell them to circulate <u>circulate</u> the Petitions— Affectionately

⤳ *Susan B. Anthony*

[*sideways on first page*] For our history send us the <u>names</u> & addresses of the most efficient workers—what is termed the <u>leaders</u>— I received your personal article—

⤳ ALS, Laura D. Gordon Collection, CU-BANC.

1. L. D. Gordon to National Woman Suffrage Association, 9 January 1877, *Film*, 19:439.

2. Upon receiving Gordon's letter to SBA, Matilda Gage wrote her a newsy letter about the year's work. She did not preserve the letter to SBA. (M. J. Gage to L. D. Gordon, 21 March 1877, Laura D. Gordon Collection, CU-BANC.)

3. ECS set out on 1 March for the Midwest.

4. To the National's annual meeting in New York.

113 ⤳ FROM THE DIARY OF SBA

[*18–21 March 1877*]

SUNDAY, MARCH 18, 1877. At Newman Ill—Pemberton House— Thought to work up Temperance speech for Mr Powells[1] church next Sunday night—but couldn't get at till I had cleaned up the letters—so wrote over 20 in all—cleared out all important ones—[2] and did nothing on my lecture—the thought of speaking in Chicago, again, is simply appalling—but I must just make a simple plain talk on Temperance ex tempore or else read my Purity lecture

1. Edward Payson Powell (1833–1915), pastor of the Third Unitarian Church in Chicago, invited SBA to preach on 25 March. (*DAB.*)

2. Among them was SBA to Sarah Williams, *Film*, 19:479.

MONDAY, MARCH 19, 1877. Hoopeston Ill     Dale Wallace     this abandoned [*illegible*][1]

Train at 9 A.M. and went to Decatur thence to Peoria—arriving at 5 P.M[2]—to hear & see Miss Helen Potter—in her personalities—she gave Ristori, Charlotte Cushman—A. E. Dickinson & John B. Gough—[3] she has marvelous powers of imitation— She had left $100. for me with Dr—↑Helen J. Underwood↓[4] at Blue Island—said it was for S B A. personally—no <u>society</u> no committee—no cause but S. B. A.

1. SBA circled this information about her cancelled lecture. Dale Wallace (1849–?) was a printer who moved to Hoopeston in 1871 and established the Hoopeston *Chronicle*. (H. W. Beckwith, *History of Vermilion County, [Illinois], Together with Historic Notes on the Northwest* [Chicago, 1879], 754–55.)

2. She reversed direction on the Indianapolis, Decatur, & Springfield Railway. From Decatur, the Illinois Midland Railway offered the most direct route to Peoria.

3. Of these personalities from the stage and lecture platform, Charlotte Cushman and Anna Dickinson have been identified. Adelaide Ristori (1822–1906) was an Italian actress, one of the leading tragediennes of Europe. John Bartholomew Gough (1817–1886) was a reformed drunkard whose lectures against drink moved countless people to sign a pledge of abstinence.

4. Helen J. Underwood was a homeopathic physician living in Blue Island, on the outskirts of Chicago, where she hosted SBA on March 24. In 1868 and 1869, when Underwood subscribed and contributed to the *Revolution*, she practiced medicine in Portage, Wisconsin. After circulating suffrage petitions to Congress, she traveled east to attend the founding of the National Woman Suffrage Association in 1869. She also earned a degree in 1872 from the New York Medical College and Hospital for Women. By at least 1874, she had moved her practice to Chicago. Her letters to the *Revolution* and remarks to the Chicago Academy of Homeopathic Physicians and Surgeons evidence strong opinions about the need to reform women's dress, principally as a matter of health. In 1905, when she made a sizable donation to the National-American Woman Suffrage Association, she lived in California. (*Rev.*, 10

September 1868, 3, 24 June 1869, and SBA diary, 24 March 1877, *Film*, 1:287, 591, 612, 19:12ff; King, *History of Homeopathy*, 3:147; *United States Medical Investigator*, n.s., 1 [1875]: 33, 34, 282–83, 415, 527, 542, 546, and 2 [1875]: 184; *History*, 5:130.)

TUESDAY, MARCH 20, 1877. Gibson Ill— $25   E. Lawry[1]

Miss Potter left P. at 3 A.M. insisted making me her guest at Peoria Hotel—& paid my bill with hers— she seems to me what dear A. E. D[ickinson] in the olden days—before her alienation by Mrs L[ivermore]'s story of my falseness to A. E. D.—[2] Have always felt that A. E. would come to her senses & put away her unjust feeling— Had a good visit— Miss P. seems a very earnest soul for equality for women—

I left at 8.45[3]—dined Fairbury & reached G. at 3.30— in mids of terrific thunder & lightning hail, snow & finally rain storm—but in spite of it—had a fair audience—so the Com. paid ↑all↓ expenses—& 40 cts over— stopped at City Hotel—Mr Sumner's—

1. Emanuel Lowry (1837–?), not Lawry, moved to Gibson City in 1875 when he bought the Gibson *Courier*. Once a schoolteacher, he trained as a printer and published papers in Ohio and elsewhere in Illinois before reaching Gibson City. He and his wife were active in the local temperance movement. (*Portrait and Biographical Record of Ford County, Illinois* [Chicago, 1892], 391.)

2. SBA alludes to events in 1872 when her close friendship with Anna Dickinson came to an end, a casualty in part of Victoria Woodhull's advent as a woman suffragist. Within weeks of Woodhull's testimony to the House Committee on the Judiciary in January 1871, both Anna Dickinson and Mary Ashton Rice Livermore (1820–1905) were spreading the word that Woodhull was unprincipled and perhaps worse. When Woodhull countered with her own rumors about sexual transgressions, her victims included Livermore. After calling on Dickinson in June 1872, SBA wrote that she "charges me with betraying her confidence" about Livermore—that is, with allowing Woodhull to learn their secrets. At the time SBA suspected a plot by Dickinson's friend and political advisor, Whitelaw Reid, behind this turn against her. It is not known how she reached a different conclusion five years later. Livermore was a very popular lecturer and former editor of the *Woman's Journal*. (*NAW*; *ANB*; Milo A. Townsend to ECS, 22 March 1871; ECS to Isabella Beecher Hooker, 1 April 1871; and SBA diary, 7 June 1872; all in *Film*, 15:493–94, 517–21, 888ff.)

3. On the Toledo, Peoria & Warsaw Railway. She reached Fairbury, sixty-seven miles to the east, before noon, and after a meal, boarded the Chicago & Paducah Railroad for the twenty-two mile trip south to Gibson.

WEDNESDAY, MARCH 21, 1877. Leroy—Ill    C. A. Bailey[1]

Had 3 hours at Farmers City Depot[2]—wrote long letter to Mrs M. J. Gage trying to soothe her suspicions that I have not always been just to her in bringing her to the front—or trying to— She is a dear good woman—but desperately misanthropic—distrusts everybody's loyalty to her & the truth—

Found letter from sister Mary—written Sat. 17th—saying she had seen niece Louise snugly in sleeping Car Friday night for Chicago— that she would leave there Tues. A.M—which if she got through all right landed her there this A.M. at 11 Oclock—& what a joy to dear sister Hannahs soul to have her only darling girl with her—it is a comfort to me to feel how happy H. must feel— Nice visiting here— Mrs [blank] [Tayer?] & Mrs Humphrey[3] met me Depot with carriage—slept at Mr [blank] Arnolds[4]—good rest & everything nice [Entries for 22–31 March omitted.]

1. This was Charles A. Barley (c. 1845–?), not Bailey, of whom a local historian wrote, "No one in Le Roy ever thinks of starting a society, company or any public undertaking, without Charley Barley's assistance." After teaching school in town for five years, in 1877 Barley sold insurance and real estate, served as town clerk, and held office in the Le Roy Library and Reading Association. (The History of McLean County, Illinois [1879; reprint, Evansville, Ind., 1976], 524, 531–35; Federal Census, 1870.)

2. She reached Farmer City on the Springfield division of the Illinois Central and waited for the Indianapolis, Bloomington & Western Railway to take her to Le Roy, a village in McLean County, fifteen miles southeast of Bloomington.

3. Possibly these were Mrs. T. A. Taylor and Mrs. N. T. Humphrey, the librarian and the president of the Le Roy Library and Reading Association. Mrs. Taylor had a millinery business. (History of McLean County, Ill., 534, 535.)

4. John H. Arnold (c. 1836–?) and his wife, Anna R. Arnold (c. 1836–?), probably ran a hotel at this date. In 1870, John kept a livery stable; in 1879, Anna occupied the Cottage Hotel. The Arnolds were both born in Ohio, which was also the birthplace of their daughter in 1859. (History of McLean County, Ill., 528, 535; Federal Census, 1870.)

⤝ The Standard Diary 1877, n.p., SBA Papers, DLC. Square brackets surround uncertain words and expansion of initials.

114   "THE SIXTEENTH AMENDMENT": LECTURE BY SBA IN MILWAUKEE, WISCONSIN

EDITORIAL NOTE: SBA spoke in the afternoon at the Academy of Music on Milwaukee Street.

[1 April 1877]

Equality of rights, she said, belongs to women as well as to men, and the best way to establish it is by a sixteenth amendment to the constitution. Senator Morton[1] wants that amendment to declare that the people shall vote directly for president; Blaine[2] wants sectarian schools not to receive state aid; the Christians want it to put God in the constitution;[3] the radicals go to the other extreme; the temperance people want the liquor traffic stopped;[4] I protest against all this and want that amendment to enfranchise women. (Applause.) We have a perfect right to demand this. During the first century of our existence man has usurped the control of affairs. I propose that we shall have something to say in the second century.

She was very severe on the Illinois Legislature for attempting to say what shall be done with the property of a man who dies leaving a wife with no children.[5] She felt convinced that the wife should get it all just as the husband does. The laws on this subject are disgraceful, she said, and so long as woman is not represented she will be robbed. This amendment is necessary to elevate human labor.

So long as any class of laborers is despised and down trodden, all labor is degraded. As it is when a woman works for an honest living she is looked down upon and loses caste in society. A married woman works and slaves from morning to night, and retains her place in society; let her husband die leaving her poor, and let her go out to earn a living. At once she loses her standing in society. This condition will never be bettered till the law declares man and woman equal, and husband and wife equal partners in all their property. The speaker gave several instances in which legislators would have voted differently if the women in their constituencies had the right of suffrage. Women now are used as the football of capitalists. When a strike occurs in a branch of labor in which women can work, women are called in and only paid half as much as the men got. She attended the first school teachers' convention in New York twenty-five years ago.[6] There were 200 gentlemen and 1000 ladies present, and the men were deploring their lack of social position. She startled pompous old Prof. Davies, who presided, by addressing him and making a speech on the subject. It was the first time a woman's voice had been heard in a public meeting. She said that the reason male teachers weren't more respected was because they did work which women also did, and thus admitted that they hadn't any more brains than a woman.

There is much talk now about civil service reform,[7] and I have waited to see if they couldn't find a capable woman somewhere. They found a German and a rebel for the cabinet,[8] a negro for United States marshal,[9] and plenty of Irishmen for high places, but nowhere have they found a place for a woman or a Chinaman. Civil service reform means picking out men who control votes for the offices. When there are clerks to be discharged in the treasury department you always find that the women are discharged; the men have votes. Individuals and corporations alike refuse to pay women as much as men both doing like work equally well. In New York the lady teachers asked that their pay should be made two-thirds that of the men. The newspapers all ridiculed the claim. The bricklayers struck for $5 a day and every political newspaper advocated the increase, and some went so far as to say "hang the capitalist." The bricklayers vote. Capitalists cannot control wages if the laborers are intelligent, and the time is coming when working men and women will see that their interests are identical.

The lecturer overhauled the national bank system and heartily denounced the bank ring. The bank ring petitioned to be exempt from taxation on their circulation, and their petition received more consideration in Congress than the women's petition.[10]

In Illinois a woman who is school superintendent gets only half as much as a man.[11] If women could vote President Hayes[12] would have found some woman, Susan B. Anthony or some other woman, to put at the head of a bureau. He's trying to conciliate everybody now, and he'd try to conciliate the women if they could vote. Fred Douglass don't know any more now than before the emancipation, but he is appointed because he represents a large colored vote.

Nine-tenths of the expense of public affairs is the outcome of intem-

perance, and while women are obliged to pay taxes they are not allowed to express their views at the ballot-box on the subject of the
liquor traffic. This is an outrage. That women should have a right to
vote on this liquor question is alone a sufficient reason for a sixteenth
amendment giving her the right of suffrage. Grog shops, brothels and
gambling shops will suffer when woman gets the ballot. In Wyoming
the women had a right to vote and sit on juries. When the first grand
jury was called half of them were women, and as soon as the disreputable women in the place heard of it they got up and traveled. They
didn't go back till women were forbidden to sit on juries.[13]

Till woman has the right to vote any woman who attempts to influence
legislation will be ridiculed. How we have been abused in the last thirty
years! Everything vile has been said of us. We haven't been abused so
badly as the temperance advocates have, but it has been bad enough. In
Grand Rapids 200 women asked to have the obscene variety theaters
closed.[14] It was laughed at, and the Council to whom it was presented
by a unanimous vote attended the worst show that night in a body.
Women can command no influence till they have the right to vote. It is
idle to work for prohibition until women have the right to vote for it.
When there are more votes for temperance than against it you will have
the temperance laws executed, and not till then. Now women are
treated just as the negroes were till 1862. Their petitions to legislative
bodies are treated with scorn.

I think a woman is justified in taking her husband's property if he is
niggardly and mean. In Sioux City, a few years ago, the women burned
down a house of ill-fame.[15] It was the only way in which they could
abate the evil. There will be but one code of morals for man and
woman. While a woman is dependent she cannot make man moral.
Make them equal before the law and he must be as moral as she. If
women could vote it would be no longer unsafe for ladies to be on the
streets at night, for they would lock up the vagabonds. If you would
control morals you must possess political and financial power.

What is wanted now is an amendment to the constitution forbidding
the States to disfranchise any citizen on account of sex; or an amendment to each State constitution granting the suffrage to women. The
last is too degraded. It requires decent women to go to the male
offscourings and ask them to grant the right of suffrage to the women.
This is true, for it is an unfortunate fact that the good men are in a

hopeless minority. The cultivated men are in favor of woman suffrage. The rum sellers, rum drinkers, gamblers and libertines are opposed to it.

Here the speaker varied the performance by saying that she would take a vote on the question then and there, and she would try the men first. She called for the ayes and noes and they were nearly equal, the ayes being a little ahead. Then she called on the ladies. There was a general outburst of feminine ayes. When she called for the noes there was a burst of silence.

She gave a little suffrage sheet, called The Ballot Box, a fine puff, and called on people to subscribe for it.

&#x224B; *Milwaukee Sentinel*, 2 April 1877.

1. Oliver Perry Morton (1823–1877), the Republican boss of Indiana, was the state's senator from 1867 until his death on 1 November 1877. A longtime advocate of reforming the Electoral College, he introduced a constitutional amendment on 5 December 1876 to provide for the direct election of the president and vice president. (*BDAC*; McPherson, *Hand-Book of Politics for 1878*, 38; Oliver P. Morton, "The American Constitution, Part II," *North American Review* 105 [July–August 1877]: 68–78.)

2. James Gillespie Blaine (1830–1893), Republican of Maine, served in the House of Representatives from 1863 until he entered the Senate in 1876. On 14 December 1875, he introduced a constitutional amendment to bar states from putting public funds under the control of religious sects or denominations, an idea also proposed by President Grant the previous week in his annual message. Many Republicans believed that by this means public schools would be freed of sectarian—especially Catholic—influence. Blaine's measure came to the floor of the House for discussion and a vote in August 1876. To the consternation of liberals, the measure protected Bible reading in public schools. (*BDAC*; McPherson, *Hand-Book of Politics for 1876*, 56, 129, 130, 240–41; James Talcott Kitson, "The Congressional Career of James G. Blaine, 1862–1876" [Ph.D. diss., Case Western Reserve University, 1971], 293–95; Ahlstrom and Mullin, *Scientific Theist*, 108.)

3. On efforts to introduce Christianity into the Constitution, see note above at first document, 10 November 1876.

4. Henry W. Blair of New Hampshire introduced an amendment on 12 December 1876 to bar the manufacture, sale, and importation of distilled alcohol after the year 1900. (McPherson, *Hand-Book of Politics for 1878*, 39.)

5. The legislature amended the rules of descent of property in the spring of 1877, though not precisely as SBA implies. The law of 1872 stated that the childless widow of a man who died intestate inherited all of his personal property and one-half of his real estate. It failed to say what happened to the other half of the real estate. The amended act of 1877 added that the remaining

property passed to the deceased's parents and siblings or their descendants. (Harvey B. Hurd, comp., *The Revised Statutes of the State of Illinois, 1883* [Chicago, 1883], chap. 39, sec. 1.)

6. For accounts of this meeting of the New York State Teachers' Association in August 1853, see *Papers*, 1:226–29, and *Film*, 7:792–803. Charles Davies (1798–1876) was educated at the United States Military Academy and spent most of his career teaching college mathematics. (*BDAmerEd.*)

7. Civil service reform, to abolish the practice of hiring public employees for their party loyalty and introduce merit systems, was endorsed by the major political parties in their platforms in 1876 and advocated by Rutherford B. Hayes in his inaugural address. (*National Party Platforms*, 51, 54; McPherson, *Hand-Book of Politics for 1878*, 41; Ari Hoogenboom, *Outlawing the Spoils: A History of the Civil Service Reform Movement, 1865–1883* [Urbana, Ill., 1961], 140–54.)

8. She refers to cabinet appointments made by President Hayes: Carl Schurz as secretary of the interior, and David McKendree Key (1824–1900), a veteran of the Confederate Army and senator from Tennessee, as postmaster general. Key's appointment was part of the Compromise of 1877 by which Hayes became president. (*BDAC.*)

9. Frederick Douglass (1818–1895) was named by President Hayes to be United States marshal for the District of Columbia in March 1877. Douglass, former slave, abolitionist, and early supporter of woman suffrage, moved from Rochester, New York, to Washington in 1872. Despite differences with ECS and SBA over the Fifteenth Amendment, he remained their friend and often attended meetings of their National association. (*DANB*; *ANB*. See also *Papers* 1 & 2.)

10. The American Bankers' Association's efforts to organize thousands of national, state, private, and savings banks and their customers to press Congress for repeal of federal taxes on bank deposits, capital, and circulation produced a flood of petitions in January and February 1877. The bankers' petitions were presented in the House and Senate at the same time as women's petitions for suffrage. Interrupting a parade of senators bearing suffrage petitions on 20 January, George G. Wright, Republican of Iowa, expressed regret that he had no "petitions of a similar character; but I have a petition from gentlemen who want to be relieved from some burdens in the way of taxation." (*Congressional Record*, 44th Cong., 2d sess., 763, 1264–65; *New York Times*, 8 February 1877.)

11. Women in Illinois became eligible for election to all school offices in 1873. Salaries were set locally, not by the statute. (*Laws of the State of Illinois, 1873*, 192.)

12. Rutherford Birchard Hayes (1822–1893) became the nineteenth president of the United States in March 1877.

13. The statute granting women their right to vote in Wyoming also granted their right to hold office, and it was the opinion of the chief justice of the

territorial supreme court, John H. Howe, that women were eligible to hold the office of juror. While Howe occupied the bench, until the fall of 1871, women served on petit and grand juries. Howe wrote that opposition came from lawyers, who found women too willing to enforce laws and punish crimes. His successors stopped the practice. (John D. W. Guice, *The Rocky Mountain Bench: The Territorial Supreme Courts of Colorado, Montana, and Wyoming, 1861-1890* [New Haven, Conn., 1972], 132; *New York Times*, 8 March 1870, 13 March 1871; *Golden Age*, 14 October 1871; *Chicago Legal News*, 12 March, 9 April 1870, 11 March 1871.)

14. SBA told this story first in October 1874, saying that last year the women were "snubbed in an effort to persuade the authorities to close the dram-shops and variety-shows." The subject of variety shows did not come before the common council of Grand Rapids at that time. In October 1875, the council granted a license for one W. B. Smith "to give variety entertainment at Smith's Opera House," over the objections of three aldermen. By July 1876, the city had filed a lawsuit against Smith, and at the council's meeting on July 31, a majority voted to revoke the license and withdraw the suit. (*Film*, 18:118-20; research by William Cunningham, City Archivist, in Common Council Proceedings, Grand Rapids City Archives.)

15. On Sioux City, see note above at 12 April 1875.

115 ᨇ FROM THE DIARY OF SBA

[*1–4 April 1877*]

SUNDAY, APRIL 1, 1877. Milwaukee Wis—$50    Chas E. Crain[1]

Mr & Mrs Stark & son & daughter[2] taking meals with Mrs Dudley[3]— Mr Dudley preaching in the Parker Memorial Hall—has a call there— Got a letter here from Mrs Stanton—she is at work in Ohio—& one from brother D. R. written a week ago to day—he has given up all hope of sister Hannahs recovery—but thinks she will live this year—but that I can do nothing but pass away weary hours—<u>but</u> that is a good deal— so am glad I have thrown all up—  Easter Sunday—only 600 in audience & my speech not a bit satisfactory—ought to have insisted on giving my Social Purity lecture—

1. Charles E. Crain, the local lecture agent, boarded in Milwaukee while working as a clerk. (City directories, 1876-77, 1877-78.)

2. The Stark family is unidentified; a number of families of that name lived in the city.

3. Marion Vienna Churchill Dudley (1844-?), a former teacher and a writer, married the pastor of Milwaukee's Plymouth Congregational Church, John Langdon Dudley, in 1872. Though she was primarily a literary writer, her speech *Suffrage for Woman: A Plea in Its Behalf, Addressed to the Senate Committee on State Affairs . . . at Madison, March 2, 1880* (1880) was well regarded. John Dudley (1812-1894), who took part in the meeting to found the state suffrage association in 1869, left Plymouth Church in 1875. He preached at Theodore Parker Memorial Hall in Boston from 1877 to 1879. (Andreas, *History of Milwaukee, Wisc.*, 578-79; Polly Longsworth, "'Was Mr. Dudley Dear?': Emily Dickinson and John Langdon Dudley," *Massachusetts Review* 26 [Summer/Autumn 1985]: 360-72; *Papers*, 2:227.)

MONDAY, APRIL 2, 1877. Beaver Dam Wis—     E. C. Pratt[1]

Left Mrs Dudley's 7.30 & found A.M. train taken off[2]—so was taken to Dr Ross Wolcotts[3]—spent day—took dinner & she took me to 3. P.M. train— Mrs Ross Wolcott gave me scorching histories of several personages—sad chapters—for poor woman nature—

Stopped with Mrs Maria L. Bracken[4]—had fine adience—Cong. Minister said no parallel between baby women & men—[5]

Received letter from Sister written Saturday A.M. March 31st—weak, trembling hand & with scalding tear drops over the page— I can hardly wait to fill Berlin before rushing to her

1. Edwin C. Pratt (1842-?), a New Yorker who came to Wisconsin as a child, farmed with his father, pursued a career as a music teacher, and served in the Civil War before moving to Beaver Dam to study law. He was admitted to the bar in 1872. (*History of Dodge County, Wisconsin* [Chicago, 1880], 593-94; Federal Census, 1870.)

2. The Chicago, Milwaukee & St. Paul Railway took her sixty miles northwest of Milwaukee to this city in Dodge County on the line's Portage branch.

3. Laura J. Ross Wolcott (1834-1915), Wisconsin's first female physician, was also the first president of the Wisconsin Woman Suffrage Association in 1869. Beginning in 1877, she was an officer of the National Woman Suffrage Association. (*Dictionary of Wisconsin Biography*.)

4. Maria L. Cowen Brackin (c. 1830-?) came to Beaver Dam from Madison County, New York, with her husband, William H. Brackin, in 1855. He was a carpenter and builder, responsible for many of the town's prominent buildings. (*History of Dodge County, Wisc.*, 575; Federal Census, 1870.)

5. Beaver Dam had two Presbyterian churches but no Congregational church.

TUESDAY, APRIL 3, 1877. Left B.D. at 9 A.M. stopped at Commercial Hotel—Horricon till 5.40 P.M.—[1] Tedious—tedious to have to wait & lose to night— No word yet from Slayton—telling whether has obeyed my order to cancel all beyond Berlin— If I close with tomorrow night shall have sent the B[allot] B[ox] 200 subscribers   enough to pay year's expenses— My nett receipts for the 9½ weeks—56 lectures—[2]

1. Reversing direction, she waited at Horicon Junction for the Chicago, Milwaukee & St. Paul main line to Berlin, thirty miles further northwest in Green Lake County.

2. Although SBA did not calculate her net receipts, it is possible to do it for her from the accounts she kept in the back pages of her diary. From the fifty-six lectures since January 29, she grossed $1,424.10. Travel and hotels cost her $226.90, and she sent $172.00 to Slayton's Lyceum Bureau, leaving net receipts of $1,025.20. (Omitted from this calculation are various small charges while on the road for stamps, paper, toiletries, and one visit to a doctor.) From her earnings, SBA repaid Ellen Sargent $90.00 she borrowed in January to get the tour started and distributed $200.00 to family members. The remainder of the money she sent to her bank in Rochester.

WEDNESDAY, APRIL 4, 1877. Berlin Wis— $30   Miss E. A. Brown—[1]

Splendid audience— But oh what fearful haste & hurry to be done on my way to my dear sister

1. Eliza A. Brown (c. 1836–?) was president of the Society of Friends in Council, No. 3, a woman's club organized in 1873 for self-improvement. SBA spoke in a course of lectures that the club launched in 1876. Brown was born in New York, arrived in Wisconsin with her family in 1843, and moved to Berlin in 1850. There she supported herself as a seamstress, until her marriage to Carlo A. Taylor in 1883. In 1880, at a joint meeting of the National and the Wisconsin suffrage associations in Milwaukee, Brown was the delegate from Berlin. (Federal Census, 1870; *Portrait and Biographical Album of Green Lake, Marquette and Waushara Counties, Wisconsin* [Chicago, 1890], 229, 266–67, 583–84; *NCBB*, June 1880, *Film*, 21:272–74.)

≈ The Standard Diary 1877, n.p., SBA Papers, DLC.

## 116  ≈  ECS TO MARGARET L. STANTON

Starlight Plantation [*Woodbine, Iowa*]   May 16th [*1877*]

Dear Maggie

I reached here yesterday. I wish you could have had a glimpse of Gat & me coming over the prairies yesterday. Imagine a long big lumber wag↑g↓on with a spring for a bed a bureau a box of groceries  two bags of flour, my trunk   a hundred trees & small fruits a bag of sundries   a box from Kit[1] & my hand bag, & some meal & grains for half a dozen other families, looming up behind us far over our heads. Moving along as if in funereal procession as the load was heavy   roads bad & head winds blowing a hurricane   my veil & hair blowing to the four points of the compass. Gat has a man now helping him plough. They set the trees all out this morning. Augusta[2] has about five hundred chickens. She made enough last year with her chickens to buy a pony & the pony has just had a colt now six weeks old. Augusta runs out   catches it herself, puts on the saddle   bridle & all & dashes off on errands in all directions. The peacocks pigeons pigs ponies chickens & cattle make quite an imposing caravan roaming on the prairies. Everybody is in bed now eight o'clock, & they will all be up at four  breakfast at five. Of course I shall not join the morning feast. When I came down this morning I had a broiled chicken some flour gems as light as a feather, stewed peaches, excellent coffee & cream as yellow as gold, & butter too as sweet as clover. Oh! if Kit could only see this cream a big quart pitcher full, & the way Gat eats is surprizing   I leave here on Monday, & have five engagements en route for home. Archy baby is dead!![3] peace to its ashes!!

[*in margins of first page*] Have you & Kit put your heads together & got me a decent pair of boots? I sent you [Minnies?] letter   I think all things considered your decision was a wise one, as to Grand Rapids Do not make any <u>business</u> <u>arrangements</u> until I see you

[*in margins of second page*] Tell Neil[4] I spent a day with Mr Holbrook,[5] & he told me about the brilliant move Neal made with Kits & Greys advice. I should think Kit knew lawyers well enough not to trust $5000 in their hands [*in margin of third page*] With love to all

~ *Mother*

~ ALS, in the collection of Rhoda Barney Jenkins, Greenwich, Conn. Variant in *Stanton*, 2:151–53. Square brackets surround uncertain name.

1. Henry B. Stanton, Jr., was known as Kit.

2. Augusta E. Hazelton Stanton (1850–?) married Gat Stanton in February 1875 in Logan, Iowa. She was born in Maine. (Stanton, *Thomas Stanton of Connecticut*, 463; Federal Census, 1880.)

3. Archibald McIntyre McMartin (1848?–1928), ECS's nephew, was a son of Duncan and Margaret Cady McMartin and a farmer in Crawford County,

Iowa. His son Archibald, the fourth of eight children, born 16 September 1876, died on 23 March 1877. (*Jasper, Marshall and Grundy Counties, Iowa*, 272; genealogical notes courtesy of Barbara McMartin, Canada Lake, N.Y., and Barbara Wood McMartin, Beaman, Iowa.)

4. That is, Daniel Cady Stanton.

5. This may be Marcellus Holbrook, a lawyer turned banker, doing business in Harrison County. (Joe H. Smith, *History of Harrison County, Iowa* [Des Moines, Iowa, 1888], 315.)

117 ≈ SBA to the Editor, "Woman's Kingdom"[1]

*[Leavenworth, Kan., after 19 May 1877]*

In a letter received from Susan B. Anthony, she corrects our statement of last week that Mrs. Mosher was her only sister,[2] when she writes: "Thanks to the good Father, she was not my only one. I have one sister left, Mary, who has taught for a quarter of a century in the schools of Rochester. There were four sisters and two brothers of us; the two married sisters have passed over the river, the unmarried sisters and the two brothers on this side. My lecturing season should have continued through April and May, but that I could not stay apart from my dear sister another day. She had insisted that I should go on through the season, but I could not, and I am very, very thankful that I did not continue my lectures another day. She was only twenty months younger than myself, and we were ever one in spirit. Though she was not in any sense a public worker she sustained me in all of my work. I shall return to Rochester and spend July and August with my only surviving sister and my aged mother, now in her 84th year."

≈ Chicago *Inter-Ocean*, 26 May 1877.

1. Elizabeth Harbert launched the Woman's Kingdom, her weekly column in the Chicago *Inter-Ocean*, on Saturday, 17 February 1877, in the newspaper's daily and weekly editions. She carried it on until 1884. In the column Harbert combined reports of women's local activities with news of national groups such as the Woman's Congress and the National Woman Suffrage Association.

2. Hannah Anthony Mosher died in Leavenworth on 11 May, with SBA at her side. Announcing her death, Harbert's column of 19 May described Hannah as SBA's "only and tenderly beloved sister."

·⟨⟶⟶⟩·

## 118 &#x2372; ECS TO MATILDA JOSLYN GAGE AND THE NATIONAL WOMAN SUFFRAGE ASSOCIATION

*[before 24 May 1877]*

Matilda Joslyn Gage—Dear Madam:— I regret that my Western engagements make it impossible for me to be present with you in the coming convention;[1] but I urge you to adopt the same two resolutions we passed at the last Washington Convention on compulsory education, and an educational qualification as the basis of suffrage.

> *Whereas*, a monarchial government lives only through the ignorance of the masses, and a republican government can live only through the intelligence of the people, therefore
>
> *Resolved*, That it is the duty of Congress to submit to the people propositions to so amend the Constitution of the United States as to make education compulsory, and to make intelligence a qualification for citizenship and Suffrage in the United States, said amendment to take effect January, 1, 1880, when all citizens of legal age, without distinction of sex, who can read and write the English language, may be admitted to citizenship.[2]

These are measures that leading men, who see their wisdom, fear to press lest they thereby jeopardize their political success.

As the women of the nation have nothing to lose, politically, in the way of place or pay, and everything to gain in the wise administration of our Government, I should like to see them pressing the question of compulsory education in every State in the Union, not only on the consideration of those legislatures likely to adopt the measure, but on Congress also, as a national duty to those States and Territories where a complete system of free schools is not yet established.

If, as a nation, we hope to celebrate the second centennial of our national life, we must give new thought to thorough education of our whole people. We should demand in our schools and colleges a knowledge of those practical branches of learning that self-government involves. Surely an intelligent understanding of the great principles of Finance, Land Monopoly, Taxes and Tariffs, the relations of Labor and Capital and the laws of Commerce are far more important in a republic than a knowledge of Homer and Virgil,[3] their descriptions of the heroes of a forgotten age, or the speculations of Dante and Milton[4] as to the sufferings of lost souls in the Inferno.

The one vital necessity to the success of our experiment of self-government is the education of our people, and in the sciences rather than foreign languages and the classics.

The same care that in the Old World is bestowed on the education of the prospective heirs to the throne, should be provided for every citizen in our republic where all are declared to be of the blood royal, all heirs apparent to the crown and scepter of the people's sovereignty.[5]

As one of the strongest motives that can be placed before the rising generation for securing the rudiments of education, let us demand an amendment to all our State and National constitutions, saying that after 1880 no person shall vote in this nation who cannot read and write the English language. It is not too much to ask that our American Kings and Queens shall be able to read the leading names and measures of the party whose ticket they vote at the ballot box.

And this measure in no way conflicts with the popular theory that suffrage is a natural right. An educational qualification does not *abolish* the suffrage for any class, as the condition is one with which all may comply, and the time given for this necessary preparation may be longer or shorter, as each State may decide.

Regulating the suffrage *equally*[6] for all classes, sexes, colors, is a very different measure in principle from abolishing it altogether for any one class, by an insurmountable qualification. When the African race were forbidden by law to read, and practically shut out of all our free schools, when the college doors were universally closed to women, and all opportunities for acquiring a knowledge of the great principles of self-government denied them, an educational qualification might have been unfair to these classes.

But as all such laws are fast becoming a dead-letter, and one class has its representatives in Congress, the State Legislatures, the Courts, and to-day has the acting Marshal of the District of Columbia,[7] and as the other has its representatives close on the heels of man in the whole world of thought, in art, science, literature, and government, the women and black men can stand the educational test quite as well as the favored "white male citizen."

This measure would also be our most effective defence against the ignorant foreign vote. It would be far easier to ascertain, when men come to register their names as voters, whether they can read and write the English language, than how long they have lived under our flag.[8]

Increasing at the rate we do now, we shall have at the end of this century a hundred millions of people. Vice, ignorance and poverty coming to us from every quarter of the globe; over 50,000 Chinese already on our Pacific slope;[9] but the entering wedge to 400,000,000 behind them, and all these masses must be educated into the rights and duties of self-government, trained to legislate wisely for the interests of a mighty people, to make and mould the institutions of a continent; or if left as they now are, to wreck our great experiment of a government of the people, by the people and for the people. It is for the women of the republic, with their growing intelligence, influence and power, to decide what our future shall be.

Hoping these resolutions may pass unanimously, and that the Convention may be successful in numbers and influence, I am very sincerely yours,

➢  *Elizabeth Cady Stanton.*

➢  Toledo *Ballot Box*, June 1877.

1. The National association held its annual meeting in New York City on May 24. As chair of the National's executive committee, Matilda Gage presided in the absence of ECS. For coverage, see *Film*, 19:504–8.

2. *Ballot Box*, February 1877, *Film*, 19:434–35.

3. Classical poets both, the Greek Homer is thought to have lived in the ninth century B.C., and the Roman Virgil lived from 70–19 B.C.

4. The Italian poet Dante (1265–1321) wrote the *Divine Comedy* about a journey through hell, purgatory, and paradise. ECS also refers to the English poet John Milton (1608–1674), author of *Paradise Lost*.

5. This paragraph with its equation between training heirs to the throne and citizens of a republic came from her popular lecture "Our Boys." See "Our Boys" manuscript, pp. 113–22, *Film*, 45:75ff.

6. The text reads "*equality.*"

7. That is, Frederick Douglass.

8. Residence and a declaration of *intent* to become a citizen qualified

foreign-born males to vote in many states. In *Minor v. Happersett* (1875), the Supreme Court, making the point that citizenship and voting rights were not joined in the United States, listed Missouri, Alabama, Arkansas, Florida, Georgia, Indiana, Kansas, Minnesota, and Texas as states with such a provision. Similar provisions also appeared in the constitutions of Michigan, Nebraska, Oregon, and Wisconsin, and in 1876 Colorado followed their example in its first state constitution. The number of states with this provision grew larger before the end of the century. See also the list in Alexander Keyssar, *The Right to Vote: The Contested History of Democracy in the United States* (New York, 2000), Table A.12.

9. The federal census of 1870 counted about fifty thousand Chinese living in California. By 1880, the state's Chinese population topped seventy-five thousand. The Chinese Exclusion Act of 1882 halted further immigration. (*Compendium of the Ninth Census*, 29; *Compendium of the Tenth Census*, 334.)

## 119 ✥ FROM DIARY OF SBA

[*7–8, 27–28 June 1877*]

THURSDAY, JUNE 7, 1877. At Leavenworth—very bright this A.M.—but at 4 P.M—raining again— a letter from Mrs Gage to day—telling of N.Y.W.S. meetings—[1] I wrote her—& Mrs Spencer—also Mrs Alida C. Avery[2]—Denver—Col—offering her to lecture for her society through September free, gratis & for nothing—

1. The New York State Woman Suffrage Association held its annual meeting in conjunction with the National's meeting on May 25.

2. Alida Cornelia Avery (1833–1908) studied medicine with Rachel and Silas Gleason in Elmira, New York, and continued her education at the Woman's Medical College in Philadelphia, the New York Infirmary for Women and Children, and the New England Female Medical College. At the opening of Vassar College, she became the professor of physiology and hygiene and the resident physician, staying until her move to Denver in 1874. She left Denver for California in 1887 to settle in San Jose, where she continued to work for woman suffrage. (*Woman's Journal*, 10 October 1908, 3 April 1909; biographical file, Special Collections, NPV.) Avery, president of the Colorado Woman Suffrage Association since its founding in 1876, sought experienced speakers to canvass the state in the month preceding the vote on a constitutional amendment for woman suffrage. As an officer of both the National and the American suffrage associations, Avery attracted not only SBA but also Lucy Stone, Henry Blackwell, Matilda Hindman, and Margaret

Campbell. On organizing the Colorado campaign, see: *Woman's Journal*, 22 January 1876, 20 January, 19 May 1877; *History*, 3:712-25; Billie Barnes Jensen, "Colorado Woman Suffrage Campaigns of the 1870s," *Journal of the West* 12 (April 1973): 254-71; Suzanne M. Marilley, *Woman Suffrage and the Origins of Liberal Feminism in the United States, 1820-1920* (Cambridge, Mass., 1996), 83-98.

FRIDAY, JUNE 8, 1877. At Leavenworth   Just 4 weeks to night at 12 Oclock—since dear sister Hannah passed out of her suffering body—it seems an age—as many months as it is weeks— Letter from Louise to day—saying Aunt A. E.[1] wanted her to stay longer [*Entries for 13-14, 22 June omitted; no entries for 9-12, 15-21, 23-26 June.*]

    1. Ann Eliza Anthony Dickinson (1814-1886), the youngest of Daniel Anthony's sisters, invited Louise Mosher to visit at 113 South Green Street, Chicago, after her mother's funeral. Louise's brother Wendell was living with the Dickinsons while he worked for the family's Albert Dickinson Seed Company. (Anthony, *Anthony Genealogy*, 218; Elinor V. Smith, comp., *Descendants of Nathaniel Dickinson* [N.p., 1978], 233-34; *Friends' Intelligencer*, 43 [1886]: 184; city directory, 1877; SBA to H. L. Mosher, 4 June 1877, *Film*, 19:509-12.)

WEDNESDAY, JUNE 27, 1877. At L— Gilles[1] drove out to Mt. Muncie[2]— Lucy E.[3] & Susie B. went with me— the cemetery seemed so <u>restful</u>— & dear Hannah's two months ago tired <u>so</u> <u>tired</u> body <u>rests</u> there—but oh so alone—so <u>away</u> from the spot where rest the bodies of her loved Father & sister Gula[4]—but I must give it up—& say farewell even to the spot that covers the last of her mortal part—& the other—<u>is</u> it where & how—thats the question!!—

    1. Gillis was an African-American coachman in Leavenworth. The census of 1870 listed E. Gillis born circa 1846 in Missouri; city directories for 1875 and 1876 listed Aaron Gillis. (With assistance from the Kansas State Historical Society.)

    2. The Mount Muncie Cemetery was Leavenworth's principal burying ground.

    3. Lucy Elmina Anthony, the oldest child of Merritt and Mary L. Anthony, was born in 1860. She may have been attending school in Leavenworth.

    4. Daniel Anthony and Guelma Anthony McLean are buried in the Mount Hope Cemetery in Rochester, New York.

THURSDAY, JUNE 28, 1877. Left Leavenworth at 5 P.M. on R.I. Train— for Rochester—N.Y—had to wait at Cameron until 1 Oclock A.M— before the H. & St Jo. train came—[1]

1. SBA began her journey home by taking the Chicago, Rock Island & Pacific Railroad from its Leavenworth terminus to Cameron Junction, Missouri, where she awaited the Hannibal & St. Joseph Railroad to Quincy, Illinois. After changing trains several more times, she reached Rochester on 1 July.

✍ The Standard Diary 1877, n.p., SBA Papers, DLC.

## 120    ✍    SBA TO ECS

*[Rochester, before 30 August]* 1877

Mrs Stanton— Did you notice the Petition of <u>Taxpaying</u> <u>women</u> of <u>New Orleans</u> to the Louisania Legislature—[1] Well the <u>prime</u> leader of it—<u>Mrs Janet Norton</u>[2]—is spending the summer <u>at</u> <u>her</u> country residence—<u>Stroudsburg</u>—<u>Monroe Co.</u>—<u>Penn</u>— She wants me to meet her in New York— I cannot—have told her of you—& of Mrs Spencer—& Mrs Lozier—her place on the <u>Lehigh</u> <u>Valley</u> R.R.— I do wish you & I could see her & infuse into her the real philosophy— I imagine she is rich— on second thought will enclose the article she sent me—& her letter—both of which I was going to send to Mrs Williams for the B.B.—[3] I want Sarah Spencer to see about her too—perhaps you will feel like making an item on her— Send <u>her</u> copies of all the documents you have—she will have time to read & ponder them up there in the mountains— I have mailed her a copy of my trial pamphlet—she seems to me a woman ~~that~~ ↑who↓ will grow & be of use—

✍    S. B. A.

*[in ECS hand]* Send to Mrs Spencer    Send documents if you have any specially Mr Hooker's Bible argument[4]

✍ ALS, on NWSA letterhead for 1877, Isabella Hooker Collection, CtHSD. Was enclosed in ECS to I. B. Hooker, 30 August 1877, *Film*, 19:525-28.

1. The petition, presented on the last day of the legislative session in April 1877, sought "equality under the law" for women who "pay half the taxes of the state without representation." One thousand women signed it. The timing of the petition in 1877 was terrible. Two legislatures and two governors vied for legitimacy in Louisiana through the winter of 1877 until President Hayes ordered the federal troops in New Orleans to withdraw their protection of the

Republican government on April 24. Democrats took over the statehouse on April 25, elected a United States senator, and adjourned on April 26. This petition and its organizers have been overshadowed by events in 1879, when a petition to Louisiana's constitutional convention resulted in an opportunity to speak to convention delegates and launched the careers of Elizabeth Saxon and Caroline Merrick. (*Woman's Journal*, 12, 19, 26 May 1877; *New York Times*, 22, 27 April 1877; Caroline Merrick, *Old Times in Dixie Land: A Southern Matron's Memories* [New York, 1901], 124–33; Carmen Lindig, *The Path from the Parlor: Louisiana Women, 1879–1920* [Lafayette, La., 1986], 36–41.)

2. Janet Norton (c. 1825–1887) was the wife of Emery E. Norton, the assignee of bankruptcy in New Orleans since 1867 and, according to the press at the time of the petition, "a very large owner of property" in her own right. After this initial contact, she kept in touch with northern suffragists. She sent a telegram to the Decade Celebration in 1878, noting new activism among Louisiana's women under the leadership of Elizabeth Saxon. A year later, Isabella Hooker reported to the National association on her consultations with Norton about seeking woman suffrage from the constitutional convention. Her attending physician at the time of her death in Stroudsburg was the suffragist Harriette Keating, who had testified before the Louisiana Constitutional Convention in 1879. Both Nortons were born in the North. Emery Norton was originally from Angelica, New York, won election to the New York State Assembly in 1851, served in the Union Army, and moved to New Orleans in 1867. Janet Norton (whose obituary gave her name as Jeannette) had two children from an earlier marriage to a Mr. Chatwick. As late as 1901, Emery Norton maintained a plantation in Louisiana as well as their large home in Stroudsburg, noted for its mountainous scenery and healthy air. (*NCBB*, August 1878, July 1879, *Film*, 20:313–21, 789–93; Stroudsburg *Jeffersonian Republican*, 3 February 1887; *New York Tribune*, 13 February 1901; *New Orleans Daily States*, 13 February 1901; New Orleans city directory, 1877 to 1880; *History of Allegany County, N.Y.* [New York, 1879], 81, 201; with the assistance of the New Orleans Public Library and the Monroe County Historical Association of Stroudsburg, Pennsylvania.)

3. Enclosures missing.

4. John Hooker, *The Bible and Woman Suffrage* (1870).

·◁═══════◈═══════▷·

121 ⤳ "THE WORKINGMAN AND HIS STRIKES":
LECTURE BY SBA IN TOLEDO, OHIO

EDITORIAL NOTE: En route to Colorado, SBA stopped in Toledo to
speak in White's Hall on Summit Street to an audience of workingmen and women. "Every available place in the main hall and the
gallery was filled to its utmost capacity," according to the *Toledo Bee*,
"until there was scarcely standing room in the spacious building,
hundreds being compelled to turn away for want of room." The
*Toledo Commercial* reported that "her views on workingmen and
their troubles were loudly applauded." (*Film*, 19:539.)

[6 September 1877]

At precisely ten minutes past 8 o'clock Miss Anthony being introduced to her audience by J. R. Fallis[1] began her lecture. She was
dressed in a rich black dress of fashionable make and her general
appearance was imposing and pleasing. Strange to say she addressed
her audience as "Gentlemen and ladies," giving the gentlemen the
preference of the first mention, which in oratorical etiquette is seldom
done. She stated that it would be her mission to speak on the uses of the
ballot box, which was the only power which the workingmen could use
to get better work and better pay. "Disfranchisement," said the speaker,
"is degradation," and after showing how degraded the miners and the
laboring class in England was before the obtaining the right to vote and
relating how they won the ballot after a long struggle,[2] with John Bright
and John Stuart Mill as their champions, she said that the women of to-
day are as degraded as respects their rights as the serfs of Russia, the
miners of England and the Chinese of the Pacific coast. "At length,
after a long fight, the ballot was placed in the hands of the laboring class
of England and into the hands of workingmen—up to that hour the
name workingman had been a title of degradation—and from that time
on, both political parties began to cater to the workingman who was
naturally allied to the party which had given him the right to vote, the
power to redress his grievances. The Tory party, however, pleaded
with the workingman and promised that it would legislate for him
better than the Liberals, but it was not until after years of persuasion

and argument that the Liberals were able to bring the working class over to their side and thus again get into power.[3]

"The Republican party was the champion of the colored man and obtained for him the right to vote. Until the Democratic party, through their editors and stump speakers, agree to legislate more for the benefit of the colored man than the Republicans do, it is not worth while for them to claim that the colored vote is divided, part of it going on the side of the Democracy."

Miss Anthony gave an account of the bread riots in England,[4] and of the recent riots in the United States.[5] She said that the latter had out Heroded Herod,[6] and that nothing in England ever equalled the Pittsburg horror.[7] But she said that they had not only made themselves better by their recent uprising, but they have made of themselves a vast political power, not to say terror.

She was loudly applauded when she said that when the workingmen put their heads together and make of the Government a demand, they will either be conceded to or both parties will take up with partial concessions. "The workingmen," said she, "hold in their hands a whip with which they make uneasy every politician that does not suit them and they do not usually fail to do it." An instance of the strikes in the mines of California was cited.[8] The Governor, a Democrat, sent out troops to put down the strikers. At the next election he was defeated by a large majority. "When I read the Associated Press report in the papers," said the speaker, "and saw that it stated that the workingmen had gone over to the Republican party because it had found that the Democrats were so corrupt, I said 'that reporter is an Idiot.' Don't put that down," said she, turning to the *Commercial* reporter. And then, as if to atone for her onslaught on the reporters, she said that they were her best friends, and made her speeches better than they were.

The Granger movement was also alluded to as another case in point. At Washington she had been introduced to numerous representatives of the Grangers, and had asked to be introduced to some representatives of the woman's crusade movement but there were none. "Why?" "Because women did not have the right to vote. If they did, there would be as many humble supplicants to ask what women would have them do, as there are to ask what the workingmen will have done." Space will not permit a further review of the lecture, the remainder dealt almost entirely on woman's rights. The speaker closed with an appeal to the workingmen to join in with the woman suffragists and they would fight their battle and work in a common cause to better their condition.

⤴ *Toledo Commercial*, 7 September 1877, SBA scrapbook 8, Rare Books, DLC.

1. John R. Fallis, of the firm Fallis & Linton, was a prominent dealer of grains in the city. (City directory, 1876–77.)

2. Whether miners were householders within the meaning of the Reform Act of 1867 was a contested point in the early 1870s in light of the fact that their employers owned their houses and collected no rent. In northeast England miners were at the center of major demonstrations from 1872 to 1874 for further extension of the franchise. (Biagnini, *Liberty, Retrenchment and Reform*, 278–88.)

3. After passage of the Reform Act of 1867, Liberals won the parliamentary election of 1868, but Conservatives, or Tories, regained control of Parliament in 1874. Liberals, led by William Gladstone, did not return to power until 1880.

4. By "bread riots," SBA probably means the wave of strikes and demonstrations led by the Chartists in the 1840s at the same time as the agitation against the Corn Laws.

5. A reference to the great strikes of 1877 on the nation's railroads. When trainmen in Toledo struck on July 23, local workers and unions called a general strike that stopped not only transportation but also manufacturing and commerce in the city for several days. A sympathetic mayor waited until July 27 to order police to stop the strike and arrest its leaders. (Robert V. Bruce, *1877: Year of Violence* [Indianapolis, 1959]; Philip S. Foner, *The Great Labor Uprising of 1877* [New York, 1977].)

6. That is, to exceed in violence the worst of tyrants, specifically Herod the Great, King of the Jews from 37–4 B.C.

7. The most violent confrontations of the railroad strikes occurred in Pittsburgh, Pennsylvania, when militia opened fire on strikers and their supporters on July 21 and 22.

8. On the strike by California miners, see notes above at 19 March 1876.

122 ⤳ SBA to the Editor, *Ballot Box*

Lake City, Col.,[1] Sept. 21, 1877.

Dear *Ballot Box*:—My meeting at this place last night surpassed all before it in numbers and enthusiasm.[2] Their largest audience chamber would not begin to hold the people. So I took my stand on a dry goods box on the court-house steps, and the ten or fifteen hundred people, mainly men, took theirs on the ground; and there with these grand old Rocky Mountains for our four walls, the blue heavens for our roof, the full moon and twinkling stars for our light, we stood and talked and listened full an hour and a half. It was a magnificent sight. No man-made temple ever contained a more attentive and respectful audience; and at the close at least three-fourths of the men shouted "Aye." Only one woman voted "No."

I am bound here to-day, because my appointment for to-night at Ouray is fifty miles across the mountain, on "*buroo*" back, by a frightfully dangerous trail, which no mountaineer would attempt in to-day's rain and hail—and at the top of the pass snow; and 125 miles around by private carriage, which would take three days, and camping out o'nights.[3] Ouray is an important mining point, but it is simply impossible for me to reach it. Tomorrow at 6 A.M. I am to take stage—no, Buck-board—for Saguache, 100 miles—a two days' journey and over the Chetope pass.[4] My next is to be at South Arkansas,[5] fifty miles "buck-board," and over the Puncho pass into the valley of the Arkansas river. But to give you a slight glimpse of our Colorado W.S. canvass experience, let me tell you: I left my home, Rochester, N.Y., September 4th; spoke that night at Somerset, sixty miles distant, to a large audience of Niagara county farmers, all jubilant with their luscious peach harvest. At 7 o'clock next morning took stage and rode seventeen miles to Lockport, spoke to a large audience and at midnight took the train for Detroit and thence to Toledo, arriving at 6 P.M. Lecturing to an immense assemblage of working men on their "strikes," and hearing them vote a solid "aye" in favor of giving to working women equal chances with themselves. At 12 o'clock took the train for Leavenworth, Kansas, via Chicago and the Rock Island railroad. Spent Sunday with my brother, D. R. Anthony, and Monday morning via the Santa Fe railroad was speeding westward over the rich and rolling prairies of Kansas.[6] Fifty years hence, when beautiful farm houses with their green blinds, their shade trees, their orchards and gardens shall dot every quarter section; when vast wheat and corn fields, interspersed with towering forests, shall break the monotony of that boundless expanse, Kansas will indeed be the farmers' paradise. And even now one is delighted at every step with the wonderful progress made in its settlement and the well-to-do look of its settlers all along the line of the railroad, which passes through the very heart of the State, and is, by the way, the very best of all the western roads.

My first point was Granada,[7] September 11th, where nobody knew that anybody there believed in Woman Suffrage. There was no hotel, no church, no school house, so I spoke in the railroad depot to a dozen men as many women and double the number of children and babies. There are only forty voters in the precinct, and a majority of those Mexicans.[8] The 12th at Las Animas—fine audience, among them a good representation from Fort Lyon.[9] At Pueblo,[10] the 13th, where I arrived at 4 P.M., no notice of my coming had been given, therefore I had to begin at the foundation of things, hire a hall, get dodgers printed and distributed, etc.[11] At last, bethinking me that the State Committee might possibly have addressed a letter to me, to somebody's care, I rushed to the postoffice, and sure enough they had; but then there was a hunt to be installed after said persons, and by 7:30 you can imagine my inspiration was of rather a sharp order; but their largest hall was packed, men standing in every available spot, and when, at the close of my speech, an immense majority of that curious crowd voted "aye" I felt better natured and right well paid for all my worry and hard work.

The 14th I spoke at Walsenburg,[12] a precinct numbering 190 voters—150 of these are Mexicans, the other forty mainly Germans. Had nearly every white man and woman of the town, and in addition some twenty or thirty Mexicans (unable to understand a word, remember,) stood braced against the wall to the very close, when the hall was cleared of the benches and the Germans had a jolly two hours of dancing and music, in which my Quaker feet could not participate.

The 15th I reached El Moro[13] at 7:30 P.M., and after the passengers had eaten their suppers the tables were cleared and I spoke in the hotel dining room to a goodly number. The 16th, Sunday, I lectured at Trinidad, where I for the first time stopped at a private house and luxuriated in a "Christian" cup of coffee, to say nothing of enjoying the society of cultivated New Yorkers.[14]

The 17th I started at 6 A.M. for Garland, over the La Veta pass[15]—the highest point yet reached by any railroad in this country—9,300 feet above the level of the sea. It is simply appalling as the narrow gauge steam-horse puffs, puffs, up, up, the heavy grades of the zig-zag road, to look to the depths below you. At 8 P.M. we reached the hardly three months old city, and at 8:30 I had eaten supper, arrayed myself and was speaking to a crowd of men, women and children, packed into the dining room of a hotel, the first nail of which was driven not over thirty days before. The 18th, was again up, breakfast eaten and aboard the stage for Del Norte[16] at 6 o'clock. We at once struck across the San Luis valley, 65 miles wide and 200 long, surrounded on all sides by high mountain ranges—evidently the bed of an immense inland sea—through alkali dust, such as only the stage line from Walula to Walla-Walla, in Washington Territory, could possibly overtop.[17] All that day, as we sped westward at the rate of eight miles an hour, the bald head of Sierra Blanca, the highest peak of the Sangre De Christo range, up and around which the railroad had wound me the day before, seemed hardly to recede from us; and when at last we had compassed the sixty-five miles its hoary head towered high above all its fellows. Del Norte is on the west side of the Rio Grande river. Here again good fortune gave me a home in a private family[18] and I was in clover; but, oh! how weary, how dusty, how utterly forlorn I entered that house—spoke in a new large M.E. church, crowded to its utmost, and again at the close a solid "aye" vote of both men and women.

At 7 P.M. of the 19th I took the stage for this city, a distance of eighty-four miles rode all that night and all the next day to 1 P.M. over the mountains and through their various passes, crossing the divide between the waters that flow into the Atlantic and Pacific—at its highest point over 11,000 feet. And the ride down that mountain pass, "Slum Gullion" they call it,[19] was the most fearful rough and tumble I ever experienced, though I returned overland from Oregon to California—nearly 400 miles—in 1871,[20] and thought I knew all in that line. And even here, in this deep ravine, just wide enough for the Gunnison river and one street on its bank, the height is still 8,500 feet. All that fearfully long, but beautiful, frosty night, the moon shone brightly and on scenery most magnificent. At midnight I alighted at Wagon Wheel Gap,[21] and with tin cup in hand trudged through the sand to the Rio Grande bank, bound to drink fresh from the pure, cold waters from the snow peaks above. It was here, where the mountains crowd up to the river's edge so closely, that Fremont, in his early survey was compelled to leave his wagons, hence the name. The rock bound sides are not only perpendicular but actually overhanging the river thousands of feet below.

Here, too, I am in luck in the delightful home of Mr. and Mrs.

Olney,[22] of the "Silver World," both in full sympathy with our movement.

The friends everywhere are very hopeful of the vote on the 2d of October, and I too might be had I not before me Michigan and Kansas; or could I imagine that the stock-men and miner, the ranchmen and mountain men of Colorado would vote any better than did the farmers of those States; but no one will be more rejoiced if they should than would

ᐊ Susan B. Anthony.

ᐊ Toledo *Ballot Box*, November 1877. Reprinted in *Woman's Journal*, 1 December 1877.

1. SBA reached Colorado on 11 September, arriving by train from Kansas to follow a schedule that kept her in the southern part of the state until election day. Lake City, the seat of Hinsdale County in the San Juan region of the state, grew rapidly in 1876 and 1877 as the commercial center of newly opened silver mines. At an altitude of nearly nine thousand feet, the town was built on a fork of the Gunnison River at the eastern base of the Uncompahgre Mountains. Information about the towns and travel described by SBA was obtained from Frank Fossett, *Colorado. Its Gold and Silver Mines, Farms and Stock Ranges, and Health and Pleasure Resorts*, 2d ed. [New York, 1880], and George A. Crofutt, *Crofutt's Grip-Sack Guide of Colorado. A Complete Encyclopedia of the State*, vol. 2 (1885; reprint, Golden, Colo., 1966).

2. See *Film*, 19:547, and Pueblo *Chieftain*, 27 September 1877. She spoke again on September 25.

3. A mining town due west of Lake City, Ouray's inaccessibility was a long-term obstacle to its growth. From their base in Denver, the organizers of SBA's tour did not know that the journey from Lake City required either a trek over a fourteen thousand foot mountain range (weather permitting) or a long loop through river valleys to approach Ouray from the north. Alida Avery chastised SBA for this decision to skip Ouray. (SBA diary, 24 September 1877, *Film*, 19:12ff.)

4. The trip took her twenty-one miles down the Gunnison River until she turned east up Indian and Beaver creeks to Fort Sanderson, where she spent the first night. On the second day, she crossed the Continental Divide through the Chochetopa Pass into the northern part of the San Juan Valley. Saguache, in the county of the same name, was a farming community largely inhabited by Spanish-speaking people. SBA spoke there on September 24. See also her further report to the *Ballot Box* in *Film*, 19:597.

5. To reach South Arkansas, then in Lake County, SBA traveled through the Poncho Pass into the upper Arkansas Valley. At this stop, her hosts told her to abandon her remaining six appointments in the south and begin the trip north to Denver. (SBA diary, 25 September 1877.)

6. Formally, the Atchison, Topeka & Santa Fe Railroad.

7. In Bent County in the plains of eastern Colorado, Granada was little more than a railroad station. SBA thought it a discouraging start: "they had never heard a lecture—seen a tract or newspaper on W.S.—" she wrote in her diary, "& this one lecture can do very little toward lifting the men out of all their traditional & educational feelings & prejudices." (11 September 1877.)

8. By "Mexicans," SBA and her contemporaries meant the large proportion of Spanish-speaking people in Colorado who became citizens of the United States by the terms of the Treaty of Guadelupe Hidalgo in 1848. The dominance of Mexicans in the region, however, was declining by 1877 as the opening of new mines and the extension of railroads brought a new population from the east and north. (William B. Taylor and Elliott West, "Patrón Leadership at the Crossroads: Southern Colorado in the Late Nineteenth Century," *Pacific Historical Review* 42 [1973]: 335–57.)

9. Las Animas and West Las Animas, four miles distant, were small towns in an agricultural area along the Arkansas River. West Las Animas was the seat of Bent County and the shipping point for cattle headed to eastern markets. Fort Lyon, a military post, was two miles north of Las Animas. For a favorable account of SBA's speech, see *Film*, 19:540. An antisuffragist from West Las Animas reported to the Pueblo *Chieftain*, 20 September 1877, that SBA convinced "everyone that it was their duty to oppose the measure. One or two more speeches of like character, will make old Bent solid against it."

10. The Santa Fe railroad reached Pueblo, eighty miles further west, in 1876. With its sister city of South Pueblo, this was the largest city in southern Colorado and a major railroad center. The Santa Fe here met the Denver & Rio Grande Railway.

11. An executive committee in Denver contacted local men and women to make the arrangements for SBA's tour and gave her the schedule to follow. One difficulty in Pueblo, SBA noted, was that "Lucy Stone did not give any notice of my coming at her meeting the week before." In addition, the editor of the Pueblo *Chieftain* used that week after Henry Blackwell and Stone spoke to start his vociferous campaign against the woman suffrage measure. SBA spoke in Chilcott Hall. (SBA diary, 13 September 1877; *Woman's Journal*, 10 November 1877; Pueblo *Chieftain*, 6 September 1877; with assistance from the Pueblo County Historical Society.)

12. Here SBA turned south, taking the Denver & Rio Grande road sixty miles to the seat of Huerfano County, a settlement of Mexican and German ranchers and farmers.

13. El Moro and Trinidad, five miles apart in Las Animas County, were old trading towns connecting southern Colorado with nearby New Mexico. Coal mining, coke ovens, and railroads were transforming both cities. While Mexicans made up a majority of the county population, English speakers now dominated the towns. At El Moro, SBA spoke in the State Hotel.

14. Her hosts were George R. Swallow (1839–?) and Hannah V. Davis

Swallow (c. 1841–?), recent arrivals from Illinois, not New York. A banker in
Trinidad, George Swallow was a founder of the city's board of trade in 1881
and the state treasurer of Colorado in 1885. (Federal Census, 1880; Michael
Beshoar, *All about Trinidad and Las Animas County, Colorado* [Denver,
Colo., 1882], 99, 106.)

15. SBA reversed direction, heading north to board the San Juan line of the
Denver & Rio Grande westward into the Sangre de Cristo Mountains and over
La Veta Pass. The tracks she traveled were completed in August 1877. Built to
serve the railroad workers, Garland was disassembled and its buildings moved
west to Alamosa in 1878. Alva Adams, later governor of Colorado, who heard
SBA speak in Garland, recalled her audience: it "was good natured, but not
sympathetic. It was made up mostly of men—of freighters, prospectors, railroad workers, merchants, gamblers and saloon men." (Reminiscences of Susan B. Anthony, typescript, SBA Library Scrapbooks, vol. 1, SBA Memorial
Library Collection, Rare Books Division, CSmH.)

16. Del Norte, the seat of Rio Grande County, sits in the San Luis Valley at
the base of the San Juan Mountains to the west and with a view to the east of
the Sangre de Cristo Mountains. Although the surrounding countryside was
populated with Mexican ranchers, the town dated to 1872 and the opening of
mines in the San Juan Mountains.

17. For this trip in Washington Territory, see SBA diary, 20 September
1871, *Film* 15:91ff.

18. SBA was the guest of Warren Richardson and his wife, who earlier
hosted Lucy Stone and Henry Blackwell. She described Richardson as "The
Baker." According to Lucy Stone, Mrs. Richardson died shortly after hosting
the lecturers. A dispatch from Del Norte to the Denver *News* claimed that as a
result of SBA's lecture at the Methodist Episcopal Church, "many who wa-
vered upon the question of woman suffrage are to-day its earnest friends; and
many who were opposed before are silenced." The reporter went on to say
that no one need fear a "solid front of southern Colorado against" the amendment. (SBA diary, 18 September 1877; *Woman's Journal*, 10 November 1877;
unidentified and undated clipping, SBA scrapbook 8, Rare Books, DLC.)

19. To reach Lake City, her stage crossed the mountains through Slumgullion
Pass, on a private toll road at an elevation of about 11,300 feet, and began a
sharp descent to the Gunnison River.

20. For her description of this earlier trip, see SBA diary, 17 November to 4
December 1871.

21. John Charles Frémont (1813–1890) led a disasterous expedition into the
Rocky Mountains in search of a route for a railroad in December 1848. Later
travelers through the narrow gap cut by the Rio Grande del Norte found
wheels thought to be left by Frémont.

22. Henry C. Olney (1842–1916) and Eugenia M. Wilde Olney (1850–1915)
married in 1875 in Dubuque, Iowa, where Eugenia taught school after gradua-

tion from Cornell College in 1869. Henry Olney, a newspaper man with the Denver *Rocky Mountain News*, bought a half interest in the Lake City *Silver World* in 1876, and the couple moved to the new town. They left Lake City for Gunnison in 1885. (Research by Michelle Holschuh Simmons, Archives, Cornell College, and Grant E. Houston, Hinsdale County Historical Society, Lake City.)

123   SBA TO ECS

Denver Col—[1] Oct. 5th 1877.

My Dear Mrs Stanton

Tell Theodore—I received his Saguache & South Arkansas packages—then turned off from the Committees appointments into more <u>populous</u> towns—but wrote friends at every point to take them from the office & distribute— I have Postal from express office of a package with <u>$7.80</u> charges on it—more than the cash value of the books— Still suppose I must pay it—rather than throw the tracts away— ↑It is a <u>box</u>— & hence costs <u>more</u>—always than a paper package—remember—↓[2]

Well the agony is over—& probably the largest <u>majority</u> yet polled against us—[3] It is worse than folly to expect to get suffrage by the state rights plan— I am to lecture here for $100. the 10th inst—next Wednesday— am mean while occupying Dr Alida C. Avery's guest chamber— which was <u>vacated</u> by Lucy & Harry the A.M. after the election[4] & I entered it that night—it is just lovely—with a South-West & North exposure— She has gone east to Woman's Congress[5]—leaving Dr Adelle Gleason[6] in charge—the daughter of Dr & Mrs Gleason of Elmira—so I have it charmingly <u>free</u> & easy— We take our miles[7] a block away—very nice indeed— My first engagement is to be at Sidney Neb. the 24th & thence East on the U.P.R.R.[8]— Sister Mary writes our dear Mother had another fall—which left her almost totally helpless & ~~nearly~~ for nearly 12 hours scarcely felt any knowledge of things—but she was about as well as before when Sister finished her letter— You know <u>this</u> is <u>the year</u> I have always felt that Mother would pass on to the beyond— Still here I am so far away—leaving <u>all</u> the care to dear faithful Mary    It is too bad—& I am constantly querying if it is right

that I should stay away— But Slayton is full of hope of great things—
& I do ↑so↓ need the pecuniary freedom that ought to come of work
now— [*sideways on first page*] Shall be here & about here till the 20<sup>th</sup>—

&#x2E5C; S. B. A—

&#x2E5C; ALS, on NWSA letterhead for 1877, Isabella Hooker Collection, CtHSD.

1. SBA reached Denver on 3 October and moved into the home of Alida
Avery at 339 Twentieth Street the next day.

2. The package contained copies of Paulina Wright Davis, *A History of the
National Woman's Rights Movement* (1871), which included ECS's speech on
"Marriage and Divorce." Noting the high freight charges in her diary, SBA
observed how like ECS it was not to know "the cost of things." (SBA diary, 5
October 1877, *Film*, 19:12ff.)

3. Preliminary returns in Denver's *Rocky Mountain News*, 4 October 1877,
indicated the defeat of the woman suffrage amendment. By the official returns
certified in November, 6,612 voters approved the measure and 14,053 did not.
It carried in Boulder County and garnered better than forty percent of the vote
in Weld, La Plata, Rio Grande, and Larimer counties. But rules of the election
worked against woman suffragists. With the exception of one statewide judicial office, only county officials were on the ballot in the election of 1877, and
the printing of ballots was left to local political parties. Moreover, it was
required that the suffrage question appear on the same ticket as county candidates. Nothing ensured that tickets approving the measure were available.
When Henry Blackwell warned supporters about this difficulty, the Pueblo
*Chieftain* accused him of tampering and reminded local officials about the
precise wording required for disapproving the amendment. Returns of ninety-
nine percent disapproval in Conejos County and ninety-five percent in Huerfano
County, to name the most extreme results, give credence to the protest by
Blackwell that some voters never had a chance to vote their approval of woman
suffrage. In Trinidad, a local woman told Congress, every ticket was printed
with "against" but none with "for" the amendment. Woman suffrage lost by
huge margins in the southern counties, which were also heavily Democratic,
and where the Pueblo *Chieftain* exploited the tension between northern and
southern Colorado by labeling woman suffrage a northern imposition on the
beleaguered south. (*Rocky Mountain News*, 10 November 1877; Pueblo *Chieftain*, 20, 23 September 1877; *Woman's Journal*, 13, 20 October, 1 December
1877; Senate, Select Committee on Woman Suffrage, *Arguments of the Woman-
Suffrage Delegates . . . January 23, 1880*, 47th Cong., 1st sess., S. Mis. Doc. 74,
Serial 1993, p. 17.)

4. Lucy Stone and Henry Blackwell joined the Colorado campaign on 3
September in Colorado Springs. SBA's route matched the early part of their
tour, but they moved quickly into northern Colorado and reached Denver
before election day. Stone wrote reports of their trip for the *Boston Globe*, and

Blackwell sent dispatches to the Associated Press that the Pueblo *Chieftain* deemed to be untruthful. Under the headline "Good-by to the Female Tramps of Boston," one of the paper's reporters wrote: "Should Massachusetts ever again undertake to manage the political affairs of a sister state, she should keep her wilted females at home, or send with them such protecting agents as have at least a character for truthfulness." (*Rocky Mountain News*, 2 September 1877; *Boston Globe*, 4, 11, 28 September, 5, 26 October 1877; Pueblo *Chieftain*, 13, 30 September, 5, 9 October 1877.)

5. Alida Avery attended the fifth annual Woman's Congress in Cleveland, Ohio, on 10 October 1877.

6. Adele Amelia Gleason (1850–1930) was the daughter of the doctors Rachel Brooks Gleason (1820–1905) and Silas Orsemus Gleason (1818–1899), who headed the Elmira Water-Cure in New York. After attending college at Elmira and Vassar and studying medicine with her parents, Adele earned her medical degree from the University of Michigan in 1875. (Necrology files, Office of Alumni Records, MiU-H; *ANB*, s.v. "Gleason, Rachel Brooks"; Weiss and Kemble, *Great American Water-Cure Craze*, 155, 157–60.)

7. Rather than cooking for themselves, they ate their *meals* (not miles) at a boardinghouse.

8. Starting from western Nebraska, SBA would reach her engagements in Kearney and Grand Island aboard the Union Pacific.

## 124 ⁀ SBA to Nancy Hall Allen[1] and the Iowa Woman Suffrage Association

Denver, Col., Oct. 14th, 1877.

My Dear Mrs. Allen:—Your letter of Oct. 11th is just here, this Sunday A.M. I had set apart to-day for writing you without fail, and now your missive helps me to keep my word with myself.

I am more sorry than I can tell that my agent has engagements for me in Nebraska from the 24th inst., and thence onward and Eastward, so it will be impossible for me to be with you at your Iowa State Woman Suffrage annual meeting. And I wish to be there all the more, now that for the third time the friends of woman suffrage have tried the "States' Rights" plan of securing it and have again the third time fearfully failed.

So far as heard from, three counties carried the question by small majorities, while all the rest lost it by large majorities.[2] The official returns will, probably show a vote of not more than 1 to 4—not a very different result from that of Kansas and Michigan—and any worse than would be that of Iowa, Massachusetts, or any other State of the Union.

The two great powers that are now solidly arrayed against the enfranchisement of woman cannot be overcome at the ballot box of any State, at least for long years to come.[3] These forces are, first, what we term the Whisky Ring, comprising not only all the men who want free whisky, but all who want free gambling houses and free brothels, as well;—all those who wish the full and free enjoyment of what are termed the "pet vices of men,"—always have voted, and always will vote against the right of their mothers and sisters, wives and daughters, to a voice in the laws and law makers that regulate society.

And the other power is the ignorant, bigoted, priest-ridden and ruled masses.

In Colorado it comprises the native Mexicans, the negroes, and the Irish and German Catholics, who, with a few noble exceptions, voted a solid "No." A week before the election I met Gov. Routt,[4] who told me the "three or four hundred negroes of Denver would give a solid vote in favor of woman suffrage." I said I hope you know whereof you speak, Governor, but I fear. The fact is, the negro vote of this city went almost solid against the amendment. "'Tis true, and pity 'tis, 'tis true,"[5] too, that we who worked so many, many years to bring freedom to the black race, must now see the men of it again and again, voting against equality of rights to women.[6]

My dear friends and co-workers of Iowa, do you not see with me, the impossibility of overcoming these great, unconvertible forces at the ballot box? In three of the most hopeful States of the Union we have marshalled the intelligent, the broad, the just, the generous voters, and seen them out-voted by their opponents three to one, each time. And I now say with the old adage, "three times and out," and appeal to you and the friends everywhere to rally to the work of petitioning Congress for a 16th amendment. Help to roll up at least a million of signatures, that our Representatives and Senators at Washington may see that we Women Suffragists have a respectable constituency in every State, and one that Congressmen may not very long ignore with impunity. The States' rights process is wholly impracticable as well as wholly unjust. The United States citizen's right to a voice in the government of the State or territory in which he or she may chance to reside is not a question of the pleasure or the displeasure of the majority of other United States citizens who like himself may be at the time sojourning in said State or Territory. The theory, though sanctioned by the Supreme Court in the case of Mrs. Virginia C. Minor, is too absurd, too unjust to be entertained by any lover of Democratic or Republican government.

National supremacy over the right to the freedom and franchise of every class of United States citizens must be established, above and beyond the power of the several States to abridge or deny on any account, save those of idiocy, lunacy and crime. No class should be compelled to beg their rights at the feet of another class. And I hope that your Legislature will not submit the question to the rank and file of the voters of your State. Iowa has its 40,000 foreign votes[7] and its whisky-ring devotees, which together with the ignorant and indifferent will make at least a two thirds' majority. The State's right to *give* or to *take* the suffrage, must be forever prohibited by a 16th Amendment to the National Constitution. I pray you, therefore, ply all your energies and money in that direction, and appoint delegates to carry to Washington—the middle of January, 1878—the largest petition ever rolled up by the liberty-loving men and women of Iowa.

Wishing you the best success in your meeting, and the strongest vote and petition for a 16th Amendment, I am most sincerely yours,

*≈ Susan B. Anthony.*

*≈ Des Moines Register,* 26 October 1877, M. J. Gage scrapbooks, Rare Books, DLC.

1. Nancy R. Hall Brace Lyon Allen (c. 1829–1881) of Maquoketa was corresponding secretary of the Iowa Woman Suffrage Association, scheduled to meet on 24 October in Des Moines. An early advocate of women's temperance activism and a member of the Woman's Christian Temperance Union, Allen worked on the campaign to gain state suffrage in 1876 and became an officer of the National Woman Suffrage Association the same year. She was a wealthy woman in her own right with substantial holdings in real estate, some of it inherited from her father, a founder of Maquoketa, and her first two husbands. She married John H. Allen, a physician, in 1857. After reading SBA's letter at the Iowa meeting, Allen reported to the *Woman's Journal,* 24 November 1877, that it "was well received, and convinced us, we had better turn our attention to secure, if possible, a sixteenth amendment to the United States Constitution. . . . Foreigners, and all who favor the 'pet vices' of the day, will never vote to enfranchise Woman." (*The History of Jackson County, Iowa, Containing a*

*History of the County, Its Cities, Towns, &c.* [Chicago, 1879], 497-98, 521, 621; James W. Ellis, *History of Jackson County, Iowa* [Chicago, 1910], 1:118, 615, 2:602; *History,* 3:39, 616, 626; *Woman's Journal,* 19 March 1881; Federal Census, 1870.)

2. SBA did not yet have the final results from the election, which showed a victory only in Boulder County.

3. The social and cultural explanations for the outcome of the Colorado election set forth by SBA in this letter were not original to her. She echoed the opinions set forth by leaders of the American Woman Suffrage Association in the week after the election. In a lecture delivered in Denver on 9 October, Margaret Campbell blamed "degraded and superstitious Mexicans of the south," "the liquor-selling and liquor-drinking interests," the Catholic church, and "the uneducated and uncultivated negroes of the north." Henry Blackwell began with the same list of enemies, writing from Denver to the *Woman's Journal,* and added Germans, southerners with slaveholding values, and "bigots, Catholic and Protestant." This unanimity among easterners who joined the campaign was not shared locally. According to the friendly editor of the *Rocky Mountain News,* the easterners had "suffered themselves to be beguiled" into believing victory was possible. No Coloradan expected victory, he wrote; neither men nor women were ready for the change. The editor of the "Woman's Column" in the same paper defended all the groups singled out by the easterners and placed blame for the defeat on the "immaturity of women" themselves. The *Boulder County News,* smug with victory in the county, traced defeat to negative votes in the southern portion of the state. The Pueblo *Chieftain* crowed that Coloradans had vindicated themselves against "certain windy fanatics" who tried "to foist female suffrage" on the state. (*Rocky Mountain News,* 4, 7, 10 October 1877, Pueblo *Chieftain,* 5, 11 October 1877, *Boulder County News,* 4 October 1877, *Woman's Journal,* 13, 27 October 1877; William B. Faherty, "Regional Minorities and the Woman Suffrage Struggle," *Colorado Magazine* 8 [July 1956]: 212-17; Marilley, *Woman Suffrage and the Origins of Liberal Feminism,* 96-98.)

4. John Long Routt (1826-1907) was named governor of the Territory of Colorado by President Grant in 1875 and won election as the state's first governor in 1876. He served until 1879. (*BDGov.*)

5. William Shakespeare, *Hamlet,* act 3, sc. 2, lines 1026-7.

6. It has not been possible to test this claim, one also made by Henry Blackwell. When the campaign opened, organizers held a large rally at Denver's A.M.E. church for the city's African-American residents. Lucy Stone mentioned the presence of African-American women at the polls on election day in Denver urging men to support suffrage. But, according to Blackwell, all their efforts influenced only the "five per cent. who are educated and intelligent" to vote for woman suffrage; "ninety-five per cent. voted and worked against us." (*Rocky Mountain News,* 2 September 1877; *Woman's Journal,* 13 October 1877; *Boston Globe,* 26 October 1877.)

7. The federal census of 1870 counted 92,865 foreign-born males over twenty-one years of age in Iowa, or thirty-two percent of the potential voters. (*Compendium of the Ninth Census*, 554.)

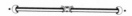

125　⇝　SBA to H. Louise Mosher and Daniel L. Anthony[1]

Denver Col— Oct. 20th 1877.

Dear Louise & Dannie

Aunt Mary wrote me ↑last Saturday↓ how sadly Louise' <u>school</u> & dancing lessons were broken into last week by her severe cold— It was too bad—and then she wrote also how she went to Dancing school with Dannie and how nicely he went through all the polite motions— How much like a <u>gentlemen</u> you will feel Dannie, when you learn how to do all those things— I am very glad Aunt Mary decided to let you both learn to "trip the light fantastic toe" this winter—and she wrote me too, how much better Grand Ma is—all of which comforted me ever so much—

Now, Dannie when is that promised letter to Aunt Susan coming— I hope it is getting written this very Saturday—or will be surely, tomorrow,— Tell ↑me↓ all about the nice boys you have got acquainted with and which you think the best— I hope ~~you~~ ↑my↓ nephew Dannie will be the <u>best</u> of the <u>very best</u> of them—

Louise, you <u>must</u> be more careful about taking those terrible colds!— are you sitting <u>too</u> <u>close</u> to a stove again—with an open window blowing down on the top of your head?— If you have to recite in a <u>cold</u> room—always put on a shawl or cape—

Does Dannie get any more colds?— I wish I could look in upon you at No 7. this very minute & see how you all are doing— <u>We</u> <u>must</u> <u>all</u> <u>of</u> <u>us</u> <u>try</u> <u>our</u> <u>best</u> <u>never</u> <u>to</u> <u>do</u> a <u>thing</u> but what <u>we</u> <u>shall</u> <u>be</u> <u>glad</u> of after it is done—& be perfectly willing to have everybody know we did it. If we always just stop a minute & think about what we a going to do, we shall be saved from wrong or foolish things— Now both of you write to Aunt Susan & just run on & tell all about everybody & everything— Mary Dobbin must write— She always tells lots of news—& that is what one likes when so far away from all one loves— affectionately

⇝　*Your Aunt Susan B*

❧ ALS, on NWSA letterhead for 1877, SBA Collection, NR.

1. Daniel Luther Anthony, the first son of Merritt and Mary L. Anthony, born in 1865, left Kansas in late August 1877 with his aunt Mary S. Anthony to be raised by her at 7 Madison Street and attend school in Rochester. Having urged Mary to undertake the task, SBA helped to cover the costs of his care. The experiment did not go well. Two days before writing this letter, SBA concluded from her sister's discouraged reports that Danny "seems to be wholly destitute of <u>moral</u> <u>sense</u>—very smart intellectually." He alternated between pledges "to try harder than ever to be a good boy" and disappearances for days at a time, leaving Mary Anthony in a state of "exhaustion." After several abortive attempts to get himself back to Kansas, he reached St. Louis in April 1878, and his family sent him the money to complete the trip. SBA tracked the story in her diary, beginning at 21 August 1877 and continuing through 25 April 1878. (*Film*, 19:12ff, 791ff.)

126 ❧ ECS TO HELEN L. POTTER

Hazleton, Pa.,[1] Sunday Oct 21st 187[7]

My dear Miss Potter,

Is it not too bad that I could not have seen you here, & enjoyed your entertainment. As you are to imitate Mrs Stanton here I thought I would tell you how I was dressed last night that you may come as near as possible    Well, I did not wear a black lace on my head, simply my hair nothing more. Black satin train  one skirt plain waist with standing ruffle, & a piece of soft blond lace[2] round the neck & running to the waist with a large cameo pin, the lace puffed a little round the pin. I am so glad to hear of your continued success. Do drop me a few lines at Tenafly, & tell me how you feel. I have often thought of the merry day we had together at my home & I do hope sometime to see you there again.[3] sincerely yours

❧ *E. C. Stanton*

❧ ALS, on letterhead of Central Hotel, ECS Papers, DLC.

1. ECS began her fall lectures in mid-October, staying in the Northeast until year's end. Hazleton, a center of coal mining, lies in the mountains of eastern Pennsylvania.
2. A lace made from raw silk, in which the threads are tied to form a pattern of hexagonals.

3. Helen Potter spent the day in Tenafly with ECS and SBA on 31 August 1876. The text of her impersonation was the Declaration of Rights from 1876, delivered, Potter wrote, "with grace, dignity and earnestness worthy the woman, and the cause she so ably represents." (SBA diary, 1876, *Film*, 18:516ff; Potter, *Helen Potter's Impersonations*, 91.)

## 127 ⤳ SBA to Clara Bewick Colby[1]

[*written above heading*] While waiting an hour for Train

Lincoln Neb. Nov. 2^d 1877.

My Dear Mrs Colby

I must have dropped a trunk key off its string—either at your house or at Mr Vails[2]—though it occurs to me—it might have been at the Depot—where I unlocked my trunk— but—if you find a key—it was rather thick & short—a little rusty withal—I wish you would put it in an envelope fast—& mail it to me—at Sioux City—Iowa Care of E. W. Skinner[3]—where I am to be the 9^th inst— The belongs to a trunk I had sent home—so did not hinder me from getting into the one I have with me— Don't worry about it—only if you hear of it—send it to me—as it will save a hunt for one to fit the trunk—or a new lock—

Well, Mr Vail—poor man—will have told you what a time he had to get me started off so early yesterday A.M— I really believe he staid up all night for fear he would not wake up early enough—and then the pouring rain—& the Buss going off & leaving him at the Depot—to foot it home in rain & mud— What a lovely woman dear Mrs Vail is— I really wanted to stay & see more of her—as I did of you—my dear Mrs Colby— Such women as you two have individual work to do—to lift the world into better conditions—& I hope you will not allow anything to estop ↑you↓ from doing what seems to be your duty— I long to see women be themselves—not the mere echoes of men— I was delighted that your "non believing" husband called at Mr Vails— Did he tell you the "mission" I laid upon him for the coming session of the Legislature?— Now won't you insist that your husband shall act for you— represent you—in the senate—& just push the 16^th am't resolution to a discussion & a vote—just as if he were disfranchised party—& not you—[4] Men owe it to us to act ↑as our↓ political proxies—so long as

they keep us locked out of our right act for ourselves— Dont you think
<u>so</u>?— ask Mr C. to please to think so this winter—

I got through—with 3 hours delay & a terribly poor breakfast at
Crete—& two hours waiting at Lincoln—& had a large ↑city↓ audience
at Seward—the rain, the mud & the dark—estopped the farmers from
driving in to attend— But the people seemed earnest—& I hope these
talks of mine is I almost fly through the country—will rouse the friends
of woman's equality to circulate our petitions—to send to Washington
an expression of <u>their wish</u> for the 16<sup>th</sup> am't to enfranchise the women
of the Republic—

Mrs Colby—do, please, write a brief letter of <u>your</u> Library work[5]—&
Lecture Course—for the <u>December</u> number of the Ballot Box—it goes
to Press about the 25<sup>th</sup> of each month—so anything you send by that
time—will be in time for the next months issue— For you—& every
woman to tell what you are doing—helps to rouse other women to do
likewise— Women want to be helped into the feeling that they <u>can</u> help
on the good works they like to see done— We have been told we
<u>couldn't</u> <u>do</u> <u>anything</u> but <u>help</u> the individual man or men of our fami-
lies—so long & so constantly—that very ↑few↓ women can of them-
selves get into any work above that— I hope I shall hear from you
often, <u>through the Ballot Box</u>, if no other way— Give my kind regards
to dear Grand Mother[6]—your husband—brother,[7] wife & Miss
Coleman[8]—& Mr & Mrs Vail— I seldom like ↑the↓ people I see so little
of, so much—so with love & hope that you will <u>keep</u> <u>up</u> the "<u>Rubadub</u>"
of <u>agitation</u>—as Daniel <u>Webster</u>—used to call <u>reform</u> <u>work</u>—[9] I am
sincerely yours

&#x223d; *Susan B. Anthony*

&#x223d; ALS, on NWSA letterhead for 1877, Clara Bewick Colby Papers, WHi.
Not in *Film*.

1. Clara Dorothy Bewick Colby (1846–1916), later editor of the *Woman's
Tribune*, graduated from the University of Wisconsin in 1869 and taught there
until her marriage to Leonard Wright Colby (1846–1925) and their move to
Beatrice, Nebraska, in 1871. Leonard Colby practiced law and won election to
the state senate in November 1876; he also owned the Beatrice *Express* for a
time, providing Clara Colby an opportunity to edit and write. Among her
projects to improve the cultural life of this frontier town, Colby arranged a
series of lectures in which SBA spoke on 31 October. (*NAW*; *ANB*; *NCAB*,
18:399; Renée Sansom Flood, *Lost Bird of Wounded Knee: Spirit of the Lakota*
[New York, 1995].)

2. Thomas Scott Vaill (1817–1892) was the Presbyterian minister in Beatrice and SBA's host. A graduate of Amherst College, class of 1840, he married Elizabeth Selden Comstock in 1844. He served churches in Iowa and Illinois until his arrival in Beatrice in 1874. Elizabeth Vaill, the mother of seven children, was the founding president of the town's Woman's Christian Temperance Union in 1880 and an officer the next year of the Gage County Woman Suffrage Association. (*History of the State of Nebraska; Containing a Full Account of Its Growth from an Uninhabited Territory to a Wealthy and Important State* [Chicago, 1882], 902, 903; on-line biographical record of class of 1840, Amherst College, Mass.)

3. Elisha Williams Skinner (1834–?) moved to Sioux City in 1872 to sell agricultural machinery and invest in real estate. (*History of the Counties of Woodbury and Plymouth, Iowa, Including an Extended Sketch of Sioux City* [Chicago, 1890–91], 691–92.)

4. SBA refers to a plan she had recently described to Elizabeth Harbert: to "set every state into a splendid agitation of the question—& that just by going into every Legislature & getting a resolution presented, discussed & voted upon—<u>recommending Congress to submit a proposition for a 16</u>[th] am't.—" The National Woman Suffrage Association adopted her idea in 1878 and supplied women with the text of petitions to state legislatures. (SBA to E. B. Harbert, 24 October 1877, and *NCBB*, August 1880, *Film*, 19:574–77, 20:313–21.)

5. In 1873 Colby and other women in Beatrice established a circulating library paid for with contributions and subscriptions. By one account, it became a project of the local Woman's Christian Temperance Union. The town took it over as a public library in 1893. (Hugh J. Dobbs, *History of Gage County, Nebraska* [Lincoln, Neb., 1918], 208.)

6. Clara Medhurst Chilton (c. 1800–1879), Clara Colby's maternal grandmother, lived with the Colbys in Beatrice. Her husband died in March 1877. (Flood, *Lost Bird of Wounded Knee*, 106ff.)

7. Clara Colby had several brothers.

8. SBA identified her as Julia Coleman, daughter of Charles Coleman of Rochester, New York. She may also have been a sister of Theodore Coleman. Theodore, his father, and his siblings left Rochester in 1859 and settled a year later in Wisconsin. He then moved to Beatrice, where he published the newspaper from 1870 until he sold it to Leonard Colby in 1875 and moved to Washington, D.C. (SBA diary, 31 October 1877, *Film*, 19:12ff; Dobbs, *History of Gage County, Neb.*, 243–46; *History of the State of Nebraska*, 902.)

9. Responding to Daniel Webster's dismissive remarks about the abolitionist movement, Wendell Phillips, speaking on 28 January 1852, referred to "a 'rub-a-dub of agitation,' as ours is contemptuously styled." Webster mentioned the rub-a-dub of the abolitionist press. (Wendell Phillips, *Speeches, Lectures, and Letters* [1863; reprint, Boston, 1891], 36.)

## 128   SBA TO ISABELLA BEECHER HOOKER

Onawa—Ia—[1] Nov. 11th 1877.

My Dear Mrs. Hooker

I have just received the Nov. Ballot Box—what a terrible blow has fallen on the heart of our dear Mrs Williams—her darling Sibyl was the child after her own mothers wish— how will the poor mother survive her loss?—[2]

But while the B.B. brought to me that sad note—it brought on another page the joyful name & word of Isabella Beecher Hooker—[3] I cant tell you how my heart bounded to see you at <u>the</u> <u>front</u> <u>again</u>—& with such a glorious <u>following</u>!— It rejoices me exceedingly—

Now I turn to <u>you</u>—to issue the call for our National—Washington Convention—the days of Thursday & Friday—Jan 17th & 18th—(See that dates match ↑I have no <u>new</u> almanac↓) are good ones— I would have the call <u>short & sharp</u>—so that every news paper will or <u>may</u> print it—[4] Of course Dear Mrs Lozier is too <u>busy</u>—as <u>I</u> am too far off—too attend to the call—and I am so delighted to find that it is <u>you</u> who stand <u>officially</u> in the place to do the correspondence— I feel that we must <u>drive</u> <u>all</u> <u>our</u> nails in the 16th am't direction— The vote of Colorado is another argument on our side for <u>national</u> protection—

You may put Mrs Stanton—Phoebe Couzins & S. B. A. down to be at ↑the↓ Washington <u>Con</u>—& of course Mrs Hooker & Olympia Brown— We must make a <u>powerful</u> <u>attack</u> upon Congress this year—it is our <u>Decade</u> <u>appeal</u>—[5] we shall doubtless have an immense petition—it seems to me it must surpass every thing we ever did in that line

I have, <u>personally</u>, put the petitions into hundreds of good earnest hands in Colorado, Nebraska & Iowa—& had Post masters & merchants—as well as many, many women—tell me they would keep the petitions in their offices & stores & get everybody to sign who called— the <u>growth</u> of <u>interest</u> in our cause is very great & rapid— I planted the Ballot Box for the coming year in <u>76</u> <u>families</u> in Colorado—& have planted it in as many more in Neb. & Iowa the past three weeks— No matter how much the Committees pay me—I close up every speech with appeal for the people to [give?] us <u>practical</u> <u>aid</u> for 16<sup>th</sup> am't—to take & sign & circulate the Petitions—& to subscribe for the B.B.—& I get from <u>3 to 10</u> subscribers every night—have an <u>average of 5</u> subscribers for my last 13 lectures—thus you see I am <u>sowing</u> other seed than [my bare?] speech—<sup>6</sup> Oh how I do wish we could take that B.B. to New York—turn it into <u>a weekly</u>—& <u>keep</u> it at <u>$1.</u> a year—then I could <u>roll</u> <u>it</u> <u>up</u>— You ↑see↓ if it were a <u>Metropolitan</u> <u>paper</u>—with a <u>National</u> <u>reputationed</u> Editor—there is scarcely any limit to the subscription list we might get for it—

The friends who take the ↑Womans↓ Journal out west here—feel that it <u>gives</u> <u>them nothing</u> <u>to</u> <u>do</u>—it is all about "<u>Hub</u>" <u>work</u>—& <u>caucus</u> <u>meetings</u>—which out here where each county has an area of all <u>Mass.</u> put together—& then <u>one</u> or <u>two</u> friends in a given town of each one of those large sections—to talk to them about attending & controlling <u>causses</u> is simply ridiculous— Those Boston people cant imagine but what ↑the things↓<sup>7</sup> <u>they</u> <u>do</u>—will be practicable every where—

They promised—at the <u>suitable</u> <u>time</u>—when their American Ex. Com. should decide it best—to advertise a <u>16</u><sup>th</sup> <u>am't work</u> of <u>their own</u> in <u>their</u> <u>own way</u>—that was ↑in↓ last August or July—when <u>Lucy</u> <u>refused</u> <u>to</u> <u>publish</u> <u>ours</u> <u>for pay</u>—sent her by Mrs Spencer—because, she said—<sup>3</sup>/<sub>5</sub> of the readers of the Journal <u>preferred</u> to work under the <u>lead</u> of the American W.S.A.— Lucy thus wrote to Mrs Sargent—& Mrs Spencer sent me verbatim copy—and still I ↑neither↓ see nor hear anything of the <u>Journal's</u> <u>announcing</u> 16<sup>th</sup> am't for themselves—<sup>8</sup> <u>Now</u> <u>Mrs Hooker</u>—we—the <u>National</u> Ex. Com. of the N.W.S.A—<u>must</u> appeal to every single <u>State</u> <u>Legislature</u>—<u>this winter</u> to pass a resolution—saying to Congress that in their opinion it is Duty of Cong. to submit proposition for 16<sup>th</sup> am't— If we can make that flank movement upon Congress—we shall bring more than double the weight of our petitions to bear upon that body—

Even at the Last winters session of the Indiana Legislature—<u>some</u> <u>idiot</u>—presented a resolution that the 14<sup>th</sup> am't enfranchised women— pressed ↑it↓ to a vote & got <u>21. votes</u> for it—& a great many more explained their "<u>No</u>"—by saying ~~they~~ <u>if</u> <u>it</u> <u>had</u> <u>been</u> directly on the <u>question</u> of the <u>right</u> of women to vote—they should have <u>voted</u>— "<u>Yes</u>" for they believed she ought to vote—<sup>9</sup> <u>Now can't you</u> <u>superintend</u> that work—or how can we compass it— I cant tell you how like a <u>caged lioness</u> ↑I feel↓—(as if <u>my</u> <u>little</u> <u>cub</u> were <u>outside</u> too) as I am

compelled to peg round here in these little towns—just for $30. a
night—to get the money to live on—when I want to be spending half
that $30. a day—to execute <u>movement</u> <u>work</u>—upon the State Legisla-
tures & upon Congress—for after all <u>Mrs Hooker</u>—we <u>reach</u> <u>more</u>
<u>people</u>—& in a <u>more</u> influential way—by getting the State Legislatures
and Congress turned <u>into</u> <u>Woman</u> <u>Suffrage</u> <u>Conventions</u> than we possibly can in School District lectures— the latter are all good—<u>but</u> too
<u>infinstesmally</u> small & <u>slow</u> <u>in</u> their results— The <u>time</u> <u>is</u> <u>ripe</u> <u>for</u>
<u>wider</u>, <u>broader</u>, <u>representative</u> <u>work</u>— Don't you see it so?— What &
how can we do to <u>set</u> <u>all</u> <u>the</u> <u>machinery</u> in motion?— I will not only do
my share of the work—but pay <u>my share</u> & more, too,—of the money to
get it done— If we can only decide on the <u>plan</u> & the persons to "boss"
it— Well do tell me what you see & feel best to undertake—& direct to
the care of H. L. Slayton— 122 La Salle st— Chicago Ill—

Since Feb. 1$^{st}$ I have sent The Ballot Box <u>350</u> <u>new</u> subscribers—and
could I have said it is <u>my</u> <u>paper</u>—with <u>Mrs Stanton</u> & <u>Mrs Hooker</u> &
<u>Mrs Gage</u>—<u>Editors</u>—I verily believe it might have been <u>3500</u> just as
easily— I tell you the time has come <u>for</u> <u>a</u> <u>National</u> <u>W.S.</u> <u>Paper</u>—
<u>fearless</u>—<u>broad</u>—Cosmopolitan—in its scope— We could just sweep
this Nation with it—[10] <u>But</u> <u>alas</u>—<u>Where is the cash</u>?— Echo answers
where? So we must do ↑with↓ the little one we have—& it is bright &
sparkling too—& all of us must help make it do more & more good
work—

⤙ S. B. A—

[*written on enclosure*] P.S. Mrs Hooker—If you cannot attend to this
Call—please send it on to Mrs Spencer at once—but I do hope the good
inspiration will be upon you to <u>write</u> <u>just</u> <u>the</u> <u>rousing</u> <u>word</u>— I want to
make it appeal to <u>every</u> <u>man</u> & <u>woman</u> who wants women to vote—of
<u>course</u> <u>not</u> to <u>pander</u> to [snub?] & snob Boston—but to invite every-
body—S. B A

⤙ ALS, on NWSA letterhead for 1877, Isabella Hooker Collection, CtHSD.
Words in square brackets obscured by ink blot.

1. SBA spent Sunday in this town in western Iowa, where she had lectured
on Saturday night.

2. Sybil Williams Hamilton (?–1877), the middle daughter of Sarah Langdon
Williams and formerly a teacher of drawing in the Toledo public schools, died
on 29 October. She had been married for about a year to James Kent Hamilton,

a graduate of Kenyon College, class of 1859, and a lawyer in Toledo. (*Ballot Box*, November 1877; *NCAB*, 18:380–81, s.v. "Hamilton, James Kent.")

3. In Hooker's letter about the meeting of the Connecticut Woman Suffrage Association in October.

4. SBA's enclosed draft of the call is omitted. For the final text, see *Film*, 19:603–4.

5. The year 1878 marked three decades since the meeting of the woman's rights convention at Seneca Falls, New York, in 1848.

6. SBA took on the responsibility of selling subscriptions to the *Ballot Box* when the paper became the organ of the National Woman Suffrage Association.

7. No caret indicates where SBA intended this interlineation to be read.

8. The American Woman Suffrage Association came to a decision about the petition drive soon after SBA wrote her complaint. Lucy Stone announced on 24 November that the executive committee had mailed sixteenth amendment petitions to every subscriber to the *Woman's Journal*; the American "has always recommended petitions to Congress for a sixteenth amendment," Stone wrote. Upon reading the announcement, SBA wrote in her diary, "glad they are driven to make that avowal at last." The committee also mailed petitions suitable for submission to state legislatures, because, Stone continued, the American "recognizes the far greater importance of petitioning the State Legislatures. . . . Suffrage is a subject referred by the Constitution to the voters of each State." Readers were urged "to give special prominence" to the state petitions.

Two weeks later, the editors gave front page space to T. W. Higginson's arguments against the amendment. Maintaining the balance between federal and state governments was, he wrote, more important than woman suffrage. No cause justified "increasing and consolidating the internal powers of the national government" by constitutional amendments. Each state "is sovereign within its own sphere," specifically with respect to suffrage; "either you must have a despotism, or you must let the separate States . . . govern their local affairs in their own way." To treat the Fourteenth and Fifteenth amendments as precedents for woman suffrage "would be a calamity."

Despite the discouraging words, one hundred and twenty petitions for the amendment, bearing more than six thousand signatures, were returned to the *Journal*'s office. Senator George F. Hoar presented them on 5 February 1878. (*Woman's Journal*, 24 November, 8 December 1877; SBA diary, 29 November 1877, *Film*, 19:12ff; *History*, 3:104; *Congressional Record*, 45th Cong., 2d sess., 747–48.)

9. SBA refers to a confusing series of events early in 1877 that culminated in a legislative vote while she visited Indianapolis in February. The Indiana Woman Suffrage Association was tracking two legislative initiatives: an amendment to remove the word "white" from the qualifications for voting, to which was added a resolution in the senate also to remove the word "male"; and a bill

to remove the legal disabilities of married women with respect to their separate property and businesses. On 2 February, at the request of the state
association, the house invited Mary Livermore to speak the next day on
property rights. But on the morning of her speech, the house considered a
resolution declaring "that the fourteenth and fifteenth amendments to the
constitution of the United States confer the right of suffrage upon all citizens
alike, regardless of sex." Livermore, who chose to speak on suffrage, dismissed the terms of the resolution at the start of her speech. Proceeding to a
vote when Livermore concluded, the house defeated the resolution twenty-
two to fifty-one. According to the *Indianapolis Sentinel*, "[m]any voted against
the resolution who expressed themselves in favor of extending the right of
franchise to women, but they objected to the wording of the resolution,
thinking a 16th amendment would be a better way to dispose of it." (*Indianapolis Sentinel*, 10, 17 January, 3, 4 February 1877; *Woman's Journal*, 3, 17
February, 24 March 1877; *History*, 3:539.)

10. Late in 1876, SBA met several times with two wealthy New Yorkers,
Susan A. King and Ellen Curtis Demorest, about creating a stock company to
revive the *Revolution*. Talks continued until the end of the year, but the plan
came to naught. (SBA diary, 25 November, 19, 25 December 1876, *Film*,
18:516ff.)

## 129 ⤳ ELLEN CLARK SARGENT TO ECS

Washington, Nov. 23^d [*1877*]

Dear Mrs. Stanton,

The call for a Convention in Washington is to be issued immediately. It is decided to hold the same on the 8^th & 9^th of Jan. 1878.

The Committee on Privileges & Elections (of the Senate) have said
they will hear from the delegates, sent from the States & Territories, on
the woman question on the 9^th of Jan. at 10.30 A.M.

We want a grand rally. You will come of course.

I want you and Miss Anthony to put up at my house. I will do as well
for you as I did last year if not better. Yours truly,

⤳ *E. C. Sargent.*

⤳ ALS, Isabella Hooker Collection, CtHSD.

130 ⚭ MARGARET L. STANTON TO ECS

[*Tenafly,*] Saturday, Nov. 24, [*1877*]

My dear Mother,

Your letter from Buffalo came to-night[1]    I will send the packages as you requested &c. &c. No, my dear, no Ballot Box in company with ten Virgins have been here.[2] There are only <u>two virgins</u> in this house, but we [boast?] four representatives of the <u>Ballot Box</u>.

In answering Mrs. Sargent's letter, if you decide to go to W., please tell her that your daughter will be with you. I should like very much to go to Washington and ↑should↓ exceedingly enjoy meeting the Sargent family. They must be so interesting, ↑judging↓ from what[3]

Good night & good bye, my beloved, it is very early in the eve'g., not later than half past seven! Yours,

⚭ *Madge*

⚭ ALS, Isabella Hooker Collection, CtHSD. Written on E. C. Sargent to ECS, 23 November, above. Square brackets surround uncertain word.

1. In a letter from Canton, Ohio, ECS told her daughter she had gone to Buffalo to visit Charlotte Mulligan, a young philanthropist gaining renown for her reformatory work with teenage boys. ECS recounted what she learned from Mulligan in "Our Boys." (ECS to M. L. Stanton, 26 November 1877, and "Our Boys" manuscript, pp. 25–42, *Film*, 19:598, 45:75ff.)

2. Margaret responds to a question about the December issue of the *Ballot Box*, which published ECS's article "The Parable of the Ten Virgins." ECS's reading of Matthew 25:1–13 as a secular parable about women and self-reliance appeared in many forms. It was the topic of her speech at the National Woman Suffrage Association convention in January 1877, though no one there reported the text; it can be found in her speech "The Bible and Woman Suffrage," below at 11 May 1879; a reporter gave the gist of a sermon with this title delivered by ECS in Washington, Iowa, on 21 February 1880; and in a condensed form, ECS retold the story as she prepared part two of the *Woman's Bible*, publishing the parable in the *Woman's Tribune*, 22, 29 June 1895, and the New York *Independent*, 16 September 1897. See *Film*, 19:431, 705–12, 21:110–111, 34:180–85, 194–202, 37:227, and *Woman's Bible*, 123–26.

3. At this point, Margaret continued her letter on the side of the sheet used by Ellen Sargent. It is not clear whether an extra sheet of her letter was lost or she forgot the drift of her sentence.

## 131 ✎ ECS TO ISABELLA BEECHER HOOKER

Canton, O. Nov 28<sup>th</sup> [*1877*]

Dear Mrs Hooker

I am glad the convention is to be on the 8<sup>th</sup> & 9<sup>th</sup> as I could not have been there a week later. Now do prepare a grand speech on some special point. I wish the Miss Smiths could be there    See that Olympia is invited in time. I shall speak on taxation for one thing.[1] I wish some one would show how degraded woman has been under all forms of religion   that would be a good theme for Olympia. Robert Ingersoll is in Washington, he should speak for us. Do invite some able men. What say you to Heywood again.[2] As Free love has done so much for you in Conn. perhaps it might do as much in the nation. I have spoken every night since I left you & oh! how tired I am    With love & kind regards for yourself & Mr. Hooker   good night

✎ *E. C. S.*

✎ ALS, on letterhead of St. Cloud Hotel, Isabella Hooker Collection, CtHSD.

1. Although ECS did not, by all reports, speak on taxation at the Washington convention, she wrote a lecture entitled "Taxation." See *Film*, 19:717–51.

2. Ezra Hervey Heywood (1829–1893), a radical reformer, anarchist, and suffragist who lived in Princeton, Massachusetts, attended the Connecticut Woman Suffrage Association meeting in October, just before his arrest by Anthony Comstock on 2 November 1877 for mailing obscene material. He had mailed a copy of *Cupid's Yokes* (1876), his critique of marriage and defense of women's rights. His trial opened on 22 January 1878, and in June, Heywood began a two-year jail sentence. (*ANB*; Martin Henry Blatt, *Free Love and Anarchism: The Biography of Ezra Heywood* [Urbana, Ill., 1989], 114–18; *Ballot Box*, November 1877.)

·⟨⟨══════⟩══════⟩⟩·

## 132 ⁓ SBA TO BENJAMIN F. BUTLER

St Charles Minn.[1] Dec. 30th 1877.

Hon. Benj F. Butler   Dear Friend

I believe I have before expressed to you my <u>rejoicings</u> because of your return to Congress by Old Essex—if not—accept them at this late day—[2] I rejoice in the presence on the floor of Congress of every man who will speak & vote for equal rights to women—and especially do I rejoice in <u>your</u> presence there this winter—

Now will you present this <u>personal</u> appeal of mine for removal of political disabilities?—[3]

Can you tell me why—if a ↑<u>traitor</u>↓ <u>man</u> may have his political disabilities under the 14th Amendment, removed by Congress,—a <u>loyal</u> <u>woman</u> may not as well?—

Now won't you look into the <u>logic</u> & the <u>law</u> of this question—and tell me how is the right way to word a petition to meet the case.

Mr Butler, you remember you told me four years ago the Repub— party would <u>not</u> take up a <u>new</u> question so long as it was sure of supremacy without doing so. Do you not think it is sufficiently in <u>doubt</u> by this time, to warrant its catching at our Woman Suffrage <u>straw</u>—if not to save its life now,—to help to resuscitate it, after it shall seem to be dead?

The <u>states</u> <u>rights</u> plan getting woman enfranchised—is <u>worse</u> than hopeless—and for our <u>men</u> <u>champions</u> & friends to longer bid us seek it there—is worse than <u>insult</u>.— If you could travel through Colorado & attempt to pursuade the <u>Irish</u> <u>Miners</u> & <u>Mountain Men</u>, the <u>Mexican</u> <u>Greasers</u>[4] and <u>Negroes</u>—as I did last September—& then come down through Nebraska, Iowa, Wisconsin, Minnesota—among the Bohemi- ans, Swedes, Norwegians, Germans—~~You~~ ↑Begging↓ <u>them</u> to vote to <u>let</u> <u>you</u> <u>vote</u>—<u>you'd</u> <u>feel</u> the insult quite as keenly as I do—[5] And you see—all these foreigners, Mexicans & Negroes, added to the <u>Whiskey</u> <u>Ring</u> & the religious bigots—in each state—make a <u>hopeless</u> majority— they <u>cannot</u> <u>be</u> <u>educated</u>—<u>nor</u> <u>carried</u> <u>forward</u> <u>except</u> <u>by</u> [s]<u>heer</u> <u>party</u> <u>force</u>—hence to <u>send</u> <u>us</u> <u>women</u> <u>back</u> [to] <u>seek</u> justice at their hands is—<u>all</u> <u>I</u> <u>have</u> <u>named</u> <u>it</u>—

I beg you—therefore—<u>push</u> a 16<sup>th</sup> Am't proposition [to] a vote in the House— <u>Divide</u> <u>the</u> <u>House</u> on it—[a]nd let us begin to take an <u>annual</u> <u>count</u> of our [fr]iends in Congress—as does the British Parliament—<sup>6</sup> [B?]y that means—we shall be able note the growth of [ou]r question from year to year— Respectfully, Gratefully

        ⋙ *Susan B. Anthony*

⋙ ALS, on NWSA letterhead for 1877, Benjamin F. Butler Papers, DLC. Letters in brackets obscured by docket.

1. She spoke in this town in the southeastern corner of the state on Saturday, 29 December, and stayed through Sunday, awaiting her next engagement in Wisconsin. (SBA diary, 1877, *Film*, 19:12ff.)

2. Butler won the election in 1876 not from his old district in Essex, to which SBA refers, but from Middlesex. The Forty-fifth Congress did not convene until October 1877.

3. Enclosure omitted. It was her handwritten petition, dated 1 January 1878, for the removal of her political disabilities, that she might be allowed to vote regardless of state law. That it is still filed with her letter suggests that Butler never submitted it to Congress. Lillie Blake and Matilda Gage submitted the first of such petitions to Congress in January 1877, and the National association recommended them as a tactic for everyone in 1878. The petitions echoed ones sent to Congress since the war by thousands of Confederates who lost political rights. Congress in turn had restored their right to hold federal office or vote. (*Congressional Record*, 44th Cong., 2d sess., 24 January, 5 February 1877, 928, 1265, 1272.)

4. The term "greaser," dating from the Mexican War, was a contemptuous term for Mexicans and Spanish-Americans. That SBA knew the term before her trip to Colorado is evident in a letter to Isabella Hooker, 1 September 1877. Anticipating election day, she predicted that "the vast majority of the Mexican 'greasers'—the miners & the other voters of that young State will doubtless vote '<u>No</u>'—& thus make a 3<sup>d</sup> demonstration of the utter hopelessness of the State's rights method of enfranchisement for Woman—" (*Film*, 19:529-35.)

5. In the agricultural states SBA names, Bohemians, Germans, Norwegians, and Swedes made up more than half of the foreign-born population and more than eighty percent of the non-English-speaking immigrants, according to the census of 1870. By 1880, the percentages had increased. SBA said nothing in her diary about the ethnic composition of her audiences on her recent midwestern tour. The Wahoo, Nebraska, *Independent*, 8 November 1877, paraphrased her as saying on 3 November that she was "done appealing to the Mikies and Greasers, who vote without knowledge like so many things, for they are invariably opposed to the ballot in the hands of women—governed

by their ignorant passion and base prejudices." (*Compendium of the Ninth Census*, 336–42; *Compendium of the Tenth Census*, 482–87.)

6. British suffrage supporters kept careful track of and publicized the division lists, or tabulation of votes, in Parliament on the Women's Disabilities Removal Bill to identify suffrage supporters and opponents.

133 ⇝ "NATIONAL PROTECTION FOR NATIONAL CITIZENS": SPEECH BY ECS TO THE SENATE COMMITTEE ON PRIVILEGES AND ELECTIONS

EDITORIAL NOTE: On January 10, Senator Aaron Sargent introduced an amendment, Senate Resolution 12, that would prohibit states from denying the franchise "on account of sex." The Senate Committee on Privileges and Elections then granted a hearing on the amendment to delegates from the National Woman Suffrage Association on Friday and Saturday, January 11 and 12. Further hearings occurred on January 14 before the House Committee on the Judiciary. "I never felt more exasperated than on this occasion," ECS recalled of the Senate hearing, due to "the studied inattention and contempt of the chairman, Senator Wadleigh of New Hampshire. . . . It was with difficulty I restrained the impulse more than once to hurl my manuscript at his head." She repeated the speech she made to the Washington convention three days earlier. Her phrase and title, "National Protection for National Citizens," was new to the sixteenth amendment campaign, but Francis Abbot used it at the National Liberal League's meeting in October 1877. Abbot listed national protection for national citizens as one of the "great national duties which had been neglected," and the phrase recurred in the league's political platform adopted in anticipation of joining the presidential campaign of 1880. Among the league's resolutions was one affirming "the paramount duty of the national government to guarantee and effectually maintain . . . the equal civil, political and religious rights of all national citizens, whether white or black, male or female, rich or poor, literate or illiterate, Christian or non-Christian."

A short portion of ECS's manuscript survives. It includes pages written for this occasion as well as pages recycled (and renumbered) from her testimony in January 1870 before the House and Senate Committees on the District of Columbia. Those same pages, based upon Francis Minor's evidence that the Constitution allowed woman suffrage, were recycled and renumbered again for Stanton's testimony to the Senate in 1888. A handwritten copy of the full text, reviewed by Sara Spencer and Isabella Hooker and marked up by typographers at the Government Printing Office, survives in the records of the Senate. The speech reproduced here is based on the printed text. Although ECS wrote on January 14 (below) that she recopied her speech for publication, the title page of *Arguments before the Committee on Privileges and Elections* indicates that all the speeches were "Phonographically Reported by J. Cover." (*History*, 3:93n; *Truth Seeker*, 3 November 1877; Ahlstrom and Mullin, *Scientific Theist*, 110–11; Washington *National Union*, 9 January 1878, Washington *Evening Star*, 9 January 1878, and "National Protection for National Citizens," *Film*, 19:1017–19, 1029–86, 20:1–232.)

[11 January 1878]

Gentlemen of the Committee:[1] In appearing before you to ask for a sixteenth amendment to the United States Constitution, permit me to say that, with the Hon. Charles Sumner, we believe that our Constitution, fairly interpreted, already secures to the humblest individual all the rights, privileges, and immunities of American citizens.[2] But as statesmen differ in their interpretations of Constitutional law as widely as they differ in their organizations, the rights of every class of citizens must be clearly defined in concise, unmistakable language. All the great principles of liberty declared by the fathers gave no protection to the black men of the republic for a century, and when, with higher light and knowledge, his emancipation and enfranchisement were proclaimed, it was said that the great truths set forth in the prolonged debates of thirty years on the individual rights of the black man, culminating in the fourteenth and fifteenth amendments to the Constitution, had no significance for woman. Hence we ask that this anomalous class of beings, not recognized by the supreme powers as either "persons" or "citizens," may now be defined and their rights declared in the Constitution.

In the adjustment of the question of suffrage now before the people of this country for settlement, it is of the highest importance that the organic law of the land should be so framed and construed as to work injustice to none, but secure as far as possible perfect political equality among all classes of citizens.[3]

In determining your right and power to legislate on this question, consider what has been done already.

As the national Constitution declares that "all persons born or naturalized in the United States, and subject to the jurisdiction thereof, are citizens of the United States, and of the State wherein they reside,"[4] it is evident—

1st. That the immunities and privileges of American citizenship, however defined, are national in character, and paramount to all State authority.

2d. That while the Constitution leaves the qualification of electors to the several States,[5] it nowhere gives them the right to deprive any citizen of the elective franchise. The State may regulate but not abolish the right of suffrage for any class.

3d. As the Constitution of the United States expressly declares that no State shall make or enforce any law that shall abridge the privileges or immunities of citizens of the United States,[6] those provisions of the several State constitutions that exclude women from the franchise on account of sex alike violate the spirit and letter of the federal Constitution.

4th. As the question of naturalization is expressly withheld from the States,[7] and as the States would clearly have no right to deprive of the franchise naturalized citizens, among whom women are expressly included, still more clearly have they no right to deprive native-born women-citizens of this right.

Let me give you a few extracts from the national Constitution upon which these propositions are based:

> (Preamble:) We, the people of the United States, in order to form a more perfect union, establish justice, insure domestic tranquillity, provide for the common defense, promote the general welfare, and secure the blessings of liberty to ourselves and our posterity, do ordain and establish this constitution.[8]

This is declared to be a government "of the people." All power, it is said, centers in the people. Our State constitutions also open with the words, "We, the people." Does any one pretend to say that men alone constitute races and peoples? When we say parents, do we not mean mothers as well as fathers? When we say children, do we not mean girls as well as boys? When we say people, do we not mean women as well as men?[9]

When the race shall spring, Minerva-like, from the brains of their fathers,[10] it will be time enough thus to ignore the fact that one-half the human family are women. Individual rights, individual conscience and judgment, are our great American ideas, the fundamental principles of our political and religious faith. Men may as well attempt to do our repenting, confessing, and believing as our voting; as well represent us at the throne of grace as at the ballot-box.

> Article 1, Sec. 9. No bill of attainder, or *ex post facto* law shall be passed; no title of nobility shall be granted by the United States.
>
> Sec. 10. No State shall pass any bill of attainder, *ex post facto* law, or law impairing the obligation of contracts, or grant any title of nobility.

See Cummings *vs.* State of Missouri (4 Wallace Rep., 278). *Ex parte* Garland (same volume).[11]

Notwithstanding these provisions of the Constitution, bills of attainder have been passed by the introduction of the word "male" into all the State constitutions, denying to woman the right of suffrage, and thereby making sex a crime. A citizen disfranchised in a republic is a citizen attainted. When we place in the hands of one class of citizens the right to make, interpret, and execute the law for another class wholly unrepresented in the government, we have made an order of nobility. Universal manhood suffrage makes all men sovereigns, all women slaves—the most odious form of aristocracy the world has yet seen.

> Article 4, Sec. 2. The citizens of each State shall be entitled to all privileges and immunities of citizens in the several States.

The elective franchise is one of the privileges secured by this section. See Corfield *vs.* Coryell (4 Washington Circuit Reps., 380), cited and approved in Dunham *vs.* Lamphere (3 Gray Mass. Rep., 276), and Bennett *vs.* Boggs (Baldwin's Rep., p. 72, circuit court U.S.).[12]

> Article 4, Sec. 4. The United States shall guarantee to every State in this Union a republican form of government.

How can that form of government be called republican in which one-half the people are forever deprived of all participation in its affairs?

Article 6. This constitution, and the laws of the United States which shall be made in pursuance thereof, . . . shall be the supreme law of the land; and the judges in every State shall be bound thereby, anything in the constitution or laws of any State to the contrary notwithstanding.

Fourteenth amendment: All persons born and naturalized in the United States, and subject to the jurisdiction thereof, are citizens of the United States . . . No State shall make or enforce any law which shall abridge the privileges and immunities of citizens of the United States.

See Federalist, Nos. 83, 84; Vattel, B. 2, ch. 17, § 282; Story's Commentaries, § 448;[13] Green *vs.* Shumway, (36 Howard's Practice Rep., p. 5);[14] Wilkinson *vs.* Leland, (2 Peters' Rep., 657); Taylor *vs.* Porter, (4 Hill's Rep., 140); People *vs.* Berberrich (11 Howard's Practice Rep., 289); Morrison *vs.* Springer, (15 Iowa, 305); Bourland *vs.* Hildreth, (26 Cal., 163, dissenting opinion of Chief-Justice Saunderson); Twitchell *vs.* Blodgett, (13 Michigan, dissenting opinion of Chief-Justice Martin);[15] Sedgwick on Constitutional Law, 537, 539.[16]

(For this list of authorities on this point I am indebted to Francis Minor, esq., of Saint Louis, one of the attorneys in the case of Virginia L. Minor *et al. vs.* Reese Happersett.)

In the discussion of the enfranchisement of woman, suffrage is now claimed by one class of thinkers as a privilege based upon citizenship and secured by the Constitution of the United States, as by lexicographers, as well as by the Constitution itself, the definition of "citizen" includes women as well as men. No State can rightfully deprive a woman-citizen of the United States of any fundamental right which is hers in common with all other citizens. The States have the right to *regulate*, but not to prohibit the elective franchise to citizens of the United States. Thus, the States may determine the qualifications of electors. They may require the elector to be of a certain age; to have had a fixed residence; to be of a sane mind, and unconvicted of crime; because these are qualifications or conditions that all citizens, sooner or later, may attain; but to go beyond this, and say to one-half the citizens of the State, notwithstanding you possess all of these qualifications, you *shall never vote*, is of the very essence of despotism. It is a bill of attainder of the most odious character.[17]

A further investigation of the subject will show that the language of the constitutions of all the States, with the exception of Virginia and Massachusetts, on the subject of suffrage is peculiar.[18] They almost all read substantially alike. "White male citizens" shall be entitled to vote, and this is supposed to exclude all other citizens. There is no direct exclusion except in the two States above named. Now the error lies in supposing that an enabling clause is necessary at all. The right of the people of a State to participate in a government of their own creation requires no enabling clause, neither can it be taken from them by implication. To hold otherwise would be to interpolate in the Constitution a prohibition that does not exist.

In framing a constitution, the people are assembled in their sovereign capacity, and being possessed of all rights and powers, what is not surrendered is retained. Nothing short of a direct prohibition can work a deprivation of rights that are fundamental. In the language of John Jay to the people of New York, urging the adoption of the Constitution of the United States: "Silence and blank paper neither give nor take away anything."[19] And Alexander Hamilton says, (Federalist, No. 83:) "Every man of discernment must at once perceive the wide difference between silence and abolition." The mode and manner in which the people shall take part in the government of their creation may be prescribed by the constitution, but the right itself is antecedent to all constitutions. It is inalienable, and can neither be bought nor sold nor given away.

But even if it should be held that this view is untenable, and that women are disfranchised by the several State constitutions, directly or by implication, then I say that such prohibitions are clearly in conflict with the Constitution of the United States, and yield thereto.

Another class of thinkers, equally interested in woman's enfranchisement, maintain that there is, as yet, no power in the United States Constitution to protect the rights of all United States citizens, in all latitudes and longitudes, and in all conditions whatever. When the Constitution was adopted, the fathers thought they had secured national unity. This was the opinion of Southern as well as Northern statesmen. It was supposed that the question of State rights was then forever settled. Hon. Charles Sumner, speaking on this point in the United States Senate, March 7, 1866,[20] said, ["]the object of the Constitution was to ordain, under the authority of the people, a national government possessing unity and power. The Confederation had been merely an agreement 'between the States,' styled 'a league of firm friendship.' Found to be feeble and inoperative through the pretension of State rights, it gave way to the Constitution, which, instead of a 'league,' created a 'union,' in the name of the people of the United States. Beginning with these inspiring and enacting words, 'We, the people,' it was popular and national. Here was no concession to State rights, but a recognition of the power of the people, from whom the Constitution proceeded. The States are acknowledged; but they are all treated as component parts of the Union in which they are absorbed, under the Constitution, which is the supreme law. There is but one sovereignty, and that is the sovereignty of the United States.

["]On this very account the adoption of the Constitution was opposed by Patrick Henry and George Mason.[21] The first exclaimed, 'That this is a consolidated government is demonstrably clear; the question turns on that poor little thing, "We, the people," instead of the States.' The second exclaimed, 'Whether the Constitution is good or bad, it is a national government, and no longer a confederation.' But against this powerful opposition the Constitution was adopted in the name of the people of the United States. Throughout the discussions, State rights were treated with little favor. Madison[22] said, 'the States are only political societies, and never possessed the right of sovereignty.' Gerry[23] said, 'The States have only corporate rights.' Wilson,[24] the philanthropic member from Pennsylvania, afterward a learned judge of the Supreme Court of the United States and author of the 'Lectures on Law,' said, 'Will a regard to State rights justify the sacrifice of the rights of men? If we proceed on any other foundation than the last, our building will neither be solid nor lasting.'["]

## A SIXTEENTH AMENDMENT.

Those of us who understand the dignity, power, and protection of the ballot, have steadily petitioned Congress for the last ten years to secure to the women citizens of the republic the exercise of their right to the elective franchise. We began by asking a sixteenth amendment to the National Constitution.

March 15, 1869, the Hon. George W. Julian submitted a joint resolution to Congress, to enfranchise the women of the republic, by proposing a sixteenth amendment, as follows:

Article 16. The right of suffrage in the United States shall
be based on citizenship, and shall be regulated by Congress, and all citizens of the United States, whether native
or naturalized, shall enjoy this right equally, without any
distinction or discrimination whatever founded on sex.[25]

While the discussion was pending for the emancipation and enfranchisement of the slaves of the South, and popular thought led back to
the consideration of the fundamental principles of our government, it
was clearly seen that all the arguments for the civil and political rights
of the African race, applied to women also. Seeing this, some Republicans stood ready to carry their principles to their logical results. Democrats, too, saw the drift of the argument, and though not in favor of
extending suffrage to either black men or women, yet, to embarrass
Republican legislation, it was said they proposed amendments for
woman suffrage to all bills brought forward for enfranchising slaves.

And thus, during the passage of the thirteenth, fourteenth, and
fifteenth amendments, and the District-suffrage bill,[26] the question of
woman suffrage was often and ably discussed in the Senate and House,
and received both Republican and Democratic votes in its favor. Many
able lawyers and judges gave it as their opinion that women as well as
Africans were enfranchised by the fourteenth and fifteenth amendments. Accordingly we abandoned, for the time being, our demand for
a sixteenth amendment, and pleaded our right of suffrage, as already
secured by the fourteenth amendment—the argument lying in a nut-
shell. For if, as therein asserted, all *persons* born or naturalized in the
United States are *citizens* of the United States, and if a citizen, according to the best authorities, is one possessed of all the rights and privileges of citizenship, namely, the right to make laws and choose lawmakers,
women, being persons, must be citizens, and therefore entitled to the
rights of citizenship, the chief of which is the right to vote.

Accordingly women tested their right, registered and voted, the
inspectors of election accepting the argument, for which inspectors
and women alike were arrested, tried, and punished, the courts deciding that although by the fourteenth amendment they were citizens,
still, citizenship did not carry with it the right to vote. But granting the
premise of the Supreme Court decision, "that the Constitution does
not confer suffrage on any one,"[27] then it inhered with the citizen

before the Constitution was framed. Our national life does not date from that instrument. The Constitution is not the original declaration of rights. It was not framed until eleven years after our existence as a nation, nor fully ratified until nearly fourteen years after the inauguration of our national independence.

But however the letter and spirit of the Constitution may be interpreted by the people, the judiciary of the nation has uniformly proved itself the echo of the party in power. When the slave-power was dominant, the Supreme Court decided that a black man was not a citizen, because he had not the right to vote;[28] and when the Constitution was so amended as to make all persons citizens, the same high tribunal decided that a woman, though a citizen, had not the right to vote. An African, by virtue of his United States citizenship, is declared, under recent amendments, a voter in every State of the Union, but when a woman, by virtue of her United States citizenship, applies to the Supreme Court for protection in the exercise of this same right, she is remanded to the State, by the unanimous decision of the nine judges on the bench, that "the Constitution of the United States does not confer the right of suffrage upon any one." Such vacillating interpretations of Constitutional law must unsettle our faith in judicial authority, and undermine the liberties of the whole people. Seeing by these decisions of the courts, that the theory of our government, the Declaration of Independence, and recent Constitutional amendments, have no significance for woman, that all the grand principles of equality are glittering generalities[29] for her, we must fall back once more to our former demand for a sixteenth amendment to the Federal Constitution, that, in clear, unmistakable language, shall declare the status of women in this republic, in the following words:

> Article 16. The right of suffrage in the United States shall be based on citizenship, and shall be regulated by Congress, and all citizens of the United States, whether native or naturalized, shall enjoy this right equally, without any distinction or discrimination whatever founded on sex.[30]

The Declaration of Independence struck a blow at every existent form of government by making the individual the source of all power. This is the sun, and the one central truth around which all genuine republics must keep their course or perish. National supremacy means something more than power to levy war, conclude peace, contract alliances, establish commerce. It means national protection and security in the exercise of the right of self-government, which comes alone by and through the use of the ballot. Women are the only class of citizens still wholly unrepresented in the government, and yet we possess every requisite qualification for voters in the United States. Women possess property and education; we take out naturalization-papers and passports and register ships. We pre-empt lands, pay taxes (women sometimes work out the road tax with their own hands), and suffer for our own violation of laws. We are neither idiots, lunatics, nor criminals, and according to our State constitution lack but one qualification for voters, namely, sex; which is an insurmountable qualification, and therefore equivalent to a bill of attainder against one-half the people, a power neither the State nor the United States can legally exercise, being forbidden in article 1, secs. 9 and 10, of the Constitution. Our rulers have the right to regulate the suffrage, but they cannot abolish it for any class of citizens, as has been done in the case of the women of this republic, without a direct violation of the fundamental law of the land. All concessions of privileges or redress of grievances are mockery for any class that has no voice in the laws and lawmakers; hence, we demand the ballot, that scepter of power in our own hands, as the only sure protection for our rights of person and property under all conditions. If the few may grant and withhold rights at their pleasure, the many cannot be said to enjoy the blessings of self-government.

William H. Seward said in his great speech on "Freedom and Union," in the United States Senate, February 29, 1860:

> Mankind have a natural right, a natural instinct, and a natural capacity for self-government; and when as here they are sufficiently ripened by culture, they will and must have self-government and no other.[31]

Jefferson said: "The God who gave us life, gave us liberty at the same time; the hand of freedom may destroy, but cannot disjoin them."[32]

Few people comprehend the length and breadth of the principle we are advocating to-day, and how closely it is allied to everything vital in our system of government. Our personal grievances, such as being robbed of property and children by unjust husbands; denied admission into the colleges, the trades, and professions; compelled to work at starving prices, by no means round out this whole question. In asking for a sixteenth amendment to the United States Constitution, and the protection of Congress against the injustice of State law, we are fighting the same battle as Jefferson and Hamilton fought in 1776, as Calhoun and Clay in 1828, as Abraham Lincoln and Jefferson Davis in 1860,[33] namely, the limit of State rights and Federal power. The enfranchisement of woman involves the same vital principle of our government that is dividing and distracting the two great political parties at this hour.

There is nothing a foreigner coming here finds it so difficult to understand as the wheel within a wheel in our national and State governments, and the possibility of carrying them on without friction; and this is the difficulty and danger we are fast finding out. The recent amendments are steps in the right direction toward national unity, securing equal rights to all citizens, in every latitude and longitude. But our Congressional debates, judicial decisions, and the utterances of campaign orators, continually falling back to the old ground, are bundles of contradictions on this vital question. Inasmuch as we are, first, citizens of the United States, and second, of the State wherein we reside, the primal rights of all citizens should be regulated by the national government, and complete equality in civil and political rights everywhere secured. When women are denied the right to enter institutions of learning and practice in the professions, unjust discriminations made against sex, even more degrading and humiliating than was ever made against color, surely woman, too, should be protected by a civil-rights bill and a sixteenth amendment that should make her political status equal with all other citizens of the republic.

The right of suffrage, like the currency and the Post-Office Department, demands national regulation. We can all remember the losses sustained by citizens in traveling from one State to another under the old system of State banks.[34] We can imagine the confusion if each State regulated its post-offices, and the transit of the mails across its borders. The benefits we find in uniformity and unity in these great interests would pervade all others where equal conditions were secured. Some citizens are asking for a national bankrupt law, that a person released from his debts in one State may be free in every other. Some are for a religious freedom amendment that shall forever separate church and state; forbidding a religious test as a condition of suffrage or a qualification for office; forbidding the reading of the Bible in the schools, and the exempting of church property and sectarian institutions of learning or charity from taxation. Some are demanding a national marriage law, that a man legally married in one State may not be a bigamist in another. Some are asking a national prohibitory law, that a reformed drunkard who is shielded from temptation in one State may not be environed with dangers in another. And thus many individual interests point to a growing feeling among the people in favor of more homogeneous legislation. As several of the States are beginning to legislate on the women-suffrage question, it is of vital moment that there should be some national action.

As the laws now are, a woman who can vote, hold office, be tried by a jury of her own peers—yea, and sit on the bench as justice of the peace, in the Territory of Wyoming, might be reduced to a political pariah in the State of New York. A woman who can vote and hold office on the school board and act as county superintendent in Kansas and Minnesota is denied these rights in passing into Pennsylvania.[35] A woman who can be a member of the school board in Minnesota, Maine, Wisconsin, Iowa, and California[36] loses all these privileges in New Jersey, Maryland, and Delaware. When representatives from the Territories are sent to Congress by the votes of women, it is time to have some national recognition of this class of citizens.

This demand of national protection for national citizens is fated to grow each and every day. The Government of the United States, as the Constitution is now interpreted, is powerless to give a just equivalent for the supreme allegiance it claims. One sound democratic principle fully recognized and carried to its logical results in our government, declaring all citizens equal before the law, would soon chase away the metaphysical mists and fogs that cloud our political views in so many directions. When Congress is asked to put the name of God in the Constitution, and thereby pledge the nation to some theological faith in which some United States citizens may not believe, and thus subject a certain class to political ostracism and social persecution, it is asked not to protect but to oppress the citizens of the several States in their most sacred rights—to think, reason, and decide all questions of religion and conscience for themselves without fear or favor from the government. Popular sentiment and church persecution is all that an advanced thinker in science and religion should be called on to combat. The state should rather throw its shield of protection around those uttering liberal, progressive ideas; for the nation has the same interest in every new thought as it has in the invention of new machinery to lighten labor, in the discovery of wells of oil, or mines of coal, copper, iron, silver, or gold. As in the laboratory of nature new forms of beauty are forever revealing themselves, so in the world of thought a higher outlook gives clearer visions of the heights man in freedom shall yet attain. The day is past for persecuting the philosophers of the physical sciences. But what a holocaust of martyrs bigotry is still making of those bearing the richest treasures of thought, in religion, social ethics, in their efforts to roll off the mountains of superstition that have so long darkened the human mind!

The numerous demands by the people for national protection in many rights, not specified in the Constitution, prove that the people have outgrown the compact that satisfied the fathers, and the more it is expounded and understood the more clearly its mechanical features can be traced to its English origin. And it is not at all surprising that, with no chart or compass for a republic, our fathers, with all their educational prejudices in favor of the mother country, with her literature and systems of jurisprudence, should have also adopted her ideas of government, and in drawing up their national compact engrafted the new republic on the old constitutional monarchy, a union where incompatibility has involved their sons in continued discussion as to the true meaning of the instrument. A recent writer says:

> The Constitution of the United States is the result of a fourfold compromise.
> Firstly, of unity with individual interests; of national sovereignty with the so-called sovereignty of States.
> Secondly, of the republic with monarchy.
> Thirdly, of freedom with slavery.
> Fourthly, of democracy with aristocracy.[37]

It is founded, therefore, on the fourfold combination of principles perfectly incompatible and eternally excluding each other; founded for the purpose of equally preserving these principles in spite of their incompatibility, and of carrying out their practical results—in other words, for the purpose of making an impossible thing possible. And a century of discussion has not yet made the Constitution understood. It has no settled interpretation. Being a series of compromises, it can be expounded in favor of many directly opposite principles.

Take, for example, the question of slavery. Even the abolitionists could not agree as to its meaning. One class insisted that slavery was unconstitutional; that the spirit and letter of that instrument was in direct antagonism to the idea of property in man. Another insisted that it was plainly recognized in the "three-fifths" representation, in article 1, section 2, and in the provision in article 4, section 2, for the return of "persons" held to service in one State escaping to another.[38]

The fathers, fresh from a seven years' struggle for liberty, having electrified the lovers of freedom the world over with their Declaration of Rights, "that all men are created equal," could not use the word "slave" in their Constitution, and thus manifest their inconsistency in practice and principle. No foreigner could understand the significance of "persons" and "all other persons" in the articles referred to, and yet these innocent words, in a Pickwickian sense, gave the slave-holder all the protection he needed to hold property in man. And not until the passage of the thirteenth, fourteenth, and fifteenth amendments did we get the national confession that until that time the Constitution was a pro-slavery document. But however the opposing principles of slavery and freedom were united in the Constitution, our late civil war opened the eyes of the nation to the fact that freedom and slavery could not exist together.

A distinguished American statesman remarked that the war of the rebellion was waged "to expound the constitution."[39] It is a pertinent question now, shall all other contradictory principles be retained in the Constitution until they, too, are expounded by civil war? On what theory is it less dangerous to defraud twenty million women of their inalienable rights than four million slaves? Is not the same principle involved in both cases? We ask Congress to pass a sixteenth amendment, not only for woman's protection, but for the safety of the nation. Our people are filled with unrest to-day because there is no fair understanding of the basis of individual rights, nor the legitimate power of the national government.

The Republican party took the ground during the war that Congress had the right to establish a national currency in every State; that it had the right to emancipate and enfranchise the slaves; to change the political status in one-half the States of the Union; to pass a civil rights bill, securing to the freedman a place in the schools, colleges, trades, professions, in hotels, and all public conveyances for travel. And they maintained their right to do all this as the best measures for peace, though compelled by war.

And now, when Congress is asked to extend the same protection to the women of the nation, we are told they have not the power, and we are remanded to the State. They say the emancipation of the slave was a war measure, a military necessity; that his enfranchisement was a political necessity. We might with propriety ask if the present condition of the nation, with its political outlook, its election frauds daily reported, the corrupt action of men in official position, governors, judges, and boards of canvassers, has not brought us to our moral necessity when some new element is needed in government? But, alas! when women appeal to Congress for the protection of their natural rights of person and property, they send us for redress to the courts, and the courts remand us to the States.

You did not trust the southern freedman to the arbitrary will of courts and States. Why send your mothers, wives, and daughters to the unwashed, unlettered, unthinking masses that carry our State elections?

We are told by one class of philosophers that the growing tendency to increase national power and authority is leading to a dangerous centralization; that the safety of the republic rests in *local self-government.*[40] Says the editor of the Boston Index:

> What is local self-government? Briefly, that without any interference from without, every citizen should manage his own personal affairs in his own way, according to his own pleasure; that every town should manage its own town affairs in the same manner and under the same restriction; every county its own county affairs, every State its own State affairs. But the independent exercise of this autonomy, by personal and corporate individuals, has one fundamental condition, viz, the maintenance of all these individualities intact, each in its own sphere of action, with its rights uninfringed and its freedom uncurtailed in that sphere, yet each also preserving its just relation to all the rest in an all-comprehensive social organization. Every

citizen would thus stand, as it were, in the center of several concentric and enlarging circles of relationship to his kind; he would have duties and rights in each relation, not only as individual but also as a member of town, county, State, and national organization. His local self-government will be at his highest possible point of realization, when in each of these relations his individual duties are discharged and his rights maintained.

On the other hand, what is centralization?

It is such a disorganization of this well-balanced, harmonious, and natural system as shall result in the absorption of all substantial power by a central authority, to the destruction of the autonomy of the various individualities above mentioned; such as was produced, for instance, when the municipia of the Roman Empire lost their corporate independence and melted into the vast imperial despotism which prepared the way for the collapse of society under the blows of Northern barbarism. Such a centralization must inevitably be produced by decay of that stubborn stickling for rights, out of which local self-government has always grown. That is, if individual rights in the citizen, the town, the county, the state, shall not be vindicated as beyond all price, and defended with the utmost jealousy, and at whatever cost, the spirit of liberty must have already died out, and the dreary process of centralization be already far advanced. It will thus be evident that the preservation of individual rights is the only possible preventive of centralization, and that free society has no interest to be compared for an instant in importance with that of preserving these *individual rights*.

No nation is free in which this is not the paramount concern. Wo to America when her sons and her daughters begin to sneer at rights! Just so long as the citizens are protected individually in their rights, the town, and counties, and states cannot be stripped; but if the former lose all love for their own liberties as equal units of society, the latter will become the empty shells of creatures long perished.

The nation as such, therefore, if it would be itself free and non-centralized, must find its own supreme interest in the protection of its individual citizens in the fullest possible enjoyment of their equal rights and liberties.

As this question of woman's enfranchisement is one of national safety, we ask you to remember that we are citizens of the United States, and, as such, claim the protection of the national flag in the exercise of our national rights, in every latitude and longitude, on sea, land, at home, as well as abroad; against the tyranny of States, as well as against foreign aggressions. Local authorities may regulate the exercise of these rights; they may settle all minor questions of property; but the inalienable personal rights of citizenship should be *declared* by the Constitution, *interpreted* by the Supreme Court, *protected* by Congress, and *enforced* by the arm of the Executive.

It is nonsense to talk of State-rights until the graver question of personal liberties is first understood and adjusted.[41] President Hayes, in reply to an address of welcome in Charlottesville, Va., September 25, 1877, said:

Equality under the laws for all citizens is the corner-stone of the structure of the restored harmony from which the ancient friendship is to rise. In this pathway I am going, the pathway where your illustrious men led—your Jefferson, your Madison, your Monroe, your Washington.[42]

If, in this statement, President Hayes is thoroughly sincere, then he will not hesitate to approve emphatically the principle of national protection for national citizens. He will see that the protection of all national citizens in all their equal rights, civil, political, and religious—not by the muskets of United States troops, but by the peaceable authority of United States courts—is not a principle that applies to a single section of the country, but to all sections alike; he will see that the incorporation of such a principle in the Constitution cannot be regarded as a measure of force imposed upon the vanquished, since it would be law alike to the vanquished and the victor. In short, he will see that there is no other sufficient guarantee of that equality of all citizens, which he well declares to be "the corner-stone of the structure of restored harmony."

The Boston Journal, of July 19, said:

> There are cases where it seems as if the Constitution should empower the Federal Government to step in and protect the citizen in the State, when the local authorities are in league with the assassins; but, as it now reads, no such provision exists.[43]

That the Constitution does not make such provision is not the fault of the President; it must be attributed to leading Republicans who had it in their power once to change the Constitution so as to give the most ample powers to the general government.

When Attorney-General Devens was charged, last May, with negligence in not prosecuting the parties accused of the Mountain Meadow massacre, his defense was, that this horrible crime was not against the United States, but against the Territory of Utah.[44] Yet, it was a great company of industrious, honest, unoffending United States citizens who were foully and brutally murdered in cold blood. When Chief Justice Waite gave his charge to the jury in the Ellentown conspiracy cases, at Charleston, S.C., in June 1, 1877, he said:

> That a number of citizens of the United states have been killed, there can be no question; but that is not enough to enable the Government of the United States to interfere for their protection.
>
> Under the Constitution that duty belongs to the State alone. But when an unlawful combination is made to interfere with any of the rights of natural citizenship secured to citizens of the United States by the National Constitution, then an offense is committed against the laws of the United States, and it is not only the right but the absolute duty of the national government to interfere and afford the citizens that protection which every good government is bound to give.[45]

General Hawley, in an address before a college last spring, said:

> Why, it is asked, does our government permit outrages in a State which it would exert all its authority to redress, even at the risk of war, if they were perpetrated under a

foreign government? Are the rights of American citizens more sacred on the soil of Great Britain or France than on the soil of one of our own States? Not at all. But the Government of the United States is clothed with power to act with imperial sovereignty in the one case, while in the other its authority is limited to the degree of utter impotency, in certain circumstances. The State sovereignty excludes the Federal over most matters of dealing between man and man, and if the State laws are properly enforced there is not likely to be any ground of complaint, but if not the Federal Government, if not specially called on, according to the terms of the Constitution, is helpless. Citizen A B, grievously wronged, beaten, robbed, lynched within a hair's breadth of death, may apply in vain to any and all prosecuting officers of the State. The forms of law that might give him redress are all there; the prosecuting officers, judges, and sheriffs, that might act, are there; but, under an oppressive and tyrannical public sentiment, they refuse to move.

In such an exigency the Government of the United States can do no more than the government of any neighboring State; that is, unless the State concerned calls for aid, or unless the offense rises to the dignity of insurrection or rebellion. The reason is, that the framers of our governmental system left to the several States the sole guardianship of the personal and relative private rights of the people.[46]

Such is the imperfect development of our own nationality in this respect that we have really no right as yet to call ourselves a nation in the true sense of the word, nor shall we have while this state of things continues. Thousands have begun to feel this keenly, of which a few illustrations may suffice. A communication to the New York Tribune, June 9, signed "Merchant," said:

Before getting into a quarrel, and perhaps war, with Mexico about the treatment of our flag and citizens, would it not be as well, think you, for the government to try and make the flag a protection to the citizens on our own soil?[47]

That is what it has never been since the foundation of our government in a large portion of our common country. The kind of government the people of this country expect, and intend to have, State rights or no State rights, no matter how much blood and treasure it may cost, is a government to protect the humblest citizen in the exercise of all his rights.

When the rebellion of the South against the government began, one of the most noted secessionists of Baltimore asked one of the Regular Army officers what the government expected to gain by making war on the South? "Well," the officer replied, laying his hand on the cannon by which he was standing, "we intend to use these until it is as safe for a Northern man to express his political opinions in the South as it is for a Southern man to express his in the North."

Senator Blaine, at a banquet in Trenton, N.J., July 2, declared that a "government which did not offer protection to every citizen in every State had no right to demand allegiance."[48] Ex-Senator Wade, of Ohio, in a letter to the Washington National Republican of July 16, said of the President's policy:

> I greatly fear this policy, under cover of what is called local self-government, is but an ignominious surrender of the principles of nationality for which our armies fought and for which thousands upon thousands of our brave men died, and without which the war was a failure and our boasted government a myth.[49]

Behind the slavery of the colored race was the principle of State rights. Their emancipation and enfranchisement were important, not only as a vindication of our great republican idea of individual rights, but as the first blow in favor of national unity, of a consistent homogeneous government. As all our difficulties, State and national, are finally referred to the Constitution, it is of vital importance that that instrument should not be susceptible of a different interpretation from every possible stand-point. It is folly to spend another century in expounding the equivocal language of the Constitution. If under that instrument, supposed to be the Magna Charta of American liberties, all United States citizens do not stand equal before the law, it should without further delay be so amended as, in plain, unmistakable language, to declare what are the rights, privileges, and immunities that belong to citizens in a republic.

There is no reason why the people of to-day should be governed by the laws and constitutions of men long since dead and buried. Surely those who understand the vital issues of this hour are better able to legislate for the living present than those who governed a hundred years ago. If the nineteenth century is to be governed by the opinions of the eighteenth, and the twentieth by the nineteenth, the world will always be governed by dead men.[50]

Without going back further than our recent elections, and the debates growing out of them as to the ultimate appeal in deciding the legal vote in the contested States, we have sufficient proof of our need as a nation of a clear understanding of our Constitution, and the underlying principles of a republican form of government. The protection we ask to-day involves the same question of State rights that now occupies and has occupied the minds of leading statesmen from the inauguration of the government.

Experience has taught us that the safety of the nation and a preservation of a real Union demand the recognition of certain universal principles of action in every State alike.

The cry of centralization could have little significance if the Constitution were so amended as to protect all United States citizens in their inalienable rights. That national supremacy that holds individual freedom and equality more sacred than State rights, and secures representation to all classes of people, is a very different form of centralization from that in which all the forces of society are centered in a single arm.

But the recognition of the principle of national supremacy as declared in the fourteenth and fifteenth amendments has been practically nullified and the results of the war surrendered by remanding woman to the States for the protection of her civil and political rights. The Supreme Court decisions and the Congressional reports on this point are in direct conflict with the idea of national unity, and the principle of State rights involved in this discussion must in time remand all United States citizens alike to State authority for the protection of those rights declared to inhere in the people at the foundation of the government.

You may listen to our demands, gentlemen, with dull ears, and smile incredulously at the idea of danger to our institutions from continued violation of the civil and political rights of women, but the question of what citizens shall enjoy the rights of suffrage involves our national existence; for if the constitutional rights of the humblest citizen may be invaded with impunity, laws interpreted on the side of injustice, judicial decisions based not on reason, sound argument, nor the spirit and letter of our declaration and theories of government, but on the customs of society and what dead men are supposed to have thought, not what they said, what will the rights of the ruling powers even be in the future with a people educated into such modes of thought and action? The treatment of every individual in a community, in our courts, prisons, asylums, of every class of petitioners before Congress, strengthens or undermines the foundations of that temple of liberty whose cornerstones were laid one century ago with bleeding hands and anxious hearts, with the hardships, privations, and sacrifices of a seven years' war. He who is able from the conflicts of the present to forecast the future events cannot but contemplate with anxiety the fate of this republic unless our Constitution be at once subjected to a thorough emendation, making it more comprehensively democratic.

A review of the history of our nation during the century will show the American people that all the obstacles that have impeded their political, moral, and material progress, from the dominion of slavery down to the present epidemic of political corruption, are directly and indirectly traceable to the Federal Constitution as their source and support. Hence the necessity of prompt and appropriate amendments. Nothing that is incorrect in principle can ever be productive of beneficial results, and no custom or authority is able to alter or overrule this inviolate law of development.

The catch phrases of politicians, such as "organic development," "the logic of events," "things will regulate themselves," have deceived the thoughtless long enough. There is just one road to safety, and that is to understand the law governing the situation and to bring the nation in line with it. Grave political problems are solved in two ways—by a wise forethought, by reformation, or by general dissatisfaction, resistance, revolution.

In closing, let me remind you, gentlemen, that woman has not been a heedless spectator of all the great events of the century, nor a dull listener to the grand debates on human freedom and equality. She has learned the lesson of self-sacrifice, self-discipline, and self-government in the same school with the heroes of American liberty. She shared the dangers of the Mayflower on the stormy sea; the dreary landing on Plymouth Rock; the rigors of a New England winter, and the privations of a seven years' war. With man she bravely threw off the British yoke, felt every pulsation of his heart for freedom, and inspired the glowing eloquence that maintained him through the century. With you, we have just gone through the agony and death, the resurrection and triumph, of another revolution, doing all in our power to mitigate its miseries and gild its glories; and now, think you, after education such as this, we have no power to weigh your arguments; that no sentiments of patriotism can ever kindle us to action; that we shall still remain silent witnesses while you crown all types and shades of manhood with those rights of citizenship denied to the most refined and educated classes of American womanhood? No, no; we feel the insult of disfranchisement more keenly day by day as we find ourselves man's equal in the world of thought.[51]

When the spirit of freedom is abroad everywhere, in the old world and the new; when men are coming up from the coal-mines of Cornwall, from the manufactories of Birmingham and Manchester, demanding new privileges;[52] when stern, frigid Russia sets 22,000,000 serfs free in a single day;[53] when 4,000,000 slaves on American soil are rejoicing in the proclamation of emancipation, and have the ballot, that scepter of power, unasked for, placed in their hands, think not the daughters of Jefferson, Hancock, and Adams will forever linger around the camp-fires of an old civilization, indifferent to the grand experiment of self-government it is our high privilege as a people to make, insensible to the dignity, power, and responsibility that belong to every citizen of a republic. No, no; woman, too, would now join the grand army of progress and help to usher in a purer and a better civilization, in which the sons and daughters of earth shall at last stand equal before the law.

⇜ *Arguments before the Committee on Privileges and Elections . . . in Behalf of a Sixteenth Amendment . . .* (Washington, D.C., 1878), 4–17.

1. Present at the hearing were: the chairman, Bainbridge Wadleigh (1831–1891), New Hampshire's Republican senator from 1873 to 1879; John Hipple Mitchell (1835–1905), Oregon's Republican senator from 1873 to 1879, 1885 to 1897, and 1901 until his death; George F. Hoar; Angus Cameron (1826–1897), Wisconsin's Republican senator from 1875 to 1885; Samuel James Renwick McMillan (1826–1897), Minnesota's Republican senator from 1875 to 1887; Benjamin Harvey Hill (1823–1882), Georgia's Democratic senator from 1877 until his death; and Eli Saulsbury. Committee members John James Ingalls and Augustus Summerfield Merrimon were absent. Wadleigh's opposition to

woman suffrage dated back at least to 1874, when he opposed universal suffrage in Pembina Territory. Hill and Saulsbury were unwavering in their opposition to suffrage and to the Lockwood bill. Mitchell was a consistent supporter of woman suffrage who voted with Aaron Sargent both in 1874 and in the months following this hearing. Cameron also voted with Sargent in 1878. (*BDAC*. For Mitchell, see also *Papers* 2.)

2. Sumner made this argument most succinctly in "Powers of Congress to Prohibit Inequality, Caste, and Oligarchy of the Skin," delivered 5 February 1869 in opposition to the Fifteenth Amendment. Congress had clear authority in the Constitution, he argued, to legislate political rights in the states without an additional amendment. (Sumner, *Works*, 13:34–52.)

3. In this paragraph, ECS quotes the resolutions written by Francis and Virginia Minor and adopted by the woman suffrage convention at St. Louis in October 1869. The quotation resumes after the next paragraph and continues through the numbered paragraphs. ECS also quotes herself, as she had appropriated the Minors' resolutions for her congressional testimony in favor of suffrage in the District of Columbia on 22 January 1870. (*Rev.*, 28 October 1869, 27 January 1870, *Film*, 2:129, 240–41.)

4. U.S. Const., amendment XIV, sec. 1.

5. U.S. Const., art. I, secs. 2, 4.

6. U.S. Const., amendment XIV, sec. 1.

7. U.S. Const., art. I, sec. 8.

8. ECS borrowed this and the subsequent references to the Constitution from the citations that Francis Minor provided to explain his resolutions. (*Rev.*, 28 October 1869.)

9. ECS wrote this paragraph for her untitled speech to the National Woman Suffrage Association in January 1873. (*Woman's Campaign*, January 1873, *Film*, 16:869–79.)

10. Minerva, the Roman goddess of wisdom, was born from the brow of her father, Jupiter.

11. Francis Minor cited the opinions of the Supreme Court in the Test Oath Cases of 1867, in which the majority relied on the Constitution's prohibition of bills of attainder and ex post facto laws to declare unconstitutional, in the first instance, a state constitutional provision and, in the second instance, a federal law. Minor contended that women's disfranchisement by states was a bill of attainder, as it punished women without judicial proceedings. In his brief to the Supreme Court in his wife's case, he asked by what warrant states inflicted "the bar of perpetual disfranchisement, where no crime or offense is alleged or pretended, and without 'due process of law.'" (Cummings v. Missouri, 4 Wallace 277 [1867]; Ex parte Garland, 4 Wallace 333 [1867]; *Rev.*, 28 October 1869; *History*, 2:720–21, 723.)

12. In *Corfield v. Coryell*, Justice Bushrod Washington defined the privileges and immunities clause of the Constitution and included among the privileges "fundamental" to citizenship "the elective franchise, as regulated by the laws

or constitution of the state in which it is to be exercised." The two other cases cited by Francis Minor, one in federal court and one in the supreme court of Massachusetts, relied on *Corfield v. Coryell* to decide questions about the power of state law over the citizens of other states. (Corfield v. Coryell, 6 Federal Cases 546 [C.C.E.D. Pa. 1823] [No. 3,230]; Dunham v. Lamphere, 69 Massachusetts Reports 268 [1855]; Bennett v. Boggs, 3 Federal Cases 221 [C.C.D. N.J. 1830] [No. 1,319]; *Rev.*, 28 October 1869; *History*, 2:725–26.)

13. This list of authorities is more extensive than what Francis Minor included in his original resolutions or his brief in Virginia Minor's case. It begins with support for his argument that states lacked authority to restrict the right of suffrage because the Constitution did not expressly give them the power. The first two references are found in the third: Joseph Story, *Commentaries on the Constitution of the United States*, first published in 1833. In section 448, Story (1779–1845) discusses the difference between "silence and abolition" in constitutional interpretation. "The truth is," he wrote, "that, in order to ascertain how far an affirmative or negative provision excludes or implies others, we must look to the nature of the provision, the subject-matter, the objects, and the scope of the instrument. These, and these only, can properly determine the rule of construction." Story cited *The Federalist Papers*, nos. 83 and 84, and Emmerich de Vattel, *The Law of Nations: Or, Principles of the Law of Nature; Applied to the Conduct and Affairs of Nations and Sovereigns*, published first in the United States in 1796.

14. Green v. Shumway, 36 Howard's Practice Reports 5, 8 (1868). Minor quoted at length from this opinion of the New York Court of Appeals in his brief to the Supreme Court. The state court found that to deprive a man of his voting rights because he could not take a loyalty oath imposed "a severe penalty, which interferes with his privileges as a citizen . . . and reduces him below the level of those who constitute the great body of the people of which the government is composed."

15. Minor's use of these cases is not known. The first three, one in the Supreme Court and two in state courts, defined limits on legislative power to deprive people of their rights of property and person: Wilkinson v. Leland, 2 Peters 657 (1829); Taylor v. Porter, 4 Hill's Reports 140 (1843); People v. Berberrich, 11 Howard's Practice Reports 289 (1855). The next three, all in state supreme courts and all concerning absentee ballots for soldiers, defined proper rules of construction for state constitutions: Morrison v. Springer, 15 Iowa Reports 304 (1863); Bourland v. Hildreth, 26 California Reports 161 (1864); Twitchell v. Blodgett, 13 Michigan Reports (1865).

16. Theodore Sedgwick, *A Treatise on the Rules which Govern the Interpretation and Application of Statutory and Constitutional Law* (New York, 1857). In a discussion of the phrase "the law of the land," Sedgwick agreed with various courts that fundamental rights and privileges could only be denied after judicial proceedings.

17. This paragraph can be found in Minor's brief to the Supreme Court, but

it and the next four paragraphs are also in ECS's congressional testimony of January 1870. ECS's manuscript ends at the word "most." (*History*, 2:721; *Rev.*, 27 January 1870.)

18. To their lists of who might vote, the constitutions of Virginia and Massachusetts added the phrase "and no other person." Virginia Const. of 1830, art. III, sec. 13, and of 1850, art. III, sec. 3; Massachusetts Const. of 1780, as amended 1821, articles of amendment, art. III.

19. John Jay, *An Address to the People of the State of New York, On the Subject of the Constitution, Agreed upon at Philadelphia, the 17th of September, 1787* (1788). Jay (1745–1829) was explaining why the Constitution did not need a Bill of Rights.

20. "Political Equality Without Distinction of Color. No Compromise of Human Rights," Sumner, *Works*, 10:282–337; quotation from pp. 304–5. This was Sumner's second major speech on the proposed Fourteenth Amendment. Quotation marks that ECS omitted are supplied within square brackets.

21. Patrick Henry and George Mason (1725–1792) of Virginia both opposed ratification of the Constitution. Sumner cited "Debates in the Virginia Convention, June 4 and 5, 1788," in Jonathan Elliot, ed., *The Debates in the Several State Conventions on the Adoption of the Federal Constitution at Philadelphia* (1836–1845).

22. James Madison (1751–1836) of Virginia was a delegate to the constitutional convention of 1787 and in 1809 became fourth president of the United States. Sumner cited "Yates's Minutes of the Debates of the Federal Convention, June 29, 1787," from the same source.

23. Elbridge Gerry (1744–1814) of Massachusetts was a member of the constitutional convention in 1787 who opposed ratification of the Constitution. Sumner cited "Yates's Minutes" of the same day.

24. James Wilson (1742–1798) of Pennsylvania was a member of the constitutional convention in 1787. Sumner cited "Yates's Minutes" for 30 June 1787.

25. 41st Cong., 1st sess., Joint Resolution, H.R. 15.

26. During debate on the District of Columbia franchise bill in 1866, senators defeated a proposal to enfranchise African-American women as well as men. See *Papers*, 2:7–10.

27. Minor v. Happersett, 21 Wallace 162, 178 (1875).

28. Dred Scott v. Sandford, 39 Howard 393, 404. Chief Justice Roger B. Taney wrote that African Americans were not included "under the word 'citizens' in the Constitution, and can therefore claim none of the rights and privileges which that instrument provides for and secures to citizens of the United States."

29. From the longer phrase, "the glittering and sounding generalities of natural right which make up the Declaration of Independence," used by Rufus Choate to disparage the Republican party, in *The Old-Line Whigs for Buchanan! Letters of Rufus Choate and George T. Curtis of Massachusetts* (Boston, 1856), 4.

30. This was not the text of S.R. 12, introduced by Aaron Sargent on January

10. Sargent's amendment read: "Sec. 1. The right of citizens of the United States to vote shall not be denied or abridged by the United States or by any State on account of sex. Sec. 2. The Congress shall have power to enforce this article by appropriate legislation."

31. *Congressional Globe*, 36th Cong., 1st sess., 914.

32. *A Summary View of the Rights of British America* (1774).

33. Reviewing the historic disagreements about the extent of national authority and the rights of states, ECS refers to the clashes between Thomas Jefferson and Alexander Hamilton; John C. Calhoun and Henry Clay (1777–1852), congressman, senator, and secretary of state; and finally Abraham Lincoln (1809–1865), sixteenth president of the United States, and Jefferson Davis (1808–1889), president of the Confederate States of America.

34. Until the introduction of national paper currency during the war, bank notes were issued by state banks. Uncertainty about the assets of the issuing banks and a lack of national standards caused their value to vary widely.

35. Kansas: Women claimed their right to vote in school districts on the basis of their first state constitution. Although excluded from voting for county superintendents, women held the office, elected by male voters. Minnesota: Voters amended the constitution in 1875 to permit women to hold school offices and vote on any measure relating to schools. Women first exercised their new rights in the spring of 1876. (Kansas Const. of 1859, art. II, sec. 23; Minnesota Const. of 1857, art. VII, sec. 8, as amended; *Woman's Journal*, 4 December 1875, 19 February, 22, 29 April, 13 May 1876; *History*, 3:652–54, 706, 710–11, 4:656, 659, 778–79.)

36. Maine: Women became eligible to hold school offices in towns and counties in 1869. Wisconsin: Legislation passed in 1875 declared women eligible for election to all county and local school offices. In at least one county, the Republican party nominated a woman for county superintendent as soon as the law took effect. Iowa: The attorney general ruled in 1869 that nothing excluded women from holding the office of county superintendent of schools, and on that basis women ran for office and won election. Ten women held the post in 1876, when a losing candidate challenged the eligibility of the woman who bested him. After a circuit court ruled in the man's favor, the legislature immediately enacted a law stating "That no person shall be deemed ineligible, by reason of sex, to any school office in the State of Iowa." California: The legislature made women eligible for all school offices in 1874. (*Woman's Journal*, 4, 25 April, 9 May 1874, 19 June, 11 December 1875, 1 April 1876; *History*, 3:360–61, 627–28, 757, 4:506, 993.)

37. Karl Heinzen, *What Is Real Democracy? Answered by an Exposition of the Constitution of the United States* (Indianapolis, Ind., 1871), 14.

38. She refers to the stipulation that three-fifths of all slaves would be counted for purposes of federal representation in the House of Representatives and to the pledge that fugitive slaves would not gain their freedom by escaping to a free state. On abolitionists and the Constitution, see Lewis

Perry, *Radical Abolitionism: Anarchy and the Government of God in Antislavery Thought* (Knoxville, Tenn., 1995), 188–204.

39. The full sentence, including what is marked as quotation, comes from Heinzen, *What Is Real Democracy?*, 15.

40. According to the Democratic platform of 1876, the nation needed "to be saved from a corrupt centralism," to which the party traced "the rapacity of carpet-bag tyrannies" in the South, fraud in Washington, misrule in local government, and economic hard times. ECS counters with an editorial by Francis E. Abbot in the Boston *Index*, 27 December 1877. Abbot was defending the National Liberal League's platform of 1877, which called for constitutional amendments to ensure "National protection for national citizens, in their equal civil, political and religious rights," universal education, and total separation of church and state. (*National Party Platforms*, 49; *Truth Seeker*, 9 November 1877; Stow Persons, *Free Religion: An American Faith* [New Haven, Conn., 1947], 120.)

41. The text of this interlude between quotations appears in ECS's speech to the National association in 1873.

42. *New York Times*, 26 September 1877. Hayes neared the end of a southern tour of reconciliation. In the list of Virginians revered by all Americans, Hayes names Thomas Jefferson; James Madison; James Monroe (1758–1831), the fifth president of the United States; and George Washington (1732–1799), the country's first president.

43. ECS paraphrases editorials in the Boston *Evening Journal*, 19 July 1877, and the *Morning Journal*, 20 July 1877, about federal authority to deploy troops against strikers on the Baltimore & Ohio Railroad. West Virginia's governor requested federal assistance on 18 July, after it was discovered that state militiamen sided with the strikers.

44. Charles Devens, Jr., (1820–1891) became attorney general of the United States in March 1877. Although his statement is unidentified, its context is evident. The Mountain Meadows Massacre, in which pioneers heading through the Territory of Utah to California were murdered by Mormons and Native Americans working in concert, occurred in 1857. Federal warrants for the arrest of participants were not issued until the Poland Bill of 1874 gave federal authorities the power to prosecute all criminal cases in the territory. On 23 March 1877, John D. Lee was executed for his part in the murders. It was assumed that more prosecutions would follow and that the line of responsibility would be traced upward through the Mormon hierarchy. In June 1877, the district attorney for the territory met with Devens and President Hayes and announced that he would bring "all the Mormon murderers to justice," not excluding Brigham Young. Young's death in August 1877 may help to explain why the federal government took no further action against the participants. (*ANB*; Juanita Brooks, *Mountain Meadows Massacre*, new ed. [Norman, Okla., 1962]; William Wise, *Massacre at Mountain Meadows: An American Legend and a Monumental Crime* [New York, 1976]; *New York Times*, 8 June 1877.)

45. U.S. v. Butler et al., 25 Federal Cases 213, 226 (C.C.D. S.C. 1877) (No. 14,700). Morrison R. Waite, as circuit justice for the Circuit Court for the District of South Carolina, presided over the trial of rioters who murdered African Americans prior to the election of 1876. They were charged under federal law for conspiracy to prevent legal voters from giving support for candidates. (George R. Rable, *But There Was No Peace: The Role of Violence in the Politics of Reconstruction* [Athens, Ga., 1984], 172–75.)

46. According to the *New York Times*, 30 June 1877, Joseph R. Hawley spoke on 27 June to alumni of Hamilton College in Utica, New York, on "Local Self-government, the Test of the Republican Experiment." It is unclear where ECS located his remarks.

47. *New York Tribune*, 9 June 1877. On June 1, the administration sent troops to the Mexican border with orders to chase marauders into Mexican territory in order to protect American citizens. The move heightened tensions between the United States and the new president of Mexico, Porfirio Díaz, who seized power in November 1876. (Kenneth E. Davison, *The Presidency of Rutherford B. Hayes* [Westport, Conn., 1972], 199–202.)

48. Trenton *Daily State Gazette*, 3 July 1877. The banquet honored New Jersey Republican George M. Robeson, secretary of the navy in the Grant administration.

49. Washington *National Republican*, 16 July 1877. Wade replied to a report that he favored the president's southern policy.

50. Most of this paragraph comes from her speech to the National association in January 1873.

51. The last two sentences of this paragraph are repeated from her congressional testimony of 1870. In the next paragraph, the clause from slaves through Jefferson, Hancock, and Adams comes from the same source.

52. ECS refers to agitation in England in the 1870s when miners and agricultural workers sought further extension of the franchise. (Biagini, *Liberty, Retrenchment and Reform*, 278–95.)

53. In 1861.

## 134 ⚡ ECS TO SBA

Tenafly, January [14?], 1878.

Dear Susan:

I suppose you are impatiently waiting to hear about the convention. [It] went off well, crowded houses as usual, and $200 in the treasury after all [bi]lls were paid. The usual successes and failures, joys and sorrows. I pre[pa]red the resolutions a week before and had them in print, so there was no [wo]rry at the last moment over them.[1] I devoted my whole vacation to the speech [to] be made before the committee. All said: "Very good."

Thursday morning, Isabella Beecher Hooker had a Moody and Sankey [pr]ayer meeting in the ladies' reception room next the Senate Chamber.[2] They [pr]ayed, sang "Hold the Fort," "Guide us, oh thou great Jehovah" and "The [Ba]ttle Hymn of the Republic," and made speeches from the tops of tables. [Se]nator Sargent said it was a regular mob. The corridors were crowded. And [al]l this while the senators were assembling for the first time after the [ho]lidays!

Mrs. Sargent and I did not attend the prayer meeting. As Jehovah [ha]s never taken a very active part in the Suffrage movement, I thought I [wo]uld stay at home and get ready to implore the committee, having more [fa]ith in their power to render us the desired aid.

At this same time a debate was precipitated in the Senate. Some[on]e rallied Senator Sargent on the mob character of his constituency. He [re]plied: "This is nothing to what you will see at this capitol, if these [wo]men's petitions are not heard."[3] Altogether it was a week of constant agi[ta]tion, and I think the result (prayer meeting, mob and all) is good.

I reached home Saturday night and found a telegram asking for my [sp]eech as the Committee intended to print it. I sat up last night until four [o']clock to copy it and sent off this morning 150 pages of manuscript. I got [so] interested in "National Protection for National Citizens" that the night [s]lipped away and I felt neither tired nor sleepy. But to-day I feel like [a] squeezed sponge and have done nothing. With love, Good-night,

≈ Elizabeth Cady Stanton.

≈ Typed transcript, ECS Papers, NjR. Later variants in same collection and in ECS Papers, DLC. All in *Film*. Also in *Stanton*, 2:153–54. The date is that assigned to the later variants. Square brackets surround letters obscured by binding.

1. The convention resolved that it was "the duty of the National Government to guarantee and effectually maintain the equal civil, political, and religious rights of all United States citizens"; that Congress should put the suffrage amendment ahead of all other business; that the proposal to introduce a sectarian God into the Constitution was "opposed to the genius of American institutions"; that church property should be taxed; and that states should make education compulsory and then, after 1885, base suffrage on literacy. An

additional resolution laid out plans to have women named commissioners to the international exposition in Paris in the summer of 1878. (*Woman's Journal*, 19 January 1878, *Film*, 19:1022–23.)

2. Isabella Hooker held a prayer meeting in the Senate Ladies' Reception Room on the morning of January 10, when Senator Aaron Sargent introduced the suffrage amendment. ECS likens the event to the revival meetings of the evangelists Dwight Lyman Moody (1837–1899) and Ira David Sankey (1840–1908). According to the Washington *Evening Star*, 10 January 1878, Hooker "offered prayer, a la Beecher, and then the ladies sang 'Guide us, oh! Thou Great Jehovah!' and repeated the Lord's prayer." Hooker stayed in Washington for several months to lobby for the amendment. She obtained extra hearings before committees of the House and Senate, and she held daily social events at the Riggs House for congressional wives and the city's leaders of society. By the middle of March, word reached SBA in the Midwest that Sara Spencer and Isabella Hooker were at odds over style and precedence. (*History*, 3:103–4; SBA diary, 10, 19 March 1878, *Film*, 19:791ff.)

3. After his introduction of the resolution for a constitutional amendment on January 10, Aaron Sargent proposed that women who favored the amendment be heard before the full Senate. A lengthy debate about Senate rules and woman suffrage ensued, pitting George Edmunds, Allen Thurman, and Thomas Bayard against Sargent and George Hoar. Two roll call votes were taken, one on Edmunds's motion to adjourn before discussing Sargent's resolution and a second on Sargent's motion itself. Ten senators voted for adjournment, and thirty-three voted with Sargent. After more debate, the Senate rejected the motion to hear the women by thirteen yeas and thirty-one nays. ECS refers to an exchange during the debate, when Senator Thurman described suffragists as laying siege to the Senate. Sargent replied: "I predict that this is only the first of a series of such assaults upon legislative bodies, not only upon the Senate but upon the House of Representatives and upon the Legislatures of the various States. This movement is getting to be very troublesome. I am aware of it. It disturbs grave Senators in their deliberations; . . . It will be more and more troublesome year by year." (*Congressional Record*, 45th Cong., 2d sess., 252, 254–55, 264–69; 45th Cong., 2d sess., Resolution, S. Mis. Doc. No. 12, Serial 1785.)

## 135 ⟶ PETITIONS TO CONGRESS

EDITORIAL NOTE: The National association circulated two petitions to Congress in 1877: for a sixteenth amendment and for relief from political disabilities. The texts here are taken from printed forms presented in the House of Representatives on 15 January 1878 and retained in the records of the House. Some senators and representatives presented petitions from their constituents as soon as the second session of the Forty-fifth Congress opened in December 1877, but the majority coordinated their presentations in January to coincide with the National's Washington convention, the introduction of the constitutional amendment, and the schedule of committee hearings on woman suffrage. The tenth of January was the principal day in the Senate, but the House of Representatives held off until the fourteenth and fifteenth. The presentations continued until early April 1878.

[15 January 1878]

## PETITION FOR WOMAN SUFFRAGE.

To the Senate and House of Representatives,
   In Congress Assembled:
The undersigned, Citizens of the United States, Residents of the State of ———, County of ———, Town of ———, earnestly pray your Honorable Body to adopt measures for so amending the Constitution as to prohibit the several States from Disfranchising United States Citizens on account of Sex.

MEN:                              WOMEN:

## PETITION OF ——— FOR RELIEF FROM
## POLITICAL DISABILITIES.

To the Senate and House of Representatives of the United States,
   In Congress Assembled:
———, a citizen of the United States and a resident of the State of ———, County of ———, Town of ———, hereby respectfully petitions your honorable body for the removal of her political disabilities, and that she may be declared invested with full power to exercise her right of self-government at the ballot-box, all state constitutions or statute laws to the contrary notwithstanding.

〜 Forms, House 45A-H11.7, 45th Cong., 2d sess., RG 233, DNA.

136 ⇜ ARTICLE BY SBA

Wyanet, Ill.,[1] April 4, 1878.

## THE NATIONAL WOMAN SUFFRAGE ASSOCIATION.

As chairman of the Executive Committee, I will say that on account of the interest and work being concentrated upon the Sixteenth Amendment petitions and Congress at Washington, we have deemed it wise not to hold the time honored May Anniversary in New York this year. It will be impossible to decide upon work, ways and means for the next year, until Congress has acted upon or failed to act upon our petitions.

Another reason is, that the 19th of the coming July is the 30th Anniversary of the first Woman's Rights Convention ever held in the world—that called by Lucretia Mott, Elizabeth Cady Stanton and Martha C. Wright, at Seneca Falls, N.Y., July 14, 1848.

Death has winnowed out very many from the ranks of our pioneer workers; but, scattered over this continent and Europe, are still left some of the earliest and noblest. Mrs. Mott, in her eighty-sixth year, Mrs. Stanton, Ernestine L. Rose, Abby Kelly Foster, Angelina Grimpke Weld, Mrs. C. I. H. Nichols, Frances D. Gage, Mrs. Tracy Cutler, Mrs. J. Elizabeth Jones, Lucy Stone, Antoinette L. Brown Blackwell, Matilda Joslyn Gage, Clemence S. Lozier, Amy Post, Sarah Pugh, Mary Grew,[2] Adelaide Thomson,[3] Mrs. Robinson,[4] &c., &c., and what a feast to the eyes and ears of the younger friends of our cause, would be the assemblage of all these and many more to talk over and rejoice over the wonderful progress of woman in the world of work, education, morals and society, since they first proclaimed the gospel of perfect and equal rights for women, civil and political.

The lecture season will soon be over, when it will be possible for our Executive Committee to meet and decide upon matters, but I should say Rochester, N.Y., would be the place, since the Seneca Falls Convention adjourned and reassembled in that city,[5] and many of the friends who attended and took part in the meeting are still living there.

⇜ *Susan B. Anthony*

&  Toledo *Ballot Box*, April 1878.

1. SBA spoke in Wyanet on April 3 and left this morning for La Moille. Her lectures continued through April 18. After a few weeks in Leavenworth and Fort Scott, Kansas, with her brothers, she escorted her brother-in-law Eugene Mosher back to Rochester in May.

2. SBA lists women prominent in the antislavery and woman's rights movements. Those not previously identified are: Angelina Emily Grimké Weld (1805-1879), abolitionist lecturer and author (whose name SBA always misspelled); Frances Dana Barker Gage (1808-1884), midwestern activist in the 1850s who moved to South Carolina during the war to work with former slaves; Hannah Maria Conant Tracy Cutler (1815-1896), a former president of the American Woman Suffrage Association who practiced medicine in Cobden, Illinois; Jane Elizabeth Hitchcock Jones (1813-1896), prominent among Ohio's reformers before the war; Amy Kirby Post (1802-1889), the central figure among reformers in Rochester, New York; and Sarah Pugh (1800-1884) and Mary Grew (1813-1896), members of the Philadelphia Female Anti-Slavery Society and leaders in local suffrage and woman's rights organizations. (*NAW*; *ANB*. See also *Papers* 1 & 2.)

3. Mary Adeline Thomson (1812?-1895) was the younger sister of Anna Thomson and SBA's frequent hostess in Philadelphia. Adeline, as she was known, was the more active reformer of the sisters, taking a part in antislavery societies and woman's rights conventions before the war and suffrage associations after. When the National Woman Suffrage Association was organized in 1869, she represented Pennsylvania on its advisory council, and in later years she was a member of the executive committee. (*Friends' Intelligencer* 52 [1895]: 109; *Woman's Journal*, 9 March 1895; *Anthony*, 1:122, 327n; assistance of the Estate of J. Edgar Thomson.)

4. Harriet Jane Hanson Robinson (1825-1911) was the widow of the Massachusetts journalist William S. Robinson, known as Warrington, and a writer in her own right. She came into the woman's rights movement after the Civil War, when she joined the New England Woman Suffrage Association, but as a mill girl at Lowell, Massachusetts, in her youth, she was another type of pioneer. This is the earliest evidence of Robinson's alliance with SBA and the National after a bitter dispute with Lucy Stone and Henry Blackwell in 1875. At the Decade Celebration she was named the National's vice president for Massachusetts. (*NAW*; *ANB*; Claudia L. Bushman, *"A Good Poor Man's Wife"*: *Being a Chronicle of Harriet Hanson Robinson and Her Family in Nineteenth-Century New England* [Hanover, N.H., 1981].)

5. After the close of the Seneca Falls woman's rights convention on 20 July 1848, a second convention took place in Rochester on 2 August.

137 ❧ SBA TO THE EDITOR, *NATIONAL CITIZEN
AND BALLOT BOX*[1]

Rochester, N.Y., May 29, 1878.

Dear N.C. & B.B:—

From the 4th of September, 1877 to the 18th of April, 1878, I lectured 148 times in 140 different towns scattered over ten States. In all of
them I urged the claims of woman's enfranchisement to the best of my
ability: and in nearly all of them I took a vote on the question, getting
almost always a unanimous "yes." At the lowest estimate my audiences
must have averaged 300, making a total number of 42,000. Then if you
will add to these the hundreds of thousands of the most intelligent men
and women who have responded "aye" to Mrs. Stanton and the scores
of lecturers who have urged the enfranchisement of women on our
Lyceum platforms the past season, you will see that the friends of our
cause are nearing the millions.

The reports of the women who circulated our Petitions, that three-
fourths of the people called upon, cheerfully signed their names, is
another evidence; also the fact that from my presenting to my audiences blank petitions almost every one of the 140 towns sent a well
filled sheet on to Congress. Another indication of growing interest may
be seen in the fact, that the bare mention, at the close of my lectures, of
the need of a newspaper to educate themselves and their children into
a true knowledge of the persons and principles of our movement, 766
women either had a dollar, or got it by the asking, and subscribed for
the *Ballot Box*. And not by any means the least of my work do I feel that
of having planted the *Ballot Box* during the past year in 766 households
of the nation.

What we now most need is to get a full public expression of the real
sentiment that already exists on the question. The method of petitioning is so tedious and so expensive in time, strength and money, not one
of which have our earnest, thinking women an over supply of, that the
result of the most herculean effort on the part of the few who can devote
themselves to it, seems almost a discouragement; and yet who can

estimate the numbers of people connected by the 300 women in the 35 States and 6 Territories who have gone from house to house and store to store circulating the petitions? One of them, Mrs. Phebe M. Kelsey,[2] devoted weeks of hardest labor in Colorado, and obtained over 2,000 signatures to her petition. But until we can devise some easier, speedier and more effective plan, I hope we shall all gird ourselves up to renewed energy, from year to year, and send into Congress larger and larger petitions until the men there shall, "from our very importunity,"[3] grant our prayer for justice.

Senator Thurman's poor plea that the 70,000 petitioners for a voice in the government did not represent the unit of more than one out of a hundred of the women of the country, merely showed his ignorance of the other 99.[4] And Senator Ingall's doubt if there were a county or township in Kansas that would give a majority vote for woman suffrage[5] only tells of his blissful ignorance that a whole decade of school houses, education and growth has passed since his State, and that, too, in spite of his and Senator Plumb's[6] active opposition in the immediate canvass, gave 9,070 votes for, to 19,857, against. But then, suppose the majority of the voters of every town, county and State are *against* equal rights for women? Who are they? The vast mass of them are the ignorant men, the bigoted men, the whiskey men, the colored men, the foreign born men. Of the 6,500 men who voted for woman suffrage in Colorado last October, I'll venture my "yankee guess" that the 500 would cover every vote from the several classes named, including too the Mexican Greasers. While the 6,000 were educated, native born, white, anti-whiskey men.

The very reason we go to Congress is that "the citizen's right to vote" shall no longer be denied to one half the people by the selfish majority of the other half.

&#x223d;  *Susan B. Anthony.*

&#x223d;  *NCBB*, June 1878.

1. Matilda Joslyn Gage took over the *Ballot Box* from Sarah Williams and the Toledo Woman Suffrage Association in time to publish the issue of May 1878 in Syracuse, New York, under the new title, *National Citizen and Ballot Box*.

2. Phebe M. Kelsey (c. 1835–?) moved to Boulder, Colorado, in 1876 or 1877 to live with her daughter, a schoolteacher, and in October 1877, she organized SBA's lecture in the town. A widow born in Massachusetts, Kelsey

lived in New York City in 1870 and described her employment as "literary." At the start of Victoria Woodhull's presidential campaign in 1872, she pledged to raise one hundred dollars. Her petition for the sixteenth amendment was submitted in the House of Representatives on 15 January 1878. (Federal Census, 1870; New York City directory, 1871 to 1876; *Woodhull and Claflin's Weekly*, 25 May 1872, and SBA diary, 12–13 October 1877, in *Film*, 16:104–9, 19:12ff; *Congressional Record*, 45th Cong., 2d sess., 349.)

3. An allusion to Luke 11:8.

4. Allen Granberry Thurman (1813–1895), Democrat of Ohio, served in the Senate from 1869 to 1881 and mounted strong opposition to any measure to enlarge women's rights, whether by suffrage or admission to the bar. SBA refers to his remark in the Senate debate on January 10: "I utterly deny that they [the suffragists] are the representatives of one-twentieth part of the women of the United States, or the one-hundredth part, my friend from Connecticut says. . . . Where are their credentials that constitute them the representatives of the women of the United States? I should like to know where they are. They are undoubtedly very worthy people. They undoubtedly have brooded over their supposed wrongs until it has almost become a mania with them to besiege Congress." (*BDAC*; *Congressional Record*, 45th Cong., 2d sess., 265.)

5. John James Ingalls (1833–1900), Republican of Kansas, served in the Senate from 1873 to 1891. While presenting petitions for the sixteenth amendment, he remarked: "I do not sympathize with the object for which the petitioners pray, and I do not think they represent the sentiments of any considerable portion of the citizens of my State, either male or female. I think that there is no county, nor city, nor ward, nor township in that State where, if this proposition were submitted to either the men or the women, it would not be voted down by a very large majority." (*BDAC*; *Congressional Record*, 45th Cong., 2d sess., 12 December 1877, p. 138.)

6. Preston Bierce Plumb (1837–1891) of Kansas, a Republican, served in the Senate from 1877 until his death. In 1867, as Kansas voters considered removing the word "male" from voting qualifications, Plumb stumped the state on behalf of the anti-female suffrage movement, and he brought his opposition to woman suffrage to the Senate. SBA refers below to the outcome of the 1867 vote. (*BDAC*; *Leavenworth Daily Conservative*, 7 September 1867; *Western Home Journal*, 26 September 1867.)

## 138 ❧ ECS TO MATILDA JOSLYN GAGE

Home, [*Tenafly,*] May 30, 1878.

Have just reached home and for the first time seen our new paper but not yet had time to read it. I like its appearance, and the name so well represents our purpose and association, that I am rejoiced that you did not hit on any other. I would however drop "the Ballot box" if not at once, after the next number, giving all the subscribers time to know of the marriage,—the two, one—and that one the *National Citizen.* It is the best name ever given a woman's paper.

❧ *NCBB,* June 1878.

## 139 ❧ SBA TO MARIETTA HOLLEY[1]

Rochester N.Y. June 26th 1878.

My Dear Bitsy Bobbitt

How glad I am to know where you are—

Enclosed is the Congressional Priv. & Elec. Com's report against our 16th Am't Petitions—[2] Samantha may have a comment to make on it— Our paper, the "National Citizen" will be sent to you—~~and~~ ↑by its↓ Editor in Chief—Mrs Matilda Joslyn Gage—and I hope you will send her any of the things <u>too good</u>—that is <u>too decidedly</u> woman suffrage for the popular press— I am so glad New York has the honor of giving such a genius on woman & of woman to the world—

I write, especially, to invite you—nay, <u>urge you</u>—to attend our 30th Anniversary of the W.R. movement— I enclose printed slip—[3] Come— in cog. if you choose—only be here— Woods Hotel—on Fitzhugh street[4]—but a few doors from the Church—is to be our Head Quarters—and your board while attending the meeting—shall be free—if you wish— But if you cannot be present, will you not send a letter to be read & printed—that we may have the influence of your name as well as good word—to start us on our 4$^{th}$ Decade—

Hoping to hear from you very soon—I am most sincerely & gratefully yours

Susan B. Anthony

I have already received favorable responses for the presence of Mrs Mott, Mrs Stanton, Mrs Gage, Mrs Spencer, Mrs Robinson—[(]widow of "Warrington"—) Frederick Douglass—Old Sojourner Truth[5]—Mrs Stowe's Lybian Sybil—almost 100 years old— It will be a gathering—such as will be worth the sight of the eyes of one who wields a pen like that of Betsy Bobbitt— S. B. A.

ALS, on NWSA letterhead for 1877, year corrected, Marietta Holley Letters, NWattJHi.

1. Marietta Holley (1836–1926), author and humorist, introduced the characters Betsey Bobbet and Samantha Allen, or Josiah Allen's wife, in *My Opinions and Betsey Bobbet's* (1873), the first in a long series of popular books. *Josiah Allen's Wife as a P.A. and P.I., or Samantha at the Centennial* appeared in 1877. Holley, who lived west of Rochester in Jefferson County, New York, made Samantha a common-sense advocate of woman suffrage and temperance with a keen ear for the absurdities of antisuffragists. (*NAW*; *ANB*.)

2. Enclosure missing. It was: Senate, Committee on Privileges and Elections, *Report*, 45th Cong., 2d sess., S. Rept. 523, Serial 1791. The unsigned report, issued on 14 June 1878, recommended that the amendment be indefinitely postponed. Its opening paragraph set the tone and infuriated suffragists. If the amendment were adopted, the authors wrote, "it will make several millions of female voters, totally inexperienced in political affairs, quite generally dependent upon the other sex, all incapable of performing military duty and without the power to enforce the laws which their numerical strength may enable them to make, and comparatively very few of whom wish to assume the irksome and responsible political duties which this measure thrusts upon them." The committee acknowledged no evidence of a public demand for woman suffrage: the small number of signatures on the petitions, they wrote, were obtained by "the efforts of woman-suffrage societies, thoroughly organized, with active and zealous managers."

3. Enclosure missing.

4. According to the call to the meeting, it was the European Hotel, at 53 Fitzhugh Street, to which guests should report. Daytime sessions of the Third Decade Celebration were held in the Unitarian Church, also on Fitzhugh Street. The Rochester woman's rights convention of 1848 met in the same church. (City directory, 1878; *Film*, 20:310.)

5. Sojourner Truth (c. 1797–1883), born a slave in New York State and freed in 1827, lived in Battle Creek, Michigan. She was active in the antebellum woman's rights movement and in the campaign for equal rights at the end of the Civil War. "Sojourner Truth, the Libyan Sibyl" was the title of an article by Harriet Beecher Stowe, published in the *Atlantic Monthly* in 1863. (*NAW*; *ANB*. See also *Papers* 2.)

## 140 ⚞ ECS TO SBA

Tenafly, June 1878.

Dearly Beloved:

It is a happy thought of mine for you to sail to Europe as soon [a]s you get ready and attend the Congress.[1] Theodore is in Paris and will [a]ct as interpreter for you.[2] See what good material you would find for a [s]peech next winter. Then, too, you can collect data[3] for our history both in [F]rance and England. I will give to the Léon Richer fund, and will [w]rite to Lizzie Miller. She will give something; so will Mrs. Phelps and [M]rs. Bullard.[4] Do give my plan serious consideration. Our society should be [re]presented at this French Congress. Lucretia Mott, Amy Post and I, will [ma]nage the Rochester Convention. Anything to get you off. Now take a broad [co]mprehensive view. When Mary is out of school, her home duties will [re]st lightly on her. I know she would willingly forego her trips for this [g]reat benefit to you and our cause. I will add to, improve, and intensify [o]ur epistle to the Congress to-morrow; but I do hope you will go over [y]ourself. Yours ever,

⚞ *Elizabeth Cady Stanton*

⚞ Typed transcript, ECS Papers, NjR. Letters in square brackets obscured by binding.

1. Word reached the United States in May 1878 that plans were underway for an international congress on woman's rights during the summer's international exposition in Paris, though the precise dates were not settled until June. Léon Richer and Maria Deraismes, France's leading advocates of woman's rights, initiated the plan, after republicans gained power in the French government in 1877 and lifted a ban on their meetings. With the congress finally set to meet on 25 July, invitations and solicitations for funds were sent to

American reformers and internationalists, including ECS. Short notice, however, caused American organizations to name delegates who were already in Europe. Woman suffrage was not on the meeting's agenda. Its five sections treated history, education, work, morals, and legislation. Richer (1824–1911), editor of the newspaper, *L'Avenir des femmes*, had worked with Deraismes for a decade, founding in 1868 their paper, then called *Le Droit des femmes*, and in 1870 the Association pour le droit des femmes. (*NCBB*, May, June, July 1878; *Woman's Journal*, 29 June, 3 August 1878; Chicago *Inter-Ocean*, 13 July 1878; Patrick Bidelman, "Maria Deraismes, Léon Richer, and the Founding of the French Feminist Movement, 1866–1878," *Third Republic/Troisième République* 3–4 [1977]: 20–73.)

2. Theodore Stanton, along with Julia Ward Howe and Mary Livermore, served in Paris on the planning commission for the congress. (Call to the Congrès international du droit des femmes, M. J. Gage scrapbooks, MCR-S.)

3. The word "data" was added to the typescript in an unknown hand.

4. That is, Elizabeth Miller, Elizabeth Phelps, and Laura Bullard.

## 141 ✎ ECS TO ELIZABETH SMITH MILLER

Tenafly, July 12, 1878.

Dear Julius:

Susan has written me how fearfully you squelched her for asking you to contribute to the expenses of the French Congress. Why, my dear, do you not know that this is one of the great events of the century for woman?—a congress at which Victor Hugo[1] will preside and in which full equality will be demanded for womanhood everywhere. Why, you should have been thankful that your attention was called to this event, and that you enjoyed the privilege of contributing your mite. I was the guilty party who suggested to Susan to ask you to join us in sending $50.[2] Sincerely,

✎ *Elizabeth Cady Stanton.*

✎ Typed transcript, ECS Papers, NjR.

1. Victor Hugo (1802–1885), French novelist and political writer, helped to plan the Congrès international du droit des femmes in Paris, and it was announced that he would preside. He did not, in fact, attend the meeting. (*NCBB*, July 1878; Chicago *Inter-Ocean*, 13 July 1878.)

2. SBA noted this sum of fifty dollars to offset expenses of the international

congress when she sent the money to Léon Richer. The National was formally thanked at the congress. (SBA diary, 1878, account page for June, *Film*, 19:791ff; *NCBB*, September 1878.)

142   THIRD DECADE CELEBRATION AT ROCHESTER, NEW YORK

EDITORIAL NOTE: The Decade Celebration opened in stages: an executive committee meeting at Mary Hallowell's house on July 17, a business meeting at the Unitarian Church on July 18, and the celebration itself on July 19. The Unitarian Church was adequate to the audience able to celebrate in the daytime, but it took the twelve hundred seats of Corinthian Hall to hold the evening crowd. In the words of a local paper, the event attracted "gentlemen recognized in society and professions as leaders" and "ladies representing the best society of our city." It also drew many of the movement's pioneers— Lucretia Mott, Sarah Pugh, Amy Post, Sojourner Truth, Frederick Douglass, Catharine Stebbins, and Elizabeth Oakes Smith—and current leaders—Clemence Lozier, Belva Lockwood, Sara Spencer, Ellen Sargent, Matilda Gage, and Phoebe Couzins. "I went to Rochester to meeting," Martha Schofield noted on her invitation from SBA, "Glorious time." ECS opened the celebration with a speech, published below. A manuscript of her speech survives, with a notation in SBA's hand that reads: "This is the poorest manuscript I ever knew Mrs Stanton to carry before an audience." That manuscript, however, may not have been the final one. ECS may have handed a cleaner and later manuscript to the press; the first, verbatim report of her speech in the local evening paper indicates significant revisions beyond those inscribed on the manuscript. The text reproduced here is that published later in the *National Citizen*, based on the local report but edited by Matilda Gage. Most of ECS's changes, from draft to emendations on the manuscript and later to published text, show repeated efforts to make her sentences shorter and more pointed, and those changes are not noted here. The notes do record shifts in wording that suggest significant rethinking of her points. (SBA to M. Schofield, 20 June 1878; *Rochester Union and Advertiser*, 19 July 1878; and ECS manuscript; all in *Film*, 20:289–92, 323–25, 334–52.)

[19 July 1878]

We are here to celebrate the third decade of woman's struggle in this country for liberty.

Thirty years have passed since many of us now present met in this same church to discuss the true position of woman as a citizen of a republic.[1] The reports of our first conventions show that those who inaugurated this movement understood the significance of the term "citizens."

At the very start we claimed full equality with man. Our meetings were hastily called and somewhat crudely conducted; but we intuitively recognized the fact that we were defrauded of our natural rights, conceded in the National constitution.[2]

And thus the greatest movement of the century was inaugurated. I say greatest, because through the elevation of woman all humanity is lifted to a higher plane of action. To contrast our position thirty years ago, under the old common law of England, with that we occupy under the advanced legislation of to-day, is enough to assure us that we have passed the boundary line—from slavery to freedom. We already see the milestones of a new civilization on every highway.

Look at the department of education, the doors of many colleges and universities thrown wide open to woman, girls contending for, yea, and winning prizes from their brothers.

In the working world they are rapidly filling places, and climbing heights unknown to them before, realizing, in fact, the dreams, the hopes, the prophesies of the inspired women of bygone centuries.

In many departments of learning, woman stands the peer of man, and when by higher education and profitable labor she becomes self-reliant and independent, then she must and will be free.

The moment an individual, or a class, is strong enough to stand alone, bondage is impossible.

Jefferson Davis in a recent speech says, "A Caesar could not subject a people fit to be free, nor could a Brutus save them if they were fit for subjugation."[3]

Looking back over the past thirty years, how long ago seems that July morning when we gathered round the altar in the old Wesleyan Church in Seneca Falls. It taxes and wearies the memory to think of all the conventions we have held, the Legislatures we have besieged, the petitions and tracts we have circulated, the speeches, the calls, the resolutions we have penned, the never ending debates we have kept up in public and private, and yet to each and all, our theme is as fresh and absorbing as it was the day we started. Calm, benignant, subdued, as we all look on this platform, if any man should dare to rise in our presence and controvert a single position we have taken, there is not a woman here that would not in an instant, with flushed face, and flashing eye, bristle all over with sharp, pointed arguments, that would soon annihilate the most skilled logician, the most profound philosopher.

Some of our opponents attack us with the same old weapons in use thirty years ago; though ever and anon, as new phases of the question have arisen, new weapons have come into use. When a number of women in this city, with Susan B. Anthony at their head, went to the polls and voted, Henry R. Selden, in his constitutional arguments in their defence before the United States, forged a good supply of Minnie guns and Columbiads,[4] which have done us good service.

The discussion of the political rights of woman involves the consideration of all the fundamental principles of republican government; hence, ours has been an educational movement, giving all those who have listened to the discussion a clearer insight into the rights of all citizens in a republic. Daniel Webster says it is fortunate for us as a nation, that different classes arise from time to time, demanding new rights and privileges, as the people thereby come to a more perfect understanding of the principles on which a republic rests.

To those of you on this platform, who for these thirty years have been the steadfast representatives of woman's cause, my friends and co-laborers, let me say our work has not been in vain. True, we have not yet secured the suffrage, but we have aroused public thought to the many disabilities of our sex, and our countrywomen to higher self respect and worthy ambition, and in this struggle for justice we have deepened and broadened our own lives, and extended the horizon of our vision.

Ridiculed, persecuted, ostracised, we have learned to place a just estimate on popular opinion, and to feel a just confidence in ourselves. As the representatives of principles which it was necessary to explain and defend, we have been compelled to study constitutions and laws, and in thus seeking to redress the wrongs and vindicate the rights of the many, we have secured a higher development for ourselves.

Nor is this all. The full fruition of these years of seed-sowing shall yet be realized, though it may not be by those who have led in the reform, for many of our number have already fallen asleep. Another decade and not one of us may be here, but we have smoothed the rough paths for those who come after us. The lives of multitudes will be gladdened by the sacrifices we have made, and the truths we have uttered can never die.

Standing near the gateway of the unknown land, and looking back through the vista of the past, memory recalls many duties in life's varied relations, we would had been better done. The past to all of us is filled with regrets. We can recall, perchance, social ambitions disappointed, fond hopes wrecked, ideals in wealth, power, position, unattained, much that would be considered success in life unrealized. But I think we should all agree that the time, the thought, the energy we have devoted to the freedom of our countrywomen, that in so far as our lives have represented this great movement, the past brings us only unalloyed satisfaction.

The rights already obtained, the full promise of the rising generation of women in our colleges and the varied industries, more than repay us for the hopes so long deferred, the rights yet denied, the humiliations of spirit we still suffer.[5]

To you, noble representative (Douglass) of a long oppressed race, who honor our platform to-day, words are inadequate to express our thanks for your steadfast, unwavering devotion to our cause. In advocating the same freedom for us as for yourselves, you have proved that to your minds liberty is the watchword, not for color and class alone, but for all humanity. Your voice, Frederick Douglass, was heard in our first convention, and but for you, I fear the resolution demanding the elective franchise for woman, would not have been adopted, as many of our friends thought the demand premature. May your voice be the first to congratulate us when our success shall be assured.[6]

And for those of you who have been mere spectators of the long, hard battle we have fought and are still fighting, I have a word. Whatever your attitude has been, whether as cold, indifferent observers— whether you have hurled at us the shafts of ridicule, or of denunciation, we ask you now to lay aside your old educational prejudices, and give this question your earnest consideration, substituting reason for ridicule, sympathy for sneers. I urge the young women especially to prepare themselves to take up the work so soon to fall from our hands. You have had opportunities for education such as we had not. You hold to-day

the vantage ground we have won by argument. Show now your gratitude to us by making the uttermost of yourselves, and by your earnest,
exalted lives secure to those who come after you a higher outlook, a
broader culture, a larger freedom than has yet been vouchsafed to
woman in our own happy land.

Much has been accomplished for the civil rights of woman. The laws
and customs touching her property, education and labor have been
essentially modified and improved, but her political rights are still
ignored.

Even England, the government our fathers repudiated, with all its
aristocratic ideas, has lifted her women above our heads. And France,
too, is just now moving in the same direction. An International Congress in the interests of woman is to be held in Paris in a few days, and
I notice among the delegates, Senators, Deputies and members of the
Conseil General of Paris, and representatives from other European
powers are to be present.

I am happy to say that one of my own sons is to represent America
and the National Woman Suffrage Association. It is a proud day for me,
my friends, when at last a man with my own blood pulsating in his heart
shall speak brave words for the freedom of woman.[7]

I would remind the gentlemen present that the enfranchisement of
woman involves your interests as deeply as our own. We are so indis-
solubly bound together that whatever degrades woman lowers the
status of man, also. Our growth is your development, our hope your
inspiration, our longings your triumph, our success your victory.[8]

EDITORIAL NOTE: At the close of ECS's speech, SBA rose to read
greetings from Wendell Phillips before speeches resumed. Fully one
hundred people wrote letters to the gathering, and the *National
Citizen* squeezed more than ninety of them into its coverage of the
event.

Boston, June 30, 1878.

My Dear Miss Anthony:

Your urgent and welcome letter, inviting me to the thirtieth anniversary of the Woman's Rights movement at Rochester, came yesterday.

Most earnestly do I wish I could be present to help mark this epoch
in our movement, and join in congratulating the friends on the marvelous results of their labors.

No reform has gathered more devoted and self-sacrificing friends. No one has had lives more generously given to its service; and you who have borne such heavy burdens may well rejoice in the large harvest; for no reform has, I think, had such rapid success. You who remember the indifference which almost discouraged us in 1848, and who have so bravely faced ungenerous opposition and insult since, must look back on the result with unmixed astonishment and delight.

Temperance, Finance—which is but another name for the labor movement—and Woman's Rights, are three radical questions which overtop all others in value and importance.

Woman's claim for the ballot box has had a much wider influence than merely to protect woman. Universal suffrage is itself in danger. Scholars dread it; social science and journalists attack it. The discussion of woman's claim has done much to reveal this danger, and rally patriotic and thoughtful men in defence.

In many ways the agitation has educated the people. Its success shows that the masses are sound and healthy; and if we gain, in the coming fifteen years, half as much as we have in the last thirty, woman will hold spear and shield in her own hands.

If I might presume to advise, I should say, "close up the ranks and write on our flag only one claim—the ballot."

Everything helps us, and if we are united, success cannot long be delayed. Very cordially yours,

⇜ *Wendell Phillips*

EDITORIAL NOTE: The Committee on Resolutions reported to the celebration on the afternoon of July 19. In a debate about resolutions a year later, Matilda Gage credited herself with writing the resolutions of 1878 about religion. According to the press, Lucy Colman, Arethusa Forbes, Amy Post, Martha Schofield, Helen Slocum, and Elizabeth Oakes Smith served on the committee. With at least three well-known freethinkers in the group—Post, Colman, and Gage herself—free thought made its way into the resolutions and occasioned a debate. (*NCBB*, June 1879, *Film*, 20:778–88.)

Upon the assembling of the Convention at 4 P.M., Matilda Joslyn Gage, Chairman of the Committee on Resolutions, which had been drafted for consideration and adoption by the association, read the following:

First—Resolved, That a government of the people, by the people, and for the people, is yet to be realized; for that which is formed, administered and controlled only by men is practically nothing more than an enlarged oligarchy, whose assumptions of natural superiority and of the right to rule are as baseless as those enforced by the aristocratic and dynastic powers of the old world.

Second—Resolved, That this claim of equal rights in determining who shall be the law makers and what shall be the laws, is not to be set aside by witless ridicule, artful evasion, masculine self-conceit, dogged resistance, or by citing long-established usage against it; but it is to be asserted and demanded with increasing emphasis, though a thousand times rejected, until its concession is fully assured.

Third—Resolved, That in celebrating our third decade, we have reason to congratulate ourselves on the marked change in woman's position within the last thirty years—in her enlarged opportunities for education and labor, her greater freedom under improved social customs, and civil laws, and the promise of her speedy enfranchisement in the minor political rights she has already secured.

Fourth—Resolved, That the International Congress called in Paris for the 20th of July, to discuss the rights of Woman—the eminent Victor Hugo its presiding officer—is one of the most encouraging events of the century, in that statesmen and scholars from all parts of the world, mid the excitements of the French Exposition, propose to give five days to deliberations upon this question.

Fifth—Resolved, That the majority report of the Chairman of the Committee on Privileges and Elections, Senator Wadleigh of New Hampshire, against a sixteenth amendment to secure the political rights of woman, in its weakness shows the strength of our reform. It is not a statesman-like argument based upon reason and conviction, but the evasion of a demagogue.

Sixth—Resolved, That the national effort to force citizenship on the Indians,[9] the decision of Judge Sawyer, in the United States Circuit Court of California, against the naturalization of the Chinese,[10] and the denial of Congress to secure the suffrage to women, is class legislation, dangerous to the stability of our institutions.

Seventh—Whereas, Women's rights and duties in all matters of legislation are the same as those of man,

Resolved, That the problems of labor, finance, suffrage, International rights, internal improvements, theology and other great questions, can never be satisfactorily adjusted without the enlightened thought of woman, and her voice in the councils of the nation.

Eighth—Resolved, That the question of capital and labor is one of special interest to us. Man standing to woman in the position of capitalist has robbed her through the ages of the results of her toil. No just settlement of this question can be attained until the right of woman to the proceeds of her labor in the family and elsewhere be recognized, and until she is welcomed into every industry on the basis of equal pay for equal work.

Ninth—Resolved, That as the duty of every individual is self-development, the lessons of self-sacrifice and obedience taught women by the Christian church have been fatal not only to her own highest interests, but through her have also dwarfed and degraded the race.

Tenth—Resolved, That the fundamental principle of the Protestant reformation, the right of individual conscience and judgment in the interpretation of scripture, heretofore conceded to and exercised by men alone, should now be claimed by women, and that in her most vital interests she should no longer trust authority, but be guided by her own reason.

Resolved, That it is through the perversion of the religious element in woman, cultivating the emotions at the expense of her reason, playing upon her hopes and fears of the future, holding this life with all its high duties forever in abeyance to that which is to come, that she, and the children she has trained, have been so completely subjugated by priestcraft and superstition.

Upon motion of Mrs. Gage the resolutions were accepted and Mrs. Stanton then announced that discussion upon them would be in order.

Mrs. Gage spoke upon the ninth and tenth resolutions, relative to the religious and natural rights which ought to be conceded to women. Though obedience and self-sacrifice had been taught as her chief duties, she said that in the experience of Frederick Douglass, who had refused obedience to tyrannical mastery, a higher type of human life and action might be found. So was it with woman, she ought to be strong enough and her ability sufficiently recognized, to warrant her in developing for herself independence of action, and freedom of thought and principle. She spoke of the false ideas which had been inculcated among womankind, restricting them not only in spiritual and intellectual culture, but also depriving them of that exercise necessary for the development of the physical frame. The protestant reformation while freeing women from certain restrictions had still continued those of a corresponding nature, and what she now most needed was to take upon herself the right inherently belonging to her, of her own private interpretation of Scripture.

Frederick Douglass said that as the doctrine of self-sacrifice was the soul of Christianity, and the soul of everything good, he would be in favor of amending this clause in the resolution discussed.[11]

Mrs. Lucretia Mott also spoke upon the same subject, distinguishing between true Christianity and theological creed. True righteousness and goodness were the only right for the correction of wrong. She believed in the Scripture, "Behold, a new heaven, and a new earth, for old things have passed away."[12] The fields were ripened for the harvest now and the churches were becoming more and more ready to do away with verbal creeds, which were such an element of dissension among them. In her closing remarks and just previous to her departure for the east she said she wished to add her expression of gratitude to the Unitarian society who had so kindly given them the use of their edifice. She spoke of the fitness of this courtesy having been extended by just such a denomination.

The convention then arose in her honor, and in behalf of all of them Frederick Douglass said to her "Good-bye."

Mrs. Stanton then spoke on the amendment which Frederick Douglass had advocated, and she said it was all very well for a man to arise and laud self-sacrifice, but when the sterner sex had tried only a portion of the self-sacrifice through which women had passed in centuries gone by, they too would be ready to advocate self-development in the place of self-sacrifice, of which they had had enough. She referred to the parable of the ten Virgins,[13] showing that only those were received who cared for themselves. What she advocated was that when any minister of the Gospel got up to preach the doctrine of woman's subjection and subjugation to man,—at such a time every woman within the church should arise and leave it.

Mrs. Lucy Colman[14] called for the reading again of the resolutions, and said she wished to preach a short sermon, and her text would be "Frederick Douglass on self-sacrifice." She might have held her peace had a woman arisen and lauded self-sacrifice for women; but when a man did so she could not. She asked why he had not sacrificed himself for the American Union and said, there was already too much of an impression abroad that humanity, and womankind especially, must be held in obedience to other powers than the God within the individual soul.

Frederick Douglass said that as he had meant it with reference to that resolution, he understood there was no conflict between the lessons of self-sacrifice and those of self-development; but the former only promoted the latter, that he had two sons in the Union army[15] and would have been there himself but they would not have him. Mrs. Colman replied that she did not refer to his entering the army, but why had he not sacrificed himself by remaining in slavery?

Mrs. Slocum[16] also spoke upon this subject, and said the point was simply this—shall self-sacrifice for woman be made worthy of her? The self-sacrifice which had been taught to woman in the past had been giving her away. It was time, now, for a woman to be first a woman; after that wife and mother, in such a position as, by self-development, they might have the judgment to know just how and what to sacrifice.

Mrs. Sands,[17] a venerable woman, arose and spoke in favor of the resolution discussed. She said that as long ago as when she was three years old, in 1803, she remembered being taught this false and overdrawn idea of self-sacrifice for woman. It was all wrong, and the change could not come too soon.

Mrs. Dundore,[18] of Baltimore, was the next speaker. She decried the Scripture teachings concerning "the rib," etc.,[19] of the garden, as well as concerning slavery of any kind, as advocated in holy writ. She believed the present teachings of the church were detrimental to the cause of woman, and thus to the common cause of humanity.

A vote upon the ninth resolution resulted in its adoption.

Mrs. Gage then moved the adoption of the remaining resolutions without discussion.

This being contrary to the desire of the convention, the resolutions were considered one by one.

Speaking upon the second resolution, Mr. Willcox,[20] of New York, said that the woman's movement was almost the only chivalrous one of the nineteenth century. In effect it said to the world, since men refuse to give women adequate protection, we purpose to arm woman with a weapon by which she could protect herself. That weapon was the ballot.

Mrs. Gage continued the reading of the resolutions one by one, and they were adopted as above, by the convention.

≈ *NCBB*, August 1878.

1. In her draft ECS echoed language from 1848: "to discuss our rights & wrongs as citizens of a republic." She altered and updated the manuscript to read as published.

2. After repeated attempts to revise this sentence, ECS struck out her work and wrote between the lines "substitute (intuitively)." She did not, however, complete the sentence in the manuscript, to explain what they had intuited in 1848. That appears only in the published text.

3. Davis spoke on 10 July 1878 in Mississippi about the South's experience of oppression by the federal government since the Civil War. The rivalry between the Romans Gaius Julius Caesar (100–44 B.C.) and Marcus Junius Brutus (85–42 B.C.) is depicted in William Shakespeare, *Julius Caesar*. (Dunbar Rowland, ed., *Jefferson Davis, Constitutionalist: His Letters, Papers and Speeches* [Jackson, Miss., 1923], 8:235; with the assistance of Lynda L. Crist, Rice University.)

4. Both were weapons—a musket and a cannon—used during the Civil War.

5. This and the previous paragraph are not in the manuscript, though an unfinished sentence on the final page suggests she planned this to be her conclusion.

6. On Frederick Douglass's part in the Seneca Falls woman's rights convention, see *Papers*, 1:75–88. ECS drafted a much longer section about the convention's uncertainty over the demand for suffrage and included in it details about her own role. By dropping it from the published text, she kept the spotlight on Douglass. In the manuscript after the Douglass tribute, ECS anticipated paying tribute to the Hutchinson Family for their years of singing at woman's rights conventions. Since none of them attended the Decade Celebration, she dropped the section. However, the *Rochester Union and Advertiser*, 19 July 1878, included in its report a short paragraph that would have introduced her tribute: "Herbert Spencer, in one of his essays, says music is the highest form of language touching deep and tender chords in our natures that respond to no other speech." Gage removed the paragraph from her report.

7. Although Theodore Stanton attended and spoke to the congress, Jane Grahame Jones was the official delegate of the National Woman Suffrage

Association. On the opening day, her sixteen-year-old daughter Genevieve charmed the audience by delivering the National's greetings in French. Theodore Stanton spoke on 28 July about the history of the movement in the United States. ECS struck from her manuscript the next paragraph, a long, sarcastic list of impossible men whom she might forgive for past insults in light of her joy over her son's part in the French congress. Her list included the male voters of New York State, the marshal who arrested SBA, Supreme Court Justice Ward Hunt, and Senator Bainbridge Wadleigh. (*Congrès international du droit des femmes. Ouvert à Paris, le 25 juillet 1878, clos le 9 août suivant. Actes. Compte rendu des séances plénières* [Paris, n.d.]; *NCBB*, September 1878; *History*, 3:896–99.)

8. Matilda Gage here reworked a confused final sentence reported in the *Rochester Union and Advertiser*: "Our growth is your development, your inspiration our hopes, your triumph, our success your victory."

9. In his first annual message, President Hayes asked Congress to pass a law that would allow Native Americans "the privileges of citizenship" if they detached themselves from their tribes and proved their ability to support their families. (Fred L. Israel, ed., *The State of the Union Messages of the Presidents, 1790–1966* [New York, 1967], 2:1350–51; Mardock, *Reformers and the American Indian*, 83, 150–67.)

10. In re Ah Yup, 1 Federal Cases 223 (C.C.D. Cal. 1878) (No. 104). Lorenzo Sawyer (1820–1891), judge of the United States Circuit Court for the Ninth Circuit in California, ruled that the naturalization laws did not permit Chinese immigrants to become citizens because Congress specifically excluded them from the category of white people. Ah Yup's application for citizenship was denied. (*DAB*.)

11. Just as it happened in Seneca Falls in 1848, so in Rochester in 1878, a prominent local minister preached against the resolutions on the Sunday after the women's meeting adjourned. At the First Baptist Church, the Rev. A. H. Strong, president of the Rochester Theological Seminary, chose as his text Genesis 2:18, "It is not good that man should be alone; I will make him an help meet for him." Strong thanked Frederick Douglass for this intervention in the convention's debate, and he reminded the congregation (and Monday's readers of the newspaper) that "all that woman has she owes to Christianity, and all that she has won has been won by the increasing power of this very gospel of self-sacrifice, which she is now called upon to reject." (Rochester *Democrat and Chronicle*, 22 July 1878, SBA scrapbook 8, Rare Books, DLC; *Papers*, 1:88–94.)

12. Rev. 21:1. Below Mott adapts Matt. 9:37–38 and Luke 10:2 about the need for workers when the harvest is ripe.

13. Matt. 25:1–13.

14. Lucy Newhall Danforth Colman (1817–1906), an old friend of Douglass who helped integrate the public schools of Rochester before the war, was the

matron of the National Colored Orphan Asylum in Washington during the war. She returned north to Syracuse to lecture and write on free thought. (*ANB*; *NCAB*, 4:229-30.)

15. Lewis Henry Douglass (1840-1908) and Charles Remond Douglass (1844-1920) enlisted in the 54th Massachusetts Infantry Regiment in 1863. (Douglass, *Papers*, 4:279n, 232-33n; John R. McKivigan, "A Black Family's Civil War," *Annotation* 28 [September 2000]:16-17.)

16. Helen Mar Almy Slocum (1826-1882) was a leader in the city and state suffrage associations of New York as well as in the National. A native of Vermont, she married Volney Peleg Slocum, a physician of Washington County, New York, in 1846. Back in Vermont around 1870, she was a leader among the state's spiritualists, but when she attended the nominating convention of Victoria Woodhull's presidential campaign in 1872 to speak about labor reform, she had returned to New York. Later that year, she and her husband moved to New York City. She took part in the first Woman's Congress in 1873 and was elected to office in the National Woman Suffrage Association in 1874. At the time of her death, Slocum chaired the executive committee of the state society and was first vice president of the New York City society. (*Woodhull and Claflin's Weekly*, 25 May 1872, *Film*, 16:104-9; *Woman's Journal*, 3 June 1882; *NCBB*, September, October 1880; Charles Elihu Slocum, *History of the Slocums, Slocumbs and Slocombs of America, Genealogical and Biographical* [Defiance, Ohio, 1908], 2:284.)

17. Catherine H. Sands, a farmer's wife from Canandaigua, New York, signed the call to the woman's rights convention at Rochester in 1853 and spoke "a few words of encouragement" at the meeting. She and her husband, James B. Sands, also hosted SBA at their home during the woman's rights canvass in 1855. At this meeting she was listed as a delegate from Ontario County. Although Sands indicated in her remarks that she was born in 1800, her age in 1850 was given as forty-five. (*Frederick Douglass' Paper*, 16 December 1853, *Film*, 7:844ff; Federal Census, 1850; *Papers*, 1:294-95.)

18. Lavinia C. Dundore, the National's key person in Maryland, organized an equal rights association in Baltimore in 1867 and represented the group at conventions in Washington until the late 1870s, when she moved to the capital. She also tried to register to vote in 1870. Not until 1886 did directories identify Dundore as a widow—variously of Henry or Harry—but as early as 1870 they listed her by her own name and occupation. In 1874, she described her business as "bounty and pension claims," to which she added an employment bureau by 1891. At the National's meeting in January 1878, Belva Lockwood spoke about a failed attempt to have Dundore appointed a constable by the District of Columbia courts. (*History*, 2:522, 542, 583, 3:73-74, 128, 151, 815, 816, 4:248; Baltimore city directory, 1870, 1871, 1873, 1874; Washington city directory, 1880 to 1892; *Woman's Journal*, 19 January 1878, *Film*, 19:1022-23.)

19. A reference to Gen. 2:22–23, in which God took a rib from man and "made he a woman" to be man's help meet.

20. John Keappock Hamilton Willcox (1842–1898), known as Hamilton, was a founder of the Universal Franchise Association in Washington and tireless worker for woman suffrage in the District of Columbia. By 1874, back in his native New York City as a writer with the *Journal of Commerce*, he took a major role in state suffrage agitation. (Columbia University, *Alumni Register, 1754–1931* [New York, 1932]; Walter Dyson, *Howard University, The Capstone of Negro Education. A History, 1867–1940* [Washington, D.C., 1941], 163, 335; *History*, 3:959–61, 4:856; *Papers*, 2:140n.)

## 143 ⤳ ECS to the Editor, *Index*

Tenafly, N.J., July 22, 1878.

To the Editor of The Index:—

Allow me to call the attention of your readers to the resolutions passed at the Third Decade Meeting of the National Woman Suffrage Association held at Rochester, July 19, which have been already sent to your journal.

I think our liberal friends will find those touching the religious element of woman's nature sufficiently broad to assure them that these women, armed with ballots, will not prove the dangerous element so many fear on the side of priestcraft and superstition.[1] The contemptuous treatment of women by the popular churches, the resolutions of synods and general assemblies as to the Divine Will in favor of woman's complete subjugation, the trials and tribulations of eminent clergymen who have recognized her equality, have at last emancipated a rapidly increasing class of women from all fear and respect for such authorities. We have really been persecuted into the higher position to which reason failed to lift us. Once more has bigotry done the world good service, by launching another class on the sea of reason.

We had a large and enthusiastic convention, the last session in Corinthian Hall continuing until eleven o'clock at night, although the heat was almost unendurable.

One of the marked features of this convention was the very respectful and complimentary tone of the entire press of the city of Rochester.

Enclosed find five dollars for *The Index*, which I find full of valuable instruction every week, and, with its reports from the various Liberal Leagues forming all over the country, full of hope for the preservation of the secular character of our government.[2] Yours with great respect,

⤳ *Elizabeth Cady Stanton.*

⤳ Boston *Index*, 1 August 1878.

1. Francis E. Abbot did indeed welcome the resolutions on religion, hailing them "with the greatest satisfaction" and blessing them as "a bold, dignified, and magnificent utterance," for which he credited ECS and Matilda Gage. He tempered his enthusiasm, however, by placing his praise at the end of a long editorial reminding his readers that freethinkers resisted universal suffrage because "the average woman is far more easily influenced by the clergy than the average man," while the clergy casts its lot with despotism. Three resolutions struck a "great and victorious blow," Abbot conceded, but now "the whole woman movement must obey the inspiration of a higher courage and a grander spirit than have been known to its past." (Boston *Index*, 1 August 1878.)

2. Local Liberal Leagues sprang up in response to Francis Abbot's call in January 1873 for secularists to organize in support of his "Nine Demands of Liberalism." By the end of 1875, there were 30 leagues across the country whose members came together in 1876 to form the National Liberal League. By 1879, the number had grown to 162 leagues. Sympathetic to their cause, ECS prepared two lectures about the league in 1877, endorsing its demand that church property be taxed and explaining its goal of complete secularization of government. Local leagues, such as those in Wausau and Manitowoc, Wisconsin, scheduled her to speak in 1878. SBA, who also found leagues willing to organize her lectures, was less enthusiastic about support from this quarter, noting in a midwestern town that Liberal League sponsorship frightened away "the religionists." (Ahlstrom and Mullin, *Scientific Theist*, 102–5, 124; *Milwaukee Sentinel*, 4, 16 March, 23 May 1878; ECS lecture on purposes of Liberal Leagues, ECS lecture on taxation of church property, and SBA diary, 11 April 1878, *Film*, 19:752–82, 791ff.)

## 144 &#126; ECS TO LUCY STONE

Tenafly N.J July 31$^{st}$ [*1878*]

Mrs Lucy Stone  Dear Madam,

We have not yet prepared the personal sketches.[1] When we do so I will gladly send you yours, & all chapters in which you are mentioned Better still if any friend of yours in whom you have confidence would prepare a biography of you, & a chapter on the work of your American association, it shall go in just as you send it.

We shall publish chapter by chapter in our paper, & invite all friends to make suggestions, & corrections as to omissions, & commissions before putting it in book form.[2]

It is our intention to be just & fair to all. Thanks for your kind mention of my daughter  She is to go to the school of oratory in Boston this winter.[3] If you would like to see each chapter before going to the paper & make suggestions I should be very happy to send them to you  you might think of something interesting of those early days to add  I would like to see your editorial on Wadleighs report. I heard it was very good.[4] With kind regards for yourself & Mr Blackwell  respt yours

&#126; *Elizabeth Cady Stanton.*

&#126; ALS, NAWSA Papers, DLC.

1. For the volume of history. Stone's query of ECS has not been found.

2. Matilda Gage announced this plan in the *National Citizen and Ballot Box* in May, stating that the first six chapters were complete and would be published serially, beginning in the issue of September 1878. (*NCBB*, May, August 1878.)

3. Harriot Stanton enrolled in Boston University's School of Oratory for the academic year of 1878 and 1879. (Research by Katherine Kominis, Special Collections, Boston University.)

4. Stone's editorial read: "The Committee on 'Privileges and Elections,' in their report against submitting a Sixteenth Amendment, urge that women are 'a dependent class,' and are not to be trusted with the ballot, because they must necessarily be so much under the control of those on whom they depend.

"I have not the report at hand, and so cannot quote its exact words; but the above is the meaning of it. This is the first time in the history of the Woman's Rights Movement, that any set of objectors or opponents have, in this bold way, used the very condition from which women are striving to be relieved, as a reason why they should not be relieved.

"There is something unspeakably hard and cruel in it. Women know that they are a subject class. Many of them never cease to feel the sting and the hurt of it. They can never cease their effort to escape. But it adds insult to injury, to have this very fact used as a cudgel by those who have subjugated us, to compel us to remain subjugated.

"This report of the Senatorial Committee should spur every woman to fresh resistance, and to redoubled activity, to conquer her right to independence." (*Woman's Journal*, 6 July 1878.)

145 &#8766; SPEECH BY SBA TO NATIONAL PARTY
        MEETING IN ROCHESTER

EDITORIAL NOTE: SBA addressed a local meeting called to fuse the Greenback and Labor Reform parties into a single National party, ready to compete in the fall elections of 1878. Born of a convention held in Toledo, Ohio, in February 1878, the new party combined Greenback proposals for paper currency with demands of labor such as reduced hours and government bureaus of labor statistics. New York's statewide party organized in July 1878, and although the party did not gain strong support in New York that year, the National party as a whole elected fifteen members of Congress and drew more than a million voters to its candidates. The *New York Times* reprinted SBA's speech (and only her speech) from coverage of the meeting in the Rochester *Democrat and Chronicle*. Because copies of the Rochester paper have not been found, SBA's reference to a previous speaker whose remarks triggered her own cannot be explained.

[1 August 1878]

Working men of Rochester and Fellow-citizens—For you all know I claim to be a fellow-citizen with the best working men in town: When your committee asked me to address the meeting this evening, I told them that I did not see how I could, for I had nothing to say. But in reply to what the last speaker has said about the approaching recognition of women in the National Government, I can only say that we are waiting for the time to come when some political party shall put a plank in its platform that will make it possible for us women with self-respect to work with that party for the public good. The very first thing for the men of this National Party to do, if they want women to help them, is to go to work and help the women. Starting out in its career, as this new party is to-day, it cannot afford to ignore this question of equal rights on the one hand, or of the disfranchisement of one-half of the people on the other. We were given to understand by the Republican Party in 1872 that we might expect a recognition at their hands as citizens, provided their campaign should terminate in success. They pressed on to re-elect Gen. Grant to the Presidency, but when other women went with me to the polls to aid them and exercise our right of franchise as American citizens, the officers of the Republican Party arrested us as criminals, and when it was found impossible to find a jury in Monroe County so dishonorable as to convict us for that act, we were taken into another county to be tried, but there the result was the same. Finding that they could not convict us by jury, they very bravely called upon a United States Judge to declare us women guilty. And though they cast into jail the Inspector of Election who permitted us to vote, we saw that he had good dinners while in prison. Fines were imposed upon us for having exercised the privilege of suffrage, but not a dollar of my fine was ever paid, or ever will be. All this from the political party which had led us to look to it for aid. When you of the new National Party are for equal rights to women, that moment I will stand on your platform, no matter whether you are for greenbacks or for silver; for free trade or protection.

⌇ *New York Times,* 4 August 1878.

## 146 &#x1F340; LUCY STONE TO SBA

Office of *The Woman's Journal*. 4 Park St., Boston, Mass.,

Aug. 7, 1878.

Miss Anthony:

The papers report you as saying at a political convention in Rochester, lately, that "the Suffragists will go for any party, of any name, that
will give us a suffrage plank." Will you send us your exact language, or
if you do not recall that, your exact meaning and oblige,

&#x1F340; *Lucy Stone.*

&#x1F340; *NCBB*, September 1878.

## 147 &#x1F340; SBA TO LUCY STONE

Rochester, N.Y., Aug. 9, 1878.

My Olden-time Friend, Lucy Stone:

To your letter of the 7th inst., asking me if I was rightly reported as
saying "the Suffragists will go for any party of any name that will give us
a suffrage plank," I answer "Yes," save that I used the pronoun "I"
instead of "the Suffragists."

I spoke for myself, alone, because I know so many of our women are
so much more intensely republican or democratic, hard-money or
greenback, free trade or tariff, prohibition or license, than they are
"*Equal Rights for all*," that they will now, as in the past, hold the
question of woman's enfranchisement in abeyance, while they give
their money and their best energies to secure the success of one or the
other of the contending parties, though it wholly ignores their just
claim to a voice in the government.

It is not that I have no opinions or preferences on the many grave
questions that distract and divide the parties; but it is that, in my
judgment, "*the right of self-government for one-half the people*" is of far

more vital consequence to the nation than any or all other questions put together.

And this has been my position ever since the abolition of slavery, by which the black race was lifted from chattelism to citizenship, and invested with civil rights equal with the best cultured, tax-paying white women of the country. Have you forgotten the cry, *"this is the negro's hour,"* that came back to us in 1866,[1] when we urged the abolitionists to make common cause with us, and demand suffrage *as a right* for all United States citizens, instead of asking it, simply *as an expedient* for another class of men? Do you not remember, too, how the taunt "false to the negro" was flung back into the face of every one of us who insisted that it was "humanity's hour," and that to talk of "freedom without the ballot" was no less "mockery" to woman, than to the "negro?"

Surely, you cannot have forgotten that it was on this very point—of having but one article in our political creed, "woman, and her disfranchised," and our welcoming the aid of every person and every party that subscribed to that article, democrat though he, or it might be—that you, yourself, in 1869, refused to affiliate with the "National Woman Suffrage Association," Elizabeth Cady Stanton, president, called the Cleveland Convention, organized the "American Woman Suffrage Association," as against the "National," and thereby divided our woman suffrage ranks from ocean to ocean.[2]

And if, in those most trying reconstruction years, I could not subordinate the fundamental principle of *"Equal rights for all"* to the republican party necessity for "Negro Suffrage,"—that is, if I would not then, in that fearful national emergency, sacrifice "the greater to the less," I surely cannot and will not to-day, hold any of the far less important party questions, paramount to that most sacred principle of our Republic. As you and I and all women are political slaves, it ill becomes us to meddle with the weightier discussions of our sovereign masters. It will be quite time enough for us, with self-respect, to declare ourselves for or against this party or that, upon the intrinsic merit of its policy, when they shall recognize us as their political equals, duly register our names, and respectfully count our opinions at the ballot box, as a constitutional right—not a high crime, punishable with "$500 fine, or six months imprisonment, or both, at the discretion of the Court."[3]

If all "the Suffragists" of all the States could but see eye to eye on this point, and stand shoulder to shoulder against any and every party and politician not fully and unequivocally committed to "Equal Rights for Woman," we should, at once, become a balance of power that could not fail to compel the party of highest intelligence to proclaim Woman Suffrage the chief plank of its platform. "In union there is strength."

And until that good day comes, I shall continue to invoke the party in power, and each one struggling to get into power, be it republican, democratic, greenback or prohibition, to pledge itself to the emancipation of our enslaved half of the people; and in turn, I shall promise to do all that a "subject" can do, for the success of the party that thus declares its purpose "to undo the heavy burdens and let the oppressed go free."[4]

To illustrate: when, six or seven years ago, the Prohibitionists and Working-men of Massachusetts, each put a Woman Suffrage plank in its platform, and each nominated for governor, Wendell Phillips,—our life long friend and advocate—"the Suffragists" of that State, putting aside all party allegiance, republican and democratic alike, should have inscribed on their banners, in letters of gold, the name of *Wendell Phillips*; and branded "traitor" on the forehead of every one of their number who spoke or voted for any other than Wendell Phillips for governor.[5] Yours as ever,

ᐊ *Susan B. Anthony.*

ᐊ *NCBB*, September 1878.

1. When Wendell Phillips became president of the American Anti-Slavery Society in May 1865 and announced his goals for Reconstruction, he added that he would not yet ask for woman suffrage, saying, "One question at a time. This hour belongs to the negro." His conviction divided abolitionists for many years. (Boston *Liberator*, 19 May 1865.)

2. Lucy Stone drafted a reply to this letter for the *National Citizen*, seizing upon SBA's characterization of the split between the National and American associations. The American was founded, she wrote, because in 1867 SBA associated with George Francis Train, who "was a lunatic and at every meeting brought only derision to the woman suffragists," and then created the impression that Train spoke "either under the auspices of the [American Equal Rights] Association or had its approval." Skipping over the founding of the National in May 1869, Stone leapt from the disagreements within the equal rights association to the start of the American in November of the same year. "The results have shown the wisdom of this action," she continued; SBA's society had associated with Victoria Woodhull, bringing "all the odium" of

her free love theories upon the cause. By making known its lack of sympathy with Woodhull, the American "was a wall of defence around the Principle itself." "To this day, both Mrs Woodhull and Mr. Train are weights which the suffrage cause" must carry. Neither the *National Citizen* nor the *Woman's Journal* published Stone's letter. (L. Stone to Matilda J. Gage, 1878, NAWSA Papers, DLC.)

3. SBA paraphrases the Enforcement Act of 31 May 1870, under which she was convicted of voting illegally in 1873. (*U.S. Statutes at Large* 16 [1870]: 140–46.)

4. Isa. 58:6.

5. SBA revives an old argument with Stone about the Massachusetts guber-natorial election of 1870, when the Labor Reform and Prohibition parties both nominated Wendell Phillips. She is in error about the platforms endorsing woman suffrage, but Phillips made clear his own support for the cause. The Massachusetts Woman Suffrage Association refused to support his candidacy, and according to Phillips, Stone and the *Woman's Journal* were rewarded by leading Republicans for that decision. (*Appleton's Annual Cyclopaedia, 1870*, 473–77; *Woman's Journal*, 22 October 1870; SBA diary, 18 December 1870, *Film*, 14:173ff; *Papers* 2:390n, 411–14.)

## 148 ॐ MARY BRAYTON WOODBRIDGE[1] TO SBA

Ravenna [*Ohio*] Aug 22[d] 1878

Miss Susan B. Anthony,

The inclosed card will explain my addressing you at this time.[2] I was made Ch[m] of the Petition Com of the W.N.C.T.U. at its last session, the petition after long discussion <u>having been provided</u>. The petition amounts to nothing.[3] Elizabeth Churchill[4] refuses to act, not being in unity with its sentiments. One member of the C[om] has never been found, & I have taken no action. I am greatly obliged to F. E. W.[5] for her [sugge]stion, & shall be most grateful [to] you for your ideas upon the subject of petitions. I was delighted with the force & form of the W.S. petition last year circulated. I am shocked at the tameness & want of scope of our temperance petitions, & begin to fear that the <u>Body</u> will never stand upon broad ground, until there is radical change in its elements. Do you take the Woman's paper "Our Union" published at Brooklyn?[6] Lest you do not I take the liberty of forwarding one, & will thank you for your opinion of the first article—[7] You may not agree with me, but I am stirred to the debths— There has been constant censorship of the press within that office since our last meeting, because forsooth, stirred by a resolution then passed,[8] there was danger that woman suffrage might creep out, or in & [the] hope it may be kept out, for women [who] [*illegible*] thus palliate sin & ↑are↓ are not com[petent] advocates of any good cause. Hoping to hear from you soon, & to receive your "ideas" in full—I am Yours Truly

⤙ *Mary A. Woodbridge*

⤙ ALS, HM 10568, Ida Harper Collection, CSmH. Square brackets surround words obscured by damage to both sides of the sheet.

1. Mary Ann Brayton Woodbridge (1830–1894), a strong advocate of woman suffrage among leaders of the Woman's Christian Temperance Union, was preparing for the union's annual meeting, where once again the argument over votes for women dominated discussions. Woodbridge founded the local union in her hometown of Ravenna, presided over the Ohio union, and in 1878, began fifteen years of service as the national union's recording secretary. (*SEAP*; *American Women*.)

2. Enclosure missing.

3. In October 1877. Woodbridge reported to the convention the committee's preference for a petition to Congress in favor of a constitutional amendment prohibiting the distillation or importation of liquor after the year 1900. The delegates would not accept it, and the committee returned later to propose a petition "for the appointment of a commission to enquire into the iniquities of the liquor traffic." (*Chicago Tribune*, 26, 27 October 1877.)

4. Elizabeth Kittredge Churchill (1821–1881) of Providence, a widow supporting young children as a writer and lecturer, helped to found the Rhode Island Woman Suffrage Association in 1868 and worked closely with the American and New England associations of Lucy Stone. She also joined the Woman's Christian Temperance Union. (*History*, 2:337, 404, 766, 820, 839, 848; 3:268, 269, 340; *Woman's Journal*, 12 March 1881.)

5. That is, Frances E. Willard.

6. *Our Union* was the official organ of the National Woman's Christian Temperance Union, published in Brooklyn, New York. When an article in favor of the home protection ballot appeared in the paper in 1878, powerful groups in the national union objected and withdrew support, causing the publication committee to ban the topic and seek the advice of the upcoming national convention. Willard's allies won the convention's support to open the paper to reports on suffrage activities and establish a column on home protection. *Our Union* later merged with the paper of the Illinois state union to become the *Union Signal*. (*Woman's Journal*, 18 January 1879; Willard, *Woman and Temperance*, 171–72.)

7. This article is not identified.

8. She referred to a resolution declaring that women should have a voice in local decisions about liquor as an extension of their responsibility for educating children. Opponents of woman suffrage within the temperance union denounced it but met defeat in a close vote on its adoption. At the meeting in the fall of 1878, opponents returned to the question and won passage of a statement that whatever individuals believed, "we deprecate the introduction of any side question, and recommend the presentation of our cause from a gospel standpoint." (*Chicago Tribune*, 28 October 1877; *Woman's Journal*, 18 January 1879.)

## 149 &#8260; ADDRESS BY SBA

Rochester, Sept. 2, 1878.

### ADDRESS OF THE
### NATIONAL WOMAN SUFFRAGE ASSOCIATION
#### TO THE
### FRIENDS OF EQUAL SUFFRAGE FOR WOMAN.

In pursuance of instructions of the annual meeting held in Rochester, N.Y., July 18th, 1878, the Executive Committee present to you the following statement of work done and to be done during the 45th Congress.[1]

#### WORK DONE.

Since the assembling of the first regular session, Dec. 3d, 1877, forty thousand men and women have petitioned Congress for a 16th amendment prohibiting States from disfranchising United States citizens on account of sex. The signatures were obtained by 1,020 women in 425 towns, 125 Congressional districts, 35 States and five Territories, and duly presented to Congress by 55 Senators and 100 representatives.

Jan. 10th, 1878, Senator Sargent of California introduced a joint resolution proposing a 16th amendment for the enfranchisement of woman.

Jan. 11th and 12th the Senate Committee reported adversely:[2] their report is now on the calendar, subject to action at the next session of Congress. The Senators endorsing it are Wadleigh, N.H.; McMillan,

Minn.; Saulsbury, Del.; Merrimon, S.C.;[3] Hill, Ga., and Ingalls, Kansas. Those in favor of the 16th amendment, Senators Hoar, Mass., Mitchell, Oregon and Cameron, Wis.; are expected to bring in a favorable minority report at the opening of the second session, December next.

Feb. 5th the House Judiciary Committee voted upon a resolution recommending our proposed 16th amendment which resulted in a tie:[4] *Yeas*, Lapham, N.Y.;[5] Lynde, Wis.; Frye, Me.; Butler, Mass.; Conger, Mich.[6] *Nays*, Knott, Ky.; Hartridge, Ga.; Stenger, Penn.; McMahon, Ohio; Culberson, Texas.[7] *Absent*, Harris of Virginia[8] who has declared himself open to conviction.

During the last session of Congress the temperance women of the nation sent up a petition of 30,000, praying for "Home Protection."[9] Though asking to have their opinions counted on the one question of licensing the liquor traffic, we may rightfully add them to our 40,000, thus making us a 70,000 prayer for the national protection of women in their citizen's right to a voice in the government.

The bill admitting women to practice before the Supreme Court unanimously reported by the Judiciary Committee and passed in the House of Representatives by a vote of 169 to 87,[10] stands upon the Senate calendar with adverse report of its Judiciary Committee to be acted upon at the coming session.[11]

The individual petitions of 300 women of the various States, asking Congress to remove their political disabilities, received no attention— were not even noticed by adverse reports—while similar petitions from nine disfranchised men were each promptly acted upon, and their political rights restored.[12]

## WORK TO BE DONE.

1st. Let all who failed to send 16th amendment petitions to Washington last winter, sign, circulate and mail them, pre-paid (letter postage, remember) to our Recording Secretary, Ellen H. Sheldon,[13] No. 1011 M. Street, N.W. Washington, D.C., on or before the 25th of November, 1878, that they may be in the hands of Senators Hoar, Mitchell and Cameron when they present their minority report, which we hope and expect will be in the first week in December. Please note, friends, that we are not asking to roll up a new petition to a new Congress, but simply to get all the new names you can to send to the 2d session of the same Congress, to add to the 40,000 presented last winter.

2d. To the 70,000 petitions for woman's right of representation now before the 45th Congress, we wish to add the weight of the opinions of the friends of woman suffrage in the Legislatures of the several States and Territories. To secure such expression, we ask the suffragists throughout the country to petition their respective Legislatures asking them to pass resolutions recommending Congress to submit a 16th amendment proposition to the States.

3d. We ask the officers of the National Woman Suffrage Association, representing the different States, to call conventions at their Capital city early in the session of their Legislature and make special effort to secure action on the 16th amendment resolution.

4th. We urge the friends, everywhere, to call public meetings, get the best local speakers, and at the close of each meeting take a *standing vote* on our 16th amendment question, duly count it and send two reports thereof, signed by the President and Secretary of the meeting to our Secretary, Ellen H. Sheldon, No. 1011 M. Street, N.W. Washington, D.C., for presentation to Congress, and two to the State Vice Pres. of the N.W.S.A. for presentation to your Legislature.

5th. Let the Temperance organizations of the country secure a vote of their members upon our question and send reports thereof duly signed by their officers on behalf of the number who desire the enfranchisement of women.

6th. Let every woman send to one of the Senators or Representatives of her State an individual petition to Congress for the removal of her own political disabilities.

7th. Let women by the hundreds and thousands each address the Senators and Representatives of her State, both in Congress and Legislature, asking them to vote for the 16th amendment resolution. Such direct personal appeals, by voice or letter, will have far more weight than the same words in form of a petition, and will compel our lawmakers to feel that we are not discouraged by their indifference or adverse reports, but instead, are stimulated to more earnest and determined efforts to secure national protection in our citizen's right to vote.

8th. Below we give forms for the several petitions[14]—we ask our friends to copy them with *ink* for themselves, in a clear, legible hand,[15] obtain signatures immediately and forward, postage paid, to the proper place and person—those for Congress to the Secretary of the N.W.S.A.,

Ellen H. Sheldon, No. 1011 M. Street, N.W. Washington, D.C., on or before Nov. 25, 1878; those for the Legislature to the Vice Pres. of the N.W.S.A. of your State, on or before Jan. 1st, 1879.

9th. For the whole thirty years of our woman suffrage work the one great hindrance has been lack of money to meet the necessary expenses, and to-day it is no exception. We need money to publish tracts, send out lecturers, hold conventions and for other manifold purposes. We therefore urge our friends everywhere to send contributions by draft on New York or by P.O. Order to our treasurer, Ellen C. Sargent, 1733 DeSales St. Washington, D.C.

10th. And last, To save the National Woman Suffrage Association the labor and expense of printing and posting the tens of thousands calls, appeals and petitions, which we have heretofore incurred, (the past year, alone, at cost of $1,000) we urge all wishing to co-operate with us to subscribe, at once, for the *National Citizen and Ballot Box*, which will hereafter be our medium of communication with friends and workers. On behalf Executive Committee N.W.S.A.

ᔥ *Susan B. Anthony, Chairman*

ᔥ *National Citizen and Ballot Box. Extra*, n.d., M. J. Gage scrapbooks, Rare Books, DLC.

1. SBA no doubt worked out the details of this appeal with Matilda Gage on her visit to Fayetteville, New York, on August 31 and September 1. (SBA diary, 1878, *Film*, 19:791ff.)

2. On these dates, the Senate Committee on Privileges and Elections held hearings on Senate Resolution 12. The adverse majority report was presented on 14 June 1878, but the Senate had not yet discussed the resolution.

3. The only member of the Committee on Privileges and Elections not yet identified is Augustus Summerfield Merrimon (1830–1892), Democrat of North Carolina, a senator from 1873 to 1879. Along with Thomas F. Bayard, Merrimon led the debate in 1874 against allowing women to vote in Pembina Territory. (*BDAC*.)

4. The House Committee on the Judiciary held two hearings on the sixteenth amendment in January before reaching an impasse on 5 February 1878 in a vote on reporting the measure to the House of Representatives. (*History*, 3:103; *New York Times*, 6 February 1878.)

5. Elbridge Gerry Lapham (1814–1890), of Canandaigua, New York, entered the House of Representatives in 1875 as a Republican and served there until he entered the Senate in 1881 to complete the term of Roscoe Conkling. He was a cousin of SBA through their grandparents, the siblings David Lapham and Hannah Lapham Anthony. (*BDAC*.)

6. Other committee members who joined Lapham and Benjamin Butler in supporting the amendment were: William Pitt Lynde (1817–1885), Democrat of Wisconsin, in the House of Representatives from 1875 to 1879; William Pierce Frye (1830–1911), Republican of Maine, who served from 1871 to 1881; and Omar Dwight Conger (1818–1898), Republican of Michigan, who served from 1869 to 1881. Frye and Conger both entered the Senate in 1881. (*BDAC*.)

7. Committee members who opposed the amendment were: James Proctor Knott (1830–1911), Democrat of Kentucky, in the House of Representatives from 1867 to 1871 and again from 1875 to 1883; Julian Hartridge (1829–1879), Democrat of Georgia, who served from 1875 until his death; William Shearer Stenger (1840–1918), Democrat of Pennsylvania, who served from 1875 to 1879; John A. McMahon (1833–1923), Democrat of Ohio, in the House from 1875 to 1881; and David Browning Culberson (1830–1900), Democrat of Texas, in the House from 1875 to 1897. (*BDAC*.)

8. John Thomas Harris (1823–1899), Democrat of Virginia, served in the House of Representatives from 1859 to 1861 and again from 1871 to 1881. (*BDAC*.)

9. This was the National Woman's Christian Temperance Union's memorial seeking a voice for women in decisions about prohibition in the territories and District of Columbia, signed by more than thirty thousand citizens. When William Frye presented it in the House of Representatives on 30 January 1878, he spoke about woman suffrage, but the memorial asked that women's views be solicited only by petition. (*Congressional Record*, 45th Cong., 2d sess., 671–72.)

10. On 21 February 1878, Benjamin Butler presented the favorable report of the House Committee on the Judiciary on H.R. 1077, the bill drafted by Belva Lockwood after she was denied admission to the Supreme Court, and he called for an immediate vote. This was the second roll call vote in the House of Representatives on women's right to practice law in federal courts, and support, as SBA indicates, had grown considerably since 1874. (*Congressional Record*, 43d Cong., 1st sess., 1 June 1874, p. 4447, and 45th Cong., 2d sess., 21 February 1878, p. 1235; Stern, *We the Women*, 216–18.)

11. On 18 March 1878, George Edmunds reported against the Lockwood bill for the Senate Committee on the Judiciary, arguing that no law barred women from practicing before the courts and that the Supreme Court should decide its own rules of admission. At the request of Senator Sargent, H.R. 1077 was placed on the calendar, and when it was called up on April 22, Sargent amended the bill and asked that it go back to the committee. On May 21, Senator Thurman presented another adverse report from the Judiciary Committee, and again Sargent asked that H.R. 1077 be placed on the calendar. On a test vote to see if the Senate would agree to discuss the bill on May 29, the senators divided evenly, twenty-nine to twenty-nine, and the bill was not debated. (*Congressional Record*, 45th Cong., 2d sess., 18 March, 22 April, 20, 29 May 1878, pp. 1821, 2704–5, 3558–59, 3889–90.)

12. On this group of successful southern petitioners for the removal of their political disabilities, see *Congressional Record*, 45th Cong., 2d sess., 5, 13, 15, 19 June 1878, pp. 4117–18, 4551, 4686–87, 4840.

13. Ellen Harriet Sheldon (1841–1890), a New York native who worked as a clerk in the War Department in Washington, signed the 1874 petition for woman suffrage in the District of Columbia, and two years later she signed the Centennial Declaration of Rights. The press first noted her presence at meetings of the National association in 1877. Named recording secretary in 1879, she held office in the National until her death. While continuing to work as a clerk, Sheldon also studied medicine at Howard University from 1879 to 1884. Although she was not listed in the city directory as a physician until 1890, she had published two books about health: *Directions for Health on a Metaphysical Basis* (1886) and *All Causation Is In the Mind. Thought, the Causative Power of the Universe* (1889). (Gloria Moldow, *Women Doctors in Gilded-Age Washington: Race, Gender, and Professionalization* [Urbana, Ill., 1987], 19, 24, 139; *Register of Federal Officers*, 1873, 1876, 1878; Daniel Smith Lamb, comp., *Howard University Medical Department, Washington, D.C.: A Historical, Biographical and Statistical Souvenir* [Washington, D.C., 1900], with assistance of Clifford L. Muse, Jr., Howard University; city directories, 1876 to 1890; Federal Census, 1880; Washington *National Republican*, 22 January 1874, E. H. Sheldon to SBA, 16, 23 August 1887, and SBA diary, 6–7 March 1890, *Film*, 17:943, 25:610–17, 627–31, 27:679ff.)

14. Petitions omitted. Those for the sixteenth amendment and for relief from political disabilities matched the texts above at 15 January 1878. The petition to state legislatures sought passage of a resolution reading: "That it is the duty of the American Congress to submit to the people of the United States through their several State Legislatures, an amendment to the Federal Constitution prohibiting the several States from disfranchising United States citizens on account of sex." In Minnesota, after the state suffrage association submitted the petition to the legislature, a majority in the senate supported the resolution, but the measure lost by five votes in the assembly. (*History*, 3:655.)

15. Further notice about handwritten petitions appeared on another page of the *National Citizen*'s "Extra" edition: "Write all petitions with ink. It is not deemed best to present printed petitions to Congress this year. In Great Britain, a printed petition is not allowed to go before Parliament, and in our Congress we found a growing objection to them last winter."

## 150 ⋙ ECS TO ELIZABETH SMITH MILLER

Tenafly, September 7, 1878.

Dearest Julius:

Maggie's wedding is to occur the 2nd. or 3rd. of October.[1] I want [y]ou to think and write me what you think we should do. If the day is warm [a]nd pleasant, we intend to have the ceremony under the trees; if not, in [t]he house. Tell me what you had at the Peterboro wedding; did you decorate [t]he house?[2] I do not care what the style in these matters is at the metro[p]olis; but I do wish to find out how we country people can have artistic, [s]imple arrangements. Maggie has been busy all day sorting her cloths and packing up what she intends to send on in advance. It has made me feel a little blue [t]o think how soon 1500 miles will stretch between us and what a serious [t]hing marriage, even under the best conditions, is with all its pitfalls. Lovingly,

⋙ *Johnson.*

⋙ Typed transcript, ECS Papers, NjR. Letters in square brackets obscured by binding.

1. Margaret Stanton was to marry Frank Eugene Lawrence (1848–1890). Lawrence was born in New York before his parents relocated to Council Bluffs, Iowa, where Margaret met him through her mother's old friends Amelia and Dexter Bloomer. "Report says," Elizabeth Harbert wrote in the press, that Margaret "who accompanied her mother on her lyceum trip last winter, has left her heart in the West, and that Frank Eugene Lawrence . . . is the happy recipient." At the time of their marriage, Frank Lawrence lived in Red Oak, Iowa, but he and Margaret soon settled in Council Bluffs. (Marriage return, New Jersey State Department of Health; Chicago *Inter-Ocean*, 22 June 1878, *Film*, 20:295; Federal Census, 1870; *History of Pottawattamie County, Iowa* [Chicago, 1883], pt. 2, p. 37.)

2. The last marriage in Miller's immediate family took place in November 1867 at Gerrit Smith's house in Peterboro, New York, between her son Gerrit Smith Miller and Susan Hunt Dixwell.

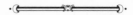

## 151   SBA to Isabella Beecher Hooker

Rochester Oct. 7, 1878

Dear Mrs Hooker

Yours of the 4th inst. is before me— I am notified that I am to begin my lecture work the 16th inst. much to my displeasure—for I had ordered "<u>no</u> work" till after Nov. elections—[1]

Then our dear Mother had a fall two weeks ago this A.M.—which affected very like the one of five years ago—when I was with you in Ct.— She has lain powerless to move her body or head—only able to move feet & legs & hands & arms—and is <u>translated</u> <u>intellectually</u> <u>back</u> to her young days, the people & the surroundings of youth— with everything strange about her—save my sister Mary & myself— But she has rallied a good deal—and the Doctor—yesterday—says she may live months & perchance years in this helpless condition— So we have a nurse—& are trying to adjust ourselves to the necessities of the hour— Still it hurts me very much to think of leaving her—for she <u>knows</u> us two girls—all she has left—and it seems cruel for me to go away—but & but—the work—the work—

So you must not depend on me— Still <u>if</u> & <u>if</u>—the <u>way</u> should be open—I should surely be with you— I hope Mrs Gage will go—her article on ↑the↓ <u>Labor</u> <u>Movement</u> <u>men</u> is <u>capital</u>[2]—they <u>care</u> only for <u>self</u>—are just as ready to take to <u>them</u> <u>selves</u> <u>womans</u> <u>chances</u> for bread—& pocket double the wages paid to the women workers by their side—as their so called Capitalists are to get all the work can out of them for as little money as possible—

So it is with the <u>Free Religionists</u>[3]— <u>Not</u> <u>one</u> of the <u>social</u>, Labor, religious ↑or↓ political reform movements has a thought of <u>woman</u> <u>as</u> <u>peer</u> <u>among</u> <u>them</u>—only for <u>Man</u> & him supreme— I have no patience with any of their pretensions—& shall [*sideways on first page*] keep my self <u>out</u> side of each & all of them—where I can <u>do</u> <u>battle</u> against their selfishness—

  S B. A.

  ALS, Isabella Hooker Collection, CtHSD.

1. Henry Slayton scheduled SBA to tour Ohio, Indiana, and New York from 16 October to 31 December 1878, speaking almost every night. In a letter now missing, Hooker probably invited SBA to attend the annual meeting of the Connecticut Woman Suffrage Association. (SBA diary, 1878, *Film*, 19:791ff.)

2. "Women, vs. the Labor Party," *NCBB*, October 1878. Gage criticized the new National party for ignoring the pleas of women, first at its founding convention in Toledo in February 1878 and again at the New York State convention in Syracuse in July. On the New York meeting, see *New York Tribune*, 25 July 1878. The National Woman Suffrage Association's posture toward the National party came up for discussion at the Washington convention in January 1879. When it was proposed that suffragists press the party to recognize "National citizenship as a kindred question with National currency, since both involve permanent justice to the laboring masses of men and women," Lillie Blake objected to attaching the suffrage movement to a party that already ignored them. Matilda Gage thought the demand improperly phrased: the party should be taught that "the question of National citizenship is one underlying National currency, as it is the vital question, and not a kindred question with the currency." The convention adopted Gage's amendment over Blake's continued objections, and the dispute surfaced again during the presidential campaign in the summer of 1880. (*NCBB*, February 1879, *Film*, 20:644–51.)

3. The National Liberal League and the New York State Freethinkers Association had both endorsed woman suffrage by this date, though neither body made it a priority. (Evelyn Anne Kirkley, "'The Female Peril': The Construction of Gender in American Freethought, 1865–1915" [Ph.D. diss., Duke University, 1993], 237–39; *Truth Seeker*, 3 November 1877.)

## 152   SBA to Rebecca Anne Smith Janney[1]

Wooster—O.[2] Nov. 2, 1878—

My Dear Friend

Pardon me for keeping your Journal so long—[3]  I mailed from Crestline, yesterday—and hope this A.M's mail delivered it to you.

And to day, I mail you a copy of "The National Citizen & Ballot Box["]—containing my letter in reply to Lucy Stone's—[4]  I hope you will not fail to read it—& wish I could hear your opinion of it. Do you not see that so long as the Republican Party—in whose ranks are our best <u>Woman</u> <u>Suffrage</u> & <u>Prohibition</u> men—<u>feel</u> <u>sure</u> of getting <u>their</u> <u>votes</u>—W.S. & Temp. plank or no plank—it will not be likely to put said planks in its platform— While if we could but hold <u>our</u> <u>Suffrage</u> & Prohibition men up to <u>voting</u> a <u>third</u> <u>party</u> <u>ticket</u>—or not voting at all— <u>until</u> the Repub. party should put <u>those two planks</u> ⏋in⏌ its platform— that would make the success of the Repub. Party <u>impossible</u>— So that just for the sake of getting back into power it would be compelled to <u>pledge</u> itself to both of our demands— Oh if I could but make our friends see eye to eye on this question—<u>this one point</u>—

At Westerville, I was the guest of President Thompson[5]—& met a warm welcome from both Mr & Mrs Thompson—& heard from them very many good words for & of Mrs Janney—

I hope you are getting better—your pale face has presented itself to me a great many times—

I hope you will be able to stir up your Columbus people to petition both state Legislature—& Congress—as recommended in our Ex. Com. Address—enclosed with Ballot Box—

I am to be in Ohio during all of this month—have my list of engagements up to the 23$^{\mathrm{d}}$ pretty nearly full—

With thanks for the reading of the Journal—but how I do wish they gave those women—<u>each</u> ⏋isolated⏌ <u>individual</u> in all the great states of the West a <u>work</u> <u>to</u> <u>do</u>—so that each could feel she could & <u>did</u> <u>help</u> on our good cause—for every woman who believes she ought to have the right to vote—<u>wants</u> to <u>help</u> <u>bring</u> the <u>day</u>—& <u>would</u> if we at the helm of the good ship would only show ⏋her⏌ how she could— Good bye— Sincerely as ever

⩗ *Susan B. Anthony*

⩗ ALS, Miscellaneous Mss.—R. A. S. Janney, NHi.

1. Rebecca Anne Smith Janney (1814–1886), a Quaker reformer from Columbus, Ohio, was active in the state association. She and SBA had known each other since the 1850s. (Biographical sketch, Janney Family Papers, OHi; SBA to R. A. S. Janney, 5 May 1853, *Film*, 7:699–702; *Woman's Journal*, 19 June 1886.)

2. SBA lectured in Wooster on this date and remained in town through the following day.

3. An issue of the *Woman's Journal*.

4. See 9 August 1878 above.

5. Henry Adams Thompson (1837–1920) and Harriet E. Copeland Thompson (?–1915) hosted SBA when she spoke at Otterbein University in Westerville, Ohio, on 28 October. Henry Thompson, a clergyman and professor of mathematics, was president of Otterbein from 1871 to 1886. He was also a frequent

candidate for public office in Ohio on the Prohibition party ticket, and in 1880 the party nominated him its vice-presidential candidate. Harriet Thompson, a painter, taught fine arts at the college. (*SEAP*; with the assistance of Stephen D. Grinch, Otterbein College.)

## 153 &#x223D; ECS TO SBA

Eagle Hotel,[1] Lebanon, [*Pa., c. 10*] November, 1878.

Dear Susan:

I met Mrs. Livermore down in West Chester. She spoke before the Institute Monday evening and I on Tuesday. Her lecture, "Beyond the Sea," is very interesting and she spoke grandly two hours. She is wonderfully magnetic.[2]

I went up to Philadelphia and heard Phillips on the "Politics of the Bay State."[3] He considers Butler's vote, 110,000, without press or party, a great triumph. He said Butler was the only statesman Massachusetts could boast who was walking in the footsteps of Wilson, Andrews and Sumner.[4] He denounced Hayes and welcomed Grant as our next president. He was applauded and hissed as usual. He closed with a tribute to Butler, and was hissed as he walked off the stage.

Hattie is delighted with the Boston University, and wishes I could have one year of its advantages. I wish I could. I do hate to go before audiences with the slip-shod preparation in which I sometimes find myself. But I suppose I shall go so to the end.

You must not ask me to give up a single possible engagement for Washington. With M's wedding and all the expenses incident to such an event, and my usual heavy family expenses during the summer, it will take all I can make to come out even by the first of June. In justice to myself I must not spend time or money on the Washington Convention. Sincerely, yours as ever,

&#x223D; *Elizabeth Cady Stanton*

&#x223D; Typed transcript, ECS Papers, NjR.

1. The Eagle Hotel stood at the corner of Ninth and Cumberland. ECS delivered "Our Girls" in the Lebanon County courthouse. This edited text is likely based on the letter SBA received on November 15 in Ohio: "splendid letter from Mrs Stanton—that did my soul good—her Hattie is a joy to her—"

(*Woman's Words* 2 [December 1878]: 307–8, and SBA diary, 1878, *Film*, 19:791ff, 20:428; with the assistance of the Lebanon County Historical Society.)

2. Mary Livermore returned from four months in Europe in September 1878 and resumed lecturing with accounts of her travels. ECS probably heard her speak on Monday, 4 November. (*Woman's Journal*, 7, 14 September 1878.)

3. Advertisements for Wendell Phillips's lecture at the Academy of Music on 7 November gave it the title "The Yardstick: Who Shall Make It?" Phillips supported Benjamin Butler's unsuccessful candidacy for governor of Massachusetts in 1878, a campaign in which Butler left the Republican party to run as a Democrat, a champion of labor, and a greenbacker. (*Philadelphia Inquirer*, 7, 8 November 1878; Hans L. Trefousse, *Ben Butler: The South Called Him Beast!* [New York, 1957], 240–41.)

4. That is, Henry Wilson, Charles Sumner, and John Albion Andrew (1818–1867), the wartime, antislavery governor of Massachusetts. (*ANB*.)

·⟨⟨═══⟩⟨═══⟩⟩·

## 154 ⤜ SBA TO ISABELLA BEECHER HOOKER

Kent, O.[1] Dec. 12, 1878

My Dear Mrs Hooker

Mr Slayton sends me your letter to him about my lecturing in Hartford— I have written him emphatically <u>no</u>— I will not thus thrust myself on any large city—besides I did speak there 5 years ago—to a pretty small audience—[2] But I have told him to leave me a day if he can to slip in & visit you— If I were sure of a full house I'd like to give my lecture—Bread & Ballot but can't run the risk of empty benches & bills to pay—

So you do not go to Covington as you thought—[3] I received your several Postals—but hadn't a day I could go there—possibly— I have written Miss Trimble & told her I would go there in February & <u>lecture</u>, too, if she could give me an audience—

Mrs Stanton is jogging around Ohio somewhere and writes me her newly married daughter Maggie is very ill in her new home at the West & she is greatly anxious about her—& may feel compelled to throw up her engagements to go to her— so it is— Marrying daughters but carries mothers back to live over their lives in anxiety for their children & children's children— This world seems made up of worriments doesn't it? But Mrs Stanton & you have had pretty smooth sailing so far as sickness & death of children—haven't you?

Well I am working eastward—& expect to have Christmas at home— just a day only—then lecture to Jan 4th then go on to Wash. to stay a week or ten days—through the Con—[4]

I tell you—it is a mistake to ease up on the friends all over the nation on the <u>work</u> of petitioning—as the course pursued has resulted— I believe if we had just <u>renewed</u> & <u>redoubled</u> our demands for them—we might have added another 40,000 to our last years petition— You ↑see↓ the women must <u>have</u> <u>some</u> <u>work</u> <u>to do</u> <u>with</u> <u>their</u> <u>hands</u> to feel they are doing <u>anything</u>— Now—will you tell me <u>what</u> you see to be the <u>best</u> <u>practical</u> <u>work</u> for us to recommend & to inaugurate— We seem <u>Lacadaisical</u>—now— <u>We</u> <u>need</u> to be <u>revived</u>—<u>in the church</u>—as they say—so as to <u>revive</u> the outside world— Goodbye & love—[5]

⇘ *S. B. Anthony*

⇘ ALS, Isabella Hooker Collection, CtHSD. Envelope addressed to Hartford, Connecticut.

1. SBA spoke in Kent, Ohio, on this date, as she neared the end of her tour through Ohio.

2. On 13 February 1874.

3. Hooker and SBA received invitations from Kate Trimble to speak in a lecture series in Covington, Kentucky, across the Ohio River from Cincinnati. A young woman, Kate Trimble was a daughter of William W. Trimble, a wealthy lawyer in Covington, and Mary Barlow Trimble, an early suffragist in the state. Kate joined the National association in 1880 and attended the Democratic National Convention that summer to lobby for a woman suffrage plank. In the fall of the year, she enrolled in the law school at the University of Michigan but left before earning a degree. She married twice: by the mid-1880s, she was known as Kate Trimble de Roode, when she wrote about state law for the Kentucky chapter of the *History of Woman Suffrage*. In 1893, she married a wealthy New Yorker, Edward J. Woolsey, after his very public and scandalous divorce, and inherited his wealth when he died in 1895. As Kate Trimble Woolsey, she published *Republics vs. Woman: Contrasting the Treatment Accorded to Woman in Aristocracies with that Meted Out to Her in Democracies* in 1903, and she used its argument as the basis for speeches she made at meetings of the National-American Woman Suffrage Association. She was still alive in 1922. (Trimble, *Trimble Families in America*, 173–74; *History*, 3:144n, 821, 4:1100, 5:31, 40, 106, 239, 280; *New York Times*, 23, 26 November, 31 December 1892, 10 October 1893, 27 October, 15 November 1895, 29 January 1896, 20 April 1913, 27 February 1922; SBA to Mary B. Clay,

29 October 1880, *Film*, 21:474–88; University of Michigan, *Catalogue of Graduates*; K. Trimble to May Wright Thompson, 14 May 1880, NWSA Collection, ICHi; research by John Boh, Kenton County Historical Society, Covington, Ky.)

4. SBA spent only a few hours in Rochester on Christmas day visiting with ECS at the home of Mary and William Hallowell. She went on to speak in Warwick, Catskill, and Rhinebeck, New York, before the New Year. (SBA diary, 1878, *Film*, 19:791ff.)

5. SBA sent this letter in an envelope left over from the supplies of the Women's Loyal National League office at Cooper Institute in New York. Under the league's return address, she wrote as a postscript: "<u>1863 & 64</u> only think of the Herculean work of the W.L.N.L. of those years"

## 155 ❧ ECS TO SBA

Waynesville, Ohio, [*before 17*] December, 1878.[1]

Dear Susan:

Well, here I am in your footsteps. The chairman of the committee has just been in to tell me how to get to Frankfort.[2] He told me all about your lecture, how much the people were pleased and how much you were pleased with your audience. I am glad you did not stay at this doleful hotel. I shall be off to-morrow, thank the Lord, and perhaps fall into something worse! I trust this is the last year that I shall take these trips.

Just home after speaking two hours and being introduced to a troop of nice Quakers. Had a fine audience, people coming in miles from the country. What a satisfaction it is to talk to these earnest people. Well, Susan, I think we have done a good deal to make women feel some new self-respect and dignity. Perhaps the world is better that we have lived and so we will not mind the hotels and early hours. I find I must get up at six to go to Frankfort. Oh!

Coming from Cleveland yesterday I met Mrs. W.,[3] and her daughter. She said she would not have our visits at her house blotted out of her life for any consideration; and hundreds of women feel the same. So we have not struggled in vain, and borne our heavy burdens to no purpose. Yours,

❧ *Elizabeth Cady Stanton*

⤳ Typed transcript, ECS Papers, NjR.

1. ECS completed her circuit through Ohio before December 17, when she headed into New York State to begin a series of lectures on December 18. Waynesville, in the Miami Valley of Warren County, was settled by a large number of Quakers from Virginia and the mid-Atlantic states.

2. When SBA lectured in Waynesville on November 15, she identified her local contacts as "Sweet & Cadwallader." Drew Sweet (1839–?) was editor and part owner of the *Miami Gazette* in Waynesville. It is not evident which of the many Cadwalladers in Warren County was Sweet's partner in arranging lectures. (SBA diary, 1878, *Film*, 19:791ff; *History of Warren County, Ohio* [Chicago, 1882], 883–84.)

3. The name left out when the Stanton children edited this letter may be that of Roselle Rebecca Watson (1821–1887), who hosted SBA in Ashtabula, Ohio, on 8 November 1878. She was the wife of Peter Hill Watson, patent attorney, former assistant secretary of war in Lincoln's administration, and former president of the Erie Railroad. Of her own visit, SBA noted "Elegant house—a cordial welcome—" It is not known when ECS visited Ashtabula. (SBA diary, 1878, *Film*, 19:791ff; research by Louise Legeza for the Ashtabula County Genealogical Society.)

## 156 ⇝ ARTICLE BY ECS

[January 1879]

### OUR HISTORY.

I am occasionally asked if writing the history of the Woman's Rights Movement *now* is not rather premature; if it would not be better to wait until the reform is carried and the lives of the pioneers rounded out, finished. I answer: by-and-by we who inaugurated this reform will have passed away and with us many of the incidents and initiative steps of the movement be forgotten, which none others can reproduce. Now is the time for the facts and for the reminiscences of its prime movers. Each generation should write the facts of its own history, a succeeding one can give its true philosophy and place each actor in her appropriate niche. Men to whose example we are ever pointed for wisdom have always pursued this plan. Macaulay[1] did not wait for Great Britain to finish her experiment of government before writing its history. Bancroft[2] is writing the history of the United States although we are but on the threshold of our national life.

Henry Wilson wrote the History of Slavery while he could gather the facts from the lips of those who took part in its overthrow.[3]

Autobiographies are reminiscences of a person's life, written by themselves, thus recording facts that in no other way could be gathered up. Prominent among recent autobiographies are those of Harriet Martineau[4] and John Stuart Mill.[5]

In the same way, we who have made this history are best fitted to write it.

⟨ E. C. S.

⟨ NCBB, January 1879.

1. Thomas Babington Macaulay (1800–1859), an English politician and historian, published five volumes of *The History of England from the Accession of James II* between 1849 and 1861.

2. George Bancroft (1800–1891), an American historian, published his *History of the United States, from the Discovery of the American Continent* between 1834 and 1875.

3. Henry Wilson, *History of the Rise and Fall of the Slave Power in America* (1872–1877).

4. Harriet Martineau (1802–1876) was an English writer and reformer and friend of the antislavery movement. Her *Autobiography*, edited by the American abolitionist Maria Weston Chapman, appeared in 1877.

5. John Stuart Mill, *Autobiography* (1873).

157 ⟨ SPEECH BY ECS TO THE NATIONAL WOMAN SUFFRAGE ASSOCIATION

EDITORIAL NOTE: ECS opened the eleventh Washington convention of the National Woman Suffrage Association at Lincoln Hall on 9 January 1879 with a short address on the political situation. In the recent elections, Democrats won control of both houses of the Forty-sixth Congress. Working against the deadline of its own demise in March 1879, the Forty-fifth Congress was in session, and its Republican Senate majority considered responses to the violence and intimidation directed against African-American voters during the election. ECS prefaced her speech with a reference to the violent rainstorm outside the convention. When "a gentleman at the hotel had asked her why it always rained during a woman's rights convention," she explained "that the heavens were weeping over woman's wrongs. It was entirely fit weather for a woman's rights convention." The text of the speech published in the *National Citizen* and reproduced here was typeset from the manuscript in ECS's hand that is now among her papers at the Library of Congress.

[9 January 1879]

For eleven consecutive years, women citizens of the United States have assembled here in Washington to ask that the principles of our government be carried to their logical results, making women equal with men before the law. And we have asked this not only for the protection of one-half the people of this nation, but for the safety of the nation itself, for every violation of a great principle is sure to be followed by its penalty. Our fathers declared the equality of the human family, but by their laws enslaved the African race, and all women. But the experiment of limiting universal principles to a favored few is ever fraught with danger; liberty for white men only, convulsed the nation for half a century; and mid the thundering cannon of a civil war the requiem of slavery was chanted round the world. Out of this baptism of blood, statesmen with clearer moral vision saw for a time a new significance in the words, justice, liberty and equality, and in the 13th, 14th and 15th amendments, declared the status of an American citizen, and the rights, privileges and immunities involved in citizenship. When learned judges, lawyers and philosophers, gave it as their opinion that woman too was enfranchised by the 14th amendment, with new hope we pondered the constitution of our country and felt that at last it was indeed the Magna Charta of our rights.

With kindling interest we listened to the eloquence of leading statesmen in their paeans to liberty, and words cannot describe the joy that filled our hearts. To realize at last the hopes so long deferred was happiness such as they only who have belonged to a disfranchised class can understand.

To make assurance doubly sure, women in many States tested their new found rights, at college doors, in the courts, at the ballot-box. Some asked the right to practice law, and were denied; some voted and were arrested; some tested their civil and political rights in the Supreme Court of the United States, and thousands petitioned Congress to declare that women were enfranchised under the 14th amendment, but they prayed and petitioned in vain. Though every great principle involved in the amendments, and all the thrilling debates of the republican party since the war, have been freighted with new hopes of freedom for all citizens, yet no sooner have the pleading voices and glowing periods of these statesmen died away, than woman learned that they had no significance for her. The Supreme Court of the United States and Congress in their decisions and arguments on the constitutional rights of woman, have alike stultified themselves and falsified both the letter and spirit of these amendments, in making them a protection for one class of citizens and a new denial of political freedom for another. We prophesied on this platform, years ago, that this violation of principle and the spirit of the amendments, the illogical decisions in our courts and the frivolous arguments in Congress on the constitutional rights of woman, must blunt the moral sense of the whole nation and ultimately imperil the liberties of the colored voters of the South; and our prophesies are fulfilled.[1] President Hayes in his last message complains[2] that the spirit of these amendments have not been faithfully fulfilled by the Southern States; and for the best of reasons, they have never been fulfilled by those who first pressed them on the nation's heart.

The South in the reorganizing of its political parties, is simply adopting the tactics of Northern politicians. Northern carpet-baggers, so-called, *"bull-dozed"* the colored men into voting the republican ticket in 1872, and Southern politicians *"bull-dozed"* the same class into voting the democratic ticket in 1878.[3]

In neither case have the purity of the ballot-box, nor the sacredness of the elections, nor the best interests of the colored voters themselves been protected. It is one thing to utter high-sounding principles and quite another to carry them into practice. I would recommend that the large appropriations made annually to the department of justice, should hereafter be applied to the education of our rulers into a knowledge of *what justice is.*

President Hayes says in his message "that all over our wide territory in the near future, the name and character of citizen of the United States shall mean one and the same thing and carry with them unchallenged security, and respect."[4]

And yet where do we see any preparation among our rulers, for the security and respect of the rights of women even in the District of Columbia, under the very shadow of the Capitol? Here in 1871 the first time the District had a republican form of government, a legislative assembly, 72 women marched to the city Hall and asked to register their names as qualified voters. This experiment of government in the District was made to swell republican power, by a solid colored vote. Intelligent American women, were crowded aside by burly African men, who could neither read nor write. Yet President Grant, who maintained the rights of freedmen in Louisiana, at the point of the bayonet, never gave a thought to the disfranchised women of the District. And yet there were 7,000 more women than men in the District at that time;[5] industrious, tax-paying, law-abiding citizens, who neither kept nor haunted the dram shops nor gambling saloons. A large part of the taxes paid for the support of the Police force, criminal and civil courts, station houses, alms house, and jail come out of the hard earnings of woman, and yet if a little vagrant, homeless, hungry girl steals a loaf of bread, a doll, or a pocket handkerchief, the jail filled with hardened criminals is the only place the District provides for her reformation, while a reform school for boys received an appropriation of $100,000 and $35,000 a year for its support.[6] And yet in view of all these outrages on women and girls President Hayes in his recent message gives them no thought, though he makes a truly paternal review of the interests of this republic great and small, from the army, the navy and our foreign relations, to the timber on the western mountains, the switches of the Washington railroad and the education of the 50 little Indians in Hampton, Virginia—from the Postal service, the Paris exposition, the abundant harvests and the possible bulldozing of some colored man in the various southern districts, to cruelty to live animals and the crowded condition of the mummies and dead ducks in the Smithsonian Institute, and yet he forgets to mention 20,000,000 women citizens robbed of their social, civil, and political rights.[7]

Hon. James G. Blaine in his speech, indicting the southern democracy, enlarges on the injustice of their treatment of colored voters, and makes a strong point on that section of the 14th Amendment, which says if colored male citizens are not permitted to vote, neither shall they be counted in the basis of representation. The Senator considers it the height of injustice to count citizens in the basis of representation when not allowed to vote, and thus compel them to swell the number of their tyrants. He says:

The colored citizen is thus most unhappily situated; his right of suffrage is but a hollow mockery; it holds to his ear the word of promise but breaks it always to his hope, and he ends only in being made the unwilling instrument of increasing the political strength of that party from which he received ever-tightening fetters when he was a slave and contemptuous refusal of civil rights since he was made free. He resembles, indeed, those unhappy captives in the East, who, deprived of their birthright, are compelled to yield their strength to the upbuilding of the monarch from whose tyrannies they have most to fear, and to fight against the power from which alone deliverance might be expected. The franchise intended for the shield and defense of the negro has been turned against him and against his friends, and has vastly increased the power of those from whom he has nothing to hope and everything to dread.[8]

But we need not go to Louisiana or South Carolina to find such injustice. The women of Maine, New England, the western, southern and middle States are all counted in the basis of representation, compelled to send hundreds of men to Congress who care nothing for their rights and interests, who wholly misrepresent them, and yet not one of all these has the right to vote. The Senator further says: "The war, with all its costly sacrifices, was fought in vain, unless equal rights *for all classes* be established in all the States of the Union." I wonder as he uttered that sentiment, if the faintest shadow of a woman fell aslant his brain!

It is a sad reflection that all these glowing sentiments of justice, liberty and equality that have thrilled the hearts of the American people for the last quarter of a century, should now have no meaning,—be but hollow mockery, naught but the stock in trade of clap trap politicians. We on this platform agree with Mr. Blaine, "that the war with all its costly sacrifices was fought in vain, unless equal rights *for all classes* be established in all the States of the Union," North as well as South. And to this end, I would recommend the Senator to begin his work in Maine. There is a large class of citizens, intelligent, refined, virtuous, whose moral power we need to have represented in the government, not only for the nation's safety, but for the more complete developement of that class itself in political, religious and social ideas. As a question of civilization, the enfranchisement of woman is of more vital importance than that of all other classes put together, as her enlightened influence would do for politics and religion what her higher education in the domestic arts has already done for social life. There is more buried wealth in the minds of the women in Maine than in all the lumber and fisheries that State can boast. And yet this large class representing so much intelligence, wealth and latent power claims no political consideration from its great Senator.

In less than sixty days the 45th Congress will have passed into history. What shall we find on its pages concerning women? That to forty thousand citizens of the United States, filling every department of art, science and literature, teachers, ministers, lawyers, "the cream of the philanthropy and intelligence of the country" as senators said upon the floor, in presenting to this Congress the petitions, asking for a constitutional amendment, protecting women citizens in their right to vote:—that the Senate Committee on Privileges and Elections gave *three minutes* to these petitioners, to the final decision of this vital question;[9] three minutes! at the close of the session, and at the close of the day, in the twilight hour, when even bats and owls begin to see clearly and to roam forth on their nightly haunts, and after this *three minutes* of consideration, two of which might have been consumed in the roll call, and the third in awaiting the arrival of the tardy chairman, this committee of the highest legislative body in the land, voted down the woman suffrage resolution 6 to 3.

They who voted in favor of the 16th Amendment are Senators Hoar, Mass.; Mitchell, Oregon; Cameron, Wis. Nays, Wadleigh, N.H.; McMillan, Minn.; Saulsbury, Del.; Merrimon, S.C.; Hill, Ga.; Ingalls, Kansas.

In the other House the Judiciary Committee were promptly in their seats. Five members of this committee, Lapham of N.Y.; Lynde of Wis.; Frye of Me.; Butler, Mass.; Conger, Mich., eminent Judges, able Lawyers and Honored Statesmen rose early in the morning, Feb. 5th, 1878 to vote Yes on the constitutional amendment for women. Five more rose early in the morning, of the same day, Knott, Ky.; Hartridge, Ga.; Stenger, Penn.; McMahon, Ohio; Culberson, Texas, to vote No on the rights of woman. The eleventh Hon. gentleman, Harris of Virginia, for some reason, did not rise that eventful morning, and there our question lies waiting for him to get up and make his toilet. In both Houses, therefore, our question is pending. In the Senate upon the calendar waiting for some brave man to call it up, and force it before that body for debate and action. In the House our question rests on that tie vote.

The days are rapidly passing and what shall be the record, on this question, of the statesmen of the 45th Congress. In each of these Houses are men of sterling integrity, who have served the men of their States faithfully and well. Yet these men have deserted them, and turned their allegiance to new heroes lifted out of obscurity by the last election.[10] To these men elected to retirement we appeal. You are writing many of you the last chapter of your public career. What page shall the mothers, and daughters of this republic find therein to which they can proudly point and say: "This was for us." As the years roll on and bring to us victory at last, the men who have helped to fight our battle will be proud of their old time loyalty to woman, and their courage in facing a false and wicked public sentiment, to so amend their laws and constitutions as to make all citizens equal before the law. The air of Washington is heavy with the wrecked hopes of disappointed statesmen, of those who led by personal ambition and party allegiance, have sacrificed principle to expediency. They only hold a place in the hearts of the people, they only are immortal, who live not for themselves alone, but for all humanity.

⤝ *NCBB*, February 1879. Also AMs in ECS Papers, DLC.

1. The sixth and seventh resolutions adopted by the convention offered this same interpretation of the connection between the rights of women and black men. Whereas "the vital principles" of the amendments "have been denied in their application to woman, by courts, legislatures and political parties," it was resolved, "That it is eminently logical that these amendments should utterly fail to protect even the male African for whom said courts, legislatures and parties declare they were expressly designed and enacted," and "That thus ever above all the short-sighted schemes of politicians will the inexorable law of justice bind humanity together, and vindicate the equal rights of all."

2. In a misreading of ECS's manuscript, the published text reads "complaining." In his second annual message to Congress on 2 December 1878, Hayes reminded the South of their pledges to enforce the amendments and went on to say that "the records of the elections seem to compel the conclusion that the rights of the colored voters have been overridden and their

participation in the general elections not permitted to be either general or free." (Israel, *State of the Union Messages*, 2:1356–57.)

3. The term "bull-doze" came into use in 1876 to describe acts of political intimidation and coercion against African Americans.

4. Israel, *State of the Union Messages*, 2:1358. Both ECS's manuscript and the published text of her speech enclose this entire paragraph in quotation marks. The marks have been moved to indicate the beginning of her quotation from Hayes.

5. The federal census of 1870 counted 62,192 males and 69,508 females in Washington. Women outnumbered men in all racial categories. (*Compendium of the Ninth Census*, 547, 548, 549, 559.)

6. Hayes, in his annual message, had asked for new appropriations to enlarge the boys' reform school. (Israel, *State of the Union Messages*, 2:1370.)

7. ECS ridicules the wide sweep of President Hayes's message, which addressed all the issues she names and more but omitted any reference to women or their suffrage. She expressed similar indignation in an interview in the *Washington Post*, 8 January 1879, *Film*, 20:641. Her paragraph was repeated in the convention's fifth resolution, with a plan to visit the president and "remind him of the existence of one-half of the American people whom he has accidentally overlooked, and of whom it would be wise for him to make some mention in his future messages." Hayes received Matilda Gage, Sara Spencer, and Emmeline Wells on January 13. They brought him a memorial asking for his support of their constitutional amendment.

At the convention, ECS's phrase about "the possible bull-dozing of some colored men in various southern districts" prompted an angry debate between Charles Purvis and Frederick Douglass. Purvis objected both to the phrase itself and to any suggestion that the "traitor" Hayes should be credited with concern about African Americans in the South: "his Southern policy has caused the slaughter of hundreds of this race alluded to as 'possibly bull-dozed,'" he proclaimed. Douglass rose to defend the president, insisting that he "should not be charged with the outrages that have followed his inauguration." The phrase was not in the president's message, although Sara Spencer said they tried to use his language in the resolutions. (*NCBB*, February 1879, and "Memorial to President Hayes," *Film*, 20:644–51, 678–81; Israel, *State of the Union Messages*, 2:1357.)

8. James Blaine urged Congress to investigate the conduct of the election of 1878. The convention's fourth resolution repeated Blaine's statement about the basis of representation swelling the ranks of the tyrants and referred to the counting of disfranchised women as "an unwarrantable usurpation of power over one-half the citizens of this Republic." (*Congressional Record*, 45th Cong., 3d sess., 11 December 1878, pp. 85–86; *NCBB*, February 1879.)

9. Presumably ECS refers to a committee meeting in June 1878 prior to release of the adverse report on June 14.

10. In the Forty-sixth Congress, the Democrats would hold forty-two seats

in the Senate compared to the Republicans' thirty-three seats. Democrats would also continue to control the House of Representatives. In the turnover, woman suffragists lost key sponsors and allies. Neither Aaron Sargent nor John H. Mitchell returned to the Senate, victims of Democratic majorities in their state legislatures. Benjamin Butler and William P. Lynde no longer sat in the House of Representatives.

## 158   ❧   SBA TO MATILDA JOSLYN GAGE

[*c. 18 January 1879*][1]

I see by the Washington *Star* that Mrs. Spencer got a hearing for the Utah Delegates.[2] Am glad of that and hope the seeing of these women will make congressmen pause before they commit them and their children to the tender mercies of outcast laws.[3] . . . I am dressing down Wadleigh in New Hampshire, and old Edmunds in Vermont.[4] They say Wadleigh is moving heavens and earth to secure his re-election next session.[5] I just wish I could take the stump in New Hampshire to defeat him. We've got to demonstrate power to kill off some of these fellows before they'll come to see, or hear, or heed us.

✒ *NCBB*, February 1879.

1. Dated after the first of the hearings in Congress obtained by Mormon women, on 17 January 1879. SBA wrote from New England, where she lectured until the end of the month.

2. Emmeline Blanche Woodward Wells (1828–1921), editor of the Salt Lake City *Woman's Exponent*, and Zina Priscenda Young Williams (1850–1931), a daughter of Brigham Young, traveled east to attend the National's convention and counter a national campaign against polygamy. In anticipation of a decision from the Supreme Court about the constitutionality of the Anti-Polygamy Law of 1862, in the case of *Reynolds v. United States*, Mormons and antipolygamists were mobilized. At a rally in Salt Lake City on 7 November 1878, antipolygamists called for a national petition-writing campaign among women to urge federal enforcement of the 1862 law, and in December, their petitions poured into Congress. The Supreme Court upheld the law of 1862 in its decision handed down on 6 January 1879. The decision emboldened sponsors of legislation pending in Congress that would dissolve polygamous marriages and repeal woman suffrage in Utah. Although the National Woman Suffrage Association steered clear of the question of polygamy at its meeting, the resolutions included one in support of women's voting rights in Utah.

(*NAW* and *ANB*, s.v. "Wells, Emmeline B."; Augusta Joyce Crocheron, *Representative Women of Deseret* [Salt Lake City, 1884], 121; *History*, 4:937; Reynolds v. United States, 98 United States Reports 145 [1879]; Edward Leo Lyman, *Political Deliverance, The Mormon Quest for Utah Statehood* [Chicago, 1986], 20–21; *Woman's Exponent*, 15 November 1878; *Woman's Words* 2 [February 1879]: 346–48, *Film*, 20:654–56.)

3. Assisted by Sara Spencer, Wells and Williams called on President Hayes, testified before the House Judiciary Committee, met informally with members of the Senate Judiciary Committee, and persuaded the speaker of the House to introduce their memorial to Congress. On each occasion they lobbied for repeal of the antipolygamy law, arguing that its enforcement would "render our children illegitimate before the world and leave ourselves and many thousands of women desolate and unprotected." Mormon men, faced with fines or imprisonment, would be forced to abandon their additional wives and children. (Washington *Evening Star*, 17 January 1879, and *Philadelphia Times*, 19 January 1879, in M. J. Gage scrapbooks, MCR-S; *Congressional Record*, 45th Cong., 3d sess., 23 January 1879, pp. 666–67; *NCBB*, January 1879; *New York Times*, 14, 21, 24 January 1879; *Woman's Exponent*, 1, 15 February 1879.)

4. At Keene, New Hampshire, on 20 January 1879, a reporter described SBA concluding her speech "with a remonstrance against returning Mr. Wadleigh to the Senate, it being her earnest desire that an avowed friend of women's rights should be his successor." George Franklin Edmunds (1828–1919) of Vermont entered the Senate in 1866 and served until 1891. An outspoken opponent of woman suffrage and woman's rights, Edmunds voted consistently against Senator Sargent's efforts to advance woman suffrage, and through the chairmanship of the Judiciary Committee, he blocked the Lockwood bill to admit women to practice in federal courts for several years. (*BDAC*; *Film*, 20:684.)

5. Bainbridge Wadleigh, whose term in the Senate would expire in March 1879, hoped for reelection when the legislature convened in June. An oversight in an amendment to the state constitution in 1877 prevented the legislature in 1878 from electing a senator in time to enter the Forty-sixth Congress in March. The governor named an interim senator to succeed Wadleigh until June, at which time the legislature elected Henry W. Blair in Wadleigh's place. (*Congressional Record*, 45th Cong., 2d sess., 10 June 1878, pp. 4353–57; McPherson, *Hand-Book of Politics for 1880*, 96–97.)

159 ⋙ MEMORIAL TO CONGRESS

[24 January 1879][1]

TO THE SENATE AND HOUSE OF REPRESENTATIVES OF THE UNITED STATES
IN CONGRESS ASSEMBLED:

Whereas more than forty thousand well-known men and women, citizens of thirty-five States and five Territories, have petitioned the Forty-fifth Congress, asking for an amendment to the Federal Constitution prohibiting the several States from disfranchising United States citizens on account of sex; and

Whereas a resolution providing for such constitutional amendment is upon the calendar in the Senate (S. Res. No. 12, second session Forty-fifth Congress), and a similar resolution is pending upon a tie vote in the Judiciary Committee of the House of Representatives; and

Whereas the women citizens of the United States are joint heirs with men of this republic, constitute one-half of the people, and have an inalienable right to an equal voice with men in the nation's councils; and

Whereas this republic is governed by opinions, and not by force of arms; and

Whereas women citizens, being denied the right to have their opinions counted at the ballot-box, are compelled to hold all other rights subject to the favor, passions, and caprices of men; and

Whereas, in answer to the appeal of so large a number of peaceable, law-abiding, honorable petitioners, it is just and courteous that the Forty-fifth Congress should express its opinion, and leave its record upon this grave question of human rights:

Therefore, we pray your honorable body to take from the calendar and pass Senate resolution No. 12 (second session Forty-fifth Congress), providing for an amendment to the Constitution protecting the rights of women citizens; and

We further pray you to relieve the House Judiciary Committee from the further consideration of the sixteenth amendment woman suffrage resolution, brought to a tie vote in that committee February 5, 1878, that it may be submitted to the House of Representatives for immediate action.

And your petitioners will ever pray.

⇘ Elizabeth Cady Stanton,
President,

⇘ Matilda Joslyn Gage,
Corresponding Secretary,

⇘ Susan B. Anthony,
Chairman Executive Committee
National Woman Suffrage Association.

⇘ Senate, *Memorial of Elizabeth Cady Stanton, Matilda Joslyn Gage, and Susan B. Anthony*, January 24, 1879, 45th Cong., 3d sess., S. Mis. Doc. 45, Serial 1833. Also in *History*, 3:130–31.

1. Very few petitions for the sixteenth amendment were presented to the third session of the Forty-fifth Congress, but the leaders of the National Woman Suffrage Association submitted this memorial in their stead. On 24 January 1879, Vice President William A. Wheeler introduced it in the Senate, and Michigan's Thomas W. Ferry obtained unanimous consent that it be read before being sent to the Committee on Privileges and Elections. On January 28, Speaker of the House Samuel J. Randall laid the memorial before the House of Representatives. There it was referred to the Committee on the Judiciary. (*Congressional Record*, 45th Cong., 3d sess., 698, 807; *Journal of the Senate*, 45th Cong., 3d sess., 158.)

160  ⇝  SBA to Lucy Webb Hayes[1]

Richmond Ind.[2] Feb. 9th 1879

My Dear Mrs Hayes

May I not address you, and ask you to help your dear husband the President—to <u>remember</u> <u>not</u> <u>to</u> <u>forget</u> <u>to</u> <u>sign</u> the bill to admit women Lawyers to the Supreme Court?[3] I cannot tell you how my heart leaped for joy yesterday morning as I read the report of the splendid Senate vote of <u>40</u> to 20 for that bill! I feel sure the President will not fail to sign it— Can you imagine what faith in truth and right must have sustained the little handful of us ~~of~~ who for a whole generation have stood before this American people—the target for the jibes & jeers of the unthinking multitudes—demanding the equal recognition of women in all the fundmental rights of our government? And now that the fruitage of the seed sowing of the thirty years begins to appear, it is not, I am sure, asking too much of the woman whose good fortune places her in the highest position in the Nation, that she shall give the influence, nay, the prestige & power of that position to crown the life efforts of the few for the ↑full↓ completetion of the experiment of a genuine republic on this continent.

Your firm & womanly stand on the custom ↑of↓ wines & other intoxicating drinks—at the "White House" dinner parties, commands the respect & admiration of all true women— And that you may declare yourself on the side of the equal recognition & counting of all Womens opinions at the Ballot-Box—not only on the question of the Liquor Traffic, but upon all questions that pertain to the weal or the woe of this republic, Is the hope and the prayer of Yours Sincerely

⤝ *Susan B. Anthony*

⤝ ALS, Lucy Webb Hayes Collection, OFH.

1. Lucy Ware Webb Hayes (1831–1889) was the first presidential wife to be referred to as the "First Lady," the first to hold a college degree, and the first to bring her own interests in reform into the White House. Although it was her commitment to temperance that gained the most press and earned her the nickname "Lemonade Lucy," she paid close attention to many issues promoted by women. She received Belva Lockwood at the White House to compliment her as soon as the Senate passed the Lockwood bill. (*NAW*; *ANB*; Emily Apt Geer, *First Lady: The Life of Lucy Webb Hayes* [Kent, Ohio, 1984], 137–38, 198–200; *History*, 3:141.)

2. As was her habit on the road, SBA took time on this Sunday to catch up on her correspondence before she continued on to a speaking engagement in Terre Haute on 11 February.

3. On 7 February 1879, Senator Joseph McDonald of Indiana moved to change the order of business and take up H.R. 1077, the Lockwood bill to admit women to practice before the Supreme Court. Over the objection of Senator George Edmunds, the Senate agreed, by a roll call vote of thirty-one yeas to twenty-nine nays, to postpone current business. After cursory remarks from Edmunds, Senators McDonald, Aaron Sargent, and George Hoar spoke for the bill, and in a second roll call vote, the Senate finally passed the measure, thirty-nine yeas to twenty nays. The bill won some unlikely support from senators who had refused to consider it a year earlier and been conspicuous in their opposition to woman suffrage. Notable among the yeas were John

J. Ingalls of Kansas, Bainbridge Wadleigh of New Hampshire, and Samuel McMillan of Minnesota. (*Congressional Record*, 45th Cong., 3d sess., 1082–84; *History*, 3:138–41.)

## 161   SBA to George F. Hoar

Richmond Ind. Feb. 9, 1879

Hon. Geo. F. Hoar   Dear Sir

The vote of the Senate on admitting women to the Supreme Court—is a most flattering one— And I hope you will lose no time in presenting your Minority ↑report↓, on our 40,000 Petition for ↑a↓ 16^th amendment—and press the proposition to a vote—[1] A discussion will do very much to advance our cause among the people at large— To know their senators & representatives favor suffrage helps the constituencies out of their prejudices—[2]

The large vote of Friday is a surprise to the friends even.—

I urge you <u>not</u> to fail to secure a discussion and vote on the <u>main</u> question, because our women, all over the country, who have been through with the drudgery of circulating petitions from year ↑to year,↓ with so little effect, and as many of them say, with <u>no</u> effect, can hardly be roused to go through the work for the 46^th Congress, unless we can have the demonstration that their last year's hard work—herculean work—has been heard and heeded at Washington.

I pray you, therefore, compel a discussion and a division of the Senate on the 16^th am't question, and thereby inspire the women of the Nation to renew their efforts in the direction of rolling up a mammoth petition the coming season to be presented to the 46^th Congress.

With many thanks for your many good words & votes for equal rights to woman   most respectfully yours

    ⚜ *Susan B. Anthony*
    *Rochester—N.Y.*

⚜ ALS, George F. Hoar Papers, MHi.

1. Hoar had presented the minority report on Senate Resolution 12 from the Committee on Privileges and Elections, signed by himself, John Mitchell, and Angus Cameron, on 1 February 1879, asking that it be printed with the

majority report. Although the report did not recommend the federal amendment, it challenged the majority's distrust of voters and disputed its dim view of women. The minority reasoned "that the American people must extend the right of suffrage to woman or abandon the idea that suffrage is a birthright." If, as some claimed, "free government has anywhere failed," they continued, that judgment proved "not the failure of universal suffrage, but the failure of masculine suffrage." (*Congressional Record*, 45th Cong., 3d sess., 808; Senate Committee on Privileges and Elections, *Views of the Minority*, 45th Cong., 3d sess., S. Rept. 523, pt. 2.)

2. On February 17, when the Senate reached Resolution 12 on its calendar, Senator Robert E. Withers of Virginia objected to taking up the matter. Aaron Sargent spoke: "Of course an objection carries it over; but I should like to ask unanimous consent of the Senate that the majority and minority reports . . . be reprinted. The edition is getting exhausted." The Senate agreed to reprint the reports and moved on to the next item on the calendar. The resolution was not taken up again in the Forty-fifth Congress. (*Congressional Record*, 45th Cong., 3d sess., 1432.)

## 162 ✍ ECS TO THEODORE W. STANTON

Indiana,[1] February 26, 1879.

Dear Theodore:—

We are to have a good convention in St. Louis the 7, 8, and 9 of May.[2] This question of woman suffrage is the coming one. We have just had a great triumph in the passage of the bill by both houses of congress giving women the right to practice law in the highest courts of the nation, and the President has signed it![3] Wadleigh last year reported against us; this year he votes for us. Blaine voted our bill straight through.[4] The action of politicians always tells which way the wind blows. Adieu, in haste,

✍ *Mother.*

✍ Typed transcript, ECS Papers, NjR.

1. In the Midwest since January, ECS was scheduled to lecture in Indianapolis on 1 March.

2. At the National's business meeting in July 1878, the members discussed whether to make the annual meeting a part of the Washington convention and give up the traditional May meeting in New York City. Unable to reach consensus, they referred the matter to the executive committee, whose mem-

bers in turn proposed that the annual meetings convene each spring but in different parts of the country. Virginia Minor organized the first of the new annual meetings at St. Louis. (*Film*, 20:313–21.)

3. President Hayes signed the Lockwood bill on 15 February, and Belva Lockwood gained admission to the bar of the Supreme Court on 3 March 1879.

4. Although Senator James Blaine took no part in the debate on the Lockwood bill, his vote in its favor was noticed because all other presidential hopefuls absented themselves from the vote. (*History*, 3:141.)

## 163  ⤳  ECS to Harriot E. Stanton

Moberly, Missouri,[1] March 21, 1879.

Dear Hattie:

I am having a hard trip through this state; night travel all the time. Last night I took the cars at twelve. No sleeping car. I had to sit upright all night with another person in the seat in a car crowded with emigrants to Kansas. It is said the emigration west was never so great, and judging from what I saw in this train, it must be so. There were babies enough to populate Jupiter and his four moons.[2]

It really made my heart sad to read the criticisms of Anna Dickinson which you sent.[3] Like the student in Longfellow's poem,[4] she forgot her high calling and thought only of making money; thus she lost her power and inspiration. Gold is good in its place, but when it becomes the primal consideration, it turns the heart to stone. Yours,

⤳  *Mother.*

⤳ Typed transcript, ECS Papers, NjR.

1. A village north of Columbia, Missouri. After the Stanton children produced a typescript of this letter, they incorporated the text of it into another and dated it 8 January 1879 in their collection of ECS's letters. See *Stanton*, 2:156–57 and *Film*, 20:738–39.

2. This was the peak of the Exodus of African Americans from the South into Kansas at the end of Reconstruction. See Nell Irvin Painter, *Exodusters: Black Migration to Kansas after Reconstruction* [New York, 1977], 184–201.

3. Possibly they refer to the attention Anna Dickinson attracted when she returned to the lecture circuit early in 1879 to speak about "The Platform and the Stage." Her contention that theater was a greater influence for good than

pulpit or press stirred the critics. (Chester, *Embattled Maiden*, 200–1; *New York Times*, 18 January 1879.)

    4. Henry Wadsworth Longfellow (1807–1882), the American poet. ECS may refer not to a poem but to a speech within Longfellow's novel *Hyperion: A Romance* (1839), in which a student warns against "wearing life away in feverish anxiety of fame." Without the patience to wait and to act regardless of approval, men "go to their graves with purposes unaccomplished and wishes unfulfilled." (Book I, chapter 8; with assistance from Albert J. von Frank.)

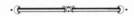

## 164  ≫   ECS to Elizabeth Smith Miller

Joplin, Missouri,[1] March 26, 1879.

Dear Julius:

    Here is Johnson down in a little mining town in southern Missouri. [I] have been wandering, wandering ever since we parted; up early and late, [s]leepy and disgusted with my profession, as there is not rest from the time [t]he season begins until it ends. Two months more containing sixty-one days [s]till stretch their long length before me. I must pack and unpack my trunk [s]ixty-one times, pull out the black silk trail[2] and don it, curl my hair, [a]nd pin on the illusion puffing round my spacious throat,[3] sixty-one more [t]imes, rehearse "Our Boys," "Our Girls," or "Home Life,"[4] sixty-one times, [e]at 183 more miserable meals, sleep in cotton sheets with these detestable [t]hings called "comforters" (tormentors would be a more fitting name) over [m]e sixty-one more nights, shake hands with sixty-one more committees, smile, look intelligent and interested in every one who approaches me, while I feel like a squeezed sponge, affect a little spring and briskness in my gait [o]n landing in each new town to avoid making an impression that I am seventy, when in reality I feel more like crawling than walking. With her best foot forward, Yours,

≫   Johnson.

≫ Typed transcript, ECS Papers, NjR. Letters in square brackets obscured by binding. Variant in *Stanton*, 2:159–60.

    1. In the southwest corner of Missouri, in an area of zinc and lead mines. The previous evening ECS delivered "Our Girls" at the Opera House. For notice of her lecture, see *Film*, 20:735.

2. A train of cloth that trailed behind the wearer.

3. Illusion lace, in this case worn gathered into a puff at her neck.

4. The manuscripts of "Our Boys" and "Home Life" are in *Film*, 20:449–616, 45:75–125. "Our Girls" is published in this volume.

## 165 ⇝ ECS TO MATILDA JOSLYN GAGE

*[Omaha, Neb.? 5? April? 1879]*[1]

Did you see in Lucy's paper of the 29th a correspondent makes some strictures on the Mormon women on our platform, which Lucy does not defend as she should.[2] If George Q. Cannon[3] can sit in the Congress of the United States without compromising that body on the question of Polygamy, I should think Mormon women might sit on our platform without making us responsible for their religious faith. If, as the husband of four wives, he can be tolerated in the Councils of the nation and treated with respect, surely the wives of only the fourth part of man should be four times as worthy of tender consideration. When the women of a whole territory are threatened with disfranchisement where should they go to make their complaint but to the platform of the National Suffrage Association? If you have not already rebuked the *Woman's Journal*, do say this much.

⇜ *NCBB*, May 1879. Variants addressed to SBA in ECS Papers, NjR, and *Stanton*, 2:160, in *Film*.

1. In the *National Citizen*, Matilda Gage prefaced this letter simply, "Mrs. Stanton enquires." The typescript prepared by the Stanton children from an unknown source shows SBA to be the recipient. That same typescript indicates Omaha at the place line and a date of "Autumn of 1879." When they published the text in *Stanton*, they assigned the date of 5 April 1879. ECS was lecturing in Nebraska in early April 1879.

2. In the *Woman's Journal*, 29 March 1879, Amanda E. Dickinson of St. Louis chastised the National Woman Suffrage Association's leaders for failing to distance themselves from the polygamous, Mormon women who spoke at the Washington convention in January. "Suffragists must deeply regret," she wrote, "any appearance of affiliation between the advocates of equal rights for Woman and those who advocate or apologize for a system which plunges her into the lowest depths of degradation."

3. George Quayle Cannon (1827–1901) served in the House of Representatives as Utah's territorial delegate from 1873 to 1881. (*BDAC*.)

166 ✎ ECS TO TRYPHENA CADY BAYARD,
HARRIET CADY EATON, AND CATHARINE
CADY WILKESON[1]

Fremont, Nebraska,[2] April 20, [1879].

Dear Sisters 1, 2, 3,

I have had a fearfully hard week and am glad that this is the Lord's day and belongs to no Lyceum Bureau. Monday I rode in an open wagon thirty miles across the prairies, spoke that evening and the next morning, and in the afternoon rode the same distance back again.[3] Then I took the car to Hastings,[4] arrived there at eleven o'clock and as there was an exciting murder trial going on, I could not get a place to sleep. So with my clothes all on, I laid on a broken-down old lounge, sleeping on the points of some springs and bumps, until one side of my body was partially paralyzed, then getting up and walking for a while before trying the other side. I thought the night would never end.

The next morning, after a meagre breakfast, I was packed into a long omnibus,—men, women, children, babies, bags, bundles, with a conceited boy of sixteen in charge of the precious cargo. He went around the corners as if the devil was after him. I expected every moment to be upset, and my expectations were realized. Dashing up to the depot, where was a crowd of men and boys all in town to attend the trial, he upset with a fearful whack, on my side, the blow coming full force on the back of my head. Many of the passengers were badly hurt and emerged with torn garments and dishevelled locks. But strange to say, I came out in order, with no scratch or bruise that I can see. But my head and back have ached ever since. Time will show whether I received any dangerous injury.[5]

Since then, I have spoken every night, travelling in the cars, each day. I am a wonder to every one for my endurance and cheerfulness. Comparing myself with most women, I have come to the conclusion that I was well born, that my parents put me together with unusual wisdom and discretion, for which I am devoutly thankful. I enjoy life under the most adverse circumstances and am in no particular hurry to be translated. Yours as ever,

~ *E. C. S.*

~ Typed transcript, ECS Papers, NjR.

1. Three of ECS's four sisters. Tryphena Cady Bayard (1804–1891), the eldest Cady daughter, lived on Fortieth Street in New York City with her husband, Edward Bayard. (Allen, *Descendants of Nicholas Cady*, 173; Gravestones, Johnstown, N.Y.; *Woman's Tribune*, 10 May 1891.) Harriet Eliza Cady Eaton (1810–1894) was widowed at age forty-five and lived with the Bayards. (Allen, *Descendants of Nicholas Cady*, 174–75; Gravestones, Johnstown, N.Y.; genealogical files, notes from Presbyterian Church Records, NJost.) Catharine Henry Cady Wilkeson (1820–?), the youngest sister and the wife of Samuel Wilkeson, also shared the house on Fortieth Street when she was not at home in Bridgehampton, Long Island. (*TroyFS*; C. H. Cady file, Emma Willard School Archives; genealogical files, notes from Presbyterian Church Records, NJost; *ACAB*, s.v. "Wilkeson, Samuel.") See also *Papers* 1 & 2 for all three sisters.

2. This seat of Dodge County lies northwest of Omaha on the Union Pacific Railroad line.

3. She delivered "Our Girls" in Hebron, Nebraska, on Monday, April 14, and stayed to organize the Thayer County Woman Suffrage Association on Tuesday morning. (*Hebron Journal*, 17 April 1879.)

4. ECS spoke in Hastings on April 10; on April 16, she returned on the St. Joseph & Denver City Railroad to await an eastbound train on the Burlington & Missouri River Railroad.

5. Noting this accident, the Hastings *Central Nebraskan*, 18 April 1879, reported that she was slightly bruised.

## 167 ~ ECS TO SBA

Woodbine, Iowa, May 4, 1879.

Dear Susan:

Here I am talking with Gat.[1] Over his sofa hang your lithograph [an]d mine, looking earnestly at each other. Gat says it reminds him of the [t]ime when we used to sit opposite each other and write, write, write calls, [p]etitions, appeals, resolutions, speeches, letters, and newspaper articles.

I have such a crick in my back that the least motion distresses [me]. I rode thirty miles yesterday across the prairies in a stiff wind and

[to]ok cold. This added to the lameness I have had in my back ever since my [up]set makes me feel very low spirited. Unless I am better tomorrow I [sh]all give up my Little Sioux appointment for the 6th. I have an engagement [a]t Cairo, Illinois, the 10th., and a dozen engagements afterwards on my [w]ay home. I cannot go through the St. Louis Convention. I feel as if one more [ou]nce of responsibility would kill me. I am sick, tired, jaded beyond des[cr]iption and the younger, fresher women must supply the enthusiasm of the [oc]casion. I do hope the Convention will go off well, and I feel guilty not [to] be there and do my part, but if you knew how I feel, you would say stay [w]here you are. I have done my best for our cause all winter, speaking [a]lmost every evening since the first of October, to ladies alone frequent[l]y in the afternoon, and preaching Sunday on the Bible position of woman. I [fe]el more like going to bed for the next month than traveling from point [to] point. Yours,

                 *Elizabeth Cady Stanton.*

  Typed transcript, ECS Papers, NjR. Letters in square brackets obscured by binding.

    1. That is, her son Gerrit Stanton.

168    REMARKS AT THE ST. LOUIS MERCHANTS' EXCHANGE

EDITORIAL NOTE: On May 10, at the conclusion of the annual meeting, members of the National association accepted the invitation of the St. Louis Chamber of Commerce to visit the Merchants' Exchange. "The appearance of so many women on the floor of the Exchange," the *Globe-Democrat* reported, "caused considerable commotion among the members, who laughed at the novelty of the thing and perpetrated huge jokes upon one another." One thousand traders stopped work to hear remarks from Phoebe Couzins, who in turn introduced ECS. When SBA was done, Elizabeth Meriwether and May Thompson made a few remarks.

[10 May 1879]

Miss Couzins then introduced Mrs. Elizabeth Cady Stanton. Mrs.

Stanton responded with great effect. What we are asking for, she said, was simply the right of self-government, exactly what you claim to-day for yourself. She felt great assurance in coming to Missouri with the demand for the suffrage, because woman has been honored in Missouri as she has in no other State. She alluded to the throwing open of the doors of medical schools here to Harriet Hosmer,[1] to enable her to study anatomy and prepare herself for her profession, and to the fact that the Law School of St. Louis was open to women,[2] and the floors of the Merchants' Exchange. Could it be because Missouri cast 60,000 Democratic majority? (Applause.)[3] She had often said to the Democracy that she thought, if they were wise, they would immortalize themselves on the future pages of history by advocating the granting of suffrage to women. While the Republican party have taken the lead in granting the right of suffrage to 4,000,000 black men, what a splendid thing it would now be for the Democratic party to immortalize themselves by giving the right of suffrage to 20,000,000 women. (Applause.) If you want to carry the election in 1880 there is no better thing that you could do than to inscribe woman suffrage on your flag. She believed it would lead them on to victory, and she believed that the Democracy at least would have the advantage of having enfranchised the more intelligent class of the two. (Applause.)

It was not so much out of place, she said, that women should meet here in the Merchants' Exchange, for the presiding genius of Commerce was represented by woman, and, indeed, were all the arts and sciences. We find that everything in all the departments of art, in philosophy, in poetry, even in justice and mercy, are all alike represented by woman.[4] She believed that when the woman idea was recognized by our nation everywhere, we should have a far more just and equitable condition of things than we had to-day. Man represents the material forces of society, woman the moral forces. Man has done his material work nobly and well, and now the world waits for the moral power of woman.

She urged that the best possible check on the extravagance of woman was to give her an education in all the arts and professions. When women understand the value of dollars they will know better how to spend them.

Miss Susan B. Anthony followed in a characteristic speech, contrasting the liberality of the Merchants' Exchange of St. Louis in opening its doors to women with the example of New York, where the Exchange was closed against her. She concluded by asking a vote on the question whether they were in favor of securing women in all their rights, privileges and immunities, by giving the right to vote through a sixteenth amendment to the Constitution. A loud yell from nearly a thousand throats answered in the affirmative. There were a few faint and hesitating noes when the negative was put.

❧ *St. Louis Globe-Democrat*, 11 May 1879.

1. Harriet Hosmer (1830–1908), a renowned sculptor, gained admission to anatomy classes at Missouri Medical College in 1850 after Harvard refused to admit her. (*ANB*.)

2. The Washington University School of Law in St. Louis admitted two women as students in 1869—Phoebe Couzins and Lemma Barkaloo. Barkaloo passed the bar examination before her graduation and withdrew without earning a degree, and Couzins graduated in 1871. Nearly two decades passed before any other women were admitted to the school. (Ralph E. Morrow, *Washington University in St. Louis: A History* [St. Louis, 1996], 57; Karen Berger Morello, *The Invisible Bar: The Woman Lawyer in America 1638 to the Present* [New York, 1986], 44–46.)

3. The Democratic vote exceeded the Republican by ninety thousand in state elections in 1878. The Democratic party, strengthened by the reenfranchisement of Confederates in 1871, took control of the state from Radical Republicans in 1872 and held it until 1904. (McPherson, *Hand-Book of Politics for 1880*, 201.)

4. On the use of female figures to represent endeavors from which actual women were excluded, see Marina Warner, *Monuments & Maidens: The Allegory of the Female Form* (New York, 1985).

169 ⤳ "The Bible and Woman Suffrage": Speech by ECS in St. Louis

EDITORIAL NOTE: At the invitation of the Rev. Ross C. Houghton, ECS spoke on Sunday evening to four thousand people gathered at the Union Methodist Church at Eleventh and Locust streets, St. Louis. Although she had delivered lectures on woman's rights and the Bible since 1867, her text in 1879 was a relatively new one, incorporating a part of her "Parable of the Ten Virgins" of late 1877 and discussing an article in the *Methodist Quarterly Review* of April

1878. She apparently regarded this report of her speech in the *St. Louis Globe-Democrat* as authoritative: she kept the clipping among her papers and corrected its errors. She also kept a nearly identical, though now incomplete, manuscript entitled "Is the Bible opposed to Woman suffrage?" The manuscript contains a few later changes, no doubt for other engagements, but more important, it indicates that the speech in St. Louis had evolved from earlier texts now missing. Nine manuscript pages of an earlier date bear multiple page numbers in ECS's hand, showing their shifting position in three different sequences; forty-one in the surviving sequence served in earlier texts as both page thirty-seven and page "35b" and so on. Those indicators, as well as other details from the manuscript, are noted in the notes to this text. (*Film*, 21:6–42.)

[11 May 1879]

As the facts of civilization must outweigh the authority of parchments, however venerable and revered; as when Science and Scripture stand opposed the latter must suffer, it is a grave mistake for those who believe the Protestant Bible to be a special inspiration of the will of God revealed to man, to use it against the progressive ideas that mark the growth of the race. Although the spirit and principles of the Bible teach justice, mercy and equality, narrow minds uniformly dwell on the letter and misquote and misapply isolated texts of Scripture, to turn this Magna Charta of human rights into an engine of oppression. Every reform that has marked the progress of the nineteenth century has been compelled to meet and conquer the objection, "The Bible is opposed to it." In the initiative steps of the temperance movement distillers and drunkards rejected the arguments of the apostles of temperance because Christ made wine, and Paul recommended Timothy and the church at Macedonia "to drink a little wine for the stomach's sake, because of their many infirmities."[1] Gerrit Smith, Edward L. Delavan[2] and others publicly vindicated the Bible against such teachings of reverend doctors of learning and position thirty years ago. When Garrison denounced slavery as a sin against God and man, these same conservatives defended it as a Bible institution.[3]

"Servants obey your masters" outweighed the Golden Rule with the teachers of the people.[4] When the Fugitive Slave Law was passed in 1850, the Northern pulpit made haste to teach that it was the duty of

Christian men and women to catch "Onesimus" wherever they found him, and send him back to the house of bondage.[5] The effort to abolish capital punishment is stoutly resisted by the same class of minds, for the same reason, though not one text of Scripture can be found in favor of our barbarous system. The labor reform also is ignored, because, say they, the Bible teaches that the extreme of riches and poverty are a blessing—a heaven-ordained plan, to call forth the virtues of humility and gratitude on one side, and pity[6] and benevolence on the other. They quote the text, "The poor ye always have with you," to show the impossibility of securing any permanent equality in human conditions.[7]

With this experience in all reforms, it is not surprising that the demand for the enfranchisement of woman should be resisted by the same class for the same reason. "The Bible is opposed to it," although nothing is said in either the Old Testament or the New in regard to republican government, universal suffrage, or the political rights of women.

In that age of the world when the masses of men, as well as women, were enslaved,[8] but little was thought of individual rights, judgment or conscience, and the great central ideas of our religion and government. Woman's position in the State was never thought of by Moses, Jesus or Paul; hence they said nothing that can be properly quoted on either side. "Obedience to the powers that be" was the one lesson of the past, alike in the State, the church and the home;[9] but "resistance to the powers that be" is the higher lesson of the new civilization, through which we shall achieve political, religious and social freedom.

In contemplating the steady march of the race, from authority to individualism, how puerile the attempt to limit human development, by isolated texts of Scripture, that have no significance whatever, beyond the period and latitude where they were first uttered; and how dishonest to so interpret special directions and injunctions as to conflict with accepted universal principles;[10] Paul's oft-quoted injunctions to woman apply chiefly to her social condition, in the one relation of wife.[11] But the enlightened, developed woman of the nineteenth century is not buried in the wife, hence her rights and duties as a woman, a member of the State, are primal to all incidental relations. The important question with us is not what, in a dark age, was supposed to be woman's position, but what the representative women of these times do themselves believe and sanction. When they read, translate and interpret the Bible for themselves they will find many views now taught unwarrantable, unfair. One might as well explore the solar system with a microscope as study history with a dictionary, or the Bible with a concordance. As well decide the spheres of Jupiter and Venus without a knowledge of the planetary world, as the true relation of man and woman for all time by the customs of the Hebrews, Greeks and Romans, or the opinions of their philosophers centuries ago. In order to form wise conclusions on any subject, one must learn what is permanent, and what is transient in human experience.

As a specimen of the puerile arguments of those who quote Bible for woman's subjection, they establish man's authority by the priority of Adam. They say Adam was made first, then Eve, and as the woman was of the man, her true position is one of subjection;[12] hence, disfranchisement in this republic. If, however, as Paul asserts, the first woman was of the man,[13] and hence her subjection, as the historical fact has been reversed ever since, and the man has been of the woman, as a logical sequence his true position is subjection; hence, all the men in this republic instead of the women should be disfranchised. But science proves that the male and female of the human family, as of all the lower animals, were a simultaneous creation. Of the different views of the creation given in Genesis that one is preferable that harmonizes with science, and represents woman as man's equal in origin and authority, and not an afterthought, called into being merely to cheer man in his hours of ease. In Genesis i, 27–28, we have the first account. "God created man in his own image, male and female created he them, and gave them dominion over the fish of the sea, the fowls of the air, and every creeping thing that moveth upon the earth"; but there is nothing said of man's authority over woman. Here the first title deeds to the boundless acres of this green earth were given alike to man and woman, the sons and daughters of God. This account of creation harmonizes with science and common sense. The masculine and feminine elements must have existed eternally together, even in the Godhead, as there could be no perpetuation of creation without their simultaneous existence in the whole world of thought and action, found everywhere in the animal, vegetable and mineral world, in the intellectual, moral, spiritual forces, the positive and negative magnetism continuing the growth and development of the universe. Our Protestant religion[14] is too wholly masculine; its severe creeds and discipline are yet to be modified and softened by woman's thought. When her soul is breathed into biblical interpretations, Westminster catechisms and the thirty-nine articles of our Presbyterian faith,[15] our theologies will reveal new lights and shadows, freed from the dark and gloomy coloring of to-day. The Catholic Church, with a wonderful adaptability, gave her children the Mother of Jesus for an object of worship. Without intending it, she has given us a feeble apotheosis of woman. Art is deeply indebted to Rome for this beneficent gift to her inspired sons. The genius of Raphael[16] dwelt fondly on the queen of Heaven, "Mary, our Mother." Swedenborg[17] also meets this hunger of the heart by giving us a divine man in whom love and wisdom represent the masculine and feminine principles. Much that is plaintive in music, sad in poetry, and pathetic in art, is the expression of the soul's instinctive sigh for a Divine Mother. We shall give a new impulse to religious thought when we uplift the veil that hides the Heavenly Mother's face, and with loving lips pray after this manner: "Our Father and Mother, who are in Heaven, hallowed be thy names";[18] and this idea of the essential oneness and completeness of man and woman is clearly set forth in the very dawn of creation, in the opening chapter of Genesis. As women, we may as well stand by that view of our advent into this stage of being, especially as the New Testament echoes back through the centuries the same declaration of woman's individual existence, not as a "helpmeet" merely, but an independent creative will power. In Galatians, iii, 28, Paul, in speaking of the power of Christianity to make all conditions equal, said: "There is neither Jew nor Greek, there is neither bond nor free, there is neither male nor female, for ye are all one in Christ Jesus." Our famous Declaration of Independence is but the re-echo of this grand principle, making all free and equal, irrespective of sex, color or condition. The scene in the Garden of Eden, which is supposed to conflict with the first account of the creation, is metaphorical and allegorical, and is found in the Scriptures of all nations. Though it is not to be understood literally, yet there is a great truth bound up in that poem, and it fully sets forth woman's power as mother of the race. Just as in her degradation the race has been dragged down to vice, crime, misery, and death, so in her elevation, shall we be lifted up again, and become as God's, knowing good and evil. That beautiful engraving of Beatrice and Dante[19] illustrates the true position of woman as the natural leader in the moral world. Beatrice tall, majestic, self-poised, in a slightly elevated position, gazes up into heaven, as if to draw her inspiration from the great soul of truth, while Dante, on a lower platform, looks up to her with a chaste and holy love; and thus the poet tells us, by the law of moral attraction, woman draws man from the hells to heaven. When we consider that woman, as the mother of the race, molds the brain and heart of all mankind, possessing a creative power second only to that of God himself; that in prenatal life every passing feeling, thought, passion of her soul are all daguerreotyped in the new life, whether for good or ill, we appreciate the blighting, dangerous influence of a literal rendering of these prophecies that make woman's highest glory her most terrible curse. As great stress is laid on the curse pronounced on woman,[20] I ask your attention to a fault in the translation. In using the word "shall" instead of "will," our English expounders have made a command of a prophecy. In the original Hebrew the verb used is "will" prophetic, not "shall" authoritative.[21] If, however, it be true, as some assert, that the majority of women prefer a state of subjection, that is no reason why an enlightened minority should accept the same condition. The fact that the few in every stage of development have protested against this slavery of sex proves a social law that can not be ignored. Whatever the theory of their true position, representative women have in all ages and nations walked outside the prescribed limits and done what they had the capacity to accomplish, and the women of the Bible form no exception. They preached, prayed, prophesied, expounded principles of government to kings and rulers, led armies, saved nations and cities by their wisdom and diplomacy, conquered their enemies by intrigue as well as courage. They communed with spirits, told fortunes, solved the mysteries of the seen and unseen, and, in great emergencies, trusting to their own strength and judgment, rose superior to the customs and conventionalisms of their times, and in no case is there a word of disapproval from prophet or apostle.

Women were among the earliest followers of Jesus, through good and evil report, ever ready to help His disciples in spreading the gospel of liberty and equality. "Honorable women not a few"[22] gild the pages of the sacred record, from Genesis to Revelation, the chosen companions of prophets and seers, of the apostles and their Master. With such independent types of womanhood as slew Abimilech and robbed Samson of his strength,[23] such as Deborah and Huldah, the Queen of Sheba, Ruth and Naomi, Esther, Vashti, Mary, Martha, Priscilla and Phoebe,[24] who shall say that the Bible teaches either by precept or example the subjection of woman? In considering the dignity and variety of their positions, we see that the representative women of the Bible ably illustrate its broad principles.

In Exodus, chapter 2, we have an account of Pharaoh's daughter sacredly guarding the life of a Hebrew child, in defiance of the King's decree that all the male children of that people should be slain, showing how naturally women act from their own judgment rather than the commandments of men.

In Exodus xv, 20, we read when the Israelites were delivered from Egyptian bondage, Miriam, the prophetess, the sister of Aaron, took a timbrel in her hand, all the women went out after her with timbrels and dances, and joined in the song of triumph and victory, thus manifesting the same love of liberty as the men by their side.

In Judges iv, 5, we find mention of Jael and Deborah, both marked characters, the one conquering the enemy with stratagem, the other with courage.[25] Deborah was a woman of very remarkable wisdom and insight, as shown in the fact that under her dynasty Israel enjoyed uninterrupted peace and prosperity over forty years.[26] When Barak, who was probably as great a general for those days as Gen. Grant is for ours, was ordered to go forth to battle, he had so little faith and courage that he refused to go unless Deborah went with him. Accordingly she led the armies of the Lord to victory.

As they journeyed along together, she seeing that Barak was pluming himself on the glory he was to reap in the coming battle, she quietly remarked, "the victory shall not be thine, for the enemy shall perish by the hand of a woman; and thus it came to pass, Sisera, the captain of the Gentile host, perished at the hand of Jael, and in the hour of victory Deborah and Jael shared with Barak in the applause of the people."

In Second Kings, xxii, 14, we are told that on finding a certain book in the temple of the Lord, Josiah, the King, sent his wise men to Huldah, the prophetess, to interpret. She did so, advised the King as to his future action, and the result proved her clear-sightedness and wisdom.

They found Huldah in the college in Jerusalem, pondering, no doubt, grave questions of State and church, of time and eternity, while Shallum, her husband, was keeper of the wardrobe. Yet we find no deprecatory remarks in the record on this invidious change of employment.

How grandly Queen Vashti stands forth in sacred history, refusing at the bidding of her King to grace with her presence the debauch of a drunken husband and reveling court. She gave up wealth, position, title, everything, rather than personal dignity.[27]

Tennyson[28] thus celebrates her love of purity rather than place:

> O, Vashti! noble Vashti! Summoned out,
> She kept her state, and left the drunken King
> To brawl at Shushan, underneath the palms.

It is curious to read what was said in the Cabinet meeting of Ahasuerus next day of Vashti's insubordination. Memucan seemed to be chief spokesman. No one condemned the action of Vashti *per se*, but for its effect on other women. Memucan, in pleading the case, said that Vashti had not only wronged the King, but the princes and all the people, and if she was not punished all women would despise their husbands. So he advised the King to give her royal estate to another, lest the ladies of Media and Persia, hearing of Vashti's contempt, should do likewise, and so Ahasuerus chose a new Queen. Esther, being more politic, managed to have her own way in all things and still keep her place.[29] She in fact ruled as well as reigned with Ahasuerus, and promoted her family and people to all the places of honor and profit. As to Job's wife, many severe criticisms have been passed on her in the pulpit, because she grew impatient under Job's intense suffering; advised him to curse God and die.[30] And yet some of our wise men are debating a similar question—whether there is any moral wrong in ending a life of pain and suffering. In Proverbs, 31, we have King Lemuel's idea of a good wife,[31] which is decidedly a strong-minded business woman, extensively engaged in merchandise—buying fields and planting vineyards. In Ezekiel, xiii, 17, 18, we find false prophets condemned.[32] "Woe to the women who betray souls for bread, who slay the souls that should not die, and save the souls that should not live." A lesson of self-reliance and personal responsibility is here taught. In Nehemiah, vi, 14, a prophetess by the name of Noadiah is mentioned. There is honorable mention of several women in the Apochrypha.[33] In the New Testament there are innumerable instances of the valued ministerial services of women, and of friendships with both Jesus and His disciples. In the first chapter of Luke we read of Mary the mother of Jesus, and her cousin Elizabeth,[34] both religious inspirational characters, who alike prophesied concerning Jesus. Mary is worshiped to this day by the largest denomination of

Christians. In Luke ii, 36, we find mention of Anna, a prophetess of great age, a widow who departed not from the temple, but served God with fasting and prayer night and day. She gave thanks publicly unto the Lord, prophesied of Christ, and spake of him to all them that looked for redemption in Jerusalem. In John iv, 7, a conversation is recorded between Jesus and a woman at the well in Samaria. He there revealed himself and the spirit of the religion he came to teach, and the nature of true marriage. His conversation with the woman was so profound and respectful, that his disciples marveled that he should spend so much time to enlighten an ignorant woman. There was something remarkable in the tenderness of Jesus for all womankind, and the devotion he inspired in all classes; the virtuous and the vicious alike worshiped at his feet. In Luke vii, 37, there is a touching picture of an outcast washing the feet of Jesus with her tears, and wiping them with the hair of her head. His disciples reproached him because they thought the woman was unworthy to touch him. His answer was remarkable alike for its wisdom and beauty.[35]

Jesus had no fear of compromising himself in the cause he represented by kindness to the most unfortunate. Many women gave Jesus freely of their substance. At the first gathering of the disciples, recorded in "The Acts," when men and women were alike filled with the holy ghost, it was announced, "This is that which was spoken by the prophet Joel; I will pour out my spirit upon all flesh; your sons and your daughters shall prophesy."[36]

Lydia, Priscilla, Persis, Julia, Tryphena, Mary and Martha[37] were all converted to the religion of Jesus and labored with the chosen disciples to spread the new gospel of love, liberty and equality, and as a proof that these women thoroughly understood its principles, we are told that when a certain man named Apollos,[38] an eloquent man and mighty in the Scriptures, came to Ephesus and taught only the baptism of John, and began to speak boldly in the synagogue, Aquila and Priscilla took him in private and expounded to him the doctrines more perfectly. The directions given to the Corinthians, i, 11, as to their appearance in praying and prophesying, apply alike to men and women;[39] and when the Apostle afterward says, "Let your women keep silent in the churches," it is evident he did not refer to preaching, as just before he had given directions how they should appear.

The wives of deacons, in several texts, should have been translated deaconesses, as women held places of honor and trust in the early church.

From all this we maintain two points: 1. That the examples given in our Bible prove an individual life and unlimited sphere for woman, in harmony with "divine will," or natural law. 2. That when Bibles are written, translated and interpreted by women, "the revealed will of God" touching their true origin and destiny will be more clearly stated. A close reading of the English translation of the Bible reveals the fact that for the general term, signifying mankind, including all humanity, women as well as men, the noun expressing man only is unfairly substituted. Just as it is in our law books. The feminine gender is never recognized in our criminal code. We find only the pronouns He, His, Him. It may be that the ancient jurists had so high an idea of woman that they made no provision for her as a criminal; but inasmuch as we are arrested, tried and hung by these masculine statutes, it is but fair that they should also secure us in all the rights, privileges and immunities as equal members in the Christian church, and as equal citizens in the American republic. A fair translation of the Epistles of Paul show that women did pray, preach and teach in the early church; and our most liberal-minded clergy, in all sects, are giving us to-day a new and higher interpretation and translation of the Scriptures as to the sphere of woman; and the Methodist Church is taking the lead. Some of its leading Bishops are pronounced in favor of woman suffrage. The *Methodist Quarterly*, April, 1878, contained an able article from the pen of the Rev. A. Hastings Ross, on "The silence of women in the churches."[40] And good Bishop Janes,[41] in the last years of his life, gave his influence in the direction of woman's elevation.

In regard to Paul's advice to women, we must remember the low, ignorant condition of the women in those Eastern nations—how disorderly they were in public assemblies, chattering with each other, playing with their children, running in and out in the midst of the exercises—disturbing in every way the solemn services. It was to them he said: "I suffer not a woman to 'chatter' in the churches."[42] "Speak" is not the fair interpretation of the Greek word "laleo," used in the original. These special epistles were given to the women of the church at Corinth, and have no significance whatever for the educated, enlightened women of our American churches in this nineteenth century.

Suppose it be an historical fact that among the Hebrews and Romans women were the slaves and subjects of man; is that a reason for their being so to-day? In those times the masses of men were slaves also; yet in this American republic they enjoy, in theory at least, political equality. Is it not fair to suppose that a higher civilization may in some degree ameliorate the condition of woman? Also suppose a few white men in power do assert that the will of God, revealed to them, teaches the rightful subjection and enslavement of black men and all women, and the few black men and women capable of reason assert that the revealed will of God to them teaches the higher truth, liberty to all. Is not the assertion of the latter class worth as much as the former? Might not a text of scripture involving the rights and interests of oppressed classes be as correctly rendered from their standpoint as from that of their masters?

Frederick Douglass, in the height of the anti-slavery struggle, once said: "Prove to me that the Bible sanctions slavery, and in the name of God and humanity I would, if possible, make a bonfire of every Bible in the universe."[43]

And so say we. Prove that the Bible sanctions and teaches the universal subjection of woman to man as a principle of social order, and we should be compelled to repudiate its authority and do all in our power to weaken its hold on popular thought. For looking over the dark past, and seeing the womanhood of all nations crushed between the upper and nether millstones of lust and superstition, and through her degradation, the disease and death that has blighted the race, we can not believe that a God of law and order, in what is claimed to be His revealed will, could have sanctioned a social principle so calamitous in its consequences as investing in one-half the race the absolute control of all the rights of the other, thus subjugating the weak to the strong, moral power to brute force, the mother to her own sons, and baptizing this holocaust in the name of the Christian religion.[44] "Every race," says a recent writer, "above the savage has its Bible. Each of the great religions of mankind has its Bible. The Chinese pay homage to the wise words of Confucius, the Brahmans prize their Vedas, the Buddhists venerate their Pitikas, the Zoroastrians cherish their Avesta, the Scandinavians their Eddas, the Greeks their Oracles and the songs of their bards," the Christians believe the New Testament to be divinely inspired, the Hebrews of our day accept with equal reverence the Old Testament,[45] and thus all along each nation has had its own idea of

God, religion, revelation; and each alike has believed its own ideas the absolute and ultimate. Much as these 'Bibles' differ in all that is transient and local, the texture of sentiment, the moral and religious principles are the same, showing a responsive chord in every human soul, in all ages and latitudes. All Bibles contain something like the decalogue; the 'Golden Rule,' written in the soul of man, has been chanted round the globe by the lips of sages in every tongue and clime.[46] This is enough to assure us that what is permanent in morals and religion can safely bear discussion and the successive shocks of every new discovery and reform.[47]

THE TEN VIRGINS.

In the first eleven verses, chapter 25 of Matthew, we have the duty of self-improvement and development, impressedly and repeatedly urged, in the form of parables, addressed to man and woman alike. The sin of neglecting and burying one's own talents, capacities, and powers, and the penalties such a course involves, are strikingly portrayed in this parable. "The kingdom of heaven is likened unto ten virgins, who took their lamps and went forth to meet the bridegroom: And five of them were wise; five were foolish. They that were foolish took their lamps, and took no oil with them. But the wise took oil in their vessels, with their lamps; while the bridegroom tarried they all slumbered and slept. And at midnight there was a cry made, Behold! the bridegroom cometh; go ye out to meet him. Then all these virgins arose and trimmed their lamps. And the foolish said unto the wise, give us of your oil, for our lamps have gone out. But the wise answered, saying, not so, lest there be not enough for us and you, but go ye rather to them that sell and buy for yourselves, and while they went to buy the bridegroom came, and they that were ready went in with him to the marriage, and the door was shut." This parable is found among the Jewish records, substantially the same as in our scriptures. Their weddings were generally celebrated at night,[48] yet this parable fairly describes the two classes of women that help to make up society in general. The ones, who, like the foolish virgins, have never learned the first important duty of cultivating their own individual powers, using the talents given them, and keeping their lamps trimmed and burning. The idea of being a helpmeet to somebody else has been so sedulously drilled into most women that an individual life, aim, purpose, ambition is never taken into consideration; they ofttimes do so much in other directions that they neglect the most vital duties for themselves. We may find in this simple parable a lesson for the cultivation of courage and self-reliance. These virgins are summoned to the discharge of an important duty at midnight, alone, in darkness and solitude. No chivalrous gentlemen there to run for oil and trim their lamps. They must depend on themselves, unsupported, and pay the penalty of their own improvidence and unwisdom. Perhaps in that bridal procession might be seen fathers, brothers, friends, for whose service and amusement the foolish virgins had watched many precious hours, when they should have been trimming their own lamps, and kept oil in their vessels. And now, as with music and banners, magic lanterns and torches, guns and rockets fired at intervals, the bride and groom with their attendants and friends numbering thousands, brilliant in jewels, gold and silver; magnificently mounted on richly caparisoned horses—for nothing could be more brilliant than were those nuptial solemnities of Eastern nations—as this spectacle, grand beyond description sweeps by, imagine the foolish virgins pushed aside in the shadow of some tall edifice, with dark, empty lamps in their hands, unnoticed and unknown. And while the castle walls resound with music and merriment, and the light from every window stream out far into the darkness, no kind friends gather round them to sympathize in their humiliation, nor to cheer their loneliness.

It matters little that women may be ignorant, dependent, unprepared for trial, temptation. Alone they must meet the terrible emergencies of life, to be sustained and protected 'mid danger and death, by their own courage, skill and self-reliance, or perish.

Again, woman's devotion to the comfort, education and success of men in general, and to their plans and projects, her self-abnegation and self-sacrifice have been so lauded, so sweetly sung by poets, philosophers and priests as the acme of human goodness and glory, that feminine vanity is quite apt to take that form of expression.

When women sacrifice themselves to educate the men of their households, and make themselves ladders by which their own husbands, brothers and sons climb up into the kingdom of light and knowledge, while they themselves are shut out from all intellectual companionship, even with those they love best—such are indeed like the foolish virgins, they have not kept their own lamps trimmed and burning; they have no oil in their vessels, no resources in themselves; they bring no light to their households, nor the circle in which they move; and when the bridegroom cometh, when the philosopher, the scientist, the saint and the scholar, the great and the learned come together to celebrate the marriage feast of science and religion, the foolish virgins, though present, are practically shut out—for what know they of the grand themes that inspire each tongue, and kindle every thought. Even the brothers and sons they have educated now rise to heights they can not reach, span distances they can not comprehend.

The solitude of ignorance, ah, who can measure its misery!

John Stuart Mill says when public sentiment demanded "a sentimental delicacy" of woman, as her most charming characteristic, women felt called upon to have turns of fainting and hysteria on all those sudden occasions when clear thought or prompt action would have been more serviceable.[49] But in the progress of civilization, as greater vigor of mind and body was called for by an improved manly taste, these graceful weaknesses went quite out of fashion. In our day, women, instead of continually fainting in men's arms, now arm and equip themselves to do battle by land and sea, buffeting the waves of vice and crime as well as old ocean, to save struggling men from death, and destruction. This parable of ten virgins is full of instruction to those whose lamps are not kept trimmed and burning, whose talents perish in their endless ministering to the animal wants of those about them. It may be a startling utterance, but nevertheless true, that a woman's first duty is to herself—to seek those conditions that will best develop her powers and capacities, that will best secure her own health, happiness and freedom. Perhaps it is equally startling to assert that womanhood is more than wifehood or motherhood, because it is a more universal fact. Hence, the discussion of this question should always turn on the rights of women, not as wives or mothers, which are incidental relations. With everything as free to woman as to man, in the world of thought and action, why may not her pet virtue, "self-sacrifice," like the ancient fainting and hysteria, give place to moral heroism, to self-reliance and self-support, to all those active virtues which would make them a new power in the work of life? In conversation with a well-educated and rather liberal woman, not long since, we chanced to speak of the lamentable patience with which women endure wrongs they could so easily escape. "Ah!" said she, "that is the Christ in woman." I felt that she was wrong in her conception of Jesus—brave, heroic, denouncing the vices and crimes, the opinions and customs of His day and generation, and He made all human relations subordinate to what He deemed His great individual work in life, the promulgation of a new religion. The sacrifice of an individual, to a great moral principle of universal interest, for the benefit of a generation, is essentially different in its essence, and infinitely higher in its grade of action, than the self-sacrifice of all women to false and degrading conditions, who from want of principle dare not defy the popular sentiment that surrounds them. Jesus bore with patience what He could not escape, but where resistance was possible He verified His words that "He came not to bring peace on earth, but a sword."[50] The one defect in Mrs. Stowe's "Uncle Tom," which well illustrates woman's misconception of her mission on earth, is the perversion of his deeply religious nature, making him through it a more abject slave, and by his example quenching, rather than kindling, the fires of liberty for his race.[51] What may be God-like for a man to do when all the consequences of his act culminate in his own person, if we can imagine such a combination of circumstances, may be most calamitous in its far-reaching results, as a precedent or principle of action. "Resistance to tyrants is obedience to God."[52] True religion sets men and women free; it does not hold them supinely down, to endure the slow, dwarfing, crippling, withering of all those powers that in their growth and development would make them like gods, knowing good and evil. Religion is a perception of the moral laws that govern the universe, a conscientious observance of them and a worshiping love of their divine Author, and of their manifestations in humanity wherever found. They are the world's saviors, who, at any personal sacrifice, seek and follow the truth; who never cringe at the feet of error to secure a transient peace and prosperity for themselves. There is no more fatal proverb to round out our lives than "anything for peace." Justice, liberty and equality first; then, and then only, will come that blessed peace that passeth all understanding.[53]

The wise virgins are they who keep their own lamps trimmed and burning, and oil in their vessels for their own use; who have improved every advantage for education, secured a healthy, happy, complete development, and entered all the profitable avenues of labor for self-support, that when the opportunities and responsibilities of life come they may be fitted fully to enjoy the one and ably discharge the other.

These are the women who to-day with telescopic vision explore the starry firmament and bring back the history of the starry world. With chart and compass they pilot ships across the mighty deep, and with skillful fingers send electric messages around the world. In galleries of art, the grandeur of nature and the greatness of humanity are immortalized by them on canvas, and by their inspired touch dull blocks of marble are transferred into angels of light. In music they speak again the language of Mendelssohn, Beethoven, Chopin, Schumann[54] and are worthy interpreters of their great thoughts. The poetry and novels of the century are theirs; they also have touched the key-note of reform in religion, politics and social life. They fill the editor's and professor's chair, plead at the bar of justice, walk the wards of the hospital and speak from the pulpit and the platform.

Such is the widespread preparation for the marriage feast of science and religion, such is the type of womanhood that the bridegroom of an enlightened public sentiment welcomes to-day, and such the triumph of the wise virgins over the folly, ignorance and degradation of the past, as in grand procession they, too, enter the temple of knowledge.

~ St. Louis Globe-Democrat, 12 May 1879; as corrected by ECS on clipping in ECS Papers, DLC.

1. Quotation from 1 Tim. 5:23. For the making of wine by Jesus, see John 2:1–10. The word "wine" was omitted from the quotation in the published report of ECS's speech. It appears in her manuscript.

2. Edward Cornelius Delavan (1793–1871) played a key role in founding the New York State Temperance Society in 1829. (ANB.) In the 1830s, in debates against those who used the Bible to excuse consumption of wine, Gerrit Smith countered that the Bible commanded people not to harm themselves. As Smith stated in published correspondence with Delavan, "Jesus Christ was not a man of science; the bible is not a book of science." Since those in the nineteenth century realized its harmful consequences, they should not drink wine. (Octavius Brooks Frothingham, Gerrit Smith, A Biography [New York, 1879], 67–69; Ralph Volney Harlow, Gerrit Smith: Philanthropist and Reformer [New York, 1939], 76–78, 87.)

3. On the debate over the Bible and slavery, see Caroline L. Shanks, "The Biblical Anti-Slavery Argument of the Decade 1830–1840," Journal of Negro History 16 (April 1931): 132–57.

4. On servants, see Col. 3:22 and Eph. 6:5. The "Golden Rule," in Matt. 7:12, reads: "Therefore all things whatsoever ye would that men should do to you, do ye even so to them."

5. Onesimus was a slave sent back to his owner by the apostle Paul, in

Philem. 10. This discussion continues in her manuscript: "Oceans of ink & eloquence were poured forth, in essays & sermons to demoralize the conscience of the nation ↑in order to maintain the slave power↓, but the first gun at Sumpter blew 'the institution' into ten thousand fragments & taught the religious world a new lesson in freedom."

6. The printed text reads "dignity"; "pity" is the more logical word in her manuscript.

7. Mark 14:7 and Matt. 26:11.

8. In the manuscript this sentence begins: "In that age of the world when the people were governed by theocracies & despotisms, when ↑the masses of↓ men as well as women, were enslaved".

9. From Rom. 13:1, "For there is no power but of God: the powers that be are ordained of God."

10. New paragraphs begin here in the manuscript: "The leading idea in our government & religion is individual rights, not man's alone, but woman's also, hence those texts of scripture based on the Jewish idea of womans have no application whatever to ~~womans~~ ↑her↓ position in this republic.

"Accepting however, the letter of Paul's injunctions to woman, they have no application whatever to her political rights, but to her social condition, in the one relation of wife."

11. By the injunctions of the apostle Paul, ECS refers to several passages used against granting women an equal voice in church and state. Paul commanded women to "keep silence in the churches," adding, "if they will learn anything, let them ask their husbands at home: for it is a shame for women to speak in church." (1 Cor. 14:34-35.) He directed wives to "submit yourselves unto your husbands, as it is fit in the Lord" and reminded them "that the head of every man is Christ; and the head of the woman is the man." (Col. 3:18; 1 Cor. 11:3.)

12. ECS points to one of the two accounts in Genesis of the creation of man and woman. The priority of Adam derives from Gen. 2:21-23, the second account, wherein God removed a rib from man and "made he a woman, and brought her unto the man." Adam responded by saying "she shall be called Woman, because she was taken out of Man."

13. 1 Cor. 11:8.

14. In the manuscript this passage begins: "The Jewish, Mahometan, & christian religions are too largely based on the masculine principle; the severe creeds & discipline of the Protestant are yet to be modified & softened by womans thought."

15. The Westminster Catechism, written during the English Civil War, and the Thirty-nine Articles, dating from the reign of Elizabeth I, defined the major Protestant faiths.

16. Raphael (1483-1520), an Italian painter, was noted for his pictures of Mary, mother of Jesus, most notably the *Sistine Madonna* (1513).

17. Emanuel Swedenborg (1688-1772), a Swedish mystic and writer, in-

spired a large religious society of Swedenborgians organized into the Church of the New Jerusalem. He wrote that man and woman were not embodiments of opposing principles but each one a combination of wisdom and love.

18. ECS revises the opening line of the Lord's Prayer, Matt. 6:9.

19. Beatrice Portinari (1266–1290), a Florentine noblewoman who inspired Dante's poetry, guides him through Paradise in his *Divine Comedy*. ECS describes a popular engraving based on the painting *Dante and Beatrice* by Ary Sheffer, an early nineteenth-century French painter. It illustrates a scene in the "Paradiso," canto 1, lines 46–54. (John Denison Champlin, Jr., ed., *Cyclopedia of Painters and Paintings* [New York, 1885], 1:371, 4:124–26.)

20. Gen. 3:16. After the Fall, God told Eve, "I will greatly multiply thy sorrow and thy conception; in sorrow thou shalt bring forth children; and thy desire shall be to thy husband, and he shall rule over thee." ECS was familiar with Sarah Grimké's statement that the so-called curse upon woman "is a simple prophecy. The Hebrew, like the French language, uses the same word to express shall and will." Grimké went on to blame translators who were "accustomed to exercise lordship over their wives" and thus read the text "through the medium of a perverted judgment"; they "converted a prediction to Eve into a command to Adam." (Sarah M. Grimké, *Letters on the Equality of the Sexes and the Condition of Woman* [1838; reprint, New York, 1970], 7.)

21. ECS continues in the manuscript: "But what a monstrous idea that woman should be cursed in her maternity. That she should have been command to multiply & replenish the earth & have ↑been↓ eternally punished for obedience to that command. And yet all the religions of the earth alike thus degrade woman making her the author of sin, taking counsel with evil one, & cursed of Heaven. Woman may trace her degradation in no small measure, to the perversion of the religious element in humanity, destroying her own self respect & the respect of man for her, by teaching the doctrine of Gods special displeasure visited on her for all time!"

22. A modification of Acts 17:12.

23. In Judg. 9:50–55, when an unnamed woman mortally wounded Abimelech, he asked to be slain by a man, "that men say not of me, A woman slew him." In Judg. 16:4–20, Delilah cut Samson's hair to make him weak.

24. ECS identifies most of these women of the Old and New Testaments in the text that follows. Those she omits are the Queen of Sheba, who visited Solomon "to prove him with hard questions," 1 Kings 10:1–10; Naomi and her loyal daughter-in-law Ruth, in the Book of Ruth; and Phoebe, the head of a Christian community near Corinth, Rom. 16:1.

25. This introduction of Jael continues in the manuscript: "Though Jael by false promises of protection induced Sisera to sleep in her tent, & when sleeping drove a nail into his temples yet in the song of triumph she is chanted as blessed above all women. The moral character of a woman's action is seldom considered so that she seconds man in all his plans & projects, but when she claims any rights, honors or privileges for herself, for her individual

happiness, or the benefit of her sex, then she is denounced for the slightest deviation from strict propriety or custom."

26. It is here that ECS began to recycle pages in her manuscript, and the pages with multiple numbers continue through her reading below of 1 Corinthians.

27. Queen Vashti's disobedience of an order by the king is told in Esther 1:9–22.

28. Alfred, Lord Tennyson, "The Princess," pt. 3, lines 1181–83. Tennyson (1809–1892) was the leading poet of the Victorian Age.

29. Esther, whose story is told in the book of the same name, replaced Vashti as queen.

30. Job 2:9–10.

31. Prov. 31:10–31.

32. ECS struck out this sentence and the two following it in her manuscript. In her quotation ECS modifies verses 18 and 19.

33. The Apocrypha consists of fifteen books found in early Christian versions of the Old Testament and sometimes still included in editions of the Bible.

34. Elizabeth was the mother of John the Baptist, Luke 1:5–80.

35. Luke 7:41–50. In conclusion Jesus said: "Her sins, which are many, are forgiven; for she loved much: but to whom little is forgiven, the same loveth little."

36. Acts 2:16–17.

37. All early converts to Christianity, Lydia appears in Acts 16:12–15; Priscilla in Acts 18:2–28, Rom. 16:3–4, and 1 Cor. 16:19; Persis in Rom. 16:12; Julia in Rom. 16:15; Tryphena in Rom. 16:12; and the sisters Mary and Martha in Luke 10:38–42 and John 12:1–8.

38. Acts 18:24–28.

39. 1 Cor. 11:4–7. The verses prescribe that while praying men should uncover their heads but women should cover theirs. Paul's directive about silence in the churches is in 1 Cor. 14:34.

40. "Silence of Women in the Churches," *Methodist Quarterly Review* 60 (April 1878): 238–68. This unsigned article criticized the biblical scholarship of five authors who opposed women speaking in churches, including Abel Hastings Ross (1831–1893), a Congregational clergyman and lecturer at Oberlin College. (*Ohio Authors and Their Books.*) The anonymous author concluded that "Paul never contemplated for one moment issuing a decree of either specific condemnation upon the order of prophetic women in the Church, or of enforcing a law of universal silence upon the Christian women of all the ages, and that he never intended to suppress the ministry of a cultured spiritual womanly influence and service in the sanctuary where Christ is to be glorified."

41. Edmund Storer Janes (1807–1876), a bishop of the Methodist Episcopal church for thirty-one years, rode the train with ECS eastward from California

in 1871, engaging in "pleasant conversations as we sat outside on the platform, day after day, and in the soft moonlight late at night." (Simpson, *Cyclopaedia of Methodism*; *Eighty Years*, 294–95.) ECS's manuscript continues after this sentence: "We are indebted to him for expunging the word obey from the Methodist marriage service. Bishop Simpson & Bishop Haven have also said brave words for the enfranchisement of woman."

42. 1 Cor. 14:34–35. In this paragraph, ECS presents a synopsis of the historical and linguistic argument advanced in the *Methodist Quarterly Review* in favor of women speaking in churches. The author described ignorant women of the East who did not listen in silence to their preachers as the specific conditions addressed by the apostle Paul, and showed that the Greek verb used by Paul meant chatter, not all speech. Lucretia Mott constructed the historical argument in a similar fashion: "Customs suited to darker ages in Eastern countries, are not binding upon enlightened society." ("Discourse on Woman, Delivered in Philadelphia, December 17, 1849," in *Lucretia Mott: Her Complete Speeches and Sermons*, ed. Dana Greene [New York, 1980], 154.)

43. In "Slavery's Northern Bulwarks," a speech delivered in 1851, Douglass disagreed with clergymen who thought the Bible sanctioned American slavery but promised "that *should* doctors of divinity ever convince me that the Bible sanctions American slavery, that Christ and his apostles justify returning men to bondage, *then* will I give the Bible to the flames, and no more worship God in the name of Christ." (Douglass, *Papers*, 2:284.)

44. A new paragraph here in the manuscript reads: "It is through the utter perversion of woman's religious sentiments that such teachings are tolerated to day. It is sad & pitiful to behold large classes of intelligent women gathering into our temples of worship to listen to sermons on woman's creation fall curse & subjection as the weaker vessel. Surely the will of God must be in the line of happiness & perfection, hence none of the positions & conditions yet realized by woman could have been projected by direct fiat from Heaven, but have been in all cases the result of causes within human controul."

45. Octavius Brooks Frothingham, *The Religion of Humanity. An Essay* (1873; reprint, New York, 1975), 60. The quotation is closed at this point in the published report of her speech; in fact ECS's direct quotation ends as indicated.

46. This sentence paraphrases Frothingham, *Religion of Humanity*, 75. The Decalogue is another term for the Ten Commandments.

47. The manuscript ends here. For more on ECS's many uses of the next section of her speech, on the Ten Virgins, see note above at 24 November 1877.

48. The information about Jewish weddings came from Adam Clarke, *Commentary on the Holy Bible*, a source ECS returned to in discussing this passage in the *Woman's Bible*. Parallel parables have not been identified.

49. "The Subjection of Women," Mill, *Collected Works*, 21:307.

50. Matt. 10:34.

51. In Harriet Beecher Stowe's *Uncle Tom's Cabin*, Uncle Tom accepts being sold from one owner to another until he is killed by his final owner, Simon Legree.

52. An epigram attributed to Thomas Jefferson.

53. Phil. 4:7.

54. Composers Felix Mendelssohn (1809–1847), Ludwig van Beethoven (1770–1827), and Robert Alexander Schumann (1810–1856), all Germans; and Frédéric François Chopin (1810–1849) of Poland.

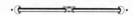

170   ECS to Matilda Joslyn Gage

Chicago,[1] May 15th [*1879*].

Dear Friend:

I reached the St. Louis Convention at the last moment, and was sorry to find that you and Olympia Brown had just gone. However I was in time to make a short speech, preside for two hours, and witness one of the most touching incidents that ever occurred on our platform.[2]

The ladies of the convention, delegates from many different states, presented our dear friend, Susan B. Anthony, two beautiful baskets of flowers, in the presence of the immense audience which had gathered through all the long sessions for three days.

Mrs. May W. Thompson of Indianapolis,[3] in presenting the flowers referred in the most happy way, to Miss Anthony's unselfish and untiring devotion to all the unpopular reforms, through long years of pitiless persecution and ridicule, and thanked her in behalf of the young womanhood of the nation, that their path had been made smoother by her brave life. Our Susan was so overcome with the delicate compliments offered her, and the fragrant flowers at her feet, that for a moment she could find no words to express her appreciation of the unexpected acknowledgement of what all American women do indeed owe her.

As she stood before that hushed audience, her silence was more eloquent than words, for her emotion was shared by all. With an effort she at last said: "Friends, I have no words to express my gratitude for this marked attention. I have so long been the target for the criticism and ridicule of our cause, I am so unused to praise and compliment, that I stand before you surprised and disarmed. If any one had come on this platform and abused all womankind, called me hard names, ridiculed our arguments or denied the justice of our demands, I should with readiness and confidence have rushed to the defence, but my Quaker education unfits me to make any appropriate reply for this offering of eloquent words and flowers, and I shall not attempt it."

Being advertised as the speaker of the evening, she at once began her address, and as that grand woman stood there and made an argument worthy a Senator of the United States, I recalled the infinite patience with which for upwards of thirty years she had labored for educational reforms, temperance, anti-slavery and woman suffrage, ridiculed by the press, arrested, tried and fined for exercising an American citizen's right to vote, misrepresented and ignored by women themselves, whose rights she had struggled to secure, with an earnestness and faithfulness worthy the martyrs in the early days of the Christian Church, I said to myself, verily the world now as ever crucifies its saviors!

Thanks to the untiring industry of Mrs. Minor and Miss Couzins the Convention was in every way a success, morally, financially, in crowded audiences, and in the fair, respectful and complimentary tone of the press. Looking over the proceedings and resolutions, the thought struck me that the National Woman Suffrage Association is the only organization that has steadily maintained the doctrine of Federal power, against state rights.[4]

The great truths set forth in the 14th and 15th amendments, of United States supremacy, so clearly seen by us, seem to be vague and dim to our leading statesmen and judges, if we may judge by their speeches and decisions. Your superb speech on state rights should be published in tract form and scattered over this entire nation.[5] How can we ever have a homogeneous government so long as great universal principles are bounded by state lines. I am homeward bound at last, after eight months of continual speaking, having filled one hundred and fifty engagements. The first of June will find me once more on the blue hills of Jersey. The prairies are beautiful in their fresh spring grass and flowers, but the valleys of the Mohawk and Hudson are more to my taste.[6] Perhaps it is well for "the young man to go west" and grow up with the country, but for women on the shady side of sixty, whose eyes have always dwelt on rocks, trees, mountains, hills and rivers, the east must ever be more congenial. As ever yours,

⇒ *Elizabeth Cady Stanton.*

&#x224b; *NCBB*, June 1879. Also in *History*, 3:147–48.

1. According to the *Chicago Tribune*, 16 May 1879, ECS was stopping at the Sherman House.

2. For local coverage of this scene, see *Film*, 20:761–63.

3. May Wright Thompson (1844–1920), later Sewall, was a cofounder of the Indianapolis Equal Suffrage Society in 1878 and its delegate to the National's annual meeting. A widow and a schoolteacher, she married Theodore Lovett Sewall in 1880 and with him established the Girls' Classical School of Indianapolis. (*NAW*; *ANB*.)

4. The first resolution adopted at the National's meeting in St. Louis, possibly authored by Virginia or Francis Minor, read: "*Resolved*, That the right of self-government through the elective franchise is the birthright of the native United States citizen, and the acquired right of the adopted citizen, being an essential attribute of citizenship, the exercise of which may be regulated, but not destroyed by legislation, in the same manner as the natural right to life and liberty and happiness may be regulated so far as not to interfere with the same rights of others." (*NCBB*, June 1879, *Film*, 20:778–88.)

5. This was Gage's speech "United States' Rights vs. State Rights," delivered at the National's Washington convention in 1879. Gage published the text in *NCBB*, February 1879, *Film*, 20:644–51.

6. Johnstown, her childhood home, lies in the Mohawk River Valley in upstate New York. The Hudson River flows near Tenafly, New Jersey.

## 171 &#x224b; SBA TO HARRIET HANSON ROBINSON

Rochester N.Y. Aug. 12th 1879.

My Dear Mrs Robinson

Yours of the 9th inst. is just here—giving me a severe rebuke—not because of its contents—but because of my failure—<u>neglect</u> perhaps— to do what I promised Mrs Gage I would do a long time ago—that is, write you with regard to the Massachusetts History Chapter—[1] But— but—well my excuse is—perfectly <u>full</u> occupation of every minute— I was summoned home from Mrs Stanton's—three weeks ago—my sister feeling that our dear Mother could not live until I should get here—but she rallied from the sinking spell—and is still alive—very feeble—and this though she has since been clear down to death again with bloody Dysentery— She has a wonderfully strong hold on life— Still it doesn't

seem possible for her to continue with us very long— And yesterday—
we got my sister started off for the sea shore—for I felt her life de-
pended on getting out of the care & sympathy of home matters— So
my time is full—yet—with the best of nurses to aid me— But to
History—

Mrs Stanton & I both feel that we cannot pledge ourselves to accept
any one's contributions, without the privilege of revision— Even the
reminiscences of Mrs Nichols were left for us to revise—cut down—or
work over—into our own style— But we felt them so simply & beautifully told—that we wished to preserve her style—[2] And thus it may be
with every one's contribution— Still, you can see—if you were putting
together a history over your own name—you would not be willing to
give up to any other person the absolute control of a part of it—
Therefore, I was, six weeks ago—to have written you—that we could
not accept Massachusetts on the terms you proposed— Mrs Stanton
has already written up the early work—down to the War—[3] And if you
have any facts or incidents that you will let us have—that we wish to
incorporate we will not only be grateful for them, but pay you for any
expense you may have been at to procure them— I am sorrier than I
can tell for the seeming injustice of Mrs Gage—& sorry that I myself
should have been the cause of the seeming—and hope you will charge
it all to me—

Of the difficulties you experience in getting at facts from the leaders
of the Boston factionists, I can fully comprehend—having had sundry
experiences with "her" in the past 12 years— When Mrs Stanton was
engaged to write a brief sketch of the W.R. movement for "Eminent
Women of the Age"—Lucy Stone refused to give her even date of her
birth—replying ↑to↓ her request—an entire forbiddal of her speaking
her name in her article—and but for Appletons Cyclopedia—and the
broad & catholic & sensible & just sister-in-law—Antoinette Brown
Blackwell—Mrs S. would have been unable to get enough to make a
paragraph—and yet—notwithstanding Lucy's narrow pig-headedness—
see how generously, and more than just—Mrs Stanton wrote up Lucys
↑in that book↓!![4]

For the whole twelve years—she has repelled everybody's efforts to
↑establish a↓ cooperate↑ion↓ with among all the suffragists, in a most
dogged manner— One after another—just as sincere as yourself—has
tried to bring about a re-union—and like yourself—always found all on

one side ready & willing to cooperate—while on the Lucy side—it was utter refusal to go or to be or to work with so and so—unless so and so would ignore and repudiate the N.W.S.A. and E. C. S. and S. B. A—[5] I could tell you the most comically little, bigotted, "mean" things—but no matter— Lucy, like the South, is incapable of understanding magnanimous overtures—(thousands of which have been ↑made↓ to her)— other than concessions—and acknowledgements of wrong on the part of the one who offers thems— She like our Southern unreconstructed, will have to be translated, I fear, before any change of feeling can be wrought in her— She suspects every ↑woman—↓ in Boston or out— east or west—who is not a narrow partisan with her—and against us of the N.W.S.A. and she cannot help it—she is so organized—I suppose— So all who cooperate & affiliate with us of the N.W.S.A. will have to act in and of themselves & their own better judgements— But enough of Lucy—

We are now going to begin getting our History into Book form—very soon—have publishing arrangements nearly completed— Shall make two volumes—the 1$^{st}$ will come down to the war— The work grows on our hands—and it is so difficult to get persons to give us the facts of their work— I am in Hopes Mrs Nichols reminiscences will help others of the old & early workers to send us like accounts of their beginnings—especially do I want such a chapter from dear, glorious Earnestine L. Rose—

When we come down to the secession of Lucy—Mrs Stanton Mrs Gage & I know all about it & its impelling causes—better than any others—save Lucy herself—& she would hardly be likely to put those that urged her on into print— It was a very picayune, ↑personal↓ persecution—on her part—such as she must be mightily ashamed of now—if she has eyes to see herself as others see he[r]

I was very glad you & daughter[6] came to Rochester Con.—was sorry not to see you at Wash. last winter and at St Louis this spring—pleas consider yourself as always invited—and always wanted—wherever the "National" holds a meeting—especially do I now ask & urge you to be at Washington at our 12$^{th}$ National Con. in that city—

I am glad to see so much effort to rouse Mass. women to register & vote—large numbers voting at the school elections will do much to stop the cry of "Women don't want to vote"!!⁷

I hope to hear from you—that you forgive Mrs Gage—for my failure

<u>to</u> <u>do</u> <u>my</u> <u>duty</u>— Please give my kind regards to your lovely daughter—
Sincerely yours

                 ⇜ *Susan B. Anthony*

[*sideways beneath signature*] N.B.—Is Lucy going to remain disfranchised rather than suffix blackwell to Stone!—or glorious Mr Garrison punned it—"sink Stone into a <u>black</u> <u>well</u>"!! either horn of the dilemma will be hard for her—but she has a capital chance to test the question— that is <u>sue</u> the <u>Registrars</u> for refusing to register—she might make a splendid case out of it in the Courts!!⁸

⇜ ALS, on NWSA letterhead for 1877, year corrected, Robinson-Shattuck Papers, MCR-S. Square brackets surround letter worn from corner.

   1. Robinson was the first, but not the last, author to challenge the working relationship between those who supplied local information for the *History* and its trio of editors. Solicited by Matilda Gage to contribute material for a chapter on Massachusetts, Robinson insisted on authorial control, while Gage maintained that the editors needed to edit and possibly rewrite all contributions. She would work with them, Robinson told Gage in May 1879, and cut her text as they required, but she would not risk her reputation as an author by allowing them to alter her prose and perhaps introduce errors into her research. Hoping for a better deal from ECS and SBA, Robinson requested that Gage present the problem to them during her next visit to Tenafly. Hearing nothing more, Robinson assumed that Gage had failed in her assignment. SBA here explains that the silence was her own fault. (M. J. Gage to H. H. Robinson, 17, 28 February, 24 April 1879, and H. H. Robinson to M. J. Gage, 18 May 1879, Robinson-Shattuck Papers, MCR-S.)

   2. The reminiscences of Clarina Nichols were published in *National Citizen*, July, August 1879, and with additional material in *History*, 1:171–200.

   3. Like other birthplaces of the antebellum woman's rights movement, Massachusetts merited a chapter in the first volume of the *History*, and it was that chapter described by SBA as nearly done. Negotiations with Robinson concerned more recent history for a chapter that appeared in the third volume under Robinson's name.

   4. This bit of history is confused: *Appleton's Cyclopaedia of American Biography* (1886–1889) did not exist when ECS wrote a sketch of Lucy Stone for *Eminent Women of the Age* (1868). SBA may refer to the more recent events surrounding biographies and the essay on woman's rights for *Johnson's Cyclopaedia*.

   5. When Robinson asked Lucy Stone to collaborate with her on a contribution to the *History*, Stone rebuffed her. She had already refused to participate in the project, she wrote, and did not want to hear about the matter again. "I am more than content to be left entirely out of any suffrage's history those

ladies may publish. I can readily understand how much they must prefer to write their own statement of their connection with Geo. Francis Train, Mrs. Woodhull, Laura D. Fair and the Mormons, and it is easy to see that they will be glad to get you, and other women, who had only regret for their action in connection with those persons, to appear with them in history." (L. Stone to H. H. Robinson, 4 March 1879, Robinson-Shattuck Papers, MCR-S.)

6. Harriette Lucy Robinson Shattuck (1850–1937) followed the family trade as a writer and shared her mother's commitment to woman suffrage. Her trip to Rochester for the Decade Celebration came just a month after her marriage. (*WWW4*; *New York Times*, 23 March 1937; Bushman, *"Good Poor Man's Wife."*)

7. On 10 April 1879, women in Massachusetts secured the right to vote for school committee members. Efforts to ensure that as many women as possible registered and voted are evident in issues of the *Woman's Journal* from June to September 1879.

8. Although Lucy Stone paid property taxes under her own name, the board of registrars ruled that she must add Blackwell to her name in order to vote. She refused, and her name was removed from the list of voters. (Kerr, *Lucy Stone*, 202–3; Wheeler, *Loving Warriors*, 259–60.)

## 172 ✎ ECS to Elizabeth Smith Miller

Tenafly, August 16, [*1879?*].

Dear Julius:

I came home early in June and found Hattie here duly installed in the third story so as to be retired for study.[1] There she has been all summer working without relaxation, much to my chagrin and disappointment. Susan spent a few weeks with us working on our history. This summer our house has been more like a school than a place for vacation recreation. [W]e generally retire about half past ten. Before going upstairs, Theodore, [H]attie and I clean up the parlors and set the table for breakfast. At half past seven we arise, breakfast at eight, after which Theodore, Hattie and I, clear away the table, wash the dishes, and set the table for lunch, make our beds, regulate things generally, and go to our rooms and read and write. At twelve, Hattie gives us all lessons in elocution. At one, we lunch, wash dishes, set the table for dinner and then do some intellectual work again. After dinner, we scrape the dishes, throw a clean towel over them and let them stand in a secluded corner until after breakfast next day, as we are dressed and in a hurry to see the sunset or enjoy the twilight hour, with walks, chats, etc., etc.

We have had no company and no drives for none of us have had time for either. Economy and elocution have been the two great arts Hattie has drilled us in this summer. She has held the purse and it is astonishing how triumphantly we have come through thus far. Yours,

~ *Johnson.*

~ Typed transcript, ECS Papers, NjR. Transcript shows year "1877," and in *Film* at that date, 19:518. Letters in square brackets obscured by binding.

1. Back from her year in Boston studying elocution and oratory, Harriot Stanton prepared herself to debut as a lecturer in the fall of 1879. It is not known why Theodore Stanton had returned from Europe.

## 173 ~ SBA TO ELIZABETH BOYNTON HARBERT

[*12? October 1879*][1]

you, alone, could go out & go through the programme, with a P.M. session free—& an evening session 25 cts admission—and make it pay you something handsome—at least I know I could—& think you could— illegible ↑ditto↓, Mrs Haggart[2]—could if she would go & do the same for Idianna—so Miss Pinney[3] of Ohio, & in almost every state there is at least one woman equal to the work—if she were only sure she could make ends meet—& a little more— Each state's Vie. Pres. of N.W.S.A. ought to do this precise work in her state—and the Vice Pres. at large ought to be free to go to the aid of first one & then anoter of the state Vice-Presidents— Oh—isn't ↑it↓ easy and splendid to do ↑up↓ great campaigns on paper and in ones day dreams as well sleeping ones—

But I declare to you, that I feel so restiff in view of the great & ↑grand↓ work of organizing our forces for most efficient cooperation, that I should bound out of this mere lecture business, here & there, scattered all over—were it not for the hungry wolf that rises before my vision— If I can get $10,000, invested in good first mortgages & 4 per cent bonds—so that I can go free—without anybody's saying Susan is reckless—& sure to go back on her friends for support when she gets broken down—then you & the world ↑will↓ see me through ↑throw↓

the Bureau's to the winds—and buckle on the harness for <u>movement</u>
<u>work</u>— and of course I should <u>do</u> <u>so</u> now, <u>if</u> <u>and</u> <u>if</u>—<u>I</u> <u>were</u> <u>sure</u> of
<u>netting</u> <u>something</u> <u>decent</u> by <u>movement</u> <u>work</u>—but you see—<u>this</u> Lec-
<u>ture</u> business <u>is</u> <u>sure</u>—and though, with my small $30— fee—not speedy—
I am able from it to contribute one & two hundred dollars in cash to the
movement work ↑each↓ year—and therefore I feel that I musn't let drop
my little <u>certainty</u> of <u>cash</u> for an uncertainty— But it does seem to me
that the women who are vastly better speakers than I ever was—or am
to day—who do not earn a dollar, any way, by staying at home, or going
away—it does seem to me amazingly strange they don't try the experiment of canvassing & I don't see why they couldn't make it pay expenses vastly better than I used to 25 years ago— Women—↑there are,
and↓ plenty of them—ambitious to be known and named as leaders of
our movement—and yet not possessed of the business tact & energy or
enterprize to make a <u>venture</u> <u>any</u> way to gain their longing—they are
<u>waiting</u> for the people to bring honors to them—without their having
sacrificed a thing to earn them— Only disappoinment & envy awaits
all such—for only such "instant in season and out of season"[4] work <u>as</u>
<u>yours</u>—work without calculating whether it is going to bring you back
a harvest of cash or Laurels—work done for the sake of <u>its</u> <u>good</u> results
to the world—will <u>ever</u> <u>bring</u> <u>honors</u>—<u>lasting</u>—to any one—a bright
sally—spasmodic—for glitter—may cause a <u>flutter</u> of praise—but it is
fleeting as the morning dew &c—

Now did I tell you how I felt about any union of Temperance women
with us Suffrage per se women     I was in Indianapolis & dined with
dear glorious Mrs Wallace[5] & saw Mrs May Wright Thompson—and
Mrs Wallace was full of the coming National Women's Temp. Con—
but told me—though she should try hard to get a <u>Suffrage</u> <u>plank</u>—a
<u>general</u> suffrage plank, adopted—she ↑had↓ but little expectation of
seeing it carried—[6] now ↑hence,↓ though <u>we</u> are ready to join them &
work for the election of any candidate pledged to both W.S. and
Temp.—<u>they</u> are not ↑ready to join us—↓ that is—not a majority and
those who are,—like Miss Willard & Mrs Wallace—would not <u>go</u> <u>with</u>
<u>us</u>—<u>if</u> <u>it</u> <u>were</u> <u>likely</u> to divide their Temp. Society—which it surely
would be very sure to do— ↑So I don't see the way—↓

But there will be a grand discussion at their annual meeting—and I
should love to see & hear the "fight" go on— Still it is doubtless better
for them—that we <u>pronounced</u> personages should leave them to <u>work</u>

out their own salvation—which wont be done until they work into suffrage a right for all women of all states—

I think about all that we can do now—is to roll up the largest petition ever sent into Congress—first—then secure a hearing before our Committee—you remember we have the promise of a special Com[7]—making the most out of our Wash. Con. and then at our May 1880 Con. at Indianapolis—to appoint strongest & ablest women on Committees to memorialize the several National President Nominating Conventions— and also to get our best speaker heard in their Con—as well as a W.S. Plank in their platform—& then after we have aliked besieged each & all—go into the canvass for the party that gives us the nearest ↑to↓ full recognition— If the Repub's could be made to believe that every one of ↑our↓ W.S. public speakers would take the stump for the Nationals,[8] or the Democrats—if either of them gave us a W.S. plank—& the Repub's did not— It would settle the question with the Repub's in the twinkling of an eye—a plank would go into their platform & Mrs Stanton & Mrs Livermore would both be not only invited but urged to address their National Convention—but, you see, the Repub's know or feel sure that nearly every individual woman of us will do all we can to help them—whether they do, or don't, help us—or promise to help us— thus you see, while our women will thus allow themselves to be used by and for the Party—while it ignores our just claims—there is no lever for us we have no fulcrum on which to plant our lever— So we must go on—like ↑the↓ boy—trying, in vain, to lift our movement by the straps of its boots, into political recognition—[9] I see no chance for us—at present—

This is a fearful scrawl—but it is all I can give you to night— I have religiously devoted this entire Sunday to doing up long neglected duties of letter answering—until my every muscle of fingers wrist & shoulder is lame—and the day has been hot—hot—like the past two weeks— I sent $50— to our N.W.S.A. Treasury yesterday—& wrote Mrs Spencer if it wasn't genuine "blood money"—it surely was "sweat money"—for ↑I↓ never ground out my lecture fees in such fearfully hot halls as the past two weeks—[10] affectionately yours

~ *Susan B. Anthony*

~ ALS incomplete, Box 2, Elizabeth Harbert Collection, CSmH.

1. With the first sheet of this letter now missing, the date is based on

references within the letter: to writing on a Sunday after SBA met with Zerelda Wallace in Indianapolis on October 7. Her location is not known.

2. Mary E. Rothwell Haggart (1843–1904), active in Indiana's suffrage movement since 1869, was a delegate to the National association's meeting in May 1879. Married in 1866 to the homeopathic physician David Haggart, she moved from western Pennsylvania to Danville, making a name for herself as an accomplished speaker, and then to Indianapolis, where she published a weekly *Woman's Tribune* in 1878 and 1879. In the 1880s, she held office in both the National and the American suffrage associations. (*A Biographical History of Eminent and Self-Made Men of the State of Indiana* [Cincinnati, Ohio, 1880], vol. 1, 7th congressional district, pp. 66–68; *Woman's Journal*, 3 July 1880, 3 September 1904; *History*, 2:860, 3:142, 175, 535–44, 551, 4:409, 411, 422–23, 428.)

3. Eva L. Pinney (1851–1916) of South Newbury, Ohio, was a founding member in 1874 of the Newbury Woman Suffrage Political Club, one of the most active suffrage groups in Ohio. Its members had tried to vote in every election since 1871. Pinney, a teacher by age nineteen, went to work about 1878 as a paid organizer for the political club in Geauga County, and at the same time she began to lecture across the state about temperance. Her speaking earned high praise at the National Woman Suffrage Association meetings in 1879 and 1880, where she was a delegate. She advertised her availability to lecture in 1881, but nothing more about her later life has been learned. She is buried with the family of a sister in East Granby, Connecticut. (*Woman's Journal*, 28 January 1878; *NCBB*, June 1881; *History*, 3:175n, 176n, 502; Florence E. Allen and Mary Welles, *The Ohio Woman Suffrage Movement* [n.p., 1952], 26–29; Geauga County Historical and Memorial Society, *Pioneer and General History of Geauga County* [Burton, Ohio, 1953], 658; Federal Census, 1870; on-line historical archive, East Granby Historical Society, Conn.)

4. An adaptation of 2 Tim. 4:2.

5. SBA lectured in Indiana in early October. Zerelda Gray Sanders Wallace (1817–1901) was president of the Indiana Woman's Christian Temperance Union and a cofounder in 1878 of the Indianapolis Equal Suffrage Society. Wallace concluded that women needed to vote after recognizing how little attention Indiana's legislators gave to women's temperance petitions, and the union endorsed her idea in 1875. Wallace worked with the National Woman Suffrage Association through the 1880s. (*NAW*.)

6. The National Woman's Christian Temperance Union convened in Indianapolis at the end of October and elected Frances Willard as its president. The members did not at this time endorse the home protection ballot. (Ruth Bordin, *Woman and Temperance: The Quest for Power and Liberty, 1873–1900* [Philadelphia, 1981], 63.)

7. On 29 April 1879, according to a report by the National Association, "the following resolution was submitted to the Committee on Rules of the United States House of Representatives:

"*Resolved*, That a select committee of nine members be appointed by the Speaker, to be called a Committee on the Rights of Women Citizens, whose duty it shall be to consider and report upon all petitions, memorials, resolutions and bills that may be presented to the House relating to the rights of women citizens."
Committtee members James Garfield, William Frye, Alexander Stephens, and Samuel J. Randall supported the idea. (*NCBB*, July 1879, *Film*, 20:814–17; *History*, 3:142.)

8. That is, the National or Greenback-Labor party.

9. SBA's boy who could not lift himself by his bootstraps illustrates one use of a proverb that also meant success requires the help of others. It later took on the metaphorical meaning that one could succeed by one's own efforts.

10. SBA to Sara Spencer, 11? October 1879, *Film*, 20:873.

## 174   SBA TO MARY B. CLAY[1]

Owenboro Ky.[2] Oct. 20th 1879

My Dear Mrs Clay

I have answered your telegram—saying I should arrive at Richmond the 25th without fail— My R.R. Guide says I can leave Bowling Green at 6 A.M. arrive at Lebanon Junction at 10 A.M. —leaving L.J. at 12.50 & arriving at Richmond ~~at~~ ↑Junction↓ 4.50 & at Richmond at 7.20—[3]

It will be a long & tedious days journey—but I can make it—and still be in pretty fair trim for my work— Now a word as to the <u>few</u> <u>minutes</u> <u>between</u> 7.20 & <u>8</u> Oclock & the platform—

All I shall want for the <u>inner</u> <u>woman</u>, will be a good cup of genuine <u>Kentucky Coffee</u>—(<u>not</u> Bourbon whiskey) not a thing to eat <u>before</u> my lecture—but after it—you may have a Kentucky <u>apple</u> <u>baked,</u> a slice of real Kentucky bread, and a glass of Kentucky "<u>blue</u> <u>grass</u>" <u>milk</u>—and though you should pile ↑before me↓ all ↑the↓ luxuries the good old state can muster—I should taste of but those three simple articles— I tell you this to put a stop to all thought of getting up every possible sort of dish to set before me— A cup of coffee <u>before</u> going on the platform—and a dish of bread & milk & baked apple after leaving it—

I am anticipating a great deal of pleasure in visiting your part of the state—& you may make all the engagements you please—that is with the dates my agent has given you—

He wrote me he had <u>offered</u> Bowling Green the 24<sup>th</sup>— Should they <u>not</u> accept it—& I have no engagement, anywhere, the 24<sup>th</sup>—I will go on to Richmond that day—

I will send you Telegram should I arrive at any other than the 25<sup>th</sup>— will anyway—so you will feel sure of me— Sincerely—

&#x1F800; *S. B. Anthony*

&#x1F800; ALS, Cassius M. Clay Papers, Manuscripts Department, KyLoF.

1. Mary Barr Clay (1839–1924) of Richmond, Kentucky, attended the National's annual meeting in St. Louis in May 1879 in order to make contact with the national suffrage movement. Named at once to be the association's vice president for Kentucky, she encouraged SBA to visit the state and made many of her arrangements. Mary, one of the daughters of Cassius M. Clay, Kentucky's famous opponent of slavery, married John Frank Herrick in 1866 but divorced him in 1872, resuming her maiden name. In 1880, she moved to Ann Arbor, Michigan, to educate her sons and soon emerged as a leader in that state's suffrage societies. Determined to bridge the split among suffragists, she also joined the American association and became its president in 1884. She contributed the report on Kentucky to the *History of Woman Suffrage*. (*American Women*; *History*, 3:818–22; Paul E. Fuller, *Laura Clay and the Woman's Rights Movement* [Lexington, Ky., 1975], 22–23.)

2. SBA was in Owensboro, not Owenboro, in western Kentucky along the Ohio River, where on this day she delivered the first lecture of her short tour into the state. She also spoke in Bowling Green, Paris, Hopkinsville, Trenton, and three times in Richmond. For coverage of Owensboro, see *Film*, 20:889.

3. She describes a trip northeastward, leaving Bowling Green on the Louisville & Great Southern Railroad, changing to the line's Knoxville branch at Lebanon Junction, and changing again at Richmond Junction to reach her destination. Richmond is south of Lexington, in the central part of the state.

## 175  &#x1F800; ECS to Frederic A. Hinckley[1]

Tenafly New Jersey  Oct 26<sup>th</sup> 1879.

Dear Mr Hinckley,

I will accept your invitation for Nov 9<sup>th</sup>, & attend the Woman suffrage convention on the 6<sup>th</sup> I am very desirous of meeting our liberal thinkers as often as possible

The greatest block in the way of our woman suffrage movement is the hold the priesthood have↑s↓ on the women "Thus saith the Lord" sent widows to the funeral pyre, holds women in harems to day, Mormon girls in polygamy, & all women in their church pews while men preach their subjection, their curse, their creation as an after-thought, for man's happiness. And yet how difficult it is to get women out of the old grooves of thought; religious prejudices are stronger than all others. With kind regards   Yours sincerely

﹖ *Elizabeth Cady Stanton.*

﹖ ALS, Charles Roberts Autograph Letters Collection, PHC.

1. Frederic Allen Hinckley (1845–1917), a Unitarian minister who led the Providence Free Religious Society, had invited ECS to speak to his congregation while she was in town to address the annual meeting of the Rhode Island Woman Suffrage Association. An officer of that association, Hinckley remained active in the suffrage movement through moves to Massachusetts, Pennsylvania, and Delaware. (*WWW1*; Lillie Buffum Chace Wyman and Arthur Crawford Wyman, *Elizabeth Buffum Chace, 1806–1899: Her Life and Its Environment* [Boston, 1914], 2:51–52.)

## 176 ﹖ SBA TO MATILDA JOSLYN GAGE

[*Cincinnati, Ohio, 1 November 1879*][1]

I have been two weeks in Kentucky, and am fully convinced the South is to be ours—(N.W.S.A,)—splendid field of operations. Why, half of Kentucky is now owned and managed by women. I went to see the widow of Cassius M. Clay.[2] She had just finished sowing eighty acres of wheat, and superintended five plows, running at the same time on a 450 acre farm. Her daughters, four of them,[3] each has 350 acres, and each manages her farm. Mary B. Clay took me over her farm. She has a tenant farmer. I tell you it does me good to see these women of Kentucky's oldest and most aristocratic families doing for themselves and their children. Indeed, I have heard it remarked over and over that hundreds and thousands of the women are actually supporting their husbands. They have more tact and sconce[4] to turn their hands and brains in line of the new order of things than the men. Oh, what a vast missionary field the South is for us; and we must go in and sow the seed.

&#x2767; *NCBB*, November 1879.

1. Matilda Gage noted the date of SBA's letter in an introduction to this excerpt. In Cincinnati to deliver a lecture and visit a cousin, SBA met on this date with the local arrangements committee of the American Woman Suffrage Association. (*Film*, 20:896–98.)

2. Mary Jane Warfield Clay (1815–1900) was not the widow but the ex-wife of Cassius Marcellus Clay (1810–1903). They divorced in 1878. Clay divided his land among his children in 1873, and their mother bought her farm from the couple's son in 1876. (*ANB*, s.v. "Clay, Cassius Marcellus"; Fuller, *Laura Clay and the Woman's Rights Movement*, 13–18.)

3. In addition to Mary Clay, the daughters were Sarah Lewis Clay Bennett (1841–1935), known as Sallie; Laura Clay (1849–1941); and Anne Warfield Clay (1859–1945), later Crenshaw. All of the Clay sisters became active in the suffrage movement. (H. Edward Richardson, *Cassius Marcellus Clay: Firebrand of Freedom* [Lexington, Ky., 1976], 31n, with assistance of the Filson Club, Louisville, Ky.; *History*, 3:818–20; Fuller, *Laura Clay and the Woman's Rights Movement*, passim; research by Ray Bonis, Special Collections, Virginia Commonwealth University.)

4. Wit or sense.

177 &#x224B; REMARKS BY ECS TO THE RHODE ISLAND WOMAN SUFFRAGE ASSOCIATION

EDITORIAL NOTE: ECS and Frederick Douglass were the distinguished guests of the Rhode Island Woman Suffrage Association at its annual meeting in Providence on 6 November. In the first of three short speeches she was asked to make, ECS followed Elizabeth K. Churchill, who spoke on the importance of personal independence in women.

[6 November 1879]

Mrs. Elizabeth Cady Stanton was next introduced. She, taking up the thread of remarks made by Mrs. Churchill, defined suffrage as a natural right. If there was an educational restriction, no one would care whether those who could not vote were educated or not.

The moment persons could vote it became important to educate them. If a man was ignorant, all the more reason why he should have the ballot in self-defence. All history and experience showed that an ignorant or non-voting class always fell under oppression. She said considerable about woman's sphere. That sphere has been said to be her home, but it was not so. A woman had no home. It belonged to some man. A woman did not own her children or even her wardrobe. And as for her home she had no ownership in it whatever. The country had just seen, in this very State, the daughter of a man, whom the nation had delighted to honor, flying with her children from her own home.[1]

She had wondered a great deal whence sprang the notion that home was a woman's sphere. She had finally traced it to this conclusion. The theory was that sin entered the world by means of woman; consequently that woman had always been in collusion with the devil. Man felt himself fully a match for the devil, but he was rather afraid of the devil, and woman too. As he could not catch the devil and put him on limits, he proceeded to catch woman and put her under all the restrictions he could devise, and this he called woman's sphere. Mrs. Stanton commented upon the apathy of woman, to what was to her a matter of vital importance, and said in giving reasons for this indifference that religious people were afraid to have women become suffragists, because as quick as they did so, they began to think, and then they became infidels. The liberals, on the other hand were rather afraid that if women could vote, they would go for stricter Sunday laws, for the Bible in the schools and all the things of that sort which Liberals did not think worth while.

She endorsed the idea of the 16th amendment, giving women suffrage, as individuals, subject to the restrictions of State laws. Many, she said, were trying to have a sixteenth amendment, for the purpose of putting God into the constitution. She thought God was there already. Wherever there was justice and goodness and truth there God was. She wanted to put woman into the constitution, adding merrily: "For if ye love not woman whom ye have seen, how shall ye love God whom ye have not seen."[2] The audience laughed and applauded, and Mrs. Stanton presently concluded her address.

~ *Providence Daily Journal*, 7 November 1879.

1. She refers to Kate Chase Sprague (1840–1899), a daughter of Salmon Portland Chase (1808–1873), former chief justice of the Supreme Court. In the late summer of 1879, she took her children and left her husband, William Sprague, a former governor and United States senator from Rhode Island,

after drunkenness and violence on his part, a suspected affair with Senator Roscoe Conkling on hers, and mutual financial problems upset their marriage. When William Sprague pointed out that if she left the marriage, she did not have the right to take the children, Kate Sprague returned home, where, it was reported, she remained "under lock and key." The Spragues divorced in 1882. (*NAW*; *ANB*; *NCBB*, September 1879.)

2. ECS modifies 1 John 4:20: "If a man say, I love God, and hateth his brother, he is a liar: for he that loveth not his brother whom he hath seen, how can he love God whom he hath not seen?"

## 178  &#8674; ECS to Elizabeth Buffum Chace[1]

[*Tenafly*] Nov. 12, 1879

I owe you an apology for not keeping my engagement with you. I wanted to talk to you about the History of Woman Suffrage which we have been publishing in the *National Citizen*. A rich lady in New York, Mrs. Elizabeth Thompson,[2] promises to publish it for us as soon as we are ready. My idea is to have some capable person in each State write a chapter on what has been done there. Would you or your daughters over your name write up Rhode Island, in as brief a manner as possible to do the work justice, giving Mrs. Davis due praise for what she did and keeping all personal antagonisms in abeyance to the grand results achieved?[3] We do not desire to give the world unimportant bickerings, and thus mar our grand movement in the eyes of future generations, but make a fair history of all that has been well done, and throw the veil of charity over the remainder.

Of course it is a task of love, as we can make no money on such a History.

If the American Association would coöperate with us in writing a great History, we will agree that Mrs. Gage and myself on one side, and you and Mrs. Howe[4] on the other, shall decide on all that shall go into the published volumes. We might add Mr. Higginson and Dr. Channing[5] if you think best. Let me know what you and your daughters think of the proposition.

&#8674; Lillie B. C. Wyman and Arthur C. Wyman, *Elizabeth Buffum Chace, 1806–1899* (Boston, 1914), 2:115–16.

1. Elizabeth Buffum Chace (1803–1899) was the president of the Rhode Island Woman Suffrage Association and a noted reformer and early supporter of William Lloyd Garrison. Although identified with the New England branch of the suffrage movement, she had worked with Paulina Wright Davis and she welcomed ECS to the recent annual meeting. ECS refers below to her daughters, author Elizabeth Buffum Chace Wyman (1847–1929), known as Lillie, and Mary Chace Cheney (1852–?), a widow engaged to marry James Pike Tolman in 1880. (*NAW* and *ANB*, s.v. "Chace, Elizabeth Buffum"; *American Women* and *WWW1*, s.v. "Wyman, Lillie B. Chace"; Wyman and Wyman, *Elizabeth Buffum Chace*.)

2. Elizabeth Rowell Thompson (1821–1899), heir to great wealth when her husband died in 1869, became a noted philanthropist, funding reform projects that ranged from temperance and labor publications to collective farming schemes, from cookery schools to women's medical schools. She called on SBA in Washington in the winter of 1879 with an offer to help underwrite publication of the *History of Woman Suffrage*, and in October 1880, she delivered a check for one thousand dollars. (*NAW*; *ANB*; *NCBB*, November 1880; *History*, 4:vii.)

3. Elizabeth Chace is credited with providing most of the information on Rhode Island for the *History of Woman Suffrage*, 3:339–50. Frederic Hinckley added his own recollections and tributes. Chace's biographers erroneously claimed she did not join in the work because of "original differences with the Stantonites." (Wyman and Wyman, *Elizabeth Buffum Chace*, 2:116.)

4. That is, Julia Ward Howe.

5. William Francis Channing (1820–1901) of Providence earned a medical degree from the University of Pennsylvania but devoted his time to invention and reform. A member of the Rhode Island suffrage association, he wrote for the *Revolution*, supported the eight-hour movement, and defended divorce. His wife, Mary, served as an officer of the National Woman Suffrage Association for fifteen years. The Channings moved to Pasadena, California, in 1884. (*DAB*; genealogical files, Grace Ellery Channing Stetson Collection, MCR-S; alumni files, University Archives and Records Center, PU.)

## 179 &#x224; "OUR GIRLS": SPEECH BY ECS

EDITORIAL NOTE: Despite the complaints she voiced about lecturing in the winter of 1878 and 1879, ECS returned to the lyceum circuit for one more season to deliver her most popular lectures, including "Our Girls." Audiences heard it in 1880 in Greenfield, Iowa, on January 24; Washington, Iowa, on February 21; Big Rapids, Michigan, on April 9; and, no doubt, in other towns not yet identified. The idea for a lecture about raising daughters came to ECS early on, when she spoke to the Seneca Falls Conversational in 1853 about "Our Young Girls" who suffered a "false system of education"; endured vacuous lives "without aim, object, plan or design"; and faced the expectation that they would be "ever young, smiling, and happy." She assigned the same title to the more elaborate speech she took on her first outing as a lecturer in December 1869. The speech bore that title through 1871, became "The Coming Girl," or, as one newspaper rendered it, "The Girl of the Future," in 1872, and shifted to "Our Girls" by 1875. The text published here is based on her undated manuscript of the speech and, to fill two small gaps, a late typescript made for ECS or her children from the same manuscript. Some pages of the manuscript date from 1870 or earlier, while varied papers and inks and renumbered pages as well as odd spacing where new and old pages meet indicate layers of revisions. The earliest report of the lecture, from Dubuque, Iowa, in December 1869, describes topics that survived her revisions: concern that girls sacrificed their health to fashion, hope that they would grow up to be not adjectives but nouns, and criticism of the marriage ceremony. By 1873, newspapers reported the lecture's lasting structure: "the coming girl will be healthy, wealthy and wise." Certain stories within the lecture also endured through the decade: the reference to watering the stock of the Erie Railroad and the swipe at Horace Greeley—both more timely in the early 1870s—are noted too in reports from 1879 and 1880. Moreover, most of the anecdotes that ECS indicated in her manuscript simply with parenthetical reminders can be expanded from newspaper reports over the course of a decade. Yet the imperfect and brief newspaper reports also make clear that ECS often added to the lecture the topics of immediate importance to her. In 1869, for example, she joined the upbringing of girls to the failure of women to rise in rebellion against the Fifteenth Amendment. In 1879, she protested the exemption of churches from taxation. At many times, she added woman suffrage to the needs of girls, and, as indicated in the end notes to the lecture, she varied her conclusions. Though the text below cannot match what audiences heard on any specific occasion, it is as close as sources allow. "Our Girls" was, in the words of Iowa's *Adair County Reporter*, a lecture that "delighted thousands of hearers in various parts of the land." (*Lily*, 1 March 1853; *Dubuque Daily Times*, 4 December 1869; St. Louis *Missouri Republican*, 29 December 1869; *Elkhart Observer*, 10 December 1873; *Indianapolis Sentinel*, 19 January 1879; Chicago *Inter-Ocean*, 22 January 1880; *Film*, 7:562–63, 14:122–23, 154–56, 17:425, 20:682, 685; *Adair County Reporter*, 15 January 1880; *Big Rapids Pioneer-Magnet*, 15 April 1880.)

[Winter 1880]

¶1    They are the music, the flowers, the sunshine of our social life. How beautiful they make our homes, churches, schools and festive scenes: how glad and gay they make our streets with their scarlet plumes, bright shawls and tartan plaids. Who can see a bevy of girls tripping home from school without pausing to watch their graceful motions, pretty faces, feet and legs, to listen to their merry words and peals of laughter. See how they romp and play with hoops and balls, with sleds and skates, wash their brothers' faces in the snow, and beat them in a race on yonder pond. These boys and girls are one to-day in school, at play, at home, never dreaming that one sex was foreordained to clutch the stars, the other but to kiss the dust. But watch awhile, and you will see these dashing, noisy, happy, healthy girls grow calm and pale and sad, and e'en though lodged in palace homes mid luxury and ease, with all the gorgeous trappings wealth can give, rich silks, bright jewels, gilded equipage, music, dancing, books, flowers, they still are listless and unsatisfied. And why? They have awakened to the fact that they belong to a subject, degraded, ostracised class: that to fulfill their man appointed sphere, they can have no individual character, no life purpose, personal freedom, aim or ambition. They are simply to revolve round some man, to live only for him, in him, with him, to be fed, clothed, housed, guided and controlled by him, to-day by Father or Brother, to-morrow by Husband or Son, no matter how wise or mature, they are never to know the freedom and dignity that one secures in self-dependence and self support. Girls feel all this, though they may never utter it, far more keenly than kind Fathers imagine.[1]

¶2    Walking in Madison Park[2] one day with my little boy, reading the signs hung on the trees, "No dogs admitted here," he remarked, "It is a good thing, mother, that dogs cannot read, it would hurt their feelings so to know that they were forbidden to walk in the parks." Yes, we said, the dogs like the girls seem to be shut out of the green pastures of life, while both alike are ignorant of the statutes by which it is done. Bruno sleeps on his master's rug in some dark street pining for the sunshine and the grass and a frolic through field and forest, without knowing his degradation published in that one invidious announcement, "No dogs admitted here," but if he should try to enter the park a smart rap on the nose would remind him that he was a dog and not a boy. So our young girls pine and perish for lack of freedom, for the stimulus of work and wages, something to rouse their ambition and love of distinction. They are clothed in purple and fine linen and in their gilded cages fare sumptuously every day, but if by chance, with some new inspiration they awake to life and go forth to claim the place in the great world that is by birthright theirs, they find at the very gates of life, at the entrance to every winding path leading to the Temple of knowledge, wealth, honor or fame, these self same little signs hung out, "No girls admitted here."

¶3    While the dogs and the girls suffer alike the penalty of the law, the degradation of the latter is greatly aggravated by the fact that they can read the signs. And what adds to the girl's humiliation, is the fact that the boy by her side reads them also, and finds out that to him alone the world is free. The universe of matter and mind is his domain, no constitutions, customs, creeds or codes block his onward way, but all combine to urge him on, his triumphs in science, literature and art are hailed with loud huzzas. He accepts the homage of the multitude as his sole right and looks with jealous eye on any girl that dares to tread upon his heels. In these artificial distinctions, boys learn their first lessons of contempt for all womankind. They naturally infer that they are endowed with some superior powers to match their superior privileges. But what avails it that here and there some proud girl repudiates these invidious distinctions, laughs at the supercilious airs these boys affect and braces up her mind to resist this tyranny of sex. She feels she is the peer of any boy she knows. She has measured many a lance on the playground and in the school, and now forsooth, shall custom make her bow to sex, to those inferior to herself. She scorns the thought, but what can one brave girl do against the world. Custom has made this type of boy, and now these grown up boys perpetuate the custom. Custom too has made the girl the slave, and subject womanhood perpetuates the custom. Man makes the creeds and codes, the constitutions, while woman is nought but a lay figure in the world, a mere appendage to lordly man, a something on which to hang his titles, name and fame. With blighted girlhood, wasted youth and vacant age, the ambition of most women we meet to-day is simply to be distinguished as the daughter, wife or mother of Gen., Hon. or Judge so and so, to shine in their reflected light, to wear their deeds and words of valor and of eloquence as their own bracelet, necklace, or coronal.

¶4  This should not be. Every girl should be something in and of herself, have an individual aim and purpose in life. As the boy approaches manhood he gathers up his forces and concentrates them on some definite work, trade or profession, has a wish, a will, a way of his own that everybody respects, hence he begins life with enthusiasm, early learns the pleasure of self dependence, growing stronger, nobler, braver, every day he lives. But alas for the girl, she leaves school with her ambition at white heat; perchance she has outstripped the foremost in the sciences and languages, she has her tools ready to carve her way to distinction. She too has a will of her own and desires the dignity and independence of self-support. But any career for a woman is tabooed by the world, and nothing that she proposes to do is acceptable to family and friends. If in spite of opposition a woman does step outside all conventional trammels, to do something that her grandmother did not do, she meets a dozen obstacles where a man does one. Surely the battle of life without any artificial trammels is hard enough, for multitudes of young men even perish in the struggle, but the girl who earns her bread, or makes for herself a name has all the boy has to surmount and these artificial barriers of law and custom in addition. Vinnie Ream.[3]

¶5  Do you wonder that so few are ready to take their rights? Multitudes of our noblest girls are perishing for something to do. The hope of marriage, all we offer girls, is not enough to feed an immortal mind, and if that goal is never reached what then? The more fire and

genius a girl has with no outlets for her powers, the more complete
is her misery when all these forces are turned back upon herself. The
pent up fires that might have glowed with living words of eloquence
in courts of justice, in the pulpit, or on the stage, are to-day consum-
ing their victims in lunatic asylums, in domestic discontent and
disgust, in peevish wailings about trifles, or in the vain pursuit of
pleasure and fashion, longing for that peace that is found only in
action. Thus multitudes of girls live and die unloving and unloved
who might have stood high in the shining walks of life a blessing to
others and themselves. I said to one of the most distinguished men
of our day not long since, your daughter has a wonderful genius for
drawing you should cultivate, it might be a source of great profit as
well [as] happiness to her. "Ah!" said he "she is interested in ragged
schools just now, that fills up her time."[4] "Yes," I replied, "but if
you should die and she be thrown on her own resources for bread,
she could not live by doing acts of charity, beside it is not wise to fill
up one's whole life with benevolence." All women were not made for
sisters of mercy and it is not best for any to watch the shadows and
sorrows of life forever. Charity is a good thing, says Sidney Smith,
but it is hard to be pitiful twenty four hours in the day.[5] I know a
beautiful girl just eighteen, full of genius, force and fire, who has had
one strong steadfast desire for years to be educated for the stage.
Her performances in private theatricals are marvellous. She has but
little thought of dress, fashion, frivolous pleasures or matrimony.
She lives in the ideal. She can give imitations to the life of Fanny
Kemble,[6] Charlotte Cushman, Ristori. She reads Shakspeare with
rare power and appreciates the nicest shades of his thought. She has
a passion for tragedy, all her desires her longings her hopes and
aspirations centre there; she thinks of the stage by day, dreams of it
by night, and in vain friends try to change the current of her thoughts,
her heart's desire, the purpose of her life. They have the power to
say her nay, to control her action, thwart her will, pervert her
nature, darken all life, but how can they fill the mighty void that one
strong passion unsatisfied makes in the human soul. The weary
hours of such a blasted life cannot be cheated with the dull round of
ordinary duties, with the puerile pleasures said to be legitimate to
woman's sphere. "The stage they say is not respectable," as if a royal
soul does not dignify whatever she touches. Have not a Siddons,

Kemble, Cushman, Kean, Rachel,[7] Ristori, made that profession honorable for all time? And what do the guardians of this girl propose for the sacrifice they ask? Can they substitute another strong purpose, will or wish as they desire? Are human souls like garden beds where passions can be transplanted as easily as flowers? Can these guardians pledge themselves, while they hold this child of genius to day in idleness and dependence, that they will surround her with comforts and luxuries her life all through? No. Fathers, Brothers, Husbands die, banks fail, houses are consumed with fire, friends prove treacherous, creditors grasping, and debtors dishonest; the skill and cunning of a girl's own brains and hands are the only friends that are ever with her, the only sure means of self protection and support. Give your daughters then the surest of all fortunes, the full developement of their own powers concentrated on some life work.

¶6 The coming girl is to be healthy, wealthy, and wise. She is to hold an equal place with her brother in the world of work, in the colleges, in the state, the church and the home. Her sphere is to be no longer bounded by the prejudices of a dead past, but by her capacity to go wherever she can stand. The coming girl is to be an independent, self-supporting being, not as to-day a helpless victim of fashion, superstition, and absurd conventionalisms.[8]

¶7 Let us consider then the reforms in her education necessary to realize the grand result. 1st She is to be healthy. As by a law of nature women mould themselves to man's ideal, we must educate our young men to demand something better than they have yet realized. All our customs and fashions, however trivial and transient, are based on the theory that woman was made simply to please man and to do this not by meeting him on the higher plane of spiritual and intellectual attraction in the world of thought, where, through ages of culture, he is supposed to dwell, and where through ignorance and inferiority she is supposed to be unable to go, but by a mere physical power such as beauty, manners, and dress can give. Hence she amuses man by an endless variety in her costume and calls out his chivalry by her seeming helplessness and dependence.

¶8 When there is a demand for healthy, happy, vigorous self-reliant women, they will make their appearance, but with our feeble type of manhood, the present supply of vanity and vacuity meets their wants. Woman, as she is to-day, is man's handy work. With iron shoes,[9] steel ribbed corsets, hoops, trails, high heels, chignons, paniers, limping gait, feeble muscles, with her cultivated fears of everything seen and unseen, of snakes and spiders, mice and millers, cows and caterpillars, dogs and drunken men, fire crackers and cannon, thunder and lightning, ghosts and gentlemen, women die ten thousands deaths, when if educated to be brave and self-dependent they would die but one. This sheer affectation of fear and feebleness men too have become so depraved in their tastes as to admire, and they really suppose that woman as she is, is Nature's work, and when they see a woman with brains and two hands in practical life, capable of standing alone, earning her own bread and thinking her own thoughts, conscious of the true dignity and glory of womanhood, they call her unsexed. But whatever his theory, the real facts of life show that man's chivalry and devotion are not manifested in proportion to a girl's need of them, but just the opposite. The beautiful highly educated wealthy heiress, who is in no hurry to marry either for a master or a home calls out ten times more chivalry than the friendless orphan girl, or the penniless widow with half a dozen children. Man's devotion is always in exact proportion to woman's actual independence!

¶9 Again when American women begin to care more for principle, than pleasing, more to be, than to seem, and understand their true dignity as citizens of a republic, they will not ape foreign customs, manners and fashions all out of joint with our theory of government. Our fashions as you all know are sent us by the French courtezans, whose life work it is to study how to fascinate man and hold him for their selfish purposes.[10] I have often wondered in fashionable parties and ball rooms if American girls with bare arms and necks had ever philosophized on the custom that required them to appear there half naked, while their brothers were modestly clothed to the very chin. This making an auction block of every drawing room, for the exhibition of our daughters' charms, and thus unduly stimulating the sensuous in our sons, is demoralizing to the virtue of the nation, dragging woman and man too down to death. It is assuming that the sexes are alike incapable of the higher and more lasting attractions of character of moral and spiritual power. (Beatrice and Dante)[11] God has given you minds, dear girls, as well as bodies and it is your duty to develope your immortal powers. Your life work is not simply to attract man or please anybody, but to mould yourselves into a grand and glorious womanhood.

¶10 The world will talk to you of the duties of wives and mothers and housekeepers, but all these incidental relations should ever be subordinate to the greater fact of womanhood. You may never be wives, or mothers, or housekeepers, but you will be women, therefore labor for the grander and more universal fact of your existence.

¶11 Speaking of the common idea that woman was made for man and not for her own happiness and enjoyment, Frances Power Cobbe,[12] a distinguished Englishwoman, says, "If it be admitted that horses and cats were made first for their own enjoyment and secondly to serve their masters, it is to say the least illogical to suppose that the most stupid of human females has been called into existence by the Almighty principally for man's benefit. Believing that the same woman, a million of ages hence, will be a glorious spirit before the throne of God, filled with unutterable love and light and joy, we cannot satisfactorily trace the beginning of that eternal and seraphic existence to Mr. Smith's want of a wife for a score of years here upon earth, or to the necessity Mr. Jones was under to find some body to cook his food and repair his clothes."[13] It is a great truth to impress on the mind of every girl that she is an independent creative will power, made primarily for her own happiness, making self-developement and self-support and the highest good of the race the end of her being. I would have girls regard themselves not as adjectives but nouns, not mere appendages made to qualify some body else, but independent, responsible workers in carrying forward the grand eternal plans in the redemption of mankind. There is a very pretty theory extant that every woman has a strong right arm on which to lean until she is safe the other side of Jordan,[14] but the facts of life conflict with the theory. We see on all sides multitudes of girls and women, matrons and maidens alike, thrown on their own resources for their daily bread, hence the importance of educating women for those positions that will secure pecuniary independence. I do not wish to undervalue domestic avocations, but the tastes of women vary as much as the tastes of men, and to educate all women for teachers and seamstresses, cooks nurses and chambermaids, is to make the supply in the home sphere greater than the demand, thus permanently to keep down wages and degrade all these branches of labour. Horace Greeley says what we most want is not women voters but 60,000 good cooks to-day in our kitchens. Well, suppose I educate my two daughters for cooks, the highest wages they can secure is $20 a month, $240 a year. A woman of refined tastes cannot live on that. Is there a harder and more monotonous life than revolving 365 days of the year round a cook stove?

¶12   The coming girl is to have health.[15]   One of the first needs for every girl who is to be trained for some life work, some trade or profession, is good health. As a sound body is the first step towards a sound mind, food, clothes, exercise, all the conditions of daily life, are important in training girls either for high scholarship, or practical work. Hence, girls, in all your gettings get health, it is the foundation of success in every undertaking. Sick men and women always take sickly views of everything and fail in the very hour they are most needed. One of the essential elements of health is freedom of thought and action, a right to individual life, opinion, ambition. The feebleness of body and mind so universal in women, may be attributed mainly to their being forever in a condition of tutelage or minority.[16] I am sure, gentlemen, you will all be glad to hear that the millenium is close at hand when you are to hear no more of headaches, earaches, sideaches, and backaches, that your homes are to be changed from the gloomy hospitals of to-day to abodes of health and happiness, when nerves are to be superseded by muscles.

¶13   It is as one of the conditions of health that the question of dress becomes one of great importance. "There was a time in the history of man," says Carlyle,[17] "when man was primary and his rags secondary, but times have sadly changed, clothes now make the man." I hope we are fast coming to that period in the history of woman when in her dress, health and freedom are to be the first considerations. As women are now rapidly asserting themselves in the world of work, an entire revolution in this respect is inevitable. A physiologist need but look at the forms of all our young girls to appreciate the violence done Nature in the small waists and constrained gait and manners of all we meet. Ordinarily a girl of fourteen is a healthy, happy, romping being, in short hair, short dress and clothes hung loosely on her shoulders, but as soon as her skirts trail and dress makers lace and tighten her clothes to form the waist as they say, a change takes place at once in her whole manner and appearance. She is moody, listless, weary, strolls when she should run, cries when she should laugh and this at the very age when she should manifest new power, vigor and enthusiasm. Much of this may be attributed to the many unnatural restraints placed on all girls, the indoor life and sedentary habits but more to her dress than any other one cause. The tight waist prevents a free circulation of the blood and action of the heart and lungs, contracts the ribs and paralyzes a belt of the nerves and muscles at least six inches in width round that part of the body. The long dress prevents all freedom of motion. When we remember that deep breathing has much to do with deep thinking we see the relation between scholarship and clothes. Girls by the style and material of their dress are practically debarred from outdoor exercise, and yet they need it as much as boys do and if well trained would enjoy it equally with them. Many a pleasant moon-light walk, or a sunset from the mountain top is sacrificed to a clean starched muslin dress or ruffled skirt, the greater often subordinated to the less, the girl forever to her clothes and the modern idea of what a woman's form should be. In looking at the beautiful paintings and statuary in the old world, I have often wondered where we moderns got our idea of the female form. It is certainly like nothing in Heaven above or the earth beneath, or the waters under the earth, for even to the mermaid is vouchsafed more breathing power than to the woman of the 19$^{th}$ century. None of the old artists have immortalized anything of the kind in marble or on canvas, and those of our times turn away in disgust from the daughters of Hancock and Adams to copy the Venus and Madonna of the past for the perfection of womanly grace and beauty.

¶14 All sensible men laugh at these wasp like waists and women themselves affect not to like them and declare, when attacked, that their clothes are perfectly loose, that they are small naturally, which is to say, that God, by way of making a variety in the human species, thought fit to lap the ribs of the American women. I do not like to interfere with the designs of Providence, but I should like to see the experiment fairly tried for one generation of hanging all woman's clothing loosely on her shoulders, that we might learn what hand God had in her present weakness and deformity. I do not believe that it is in harmony with God's laws that any woman should move up and down the earth with her ribs lapped. And the fact the mass of American women are diseased, old before they are thirty years, proves that some great law is violated. (West Point[18] Ann Arbor[19]). I conjure every girl in the sound of my voice, if she desires a healthy, happy old age, to attend to this question of dress at once, to have her clothes hung loosely on her shoulders and not dragging down as now on her vital organs, and to have her skirts above her boot tops that she may run up and down stairs with freedom, walk in all kinds of weather and be ready for any outdoor pleasure that may offer. If a girl must always change her dress for a walk, ten to one she will give up the walk and plead some other excuse for doing it. Exercise to be pleasant and profitable must be regular and to make it so, one must have a convenient comfortable dress. Young girls are moved about three times a year to walk five miles to some water-fall or hill-top. From the sense of weariness that follows such an effort in long dresses and laced boots, they infer that walking does not agree with them. When I was a girl with a short dress, round hat and a pair of light boots made precisely like my Father's, I used to walk five miles before breakfast, or ride ten miles on horseback, and to those early habits and the fact that my ribs were not lapped by tight lacing, I am indebted for a life of uninterrupted health and happiness. A man's boot is preferable to those made for women because the pressure is equal on the whole foot, and the ankle has free play. Health is the normal condition for all women, weakness, disease, pain and sorrow are the results in all cases of violated law. There is nothing more absurd and untrue than all the talk we hear of the natural weaknesses and disabilities of woman,[20] and so long as physicians continue to teach this theory, women instead of having a feeling of guilt, when their children or themselves are always out of health, they will continue to throw all their sins on a mysterious providence. With the scientific education of our youth of both sexes, and a strict observance of the great immutable laws of life, another generation might show as marked a change in the human family as we already observe in the lower animals, which science has done so much to improve during the last century.

¶15 Remember, girls, you have an inalienable right to be healthy and happy and it is your duty to secure these blessings. A sound body is to the mind what a good foundation is to a house. Napoleon[21] once said you cannot make a soldier out of a sick man, neither can you make a wise, kind woman out of a girl whose vital organs have been displaced with tight lacing and whose feet have been cramped with tight shoes. I have no hope that woman will ever remedy these things herself. I look to Fathers, Husbands, and Brothers to inaugurate some grand reform in this direction and unless it is done speedily, the higher orders of refined, cultivated American womanhood must give place to the sturdier foreign races. If you appreciate the effect of American institutions on character as highly as I do, you would feel that this would be a great calamity, for I consider the women of this republic, in beauty, intellect, moral power, and true dignity, superior to any type of womanhood that the world has yet seen and perhaps it might not be amiss in passing to say the same of our men also. There was nothing in all Europe that pleased me more than the self possession of Americans in moving about among the Kings, Queens and nobles of the old world. The unconscious way in which Americans ignore all distinctions is a matter of surprize and astonishment to the middle classes who always manifest in the presence of the nobility the most pitiful unrest and obsequiousness. (Anecdotes Bull[22] at Naples Duchess of Sutherland[23]) We never fully appreciate the beneficent results of our republican theory, that all men are created equal until we see our people in contrast with the cringing masses in the old world. It is because I love my country and believe in its free institutions that I desire to see this government maintained and perpetuated as it only can be by baptizing its women into the spirit of freedom and equality. As I look to the young girls of this nation for the grand work of the future and as it is impossible to rouse the sick, the weak or the lazy to enthusiasm on any subject, to high purpose or noble action, I urge you one and all to study the laws of health and obey them, that you may bravely do your part in the future in maintaining the strength, virtue, honor, and dignity of this government. Remember woman's sphere is wherever her sires and sons may be summoned to duty.

¶16   Another reason why you should observe all the laws of health is that you may be beautiful. All girls desire to be so, yet they take every means to defeat their desires. I suppose you have all read the recipes for beauty in our daily papers. Here is one I cut from a N.Y. paper. "Beautiful women." "If you would be beautiful, use Hagan's

Magnolia balm.[24] It gives a pure, blooming complexion and restores
youthful beauty. Its effects are gradual, (so gradual you never see
them) natural, perfect.[25] <It removes blotches, pimples, tan, sunburn, freckles, and redness. (Wonder if it would take the redness
from the noses of our sires and sons? If so I hope they will all get a
bottle for I hate a red nose.) The Magnolia Balm makes the skin
smooth and pearly, the eye bright and clear, the cheek glow> with
the bloom of youth and imparts a fresh plump appearance to the
countenance." How pray can an external wash make the face plump,
and as to the eye a few ideas on any subject, dear girls, will make
your eyes brighter and clearer, than a dozen bottles of Balm. Again,
the recipe says, "The Magnolia will make a lady of thirty look like a
girl of sixteen." Now what sensible woman of thirty, with all the
marks of intelligence and cultivation that well spent years must give,
would desire to look like an inexperienced girl of sixteen? The
papers are full of these quack remedies for wrinkles and grey hairs,
old age and disease and the fact that men can afford to advertize
these nostrums everywhere shows that there must be fools enough
among womankind to believe them. Pray waste no money in cosmetics, they are worse than useless, they are positively injurious. White
lead enters more or less into the compounding of all of them.[26]
Several physicians have told me of different young ladies dying in
our midst with paralysis from the constant use of cosmetics and hair
dyes.

¶17   Now I think a woman has as good a right as a man has to grow old
and have freckles and tan and sunburn if she chooses. When it is
only through age that one gathers wisdom and experience, why this
endless struggle to seem young? I will give you a recipe, dear girls,
for nothing that will prove far more serviceable in preserving your
beauty than Hagan's Magnolia Balm at 75 cts a bottle. While his is
only skin deep mine will preserve your beauty of body and soul until
like the old family clock in the corner the machinery runs down to
work no more forever. For the hair, complexion, and clear bright
expression of the eye, there is nothing you can do like preserving
your health by exercising regularly, breathing pure air in all your
sleeping and waking hours, eating nutritious food, and bathing
every day in cold water. Not three times a day as one of the Cincinnati papers reported me,[27] that would wash all the constitution out

of you. Don't imitate our financiers, the Vanderbilts and the Fisks,[28] who water their stocks so freely as to take all the value out of them. Eat rare roast beef and vegetable, good bread and fruits, do not munch chalk, clay, cloves, india rubber, pea-nuts, gum, and slate pencils, always chewing, chewing, chewing, like a cow with her cud.[29]

¶18 Remember that beauty works from within, it cannot be put on and off like a garment, and it depends far more on the culture of the intellect, the tastes, sentiments, and affections of the soul, on an earnest unselfish life purpose to leave the world better than you find it, than the color of the hair, eyes or complexion. Be kind, noble, generous, magnanimous, be true to yourselves and your friends, and the soft lines of these tender graces and noble virtues, will reveal themselves in the face, in a halo of glory about the head, in a personal atmosphere of goodness, and greatness that none can mistake. To make your beauty lasting when old age with the wrinkles and grey hairs come and the eyes grow dim and the ears heavy, you must cultivate those immortal powers that gradually unfold and grasp the invisible as from day to day the visible ceases to absorb the soul.

¶19 "There is a knowledge of the truth," says Plato,[30] "that gives rest to the soul and thus saves life." But the mere capacity for this knowledge unsatisfied, gives the soul not rest but restlessness. Your life work dear girls is not simply to eat, drink, dress, be merry, be married and be mothers, but to mould yourselves into a perfect womanhood. Choose then those conditions in life that shall best secure a full symmetrical developement. We cannot be one thing and look another. There are indelible marks in every face showing the real life within. One cannot lead a narrow, mean, selfish life and hide its traces with dye, cosmetics, paint and balm. Regard yourselves precisely as the artist does his painting or statue, ever stretching forward to some grand ideal. Remember that your daily, hourly lives, every impulse, passion, feeling of your soul, every good action, high resolve and lofty conception of the good and true, are delicate touches here and there gradually rounding out and perfecting in yourselves a true womanhood. Oh! do not mar the pure white canvas or marble statue with dark shadows, coarse lines, and hasty chiseling.

¶20 Idleness, frivolity, ill nature, discontent, envy, jealousy, hatred, backbiting, and malice, all outbursts of ill temper and indulgence in low passions, leave their marks and shadows on the face, that no balm can chase away no artifice conceal. What we are is revealed in the expression and features of the face.

¶21 2^{nd} In the second place the coming girl is to be wealthy, that is she is to be a creator of wealth herself. I urge upon the consideration of all thinking parents guardians and teachers the necessity of educating girls under their care to some profitable life work, some trade or profession. There cannot be too much said on the helpless condition in which a girl is left, when thrown alone on the world, without money, without friends, without skill or place in the world of work. One half the stimulus to a girl's education is lost in the fact, that she has no aim or ambition in the future. Boys may be Doctors, Clergymen, Lawyers, editors, Poets, Painters, Presidents, Congressmen, Senators, anything and everything, be what they can, go where they can stand; but girls must be wives and nothing more, and if they are not wives, most people consider their lives failures. Now I want to raise the standard for old maids, and teach girls two things, that marriage as a profession nine cases in ten proves a sad failure because the wife is pecuniarily dependent. To be independent she must have some trade or profession, beside that of the wife, mother, and housekeeper, as only in the happiest and most lasting relations are these offices honored and remunerated. Beside in the most fortunate marriages women are not secure against want, for good husbands sometimes die bankrupt, leaving a young wife with half a dozen little children to provide for, helpless, friendless, alone, with no trade or profession by which she can gain a livelihood, and worse than all, with the feeling that labor is a degradation, that it is more honorable for a woman to live on the bounty of another, beg bread or sell herself for a home either in marriage or out of it, than it is to work side by side with her brother anywhere and maintain a lofty independence. A mighty multitude of women find themselves in this position in all our large cities. Over fifty thousand in N.Y. alone earn their daily bread by the needle and below these are deeper depths, where dwell the daughters of vice and folly, a vast throng God only knows how many, over whom society draws the veil of forgetfulness, or before that sad problem stands hardened or appalled. Full three fourths the girls before me will be called at some period of their lives to support themselves. Shall we prepare them for the facts of life, its real emergencies, or sacrifice them to a theory? To-day perchance your daughters rest at ease in your palace homes, to morrow misfortune comes as it may to all. Your bonds, deeds, mortgages, change hands, your house, furniture, books, pictures, all your household Gods are put up at auction to the highest bidder, sick, sorrowful, disappointed, weary of life, the grave welcomes you to rest, but leaves your helpless wife and daughter to begin alone the hard struggle of life. Go to the departments of Washington and what do you find there, a large majority of the female clerks from the first families in the land. Go to the mercantile establishments, the garrets and cellars of our metropolis, the sinks of iniquity and vice, the busy marts of trade in your own city and there too are the daughters and sisters of Supreme Court Judges, Presidents, Senators, Congressmen, Priests and Bishops.[31] Talking with one of these not long ago, one who in my girlhood moved in the first families of this state, now a miserable outcast in the haunts of vice, oh! said she, if my Father had educated me to self support I should never have been here.

¶22    Remember vice recruits her palsied ranks not from the children of toil, but from the gay, the fashionable the helpless, those who know not how to work, but yet must eat. The stern question presses itself on our consideration, what can these soft, white hands and listless brains do for an honorable support? Make shirts at twelve cents apiece in a New York garret? Teach school at thirty dollars a month and pay six dollars a week for board, go out to service as waitresses and chambermaids at twelve dollars a month and be on the jump sixteen hours out of the twenty four, or marry a millionaire who drives fast horses, drinks good whiskey, puffs tobacco smoke in her face, and reminds her every day that he married a pauper and expects her to act with becoming humility? Give a man says Alexander Hamilton a right over my subsistence and he has a power over my whole moral being.[32] When a woman marries a man for a home, for silks, jewels, equipage, she not only degrades herself, but sacrifices him. The sweet incense of love never rises from such altars and the fruit of such unions is blighted ere it blooms.

¶23    Instead of this sad picture, we will suppose that your daughters educated in freedom like your sons, looking forward to some life work for self-support, had each chosen a trade or profession. One is a skillful telegraph operator making $15 or $20 a week, another is notary public, or commissioner of deeds with daily fees. Another is a Homeopathic Physician with an income of $5000 a year. Another having gone through a thorough collegiate and theological course of study is an able Divine preaching in a pleasant place on $2000 a year.[33] One is in your post office on $3000 a year and another is President of the United States with $25000 a year. Are not any of these positions better than teaching a school for a mere pittance, or running a sewing machine in a N.Y. garret with the gilded hand of vice ever beckoning her to ease and plenty in the paths that lead to infamy and death? Oh! Fathers, Husbands, Brothers, sons this question of woman's work and wages may lie nearer your hearts to-morrow than it does to-night. By some sudden turn in the wheel of fortune, your daughters, sisters, wives may stand face to face with the stern realities of life. If in obedience to the tyrant custom you have left them unprepared for such an emergency, and pressed with poverty and temptation they are drawn down the whirlpool of vice, their destruction lies at your door. To-day men are ashamed to have the women of their households enter into any kind of profitable labor, because work is supposed to degrade them. This has a depressing influence on all women who are compelled to support themselves, and only when the daughters of the rich are educated to self-support will labor be honorable for all women. Every Father has it in his power to educate his daughter in his own trade or profession and it is his solemn duty to do it be he doctor, lawyer, banker, jeweller, or dentist.

¶24 The study of theology is peculiarly adapted to woman should her tastes draw her to that profession, as its duties are chiefly thought, research, teaching and sympathy, and its pursuit seldom leads one into the public and disagreeable walks of life. After a thorough collegiate course and a few years reading under the care of a judicious Father, a gifted and devotional woman might stand unrivalled as a preacher of excellence and power. Without preparation women in all ages have preached the best gospel of their times. It was a woman, Elizabeth Fry[34] who first went down into that pandemonium of misery and horrors Newgate, London, and by her eloquence wrought such changes in the character and surroundings of the unhappy criminals as to fill the wise men of her day with admiration and amazement. The mother of Wesley[35] often preached in the absence of her Husband and Adam Clarke says she was "an able Divine." The Methodist church has long recognized the fact that in the outpouring of God's spirit there is no distinction of sex. At one time a great revival occurred in the church of Wesley in his absence. When he heard that the women as well as the men were all talking in the assembled congregation he hastened home to stop such irregularities. But his mother told him to wait and watch, for, said she if these women bring sinners to repentance they are as much called of God as you are.[36] Seeing that Wesley was under great concern of mind on this point, a friend remarked to him one day, if a cock might rouse the slumbering conscience of a Peter, or an ass warn Balaam of his danger, why may not a woman reprove a man of sin.[37]

¶25  Many of our wealthy merchants too have daughters suffering for something to occupy their minds, yet their Fathers hire clerks to do the very things for which their daughters could be easily trained. Most girls could learn the laws of barter, to keep books in a mercantile establishment, and with practise buy and sell with as much skill as their brothers. As to the profession of medicine "the fair sex" have already taken that by storm. There are medical colleges for girls in most of our great cities, several old established institutions are recently opened to them,[38] many have graduated and are already in a lucrative practise of the healing art. All over the country women are already making from $2000 to $10,000 a year. Is it not better thus to use their brains and secure pecuniary independence, delegating household cares to others, than to be dependent drudges all their days—to have perchance a few hundreds left them by husbands as long as they remain their widows. Michigan woman.

¶26  There too is the legal profession, and if the elevating, purifying influence of woman is needed anywhere, it is in our courts of justice, especially in those cases involving the interests of her own sex. In Shakspeare's "Merchant of Venice" we see how superior the ready wit, intuition and keen sympathy of a Portia was to the lumbering logic of the Antonios by her side.[39] In portraying real wrongs before grave and reverend Judges would she be more out of her place than acting imaginary ones on the stage? Would not the study of Blackstone and Kent's commentaries[40] enlarge their minds and be of more practical benefit, than the Magazine of fashion, the last novel, or hours every day devoted to the needle? Would not daily talks in a lawyer's office with sensible men, with bankers, merchant, farmers, on the practical business of life, on statute law, land titles, taxes, bond mortgages and usury for which they might receive a fee of $25 or $50 be far more rational than a three hours unprofitable talk with a dandy on the little nothings of fashionable life? Do you complain of the publicity of such a position? Is a lawyer's office with a dozen clients all sober men engaged in the practical business of life, where your daughter may sit plainly and completely dressed, pen and book in hand, as public as a ball room where assembled hundreds may look at her as she moves about immodestly dressed now in the mazy dance,[41] taking anybody by the hand, and now in the giddy waltz, whirling in the arms of some licentious debauchee? Your daughter could attend to all a lawyer's business without taking the hand or inhaling the breath of a client, but there is no place where she is subject to such intimate approaches as in fashionable life, and no place where one meets a more sensual type of manhood.

¶27  To train your daughter to a good trade or profession is far better than to leave her an unhappy dependent or a fortune without the necessary knowledge to take care of it. Every thinking man must see how entirely a woman's virtue and dignity are involved in her pecuniary independence.

¶28  Encourage your daughters, sisters, wives, to enter into all honest and profitable employments, not only for their own personal happiness, but for the safety of public morals, for thus only can you strike a blow at licentiousness and excess that shall be seen and felt throughout the land. Girls see all this more readily than their parents. I am in daily receipt of letters from them from all parts of the country expressing the strongest desire for education and profitable work but unfortunately these are the very girls who have no means to carry out their desires. Those who have rich parents and could be thoroughly educated are so enervated by ease and luxury, and the firm faith that hardship and trial can never come to them, that they have no motive stimulating them to effort. But say some would not all this conflict with what seems to be the special destiny of girls, marriage and maternity? When women are independent and self supporting fewer will enter the marriage relation with the present gross conceptions of its rights and duties, for the coming girl is to be wise as well as healthy and self-supporting.

¶29   In the higher civilization now dawning upon us, the love element of pure, refined women, guided and controlled by conscience, science, and religion will find higher purer outlets for its forces, giving us that glorious period when old maids will be honored and revered. The world has always had its Marys as well as Marthas,[42] women who preferred to sit at the feet of wisdom to learn science and philosophy rather than to be busy housewives, mothers of ideas, of music, poetry and painting, rather than of men. All honor to the Mary Carpenters, Florence Nightingales, Maria Mitchells, Harriet Hosmers, Louisa Alcotts, Rosa Bonheurs,[43] Anna Dickinsons, Susan B. Anthonys and the long line of geniuses, saints and philanthropists who have devoted themselves to art, religion and reform. Again no girl should marry until she is at least twenty five years of age as she does not reach physical maturity before that time. Thus many years could be devoted to reading, thought and study, to a preparation for that higher companionship of the spirit and intellect with pure, cultivated, scholarly men.

¶30   If Husbands found this companionship in their wives in science, philosophy and government, our whole social life would be refined and elevated and marriage be a far more happy and permanent relation than it is to-day. But marriage has thus far been based wholly on the man idea, a condition of subjection for woman. The Methodist church has taken the initiative step to the higher idea. I understand that by an act in their ecclesiastical councils they have dropped the word "obey" from their marriage ceremony.[44] All praise to the Methodist church! When women have a proper self-respect, a laudable pride of sex, they will scout all these old barbarisms of the past that point in any way to the subject condition of woman, in either the state the church or the home. Until all other sects follow her example, I hope all girls will insist on being married by the Methodist ceremony and clergyman.[45]

¶31   The Episcopal marriage service is more at loggerheads with time than any other now extant in civilized nations. It not only still clings to the word obey but it has a most humiliating act in giving the bride away.[46] I was never more struck with its odious and ludicrous features than on once seeing a tall, queenly looking woman magnificently arrayed, married by one of the tiniest priests that ever donned a surplice and gown, given away by the smallest guardian that ever watched a woman's fortunes, to the feeblest bluest looking groom that ever placed a wedding ring on bridal finger. Seeing these Lilliputs round her I thought when the little priest said "who gives this woman to this man" that she would take the responsibility and say I do, but no there she stood calm serene like an automaton, as if it were no affair of hers while the little guardian placing her hand in that of the little groom said I do. Thus was this stately woman bandied about by these three puny men all of whom she might have gathered up in her arms and borne off to their respective places of abode. But women are gradually waking up to the degradation of these ceremonies. Not long since at a wedding in high life, a beautiful girl of eighteen in the response was suddenly struck dumb at the word "obey." Three times the Priest pronounced it with an emphasis and holy unction each time slower, louder than before, though the magnificent parlours were crowded, a breathless silence reigned. Father, Mother and Groom were in agony, the bride with downcast eyes stood speechless, at length the Priest slowly closed his book and said the ceremony is at an end.

¶32 One imploring word from the groom and a faint "obey" was heard in the solemn stillness. The Priest unclasped his book and the knot was tied. The congratulations, feast and all went on as though there has been no break in the proceedings, but the lesson was remembered and many a rebel made by that short pause. Now I think that all these reverend gentlemen who insist on the word obey in the marriage service should be impeached in the supreme court of the United States for a clear violation of the 13th amendment to the Federal constitution, which says there shall be no slavery or involuntary servitude in the United States.[47]

¶33 An old German proverb says that every girl is born into the world with a stone on her head. This is just as true now as the day it was first uttered.

¶34 Your creeds, codes, and conventionalisms have indeed fallen with crushing weight on the head of woman in all ages, but nature is mightier than law and custom, and in spite of the stone on her head, behold her to-day close upon the heels of man in the whole world of thought, in art, science, literature and government. Where has the world produced an orator that could draw such audiences and hold them spell bound as did our own Anna Dickinson at the tender age of seventeen. In science we have Caroline Summerville[48] and Maria Mitchell, in political economy Harriet Martineau. In art Angelica Kauffmann,[49] Harriet Hosmer and Rosa Bonheur, who refused admission into the universities of France, studied anatomy in the slaughter houses of Paris and has given us the most wonderful painting of animal life that the world has ever seen. In literature we have Elizabeth Barrett Browning[50] the Shakspeare of our age, George Sand, Charlotte Brontë and Harriet Beecher Stowe, who have produced the most popular novels of the century. All these and many more have risen up in spite of the stone on their heads and walked forward as easily as did Samson[51] <into the gates of the city.

¶35 Educate the world into higher thoughts and affections. Children of the brain are more needed for the ushering in of the higher civilization than those of the flesh alone.

¶36 That beautiful myth of the goddess Minerva springing from the brain of her Father,[52] fully armed and equipped for the battle of life, has a deeper significance than the world dreams of today.>[53]

~ AMs, ECS Papers, DLC; typescript, scrapbook 2, Papers of ECS, NPV. Word in square brackets supplied by editors.

1. An *X* at the end of this paragraph may indicate that ECS intended to insert new material. ECS's next "paragraph" covers twenty-two manuscript pages, but the editors have introduced breaks in the text.

2. Madison Square was a fashionable park in New York, bound by Fifth and Madison avenues between Twenty-third and Twenty-sixth streets.

3. Vinnie Ream's name in the manuscript reminded ECS to tell an anecdote. When Congress commissioned Ream (1847–1914) in 1866 to sculpt a statue of Abraham Lincoln for the Capitol, their choice of such a young woman led to harsh public attacks on Ream's worthiness for the assignment. In an early version of this lecture, ECS reportedly "paid a tribute of praise to Vinnie Ream, who had met with such opposition from all the world, and hounded by the press. The statue of Lincoln is a perfect likeness of an ungainly man." (*NAW*; *San Francisco Chronicle*, 15 August 1871, *Film*, 15:708.)

4. Ragged schools provided education for the poorest children.

5. Sydney Smith (1771–1845), the English cleric and wit, wrote in 1810 about female education: "Nothing, certainly, is so ornamental and delightful in women as the benevolent affections; but time cannot be filled up, and life employed, with high and impassioned virtues. . . . Compassion, and every other virtue, are the great objects we all ought to have in view; but no man (and

no woman) can fill up the twenty-four hours by acts of virtue." (*Wit and Wisdom of the Rev. Sydney Smith, Being Selections from His Writings and Passages of His Letters and Table-Talk* [New York, 1856], 143–44.)

6. Like Charlotte Cushman and Adelaide Ristori, Frances Anne Kemble (1809–1893) was a celebrated nineteenth-century actress.

7. More actresses, these were Sarah Kemble Siddons, Rachel (1820–1858) of France, and Ellen Tree Kean (1805–1880) of England.

8. ECS ended her twenty-two page paragraph here.

9. By "iron shoes" ECS may mean shoes that squeezed the foot into an unnatural configuration to make it look dainty. (With assistance of Nancy E. Rexford, Danvers, Mass.)

10. For an earlier reference to the unsuitability of French fashions for American women, see *Papers*, 1:180. At this point in her manuscript, ECS drew a symbol that may have indicated to turn over her page. She had, however, struck out a passage on the verso about the Franco-Prussian War. It reads: "I have hoped that one of the good results of the late war might be more rational & economical fashions. As the French are to be compelled to pay the Germans $240,000,000, I suppose it would be the height of presumption for American women to invent their own fashions."

11. This notation for an anecdote refers to the same engraving of Beatrice and Dante described in her speech "The Bible and Woman Suffrage" above at 11 May 1879. A report of "Our Girls" in 1869 used the identical language to tell the story. Then, according to the reporter, "Mrs. Stanton said she would not place woman above man's head nor beneath his feet, but would draw a line half way between Dante and Blackstone, and place her by his side." (Quotation from *Cincinnati Daily Gazette*, 31 December 1869; other reports in *Dubuque Daily Times*, 4 December 1869, and *Cincinnati Daily Enquirer*, 31 December 1869, all in *Film*, 14:122–23, 162–63.)

12. Frances Power Cobbe (1822–1904) was an English writer and reformer. ECS quotes her essay "The Final Cause of Woman," in *Woman's Work and Woman's Culture*, ed. Josephine E. Butler (London, 1869), 22–23.

13. Cobbe's passage continues in the manuscript, but ECS drew lines across it: "'If these ideas be adsurd then it follows that we are not arrogating too much in seeking elsewhere than in the interests of man the ultimate reason of the creation of woman.'"

14. An expression for death or the afterlife.

15. ECS squeezed this sentence into the margin at the top of her page, as if it were a subtitle.

16. A draft of these two sentences on manuscript page forty-five appears, struck out, on the verso of page thirty-five above.

17. ECS probably alludes to *Sartor Resartus: The Life and Opinions of Herr Teufelsdröckh* (1836) by the Scottish essayist Thomas Carlyle (1795–1881). She does not, however, quote directly from the book. For an earlier instance of ECS using the same phrases, see "Our Costume," July 1851, *Film*, 7:100.

18. ECS's anecdote about West Point appears in reports of the speech in 1869, 1873, and 1878. "The cadets at West Point once threw aside their suspenders and fastened their garments around the waist. In a few weeks a disease broke out which was unaccountable. When it was suggested that the waistband had somewhat to do with it, the suspenders were resumed, and soon the disease disappeared." (Quotation from *Woodhull and Claflin's Weekly*, 8 November 1873; other reports in St. Louis *Missouri Republican*, 29 December 1869; *Cincinnati Daily Enquirer*, 31 December 1869; *Woman's Words* 2 [December 1878]; all in *Film*, 14:154–56, 162, 17:399, 20:428.)

19. Her anecdote about Ann Arbor is told in a report of the lecture in 1870: "When on a visit to the University of Ann Arbor, Mrs. Stanton had a discussion with one of the Professors on the difference between the mode of training boys and girls. He said girls could not endure so much as boys, and she thought they could endure more, and suggested that if boys of the University were laced and pinched and cramped by dress as girls are, they would soon languish and die." (*Grand Rapids Daily Eagle*, 12 January 1870, *Film*, 14:523.)

20. ECS marked the manuscript here for an insertion that completes this sentence. The text appears on the verso of the preceding page.

21. Napoléon Bonaparte (1769–1821), emperor of France.

22. This unidentified anecdote probably concerned Ole Bornemann Bull (1810–1880), a Norwegian violinist who made his final tour of the United States in 1880.

23. Harriet Elizabeth Georgiana Leveson-Gower, Duchess of Sutherland (1806–1868), asked to meet the American abolitionists after the World's Anti-Slavery Convention of 1840. In *Eighty Years*, ECS described how nervous her visit made the English middle class and how easily Lucretia Mott greeted the duchess (86–87).

24. Hagan's Magnolia Balm was a popular skin lightening product patented by the Lyon Manufacturing Company of Brooklyn, New York. Advertised as a "Liquid Toilet Powder," it promised to remove blemishes and make "a *lady of thirty appear but twenty*." (Flyers from Warshaw Collection of American Business, AC 060, National Museum of American History, DSI, courtesy of Martha Lawrenz; Kathy Peiss, *Hope in a Jar: The Making of America's Beauty Culture* [New York, 1998], 42–43.)

25. Here, on a page that ECS renumbered "70–71," something was cut or torn from the sheet, and two parts rejoined. The text in angle brackets, continuing the text of the advertisement, appears in the typescript of this speech.

26. White lead was used in paints, pottery glazes, and cosmetics. Prolonged exposure to it in hair dyes and face powders caused lead poisoning. (Peiss, *Hope in a Jar*, 21; P. A. Monsegur, *Hair Dyes and Their Applications* [London, 1915], 36–37.)

27. *Cincinnati Daily Enquirer*, 31 December 1869.

28. James Fisk (1834–1872) and Cornelius Vanderbilt (1794–1877) were

financiers whose manipulation of stock ruined the Erie Railroad in the late 1860s.

29. This list of things to munch on in lieu of nutritional food was a familiar one to physicians treating adolescent girls. On such eating habits, see Joan Jacobs Brumberg, *Fasting Girls: The Emergence of Anorexia Nervosa as a Modern Disease* (Cambridge, Mass., 1988), 175–77.

30. Plato (c. 428–348 B.C.), Greek philosopher, expresses this idea in *Phaedrus* at 248B–248C. (With assistance of Robert Bolton, Rutgers University.)

31. ECS marked her sheet here for an insertion. The sentence that follows appears on the verso of the preceding page.

32. *The Federalist Papers,* no. 79.

33. The manuscript shows that ECS often tailored this sentence to name the place where she spoke, and the place names she added indicate that this sheet of the manuscript dated back to 1870. The original text read "place like Peoria," Illinois, where she delivered the speech on 14 March 1870; subsequently she wrote "Alfred Centre," New York, for 24 June 1870, and "a charming city like San Francisco" for 14 August 1871.

34. Elizabeth Gurney Fry (1780–1845), English prison reformer.

35. Susanna Annesley Wesley (1669–1742) was the mother of John Wesley (1703–1791), the founder of Methodism. Adam Clarke wrote of her: "If it were not unusual to apply such an epithet to a *woman*, I would not hesitate to say she was an able divine!" (*Memoirs of the Wesley Family; Collected Principally from Original Documents* [New York, 1824], 291.)

36. This story from Clarke, *Memoirs of the Wesley Family,* 286, is told not about women but about male lay preachers.

37. Matt. 26:69–75, and Num. 22:23–33. Here ECS drew a symbol as if to indicate an insertion. On the verso of the page, this passage is written: "In the light of the present day with women talking on every subject, we look back with wonder that her right was ever doubted   Yet in the time ⸢of⸣ Shakspeare a woman was not allowed to tread the boards of the stage. All his fine female characters were performed by men   Ophelia Desdimona & Juliet"

38. After the University of Michigan opened its previously all-male medical school to women in 1870, a handful of other schools did likewise over the next decade. (Thomas Neville Bonner, *To the Ends of the Earth: Women's Search for Education in Medicine* [Cambridge, Mass., 1992], 140.)

39. In Shakespeare's *The Merchant of Venice*, Portia acts as Antonio's lawyer against Shylock's claim for a pound of flesh.

40. James Kent (1763–1847) published his four-volume *Commentaries on American Law* between 1826 and 1830.

41. The mazy dance, a description derived from the complex, maze-like patterns traced by the dancers, was by this date a generic term for social dancing that involved groups of couples.

42. In Luke 10:38–42, Martha busied herself about the house, while her sister Mary studied at the feet of Jesus.

43. Accomplished single women, these were Mary Carpenter (1807-1877), English educator and prison reformer; Florence Nightingale (1820-1910), pioneer English nurse; Louisa May Alcott (1832-1888), American writer; and Rosa Bonheur (1822-1899), French painter.

44. In 1864, the General Conference of the Methodist Episcopal Church removed the word obey from the marriage ceremony. (With the assistance of Tracey Del Duca, General Commission on Archives and History, United Methodist Church.)

45. This sentence was added in the margins beneath the previous paragraph and sideways up the page. A different manuscript of this section, beginning with "All praise to the Methodist Church" and continuing through paragraph thirty-two, survives because ECS recycled the pages into a chapter of her reminiscences in 1890, in *Film*, 28:718-25. The passage is also to be found in *Eighty Years*, 295-96.

46. The ceremony followed the protocol set forth in 1871, in a revision of the Episcopal Prayer Book. Inclusion of the word obey and the practice of giving in marriage predated the establishment of the Episcopal church in the United States. (Research by Jennifer Peters, Archivist for Research and Public Service, Archives of the Episcopal Church.)

47. On the verso of the sheet that ends with this paragraph, ECS at some time wrote: "If we would make the home what it should be our first duty is to base it on the republican theory".

48. ECS combines the names of British astronomers Caroline Lucretia Herschel (1750-1848) and Mary Fairfax Somerville (1780-1872).

49. Angelica Kauffmann (1741-1807), Swiss painter.

50. To the French George Sand and American Harriet Beecher Stowe, ECS adds the English novelist Charlotte Brontë (1816-1855) and poet Elizabeth Barrett Browning (1806-1861).

51. ECS's manuscript ends here. Judg. 16:1-3 recounts this story of Samson.

52. Minerva, goddess of wisdom, was not born of a mother but sprang full grown from the head of Jupiter.

53. Like her notes to insert particular anecdotes, ECS's concluding sentences may be more suggestion than literal text. Newspaper coverage of this lecture indicates that she varied her perorations, sometimes adding a fourth element—political rights—to the health, wealth, and wisdom that held the keys to woman's happiness. In Grand Rapids, Michigan, in January 1870, "[s]he wound up her lecture by a beautiful peroration, in which she alluded to the artist, who, in a foreign land, found a beautiful block of marble, embedded in the dirt and dust. He commenced clearing away the dirt and cleaning off the dust, and when asked what he was doing, replied that he was going to set free the angel that was imprisoned within that block. He had the block moved to his studio, and set to work with his fine instruments, and patiently worked days, months and years on the block, until at length the angel was released from its imprisonment, and stood forth in all its loveliness. So it is with our

young girls. Your life work is not to build up false works and customs, but to set free the angel that is imprisoned within you." (*Grand Rapids Democrat*, 12 January 1870, *Film*, 14:522.)

In San Francisco in August 1871, "Mrs. Stanton concluded her address by describing the wonders she had recently seen at Yosemite, the Geysers and other places she had visited; how the thought came across her that in such spots as these would be the place to experiment on a higher civilization, where the women would have equal liberty, and an equal place and pay in the world of work and all the rights and privileges of citizenship, for nothing else would ever make institutions worth such a paradise to dwell in." (*San Francisco Chronicle*, 15 August 1871, *Film*, 15:708.)

In Canton, Ohio, in 1875; in Milwaukee in 1877; in Indianapolis in 1879; and in Washington, Iowa, in 1880, she dealt at length with political rights. At the last place, a reporter wrote: "When our girls become both healthy and wealthy, they will be wise—wise enough to know their political rights, and to demand and secure them, and to use them rightly and well. And now having floated out of the river and bay into the wide ocean of 'women's rights,' she turned on steam and set all the sails alow and aloft, and just went flying for a half hour or so, taking up all the stock objections and answering them with great good humor and right enjoyable wit. She poked fun at the property laws which, after a wife worked 12 to 18 hours out of the 24 for years, recognized her as the ward of her 'provider' who might leave to her, in his will, the property she helped to earn, to use so long as she remained his widow! She chuckled at the legislators who, classing women with criminals, lunatics, idiots and negroes, denied the privilege of voting, but lately called the negroes into the kingdom and left her without, where, I suppose, is weeping and wailing and gnashing of teeth, if not cussing and hair-pulling,—still classed with the c., l. and i. aforesaid. At least they might have let negroes and women into the kingdom at the same time. She ridiculed the notion that women's voting would corrupt politics. But the women could vote at a place apart from the men; let them at least go the polls at churches, and vote under the eye of pastors! She wants women to vote, so that saloons and brothels may be banished, doors of opportunity may be opened to save women from lives of shame, &c.; but she admits that the great trouble with the movement is, the reluctance of the sex themselves." (Quotation from *Washington County Press*, 25 February 1880; other reports in *Canton Repository*, 12 February 1875; *Milwaukee Sentinel*, 16 April 1877; *Indianapolis Sentinel*, 19 January 1879; all in *Film*, 18:305, 19:487–88, 20:682, 21:110–11.)

## TEXTUAL NOTES

¶1   *l.* 8     their brothers faces in the snow
    *ll.* 16–17   And why. They have awakened
    *l.* 22     guided & controlled ↑by him↓,
    *ll.* 23–24   no matter how wise or mature they are never

*l.* 26 keenly than kind Fathers ~~ever~~ imagine.

¶2 *l.* 2 admitted here" ↑he↓ remarked,

*l.* 5 the dogs like the ~~women~~ ↑girls↓ seem

*l.* 12 was a dog & not a ~~man~~ ↑boy↓.

¶3 *l.* 1 the dogs & the ~~women~~ ↑girls↓ suffer

*ll.* 14–15 girl repudiates these ↑invidious↓ distinctions ↑,↓ ~~of sex~~

*ll.* 21–24 boys perpetuate the custom. ↑Custom too has made the girl the slave & subject womanhood perpetuates the custom↓ ~~They~~ ↑Men↓ ↑Man↓ make↑s↓ the creeds & codes ↑the constitutions↓,

¶4 *l.* 1 beg. ~~Now t~~↑T↓his ~~ought~~ ↑should↓ not ~~so to~~ be.

*l.* 4 on some definite ~~purpose~~ ↑work↓, trade or

*ll.* 6–7 self dependence, ~~& grows~~ ↑growing↓ stronger nobler, braver, every day ~~that~~ he lives.

*ll.* 8–9 at white heat; ↑perchance↓ she has outstripped

*ll.* 13–14 If in spite of ~~all~~ opposition a woman

*l.* 20 ↑Vinnie Ream↓

¶5 *l.* 1 ready to take their rights. [*passage struck out*] Oh! men of the republic strike off these chains, the distinctions that God has made he will maintain, he needs none of your puny legislation to vindicate his wisdom or carry out his will.

*l.* 14 ~~We~~ ↑I↓ said to one of

*l.* 15 not long since your daughter has a wonderful

*ll.* 16–17 it might be ↑a↓ source of great profit as well happiness to her.

*l.* 18 "Yes," ~~we~~ ↑I↓ replied,

*ll.* 20–21 not wise to fill up ones whole life

*ll.* 33–34 thinks of the stage by day dreams of it by night,

*ll.* 34–35 thoughts, her hearts desire,

*l.* 40 puerile pleasures ↑said to be↓ legitimate

*ll.* 43–44 profession honorable for all time.

*l.* 46 will or wish as they desire.

*l.* 47 transplanted as easily as flowers.

*ll.* 50–51 Fathers Brothers Husbands die,

*ll.* 53–55 & cunning of ~~our~~ ↑a girls↓ own brains & hands, are the only friends that are ever with ~~us~~ ↑her↓, the only sure means of ↑self↓ protection

¶7 *ll.* 9–10 to dwell, & ↑where through ignorance & inferiority↓ she ↑is supposed to be↓ unable to go,

*l.* 12 amuses man by ~~her~~ ↑an↓ endless variety

¶8 *ll.* 2 –3 with our ~~present~~ feeble type of manhood,

*ll.* 3–4 their wants. ↑Woman, as she is to-day is man's handy work.↓

*l.* 6      paniers, limping gate, feeble muscles,

*ll.* 8-9      cows & catepillars, dogs & drunken men, fire crackers & canon, thunder & lightening,

*l.* 13      is Natures ~~handy~~ work,

*l.* 14      two hands in practical ~~work~~ ↑life↓,

*ll.* 17-18      her unsexed. ↑~~However~~ But whatever his theory↓ ~~T~~↑t↓he real facts of life show that man's chivalry & devotion ~~is~~ ↑are↓ ~~never~~ ↑not↓ manifested

*l.* 21      ten times ~~the~~ ↓more↓ chivalry

¶9   *l.* 1 beg.      ↑Again↓ When ↑American↓ women begin to care

*l.* 14      draging woman & man too down to death.

*ll.* 18-19      immortal powers. your life work, is not to attract ↑simply↓ man or please

¶11   *l.* 2      & not for ↑her↓ own happiness & enjoyment, Francis Power Cobbe

*l.* 18      mere appendages ↑made to qualify some body else↓, but

*ll.* 28-30      educate all women for ↑teachers & seamstresses↓ cooks ↑nurses↓ & chambermaids, is to make the supply in ~~that branch of labor~~ ↑direction↓ ↑the home sphere↓ greater

*ll.* 31-32      wages & degrade ~~that~~ ↑all these↓ branch↑es↓ of labour↑.↓ ~~which is the fact to day.~~

*l.* 37      day of the year round a cook stove.

¶12   *l.* 4      food, cloths, exercise, all the conditions

*l.* 17      to be superceeded by muscles.

¶13   *l.* 4      changed, cloths now make the man."

*l.* 11      manners of ~~nearly~~ all ~~the girls~~ we ~~see~~ ↑meet.↓

*l.* 14      tighten her ↑clothes to↓ form the waist

*l.* 19      the many unnatural restra↑i↓nts placed

*ll.* 34-35      where ~~the~~ ↑we↓ moderns got ~~their~~ ↑our↓ idea

*l.* 39      in marble or on canvass, & those of

¶14   *ll.* 2-3      that their cloths are perfectly loose,

*ll.* 15-16      to have her cloths hung loosely

*l.* 28      made precisely like my Fathers,

*l.* 31      indebted for a life of ↑un↓interrupted

*ll.* 42-43      observance of ↑the↓ great immutable laws of life, another generation ~~will~~ ↑might↓ show as marked a change

¶15   *ll.* 2-3      sound body ↑is↓ to the mind ~~is~~ what a good

*l.* 11      place to the sturdier ↑foreign↓ races.

*l.* 23      Sutherland) ~~Such are the results of our free institutions.~~

¶16   *l.* 16      a dozen bottles of ~~Blam~~ ↑Balm↓.

*l.* 20      desire to look like ↑an↓ inexperienced girl of sixteen.

*l.* 25      worse than useless they are positively

*ll.* 27-28      ladies dying ↑in our midst↓ with paralysis

¶17   *ll.* 5-6      preserving your beauty ~~of body & soul~~ than

|  |  |  |
|---|---|---|
| | *ll.* 8–9 | the machinary runs down to work |
| | *ll.* 13–14 | one of the Cincinnatti papers reported |
| | *ll.* 14–15 | constitution out of you, dont imitate our |
| | *l.* 17 | Eat ~~good~~ rare roast beef & vegatable |
| | *ll.* 18–19 | clay, cloves, ↑india rubber, pea-nuts, gum,↓ & slate pencils, |
| ¶18 | *ll.* 2–3 | far more on ↑on the culture of the intellect↓ the tastes, |
| | *ll.* 3–5 | of the soul ↑on an earnest unselfish life purpose to leave the world better than you find it↓, than the color |
| ¶19 | *l.* 3 | for this knowledge Unsatisfied, gives the soul |
| | *l.* 7 | full symetrical developement. |
| | *l.* 10 | and balm, ~~best secure a full symetrical developement.~~ |
| | *ll.* 12–13 | daily, hourly ~~life~~ ↑lives↓, |
| | *ll.* 17–18 | lines, & hasty chisseling. |

[*entire paragraph after 20 is struck out*] We cannot be one thing & look another. There are indelible marks, in every face showing the real life within. Do not imagine that you ↑can↓ lead a narrow mean selfish life, & hide it with dye cosmetics, paint & balm.

|  |  |  |
|---|---|---|
| ¶21 | *ll.* 2–4 | urge ↑upon↓ the consideration of all thinking parents ↑guardians↓ & teachers ~~on~~ the necessity of educating girls ↑under their care↓ to more profitable |
| | *l.* 36 | or sacrifice them to a theory. To-day |
| | *l.* 37 | your palace homes ~~clothed in purple & fine linen & faring sumptuously,~~ to morrow |
| | *l.* 41 | the grave ~~closes over~~ ↑welcomes↓ you |
| | *ll.* 43–44 | & what do ↑you↓ find there |
| | *l.* 45 | Go to the ~~slop shops~~ ↑mercantile establishments,↓ |
| | *ll.* 46–47 | iniquity & vice, ↑the busy marts of trade in your own city↓ |
| | *ll.* 48–49 | Congressman ↑Priests & Bishops↓ |
| | *l.* 50 | families of ~~the~~ ↑this↓ state, |
| ¶22 | *ll.* 5–6 | do for an honorable support. Make shirts at twelve cents apeice |
| | *ll.* 10–11 | drinks ~~poor~~ ↑good↓ whiskey, puffs tobacco smoke in her face, & reminds ↑her↓ every day |
| | *ll.* 12–13 | act with becoming humility. Give a man ↑says Alexander Hamilton↓ |
| | *l.* 16 | rises from such ~~unions~~ ↑altars↓ |
| ¶23 | *ll.* 13–14 | paths that lead to infamy & death. Oh! |
| ¶24 | *l.* 3 | its pursuit ↑seldom↓ leads one |
| | *ll.* 20–21 | if these women ~~call~~ ↑bring↓ sinners |
| | *l.* 25 | may not a woman reprove ↑a man of↓ sin. |
| ¶25 | *ll.* 5–6 | much skill as ~~her~~ ↑their↓ brother↑s↓. |
| | *ll.* 8–9 | institutions are ↑recently↓ opened to ~~girls~~ ↑them↓, |
| | *l.* 15 | remain their widows. ↑Michigan woman↓ |

¶26  *l.* 8       imaginary ones on the stage. Would
      *l.* 9       and Kents commentaries
      *l.* 11      every day devoted to the needle
      *l.* 16      nothings of fashionable life
      *l.* 17      Is a lawyers office
      *l.* 23      of some licentious debauchee. Your
¶27  *l.* 1 beg.  To train your daughter to ↑a↓ good trade or profession
      *ll.* 4–5    dignity are involved in ~~their~~ ↑her↓ pecuniary independance
¶28  *l.* 6       letters from ~~young girls in~~ ↑them from↓ all parts
¶29  *l.* 1 beg.  3ʳᵈ ~~The coming girl is to be wise~~
      *l.* 2       guided & controulled by conscience
      *ll.* 9–11   Nightengales, Maria Mitchells, Harriet Hosmers Louisa
                   Alcotts, ↑Rosa Bonheurs↓ Anna Dickinsons Susan B.
                   Anthony's & ~~Belle Bush's~~
      *l.* 12      art, religion & reform. [*passage struck out*] It is as absurd
                   to educate all ~~women~~ ↑girls↓ for wives & nothing more as
                   it would be to educate all boys for husbands & nothing
                   more
      *l.* 14      maturity ~~until~~ ↑before↓ that time.
¶30  *ll.* 2–3    in science philosophy & government
¶31  *ll.* 8–9    feeblest blueist looking groom
      *l.* 17      women are ↑gradually↓ waking up
      *l.* 18      at a wedding in ↑high life↓
      *ll.* 23–24  Father Mother & Groom were in agony, the bride with
                   downcast eyes stood speechles,
¶32  *l.* 6       all these revrened gentlemen
      *l.* 10      servitude in the united states.
¶34  *ll.* 9–10   Angelica Karfmann,
      *l.* 15      Charlotte Brontè
      *l.* 18      as easily as did Sampson

180  ⤳  PETITION TO CONGRESS

EDITORIAL NOTE: In 1879, the National association circulated three,
newly worded petitions, seeking from Congress a sixteenth amendment and relief from political disabilities and from state legislatures a
resolution in support of the amendment. The first of these, printed
below, offered new language for the amendment, language that was
echoed in Senate Resolution No. 65, introduced by Senator Thomas
W. Ferry on 19 January 1880, and in House Resolution No. 175,
introduced by George B. Loring the next day. Questioned about the

change in wording by a member of the House Committee on the Judiciary, Sara Spencer answered that the new text was "the concentrated wish of the women of the United States." She went on to say that petitions sent to Congress in previous years had asked for three different forms of amendment and that she "concentrated" them into one text. Presentation of the petitions started on 14 January 1880 and continued on the fifteenth and nineteenth in the Senate, where forty-seven senators presented petitions signed by more than twelve thousand people. In the House, due to an objection, the petitions were not read, but members continued to submit them to the clerk on the fifteenth and sixteenth. In both houses, the petitions were referred to the Committee on the Judiciary. (*History*, 3:154; *Congressional Record*, 46th Cong., 2d sess., 312–14, 335–37, 362–63, 374–75, 377–78, 380, 418; House Committee on the Judiciary, *Woman Suffrage—Arguments before the Committee on the Judiciary*, 46th Cong., 2d sess., H. Mis. Doc. 20, Serial 1929, p. 10, *Film*, 21:84ff.)

[*14 January 1880*]

## WOMAN SUFFRAGE PETITION TO CONGRESS
## FOR
## A SIXTEENTH AMENDMENT
## TO THE NATIONAL CONSTITUTION.

To the Senate and House of Representatives of the United States, In Congress Assembled:

The undersigned, Citizens of the United States, Residents of the State of ———, County of ———, Town of ———, earnestly pray your Honorable Body to submit to the several States the following Amendment to the National Constitution.

### ARTICLE XVI.

Sec. 1. The right of suffrage in the United States shall be based on citizenship, and shall be regulated by Congress, and all citizens of the United States, native or naturalized, shall enjoy this right equally, without any distinction founded on sex.

Sec. 2. Congress shall have power to enforce this article by appropriate legislation.

MEN:                                    WOMEN:

☙ From *Plan of Woman Suffrage Organizations, For Nation, State, County, Town and Ward*, Tract No. 2, circular, NWSA Collection, ICHi.

181　❧　EXECUTIVE SESSIONS OF THE NATIONAL WOMAN SUFFRAGE ASSOCIATION

[23–24 January 1880]

RESOLUTIONS ADOPTED AT EXECUTIVE SESSION OF NATIONAL WOMAN SUFFRAGE ASSOCIATION, HELD IN SENATE LADIES' ROOM AT CAPITOL BUILDING, FRIDAY, JANUARY 23, AT 1 P.M.[1]

*Resolved*, That a new brief appeal to the women of the United States, describing the present status of the pending Sixteenth Amendment in Congress, be immediately prepared by the Corresponding Secretary of this Association and issued to active friends of woman suffrage and to towns not reached by former documents.[2]

*Resolved*, That the sum of two hundred dollars be and hereby is appropriated out of the treasury for the use of the Corresponding Secretary for labor at her discretion.

RESOLUTIONS ADOPTED AT THE EXECUTIVE SESSION OF NATIONAL WOMAN SUFFRAGE ASSOCIATION, HELD IN JUDICIARY COMMITTEE ROOM, U.S. HOUSE OF REPRESENTATIVES, SATURDAY, JANUARY 24, 1880, AT 1 P.M.

*Resolved*, That a committee of three be appointed by the Chair (Miss Anthony) to draft a Presidential Campaign appeal to the women of the United States, on behalf of the National Woman Suffrage Association.[3]

Miss Anthony appointed as such committee, Mrs. Blake of New York, Mrs. Saxon[4] of La., Mrs. Spencer of Washington.

*Resolved*, That the National Woman Suffrage Association send a delegate from each State and Territory to each of the three great presidential nominating conventions.

*Resolved*, That we hereby request each State suffrage association to elect an alternate to each presidential nominating convention.

*Resolved*, That the officers of this Association are hereby appointed delegates to the three presidential conventions.

*Resolved*, That an Auditing Committee of three be appointed by the Chair.

The Chair appointed as Auditing Committee, Mrs. Stebbins, Mrs. Lockwood, Mr. Wm. O. Denison.[5]

*Resolved*, That an address be prepared for presentation to each Presidential Nominating Convention, the Chair to select the person to prepare such addresses.[6]

A resolution was also passed appointing Wednesday and Thursday, May 27 and 28, as the time of holding the Annual Convention in Indianapolis, provided such dates did not prevent attendance upon the Democratic Nominating Convention, not yet appointed.

⇔ *NCBB*, February 1880.

1. The National's Washington convention opened in Lincoln Hall on the morning of January 21 and continued through January 22. The Senate Ladies' Room, a reception area near the Senate Chamber, was made available as a courtesy for a few years. Before 1886, new facilities were made available—in the basement. (*History*, 3:70.)

2. This "Appeal to Women Citizens of the United States, Tract No. 1," reporting on congressional events and imploring women to send more petitions, is in *Film*, 21:106–8.

3. Headed "Women, Read!" and numbered as tract four, this appeal urged women to attend all local and state primary meetings and political conventions, ask for the opportunity to speak on a resolution in support of woman suffrage, and seek nominations to the next higher political convention. The tract also reported the decision below to select delegates from each state and territory. See *Film*, 21:115–16.

4. Elizabeth Lyle Saxon (1832–1915), a southern writer who settled in New Orleans after the war, was president of the city's Ladies' Physiological Association. In 1879, she led the effort to petition the state constitutional convention for woman suffrage. Moving north late that year, she became a popular lecturer for the National association. (*NCAB*, 16:207; *American Women*; Lindig, *Path from the Parlor*, 43–44.)

5. William O. Denison (c. 1830–?), husband of Ruth Carr Denison, held a position as clerk in the Treasury Department until 1880, when he left to open his own real estate agency in Washington, D.C. (Federal Census, 1870; *Register of Federal Officers*, 1863 to 1875; city directories, 1880, 1881.)

6. The National's memorials to the Republican, Democratic, and Greenback-Labor parties are in *Film*, 21:267–70, 292–93, 308–11.

## 182  &#x223D; TESTIMONY OF SBA BEFORE THE HOUSE COMMITTEE ON THE JUDICIARY

EDITORIAL NOTE: Sara Spencer arranged two hearings before congressional committees for delegates to the National's Washington convention. SBA spoke on both occasions and was allotted the longest time, but Spencer also arranged for the committees to hear from less well-known women, representing different regions and ranging in age from twenty-four-year-old Jessie F. Waite of Chicago to eighty-eight-year-old Julia E. Smith of Connecticut. At the hearing before the House Committee on the Judiciary on Saturday, January 24, SBA was preceded by Emma McRae, Jessie Waite, Catharine Stebbins, Elizabeth Saxon, Lillie Blake, Matilda Gage, and Phoebe Couzins.

[24 January 1880]

Mr. Chairman and Gentlemen of the Committee:[1] I did not propose to make any argument, but simply to call the attention of the committee to the fact that disfranchisement is not only political degradation, but that it is also social, moral, and industrial degradation. It does not matter whether the class affected by disfranchisement is that of ignorant, intemperate, or vicious men—the serfs in Russia, the negroes on our plantations before the war, the Chinamen on our Pacific coast to-day—or the intelligent, educated women of this Republic, disfranchisement works precisely the same results. If we could make the men and women of this republic realize for a moment that the results of disfranchisement to woman are the same as the results of disfranchisement to all the different classes of men I have named, we should not have to wait for another Congress before the proposition for a XVIth amendment would be submitted. But the difficulty is that each man to whom we appeal fails to appreciate the consequences of this law of disfranchisement or to realize the degradation which it entails. I have endeavored, in my arguments, to show that disfranchisement is the cause of woman's degradation in the world of labor; that it is because of it that she is doomed, everywhere doomed, to remain in the subordinate departments of labor, in the school-house, everywhere; that she is doomed to do her work for half pay, always as a subordinate, as I have said, and without any promotion. If men could only believe that the fact of that position of woman in the world of work was due to her disfranchisement, we should not have one session of Congress pass without a proposition for an amendment. But the people do not believe it; and yet, as some of the ladies have shown here, it is the cause of woman's degradation in labor everywhere.[2] We are here to ask that woman may have the power of the ballot; that when she speaks she shall be respected; that when women workers in the factories and shops, the teachers in the school-houses, shall combine together to demand better wages of the capitalists; the political editors of the newspapers in a community will feel that if they speak on the side of the capitalist and against the workingwomen their party will lose the votes of those workingwomen at the next election. With the ballot in the hands of all the millions of factory women and workingwomen in this nation, you can perceive at once that they have a power by which they, like the workmen of the nation, can decide what work they will do, what prices they will be paid, and what positions they will occupy. Then, as to the government departments of which some one here has spoken,[3] the facts are that all over the country there are hundreds of thousands of civil service offices; that many of the women of this republic are well qualified to do the work in those departments, but stand very little chance to get a fair quota of those appointments at the hands of members of Congress, members of the state legislatures, and "the powers that be" everywhere—this, not because men are unjust, not because many of the members of Congress here at Washington would not be glad to have women appointed to the various positions of work, but because it is an utter impossibility, politically speaking, for them to secure places. Governments cannot afford to give good places, good work, or good offices to persons who cannot help to make government. So long as woman holds in her hands no power to help make this government, no member of Congress can afford to advocate equal pay and equal place for women in the departments. The best of our friends, as members of this committee, know that, on the floor of Congress, when we have asked them to ordain that women workers shall be paid equal wages with men, they have told us that to pass such a law, and enforce it, would be to drive all the women out of the departments, because the only excuse that the government now has for employing them is that it is a matter of economy to the government. Now, what we ask is that women shall have this power of appeal to the self-interest of the government office-holders and to the government itself. We ask that woman shall have the ballot that she may come within the body-politic, and there become joint heir with her brothers for all the good things that are to be disposed of at the hands of the government.

This disfranchisement is not only an industrial and a social, but a moral degradation. Why, gentlemen of the committee, did you ever stop to think of what disfranchisement says to each and every one of these women here to-day and to each and every one of the women under this proud flag? It says, *non compos*, your judgment is not sound, your opinions are not worthy to be counted up in what men call "public sentiment," "the crystallizing of the popular will into law." While that is true of all women, let me put before you the other side. Enfranchisement says to every man, poor or rich, ignorant or learned, drunk or sober—to every man outside the State's prison or the lunatic asylum—"your judgment is sound, your opinion is worthy to be counted." And you gentlemen, all of you, recognize the fact that the equal counting and equal recognition of men's opinions establishes in this country that good thing which we call "political equality"—each and every man equal to each and every other man. The opinion of the most ignorant ditch-digger in the country, on election day, counts for just as much as that of the richest and proudest millionaire. It is a good thing, gentlemen; and we women suffragists, believe in the principle of democracy and republicanism, in the equal recognition of all men; but while that principle establishes the equal and just recognition of all men among men, we at the same time recognize that it establishes between the sexes that hateful thing of inequality; that it makes all men sovereigns and all women subjects; that it makes all men, politically, superiors and all women inferiors. And there is no amount of training, education, or discipline that can ever educate an ignorant man or a small boy to the belief that that is not the discrimination. This ignoring of women's opinions politically is not grounded upon intellectual inferiority. The more ignorant the man the better he feels convinced that he knows more than the most intelligent woman in the country. Intelligent men know that the great work of this republic from the beginning has been the sloughing off, little by little, of the old feudalistic ideas of caste, until at last we have this grand idea of self-government. We women know that those who are engaged in this movement are struggling with might and main to lift the women, through the XVIth amendment, upon the same platform with intelligent, cultivated man, who does respect an intelligent, cultivated woman, whom the ignorant man does not comprehend and has no appreciation of.

I will give you an illustration of my meaning. There are three ladies in this room to-day from the State of Iowa.[4] One of those ladies pays more taxes in the city of Maquoketa, in which she resides, than do the whole twelve men who are the members of the common council of her city. Those three women, in the city of Maquoketa, and the county of Jackson, have been at the very head and front of the Women's Christian Temperance organization in that city. They have prayed, petitioned, and done everything to shut up the grog-shops in their community which a disfranchised class can do—which is exactly nothing. On election morning, the question of license or no license is to be voted on in that city. My friend, Mrs. Allen, and other ladies who work with her have paid into the treasury of the county of Jackson no small amount of taxes for the support of the victims of the idiocy and crime which are the outgrowth of the liquor traffic. My friend, Mrs. Allen, is standing on the street on election morning, and in another quarter there stands an ignorant man, a man who by his drunkenness has caused to be sold under the hammer the farm he inherited from his father, whose every dollar of property is gone, whose wife and children are houseless and homeless and he a pauper in the county-house, supported at the public expense. He knows that three-fourths of the money taken from Mrs. Allen's and those other ladies' taxes goes to support him and other like him in his and their necessities. He looks at that woman; he sneers at her education, her standing, her fine clothes, her self-respect, at everything she possesses; he envies her; but at last he bethinks himself. He folds his arms and with utter complacency exclaims, "Yez can sing, yez can shout, yez can pray, yez can petition agin rum; but, *be jabers, yez* can't go to the ballot-box and vote agin it. I can vote for free whisky and you can't help yourselves." Now, gentlemen of the committee, do you not see how that little fact, that that ignorant pauper's opinion is thus respected and counted that day, while that intelligent tax-paying woman's opinion is ignored, educates that ignoramus into a feeling of superiority over that woman? Nothing but an amendment of the Constitution of the United States, saying that that woman's opinion shall be respected and counted, will ever educate that man to respect her. The secret, underlying cause of the disrespect which men often show toward women—the slighting manner in which coarse, rude men are wont to speak of woman—lies in the fact of woman's opinion being ignored in the deciding of all the great questions involving the conditions or surroundings of society and the government.

Then look at the boys of this generation. Before the boy's head reaches the level of the table, he learns that he is one of the superior class and that when he is twenty-one years old he will make laws for Mrs. Saxon, Mrs. Gage, and all these ladies who are mothers. His mother teaches him all the requisites for success in after life. She says: "My son, you must not chew, nor smoke, nor gamble, nor swear, nor be a libertine; you must be a good man." The boy looks his mother in the face, unbelievingly, and, perchance, at his father, who is guilty of every one of the vices which the mother says he must avoid if he would become a great man. Perhaps he sees the minister of his mother's church walking the street with a cigar in his mouth. Then he looks to Congress. It may have been a slander—nevertheless it was a newspaper report, and I use it as an illustration—that the Forty-fifth Congress, at its close, had but one sober man on its floor, and he was a black man (Cain) of South Carolina.[5] I do not say that that was true, but I give it as I heard it. If the boy goes into court, he sees the judge, with a good-sized spittoon by his side and half filled. Now, what does the boy say when he looks up to his mother? He says, "O, nonsense! mother, you don't know what you are talking about; you're only a woman."

If you would have that boy respect his mother, your laws will first have to respect her. Laws do more to educate and develop public sentiment than you, whose business it is to make laws and constitutions, are doing to-day. Therefore, as a matter of educating ignorant men and small boys in a just and respectful appreciation of woman, I ask you not to bury this petition of ours, but to do something to awaken an agitation and discussion of our request on the floors of Congress.

Allow me to make one further observation. Since the days of Fremont and Jessie,[6] women have been very politely invited to attend Republican meetings. All of you Republicans know how the women filled up your empty benches in those days and made your conventions look very respectable indeed. By and by the Democrats came into line and the conventions of both parties often contained as many women as men. Then the poor stump orators are put to their wit's end upon the woman question. They can, without difficulty, frame paragraphs to suit every class of human beings who have a ballot; they can appeal alike to the rumsellers and the temperance men, to the Irishmen, the Germans, the Swedes, the Bohemians, and since the XVth amendment, to the negroes. Every politician can promptly show why his own party is the one for which the particular class to which he addresses himself should vote. Finally he comes to the inevitable woman and, realizing that he must say something on that point, says: "I am glad to see the ladies here to-night, am always glad to have them in my audiences; they are a sort of inspiration, enable me to make a better speech; the fact is, gentlemen, I rather like the ladies, for my mother was a woman—God bless her." Now, gentlemen, don't you believe that if under those bonnets there were voters, those voters would soon cause that orator and his party, whether in or out of power, to suddenly discover there were some brains under there? You see that we want this power to appeal to the instinct of self-interest in this government; and if this committee does not do itself the honor to report a proposition for a XVIth amendment, some succeeding committee will do itself that honor. The tide is moving, it cannot be swept back. I beg you, in the name of justice, humanity, and mercy, that you will not keep woman coming back here for the next thirty years as she has been kept coming here for the last thirty years.

I hope too, that you will help us all you can. We, who are agitating this movement, are not a moneyed class. I trust that you will submit a resolution directing that the reports of this hearing shall be printed at the government expense.[7] I would also urge the importance of your presenting the proposition for a XVIth amendment before Congress because it will create an agitation and discussion which may educate not only the members of Congress but their constituencies on this question.

⌇ House, Committee on the Judiciary, *Woman Suffrage—Arguments before the Committee on the Judiciary*, 46th Cong., 2d sess., H. Mis. Doc. 20, Serial 1929, pp. 18–22.

1. Only half of the fourteen members of the House Judiciary Committee attended the hearing, chaired by the same John T. Harris whose absence from a meeting in 1878 left the committee locked in a tie vote on the sixteenth amendment. Also in attendance were Elbridge Lapham and five new members of the committee: Edwin Willits (1830–1896), Republican representative of

Michigan from 1877 to 1883; David Browning Culberson (1830–1900), Democratic representative of Texas from 1875 to 1897; Nathaniel Job Hammond
(1833–1899), Democratic representative of Georgia from 1875 to 1897; Charles
Grandison Williams (1829–1892), Republican representative of Wisconsin
from 1873 to 1883; and William McKinley (1843–1901), Republican representative of Ohio from 1877 to 1884 and 1885 to 1891, later president of the United
States. (*BDAC*; *NCBB*, February 1880, *Film* 21:69.)

2. The economic impact of disfranchisement was a topic in the arguments
of Emma McRae and Jessie Waite.

3. Mary Emma Montgomery McRae (1848–1919), who led off the hearing,
described a clerk in her local post office whose position was given to a man as
a political favor. Emma Mont. McRae, as she preferred to be known, had
attended her first Washington convention. She was the principal of a high
school in Muncie, Indiana, and married to the school superintendent, Hamilton
S. McRae. She was also an organizer of the local woman's club and a regular
lecturer at teachers' institutes. After her husband died in 1887, McRae joined
the faculty of Purdue University as professor of English literature and lady
principal, and in 1896, she earned a master of arts from the College of Wooster.
(*Biographical History of Indiana*, vol. 1, 6th congressional district, 54–57; T.
B. Helm, *History of Delaware County, Indiana* [Chicago, 1881], 58, 166–67,
187–88; with assistance from Katherine M. Markee, Special Collections, Purdue
University, and Denise Monbarren, Special Collections, College of Wooster;
House, Committee on the Judiciary, *Woman Suffrage—Arguments before the
Committee on the Judiciary*, 46th Cong., 2d sess., H. Mis. Doc. 20, Serial
1929, p. 2, *Film*, 21:84ff.)

4. One of the women, Nancy Allen of Maquoketa, spoke at the Senate
hearing on January 23 about the injustice of taxation without representation
and the obstacles to obtaining temperance legislation. (Senate, Select Committee on Woman Suffrage, *Arguments of the Woman—Suffrage Delegates
before the Committee on the Judiciary of the United States Senate, January 23,
1880*, 47th Cong., 1st sess., S. Mis. Doc. 74, Serial 1993, p. 10, *Film*, 21:70ff.)

5. Although the stenographer added the name of Richard Harvey Cain
(1825–1887) of South Carolina to the text, SBA probably refers to reports of
the final days of the second session of the Forty-fifth Congress when another
African-American member of Congress from South Carolina was singled out
for praise. Then, only Joseph Rainey (1832–1887) completed the work of his
committee amidst drunk and rowdy colleagues. (*BDAC*; unidentified clippings, 17–20 June 1878, SBA scrapbook 8, Rare Books, DLC.)

6. Jessie Ann Benton Frémont (1824–1902), wife of John C. Frémont, was
active in her husband's campaign for president as the first Republican candidate in 1856. (*NAW*; *ANB*.)

7. Elbridge Lapham took this request to the floor of the House on February
3 and moved that the women's arguments be printed at congressional expense. After some debate, his motion passed. (*Congressional Record*, 46th
Cong., 2d sess., 680–81.)

183   ॐ   SBA to Margaret Stanton Lawrence

*[after 24 January 1880]*[1]

Miss ↑W.↓ is a Graduate from the Chicago University—and a very superior scholar—and destined to make a grand mark for woman—[2]

We had two hearings—the Senate Judiciary Com—Friday A.M. & the House [Judiciary Com]—Saturday—[A.M.]— Oh, dear—I wish I had patience to tell—or you to read— But ↑on↓ the Senate Com—were Thurman of Ohio—Edmunds of Vt—Davis of Ill—Bayard of Del— McDonald of Ind[3]—just a quorum & no more present—but a straw— On the street Car—Senator Edmunds got up & coming ↑across↓ to me said—Miss Anthony—I want to say to you what in the rush at close of hearing I did not—that is—that I listened to your argument with great pleasure & interest—it was unanswerable—though I may not yet be able to quite assent to all of your conclusions— The committee wanted exactly what you ↑gave them,↓ argument—not platform rhetoric & oratory— I can't half convey to you, the import & hearing—but Mrs Gage pronounces it the greatest "straw"—politically—ever floated to us— Then Senator Conkling[4] told Mrs Blake that—"for a year & a half he had been giving our question serious thought & it must be met—["]

Geo. W. Julian called on me— He said he had never before seen & heard such cordial commendation of our demand—

~~I hope~~—oh yes—Mrs Gage made a 30 minutes argument before the House Com—and I was never prouder of your own mother's grand utterances before Honorable M.Cs than was I of Mrs Gage—it seemed as if she was wholly lifted out of and beyond herself—it was a close & consecutive historic argument[5]—& our dear Phebe seemed perfectly inspired not only before the Committee—but in every utterance before the Convention— I never saw her so completely swallowed up in the sublime thought she was advocating—as the evening she gave the moral bearing of our movement—no pen or tongue ever touched the depths of our social demor↑al↓~~izattion~~alization with such deep, religious consecration as did Phebe that night— What added to the impressiveness was that Phebe's health is really ↑in a↓ very critical condition—her hands & feet are all grown out of shape—& almost out of joint—with inflamatory rheumatism—and we, who knew the facts of her condition—felt every minute that this <u>might</u> <u>her</u> <u>last</u> <u>presence</u> <u>among</u> <u>us</u>—there was scarce a dry eye—either on the platform—or in the audience— I did so wish dear Hattie were with us—that we might have seen & felt that we had a new force consecrated to our move-ment—grander & greater than any who have ever yet planted them-selves on our platform— I tell you, darling Maggie—this great movement for the redemption of woman from the curse of the ages—"subjection to man"—inaugurated thirty two years ago by your mother & the venerated Lucretia Mott—is the grandest and greatest reform of all time—and destined to be thus regarded by the future historian—and your mothers <u>grand</u>-children & <u>great</u> <u>Grand</u> children, if <u>not</u> <u>her</u> <u>own</u> children—will thus regard it—

⤳ AL incomplete, Blanche Ames Papers, MCR-S. Marked in unknown hand, "To Margaret Stanton Lawrence, 1892." Bracketed words supplied by editors where SBA used ditto marks to repeat the words on the previous line of her letter.

1. A page (or more) of this letter is missing. It is dated with reference to the congressional hearings on 23 and 24 January, but SBA's location is not known. She left Washington for Philadelphia, and then, through February and March, she stayed in western New York and Pennsylvania to be within reach of her mother. Her diary for 1880 has not been found.

2. She referred to Jessie Fremont Waite (1856-?), the eldest daughter of the Illinois suffragists Charles B. and Catharine Van Valkenburg Waite. Waite attended the National's convention as the delegate from the Illinois state association and spoke to the House Committee on the Judiciary. Later in life, as Jessie Waite Wright, she presided over the District of Columbia Woman Suffrage Association from 1906 to 1908. (*Women Building Chicago*, s.v. "Waite, Catharine Van Valkenburg"; Patricia R. McMillen, "Catharine Van Valkenburg Waite," *Bar None: 125 Years of Women Lawyers in Illinois*, ed. Gwen Hoerr McNamee [Chicago, 1998], 47–50; *History*, 3:151, 161, 190, 254, 6:105.)

3. Allen G. Thurman, George F. Edmunds, and Thomas F. Bayard were joined by David Davis (1815–1886), former justice of the Supreme Court and Democratic senator from Illinois from 1877 to 1883, and Joseph Ewing McDonald (1819–1891) of Indiana, Democratic senator from 1875 to 1881. Davis, a consis-tent opponent of greater rights for women, fit well among his fellow committee members. McDonald had defied the committee by supporting the Lockwood bill and helping to ensure its passage. (*BDAC*.)

4. Roscoe Conkling (1829–1888), reported to be too ill to attend the Senate

hearing, was the leader of New York's Republican party and a senator from 1867 to 1881. He often presented suffrage petitions from his constituents, but he did not endorse their aims. In recorded votes, he opposed universal suffrage in Pembina in 1874, opposed allowing women to address the Senate and debating the Lockwood bill in 1878, and absented himself when the Lockwood bill came to a vote in 1879. (*BDAC*. See also *Papers* 2.)

5. See House, Committee on the Judiciary, *Woman Suffrage—Arguments before the Committee on the Judiciary*, 46th Cong., 2d sess., H. Mis. Doc. 20, Serial 1929, pp. 10–14, *Film*, 21:84ff.

## 184 ๛ SBA to Sara Andrews Spencer

*[before 25 March 1880]*[1]

I want the rousingest rallying cry ever put on paper—first, to call women by the thousand to Chicago; and second, to get every one who can not go there to send a postal card to the mass convention, saying she wants the Republicans to put a Sixteenth Amendment pledge in their platform. Don't you see that if we could have a mass meeting of 2,000 or 3,000 earnest women, June 2, and then receive 10,000 postals from women all over the country, what a tremendous influence we could bring to bear on the Republican convention, June 3? We can get Farwell Hall[2] for $40 a day, and I think would do well to engage it for the 2d and 3d, then we could make it our headquarters—sleep in it even, if we couldn't get any other places.

Besides this, I want to make the best possible use of all our speakers between June 3 and 21, when we shall have a mass meeting in Cincinnati, the day before the Democratic convention. My proposition is that I, as vice-president-at-large, call conventions of two days each at a number of cities. We could divide our speakers and thus fill in the entire two weeks between Chicago and Cincinnati with capital good work. How does the plan strike you? Can we summon the women from the vasty deeps[3]—or distances? Can we get 5,000 or 10,000 to send on their postals? Do the petitions still come in? How many thousands of appeals and documents have you had printed and how many have you sent out?[4]

๛ *Anthony*, 2:515. In *Film* at March? 1880.

1. Dated with reference to plans for a mass meeting of women in Chicago. On March 24, SBA learned from Matilda Gage that arrangements for the National association to rent Chicago's Farwell Hall were complete, as noted in the letter that follows this one.

2. Farwell Hall, located at 148 Madison Street in Chicago, could seat well over one thousand people.

3. From William Shakespeare, *Henry IV*, part 1, act 3, sc. 1, line 150.

4. According to information in the tracts issued by the National association during the sixteenth amendment campaign, one thousand dollars was spent to mail tens of thousands of petitions and appeals in the year leading up to September 1878, but this fell far short of the goal set in 1877 to reach one hundred thousand people. An additional sixty-six thousand documents were issued between July 1879 and February 1880 and sent to twenty thousand postmasters for distribution. The campaign committee estimated this left twenty-five thousand towns without any information about the campaign. ("Appeal to the Women Citizens of the United States, Tract No. 1," *Film*, 21: 106–8.)

## 185   SBA TO ELIZABETH BOYNTON HARBERT

Rochester N.Y. M'ch 25/80

My Dear Friend

Yours of Tuesday is just here this noon— We had already decided to take Farwell Hall for June 2$^{d}$—as I learn from letter from Mrs Gage awaiting me here, on return, yesterday—[1] So I am very sorry that you should have to be at the trouble of going down to the city for that— We get ↑Farwell Hall for↓ $40— and they require $20. <u>pre</u>-payment—

I am very happy to say, too, that our glorious Chief has re-considered and now declares her resolve to stand at our head, not only through Indianapolis—but through <u>Chicago Mass Con</u>. June 2$^{d}$—and the Repub. Con. June 3$^{d}$— So now ↑with Mrs Stanton↓ we shall all feel fully armed for whatever shall present itself to us as <u>the thing</u> to be said or done— I am very sorry to hear of your ill health—and pray you, now that ↑you↓ are feeling thus—not to overdo—if you can possibly help it—

Dr Wolcott & Olympia Brown have decided upon a Wisconsin State Con—June 4$^{th}$ & 5$^{th}$—and I am getting others fixed as rapidly as possible—and hope ↑to↓ make our large force of speakers from all sections—do good service for the cause—through June— We are arranging for a good hall at Cincinnatti June 21^st—

I had hoped the Indianapolis↑na↓ State annual meeting would have been called at Indianapolis—the day previous to our National Con. so that the friends could have compassed both meetings at one bill of expense of time & money— But, no matter,—the State has enough speakers with you—to ensure success—[2]

We shall have our Delegates to the Repub. Con.—all the same as in 1876— But in addition very many more, than they—will be gathered near by—to be & to do what seems the true & right thing then & there—which I cannot at this distance see— But ever since my first experience in 1868—I have longed for unison of thought and action— to concentrate ↑our forces↓ upon Every Presidential nominating Convention—& I hope, this year, to see it carried out & up to each of the great national gatherings— And I know—though you may not quite see the way clear, as those of us at Washington seemed to feel ↑best↓ and agree upon—you will join heartily in hoping & helping it to the best good for our cause— I hope you will soon be in your full health again— With Love as ever yours

~ *Susan B. Anthony*

~ ALS, A-68 Mary Earhart Dillon Collection, Series III, Box 2, MCR-S.

1. She returned from a lecture on March 22 in Pittsburgh, Pennsylvania. (*Film*, 21:132.)

2. Rather than scheduling their annual meeting around the National's annual meeting on May 25 and 26 in Indianapolis, the Indiana Woman Suffrage Association called its meeting for June 16 and 17 in Lafayette.

186 ❧ ANNOUNCEMENT OF A MASS MEETING IN CHICAGO

[April 1880]

A MASS MEETING FOR ALL WOMEN
WHO WANT TO VOTE
WILL BE HELD AT FARWELL HALL,
148 MADISON ST. BETWEEN CLARK AND LA SALLE STREETS,
CHICAGO, ILL.,
WEDNESDAY, JUNE 2D, 1880.
AT 10 A.M., 2.30 AND 8 P.M.

Every woman in the United States who sees or hears of this call is most earnestly invited to be present at this meeting. If this is impossible, she is urged to send a letter or postal, with her name and wish expressed in her briefest and strongest manner, addressed to

Elizabeth Cady Stanton,
President N.W.S.A.,
Care 476 West Lake St., Chicago, Ill.

Letters or Postals *certain* to reach Chicago on June 2d, can be addressed Farwell Hall.

Now let us receive at least twenty thousand postals, and let them be sent in ample time to reach our meeting at Farwell Hall in season.

The best speakers in the United States will be present. Our delegates will proceed from this meeting to the Republican Nominating Convention, to present our demand for their insertion of the following plank:

*Resolved*, That the right of suffrage inheres in the citizen of the United States and we pledge ourselves to secure protection in the exercise of this right to all citizens, irrespective of sex, by an amendment to the National Constitution.

Let us meet together and by overwhelming force of numbers show our earnestness and our determination to secure for ourselves the acknowledged right of self-government.

&#x2AE0; *Susan B. Anthony,*
*Vice-Pres. at Large, N.W.S.A.*
&#x2AE0; *Matilda Joslyn Gage,*
*Chairman Executive Com. N.W.S.A.*

All papers friendly to woman's demands are requested to copy this call. Women are everywhere urged to give it wide circulation.

&#x2AE0; *NCBB,* April 1880.

## 187 &#x2618; SBA to John Anthony and Elizabeth Wadsworth Anthony[1]

Rochester N.Y. April 4/80

Dear Uncle John & Aunt Eliza

Our dear Mother passed away yesterday morning after an illness of ten-days, from a severe cold—and will be buried Tuesday afternoon at 3 Oclock— We should like to have you with us that hour—but should you get this in time—you may be in spirit—though not in body— Brothers Daniel and Merritt are on the way—and will arrive tomorrow afternoon—

Mother has been very comfortable most of the Winter—and when I was at home last February she seemed to enjoy visiting with me more than for a great many months— I got home now just the next day after she was taken ill—and it is a great comfort to me that I could be with her & help do for her in her last days— Sister Mary will now be left without any care and will be very, very lonely— For 17 years and five months— (ever since dear fathers death) Sister Mary has been "instant in season and out of season"[2] in her watchfulness over our dear Mother—

How are both of you this winter— I have not forgotten my ride out to see you last year—and what a good visit I had—[3] I heard that uncle John had been to Adams[4] last summer. But could hardly believe it possible he could go there, and not call at Rochester to see our dear

Mother— If you can't get about writing me—tell Jessie[5] she must do it for you. I remember her sweet face pleasantly—

Give our kind regards to all the boys[6] & to Jessie— From your affectionate niece

ᔥ Susan B. Anthony

ᔥ ALS, AF 15(2), Anthony Family Collection, CSmH.

1. John Anthony (1800–1882), SBA's uncle, lived in Coleta, Illinois, with his wife, Elizabeth Wadsworth Anthony (1806–1892). (Anthony, *Anthony Genealogy*, 198–99; SBA diary, 23 April 1892, *Film*, 29:655ff.)

2. 2 Tim. 4:2.

3. SBA was in Illinois in February and December 1879.

4. Members of the Anthony family regarded Adams, Massachusetts, where two of SBA's great-grandfathers settled in the eighteenth century, as their homestead.

5. Jessie Anthony (1856–1916?) was John's granddaughter. Joseph Anthony, her father, retired as an engineer on the Boston & Albany Railroad in order to farm in Coleta near his father after the death of his second wife left him with four young children to care for. He and his children later moved to California. (Anthony, *Anthony Genealogy*, 198–99; Brief Account of Joseph Anthony, Sr., typescript, MNS-S.)

6. The boys were Joseph Anthony, Jr., (1863–?) and Horace G. Anthony (1865–?), half brothers of Jessie. (Anthony, *Anthony Genealogy*, 198–99.)

188 ᔥ SBA TO SARA ANDREWS SPENCER

[*Rochester, c. 20 April 1880*][1]

A letter from Mrs. Stanton tells of her being on the verge of pneumonia, and rushing home to rest and recruit. She is better and, since she has been to the dinner-table, I infer she is well enough to begin to work up the thunder and lightning for Indianapolis and Chicago. Now won't you at once scratch down the points with which you want to fire her soul and brain, and get her at work on the resolutions, platform and address? She won't go out to lecture any more this spring, and if you will only put her en rapport with your thoughts she will do splendid work in the herculean task awaiting us.

It is simply impossible for me to go to her at present, and we must all give her our ideas in the rough, from time to time, and let her weld them together as best she can; and then, as she says, when we meet in Indianapolis we all will put in our happiest ideas, metaphysical, political, logical and all other "cals," and make these the strongest and grandest documents ever issued from any organization of women. It does seem to me that if we can succeed in grinding out just the right appeal, demand, or whatever it may be called, the Republican convention must heed us. At any rate, we will do our level best at a strong pull, a long pull and a pull all together to compel them to surrender.

I enclose my list of May lecture engagements.[2] I shall be able to help in money from them soon, and better than I could in any other way. I watch both Congress and our State legislatures, but the "scamps" are vastly better at promising than fulfilling. The politicians, of course, expect all this flutter and buncombe about doing something for women in New York—in California—in Iowa[3]—is going to spike our guns[4] and make us help the Republican party to carry all before it; but we must not be thus fooled by them.

&#x223D; *Anthony*, 2:516. In *Film* at April 1880.

1. Dated with reference to ECS's illness. On 20 April, SBA learned that ECS had returned to Tenafly. (SBA to Elizabeth Harbert, 20 April 1880, *Film*, 21:150.)

2. Although her list is missing and her diary gone, SBA's lecture stops included Waynesburg, Pennsylvania, on May 9, and Carrollton, Ohio, sometime before May 19.

3. In New York in February 1880, the Republicans enacted a law making women eligible to serve as school officers and to vote at school meetings. In California, SBA may refer to the efforts of James L. York, Republican assemblyman from Santa Clara, who came close to gaining school suffrage for women in March 1880. The bill passed the assembly on March 24, but on reconsideration the next morning, seven members changed their votes and defeated it. A simple majority in the state senate also passed a constitutional amendment for woman suffrage, but the measure required a two-thirds vote. In Iowa, the Republican legislature returned to the state's perennial constitutional amendment for woman suffrage, which on this occasion passed in the house but lost in the senate. Instead, women gained by new legislation the right to hold the office of county recorder. (*History*, 3:423-25, 625, 627; *Woman's Journal*, 7, 21 February, 27 March, 10, 17 April 1880; *NCBB*, March 1880; with the assistance of the State Law Library of Iowa and of Lucy Barber, California State Archives.)

4. That is, to render their guns unserviceable by blocking them with a spike.

189 ❧ ECS TO SARA ANDREWS SPENCER

Tenafly April 25th [*1880*]

My dear Sarah,

A severe cold that made it impossible for me speak sent me home from the west a week ago. I have a hacking cough & am very hoarse, & whether I shall be able to go to Indianapolis remains to be seen.

However I will do all the work I can in helping to get documents ready to hurl at the politicians & the people. I write to ask you to start in time to spend a few days with me & together we will get up the best resolutions, appeals   addresses &c &c that we can, so that you need not be taxed with any extra work in the conventions    It is impossible to get up satisfactory documents in a hurry. Send me what you have thought of as points for resolutions & address to conventions & I will put my mind to it at once.

I appreciate fully the great work you have done in Washington, & have been much interested in your letters in Nat. Cit.[1] I met some ladies & gentlemen in Big Rapids Michigan[2] who attended the convention last winter at Wash. They were greatly pleased. They are people of wealth & I think if you would write them you might get some money. They were specially pleased with you. They are very rich & liberal.

Mrs. Delos A. Blodgett[3]      Hersey Michigan

Mrs. Thomas B. Stimson[4]    Big Rapids Michigan

Now just ask them for some money to carry on those western conventions, to pay expenses of speakers &c &c & I think you will get it. With kind regards   sincerely yours

❧ *Elizabeth Cady Stanton.*

❧ ALS, Knollenberg Collection, Manuscripts and Archives, CtY.

1. Sara Spencer began writing a column on national politics and congressional action for the *National Citizen* when she joined the paper in August 1879 as the Washington corresponding editor.

2. ECS spoke in Big Rapids, Michigan, on April 9, 10, and 11. (*Big Rapids Pioneer-Magnet*, 1, 8, 15 April 1880.)

3. Jane, or Jennie, Wood Blodgett (?–1890) was the wife of Delos Abiel

Blodgett (1825–1908), a major figure in Michigan's lumber business, a banker, and a delegate to the Republican National Convention in 1880. Hersey, Michigan, is north of Big Rapids. (*NCAB*, 6:77; *New York Times*, 2 November 1908.)

4. ECS may refer to Mrs. Thomas D. Stinson, whose husband was a farmer and former city alderman in Big Rapids. (*Portrait and Biographical Album, Mecosta County, Mich.* [Chicago, 1883], 644; Federal Census, 1860.)

## 190 ⤳ ALBERT D. HAGER[1] TO ECS

Chicago, May 19 1880.

Mrs. E. C. Stanton   Prest. N.W.S.A. 476 W. Lake St.
Dear Madam,

I write you in behalf of Chicago Historical Society and with the hope that you will obligingly secure for and present to this Society a full manuscript record of the Mass Meeting to be held in Farwell Hall in this city June 2, 1880, duly signed by its officers.

We hope too that you will also do the Society the great favor, to deposit in its archives all the letters and postals which you may receive in response to your invitations to attend that meeting.[2]

This meeting may be an important one and long to be remembered. It is hard to measure the possibilities of 1880. I hope this meeting will mark an epoch in American history equal to the convention held in Independence Hall in 1776. How valuable would be the attested manuscript record of that convention and the correspondence connected therewith. The records of the Farwell Hall meeting may be equally valuable one hundred years hence. Please let the records be kept in the city in which the Convention, or Mass Meeting is held.—

I am a republican. I hope the party to which I belong will be consistent. On the highest stripe of its banner is inscribed "Freedom and Equal Rights." I hope the party will not be so inconsistent as to refuse to the "better half" of the people of the United States, the rights enjoyed by the liberated slaves at the South. The leaders should not be content to <u>suffer</u> it <u>to be</u> so—but should work with a will to make it so. I have but little confidence in the sincerity of the man who will shout himself hoarse about "shot guns" and "intimidation" at the South, when ridicule and sneers come from his "shot gun" pointed to those who advocate the doctrine that our mothers, wives and sisters are as well qualified to vote & hold official position as ⁺the⁺ average senegambian of Mississippi—[3]

We should be glad to have you and your friends call at these rooms which are open and <u>free</u> <u>for</u> <u>all</u>. Very Respectfully

⤙ *A. D. Hager*
*Librarian*

⤙ ALS, on Chicago Historical Society letterhead, NWSA Collection, ICHi. Also in *History*, 3:179n.

1. Albert David Hager (1817–1888), formerly state geologist of Vermont, became secretary and librarian of the Chicago Historical Society in 1877. The society was founded in 1856 and suffered greatly in the Chicago Fire of 1871, losing most of its collections and library at Dearborn Avenue and Ontario Street. By 1880 the society occupied new rooms on Dearborn. (Andreas, *History of Chicago*, 2:513–14, 3:410–14; William Stewart Wallace, *A Dictionary of North American Authors Deceased before 1950* [1951; reprint, Detroit, Mich., 1968].)

2. When the postals and letters were deposited in the Chicago Historical Society in the fall of 1880, Hager complained about the absence of letters from the movement's leaders. Nonetheless the society retained the gift as its National Woman Suffrage Association Collection, available in *Film*, reels four and five. (Matilda J. Gage to Albert D. Hager, 30 October 1880, NWSA Collection, ICHi.)

3. Hager may have had a specific politician in mind, but the juxtaposition of strong rhetoric about protecting the voting rights of African-American men in the South and indifference to the voting rights of women characterized all the Republican "Stalwarts" who aspired to win the party's nomination. At this date, Ulysses S. Grant was chief among them. The Stalwarts opposed the southern policy and conciliatory gestures of President Hayes. "Senegambian," referring to the region of West Africa near the Senegal and Gambia rivers, was an American colloquial term for any African American.

## 191 ❧ ECS TO SBA

Tenafly, [*c. 21 May 1880*][1]

Dear Susan:

And now let me say one word about officers. Make Mrs. Wallace [p]resident. The West should have the leading officers. Do not let my name [co]me up for consideration, as I <u>positively decline</u>. My work in conventions is [a]t an end; they are distasteful to me.[2] Let those who enjoy them have the [h]onors as well as the labors. Yours as ever,

❧ *Elizabeth Cady Stanton.*

❧ Typed transcript, ECS Papers, NjR. Transcript is erroneously dated 20 August 1880. In *Film* at 25 May 1880 with proceedings of NWSA meeting. Letters in square brackets obscured by binding.

1. The date is based on ECS's remark to Theodore Stanton (in the next letter) that she received a letter from SBA on 21 May, and the fact that her letter reached SBA in Indianapolis before the National's meeting on 25 May.

2. At the annual meeting, Phoebe Couzins called for ECS's reelection, noting that it was "chronic with Mrs. Stanton to resign and then come up and take her place as President." ECS had earlier announced that she would not return to the lyceum circuit. She did stop lecturing, but she kept a busy schedule of conventions through the first half of 1881. (*Indianapolis Sentinel*, 27 May 1880, and Chicago *Inter-Ocean*, 6 March 1880, *Film*, 21:118, 190.)

## 192 ❧ ECS TO THEODORE W. STANTON

Tenafly, May 21, 1880.

My dear Theodore:—

Since the Monday after you left[1] until to-day, I have been busy writing appeals, resolutions, etc., etc., for the seven conventions Susan has planned to hold in western cities.[2] I had a letter from Susan this morning appealing to my conscience, my friendship, everything noble and tender in the human soul, to take the first train for Indiana. But I shall remain at home to listen to my own coaxing whippoorwill in the evening hour and my own birds that in chorus, with glad songs, usher in the morning hour; that is, not being awake, I let them do what they choose at the break of dawn, taking it for granted that they will follow out the law of their being, as I do mine.

I have finished "Nana" and am now deep in "The Lady of the Aroostock."[3] The <u>Sun</u>, as well as all the other papers, is full of fears and hopes of Grant's success or defeat. Logan has carried everything in Illinois with a high hand for Grant.[4] One hundred and eighteen Republicans signed the letter asking for 76 seats in the Chicago convention for women delegates.[5] Judge Church[6] has died suddenly with apoplexy. Your father wrote a two-column sketch of him for the <u>Sun</u>, and in the same paper your uncle Sam Wilkeson has written a chapter of Weed history and given him an awful scorching.[7] With love and kisses,

&#x223D; *Mother.*

&#x223D; Typed transcript, ECS Papers, NjR.

1. Theodore Stanton sailed for Europe with his sister Harriot in May 1880 to begin work as the Berlin correspondent for the *New York Tribune*. (Ellen Carol DuBois, *Harriot Stanton Blatch and the Winning of Woman Suffrage* [New Haven, Conn., 1997], 33, 35–48.)

2. In addition to the National's annual meeting and its mass meeting in Chicago, SBA planned two-day conventions in the Midwest, sponsored jointly by the National and state associations. These were Milwaukee, Wisconsin, June 4; Bloomington, Illinois, June 7; Grand Rapids, Michigan, June 14; and Lafayette, Indiana, June 16. Meetings in Detroit and Ann Arbor, Michigan, were announced, but both were cancelled. (*History*, 3:184; *NCBB*, May, June 1880.)

3. The typist working from the lost manuscript recorded ECS's handwriting thus: "'Zana' (?) and am now deep in 'The Lady of the Aroustook.'" ECS referred to Émile Zola, *Nana* (1880), and William Dean Howells, *The Lady of the Aroostook* (1879).

4. ECS refers to the New York *Sun*, where Henry B. Stanton was an editorial writer. John Alexander Logan (1826–1886), one of Ulysses Grant's campaign managers and a United States senator from Illinois, outraged the press and party officials by his efforts at the state Republican convention to bar anti-Grant members from Illinois's delegation to the Republican National Convention. (*New York Tribune*, 20 May 1880; *BDAC*.)

5. A majority of Republican senators and representatives signed a letter to the National Republican Committee asking that seventy-six seats at the nominating convention be provided for the National Woman Suffrage Association. Interviewed after he delivered the letter, Senator Thomas W. Ferry reported

that the chairman of the committee was "pledged in its favor." (*NCBB*, May 1880; *Chicago Evening Journal*, 20 May 1880; *History*, 3:176–77.)

6. Sanford Elias Church (1815–1880), a former Democratic assemblyman and lieutenant governor of New York, was chief judge of the state's Court of Appeals from 1870 until his death. In his "Recollections of Sanford E. Church," Henry Stanton recalled their encounters in antebellum state politics. (McAdam, *Bench and Bar of New York*, 1:279; New York *Sun*, 18 May 1880.)

7. Thurlow Weed (1797–1882) had been the undisputed leader of New York's Whig party and a powerful journalist who only reluctantly joined the Republican party. In a full-page article signed "Genesee," Wilkeson reviewed and reprinted large extracts from a recent pamphlet about an early episode in Weed's career, when he led the Antimasonic party in New York. (*ANB*; New York *Sun*, 16 May 1880.)

EDITORIAL NOTE: Woman suffragists responded in considerable numbers to the National's appeal for a show of strength at the Republican National Convention. Across the country they read the call for written messages issued in April and sent postcards and letters expressing their wish to vote—seventeen hundred in all, many of them bearing dozens of signatures gathered in families and neighborhoods. As Albert Hager noted with disappointment, the letters came from unknown women, many of them making their first political statement. Experienced, local leaders arrived as delegates to the mass meeting from the District of Columbia and twenty-three states, including Minnesota, Colorado, Oregon, and South Carolina. Virginia Minor led the large delegation from Missouri, while newcomer Helen M. Gougar headed the group from Indiana.

The sharp division in the Republican party between supporters of Ulysses S. Grant, on the one hand, and James Blaine or John Sherman, on the other, posed an unusual challenge for the women. When they began calling on Republican delegates on the afternoon of May 31, they were received politely by men they knew from local, state, and federal governments. Roscoe Conkling, no friend of woman suffrage, nonetheless received SBA in his rooms at the Sherman House. Lillie Blake called on delegates from New York, Maine, North Carolina, and Connecticut, only to conclude: "Found many friends of our movement, but no reliable support." "Our golden opportunity went by the first day," Sara Spencer wrote to James Garfield on June 7. "Our friends in the different state[s] counselled with their delegations and decided that in the present condition of the party our issue must not be put before the Convention."

On May 31 also, the National Republican Committee met and "laid over" the request from Senate and House Republicans to allot tickets on the floor of the convention to the women, while committee members weighed competing demands for seats from the press, campaign contributors, and veterans. Later the committee offered suffragists ten tickets to seats among the distinguished guests at the back of the platform, and various state delegations provided a few additional seats.

At Farwell Hall, the National's mass meeting opened on June 1 with SBA in the chair and attracted such large crowds to its three sessions each day that the association extended it to last through June 3. People moved back and forth between the meeting and the parlors at the Palmer House that Potter Palmer provided to the association for their appointments with Republican delegates. Some delegates, like Frederick Douglass, left the convention to show their support at the mass meeting.

Until the Republicans were done, leaders of the National worked hard to find a delegate willing to propose they address the nominating convention directly, hoping that chairman George F. Hoar would honor their request in due time. At one moment Hoar indicated he would accept a resolution to hear them if it came from James Garfield, and Garfield was rumored to have consented, but no resolution was offered.

Resistance from the Republican platform committee left the bitterest memories. Belva Lockwood and Cornelia Scarborough gained a short hearing on the afternoon of June 2, when they read the National's memorial and plank, and the chairman indicated he would set a time to hear arguments in its favor. It was late that evening when he sent word to Farwell Hall that the committee would immediately receive the women in the smoking rooms of the Sherman House. SBA left the podium and, in company with Sallie Clay Bennett and Lillie Blake, answered the summons. Held to five or ten minutes, she read the plank and made a short case for national protection, closing with a request that the committee vote on her proposal. The chairman refused to poll the committee and proceeded to take up a long list of political projects. "We left," Blake wrote in her diary, "indignant, humiliated and insulted." (*Chicago Tribune*, 1 June 1880; *Chicago Evening Journal*, 1 June 1880; *New York Times*, 2, 3 June 1880; "Woman's Kingdom," Chicago *Inter-Ocean*, 12 June 1880; Blake and Wallace, *Champion of Women*, 137–38; S. A. Spencer to J. A. Garfield, 7 June 1880, Garfield Papers, DLC; *History*, 3:175–80; NWSA Collection, ICHi, in *Film*, reels 4–5; *Film*, 21:248–69.)

## 193 ⇝ REMARKS BY SBA TO WOMAN SUFFRAGE MEETING IN MILWAUKEE, WISCONSIN

EDITORIAL NOTE: The first in the series of meetings called by the National Woman Suffrage Association in conjunction with midwestern state associations opened in Milwaukee's Academy of Music on the evening of 4 June 1880. While Phoebe Couzins, Sara Spencer, and Matilda Gage stayed in Chicago to attend the Republican National Convention, SBA traveled to Wisconsin with Elizabeth Meriwether, Elizabeth Saxon, Olympia Brown, and the sisters Julia and Rachel Foster. She responded to Mathilde Anneke's welcoming address, though Anneke spoke in German. The meeting continued through June 5.

[4 June 1880]

Susan B. Anthony followed with a response. As the grand old lady came upon the stage she was greeted with outbursts of enthusiasm, and during the recital of statements in favor of women's suffrage, as she believes them, she was not unfrequently applauded. She began by thanking the audience for their hearty greeting, and then launched into the question of so much moment to her. The question of women's suffrage, she said, was a broad one. It was the underlying question of the government, not only as regards women, but the whole human race. It was no new subject which they were agitating, the simple demand of practically applying the fundamental principles of our government to one-half of its people. They came to insist that the women are a part and parcel of the nation, and all they ask is that this one-half may be counted in. They demand this, not as women, but as citizens and human beings. The great question, when first agitated in 1853, was done after serious thought, and the speaker if she went into the details would prove that Madame Anneke and herself were not very young. Madame Anneke was one of the first women who had taken a decided stand in favor of women's suffrage, and when the speaker first listened to her thirty years ago she understood not a word of the speech until it was translated to her.[1] Madame Anneke, Miss Anthony said, is a woman who had ridden on the battle-fields of Germany with her husband, and over the same ground did Carl Schurz ride.[2] These two came to the United States to avoid oppression. Carl Schurz to-day takes a high position in the country and takes part in framing the laws of the nation. He walks clear up to the door of the White House, where he is to-day. But where is Madame Anneke? She comes here to-night with not as many rights as she had when she landed in America. Schurz on the other hand stands looking down and says to this woman, "I'll be citizen; I'll be lawyer; I'll be master; you'll be my subject. I shall dictate." Is this not humiliating; is it not unjust? What we demand then is that when foreign women come to this country they shall have the same privileges as foreign born men when they land upon our shores. Under the shadow of this great flag of ours I say it is an insult, an outrage, to stand by and see Carl Schurz say to Laura Ross Wolcott, "Be my subject, while I occupy the highest position." We want the principles enunciated by this government to be carried out to a logical conclusion.

Thirty years ago when we began this question of Women's Emancipation there was not a single state in which married women had a right to their wages. Every dollar belonged to her husband. The guardianship of the children absolutely to the father; but the laws have been changed wonderfully. Just look at the progress made in thirty years. Married women have now the right to control property which they inherit. Laws have been made to protect women. One change has not been made, however, and that is the old Blackstone law which makes man and wife one, and that one, man. Thirty years ago women were debarred the privileges of education. Now colleges are thrown open to them. They have equal advantages with the men. Forty women are educated and admitted to the bar.[3] Thirty years ago we had one doctor, and when she received her diploma and passed out of the medical institution a resolution was passed that no women should ever enter there again.[4] It is the same as regards ministers, same in the trades and navigation. What has been accomplished is the result of hard, persevering, determined work. But success has followed our efforts.

The speaker reminded women that Fred Douglass said to the negroes "Get money."[5] She too would say to the women "Get money," then get the ballot, for both are powerful. She claimed that the woman's rights platform was broad and Catholic, and its earnest supporters were neither Protestant or Catholic, sectarian or non-sectarian, but all com-

bined, if one can understand. They knew no Jew, no Greek, no nothing, in fact they were nothing.[6]

&#x2E13; *Milwaukee Sentinel*, 5 June 1880.

1. At the woman's rights convention in New York City in September 1853.
Anneke spoke in German, and Ernestine Rose translated for the audience.
(*History*, 1:571–73.)

2. Fritz Anneke (1818–1872) commanded a revolutionary army unit during
the Revolution of 1848 in Germany, with his wife, Mathilde, as his orderly and
Carl Schurz as his aide-de-camp. SBA told this story in her biography of
Anneke for *Johnson's Cyclopaedia*. (A. E. Zucker, ed., *The Forty-eighters:
Political Refugees of the German Revolution of 1848* [New York, 1950], 272–
73; *Dictionary of Wisconsin Biography*; *Film*, 20:626.)

3. According to the *Albany Law Journal*, twenty-six women were admitted
to the bar in the United States between 1869 and 1879. The 1880 census
recorded seventy-five women lawyers. (*Chicago Legal News*, 24 May 1879;
*Statistics of Population, Tenth Census*, 744.)

4. After Elizabeth Blackwell (1821–1910) received the first medical diploma
awarded to a woman in the United States, from New York's Geneva Medical
College in 1849, her sister Emily (1826–1910) sought admission but was rejected because the faculty decided that female students threatened the school's
reputation. Emily earned her degree from Western Reserve University. (*NAW*;
*ANB*; James J. Walsh, *History of Medicine in New York: Three Centuries of
Medical Progress* [New York, 1919], 1:314–15.)

5. At an event celebrating the passage of the Fifteenth Amendment in 1870,
Frederick Douglass advised the newly enfranchised black men to "get education and get money in your pocket, and save it, for without it you will never be
an independent voter." (*Baltimore American and Commercial Advertiser*, 20
May 1870, from on-line newspapers, Maryland State Archives.)

6. An allusion to Gal. 3:28.

## 194 &#x2933; ECS TO HARRIOT E. STANTON

Tenafly, June 8, 1880.

Dear Hattie:

Well, the Republicans have at last chosen their leader, Garfield of
Ohio.[1] A self-made man, graduated as a boy on the tow-path of a canal,
worked up to be a Campbellite preacher, from religion to politics, from
one vote in the convention, he climbed up to the requisite 379. The

Blaine men gave him the nomination; when they saw after many ballotings that they could not nominate Blaine, they agreed on Garfield. Your father says he will be a very vulnerable candidate, as he was mixed up with the Crédit Mobilier, the "salary grab," etc., etc. Poor man! What a sifting he will get now. The nation will know before the election, who and what Garfield is. The convention has been in session a whole week. Garfield presented Sherman's[2] name and it is said did finely. It is said that for length of time, excitement and bitterness, it is unprecedented in our political history.

Neal[3] and I sat up late last night until after twelve, as he was down at the telegraph office waiting for news, and I here waiting for him. When at last he came, I ran from the back room to let him in and fell over a pail of water Amelia[4] had left standing on the round mat. It was clean drinking-water too. But you can imagine my plight. Your father rushed out of bed, either to sympathize with me, or to hear the political news, or both.

Having inaugurated an era of accidents, we seem bent on keeping them up. This morning Neal took it into his head to take down the well-sweep, which would have required the aid of a strong man. But he persuaded Amelia to stand on the cistern and hold the pole until he went up with a ladder and unhooked it. What he did I cannot explain, but as soon as they were both in position, the pole fell in one direction and Amelia, instead of letting go at once, hung on tighter than ever, to save the pole, I suppose; and off she flew with it; while Neal and the ladder tumbled in another direction. They were not much hurt, but all of us were greatly frightened. Though a dangerous performance, it was so comical that we all laughed heartily after recovering from our fright. With much love and many kisses for all of you,

&#x2ABD; *Mother*

&#x2ABD; Typed transcript, ECS Papers, NjR.

1. James Abram Garfield (1831–1881) of Ohio, a member of the House of Representatives from 1863 to 1880, emerged as the compromise candidate of delegates opposed to the reelection of Ulysses S. Grant. After thirty-five inconclusive ballots at the Republican National Convention, delegates committed to James G. Blaine changed their votes and Garfield won the party's nomination early in the afternoon of June 8, with 399 votes to Grant's 306. Implicated in both the Crédit Mobilier and Salary Grab scandals of the 1870s, Garfield eluded formal censure, but his public image remained tarnished. (*ANB*; McPherson, *Hand-Book of Politics for 1880*, 191–92.)

2. John Sherman (1823–1900) of Ohio, a Republican representative from 1855 to 1861, senator from 1861 to 1877, and secretary of the treasury since 1877, was himself a candidate for the nomination. Garfield was his campaign manager at the convention. (*BDAC*.)

3. Daniel Cady Stanton.

4. Amelia Willard (c. 1835–?) went to work for the Stantons at age sixteen in Seneca Falls and became the family's housekeeper. "She was," Gerrit Stanton wrote, "not only the overseer of the inside help, but the garden help had to suit her as well." She died in Ypsilanti, Michigan, at age ninety-six. (*History*, 3:477n; *Eighty Years*, 203–5; G. Smith Stanton, "How Aged Housekeeper Gave Her All to Cause of Woman Suffrage," unidentified and undated clipping, Seneca Falls Historical Society. See also *Papers* 1 & 2.)

## 195 ➽ INTERVIEW WITH SBA IN CINCINNATI, OHIO

[*24 June 1880*]

After five long weeks of indefatigable labor in trying to have a plank inserted in the platform of either of the political parties, the women of the National Suffrage Association have failed.[1] They have worked almost incessantly for weeks, and were found last night seeking a little rest previous to leaving for their different homes.

Miss Anthony, in a conversation, said: "The Democrats have left us without a platform, just as the Republicans did. They said they would protect every citizen in the right to the ballot, but refused to place in their platform this plank:

> *Whereas*, Believing in the self-evident truth that all persons are created with certain inalienable rights, and that for the protection of these rights governments are instituted, deriving their just powers from the consent of the governed; therefore
>
> *Resolved*, That the Democratic party pledges itself to use all its powers to secure to the women of the nation protection in the exercise of their right of suffrage.

"Our next movement will be to question each nominee for any office in the State, and ascertain whether he is in favor of giving the ballot to women, and if he is not, we all intend to bring our influence to bear to

defeat his election, no matter who he is, or for what office he is nominated. The women of the association are all going to their homes with
this determination. We will support any man, or any party, that is in
favor of giving us the right of suffrage."[2]

↢ *Cincinnati Daily Gazette*, 25 June 1880.

1. Democrats at their national convention in Cincinnati, held June 22 to 24,
welcomed representatives of the National Woman Suffrage Association with
considerably more warmth and grace than had the Republicans in Chicago,
but the platform committee made no recommendation about woman suffrage
to the convention. From headquarters provided by the party, SBA, Lillie
Blake, Matilda Gage, Elizabeth Meriwether, Elizabeth Saxon, Sara Spencer,
Kate Trimble, and others fanned out to talk to the delegates as they arrived in
the city. The platform committee heard the National's speakers for more than
an hour. Escorted to the stage of the full convention by the mayor of Chicago,
SBA presented a copy of the National's memorial to the Democrats and stayed
on stage while the clerk read it aloud. A large bloc of seats were reserved for
the woman suffragists' use on the convention floor. (*Film*, 21:306–10; *NCBB*,
June 1880; *Woman's Journal*, 28 August 1880; *Cincinnati Daily Gazette*, 25
June 1880; Blake and Wallace, *Champion of Women*, 139–40.)

2. The reporter next called on Matilda Gage and Lillie Blake. Gage agreed
that no party won suffragists' loyalty, and she predicted, "we shall hold
ourselves as a balance of power against any candidate for office who is not for
us." Blake revealed a leaning toward the Democratic party "on account of the
way we were treated in Chicago by the Republicans," but she said she could
not support the candidacy of General Winfield Scott Hancock.

196 ↣ SBA TO FREDERIC A. HINCKLEY

Rochester N.Y. July 23, 1880

Dear Friend Hinckley

Mrs Stanton forwards me your Postal of the 15th—

We have required the petitions to be <u>written</u> <u>with</u> <u>ink</u> at head of the
sheets— The "enemy" came to making <u>disagreeable</u> criticisms of
<u>printed</u> <u>forms</u>—so last year we required each person to make a copy for
himself—

I send you two forms— It really makes but little difference—which
is used—these are those of we circulated to the 45 & 46 Congresses—[1]

I am glad you of R.I. are going to take hold of the <u>National</u> <u>Constitu-</u><u>tional</u> <u>Guarantee</u> plan of work—

I cant lay my hand on our series ↑of↓ leaflets—our last edition is exhausted—but we shall keep all necessary forms of petition, the N.W.S.A. Constitution & list of Officers for each state—with form of Constitution for local societies, and instructions relative to them—<u>standing</u> on the 4<sup>th</sup> page of the <u>National Citizezen,</u> hereafter, so that any copy of that paper sent to a person, will carry all instructions as to the different kinds of work— The day has come when every one intellectually convinced, must be made to feel it their duty to <u>practically</u> help— Our cause has <u>plenty</u> of <u>latent</u> <u>feeling</u> to carry it to success—but thus far we fail to secure any just expression of it—

Nearly every republican we talked with at Chicago—<u>personally</u> believed in suffrage for women—and yet we could ↑not↓ secure an expression of that general sentiment in their Platform—

The vast majority of the Greenback Labor Convention were <u>outspo-</u><u>ken</u> & warm in their <u>individual</u> belief—and yet they almost failed to secure a full expression—↑it was only↓ at the last moment—after daylight of their all nights session—a good resolution—but still only <u>one</u> <u>half</u> <u>the</u> <u>full</u> <u>idea</u> we asked of them—was adopted by an overwhelming majority—[2]

And with the democrats—it was surprising to us all, how many of them expressed <u>personal</u> sympathy— Even Watterson[3] of Louisville Journal declared himself, <u>fully</u> on our side—in presence of their entire Resolution & Platform Committee—and I said to them there in their hearing gave to us—"Gentlemen if you could believe that a W.S. plank in your platform would ensure your triumph, it ↑would↓ be put in"— they all responded "surely it would"—but we <u>cannot</u> make either of the parties great or small, except the Prohibitionists,[4] believe, <u>recognition</u> of Political equality for women will <u>help</u> them to <u>votes</u>—on the other hand <u>all</u> are <u>afraid</u> <u>such</u> <u>recognition</u> would lose them <u>votes</u>— It was very ludicrous to see & hear the <u>Greenbackers</u>—the <u>minority</u> of them to be sure—Karney[5] ↑one↓ of them—gravely repeating the great partisans response—"<u>We</u> <u>cant</u> <u>afford</u> <u>to</u> <u>shoulder</u> the additional load"—

Mr Hinckley—wont you give me your idea—as to what should be the platform—the position—of all true women & their co-workers—to the political parties during this Presidential canvass— In view of the fact that <u>neither</u> of the <u>two</u> great parties—<u>one</u> of which is likely—<u>sure</u> to win—have given woman <u>any</u> <u>mention</u>—and the <u>two</u> <u>small</u> <u>third</u> <u>parties</u> have given very good & fair mention—full <u>assertion</u>— The resolutions of the Greenback Convention were two—the first was—"That ~~all~~ ↑every↓ citizens of due age and not ~~convi~~ a felon should be entitled to the franchise"—and recomended ↑that↓ the whole question ↑be↓ remanded to the states— The second was—"That the right of self-government inheres in the individual as the fundamental principle of our govern-ment, and we hereby pledge ourselves to secure by Constitutional Amendment, the right of suffrage to the women of the nation"— both were adopted by roll call of states—& by large majorities— <u>But</u> they <u>were</u> <u>not</u> <u>presented</u> by the regular platform Committee—the latter was in his hands—but he being opposed to it—would not report it—then individual members thrust it upon the Con—& it was adopted as the <u>voice</u> of the majority—[6]

Had the Republicans ~~or Democrats~~ done half as much—we should have been ready to have shouted for them— I won't say <u>Democrats</u> for all of us—but now, thus far, our women seem to ignore the fact of the <u>Green</u>-back recognition— I am waiting to get the opinions of each & all on the question—and hope to get yours—

I presume you take the National Citizen—I hope you do at least— and so are in way of seeing what the N.W.S.A. proposes—

Though I haven't seen you personally, that I remember—I feel that I know you—having seen your name among the New-England friends so long—and this must be my apology for thus trespassing upon you this long scribble—

I have taken the lib[erty] to mail to you a copy of the Court Report of my Trial for voting in 1872—also—a copy of Senator Sumners pre-sentation of our first installment of Emancipation in 1863—and forms of petition we circulated in this state in 1854 & /53[7]

I wish we could roll up such a mammoth petition for woman—as we did for the negro— How is it possible to rouse all the friends of all the states to unite upon <u>one</u> <u>petition</u> for one thing to one session of Con-gress?— Such an <u>exhibition</u> of our strength would do much to estop the retort so aggravating—that "only a <u>few</u> <u>women</u> want to vote"—

What we most need, now, <u>united</u> <u>action</u> in one <u>given</u> direction— organized action— The time was, perhaps, when the friends might excuse themselves with individual work in their respective localities— but it seems to me—that, now, we need to rouse every man & woman who believes in woman's enfranchisement—to show hands, and more, join hands—in the very best devised practical work—to secure it—and I think by National Prohibition in line with the 14$^{th}$ and 15$^{th}$ amendments—

Do you see any hope of any such combination & cooperation of all our forces?— Most sincerely yours

⇘ *Susan B. Anthony*

⇘ ALS, Charles Roberts Autograph Letters Collection, PHC. Square brackets enclose letters lost when pen ran dry.

1. Enclosures missing. The petitions were those above at 15 January 1878 and 14 January 1880. Hinckley's decision to work with the National rather than the American suffrage association was announced in the *Woman's Journal*, 21 August 1880.

2. Matilda Gage, Sara Spencer, Lucinda Chandler, and SBA all spoke at the Greenback-Labor party convention in Chicago on June 9 and 10. The platform committee reported nothing on woman suffrage, but through a procedure that allowed delegates to introduce additional planks and vote on them from the floor, the convention adopted two resolutions quoted by SBA further along in this letter. The second of these used wording proposed by the National association to all the party conventions, but the Greenback party omitted an extra provision that the National asked the small parties to adopt: "we further pledge ourselves that whenever we hold the balance of power we will maintain this principle of woman's right to the ballot, steadfastly refusing all affiliation with other parties unless they concede this principle." (*Film*, 21:285–93.)

3. Henry Watterson (1840–1921), the well-known editor of the *Louisville Courier-Journal*, chaired the platform committee at the Democratic National Convention. (*ANB*.)

4. The Prohibition party's platform demanded that the right of female citizens to vote be recognized. The chairman of the party's national committee invited the National Woman Suffrage Association to participate in its nominating convention in Cleveland on June 17, and the association chose Phoebe Couzins to represent them. (James Black to National Woman Suffrage Association, 8 June 1880, *Film*, 21:284; *National Party Platforms*, 60.)

5. Denis Kearney (1847–1907), a delegate from California, objected loudly each time the Greenback-Labor convention agreed to hear from an advocate of woman suffrage. Kearney, who emerged as a leader of the anti-Chinese Workingmen's party in California in 1877, was sent to the convention by the rapidly disintegrating party. (*ANB*; Ira B. Cross, *History of the Labor Movement in California* [Berkeley, Calif., 1935], 125–27.)

6. Edward Hooker Gillette (1840–1918), chairman of the Greenback-Labor party's platform committee and a member of Congress from Iowa, brought no

woman suffrage plank to the floor of the convention. (*BDAC*; *Film*, 21:285–93.)

7. She sent the *Account of the Trial of SBA*; *The Prayer of One Hundred Thousand*, the Women's Loyal National League publication of Charles Sumner's speech of 9 February 1864; and copies of the printed petitions circulated in New York in 1853 and 1854 asking for "Just and Equal Rights of Women" and "Woman's Right to Suffrage." (*Film*, 7:853–54; 10:746–49; 17:103ff.)

# 197 ✍ ECS to Amelia Jenks Bloomer[1]

Tenafly N.J.  July 25th [*1880*]

Dear Mrs Bloomer

Your letter & paper received. I was quite amused with Mary Bull's article[2]

The only point that vexed me was the suggestion that I was not well formed. If I remember aright in those days I was ↑not↓ beyond the becoming point of plumpness. Again she seems to think that no one can have a higher motive in doing anything than the love of notoriety. But so long as we cannot make ↑men↓ & women to order we must let them say & write what they please    The article is full of mistakes but I have long since ceased to correct misstatements, it is of no use. I am now in the full enjoyment of my own home. Maggie & Franks sister[3] have been with me since the 1st of June, the former will probably remain until the 1st of October, unless Frank finds his solitude unendurable Theodore & Hattie went to Germany in May. As Theodore is engaged to the daughter of our minister[4] at Berlin they have the opportunity of frequently meeting at his house, some of the distinguished people of the old world. Hattie will remain abroad two or three years to travel read & study for her profession, unless caught in the trap of matrimony, from which Good Lord deliver her. If our girls would only use their freedom for culture & travel until they are thirty, we should have grander women, & children than we now do

The sickly snubbed women I see all over our land fully explains the dearth of great men    What can we do to keep girls out of the pitfalls of matrimony? Echo answers, what?

Just had a long letter from Susan, she is coming here the 1st of ~~December~~ ↑September↓ to remain four months to help me get out the

1$^{st}$ volumn of our history. If you see Mrs Lawrence[5] tell her that Mrs Monell is well & cheerful, her trip has been of great benefit to her both mentally & physically. She is a fine looking woman & much admired. With kind regards for yourself & Mr Bloomer  [*written crosswise over text*] sincerely yours

⇝ *Elizabeth Cady Stanton*

⇝ ALS, Amelia Bloomer Papers, Seneca Falls Historical Society.

1. Amelia Jenks Bloomer (1818–1894), publisher of the temperance paper the *Lily* and popularizer of the reform costume bearing her name, lived in Seneca Falls in 1848 and moved to Council Bluffs, Iowa, in 1855. Her husband, Dexter Chamberlain Bloomer (1816?–1900), a lawyer and local Republican activist, served twice as mayor of Council Bluffs. (*NAW*; *ANB*; Edward H. Stiles, *Recollections and Sketches of Notable Lawyers and Public Men of Early Iowa* [Des Moines, Iowa, 1916], 893–94; Benjamin F. Gue and Benjamin F. Shambaugh, *Biographies and Portraits of the Progressive Men of Iowa* [Des Moines, Iowa, 1899], 1:452–53.)

2. Mary Sherwood Bascom Bull (1835–1881) grew up in Seneca Falls, New York, the daughter of Ansel Bascom, a lawyer and local political leader. Her father took Mary with him to the woman's rights convention in 1848. Mary Bull's article, "Woman's Rights and Other 'Reforms' in Seneca Falls," appeared first in the journal *Good Company* and was then reprinted, among other places, in the *Woman's Journal*, 14 August 1880. Bull described ECS as "stout, short, with her merry eye and expression of great good humor," and Amelia Bloomer as "rather plain." But in their bloomer costumes, it was Bloomer who "had a far better figure for the dress"; no scarecrow had ever been "better calculated to scare all birds, beasts and human beings than was Mrs. Stanton in the Bloomer dress." Bull also described reform as a search for novelty: woman's rights "had the great merit to Mrs. Stanton of being new if nothing more." ECS welcomed the arrival of the bloomer costume because, Bull explained, she "had worn the gloss of novelty off from most of her themes and was sighing for a new sensation, a new reform." (Edward Doubleday Harris, *A Genealogical Record of Thomas Bascom, and His Descendants* [Boston, 1870], 62; Mary Bull, "'Woman's Rights and Other Reforms in Seneca Falls': A Contemporary View," ed. Robert Riegel, *New York History* 46 [January 1965]: 41–59.)

3. Ella M. Lawrence Monell (1851–?) was Frank Lawrence's younger sister. She married John Monell in 1871 and lived in Omaha. (*History of Pottawattamie County, Iowa*, pt. 2, p. 37.)

4. Theodore was engaged to marry Clara White (c. 1858–1907), the daughter of Andrew Dickson White (1832–1918), first president of Cornell University. White was named minister to Germany by President Hayes in 1879. When they broke their engagement, Clara married Spencer Baird Newberry,

a recent graduate of Cornell who was also in Berlin for post-graduate work in chemistry. (*ANB*; Glenn C. Altschuler, *Andrew D. White—Educator, Historian, Diplomat* [Ithaca, N.Y., 1979], 48, 262, 277; *NCAB*, 10:71–72.)

5. Lara M. Rockwell Lawrence (c. 1822–?), the mother of Frank Lawrence and Ella Monell, moved from New York to Council Bluffs in 1868 with her husband, Noah D. Lawrence, a physician. (*History of Pottawattamie County, Iowa*, pt. 2, p. 37; Federal Census, 1870.)

## 198 &#x223D; ECS TO SBA

Tenafly, July 26, [*1880?*][1]

Dear Susan:

As to the History, sit right down and write everything you can [rem]ember of yourself, and write objectively just as you would of another pe[rso]n. The moment you left me last summer, I packed the whole thing away and [h]ave never put pen to paper since. I cannot work on the big job alone. [Y]ou have done convention work enough. Leave these state conventions to [t]hose who have each in turn wished you and me out of their way;[2] so do let [t]hem alone, for a short season, at least until we can finish that History. [A]s soon as you come, we will begin at once with the printer. Working under [p]ressure with him hurrying us up, we shall do something. That is the only [w]ay we can be made to do our level best. We must go at it religiously, and [n]ot turn aside one hour for anything. Affectionately,

&#x223D; *Elizabeth Cady Stanton.*

&#x223D; Typed transcript, ECS Papers, NjR. Misdated [1877?] in *Film*, 19:517.

1. The references in this letter to interrupted work on the *History of Woman Suffrage* "last summer," to the competing claims on SBA's time, and to ECS's commitment to complete the work, all fit best with what is known about their collaboration in 1880.

2. Under pressure from New York State suffrage leaders, SBA intended to join a statewide canvass leading up to the New York school elections on October 12. Both national and state suffrage leaders were anxious that women turn out in large numbers to exercise their new privilege of voting in school elections. In the words of Lillie Blake, suffragists needed "such a response at the elections in October as shall everywhere show our opponents that women do wish to vote." (*History*, 3:424–31; *NCBB*, August 1880.)

199 ⇝ SBA to Catharine Fish Stebbins

*[before August 1880]*

I have loaned the *Woman's Journals* of the past two months and read up its various criticisms and flings, and must say they are in the main very weak, if not wicked.[1]

Why didn't we old abolitionists chide the slave for cheating his master out of his property when he stole himself. The fact is, no man feels the theft, the great conspiracy he is a part of, in robbing women of their birthright to a voice in the government. I, personally, might not do exactly what Miss King[2] did, but nevertheless, it ill becomes any one of the ruling class, who tax her vast real estate on the Boulevards of New York, while they deny her the only weapon of defence, to taunt her with dishonesty.

Do you not see, my dear friend, that this exceeding conscientious-ness on the part of the republicans and Blackwells is but the necessity for a *new scare*, a new fling at us of the National Woman Suffrage Association? It used to be "False to the negro!" then "Free Love!!" and now those bugaboos have lost their power to frighten timid women, they resort to "*Honesty*" or rather lack of it, in women's ways of protecting themselves. The whole matter comes down to about the same fine point as that of non-resistance,—asking, "whether a man would be justified in killing another whom he saw aiming a bullet at the heart of his child" it would be violation of the extreme principle of non-resistance.[3] So with Miss King's case. The New York senator,[4] whom she was trying to defeat, had worked against her very life, financially, at Albany, and would, if returned, continue the same; it was to her, as she felt, financial death, and she used every weapon she possessed to save herself—she called public meetings, printed and circulated appeals, gave good suppers to the poor laboring men voters, and to make sure, when still doubtful, she gave the poor man's wife a calico dress or a sack of flour, *never a drop of whiskey*—and I cannot sit in judgment against her. Each woman must be left to work out her own problem of freedom as best she can; I shall not criticise the methods of any one of them, for I do not know what I should do were I in the place of any other than myself. But of this I am sure, desperate, and more desperate things are sure to be done as women come more and more into a true sense of the injustice of their position of disfranchisement. It is grievous, it is humiliating, it is degrading, and should not be submitted to another hour by any woman with two grains of self-respect. Do you not see that if it were any class of educated, property-holding men, they would not only buy ignorant men to represent them at the ballot-box, but they would rise in rebellion, devastate the land, and slay all men who denied them their right to a voice in the government? No, I cannot condemn any woman for using any and every weapon she can wield for the gaining of her right to freedom and the franchise. "Liberty or Death," is as heroic and grand a watchword for the women of to-day as it was for the men of yesterday. The men of the Revolution *stole other people's tea* in Boston Harbor and we build monuments to their courage, honor and honesty, you see it is a fine point of morals for enslavers and champion thieves to preach honesty and integrity to their victims in their methods of escaping from their despots, or regaining their stolen property.

But, say you, the present generation of men are not responsible for the condition of things. That depends. All who suffer the conditions to continue without effort to change, *are* guilty of the crime, hence every republican like every democrat, who, without protest goes with his party in its silence on this gross injustice, is guilty, as if he were one of the original plotters against equal rights for women. *Senator Hoar silent* in the Chicago Convention made himself a party to the great crime against the women of this nation. How can we make even our very best friends see and feel that it is their duty to act for women as they would if it were themselves who were denied their right.

⤙ *NCBB*, August 1880.

1. The *Woman's Journal* launched several offenses against the National Woman Suffrage Association after the presidential nominating conventions. By reprinting items from the Democratic press, the editors spread the erroneous reports that the National's leaders would campaign for the Democratic candidate. To those stories they added editorials condemning the National for its willingness to talk to parties other than the Republican and subordinate other national issues to woman suffrage. Unfaithful and selfish women would not win party support, wrote Henry Blackwell: politicians would ignore their

claims if women "seem[ed] to play fast and loose with political parties. . . . A woman who goes from the Convention of one party to that of another, and still another, no matter how pure her motives may be, will be likely rejected by all." At the same time, the editors chastised New York suffragists for allegedly buying votes in the state election of 1879. This flap, addressed by SBA below, stemmed from the decision to campaign against the reelection of both Governor Lucius Robinson, who vetoed a bill to make women eligible for school offices, and a state senator, who opposed and ridiculed woman's rights. After both men met defeat, the *National Citizen* boasted that Susan King "spent money like water" in the campaign and quoted King as saying that women should buy their freedom. In May 1880, repeated references to King's actions led Lucinda Chandler to ask if King had bought votes; Matilda Gage not only reported that yes, King bought votes, but also that she, Gage, commended the action. At the mass meeting in Chicago in June, when Chandler asked the National to condemn King's behavior, SBA defended her. In July, the *Woman's Journal* took up the criticism in editorials and articles. (*NCBB*, November 1879, February, April, May 1880; *Woman's Journal*, 26 June, 17 July 1880; *Chicago Evening Journal*, 2 June 1880; *Chicago Tribune*, 3 June 1880, *Film*, 21:249–50.)

2. Susan Ann King (1817–1898), a New York City businesswoman and the sister of a Tammany Democrat, spent some of her fortune in 1879 in the effort to defeat candidates hostile to woman suffrage. What caught especial attention was the entertainment she offered to local voters at her house on 105th Street to campaign against her state senator. King boasted after the election that the law against bribing voters did not apply to women. Born in Gorham, Maine, King had moved to New York City by 1860 and, along with her brother, made a fortune from real estate. By the early 1870s, she pursued philanthropic activities intended to expand women's employment. With Ellen Demorest, she formed the Woman's Tea Company and made several trips to China to select tea. In 1871, the company's "Mandarin Tea" could be purchased at Demorest's Emporium on Broadway, and its "lady agents" canvassed the country, soliciting sales. King was an officer of the New York State Suffrage Association and a member of the National association's executive committee. (Hugh D. McLellan and Katharine B. Lewis, *The History of Gorham, Maine* [1903; reprint, Camden, Me., 1992], 605–6; *History*, 3:417–19, 422–23, 431; *NCBB*, November 1879, April, May, July 1880; Blake and Wallace, *Champion of Women*, 132–34; Federal Census, 1860, 1870, 1880; Ishbel Ross, *Crusades and Crinolines: The Life and Times of Ellen Curtis Demorest and William Jennings Demorest* [New York, 1963], 128–39.)

3. SBA here uses the term nonresistance as a synonym for nonviolence, but she alludes to a movement among Garrisonian abolitionists that renounced human government because it was based on force and violence. (Perry, *Radical Abolitionism*, 55–91.)

4. Thomas Charles Edward Ecclesine (1846–1895) incurred the wrath of

suffragists in 1878 when he opposed bills for their enfranchisement and relief from taxation, and he became a target of their political influence in his bid for reelection to the state senate in 1879. An Irish-born graduate of Columbia College and Columbia Law School and a New York City Democrat, Ecclesine won election to the state assembly of 1877 and to the state senate of 1878. (Columbia University, *Alumni Register*, 246; Charles G. Shanks, *The State Government for 1879. Memorial Volume of the New Capitol* [Albany, 1879], 53; *History*, 3:419-20, 423; *NCBB*, April 1880; *Woman's Journal*, 13 April 1878.)

200 &#x223D;&#x223D;   SBA TO ELIZABETH BOYNTON HARBERT

Rochester N.Y. August 5, 1880

My Dear Friend Lizzie B. H.

Your 5 or 6 Inter Oceans are here—and letter of the 27th Ult—also a letter of weeks ago—which is going the rounds among the members of our N.W.S.A. to read and to give their opinions to me upon—at latest report it had reached Mrs Spencer—

I thought I had answered the main points of your first letter[1]—and told you that I considered your head "<u>level</u>" on the main question— that is our <u>non</u>-action for either of the two great parties. As to the two small ones— Since neither of them made a pledge to <u>carry</u> Woman Suffrage <u>with Greenbacks,</u> or <u>with Prohibition,</u> wherever it went as a balance of power, and since no &#8593;third&#8595; par~~ties~~&#8593;y&#8595; <u>can</u> be anything to us <u>politically</u> except it does thus make our question equally and on all occasions its test of affilliation, we cannot give aid or comfort to either the Greenback or Prohibition party.— We can only look over the whole list of nominees of the four parties—and do all in our power to <u>defeat</u> every candidate opposed to Woman Suffrage—no matter whether Repub. or Dem. Green. or Prohibition—as Miss King killed of the N.Y. Sena-tor last fall— the men of neither party <u>believes</u> <u>enough</u> in our <u>power</u> to <u>help them</u> to give us the plank we demanded— <u>Politically</u> our outlook is dark as ever—but morally it is hopeful—more hopeful than ever— The large numbers of the <u>men</u> of all the parties—<u>Democratic</u>, with the rest—indicates the moral & intellectual advance— But none of them, except the two <u>small</u> feel that we can <u>help them</u> into power—<u>and</u> <u>they</u> cant <u>help us</u> to the ballot—so there we stand— If the Prohibitionists had the speakers and the money to make a thorough canvas—or we had the money—but they haven't & we haven't— And then beside, what discourages me about women—scarce one of them but, after all, cares more for <u>her</u> <u>love</u> of ↑the↓ <u>political</u> <u>party</u>—Repub. Dem. or Greenback than for <u>her</u> <u>own</u> <u>political</u> rights—

I see Mrs Blake is asking the <u>National</u> Democratic Committee for something—[2] Mrs Spencer says she is going into the Greenback Canvass[3]—and I dare say some of our women are fixing to go into the Republican canvas— We cant <u>make</u> <u>our</u> <u>W.S.</u> <u>army</u> <u>to</u> <u>the line</u>—or any one line— I feel the Repub. party deserves to die for its falseness to principle—but I do not see any <u>better party</u> struggling to take its place— I can but feel that the safest been men of the nation are <u>in</u> the republican ranks—but all of the parties are false to woman—

I shall be very glad to hear from Miss Willard—whether she and her C.T. hosts are going into the Prohibition Canvass—[4] I do not see how <u>they</u> <u>can</u> do otherwise—and as you say—<u>no</u> suffrage woman <u>can</u> <u>work</u> for any other party but that & the Greenback—but then some of our women <u>oppose</u> <u>Prohibition</u> and then <u>hate</u> that <u>party</u> because its leaders are, so many of them, working to put <u>God</u> in the Constitution—

General Weaver[5]—Mrs Spencer says—is a strong suffragist— I do not know about Neal Dow[6]—but imagine he is—

My plan for next winter is to work in N. York in School Suffrage through November—and in the east till the Washington Con. in Jan. and after that make a southern tour— I surely have written you about all this in reply to your letter— Didn't you get it—

You will see that I am as much at sea as to our true work as you or any one can possibly be— I do not see any way in which we W.S. women can <u>mass</u> <u>enough</u> <u>speakers</u> to make ourselves felt for <u>any</u> <u>party</u>— as I said neither the Greenback nor the Prohibition have the money to <u>enable</u> us to help them—

Mrs Gage was here a week ago—and she sees no way we can make a power of ourselves—only for each one of us in o̶u̶r̶ ↑her↓ locality to find out our enemies & do what she can to defeat them—

I sent Mrs Gage your last Kingdom— I was delighted with <u>your</u> disposal of the growlers—& I told her I hoped she would copy it in N.C.— I have read up the Woman's Journal flings & criticisms— (borrowed the papers I do not take it) and they are too weak and too wicked for anything or anybody decent— They <u>do</u> <u>nothing</u>—give no

<u>plan</u> of work to the people—but growl—↑and↓ they surely do enough of
that—

I have a most remarkable letter from Mrs Chandler—[7] Who tells me
we snubbed the working women of Chicago— I surely heard nothing
of any such— Then I find Mrs Bishops[8] open letter in the Inter Ocean
to you— Isn't it marvelous how impossible it is to do what everybody
feels satisfied with?— I surely would not have refused any representave
sent by 76 or more or less working women— If Mrs B. had been very
wide awake before—she would have known that there had been a W.S.
society in Chicago— Well good night— Tell Miss Willard I want to
hear from her what & how she sees the way to do— affectionately yours

⤙ *Susan B. Anthony*

⤙ ALS, Box 2, Elizabeth Harbert Collection, CSmH.

1. None of Harbert's letters in this exchange survives, but SBA's earlier
letter of 7 July 1880 is in *Film*, 21:317–24.

2. When Lillie Blake returned from the Midwest, she was frequently reported as saying that the Democratic candidate might still express himself in
favor of woman suffrage despite the silence of the party's platform. At some
point during the campaign, she also offered her services to the New York State
Democrats. (*New York Herald*, 3 July 1880; Blake and Wallace, *Champion of
Women*, 140–41.)

3. By this date, SBA had seen a letter by Sara Spencer that was finally
published in the *Woman's Journal*, 28 August 1880. According to Spencer,
she wrote it in June and sent it to the *National Citizen*, but SBA and Matilda
Gage refused to publish it. In the letter, Spencer described the responses of
each political convention to the delegations of woman suffragists and concluded, "I believe our allegiance as Woman Suffragists is due to the Greenback Labor party." (Sara Spencer to James A. Garfield, 5 September 1880,
Garfield Papers, DLC; *Woman's Journal*, 28 August 1880.)

4. In fact, Frances Willard supported James Garfield in the election. (Earhart,
*Frances Willard*, 211–12.)

5. James Baird Weaver (1833–1912) of Iowa was the presidential candidate
of the Greenback-Labor party. He was elected to the House of Representatives as a Greenbacker for one term in 1879. (*BDAC*.)

6. Neal Dow (1804–1897) was the presidential candidate of the Prohibition
party. Active in temperance reform since 1824, Dow was the architect of the
Maine Law, the model for prohibitory legislation to ban alcohol. (*ANB*.)

7. Lucinda Banister Chandler (1828–1911) was a reformer well known for
her ideas about enlightened motherhood, women's control of their bodies,
and a uniform sexual standard for men and women. She had been active in the
National Woman Suffrage Association since 1872 and attended the mass meet-

ing in Chicago. There and through the summer, she made it her mission to publicize and criticize the association's support of Susan King and her use of gifts in the election of 1879. Her missing letter referred to another controversy at the mass meeting about the reception of delegates from a local union of women. Chandler was also a voting delegate to the Greenback-Labor party convention. (*ANB*.)

8. Julia Howard Bishop, known always in the press as Mrs. O. A. Bishop, was married to Orris Addison Bishop, a war veteran, pattern maker, and socialist. She too was a voting delegate to the Greenback-Labor convention, part of the Socialist Labor party contingent, with credentials from Chicago Working Women's Union No. 1. At the National's mass meeting, according to the *Chicago Tribune*, "Mrs. Bishop, a local female Communist, attempted to make a speech but Miss Anthony quietly squelched her, and she sat down." Bishop's letter, dated 22 June 1880, had in fact not yet appeared in Harbert's column. SBA enclosed her copy with this letter, and Harbert published it on 14 August. Bishop made two complaints: that Illinois and Chicago lacked suffrage associations and that the Working Women's Union's delegates were not recognized at the meeting. Harbert, who explained to readers that the letter had only now come to her attention, corrected Bishop about the matter of local suffrage societies and apologized for the mistake of not recognizing the union. She also quoted this letter from SBA. (*Chicago Tribune*, 12 April, 16 July 1880; city directory, 1880; on-line archive of Kane County, Illinois, marriages; with assistance of Richard Schneirov, Indiana State University; *Chicago Tribune*, 2 June 1880, and "Woman's Kingdom," Chicago *Inter-Ocean*, 14 August 1880, *Film*, 21:248, 353.)

## 201  ⤳  INTERVIEW WITH SBA IN ROCHESTER

[*13 August 1880*]

Our esteemed townswoman, Miss Susan B. Anthony, is at present sojourning at her home on Madison street, in this city. A Democrat and Chronicle reporter who had a pleasant conversation with her last evening, learned as a positive fact, emphasised by Miss Anthony's own lips, that she is not now in Colorado, as some of the newspapers insist on having it; that she has not been to visit Hancock,[1] in company with Mrs. Blake, of New York, or anybody else, and that she is not "now organising the campaign for Garfield in Western New York," as several other newspapers are bound to have it. She disclaims the statement that she is to work in the presidential campaign for Garfield, Hancock, or anybody else, or that the National Woman Suffrage association is going to work for any presidential nominee or party not pledged to the enfranchisement of woman.[2] Miss Anthony says:

"I hate the state rights dogma, and the only thing that could make me willing to see the Democratic party in power, even for one term, would be its pledge to support a sixteenth amendment for woman suffrage. I surely wouldn't work for the Devil—the states rights party—unless he pledged himself to free women from their political slavery. I am going to engage in canvassing the state of New York on the school suffrage question, and I will do all I can to influence men to vote for every candidate who is in favor of woman suffrage, and to defeat every candidate opposed, whether Democratic or Republican."

⚝ Rochester *Democrat and Chronicle*, 14 August 1880, SBA scrapbook 9, Rare Books, DLC. This was widely reprinted in other newspapers.

1. Winfield Scott Hancock (1824–1886), a career military man and hero of the battle at Gettysburg, was the presidential candidate of the Democratic party. On this day in New York City, he met with Lillie Blake, Susan King, and Helen Slocum, representing the New York City Suffrage Society, to discuss his personal views of woman suffrage. (*ANB*; New York *Sun*, 14 August 1880, in SBA scrapbook 9, Rare Books, DLC; Blake and Wallace, *Champion of Women*, 140–41; *Woman's Journal*, 28 August 1880; *NCBB*, September 1880.)

2. SBA responded to an interview published in the New York *Evening Telegram*, 10 August 1880, in which it was claimed that all of New York's leading suffragists had endorsed General Hancock and that SBA would campaign against James Garfield in the western part of the state. The interview was picked up by papers elsewhere in the country, though rarely with the denials and corrections sent to the press by Clemence Lozier and Lillie Blake. Blake was quoted as saying of SBA's meeting with Garfield, "'She had not talked with him ten minutes when she found out that he was dreadfully opposed to women's rights.'" Implying that a reporter had also spoken to SBA, the article summed up her views: "She made up her mind that Garfield was not the proper man to fill the important position of Chief Magistrate of the nation at the time she visited him at his home in Ohio, and she advised all her friends in the women's rights movement to urge their husbands and brothers to vote for Hancock." (New York *Evening Telegram*, 10, 12, 13 August 1880; *Woman's Journal*, 28 August, 4 September 1880.)

202 → SBA TO JAMES A. GARFIELD, WITH
ENCLOSURE

Rochester N.Y. Aug. 16^th 1880.

Hon James A. Garfield  Dear Sir

The Associated Press busies itself reporting Susan B. Anthony's interview with Gen. Garfield—and her saying that "he was opposed to Woman Suffrage," that "he would veto any bill passed by Congress" &c. &c—that "she was going to work in the Canvass for Gen. Hancock"— that she was one of the party who interviewed Gen. Han.[1]

I really care very little for any or all of it—except that which reports so discreditably as regards my private interview with yourself at Mentor—[2] I have made no public mention of it—but one or two ↑have done so,↓ to whom I have privately expressed my regret that you could not give me some direct and possitive word,— ↑as↓ that you would mention woman Suffrage in your letter of acceptance as a question claiming political consideration, or that you would recommend to Congress, in case you were elected, the submission of a 16^th Am't proposition to the several Legislatures, thereby throwing the responsibility of the woman suffrage question upon the States,—or in some way, giving to me an intimation of your wish that our demand should be fully & fairly adjudicated upon by the highest tribunals—Congress and the several State Legislatures.

I regret exceedingly that any one should cite my name as regards your position on the w.s. question.— It is done wholly without my consent—and I vastly more ↑[regr]et↓ that as reported—they entirely falsify any statement made by me.— For I do not believe that you would veto a w.s. bill, nor in any way hinder its enactment.

My position & that of the N.W.S. Association is—to work for the success of no party, nor no candidate, unless the party or the candidate is publicly pledged to work for the emancipation of woman from political slavery, and since neither of the great parties, nor their candidates are ↑thus↓ pledged I ↑shall↓ work for neither—

But if I were compelled to declare for one or the other, while both stand with their heel on the neck of woman, it would surely not be for the one clamoring for "States Rights"—for I hate that Dogma, and hold that the State should no more be allowed to disfranchise U.S. citizens, than to enslave them. The only thing that could influence me to work for the success of the Democratic Party would be a pledge from it, solemn & solid, to add another amendment to the National Constitution, forever forbidding the States from disfranchising U.S. citizens—except for crime, idiocy or lunacy—

It is impossible for you to comprehend the trial it is to my political instincts, to withhold my most earnest word and work for the success of the Republican Party in this campaign—and especially for the success of yourself— All that I read of you, your relations to freedom in all the war period—make me long for the freedom to rush into the thick of ↑the↓ battle—but then comes the stern fact—I and all of my half of the people are political slaves—and neither the Republican Party nor its nominee give promise of freedom to us!! Self-respect,—respect for my sex;—self-justice,—justice to my sex, all bid me be silent, until the party and the man appear pledged to "undo the bands and let the oppressed go free."[3]

On the first of September, I begin a canvass of the state of New York, especially to rouse the women to a sense of their duty to vote at the October School meetings, as they are entitled to do under the new law—and I should be more than glad if I had some good word to drop for you at each of my meetings—I mean from you.

Now can you not, will you not, give me a letter—stating that you feel it the duty of Congress to submit a proposition for a 16th Am't to prohibit ↑the states from the↓ disfranchisement↑ing↓ of women by the states—that the question may be brought into a position to be acted upon by the representative men of the several States. You see our movement stands at a dead-lock until Congress will thus make it possible for the states to pass upon it.

You are a sagacious politician—and a statesman—and one, too, believing in the principle of equality of rights for all—and I am sure you must be able to see some way in which you can say the word to me that shall make it possible for me to speak and to urge all women to speak and all men to vote for you—because in your elevation to the Presidency lies the strongest—the only hope of political aid in the emancipation of Woman. With great respect   Sincerely yours

⤺ *Susan B. Anthony*

P.S.—Aug. 17<sup>th</sup> Still other word comes to me of the public action & talk of some of our <u>woman</u> <u>suffrage</u> <u>women</u>—this morning—which decides me to send you the enclosed <u>official</u> request—and I do hope you will be able to see it both wise & expedient—for to give me a most full & clear reply—& that, too, such that I can at once make <u>counter</u> statement—as to all the newspaper gossip that S. B. Anthony & all of the N.W.S.A. are going to work for Hancock because of his <u>suave</u> <u>word</u>—<u>polite</u> <u>bow</u> to a delegation of woman suffrage ladies— Hoping you will pardon my importunity—& believe me in serious anxiety to be able to <u>work</u> <u>for</u> the <u>nation</u> with a capital N.— S. B. A.

⚞ ALS, on NWSA letterhead for 1880, James A. Garfield Papers, DLC. Letters in square brackets torn from corner.

## ENCLOSURE

Rochester N.Y. Aug. 17<sup>th</sup> 1880.

Hon. James A. Garfield   Dear Sir

As Vice President at Large of the National Woman Association, I am instructed to ask of you, as nominee of the Republican Party for President, if you in the event of your election, would in your address to Congress, recommend the submission of a 16<sup>th</sup> Amendment of the National Constitution, prohibiting the states from the disfranchisement of United States citizens on account of sex.

The claim of our N.W.S. association for <u>National</u> <u>protection</u> of <u>Women</u> in their right to a voice in the government can be met in no other way than that named above, and in no other ↑way↓ can our question be acted upon <u>by</u> <u>the</u> <u>people</u> of the <u>Nation</u> through their representatives in their several state Legislatures.

Hoping that you will give me a favorable and an immediate reply—I am respectfully yours

⚞ *Susan B. Anthony*

⚞ ALS, on NWSA letterhead for 1880, James A. Garfield Papers, DLC.

1. That is, the interview in the New York *Evening Telegram*, 10 August 1880.
2. The date of SBA's meeting with James Garfield at Mentor, Ohio, is not known. When she left Cincinnati on June 25, she changed trains at Cleveland

for Willoughby, Ohio, where she was scheduled to lecture on Saturday, June 26. Willoughby is close to Mentor, and it is likely that she saw him over that weekend. According to the *National Citizen*, she called on him "to learn from his own lips, how he, the candidate of a great party, individually looked upon the demand of woman for 'additional rights'" and she found him "'not convinced.'" (Blake and Wallace, *Champion of Women*, 140; *Cincinnati Commercial*, 25 June 1880, *Film*, 21:313; *NCBB*, July 1880.)

3. From Isa. 58:6.

203 ⤳ SARA ANDREWS SPENCER TO ECS

Washington, D.C., Aug. 17, 1880.

To Mrs. Elizabeth Cady Stanton, President National Woman Suffrage Association:—

Dear Madam.—I herewith tender to you my resignation as Corresponding Secretary of the National Woman Suffrage Association and also as member of that organization, to take effect upon your receipt of this letter. My duties in the college will be resumed next Monday, and I should be glad to turn over the correspondence of the N.W.S.A. to my successor at the earliest day you may find it convenient to name.[1] Very Respectfully,

⤳ *Sara Andrews Spencer.*

⤳ *NCBB*, September 1880.

1. In a later letter to James Garfield, written after the *Woman's Journal* had published her article about the need for suffragists to support the Greenback-Labor party, Spencer explained that the rejection by SBA and Matilda Gage of that article led her to resign. She also quoted ECS as saying that Spencer's was "a fair, just statement and ought to have gone out to our Association." Spencer further told Garfield that she would organize a "new and more hopeful and efficient organization." (S. A. Spencer to J. A. Garfield, 5 September 1880, Garfield Papers, DLC; *Woman's Journal*, 28 August 1880.)

## 204 ↭ ECS TO SBA

Tenafly, August 18, 1880.

[D]ear Susan:

Well then you have changed your plans about work this fall. I thought [y]ou and I were to devote ourselves religiously to History for four months [a]nd get the first volume published by Christmas. And now you fly off at [s]omething else.

I enclose you Mrs. Blake's letter.[1] I answered that I thought we had sat [on] a limb of the Republican tree singing "suffrage if you please" like so [m]any insignificant humming birds quite long enough, and I was ready for [a]ny change of base that would undermine a solid male dynasty. Good night, Yours as ever,

↭ *Elizabeth Cady Stanton.*

↭ Typed transcript, ECS Papers, NjR. Letters in square brackets obscured by binding.

1. Enclosure unidentified.

## 205 ↭ JAMES A. GARFIELD TO SBA

Mentor, Ohio   Au 24/80

Copy   Private

Dear Miss Anthony

Your letter of the 17th inst came duly to hand. I take the liberty of asking your personal advice before I answer your official letter.

I assume that all the traditions and impulses of your life lead you to believe that the Republican party has been ~~the~~ ↑and↓ is more nearly in the line of liberty than its antagonist the Democratic Party. And I know you desire to advance the cause of women.

Now in view of the fact that the Chicago Convention has not discussed your question do you not think it would be a violation of the trust they have imposed in[1] me to speak of as their nominee and add to the present contest an issue that they have not raised?

Again if I answered your questions on the ground of my own private opinion I shall be compelled to say that while I am open to the freest discussion and ~~fullest~~ ↑fairest↓ consideration of your question I have not yet reached the conclusion that it would be best for ↑the↓ women ~~illegible~~ ↑of↓ the country that she should have the suffrage. I may reach it but whatever time may do to me that fruit is not yet ripe on my tree    I ask you ~~however~~ ↑therefore↓ for the sake of your own questions do you think it wise to pick my apples now.

Please answer me in the frankness of personal friendship    With kindest regards I am Very Truly Yours

⤜  sd J A Garfield

Miss Susan B Anthony   Rochester N.Y.

⤜ Hw copy, James A. Garfield Papers, DLC. Also in *History*, 3:185–86, dated 25 Aug 1880.

1. The text in the *History of Woman Suffrage* reads "reposed in"; whether editors fixed Garfield's prose there or the copyist erred here is not known.

## 206  ᔰ  ARTICLE BY ECS

[September 1880]

The last number of *National Citizen* delights my heart. It bristles all over with indignation and rebellion politically, religiously and socially. The arraignment of the republican party, both in its legislative and judicial action is just and timely.[1] I think we have sat on a limb of the republican tree, singing "suffrage if you please," like so many insignificant humming birds, quite long enough. And now in view of the cool treatment our delegates received at Chicago, and the questionable attitude of Gen. Garfield, why not turn our ears to more hopeful opinions in other directions.

I understand that the democratic party received our national delegates with great courtesy at Cincinnati, and that the officers of the New York state association were graciously received at his residence, by Gen. Hancock, and that he enlarged and improved his printed declaration by saying on that occasion, "I believe in a free ballot for all people, *women* as well as men."[2] Now if he actually said "women," in a round, clear tone, without any nervous twitching, as if the word stuck in his throat, or as if struggling with a half-fledged idea, I think the chosen leader of the democracy is worthy our "respectful consideration."

I see the republican press is inviting our attention to the following utterance from Gen. Garfield, as if it should be highly satisfactory to woman suffragists.

> Laugh at it as you may, put it aside as a jest if we will, keep it out of Congress or political campaigns, still the woman question is rising in our horizon larger than the size of a man's hand; and some solution ere long, that question must find. I have not yet committed my mind to any formula that embraces the whole question. I halt on the threshold of so great a problem; but there is one point on which I have reached a conclusion, and that is that this nation must open up new avenues of work and usefulness to the women of the country, so that everywhere they may have something to do. This is just now infinitely more valuable to them than the platform or the ballot box.[3]

The formula that embraces the civil, political, religious, social freedom of every citizen in a republic, is not a question on whose threshold the mind of an American statesman in the 19th century should halt. If the republican nominee has not committed his mind to the great fundamental principles of our government: "No just government can be formed without the consent of the governed," "Taxation without representation is tyranny," he is not fit to fill the highest office in our republic.

However Gen. Garfield may estimate the comparative importance of occupation, a trade or a profession with enfranchisement, let us assure him there are some women in this nation sufficiently developed under the genius of our free institutions to appreciate the sacred rights of citizenship,—the right of trial by a jury of one's peers; the rights of person and property; the right to a voice in the laws, and the rulers under which we live; the right to be represented in government; all summed up in the right to vote. We consider this right to express our wants and wishes at the ballot box, "infinitely more valuable" than the right to earn our bread at the sewing machine, in the school-house or the sub-treasury at Washington.

With the ballot in her hand, the woman citizen has the power to open for herself new avenues of work and usefulness, and to secure new dignity and self-respect. Had Gen. Garfield belonged to a disfranchised class, the wings of his ambition and success would have been sorely clipped. Ostracised in constitutions, Bibles and the statute laws of every state of the union, as a subject, an inferior, a pariah, he would have found his struggles to manhood threefold harder than they were. Would the simple right to work in a New England manufactory, without the right to vote, ever have given Frederick Douglass the power to command the office of U.S. Marshal of the District of Columbia, or an honored place on the platform of the republican national convention in Chicago? "No, no, the ballot is the crown of honor, the scepter of power; it is," said Charles Sumner, "the columbiad of our political life, and every citizen who holds it is a full armed monitor."[4]

To vote the democratic ticket, it is said, is to surrender our government to a "solid south."[5] Intertwisted, intertwined as are the interests of all sections of our country, any legislation in which all the people are not of one mind is to be deplored, but to the women of this republic a "solid south" is not fraught with half the danger that must come from a *solid male dynasty*, north, south, east, west, everywhere.

&#8620; *NCBB*, September 1880.

1. In the *National Citizen*, August 1880, Matilda Gage wrote two forceful editorials about women and the Republican party: "Woman Idolaters" and "Professed Friends." In the first she reviewed the long history of betrayals by the party and urged women to "break it in pieces. It is liberty you want, not party." In the second she replied to the editors of the *Woman's Journal* that it was the sole aim of the National association to secure woman suffrage, not to protect parties or other principles. "When woman loves freedom for freedom's sake," Gage wrote, "she will not ask the name of the party which secures it to her."

2. When Winfield Scott Hancock accepted the Democratic presidential nomination on 29 July 1880, he wrote, "It is only by a full vote, free ballot, and fair count that the people can rule in fact, as required by the theory of our government. Take this foundation away, and the whole structure falls." When Lillie Blake met with him on August 13, she asked, according to the New York *Sun*, "if he considered women as 'people.'" "Undoubtedly" was his reply.

Blake went on to say that the woman suffragists asked no more than his letter of acceptance already stated. "'I am perfectly willing,' said Gen. Hancock, 'that you should say I take my stand on that paragraph in my letter of acceptance.'" (*New York Times*, 31 July 1880; New York *Sun*, 14 August 1880, in SBA scrapbook 9, Rare Books, DLC; Blake and Wallace, *Champion of Women*, 140–41.)

3. The *Woman's Journal*, 31 July 1880, included this quotation from James Garfield's address at commencement exercises of 1869 at the Spencerian Business College in Washington within an article entitled "The Education of Garfield."

4. "Equal Rights of All," Sumner, *Works*, 10:224.

5. The phrase appeared in the Republican party platform. (*National Party Platforms*, 62.)

207  ⇒  ECS, SBA, AND MATILDA JOSLYN GAGE TO SARA ANDREWS SPENCER

Tenafly, N.J., Sept. 1, 1880.

Sara Andrews Spencer:—

Dear Madam.—Your resignation of the office of Corresponding Secretary of the National Woman Suffrage Association was duly received, and after consultation with members of the Executive Committee, was accepted, and Ellen H. Sheldon appointed to fill the place, to whom you will please deliver all the books, papers, letters, furniture and all matter and property belonging to the National Woman Suffrage Association. Very respectfully,

⇒  *Elizabeth Cady Stanton, President.*

⇒  *Matilda Joslyn Gage, Ch. Ex. Com.*

⇒  *Susan B. Anthony, Vice Pres. at Large.*

⇒ *NCBB*, September 1880.

208 &#8766; SBA to Rachel G. Foster[1]

Rochester N.Y. Sept 7th 1880.

My Dear Rachel

Crowd all the engagements you have into those last two weeks of this month, if possible—and then don't try to make any more for me until after this Presidential campaign is over— It is always a very bad time— I do not believe Geo. Wm Curtiss, or Wendell Phillips, or any one could get a crowd at 50 cts admission in this City or any other in the Nation now— You—the very best orators in the Nation are speaking everywhere—with <u>open</u> <u>doors</u>— We had "<u>the fool</u>" Tourgee[2]—here the other night—with our vast City Hall packed— And, in view of the surfeit ↑of lecturing↓ every town will get this autumn—I think it will be the wise thing for me to give my time to working upo[n] the History of the W.R. movement with Mrs Stanton—up to the time of the Washington Con—the middle of January—and that will leave you to work me into Feb. March & April of 1881—just as closely as you please—through the south if you like— I wish there were some strong, energet, <u>business</u> woman to just engineer and financier me through the Southern states— perhaps your Bureau Business may permit you just to go with me—but I should fear it would be too much for you physically—

If you have seen dear Sarah Pugh—who has just visited Mrs Stanto[n] at Tenafly[3]—she has told you what we all feel—& that is that Mrs Stanton is <u>now</u> <u>at</u> leisure and <u>in</u> <u>the</u> <u>mood</u> of writing on <u>the</u> <u>history</u>— and that—as <u>she</u> nor I have any lease of such conditions—it is Miss Pughs judgement—as well as my sisters & mine—that it is my duty to go to Mrs Stanton and make the most of the coming three months— I hope this will not disappoint you— I have been fearfully divided in my feelings as to what was my <u>first</u> <u>duty</u>—all along— Mrs Gage & Mrs Blake so sure <u>it</u> was to work for school suffrage in New York—Mrs Stanton that it was to go to her to work on history—& I wanting to both—and <u>too</u> distracted to anything—

I have a letter from Mrs May Wright Thompson—she will be in New York City about the first of October—& wants, very much, that we shall call an Ex. Com. Meeting there—& get together as many as possible to talk over & plan to make our next Jan. Wash. Con. the best we can— Would it be possible for you & Julia to go there?—an[d] we ought to have one or two of our Washington City women there too— I suppose Mrs Spofford[4] is still in Maine— I will write her & see if she cannot make it so she can be with us— She writes me Mrs Spencer has cut her—not having written her since she left—

If you give me nothing after Sept. 30th I shall then go direct to Tenafly—or rather New York— Phebe Couzins is in Boston too—attending Social Science meeting—[5] Both she & Mrs Thompson are glad Mrs Spencer has resigned— Mrs Stanton has accepted the resignation—with her own & Mrs Gage's & my signatures to her letter—and instructed her to turn over all property of the N.W.S.A. to Mrs Ellen H. Sheldon—who is to act as Cor. Secy. until the Ex. Com. meet—

Either you or I must go on to Washington a week or two before date of Con—and attend to matters— Indeed we ought to engage our Hall right away— Jan 13th & 14th will be the best days—I guess—though may come in "Prayer Week"— If not the Thurs & Frid—13 & 14—then Tues. & Wed. the 18 & 19 of Jan—but that brings us too late—I fear—Mrs Spencer always insists upon it that the very first week is best—bu[t] I think the 2[d] is— You see New Years coming on Saturday—Congress wi[ll] most likely open on Tues. or Wed. the 4 or 5th but may not till Monday the 10th—therefore Thursday the 14th & Frid the 6th will be likely to catch them at latest— Then, after the Con.—I would like a few days to stay in Washington & look after our Congress prospects— With Love to Mother[6] & sister affectionately yours—

⇒ *S. B. A—*

⇒ ALS, on NWSA letterhead for 1880, SBA Papers, DLC. Letters in square brackets obscured at margins.

1. Rachel G. Foster (1858–1919), later Avery, was trying her hand as a lecture agent, arranging SBA's engagements. Rachel and her sister, Julia T. Foster (c. 1849–1890), were sent by Philadelphia's Citizens' Suffrage Association to the National's Washington convention in January 1879, and they were immediately recognized for their efficiency and willingness to work. Both sisters were independently wealthy. (*NAW* and *ANB*, s.v. "Avery, Rachel G. Foster"; SBA to R. G. F. Avery, 18 November 1890, *Film*, 28:737–41.)

2. Albion Winegar Tourgée (1838–1905), a northern Radical Republican, served as a superior court justice in North Carolina from 1868 to 1874 and

stayed in the state until 1880, trying to protect the legal gains of Reconstruction. SBA refers to the title of his autobiographical novel, *A Fool's Errand* (1879), the basis of campaign speeches he made for James Garfield. (*ANB*.)

3. On this visit to see both ECS and Henry B. Stanton, see *Memorial of Sarah Pugh. A Tribute of Respect from Her Cousins* (Philadelphia, 1888), 133.

4. Jane H. Snow Spofford (1828–c. 1905) became the treasurer of the National association when Ellen Sargent returned to California in 1879. Raised in Hampden Corners, Maine, she married Caleb Wheeler Spofford of New Hampshire. Caleb Spofford became a proprietor of the Riggs House, at Fifteenth and G Streets, Northwest, in Washington, D.C., about 1877 and the sole owner a year later. With the hotel at her disposal, Jane Spofford became the National association's hostess in Washington, opening public rooms for receptions, discounting rates for delegates to the conventions, and reserving space for SBA to stay in the city for long periods of time. She was also active in city societies and represented the District suffrage association at the National's meetings. By 1892 the Spoffords had moved out of the hotel, which was then managed by the Riggs House Company. Although her husband stayed in Washington, Jane Spofford spent much of her time thereafter in Maine, caring for her mother. Her death was noted at the National-American Woman Suffrage Association convention in 1906. (Jeremiah Spofford, *A Genealogical Record, Including Two Generations in Female Lines of Families Spelling the Name Spofford, Spafford, Spafard, and Spaford* [Boston, 1888], 247; research by Katherine W. Trickey, Bangor, Me.; *History*, 3:98–99, 260, 4:387, 571, 689, 5:180; city directories, 1877 to 1892.)

5. The American Social Science Association met in Saratoga, New York, not Boston. (*New York Times*, 11 September 1880.)

6. Julia Manuel Foster (?–1885) was the wealthy widow of J. Heron Foster, publisher of the Pittsburgh *Daily Dispatch*. According to ECS, she was a servant in the Cady household in Johnstown, New York, in her youth. Sometime after 1870, Julia Foster moved with her daughters to Philadelphia. (Federal Census, 1870, for Pittsburgh; Samuel W. Durant, *History of Allegheny Co., Pennsylvania* [Philadelphia, 1876], 127, 128, 138; Adelaide Mellier Nevin, *The Social Mirror; A Character Sketch of the Women of Pittsburg and Vicinity* [Pittsburg, Pa., 1888], 30; *Anthony*, 2:701; ECS to Clara B. Colby, c. 5 February 1896, *Film*, 35:541–50.)

209 ⤳ SBA TO JAMES A. GARFIELD

Rochester N.Y. Sept. 9th 1880.

Hon. James A. Garfield   Dear Sir

Yours of the 25th ult. has waited these many days, simply because I didn't know what to say to you in reply.

1st The Republican Party did run well for a season in the "line of liberty."— But, also, since 1870, its Congressional enactments, majority reports, Supreme Court Decisions, and now its Presidential platform,[1] show a retrograde movement—(not only for woman, but for men of color) limiting the power of the National Government in the protection of United States Citizens against the injustice of the States, until what we gained by the sword is lost by political surrenders. We need nothing but a Democratic administration to demonstrate to all Israel and the Sun the fact,—the sad fact,—that all _is_ _lost_ by the Republican Party,—not _to_ _be_ _lost_ by the Democratic Party. I mean, of course, the _one_ _vital_ _point_ of _Supremacy_ of the United States government in the protection of citizens in their right to vote, and in the punishment of states, or the inhabitants of States, for depriving citizens of the exercise of their right to vote.— The first and fatal step, was denying the application of the great principle ⸙of⸙ equality of rights to women, and to men of foreign-birth in Rhode Island.[2] After conceeding the state's right to supremacy over those two classes, inch by inch has slipped away, until it is only _in_ _name_ that the Republican Party is now the party of _National_ _Supremacy_. _Grant_ could not protect the negro's ballot in 1876, and _Hayes_ cannot in 1880—nor can Garfield in 1884— For the Sceptre has departed from Judah!—[3]

2d For the candidate of a party to _add_ to the discussions of the contest an issue unauthorized or unnoted in its platform, when that issue was one vital to its very life,—would, it seems to me be the grandest act imaginable. And for doing that very thing with regard to _protection_ _of_ _the_ _negroes_ _of_ _the_ _south,_ _you_ are _to-day_ receiving more praise from the best men of the party, than for any and all of your utterances inside the line of the platform. And I _know,_ if you had in your [let]ter of acceptance, and in [N]ew-York speech,[4] spoken the one word of and for "<u>Perfect</u> <u>equality</u> <u>of</u> <u>rights</u> <u>for</u> <u>Women</u>, <u>civil</u> <u>and</u> <u>political</u>"—you would ↑have↓ touched an electric spark that would have fired the heart of the women of the entire nation, and made the triumph of the Republican Party more grand and glorious than any it has ever seen.

3^d As to picking fruit before it ripens!!— Allow me to remind you that very much fruit is <u>never</u> <u>picked</u>.— Some gets worm-eaten and falls to the ground; [som]e rots on the trees before it ripens;—some, too slow in maturing, gets bitten ↑by↓ the early frosts of Winter;—while some ripe, rich, rare apples hang un-picked, frozen and worthless on the leafless trees of Winter!!

But really, Mr Garfield, if, after passing through ↑the↓ war of the rebellion and your sixteen years of service in Congress,— if, after seeing, and hearing, and repeating over and over again, that no class ever got justice and equality at the hands of any government, except it had the power, the ballot, to clutch them for itself,— if, after all your opportunities for growth and developement, you cannot yet see the truth of the great principle of <u>individual</u> <u>self-government</u>,—if you have only reached the principle of <u>class</u>-<u>government</u>, and that, too, of the most hateful and cruel form,—bounded by sex,— there must be some radical defect in tree or fruit. And the more is the pity, because in the Democratic Party and its nominee there is <u>no</u> <u>hope</u> <u>whatever</u>—the root itself being defective, if not altogether <u>rotten</u>.— For neither of the two great parties, therefore, can women, with true self-respect, enter into this Presidential cavass.

No matter which party shall administer the government, women will continue to get only subordinate positions and half-pay under it;—not because of the party's or the President's <u>lack</u> of chivalric regard or love of justice for woman, but because, in the nature of things, it is impossible for any government to protect any disfranchised class in equality of chances. The point I want to gain is <u>political</u> freedom and equality for women.

But pardon this long tresspass upon ↑your↓ time and patience—and please bear in mind, that it is not for the many <u>good</u> things the Republican Party and its nominee have done in extending the area of liberty, that I criticise them, but because they refuse to go forward and admit women citizens to equal rights with their brothers.

I do not ask you to go beyond your own convictions—but I do most earnestly beg you to look at this question and decide upon it, from the stand-point of woman—alone—without father, brother, husband, son— battling for bread, it is for the millions ⌐of⌐ <u>un</u>loved, <u>un</u>protected, <u>un</u>cared for women that I plead for the ballot in the hands of all women—

With great respect for your frank and candid talk with one of the disfranchised—I am Sincerely yours

    *Susan B. Anthony*

  ALS, on NWSA letterhead for 1880, James A. Garfield Papers, DLC. Letters in square brackets torn from corners. Also in *History*, 3: 186–87.

1. The Republican party platform of 1880 backed away from language in its platform of 1876 about enforcing the amendments of Reconstruction to secure "to every American citizen complete liberty and exact equality in the exercise of all civil, political, and public rights." It did castigate the Democrats for obstructing voting (though the examples were northern and the victims white), but in its pledge to achieve "equal, steady and complete enforcement of the law, and the protection of all our citizens in the enjoyment of all privileges and immunities guaranteed by the Constitution," it avoided political rights. (*National Party Platforms*, 53–54, 62.)

2. SBA refers to the decision of the Senate Committee on the Judiciary in 1870 that neither the Fourteenth nor the Fifteenth Amendment had any bearing on Rhode Island's requirement that naturalized male citizens meet a property qualification in order to vote, a qualification not required of native male citizens. The committee reported that on questions of nativity rather than race the states were at liberty to decide for themselves what was necessary for "security and good order in society." (McPherson, *Hand-Book of Politics for 1874*, 215–16.)

3. Gen. 49:10.

4. In accepting the Republican nomination on July 10, Garfield went beyond the party's platform by insisting that the nation had the authority to protect the methods of electing members of Congress and warning that national reunification required that "every citizen, rich or poor, white or black, is secure in the free and equal enjoyment of every civil and political right guaranteed by the constitution and the laws." A month later, addressing Union Army veterans in New York City, he reminded the crowd that "[w]e have seen white men betray the flag and fight to kill the Union, but . . . you never saw a traitor under a black skin." Cheers greeted his call for the nation to "stand by these black allies of ours." (*New York Times*, 13 July, 7 August 1880.)

## FAMILIES OF SBA'S SIBLINGS

The names and relationships of older members of the Anthony and Cady families and of the Stanton children may be found in the appendix to volume 1 of this edition. This chart identifies SBA's nieces and nephews and their children as of the year 1880.

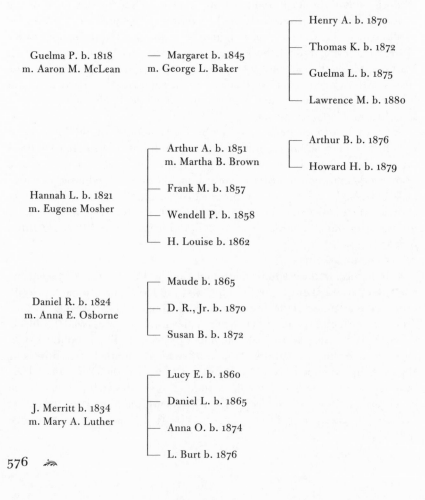

Guelma P. b. 1818
m. Aaron M. McLean

— Margaret b. 1845
m. George L. Baker

┌ Henry A. b. 1870

├ Thomas K. b. 1872

├ Guelma L. b. 1875

└ Lawrence M. b. 1880

Hannah L. b. 1821
m. Eugene Mosher

— Arthur A. b. 1851
m. Martha B. Brown

┌ Arthur B. b. 1876

└ Howard H. b. 1879

— Frank M. b. 1857

— Wendell P. b. 1858

— H. Louise b. 1862

Daniel R. b. 1824
m. Anna E. Osborne

— Maude b. 1865

— D. R., Jr. b. 1870

— Susan B. b. 1872

J. Merritt b. 1834
m. Mary A. Luther

— Lucy E. b. 1860

— Daniel L. b. 1865

— Anna O. b. 1874

— L. Burt b. 1876

# ❦ Appendix B

Officers of the National Woman Suffrage Association, 1872 to 1880

Officers were named at the annual meeting, usually held in May of each year. In 1878 it took place in July.

## ❦ 1872

Letterhead and constitution at 13 August 1872, *Film*, 16:333–35.

| | |
|---|---|
| *President* | Susan B. Anthony |
| *Chairman*, Executive Committee | Matilda Joslyn Gage |
| *Corresponding Secretary* | Jane Grahame Jones |
| *Foreign Corresponding Secretary* | Laura Curtis Bullard |
| *Recording Secretary* | Mary Fenn Davis |
| *Treasurer* | Ellen Clark Sargent |

## ❦ 1873

Annual meeting at 6 May and letterhead at 15 December 1873, *Film*, 17:68, 447.

| | |
|---|---|
| *President* | Susan B. Anthony |
| *Chairman*, Executive Committee | Elizabeth Cady Stanton |
| *Corresponding Secretary* | Jane Grahame Jones |
| *Foreign Corresponding Secretary* | Laura Curtis Bullard |
| *Recording Secretary* | Mary Fenn Davis[1] |
| *Treasurer* | Ellen Clark Sargent |

## ❦ 1874

Annual meeting at 14 May 1874 and letterhead at 10 March 1875, *Film*, 18:11, 342.

| | |
|---|---|
| *President* | Martha Coffin Wright |
| *Chairman*, Executive Committee | Susan B. Anthony |

| | |
|---|---|
| *Corresponding Secretary* | Isabella Beecher Hooker |
| *Recording Secretary* | Lillie Devereux Blake |
| *Treasurer* | Ellen Clark Sargent |

## ⇜ 1875

Annual meeting at 11 May and letterhead at 27 September 1875,
*Film*, 18:404, 453.

| | |
|---|---|
| *President* | Matilda Joslyn Gage |
| *Chairman*, EXECUTIVE COMMITTEE | Susan B. Anthony |
| *Corresponding Secretary* | Isabella Beecher Hooker |
| *Recording Secretary* | Henrietta Paine Westbrook |
| *Foreign Corresponding Secretary* | Mathilde F. Wendt |
| *Treasurer* | Ellen Clark Sargent |

## ⇜ 1876

Letterhead and constitution at 3 July 1876, *Film*, 18:856–58.

| | |
|---|---|
| *President* | Elizabeth Cady Stanton |
| *Chairman*, EXECUTIVE COMMITTEE | Matilda Joslyn Gage |
| *Corresponding Secretary* | Susan B. Anthony |
| *Recording Secretary* | Lillie Devereux Blake |
| *Foreign Corresponding Secretaries* | Laura Curtis Bullard |
| | Jane Grahame Jones |
| *Treasurer* | Ellen Clark Sargent |
| CAMPAIGN COMMITTEE–1876 | Susan B. Anthony |
| | Matilda Joslyn Gage |
| | Phoebe W. Couzins |
| | Olympia Brown |
| | Jane Grahame Jones |
| | Abigail Scott Duniway |
| | Laura De Force Gordon |
| | Annie Nowlin Savery |
| RESIDENT CONGRESSIONAL COMMITTEE | Sara Andrews Spencer |
| | Ellen Clark Sargent |
| | Ruth Carr Denison |
| | Belva McNall Lockwood |
| | E. D. E. N. Southworth |

## ⚹ 1877

Letterhead and constitution at 1 September 1877, *Film*, 19:529.

| | |
|---|---|
| *President* | Clemence Harned Lozier |
| *Chairman*, EXECUTIVE COMMITTEE | Susan B. Anthony |
| *Corresponding Secretary* | Isabella Beecher Hooker |
| *Recording Secretary* | Lillie Devereux Blake |
| *Treasurer* | Ellen Clark Sargent |
| *Foreign Corresponding Secretaries* | Laura Curtis Bullard |
| | Jane Grahame Jones |
| RESIDENT CONGRESSIONAL COMMITTEE | Sara Andrews Spencer |
| | Ellen Clark Sargent |
| | Ruth Carr Denison |
| | Rosina M. Parnell |
| | Mary Ann Shadd Cary |

## ⚹ 1878

*National Citizen and Ballot Box*, September 1878.

| | |
|---|---|
| *President* | Elizabeth Cady Stanton |
| *Chairman*, EXECUTIVE COMMITTEE | Susan B. Anthony |
| *Corresponding Secretary* | Matilda Joslyn Gage |
| *Foreign Corresponding Secretaries* | Jane Grahame Jones |
| | Laura Curtis Bullard |
| | Margaret M. J. Miller[2] |
| *Recording Secretaries* | Lillie Devereux Blake |
| | Ellen H. Sheldon |
| *Treasurer* | Ellen Clark Sargent |

## ⚹ 1879

*Appeal to Women Citizens of the United States, Tract No. 1*, September 1879, *Film*, 20:864–65.

| | |
|---|---|
| *President* | Elizabeth Cady Stanton |
| *Chairman*, EXECUTIVE COMMITTEE | Matilda Joslyn Gage |
| *Corresponding Secretary* | Sara Andrews Spencer |
| *Foreign Corresponding Secretaries* | Laura Curtis Bullard |
| | Jane Grahame Jones |
| *Recording Secretary* | Ellen H. Sheldon |
| *Treasurer* | Jane Snow Spofford |
| *Vice President at Large* | Susan B. Anthony |

## ❦ 1880

*National Citizen and Ballot Box*, June 1880.

| | |
|---|---|
| *President* | Elizabeth Cady Stanton |
| *Chairman*, EXECUTIVE COMMITTEE | Matilda Joslyn Gage |
| *Corresponding Secretary* | Sara Andrews Spencer |
| *Foreign Corresponding Secretaries* | Laura Curtis Bullard |
| | Mathilde F. Wendt[3] |
| *Recording Secretary* | Ellen H. Sheldon |
| *Treasurer* | Jane Snow Spofford |
| *Vice President at Large* | Susan B. Anthony |

### EXECUTIVE COMMITTEE MEMBERSHIP

Sources are same as above; no list of committee members in 1874 has been found.

Nancy Hall Allen (Iowa), 1876, 1877

Susan B. Anthony (N.Y.), 1875, 1877, 1878

Lillie Devereux Blake (N.Y.), 1872, 1875

Marian Carr Bliss (Mich.), 1879, 1880

Olympia Brown (Conn. & Wis.), 1872, 1873, 1875, 1876, 1877, 1879, 1880

Carrie S. Burnham (Pa.), 1875

Mary Ann Shadd Cary (D.C.), 1878, 1879, 1880

Mary B. Clay (Ky.), 1879, 1880

Lucy Danforth Colman (N.Y.), 1878

Helen M. Cooke (N.Y.), 1877

Phoebe W. Couzins (Mo.), 1877, 1878, 1879, 1880

Lavinia C. Dundore (Md.), 1878

Abigail Scott Duniway (Ore.), 1872, 1875, 1877, 1878

Martha L. Fort (Ga.), 1879

Matilda Joslyn Gage (N.Y.), 1872, 1876, 1877, 1879, 1880

Nannette Ellingwood Gardner (Mich.), 1872

Mary Fowler Gilbert (N.Y.), 1875

Mary Hampton Godbe (Utah), 1879, 1880

Laura De Force Gordon (Calif.), 1872, 1873, 1875

Ann Jarvis Greely (Me.), 1879, 1880

Frances Robinson Hallock (N.Y.), 1873, 1875

Mary Post Hallowell (N.Y.), 1878

Elizabeth Boynton Harbert (Ill.), 1877, 1878

Isabella Beecher Hooker (Conn.), 1878

Mary Vance Humphrey (Kan.), 1879, 1880

Bessie Bisbee Hunt (N.H.), 1879, 1880

Jane Grahame Jones (Ill.), 1875

Phebe Hoag Jones (N.Y.), 1876

Harriette Harned Keating (La.), 1880

Susan A. King (N.Y.), 1877, 1878

Sarah Browning Knox-Goodrich (Calif.),[4] 1878, 1879, 1880

Orra Gray Langhorne (Va.), 1879, 1880

Emily J. Leonard (Conn.), 1879, 1880

Augusta Lilienthal (N.Y.), 1879, 1880

Belva McNall Lockwood (D.C.), 1877, 1878, 1879

Helen M. Loder (N.Y.), 1878, 1879, 1880

Elizabeth Edwards Loomis (Ill.), 1872, 1873

Clemence Harned Lozier (N.Y.), 1873, 1875, 1876, 1879, 1880

Ada W. Lucas (Neb.), 1879, 1880

Buell Drake McClung (Ala.), 1880

Mary F. Mann (La.), 1879

Virginia L. Minor (Mo.), 1875

Louisa M. Oliver (Ark.), 1879, 1880

Rosina M. Parnell (D.C.), 1880

Sarah Clinton Perkins (Vt.), 1879, 1880

Elizabeth B. Phelps (N.Y.), 1875, 1876

Sarah Pugh (Pa.), 1872, 1873, 1875

Harriet Purvis (Pa.), 1877

Marilla Young Ricker (N.H.), 1877, 1878

Annie Nowlin Savery (Iowa), 1877

Cornelia Hartley Scarborough (Pa.), 1878, 1879, 1880

Harriette Robinson Shattuck (Mass.), 1878, 1879, 1880

Lewia C. Smith (N.Y.), 1877

Sara Andrews Spencer (D.C.), 1878

Elizabeth Cady Stanton (N.J.), 1873

Catharine Fish Stebbins (Mich.), 1875, 1877, 1878

May Wright Thompson (Ind.), 1880

M. Adeline Thomson (Pa.), 1876, 1877, 1878, 1879, 1880

Sarah Armstrong Wallis (Calif.), 1877

Mathilde F. Wendt (N.Y.), 1872, 1873, 1876, 1878

Henrietta Paine Westbrook (Pa.), 1876

Charlotte Beebe Wilbour (N.Y.), 1872, 1873, 1875

Sarah Langdon Williams (Ohio), 1875, 1876, 1877, 1878

Laura Ross Wolcott (Wis.), 1877, 1878

1. The press reported of the annual meeting that Lillie Devereux Blake and Anna Rice Powell were named recording secretaries, but that information appears nowhere else during the year. They may have acted in that capacity at the meeting itself.

2. Miller's name did not appear on the earliest lists of the year's officers, in *Rochester Union and Advertiser*, 19 July 1878, and *Woman's Words* 2 (August 1878). Late additions to the executive committee were Lucy Colman, Lavinia Dundore, and Sarah Williams.

3. The annual meeting in 1880 amended the slate of officers proposed by the nominating committee, rejecting Rachel G. Foster and returning Sara Spencer to her post as corresponding secretary and, according to the *National Citizen*, changing one foreign corresponding secretary. Although lists differ, it appears that Laura Curtis Bullard replaced Jane Grahame Jones.

4. Sarah Knox became Sarah Knox-Goodrich between her first and second selection to the executive committee, when she remarried.